The Ernst & Young
New York, New Jersey, Connecticut
State Tax Guide
1993

The Ernst & Young
New York, New Jersey, Connecticut
State Tax Guide
1993

Ernst & Young

John Wiley & Sons, Inc.
New York • Chichester • Brisbane • Toronto • Singapore

The text is printed on acid-free paper.

This publication is designed to provide accurate and authoritative information in regard to the subject matter covered. It is sold with the understanding that the publisher is not engaged in rendering legal, accounting, or other professional services. If legal advice or other expert assistance is required, the services of a competent professional person should be sought. *From a Declaration of Principles jointly adopted by a committee of the American Bar Association and a Committee of Publishers.*

Library of Congress Cataloging in Publication Data:
ISSN 1065-7312

ISBN 0-471-58045-7

Printed in the United States of America

10 9 8 7 6 5 4 3 2 1

Contents

Part II   NEW JERSEY   NJ-1

Part III CONNECTICUT CT-1

The Ernst & Young Editorial Board

Tax Watch

A Letter from Ernst & Young

November, 1992

This country was established under the rallying cry of "no taxation without representation." Two hundred years later, we find that taxation *with* representation is not a pleasurable alternative. In part this is because tax rates are high. In part it is because taxes are not simple. Preparing one's tax return for the April 15 filing is a task that for most approaches herculean proportions.

Adding to the complexity is that our system of federalism requires that taxpayers file two sets of returns—one for Uncle Sam and one for the separate states. Virtually all states impose individual income tax obligations. Only a handful—Alaska, Florida, Nevada, South Dakota, Texas, Washington, and Wyoming—do not tax personal income. And since each state creates its own unique tax code, filing one's state return is not an easy or routine task. Indeed, the growing complexity of state tax filing obligations has spawned an industry of professional state tax preparers and planners, something that was practically unheard of several years ago.

Several factors have combined to push state taxation into the forefront:

- Federal policy has had a significant impact. The drastic reduction of federal tax rates has focused the spotlight on state taxes as a percentage of the total tax exposure. Moreover, as the federal government has cut back, there is a perception that the resources available to the state have been depleted, thereby putting pressure on each state to raise its own funds.
- Under the doctrine of the separation of powers, the states are independent in matters involving their own treasury. Accordingly, state tax codes do not necessarily follow the federal provisions. There are thus 40 *different* state tax codes that are being administered by the state governments.
- Politics also enters into it. Most politicians are promising "no new taxes" while finding ways to squeeze additional revenue from the existing tax base, without resorting to a tax increase. For example, the tri-state jurisdictions of New York, New Jersey, and Connecticut all amended their sales tax laws to cover the mail order industry. This happened despite a recent Supreme Court decision that protected the industry! In this case, we have state legislatures unilaterally repealing a Supreme Court decision to protect the interests of a powerful industry and the effect is being felt by taxpayers.
- Unlike the voluminous Internal Revenue Code designed to guide taxpayers through the federal filing process, the state tax codes tend to be much more general in nature and far less extensive in explanation. Since there is no official drafting of state tax laws for either New York, New Jersey, or Connecticut, the states are free to take considerable berth with dictating tax policy—leaving the unwary taxpayer at their whim.
- The states have become very aggressive in enforcing the tax laws in the form of increasing audits. As anyone who has recently experienced a state tax examination knows, the auditors are extremely zealous. Auditors are quick to impose penalties on any taxpayers who have made errors, even if unwittingly, on their return. Increased audit activity, narrow interpretation of the law, and swift imposition of penalties are all revenue raisers for the states.

We in our practice have found that the only antidote to state tax complexity is an educated consumer. That is the purpose of this book—to remove the scales from the taxpayer's eyes, enabling you, the reader, to meet your New York-New Jersey-Connecticut tax filings in the most simple and least painful manner possible.

Ernst & Young

How to Use This Guide

The Ernst & Young New York, New Jersey, Connecticut State Tax Guide 1993 is the first book to address the preparation of individual tax returns for filers in New York, New Jersey, and Connecticut. It is an easy-to-use guide that explains, in clear and simple language, everything you'll need to know about filing state income tax returns for these three states. Designed to eliminate worry and confusion about your state tax return, it leads you step-by-step through preparing your return. It also tells you about the schedules and other documents to attach.

This book is much more than just a tax return preparation guide. It also provides you with all you need to know *before* you fill out your return, including information on your filing status and figuring out who your dependents are. In addition, it helps you decide whether to file as a resident, part-year resident, or nonresident. You can also use it as a convenient reference tool throughout the year. Examples, special worksheets, and our unique Tax Organizer will help you plan the way the experts do!

Other special features of this guide are:

- **Separate parts for New York, New Jersey, and Connecticut filers:** If you file a tax return in only one of these states, you can read as much, or as little, about the other states as you wish. However, if you are filing as a **resident** of one state and as a **nonresident** wage-earner in another, our state-by-state organization will save you time.
- **Changes in the Tax Law:** Even if you've prepared your own return in the past, you'll benefit from our up-to-the-minute information on changes in the laws of all three states.
- **TaxPlanners, TaxSavers,** and **TaxAlerts** have been included in appropriate places throughout the book. *TaxPlanners* outline strategies that help you plan better for the upcoming year; *TaxSavers* are tips that help you slash your tax bill this year and next—legally; and *TaxAlerts* give you important filing advice about things to consider as you prepare your returns.

- **Sample Filled-In Forms:** To help you fill out your return line-by-line, we've included filled-in examples of the primary forms for each state to refer to when completing your own forms.
- **Abandoning Your Domicile Checklist:** If you've recently moved from a high-tax to a low-tax (or no-tax) state, this *Checklist* alone may be worth the price of this book! It tells you what you need to know to avoid being taxed as a resident of your former home state *after* you've moved. It shows you exactly what steps to take and what documents you need to keep, to convince state taxing authorities that you've relocated.
- **Estimated Taxes and Withholding:** We've included a chapter to help you understand how estimated tax payments and withholding of tax works to avoid tax penalties and help you "pay as you go."
- **What to Do If Your Return is Examined:** Our special chapter on state tax audits are designed to help you avoid panic and costly mistakes in dealing with the tax authorities. We tell you exactly what to expect if you are audited, how to prepare for the tax examiner, what rights you have if you disagree with an assessment of additional tax, and how much time you have to protest an assessment.

And much more! This book draws on the combined state and local tax experience of partners and professionals at Ernst & Young.

Also available is *The Ernst & Young Tax Guide 1993*, to help you prepare and file your 1992 federal tax return. We welcome your suggestions about how to make this book even better! Please write to us in care of our publisher, John Wiley & Sons, 605 Third Avenue, New York, New York 10158. And here's to a hassle-free April 15!

Note: Although every effort has been made to include the most up-to-date information, we advise that you use this guide in conjunction with the official 1992 instructions.

1993 New York Personal Income Tax Calendar

Date in 1993	Action Required
January 15	Last installment of 1992 estimated tax payment due if you expect to owe over $100 in tax after withholding and credits. Use Form IT-2105.
February 15	Employer must give employee statement of amount withheld for 1992.
February 28	Information return due reporting payments of $600 or more to any New York State or City taxpayer in 1992.
April 15	Personal income tax return and payment of tax due. Residents use Form IT-100, IT-200, or IT-201. Nonresidents and part-year residents use Form IT-203. To receive an automatic four month extension of time to file the return, Form IT-370 must be filed by this date. First installment of estimated tax payments due if you expect to owe over $100 in tax for the year after withholding and credits. Use Form IT-2105.
June 15	Second installment of estimated tax payments due if you expect to owe over $100 in tax for the year after withholding and credits. Use Form IT-2105.
August 15	Automatic four month extension period for filing return ends.
September 15	Third installment of estimated tax payments due if you expect to owe over $100 in tax for the year after withholding and credits. Use Form IT-2105.
October 15	Last day to file return if six month extension has been granted by Commissioner.

1993 New Jersey Personal Income Tax Calendar

Date in 1993	Action Required
January 15	Last installment of 1992 estimated taxes due. Use Form NJ-1040ES.
February 15	Employer's statement of amount withheld must be sent to employee.
April 15	Personal Income Tax return and payment due. Residents file Form NJ-1040. Nonresidents file NJ-1040NR. Declaration of estimated tax and first installment payment are due if your personal income can reasonably be expected to exceed $100 after withholding and credits. Use Form NJ-1040ES.
June 15	Second estimated tax installment payment is due if your personal income can reasonably be expected to exceed $100 after withholding and credits. Use Form NJ-1040ES.
August 15	End of extension period if based on receiving federal extension.
September 15	Third estimated tax installment payment is due if your personal income can reasonably be expected to exceed $100 after withholding and credits. Use Form NJ-1040ES.
October 15	Last day to file return if six-month extension has been granted using Form NJ-360.

1993 Connecticut Personal Income Tax Calendar

Date in 1993	Action Required
January 15	Last installment of 1992 estimated tax payment due if you earned more than $1,000 in 1991 on which no tax was withheld. Use Form CT-1040ES.
January 31	Employer statement of amount withheld from wages must be sent to employee.
April 15	Personal income tax return must be filed and tax paid. Residents use Form CT-1040. Nonresidents and part-year residents use Form CT-1040NR/PY. First installment of 1993 estimated tax payment due if you are not paying tax through withholding or expect to earn over $1,000 on which no tax will be withheld. Use Form CT-1040ES.
June 15	Second installment of estimated tax payment due if you are not paying income tax through withholding or expect to earn over $1,000 on which no tax will be withheld. Use Form CT-1040ES.
September 15	Third installment of estimated tax payment due if you are not paying income tax through withholding or expect to earn over $1,000 on which no tax will be withheld. Use Form CT-1040ES.
October 15	Last day to file return if six-month extension has been granted using Form CT-1040EXT.

Organizing Your Records

Note: This section will be useful whether you are filing in New York, New Jersey, or Connecticut. It will also help you get organized to prepare your federal income tax return.

Getting Started

All during the year, you may receive different forms, such as Form W-2, *Wages and Tax Statement*, or statements from your stock broker, that you will eventually need to file your tax return. If you are like most people, you stick these pieces of paper in a drawer somewhere, out of sight and out of mind. When the time comes to fill out your tax return, you discover that the various pieces of information you've accumulated don't have any obvious connection with the line items on your *blank* tax returns. To make matters worse, you realize that you cannot find some of the information you need. It is now up to you to locate this information. At this point, you not only need to know where to look, you also need to know what you are looking for. To make this process easier, the following charts and schedules will help you identify and organize the information you need to prepare your tax return.

Information for your tax return may come from many sources. The most common sources of information and the items they substantiate are listed below. The Individual Tax Organizer that follows should make the preparation of your tax returns easier by helping you to organize this data.

Item on Your Return	Source of Information About the Item
1) Wages and salaries	W-2 forms; usually provided by your employer
2) Dividends and interest	Form 1099-Div and Form 1099-Int; usually provided by a bank or company that pays you dividends or interest
3) Capital gains and losses	Your broker's statements for purchase and sale of assets, such as stocks or real estate, you disposed of during the year; Form 1099-B, usually provided by the broker who sold the assets
4) Business income from sole proprietorships, rents, and royalties	Books and records from your business
5) Business income from partnerships, estates, trusts, and S corporations	Form K-1; usually provided by your partnership, estate, trust, or S corporation
6) Unemployment compensation	Form 1099-G; usually provided by the governmental agency paying your unemployment compensation
7) Social Security benefits	Form SSA-1099; usually provided by the federal government
8) State and local income tax refunds	Form 1099-G; usually provided by the state or city that refunded the taxes
9) Original issue discount	Form 1099-OID; usually provided by the issuer of a long-term debt obligation
10) Total distributions from retirement or profit-sharing plans or from Individual Retirement Arrangements (IRA's)	Form 1099-R; usually provided by the trustee for the plan making the distribution
11) Annuities and retirement pay	Form W-2P; usually provided by the trustee for the plan making the payment
12) Barter income	Form 1099-B; usually provided by the barter exchange through which property or services were exchanged
13) Gambling winnings	W-2G
14) Moving and employee business expenses	Receipts and canceled checks and federal Form 4782, if moving expenses are paid or reimbursed by your employer
15) Medical expenses	Receipts and canceled checks
16) Mortgage interest expense	Form 1098 or mortgage company statement; usually provided by mortgage company
17) Business and investment interest expense	Canceled checks and brokers' statements
18) Real estate taxes	Receipts and canceled checks or mortgage company statement
19) Other taxes	Receipts and canceled checks
20) Contributions	Receipts and canceled checks
21) Residency status	Diary and corresponding documentation

TAXALERT: It is always a good idea to complete your federal tax return before preparing your state return(s). If you file in New York or Connecticut, the starting point for computing taxable income will be your federal adjusted gross income. If you file in New Jersey, many of the items will be identical on both returns. In addition, it may be necessary to attach federal schedules, such as Schedule C, *Profit or Loss From Business*, to your state return.

Individual Tax Organizer

The following schedules should help you organize the data you need to prepare your 1992 income tax returns. They are intended only to provide general guidelines and should not be regarded as all-inclusive.

PERSONAL DATA

Last name _____

First name _____ Spouse's _____

Social Security number _____ Spouse's _____

Marital status at year-end: ☐ Married   ☐ Single   ☐ Widowed after 1989   ☐ Divorced   ☐ Married but separated

Are you blind?   Yes ☐   No ☐   Spouse?   Yes ☐   No ☐

Note: If a joint return is to be filed, the words "you" and "your," as used throughout this organizer, include your spouse.

DEPENDENTS

Name	Dependent child (y/n)	Other dependent	Dependent attending college	
			Full time student (y/n)	# of months of full time study

COMPENSATION

Indicate recipient: H—Husband; W—Wife

H W	Employer Name	State gross earnings	City gross earnings	NYS tax withheld

H W	NYC tax withheld	City of Yonkers tax withheld	NJ tax withheld	CT tax withheld	Other

Notes

DIVIDEND AND INTEREST INCOME

Report all dividends received by you or for your account on forms 1099-DIV or other information statements received.

Report all interest received by you or for your account on Forms 1099-INT or other statements of total interest received.

If you invested in a tax-exempt municipal bond fund, *note the fund's schedule of percentage income and assets related to each state.* If you invested in a mutual fund that receives interest from US government obligations, note the percentage of the fund invested in this manner and the percentage of US government interest.

Example—New York Resident

Mary holds shares in a fund that invests 40% of its assets in United States Treasury bills and the other 60% of its assets in certificates of deposit. Because of New York's special rules relating to the allocation of such income, Mary cannot characterize 40% of this distribution as income from US obligations.

Example—New Jersey Resident

Scott holds shares in a fund that invests 50% of its assets in obligations of the State of New Jersey. Distributions from this fund cannot be characterized as tax-exempt interest income because this fund is not a "qualified investment fund" for New Jersey purposes.

Example—Connecticut

Jane receives income from a regulated investment company which invests in obligations of many states, including Connecticut. Assuming that 80% of the distribution is from Connecticut obligations, this percentage would be characterized by nontaxable state income. The other 20% would be characterized as income subject to Connecticut tax.

Dividend Income

Indicate ownership: H—Husband; W—Wife; J—Joint.

H W J	Name of corporation	Indicate T (taxable), C (capital gains, or N (nontaxable)	Dividends received
	Investment funds holding resident state investments.		
	Investment funds holding other states investments.		
	Investment funds holding US government obligations.		

Interest Income

Indicate ownership: H—Husband; W—Wife; J—Joint.

H W J	Savings accounts, credit unions, and certificates of deposit	Amount
	US savings bonds and other U.S. government securities	
	Corporate bonds	
	Other interest (i.e., from partnerships)	
	Interest on state & local obligations issued by resident state or local authority	
	Interest on state & local obligations issued by other states	
	Interest received on tax refund	
	Bank charges for early withdrawals	

SALE OF STOCKS AND BONDS

Indicate: H—Husband; W—Wife; or J—Joint.

Note: Gross proceeds from sales reported here should reconcile to Forms 1099-B received from your broker. You may need to explain any discrepancies if you receive inquiries from governmental agencies.

H W J	Description (include number of shares, common or preferred, and par value of bonds)	Date		Gross sales price[1]	Cost or other basis plus expenses of sale[2]	Gain or (loss)
		Acq.	Sold			

H W J	Description CT resident only—Notes, bonds or other Connecticut obligations	Date		Gross sales price[1]	Cost or other basis plus expenses of sale[2]	Gain or (loss)
		Acq.	Sold			

[1]List proceeds of sale or cash received in lieu of fractions on receipt of stock rights or stock dividends.

[2]The basis of stock should be decreased by all nontaxable dividends and increased by any reinvested dividends.

SALE OF OTHER PROPERTY

H W J	Description	Date Acq.	Date Sold	Gross sales price[1]	Cost or other basis plus expenses of sale	Depreciation or depletion	Gain or (loss)

SALE OR PURCHASE PRICE OF RESIDENCE

Did you sell your residence during the year? ☐ Yes ☐ No

Have you ever postponed any gain on the sale or exchange of a principal residence? ☐ Yes ☐ No

If you sold your principal residence at a gain during the year, you may elect once in your lifetime to exclude up to $125,000 of the gain from income if you lived in such residence for 3 out of 5 immediately preceding years and you were at least 55 years old on the date of sale. If you meet these requirements, do you wish to make this election for the sale? ☐ Yes ☐ No

Did you purchase and occupy a new house, condominium, or other residence during the year? ☐ Yes ☐ No

If you did not purchase a replacement residence, do you intend to do so and make it your principal residence within 2 years from the sale of your former residence? ☐ Yes ☐ No

Notes

INSTALLMENT SALES

Did you make sales during the year for which the receipt of all or part of the sale price was deferred until future years?　　□ Yes　　□ No

Has your residency status changed since the time of this sale?　　□ Yes　　□ No

Amount of cash received in the current tax year _____

Was other property received? Describe. _____

_____

Was any mortgage or other indebtedness assumed by purchase? Describe. _____

_____

Interst rate on installment obligation _____

Did you collect on any installment obligations from sales made prior to 1992?　　□ Yes　　□ No

Was any amount previously taxed by any state or local government? If so, please describe below.

Notes

_____

_____

_____

_____

_____

_____

_____

_____

_____

_____

_____

_____

_____

RENT AND ROYALTY INCOME

	Property A	Property B
Did you actively participate in the operation of the rental activity during the year?	☐ Yes ☐ No	☐ Yes ☐ No
Location and description of property[1]		
Gross rents and royalties received		
Expenses		
Advertising		
Auto and travel		
Cleaning and maintenance		
Commissions		
Depletion		
Depreciation		
Insurance		
Legal and accounting		
Management fees		
Mortgage interest		
Other interest		
Repairs		
Supplies		
Taxes, personal property		
Taxes, real estate		
Utilities		
Wages and salaries		
Windfall profits tax withheld		
Other		

[1]If you or your family used the property as a permanent residence, indicate the total days held for rent but not rented, total days rented, and total days you or your family used it.

Notes

PARTNERSHIP (P), SMALL BUSINESS CORPORATIONS (S), AND ESTATES AND TRUST (E/T)

Retain all Forms K-1 or other information relating to entity listed below.

P S E/T	H W J	Name	Taxpayer Identification Number	Ordinary Income	Real estate income	Interest	Other

State in which income is derived	State adjustment	Description

Notes

BUSINESS OR PROFESSIONAL INCOME

Employer ID number (not
Business name and address _____ Social Security number) _____

Principal business activity _____ Product _____

Gross sales or receipts _____

Returns and allowances _____

Other income (describe)

_____ _____

_____ _____

_____ _____

_____ _____

Inventory at beginning of year	_____	Interest	
Merchandise purchased for resale	_____	Mortgage	_____
Withdrawals for personal use	_____	Other	_____
(if any)		Laundry and cleaning	_____
Cost of labor	_____	Legal and professional fees	
Materials and supplies	_____	Office expense	_____
Other costs (attached schedule)	_____	Pension and profit-sharing plans	_____
Inventory at end of year	_____	Rent on business property	_____
Advertising	_____	Repairs	_____
Bad debts from sales or services	_____	Supplies (not included above)	_____
Bank charges	_____	Taxes	_____
Car and truck expenses	_____	Travel, meals, and entertainment	
Commissions	_____	Travel	_____
Depletion	_____	Meals and entertainment	_____
Depreciation	_____	Club dues	_____
Dues and publications	_____	Utilities and telephone	_____
Employee benefit programs	_____	Wages (not included above)	_____
Freight (not included above)	_____	Other expenses (specify)	_____
Health insurance	_____	_____	_____
Insurance (other)	_____	_____	_____
	_____	_____	_____
	_____	_____	_____

Do you conduct your business in more than one state? ☐ Yes ☐ No

If yes, the following schedule may help you to organize your business records.

Property

Real estate that you own (average cost)	_____	_____	_____	_____
Accumulated depreciation (average)	_____	_____	_____	_____
Tangible personal property that you own (average cost)	_____	_____	_____	_____
Accumulated depreciation (average)	_____	_____	_____	_____
Real estate that you rent	_____	_____	_____	_____
Tangible personal property that you rent (annual rent)	_____	_____	_____	_____

Receipts

Sales of tangible personal property	_____	_____	_____	_____
Services	_____	_____	_____	_____
Payroll	_____	_____	_____	_____

TaxAlert

If you are a nonresident and you conduct your business in and out of New York State and maintain separate books and records, you may be able to base your apportionment on these books and records.

Notes

_____

_____

_____

_____

_____

_____

_____

_____

_____

PENSION AND ANNUITY INCOME

Did you receive any payments from a retirement plan? ☐ Yes ☐ No

If yes, provide the amount received during the year and any taxes withheld. _____

Did you roll over a profit-sharing or retirement plan distribution into another plan? ☐ Yes ☐ No

What was the starting date of your annuity? _____

What is the amount received in the current taxable year? _____

Did you receive any IRA distributions during the year? ☐ Yes ☐ No

OTHER INCOME

Description	Amount
Alimony or legal separation payments received	
Director's fees	
Disability payments	
Executor's or trustee's fees	
Insurance proceeds (describe)	
Other tax refunds not shown elsewhere	
Unemployment insurance compensation	
Social Security benefits	
Reimbursed moving expenses	
Other[1]	

[1]Other income may include, but is not limited to, prizes, cancellation of debts, gambling winnings, jury fees, punitive damages, receiver's fees, and certain tuition paid by an employer.

DEDUCTIONS

ADJUSTMENTS TO INCOME

Alimony or legal separation payments made in current taxable year _____

    Recipient's last name _____ and Social Security no. _____ – _____ – _____

Penalties for early withdrawal of savings _____

Individual Retirement Arrangements (IRA's)[1]

Did you contribute to your own IRA?	☐ Yes	☐ No
Did you participate in a retirement plan maintained by your employer?	☐ Yes	☐ No
Did your spouse contribute to his/her own IRA?	☐ Yes	☐ No
Did your spouse participate in a retirement plan maintained by his/her employer?	☐ Yes	☐ No
Did your spouse contribute to a spousal IRA?	☐ Yes	☐ No
	Yours	Spouse's
If yes, indicate amount contributed for the current taxable year.	_____	_____

Self-employed Keogh (HR-10) plan

    Amount contributed _____ _____

Disability income

Did you receive any disability payments this year?	Yourself	☐ Yes	☐ No
	Spouse	☐ Yes	☐ No

[1]Depending on your (and your spouse's) income level and whether you (or your spouse) are an active participant in an employer-maintained retirement plan, your IRA deduction may be limited.

Notes

_____

_____

_____

_____

_____

_____

_____

_____

_____

_____

1992 PAYMENTS OF STATE INCOME TAXES

Payments towards 1992 tax liability	NYS	NYC	Yonkers	NJ	CT	Other
Overpayment credited from 1991 return	___	___	___	___	___	___
Estimated Payments	___	___	___	___	___	___
April 1992	___	___	___	___	___	___
June 1992	___	___	___	___	___	___
September 1992	___	___	___	___	___	___
January 1992	___	___	___	___	___	___
Withholding	___	___	___	___	___	___
Extension payments	___	___	___	___	___	___
Other						
___	___	___	___	___	___	___
___	___	___	___	___	___	___
Total	___	___	___	___	___	___

TaxAlert

If you file an income tax return in more than one state, complete your nonresident return(s) before preparing your resident return. This will enable you to compute the credit for taxes paid to other jurisdictions.

MISCELLANEOUS

GIFTS

Did you make gifts of a value exceeding $10,000 to any one person?	☐ Yes	☐ No
Did you make any gifts of a future interest during the year (that is, a gift whose possession, use, or enjoyment is restricted until some future time)?	☐ Yes	☐ No

Notes

_____

_____

_____

_____

_____

NEW JERSEY

MEDICAL EXPENSES

Note: You will qualify for this deduction *only* if your total unreimbursed medical expenses exceed 2% of your New Jersey gross income.

List even if reimbursed	Amount
Medical or health insurance premiums (including amounts paid by payroll deductions)	
Medicare premiums	
Prescription drugs and insulin	
Doctors and dentists	
Hospitals	
Other medical expenses	
Reimbursements for medical expenses through insurance or other sources	

1. Medical expenses deductible within the specified limits in addition to doctor and hospital bills include, but are not limited to, artificial limbs, eyeglasses, elevators, X-rays, special shoes, laboratory costs, blood donor expenses, and certain doctor-prescribed trips. Include transportation for medical care (e.g., cab, bus, and train fares and use of personal auto at 9¢ per mile plus parking fees and tolls). Also include amounts paid for lodging while away from home primarily for medical care.

TaxAlert

If you are divorced or separated, have a child, and paid medical expenses for that child, include these amounts whether or not you are entitled to the dependency exemption.

TAX PREPAYMENTS

Excess New Jersey unemployment insurance withheld .... _____

Excess New Jersey disability insurance withheld... _____

INTEREST EXPENSES

If you prepaid any interest or paid any interest on property under construction, please indicate (✓).

Item	Payee	Amount
Home mortgage paid to financial institutions		
Home mortgage paid to individuals[1]		
Mortgage points on principal residence[2]		
Prepayment penalty on loans		
Brokerage accounts		
Investment interest		
Other (itemize)		

1. Furnish name(s) and address(es).
2. Include only points, including loan-origination fees, on the purchase or improvement of your principal residence.

CHARITABLE CONTRIBUTIONS

In addition to outright gifts of cash or property, deductible contributions also include out-of-pocket expenses incurred for charity, e.g., transportation (auto mileage may be claimed at 12¢ per mile), meals and lodging away from home, and cost and upkeep of special uniforms and equipment required in the performance of donated services.

If you have sold any property to a charity for less than the property's fair market value, please provide details.

Cash Contributions

Recipient	Amount[1]	Recipient	Amount[1]

Noncash Contributions

Recipient	Amount[1]	Recipient	Amount[1]

1. If you do not have a receipt, canceled check, or other written evidence, please indicate (✓).

If total noncash contributions have a value in excess of $500, please provide the following information:
the name and address of the donee; the date of the gift; a description of the property, how it was acquired by you, and when it was acquired by you; your tax basis; its value at the time of the donation and how the value was ascertained. Indicate (✓) if any property was held by you for less than one year.

If you made noncash contributions of property in excess of $5,000 in value use Form 8283, *Noncash Charitable Contributions*, with Section B, *Appraisal Summary*, completed.   □ Yes   □ No

CASUALTY LOSSES

Note: You will qualify for a deduction for a personal casualty loss only if it exceeds 10% of your adjusted gross income.

Casualty losses include such items as losses from auto collisions; damage from storms, fires, and floods; as well as damage from vandalism, theft, and other casualties.

Describe the casualty loss and its approximate date and location. _____

_____

_____

_____

_____

Indicate (✓) type of property: _____ business _____ investment _____ personal

Was the casualty loss reported to the police?   □ Yes   □ No

Was the loss covered by insurance?   □ Yes   □ No

If yes, what was the date of the final settlement?   _____

What was the cost or other tax basis of the property?   _____

What was the date of purchase of the property?   _____

What was the approximate fair market value before the casualty?   _____

What was the approximate fair market value after the casualty?   _____

What insurance reimbursement have you received, or do you expect to receive, if any? _____

OTHER DEDUCTIONS

Note: In general, you will qualify for a federal deduction only if your total other miscellaneous deductions exceed 2% of your adjusted gross income.

Item	Amount	Item	Amount
Investment expenses: Auto expense		Educational expense (to maintain or improve skills required by employer)	
Investment counsel fees		Entertainment[1]	
Safe deposit box		Tax advice/return fees	
Dues and subscriptions		Union dues	
Telephone		Dues for professional organizations	
IRA fees		Business publications	
Other		Office-in-home expenses	
		Other	

1. Only 80% of entertainment expenses are deductible.

MOVING EXPENSES IN CONNECTION WITH EMPLOYMENT

Have you incurred moving expenses in connection with starting work at a new permanent location? ☐ Yes ☐ No

If yes, you will need to furnish details of expenditures and reimbursements, including moving and travel expenses, selling cost of former residence, house-hunting expenses, and temporary living expenses at the new location. (State reimbursements for meals separately.) Use Form 4782 or other information in this connection, if any, received from your employer.

What is the number of miles from your old residence to your new workplace? _____

What is the number of miles from your old residence to your old workpalce? _____

Notes

_____
_____
_____
_____
_____
_____
_____
_____
_____
_____
_____
_____
_____
_____

EMPLOYEE BUSINESS EXPENSES

Were you reimbursed for any business expenses incurred in connection with the performance of services for your employer? ☐ Yes ☐ No

If yes, answer the following questions:

A. Are you required to return reimbursement to the extent it exceeds expenses? ☐ Yes ☐ No

B. Are you required to submit itemized supporting documentation to your employer? ☐ Yes ☐ No

If you answered yes to the above questions and your reimbursement does not exceed your expenses, you are generally not required to report the reimbursement and expenses on your return. However, if your reimbursement does not equal your expenses, or if you answered no to questions A and/or B, report below the total reimbursements and expenses for the year. Certain other business expenses, even if not reimbursed, may also be deductible.

Employee business expenses   Amount

Auto rental   _____

Fares for airplanes, taxicabs, trains, etc.   _____

Lodging   _____

Meals and entertainment

    Reimbursements for meals and entertainment included in W-2   _____

    Reimbursements for meals and entertainment *not* included in W-2   _____

    Unreimbursed meals and entertainment   _____

Office-in-home expenses   _____

Professional dues   _____

Stationery, postage   _____

Telephone   _____

Other (describe) _____   _____

_____   _____

_____   _____

_____   _____

_____   _____

_____   _____

_____   _____

Total amount reimbursed (Do not include any amounts that were reported to you as wages in Box 10 of Form W-2.)   _____

Do you have substantiation (described below) for travel and entertainment expenses? ☐ Yes ☐ No

Information that must be available includes:

- Amounts spent
- Dates of departure and return for each trip and the number of days spent on business
- Dates of entertainment
- Places of entertainment or travel
- Dates and descriptions of business gifts
- Business purposes of the travel, entertainment, or business gifts
- Business relationships with the persons entertained or to whom gifts were made

AUTOMOBILE EXPENSES

Mileage information

	Car 1	Car 2
Number of months used for business during the year	_____	_____
Total mileage (include personal miles)	_____	_____
Business mileage portion of the total mileage	_____	_____
Commuting mileage portion of the total mileage	_____	_____

Total actual expenses (business and personal for months used for business)

	Car 1	Car 2
Gasoline, oil, lubrication, etc.	_____	_____
Repairs	_____	_____
Tires, car washes	_____	_____
Insurance	_____	_____
Taxes	_____	_____
License	_____	_____
Parking fees and tolls (business portion only)	_____	_____
Other (describe) _____	_____	_____
_____	_____	_____
_____	_____	_____
_____	_____	_____
_____	_____	_____
_____	_____	_____
_____	_____	_____
_____	_____	_____
_____	_____	_____
_____	_____	_____
_____	_____	_____
_____	_____	_____
_____	_____	_____
_____	_____	_____

Auto Depreciation

Year, make, model	Cost	Date acquired
Car 1 _____	_____	_____
Car 2 _____	_____	_____

Was either car used for commuting? ☐ Yes ☐ No

  If yes, what is the round-trip distance normally commuted? _____

If your employer provided you with an auto, was it available for personal use in off-hours? ☐ Yes ☐ No

Was another auto available for personal use? ☐ Yes ☐ No

Do you have adequate or sufficient evidence to justify the deduction for the vehicles? ☐ Yes ☐ No

  If yes, is the evidence written? ☐ Yes ☐ No

I | New York

1 | Changes in the Tax Law

This chapter summarizes and highlights recent personal income tax developments in New York.

Tax Rates

The tax cut that was scheduled for tax year 1992 was postponed until April 1, 1993. The 1991 rates will continue to be in effect for tax year 1992. The 1992 tax rates for state residents are as follows:

Married filing joint returns and qualifying widow(er)s

If your New York taxable income is:	The tax is:
Not over $11,000	4% of the New York taxable income
Over $11,000 but not over $16,000	$440 plus 5% of excess over $11,000
Over $16,000 but not over $22,000	$690 plus 6% of excess over $16,000
Over $22,000 but not over $26,000	$1,050 plus 7% of excess over $22,000
Over $26,000	$1,330 plus 7.875% of excess over $26,000

Heads of households

If your New York taxable income is:	The tax is:
Not over $7,500	4% of the New York taxable income
Over $7,500 but not over $11,000	$300 plus 5% of excess over $7,500
Over $11,000 but not over $15,000	$475 plus 6% of excess over $11,000
Over $15,000 but not over $17,000	$715 plus 7% of excess over $15,000
Over $17,000	$855 plus 7.875% of excess over $17,000

Single, married filing separately, and estates and trusts

If your New York taxable income is:	The tax is:
Not over $5,500	4% of the New York taxable income
Over $5,500 but not over $8,000	$220 plus 5% of excess over $5,500
Over $8,000 but not over $11,000	$345 plus 6% of excess over $8,000
Over $11,000 but not over $13,000	$525 plus 7% of excess over $11,000
Over $13,000	$665 plus 7.875% of excess over $13,000

Standard Deduction

Increases in the standard deduction amounts, scheduled for 1992, were postponed until the 1993 tax year. The 1991 standard deductions will continue in effect for 1992. These amounts are as follows:

Filing Status	Standard Deduction
Single dependent individuals	$2,800
Single (and you cannot be claimed as a dependent)	$6,000
Married filing joint return	$9,500
Married filing separate return	$4,750
Head of household (with qualifying person)	$7,000
Qualifying widow(er) with dependent child	$9,500

Estimated Payments

The requirements for making estimated tax payments were changed, effective January 1, 1992, to conform to recently enacted federal tax changes. The new rules require certain taxpayers to make estimated tax payments equal to at least 90% of their *current* year's expected tax liability. In the past, if your income increased substantially, you could avoid paying a penalty by making estimated tax payments based on your tax liability for the previous year.

You are subject to these new rules if:

- Your New York adjusted gross income increases by more than $40,000 over the prior year ($20,000 for married, filing separately);
- Your New York adjusted gross income is over $75,000 in the current year ($37,500 for married filing separately); or
- You made an estimated tax payment during any of the three preceding tax years or were assessed a penalty for failure to pay estimated tax for such years.

The following exceptions apply:

- Any gains from involuntary conversions or from the sale of a principal residence are not taken into account in determining whether your adjusted gross income increased by more than $40,000 or in computing your estimated tax liability for the current year;
- If you are an owner of a less than 10% interest in an S corporation or partnership (other than as a general partner), you may use your previous year's income from those entities to determine whether your adjusted gross income increased by more than $40,000, or in computing your estimated tax liability for the current year; and
- If your annualized adjusted gross income is estimated to be within the $40,000 and $75,000 threshold amounts (as previously described) for the first quarter of the new taxable year or for any other quarter, you may base your estimated tax payments on 100% of last year's tax liability.

2 | The Income Tax Return

Who Must File

The following individuals must file a New York State income tax return:

- Resident individuals;
- Nonresident individuals with income from New York sources;
- Part-year resident individuals;
- Partners with income from a partnership that does business in New York;
- Nonresident shareholders in a New York S corporation;
- A fiduciary of a trust or estate with New York source income; and
- A beneficiary of an estate or trust with New York source income.

New York Resident Individuals

New York requires any person who is a New York State resident and files a federal income tax return to file a New York State personal income return. However, even if you did not file a federal income tax return, you still have an obligation to file a New York State tax return if you meet *all* of the following criteria:

- You are single; and
- You can be claimed as a dependent on another taxpayer's federal return; and
- Your federal adjusted gross income, plus your New York additions, is more than $2,800.

If you cannot be claimed as a dependent, but your federal adjusted gross income, including New York additions, is more than $4,000, you must file a New York State income tax return.

Example
Jack is a 22-year-old student who lives with his parents in New York State. Jack has a part-time job in a doctor's office. In 1992, Jack earned a total of $3,200 at his part-time job. He has no other income. Jack is not required to file a federal income tax return. However, Jack is still required to file a New York State income tax return because his federal adjusted gross income, including his New York additions, is more than $2,800.

Your federal adjusted gross income is your total income after federal adjustments—such as deductions for IRAs, self-employment taxes, and Keogh retirement plans—have been made. It is the amount you reported on Line 31 of your federal income tax return. The New York additions to federal adjusted gross income are explained in Chapter 3, *Calculating Your Taxable Income*. Typically, they consist of certain types of federally tax-free interest income and state or local income tax refunds.

As a New York State resident, you will also be required to file a state income tax return if you would like to claim a refund of any New York State, New York City, or Yonkers taxes that were withheld from your paycheck or paid as estimated taxes. If you are subject to the New York State minimum income tax or the special tax on lump-sum distributions, you must file a state income tax return as well.

The New York State minimum income tax is based on your federal tax preference items, reduced by New York's specific deduction and some modifications. Federal preference items include items such as a charitable deduction of appreciated property, tax-exempt interest on certain private activity bonds, and accelerated depreciation or amortization on certain property.

Special tax rules apply to payments from qualified retirement plans or profit-sharing plans that qualify for treatment as lump-sum distributions. (For more information on the minimum income tax or the tax on lump-sum distributions, see the section on *Other Resident Taxes* in Chapter 4, *How to Figure Your Tax*.)

Example
Bob was unemployed for most of 1992 and was not eligible for unemployment benefits. In mid-November, Bob found a job at the local drug store. Bob's weekly salary is $250 before taxes are withheld. Bob is married and files any tax returns he is required to file jointly with his wife, Sue. At the end of 1992, Bob and Sue's federal adjusted gross income plus New York adjustments was approximately $1,500. Even though they are not required to file a New York income tax return because their total income was less than $4,000, Bob and Sue should still file a New York income tax return to claim a refund of any New York State or City income taxes that Bob's employer may have withheld.

TaxPlanner: If you are under age 18, over age 65, or a full-time student under age 25, you may not need to have New York taxes withheld from your paycheck. If you know that your New York income for the year will be less than the minimum amount applicable for your filing status and you had no New York income tax liability in the prior year, ask your employer for Form IT-2104-E, Certificate of Exemption from Withholding. If you complete this form and give it to your employer, he or she will not be required to withhold New York State, New York City, or Yonkers taxes from your paycheck.

The New York residency rules are discussed in detail later in this chapter.

Nonresidents and Part-Year Residents

New York requires any person who is a nonresident or a part-year resident of the state with income earned in New York to file a New York State nonresident income tax return (Form IT-203). You are subject to this requirement if you meet *any* of the following criteria:

- You have income earned from sources inside the State of New York, and the sum of your federal adjusted gross income plus your New York additions (items that must be added to federal gross income, according to New York State law) is more than your New York standard deduction (see table to follow); or
- You are claiming a refund of any New York State, New York City, or Yonkers income taxes that were withheld from your paycheck; or
- You are subject to the minimum income tax on federal tax preference items derived from or connected with New York sources; or
- You are subject to a separate tax on any lump-sum distributions derived from or connected with New York sources; or
- You incurred a net operating loss for New York State personal income tax purposes without incurring a similar net operating loss for federal income tax purposes.

(For more information on net operating losses, see the section on *Additions and Subtractions*, in Chapter 3.)

New York Standard Deduction. Your New York standard deduction is based on your filing status and your status as a dependent. The table below lists the available New York standard deductions, for purposes of deciding whether or not you will be required to file the nonresident tax return, Form IT-203. A full discussion of the deduction is contained in Chapter 3. Please note that the deduction is subject to change each year.

New York Standard Deduction Table
-Nonresidents and Part-Year Residents-

If your Filing Status is	Your New York Standard Deduction is
Single, and you can be claimed as a dependent on another taxpayer's federal return	$2,800
Single, and you cannot be claimed as a dependent on another taxpayer's federal return	$6,000
Married filing joint return	$9,500
Married filing separate returns	$4,750
Head of household	$7,000
Qualifying widow(er)	$9,500

Example

Mimi and Joe are married and file a joint federal return. From January until November, 1992, Mimi and Joe lived and worked in Iowa. In November, Mimi and Joe moved to New York City to begin new jobs in the Big Apple. From November through December, Mimi

and Joe earned a total of $8,400 in salary. Their total federal adjusted gross income for the year was $45,000. They had no New York additions. Mimi and Joe must file a Form IT-203 even though their New York source income is less than their New York standard deduction. They must compare their *federal* adjusted gross income for the year plus any New York additions to their New York standard deduction to determine whether or not they must file a New York State income tax return.

Nonresident Shareholder of S Corporation. In New York an S corporation shareholder assumes the obligation to pay tax individually on S corporation income. Therefore, if you are a nonresident shareholder of a New York S corporation, you must file a New York nonresident income tax return. You must include in your New York adjusted gross income your pro rata share of the S corporation's income, loss, and deduction.

Commuters to New York City or Yonkers

If you file a New York State resident income tax return, but you are not a New York City or Yonkers resident, you must pay a city nonresident earnings tax if you earned income from wages or self-employment in either city. If you and your spouse are nonresidents of New York City and Yonkers, and both of you receive income from either place, you must file separate city nonresident earnings tax forms. You cannot file either return jointly. These forms are due at the same time as your state return and must be attached to the state return. (For more details, see the sections, *Which Forms to Use* and *Where to File*, later in this chapter.)

Example

Sid and Lisa are married and live on Long Island. Both Sid and Lisa work in offices located in New York City. On or before April 15, when Sid and Lisa jointly file their New York State income tax return, each spouse must file his or her own Form NYC-203. However, they may receive a credit against their New York State income tax if they itemize their deductions.

Partnerships

Partnerships are not subject to the New York State personal income tax. However, individual partners may be subject to income tax on their shares of the partnership's income. If you are a partner in a partnership and a New York State resident, your share of the partnership's income is included in New York taxable income. If you are a nonresident partner in a partnership that has business activity in New York, New York can tax you on the partnership income derived from New York sources. If the partnership earns any income connected with a New York State activity or has a resident partner, it is required to file an information return (Form IT-204, Partnership Return). The items of income or loss, deduction, or adjustment shown by the partnership on its Form IT-204 are transferred to each partner's individual resident or nonresident return, based on the partner's share of the partnership's income.

If your partnership conducts a business in New York City, it may also be required to file a City of New York Unincorporated Business Tax Partnership Return (Form NYC-204). (See the section on *Unincorporated Business Tax* in Chapter 7.)

Partnerships doing business in Yonkers and having partners who are not Yonkers residents must file Form Y-204, City of Yonkers Nonresident Partner Allocation.

Estates and Trusts

New York looks to the decedent's residence to determine whether or not intangible personal property is subject to New York estate taxation. Intangible property includes items such as stock certificates, bonds, promissory notes, and contract rights. Real and personal property is taxed in New York only if it is actually located there.

Generally, estates and trusts that are subject to federal income tax are also subject to the New York State personal income tax. A fiduciary or trustee for an estate or trust must file a New York State Fiduciary Income Tax Return (Form IT-205). Each beneficiary of an estate or trust must include his or her share of the estate or trust income on his or her individual income tax return. Resident beneficiaries must include *all* income from the estate or trust. Nonresident beneficiaries only include income from New York sources.

When an Individual Dies

If a taxpayer dies before filing a New York State return, his or her executor, administrator, or spouse must file a return on behalf of the deceased. If the deceased person and his or her surviving spouse filed a joint federal return, a joint New York State return may be filed for 1992 and 1993. However, if the deceased person and his or her surviving spouse were nonresidents filing a joint federal return, and only one of them had New York income, the surviving spouse may choose whether to file jointly or separately for New York purposes. For two years following the date of death, the surviving spouse is allowed the filing status of "surviving spouse."

TaxAlert: If you are the spouse or close family member, but not a named executor or administrator of a deceased taxpayer's estate and you want to claim a tax refund for the deceased taxpayer, you may have to file a Survivor's Affidavit (Form AU-281.17).

Members of the Armed Forces

If you are a member of the Armed Forces and a New York State resident, the amount of your military pay that is subject to federal income tax is also subject to New York State income tax. This is true whether you are based in or out of New York. However, if your permanent home was outside New York State when you entered the military, your military pay is not subject to New York State tax. You will not have to file as a New York State resident merely because you have been assigned to duty in New York State and have established a place to live while on assigned duty.

TaxAlert: If you are a New York nonresident on assigned military duty, any income you or your spouse earn in New York, other than military pay, may be subject to New York State income tax. This may include your spouse's salary or any money you earn from an off-duty civilian job. So-called "passive" income, such as dividends, interest, or rental income from property outside New York, will not be subject to tax. (For more information, see the sections for *Nonresidents* in Chapter 3.)

Example

Ken and Linda are residents of the state of Washington. Ken enlisted in the army in Washington and was stationed at Fort Totten in New York. Ken and Linda moved to New York, where they live on the military base. Ken earned $42,000 in military pay. They had no other income. Because military personnel and their spouses are generally considered to remain residents of the state in which they resided when they enlisted, Ken and Linda are not considered New York residents and do not have to file a New York return. However, if Linda is employed by a New York company, any income she earns from this job must be reported on a New York nonresident return (Form IT-203).

Determining Residency/Domicile*

Are you a resident of New York State for personal income tax purposes? The answer to this question can have far-reaching personal income tax implications. The distinction between resident and nonresident status is crucial. Generally, residents are subject to income tax on both earned income such as wages, and unearned income such as dividends, interest, and capital gains. Nonresidents, by contrast, pay income tax only on income from New York sources.

Determining Residency

You may be subject to the New York income tax on residents even if you are not considered a resident for other purposes. For income tax purposes, you can be considered a resident even if you were not *domiciled* in New York. If you maintained a *permanent home* in New York during most of the taxable year, you will be treated as a resident taxpayer. In other words, if you meet either one of the following criteria, you will be required to file a New York resident tax return.

A. Your domicile is not New York but you maintain a permanent home in New York and spend more than *183 days* in New York during the year.

Exception: If you are a member of the Armed Forces, and your domicile is not New York State, you are not considered a resident under this definition.

B. Your domicile is New York, unless you satisfy *all three* of the conditions noted in *either* of the Exceptions that follow.

Exception: (All three conditions must be met.)

1. You did not maintain a permanent home in New York State at any time during the taxable year.
2. You maintained a permanent home outside New York State during the taxable year.
3. You spent 30 days or less in New York State during the taxable year.

Example

Vivian claims New York as her domicile. She maintains a permanent home in Pennsylvania and she does not maintain a permanent home in New York. During 1992, Vivian spent 29 days in New York. Vivian is not a New York resident for the 1992 tax year.

Exception: (All three conditions must be met.)

1. You were in a foreign country for at least 450 days during any period of 548 consecutive days.
2. You spent 90 days or less in New York State during this 548-day period, and your spouse (unless legally separated) or minor children spent 90 days or less in New York during this 548-day period in a permanent home that you maintained.

*Note: The same rules apply for New York City.

3. You were present in New York State for no more than a limited number of days during the nonresident portion of the year in which the 548-day period either began or ended.

This limit can best be illustrated by the following formula:

$$\frac{\text{Total number of days in the nonresident period}}{548}$$

$$\times \ 90 = \left\{ \begin{array}{l} \text{Maximum number of} \\ \text{days allowed in New York State} \\ \text{during the nonresident period} \end{array} \right.$$

Example

Mr. and Mrs. James Kirk have been domiciliaries of New York since 1985. Since 1985, they have lived in a cooperative apartment, which they own. On January 1, 1990, the Kirks left for the Orient. Due to their fancy for Chinese food, the Kirks remained in China for a year and a half. They returned to the United States on June 1, 1992. During 1992, the Kirks made their only return visit to New York and spent two weeks visiting friends. Mr. and Mrs. Kirk will not be considered New York domiciliaries because:

1. They were in a foreign country for at least 450 days out of a period of 548 consecutive days (January 1, 1990–June 1, 1992 = 882 days).
2. They spent fewer than 90 days in New York.
3. During the nonresident portion of the year in which the 548-day period ended, they were only present in New York for 14 days. Using the above formula,

$$\frac{152*}{548} \times 90 = 25 \text{ days},$$ shows that their number of days in residence is 11 days fewer than the maximum number of days allowed in New York State for the 1992 tax year.

*January 1, 1992–June 1, 1992 = 152 days.

Determining Domicile

Your domicile is the place that you intend to be your permanent residence. Once your domicile is established, it continues until you move to a new location with the genuine intention of making it your fixed and permanent home. If you move to a new location but intend to remain there only for a limited time, your domicile has not changed. This is true even though you may have sold or disposed of your former home. To abandon a New York domicile, you must establish a residence in a new locale with the intention of making it permanent.

If you assert a change of domicile, the burden of proof is upon *you* to show that the necessary intention existed. You must demonstrate by what the courts call "clear and convincing evidence," or proof that would leave no doubt in the mind of the person making the decision, that you intended to change your domicile. Your ties to the new residence must be permanent. In determining intention, your declarations will be given due weight, but they will not be conclusive if they are contradicted by your conduct. For example, registering to vote in another state is important. However, it does not necessarily prove you have changed your domicile, especially if other facts indicate that you registered merely to escape taxation as a New York resident. (See *Abandoning Your Domicile Checklist* on page NY-9.)

You can have only one domicile. If you have two or more homes, your domicile is the one that you regard as your permanent home. In determining an individual's intention, the length of time customarily spent at each location is important, but not necessarily conclusive. Other factors may include comparing the sizes of your two homes, their furnishings, and so forth.

EXCEPTION: Students are not usually considered residents of the state in which they attend school, as long as they have a permanent home somewhere else.

Example

Mr. Green, an executive of ABC Hardware, Inc. in Purchase, New York was temporarily assigned to the Boca Raton, Florida branch office for three years. His boss made it clear that Mr. Green was assigned to Boca Raton only "to get some experience in how the branch offices work" before returning to the executive fast track in Purchase. Mr. Green bought a home in Florida and enrolled his children in school there. Mrs. Green joined the local garden club. After his assignment in Florida was finished, Mr. Green returned to his job in New York. He remained a New York domiciliary and resident throughout the three-year period, because he always intended to return to New York.

Generally, domicile is the same for you and your spouse unless you are separated. If each of you has your own separate domicile, you will be treated separately for tax purposes even if you have no judgment or decree of separation. A child's domicile is ordinarily the same as that of his or her parents. When parents have separate domiciles, the domicile of the child is generally the domicile of the parent with whom the child lives for the major portion of the year.

Domicile is not dependent on citizenship. An immigrant who has permanently established his or her home in New York State is domiciled here, regardless of whether he or she has become a United States citizen or has applied for citizenship. A United States citizen, however, will not ordinarily be considered to have changed his or her domicile because of a temporary stay in a foreign country.

If you are a United States citizen domiciled in New York State and you go abroad because of an assignment by your employer or for study, research, or recreation, you do not lose your New York State domicile, unless it is clear that you do not intend to return to New York.

Example

Phil is an accountant who always wanted to be a pastry chef. He makes his permanent home in New York City, where he intends someday to open a trendy café. To further his lifelong dream, he takes a year's leave of absence to work as an apprentice in a restaurant in Paris. For tax purposes, Phil continues to be domiciled in New York.

There is no magic formula that you can follow to demonstrate that your domicile has changed. However, when tax authorities question your domicile, they consider carefully whether your place of habitation has the range of sentiment, feeling, and permanent association attached to it that people normally attach to their homes. They pay less attention to merely formal declarations of an individual concerning his or her domicile.

Permanent Home

A permanent home is a dwelling place that you maintain permanently, whether or not you own it. Your permanent home can be a dwelling owned or leased by your spouse, as well as yourself. Nevertheless, a camp or cottage that is not winterized or has no kitchen, such as a vacation bungalow, will not be considered a permanent home.

A home is not considered permanent if it is maintained only during a temporary stay for the accomplishment of a particular purpose.

Example

Lawrence is domiciled in California and is assigned to his employer's New York State office for a fixed and limited period of time. After that, he is expected to return to California. Lawrence takes an apartment in New York during this period and spends more than 183 days of the tax year in New York. Lawrence is not a New York resident, since his apartment in New York is not considered a permanent home. He could still, of course, be taxable as a nonresident.

TaxPlanner: If you are an employee or foreign national on temporary assignment in New York, ask your employer to draw up an employment contract for you. It should cover a specific period of time (generally, less than five years) and should state the purpose of your assignment. The contract should clearly establish that you will return to your previous office upon completing your assignment.

Days Within the Jurisdiction

The counting of days within New York in a taxable year is crucial under the tests for residency as set forth above. If you are not domiciled in New York but you maintain a permanent home in the state, you will be considered a nonresident for filing purposes only if you spend fewer than 184 days in New York. A New York domiciliary who does not maintain a permanent home in New York and maintains a permanent home elsewhere will be considered a nonresident if he spends 30 days or fewer in New York.

TaxPlanner: If you maintain a home in New York and spend time there, you may be interested to know what you can do to help substantiate your nonresident status. Many tax experts suggest keeping a detailed diary and receipts that can help you prove you were not in New York for more than 183 days. The diary must account for your whereabouts on all 365 days of the calendar year. If you were present inside New York for any part of a calendar day, whether for business or pleasure, you must count it as a day spent within New York. This is a vital point. It does not matter if you spent the night or a full 24-hour period in New York. Any part of a day constitutes a "day" for purposes of the residency test.

Exception: If you were in New York solely for the purpose of boarding a plane, ship, train, or bus for travel outside New York, you do not have to count that day as a day spent in New York. Similarly, you do not have to include a day on which you merely traveled through the state to an out-of-state destination. However, if you travel to the airport after spending the night in your New York apartment, it will count as a "day spent in New York."

Abandoning Domicile

To abandon a New York domicile, you must establish by clear and convincing evidence that you intend to remain permanently in the new jurisdiction.

Example

Charlie was born and raised in Queens, New York. After their divorce, Lucy, his former wife, continued to live in their home in Queens. Charlie moved into a one-bedroom apartment in Manhattan. Some years later, after spending several winters in Florida, Charlie moved into a large, luxurious, custom-built condominium in West Palm Beach. In addition, Charlie filed a declaration of domicile in Florida, established social ties there, raced horses for a hobby in Florida and, later, executed a Florida will.

Even though Charlie spent most of his time in Florida after moving into the condo, he continued to receive passive investment income from two New York businesses. He tried to buy Florida franchise rights from a popular restaurant chain, but this venture ultimately fell through. Occasionally he returned to New York, where he stayed at his apartment.

In this instance, Charlie had changed his domicile from New York to Florida. He was able to prove that he intended to return to his Florida condominium whenever he was away. He treated his condo, rather than the small apartment he continued to rent in New York, as his home. His active business interests as well as most of his personal and leisure interests centered around his life in Florida. Indeed, there was only a limited connection between Charlie and the State of New York.

TaxSaver: A declaration of domicile is generally a preprinted form on which you declare that you intend a particular location to be your domicile. This form must be signed by you and your spouse, if you are married. The declaration of domicile must be filed with your new state, if your new state permits this.

Example

Mr. and Mrs. Sacco purchased a home in Florida in 1981 and filed a declaration of Florida domicile in 1982. In 1983, they registered to vote in Florida. Their tax returns for 1982 through 1985 listed Boca Raton as their home address. They belonged to several tennis clubs in Florida, maintained a checking account there, and spent most of their time there.

Mr. Sacco had lived in New York for many years before moving to Boca Raton. He was the founder of a successful New York architectural firm and continued to make all major business decisions for the firm. This caused him to spend a significant amount of time in New York. The couple also kept their New York home.

Mr. and Mrs. Sacco did not change their domicile. Their formal declaration and ties with Florida were insufficient to overcome Mr. Sacco's involvement in his New York business and the couple's maintenance of a home in New York. The most significant evidence was Mr. Sacco's continued overall control of his New York business, a fact that made it difficult to prove that the couple had abandoned their New York domicile.

Abandoning Your Domicile Checklist

Each of the following items represents a step you can take to establish a change in domicile. Check off each action that you take. Keep this list with your permanent records. Remember that, in the final analysis, your domicile is a subjective matter, based on sentiment and associations. No one step on our checklist will automatically guarantee you success in changing your domicile for tax purposes.

1. _____ Purchase a home or an apartment in the new state. If you choose to rent instead, execute a lease for as long a term as possible and spend more time in the new state than you spend in New York.

2. _____ Even if you maintain living quarters in New York, move as much personal property as possible to your new home, especially things with personal or sentimental value—for example, your family pictures.

3. _____ Open a safe deposit box and transfer all valuables and pertinent papers which were held in your New York safe deposit box. Close your New York safe deposit box.

4. _____ Make new friends.

5. _____ If applicable, file resident income tax returns in the new state and claim any homestead rebates that may be available.

6. _____ Maintain important papers, such as birth certificates, Social Security cards, marriage and divorce records, and copies of tax returns, at the new location.

7. _____ Register to vote in the new locality, vote there in the next election, and notify the New York Board of Elections that you have relinquished the right to vote in New York.

8. _____ Obtain a driver's license in your new domicile and cancel your New York driver's license.

9. _____ Register your car in the new state and cancel your New York vehicle registration.

10. _____ Transfer major bank accounts to banks in the new state and close former accounts.

11. _____ Execute a new will and have it signed and probated in the new state. This means that the laws in your new state will be used to determine whether or not the will is valid.

12. _____ File a change of address form with the Internal Revenue Service. Show your new address on your next federal income tax return (Form 1040) and on all future federal tax returns. File them with the IRS office indicated for your new address.

13. _____ Send letters of resignation to all your former New York clubs and organizations.

14. _____ Join as many local organizations and clubs in your new state as possible.

15. _____ Do not renew any New York theater, ballet, or opera subscriptions. Any subscriptions that you have already paid for should be cancelled, if possible. Many organizations will accept donations of previously purchased tickets. If you donate your unwanted tickets, you may be able to include the donation in your charitable contributions for federal income tax purposes.

16. _____ Inform all credit card companies, frequent flyer affiliates, and similar organizations of your change of address.

17. _____ Change all your magazine subscriptions to your new address.

18. _____ If you continue to maintain a home or apartment in New York, arrange for your New York utility bills to be sent to your new address.

19. _____ Open charge accounts in your new state with local vendors, such as service stations, florists, bakeries, and department stores.

20. _____ Establish relationships with doctors and dentists in your new locality.

21. _____ Establish a relationship with a local stockbroker in your new state.

22. _____ Use a local insurance broker and utilize his or her services.

23. _____ Send change of address forms to everyone you can think of, including the Social Security Administration, New York doctors and dentists, and professional advisors. Notify your New York post office to forward all mail to your new home address.

24. _____ Apply for a new passport using your new address, even if your current passport has not expired.

25. _____ Cancel your subscriptions to cable television stations in New York and subscribe to pay channels in your new locality.

26. _____ Buy a cemetery plot in your new state and surrender any New York plot you may own.

27. _____ Arrange to have all federal income tax forms, such as Forms W-2 and 1099, mailed to your new address.

28. _____ File a declaration of domicile in the new state, if your new state permits this. Florida is among the states that provide for filing such a declaration.

TaxPlanner: Proving abandonment of your New York domicile is not easy. The New York Department of Taxation believes each case is unique. It bases each determination on the facts and circumstances of a particular taxpayer's case.

If your return is chosen for audit, the Department will generally send you a New York State personal income tax questionnaire to complete. This questionnaire is used to determine whether or not your status as a resident bears further review. Keep in mind that it is your responsibility to have available adequate records for examination. If you have a professional tax advisor, you may wish to consult him or her before completing the tax questionnaire. Be sure to answer the questionnaire truthfully.

The preceding *Abandoning Your Domicile Checklist* may be helpful in evaluating whether or not you have established a change in domicile and should be filing as a nonresident. However, it is not intended to be exhaustive. Each person's separate and unique situation determines his or her domicile.

Nonresidents

If you were not a resident of New York State but you received income from New York sources during the year, you may be subject to New York State personal income tax. If you moved into or out of New York during the tax year, you may be subject to tax as a part-year resident.

You are a nonresident for New York State purposes if you were not a resident for any part of the year. You are a part-year resident if you meet the definition of a resident or nonresident for only part of the year. See *Determining Residency/Domicile* earlier in this chapter if you need help determining whether you are a resident or not.

New York Source Income—Nonresidents
To calculate your New York source income as a nonresident, you must determine what portion of your federal adjusted gross income is attributable to activities conducted in New York. New York source income for a nonresident includes income, gains, losses, or deductions included in federal adjusted gross income from:

- Services performed in New York;
- A business, trade, profession, or occupation carried on in New York;
- Real or tangible personal property located in New York;
- Your share of a New York S corporation's income or loss apportioned to New York;
- Your share of income or loss from a partnership that is sourced to New York; and
- Your share of income from an estate or trust that is sourced to New York.

Exception: New York source income of a nonresident does not include income from the following sources, even if the item was included in your federal adjusted gross income:

- Annuities and pensions that meet the definition of an annuity, unless the annuity is employed in or used as an asset of a business, trade, profession, or occupation carried on in New York. (Annuities are discussed in detail in the section called *Special Problems in Attributing Income,* included in Chapter 3.);
- Interest, dividends, or gains from the sale or ex-

change of intangible personal property, unless the property was used in carrying on a business in New York;
- Compensation you received for active service in the United States military;
- Your income as a shareholder of a corporation that has not elected to be taxed as a New York S corporation;
- Compensation you received from an interstate rail carrier, interstate motor carrier, or an interstate motor private carrier for regularly assigned duties performed in more than one state;
- Your distributive or pro rata share, for federal income tax purposes, of income, gain, loss, or deduction from an insurance business doing business as a member of the New York Insurance Exchange; or
- Investment income of a resident estate or trust if the estate or trust is not involved with any business.

Example
Scott lives and works as a carpenter in Pennsylvania. During 1992 Scott had income from sources within both Pennsylvania and New York. The following chart shows how Scott, as a nonresident, should report his income to New York State:

Income Source	Income	Reportable to NYS
Carpenter services performed in Pennsylvania	$40,000	No
Carpenter services performed in New York	$10,000	Yes
Sale of land located in New York	$ 5,000	Yes
Estate income from New York sources	$ 2,000	Yes
Payment by U.S. Army for one week services in the Reserve Corps at Fort Hamilton, Brooklyn	$ 1,000	No
Dividends from an investment in stock of corporation located in New York City	$ 500	No

When he files his New York nonresident return, Scott will be required to report $17,000 of income ($10,000 + $5,000 + $2,000 = $17,000) as income from New York State sources.

New York Source Income—Part-Year Residents
If you are a part-year resident, you will be taxed on all income you receive while you are a New York State resident. You will also be taxed on all income from New York sources that you receive while a nonresident, plus any adjustments for special accruals. The total of these two amounts is your New York source income. (For a discussion of special accruals, see the section titled *Attributing Income to New York—Sourcing Rules* in Chapter 3.)

Part-year residents should use the *Part-Year Resident Income Allocation Worksheet*, reproduced in Chapter 3. This worksheet will assist you in determining your New York source income for the entire taxable year.

Married Taxpayer's Filing Status Election

Before 1991, New York State required a nonresident with no New York source income to file a joint New York State tax return with a nonresident spouse who earned income in New York if the couple filed a federal income tax return jointly. This practice has recently been ruled unconstitutional by New York courts. If you and your spouse are nonresidents who filed a joint federal tax return, but only one of you has New York source income, you may choose whether to file jointly or separately. If you filed jointly for previous tax years, you may be entitled to a refund.

Looking at the Options

If one spouse is a resident of New York and the other spouse is a nonresident or a part-year resident, you must file separate returns, regardless of how you filed for federal purposes, unless you both elect to file as New York residents. If you are both nonresidents with New York source income or part-year residents, your filing status for New York will generally be determined by how you filed for federal purposes. However, you may have some choice in the matter. Refer to the two charts on page NY-13 to see what your options are.

Special Rules for Members of the Armed Forces

If you are a member of the United States Armed Forces, your residency status depends upon where your permanent home, or domicile, is located. Generally, your domicile does not change if you are serving temporarily in the Armed Forces.

If your permanent home was in New York State when you entered the military, you are still considered a New York State resident, even if you are stationed in another country or state. You must file your return as a New York State resident. However, if you meet all three conditions under Group A or Group B in the residency section of this guide you may file as a nonresident. (See the section *Determining Residency* earlier in this chapter.)

Generally, if your permanent home was outside New York when you entered the Armed Forces, you will not be considered a New York State resident. This is true even if you are assigned to duty in New York State and your living quarters are on or near your base. Any income you receive from the military is not considered income from New York sources and is not reportable to New York. However, if you receive any other income from New York sources, you may be subject to tax as a nonresident. See *Who Must File* at the beginning of this chapter.

Example

Private Walter of the U.S. Army and his wife, Dorothy, are stationed at Fort Hamilton in Brooklyn, New York, and live on the military base. Walter and Dorothy are residents of Montana. To supplement his military pay, Walter works as a car mechanic on weekends at a local garage. Dorothy is an accountant for a New York City accounting firm. Walter's military income is not taxable by New York State. However, his income from the garage and Dorothy's income from her job will be taxable by New York State.

U.S. Nonresident Aliens

Nonresident aliens who are required to file a federal income tax return (Form 1040NR, U.S. Nonresident Alien Income Tax Return) may be required to file a New York nonresident return. The filing requirements are the same as for a nonresident or part-year resident.

Deceased Taxpayers

The executor, administrator, or spouse of a deceased nonresident or part-year resident of New York must file a New York State nonresident or part-year resident return if the taxpayer died before filing his or her tax return and would otherwise have been required to file the return.

Nonresidents of New York City

If you earned some or all of your income in New York City and you were not a resident, you must file Form NYC-203 (*City of New York Nonresident Earnings Tax Return*). This form is due at the same time as your New York State return and must be attached to the state return.

Form NYC-203 can only be filed on a separate basis. If you are married and both you and your spouse earn income in either city, you must each must file your own return.

Nonresidents of Yonkers

The rules for filing a Yonkers nonresident income tax return are exactly the same as those for filing a New York City nonresident return. However, instead of filing Form NYC-203, you file Form Y-203 (*City of Yonkers Nonresidents Earning Tax Return*).

Filing Status

Note: Except as noted, the following general rules for determining filing status detailed for New York are also applicable to New Jersey and Connecticut.

Introduction

Your choice of filing status determines the effective, or true, rate of tax you will pay on your income. It determines whether you are entitled to certain exemptions, credits, and deductions. Your filing status also dictates the amount of income you can earn before you are taxed at all. The basis for determining filing status is your marital and family situation.

In *nearly* all cases, you must use the same filing status on your state income tax return that you used on your federal income tax return or would have used for federal income tax purposes if you were not required to file a federal return.

The five possible filing statuses for federal and New York State purposes are:

1. Single;
2. Married filing jointly;
3. Married filing separately;
4. Head of household (with qualifying person); or
5. Qualifying widow(er) with dependent child.

Your filing status for the entire year is determined by your status on the last day of your tax year. For most individuals, that day is December 31.

TAXPLANNER: If events occur during the year to change your filing status, you may *not* file under a different filing status for each portion of the year. Your status at the end of the tax year governs your filing status for the entire year.

Different tax rates apply to different filing statuses. To determine your tax properly, be sure to use the column in the New York State tax table or tax rate schedule that corresponds with your filing status.

Single

Your filing status is *single* if you are unmarried, divorced under a final decree, or legally separated under a separate maintenance decree as of the last day of the taxable year, provided you do not qualify to file as either *head of household* or *qualifying widow(er) with dependent child* (see following discussion of each of these two cases). Generally, the effective tax rate for single taxpayers is higher than for married couples filing jointly, heads of household, or qualifying widow(ers).

Choose the *single* filing status by checking box 1 of Item A of Forms IT-100, IT-201, and IT-203 or Item B of Form IT-200. Single taxpayers are not entitled to take any personal exemption for themselves and are limited to a specified New York standard deduction, if not itemizing deductions. This standard deduction is reduced if you can be claimed as a dependent on someone else's return. (See the following section on *Personal Exemptions and Dependents* and the section on *Deductions* in Chapter 3.)

Married Filing Jointly

You may choose *married filing jointly* as your filing status if you are married and both you and your spouse agree to file a joint return. To select *married filing jointly* as your filing status, check box 2 in Item A of Forms IT-100, IT-201, and IT-203 or Item B of Form IT-200. Figure your tax by using the *Married Filing Jointly* column of the New York State tax table or tax rate schedule.

You are considered married for the whole year if on the last day of the tax year you are *either:*

1. Married and living with your spouse as husband and wife;
2. Married and living apart from your spouse, but not under a court-ordered decree of divorce or separate maintenance;
3. Separated under an interlocutory (not final) decree of divorce; *or*
4. Widowed during the year and you did not remarry before the close of the tax year. If you remarried during the year, you are considered married if you fall under one of the categories listed in 1, 2, or 3 above.

EXCEPTION: Certain married individuals living apart may be considered unmarried and eligible to file a separate return as *head of household*. You will not be eligible for this filing status unless your spouse was not a member of your household during the last six months of the tax year. Also, your household must be the principal home of a qualified dependent child. (See *Head of Household*, to follow, for more information.) If you qualify as *head of household* instead of *married filing separately*, you will receive a higher New York State standard deduction and household credit. Furthermore, you will be entitled to use the more favorable rates that apply to *head of household*.

TAXPLANNER: If you and your fiancé are planning a winter wedding and one of you has significantly more income than the other, December is generally a better choice than January if you want to save on taxes. This is because married taxpayers who file joint returns generally enjoy more favorable tax rates than single individuals. If both of you have similar incomes, you may wish to consider postponing the marriage until January. Because New York State uses a graduated tax rate structure, you will generally end up with less combined income taxed at the highest rate than you would if you filed a joint return. If you or your spouse were a nonresident of New York for any part of the year, you may also need to consider how a change of residence will affect your taxes.

TAXPLANNER: *When to get divorced.* December is generally a better month to separate from a tax standpoint if both spouses have similar incomes. This way, you can file separate returns for the entire year. Since New York State uses a graduated tax rate structure, you will generally end up with less combined income taxed at the highest rate than you would if you filed a joint return. If your combined New York adjusted gross income is more than $100,000, you may need to consider the impact of the itemized deduction adjustment. January is usually a better choice if one of you has considerably more income than the other and you *both* want to save on taxes.

Filing a Joint Return. When you file a joint return, all items of income and expense for you and your spouse are combined. You may file a joint return even if one spouse has no income or deductions. Married taxpayers who file joint returns enjoy more favorable tax rates than married taxpayers who file separately. In addition, you may qualify for certain tax benefits, such as the New York State child and dependent care credit, that are not available to people with other filing statuses.

If you are filing a joint return, both you and your spouse *must* use the same accounting period, although you may use different accounting methods. Your *accounting period* is the period that you will use for tax reporting purposes—usually a calendar year. Your *accounting method* is the manner in which you keep track of your income and expenses and can be either the cash or the accrual method.

TAXALERT: If you file a joint return, both you and your spouse may be held jointly and individually liable for the entire tax due plus any interest or penalty due on your joint return.

TAXALERT: In certain cases, New York State has the authority to garnish any refund that may be due to you in order to satisfy debts such as a defaulted student loan or past-due child support. If you do not want to apply your part of a refund to debts your spouse may have incurred, complete Form IT-280, *Nonobligated Spouse Allocation* and attach the *original* to your return. Once you have filed your return, you cannot file an amended return to disclaim your spouse's debts. However, you will be notified if your refund is being applied against your spouse's debt. If you receive such a notice, you will then have ten days from the date of the notice to file Form IT-280.

If your spouse died during the year and you filed a joint federal income tax return, you can still file a joint New York State return. If you are claiming a refund for a deceased taxpayer and are not an executor or administrator of the person's estate, you may have to file Form AU-281.17, Survivor's Affidavit.

If you obtain a court decree of annulment, you must file as either *single* or *head of household* for that year. If you are required by federal law to file amended returns adjusting your filing status for all open tax years affected by the annulment, you must also file amended New York State returns within 90 days from the date you amend your federal return. (See Chapter 6, *Refunds (Amended Returns)*.)

Signing a Joint Return. In order for a joint return to be processed, you and your spouse must both sign it. If your spouse is away from home, you should prepare the return, sign it, and send it to your spouse to sign so that it can be filed on time. If your spouse cannot sign the joint return for any reason, you may sign it on behalf of your spouse if he or she gives you a valid Power of Attorney. This is a legal document giving you permission to act for your spouse. Your lawyer or accountant should be able to supply you with the proper form and instructions. Attach the Power of Attorney to your return. You can use Form DTF-14, Power of Attorney (Individual).

Married Filing Separately

Married taxpayers may choose *married filing separately* as their filing status by checking Box 3 of Item B on Form IT-200 or Item A of Forms IT-100, IT-201, or IT-203. You may prefer this method if you want to be responsible for your own tax or wish to avoid interest and penalties that your spouse may incur. You may be required to use this filing status if your spouse does not agree to file a joint return.

Unless you are *required* to file separately, you should figure your tax under both methods to make sure you are using the method that results in the lower combined tax. When you are married and file a separate New York return, you must compute your New York return using only *your own* items of income and deductions, computed as if you had filed separate federal returns. Generally, you will pay a greater total combined tax by filing separate returns. This is because there is a higher effective tax rate for married persons filing separately.

If you live apart and meet certain tests, you may be *considered unmarried* for federal and state tax purposes and file as *head of household* even though you are not divorced or legally separated. (See *Head of Household*, to follow, for more information.)

If you file as *married filing separately*, you must write your spouse's full name and Social Security number in the spaces provided. Figure your tax by using the *Married Filing Separately* column of the New York State tax table or tax rate schedule.

Joint vs. Separate Returns for Married Taxpayers

Separate Federal Return. If a husband and wife filed separate federal returns, each spouse having New York source income must file a separate New York State return.

Joint Federal Return. If a husband and wife filed a joint federal return, they must file a joint New York State return if:

- Both the husband and wife are nonresidents and *both* have New York source income; or
- One spouse is a part-year resident and the other is a nonresident with New York source income; or
- Both spouses are part-year residents.

EXCEPTIONS: If a husband and wife filed a joint federal return, each spouse may file a *separate* New York State *nonresident* return (Form IT-203) if:

- Both spouses are nonresidents but only one has New York source income; or
- One spouse is a part-year resident and the other is a nonresident with *no* New York source income.

If you and your spouse filed a joint return for federal purposes and one of you is a New York State resident and the other is a nonresident or part-year resident, you may file separate New York State returns using *married filing separately* as your filing status. The New York State resident spouse may file either Form IT-200 or IT-201; the nonresident must use Form IT-203 if he or she is required to file a New York return. However, you may both elect to file a joint New York State *resident* return, using Filing Status 2 on either Form IT-200 or Form IT-201.

If you are eligible to elect a filing status, you should compute your tax under the different options in order to determine which would be more advantageous. Generally, it is more favorable to file separate New York State returns if the spouse with the lower federal income has New York source income. If the spouse with the higher federal adjusted gross income has New York source income or if the other spouse has no federal adjusted gross income, you may pay less tax if you file a joint return.

Both Spouses Nonresident

Federal Filing Status	New York Source Income Received by	New York Filing Status
Separate	Both Spouses	Separate
Joint	Both Spouses	Joint
Separate	One Spouse	Separate
Joint	One Spouse	**Choose Joint or Separate**

One Spouse Nonresident and the Other One Part-Year Resident

Federal Filing Status	Nonresident Spouse Receives New York Source Income	New York Filing Status
Separate	Yes	Separate
Joint	Yes	Joint
Separate	No	Separate
Joint	No	**Choose Joint or Separate**

TAXSAVER: If your New York filing status is *highlighted* in the chart above, compute the tax due under both filing statuses to determine which status results in the lower tax. Indicate that filing status on your return.

TAXALERT: Because of a recent court ruling, New York State can no longer require a nonresident with no New York State source income to file a joint New York State nonresident tax return solely because that person's nonresident spouse earned New York income and the couple filed a joint federal income tax return. This decision applies to 1991 and future years as well as previous tax years that are still open under the statute of limitations. (See the section, *Statute of Limitations*, in Chapter 8.) If you would have paid less tax if you had filed a separate New York State nonresident return in any of the three preceding tax years, you should file an amended Form IT-203 to claim a refund for that tax year.

Head of Household

In order to qualify as *head of household*, you cannot be married or be a surviving spouse at the close of the tax year. If you are a widow or widower, you may not use the *head of household* rates for tax years in which you are eligible to use the joint tax rates under *qualifying widow(er)*. In addition, you must maintain as your home a household which, for more than one-half of the tax year, is the principal home of one or more of the following:

1. A son or daughter, a stepchild, a grandchild, an adopted child, or a foster child. If any such person is married on the last day of the tax year, you must qualify to claim him or her as a dependent. If the person is unmarried, he or she does not need to qualify as your dependent in order for you to use the head of household filing status;
2. Any other relative eligible to be claimed as a dependent, except those eligible to be claimed by virtue of a multiple support agreement.

EXCEPTIONS: It is still possible for you to qualify as *head of household* if your dependent parent lives elsewhere, such as in a rest home or home for the aged, provided you maintain your parent's household.

You are considered to "maintain a household" only if you furnish, with funds that can be traced to you, more than one-half of the cost of maintaining a home during the year. Costs of maintaining a household include property taxes, mortgage interest, rent, utility charges, upkeep and repairs, property insurance, domestic help, and food consumed on the premises. They do not include the cost of clothing, education, medical treatment, vacations, life insurance, or transportation.

A married taxpayer will be considered unmarried and eligible for *head of household* status if his or her spouse was not a member of the household for the last six months of the tax year and if the household is the principal home of a dependent child.

To choose *head of household* as your filing status, check either Box 3 in Item A on Form IT-100 or Box 4 in Item B of Form IT-200 or Item A of Forms IT-201 and IT-203. Figure your tax by using the column labeled *Head of Household* in the New York State tax tables or tax schedule.

Qualifying Widow(er) with Dependent Child

If you are a surviving spouse with a dependent child, you may be able to use *qualifying widow(er) with dependent child* as your filing status in the next two years, provided you have not remarried. This filing status entitles you to use joint return tax rates, the highest standard deduction amount (provided you do not itemize), and other deductions and credits for the two years following the death of your spouse.

In order to qualify for this filing status, you must have a child, stepchild, adopted child, or foster child who qualifies as your dependent for the tax year and you must have paid more than half the cost of maintaining a home in which both you and the child resided for the *entire* year, except for temporary absences.

Death or Birth. If the dependent who qualifies you to file using *qualifying widow(er) with dependent child* is born or dies during the year, you may still be able to claim that filing status. You must, however, have provided for more than half of the costs of maintaining a home that was the dependent's main home during the entire part of the year he or she was alive.

To select *qualifying widow(er) with dependent child* as your filing status, check either Box 4 in Item A on Form IT-100 or Box 5 in Item B on Form IT-200 or Item A on Forms IT-201 or IT-203. Figure your tax by using the *Qualifying Widow(er)* column of the New York State tax tables or tax schedules.

Summary of Filing Status Options

Marital Status	Filing Status
Single (including divorced and legally separated at end of year)	Single or Head of household
Married with a child and living apart from your spouse during the last six months of the year	Head of household
Married and living with your spouse at the end of the year (or on the date your spouse died)	Married, joint return or Married, separate return
Married, *not* living with your spouse at the end of the year (or on the date your spouse died)	Married, separate return or Married, joint return
Widowed before this year and not remarried during the year	Single or Head of household or Qualifying widow(er) with dependent child

Filing Status—New York City and Yonkers

Your New York City *resident* filing status is the same as your filing status for New York State purposes. Filing statuses do not apply for purposes of the Yonkers resident income tax surcharge. Use the corresponding column to the filing status you used to determine your New York State tax liability in order to find the amount of your tax in the *City of New York Tax Table* or *Tax Schedule*.

Filing statuses do not apply for purposes of the New York City and Yonkers nonresident earnings taxes.

TaxAlert: If you and your spouse are filing a joint resident or nonresident New York State income tax return, you must each file a *separate* NYC-203 to report any earnings in New York City.

Personal Exemptions and Dependents

The use of exemptions is based in part on the concept that a taxpayer with very little income should be left with enough money after taxes to support self and family. New York only allows exemptions for your dependents. Personal exemptions for you, and for your spouse if you are married, cannot be claimed on your New York return. Both resident and nonresident filers are allowed dependent exemptions. New York follows federal rules concerning who qualifies as a dependent.

Who is a Dependent?

For federal purposes, a person is considered your dependent if, with respect to that person, you meet the following five tests. *All* of the tests must be met:

1. Support Test;
2. Member of Household or Relationship Test;

3. Gross Income Test;
4. Joint Return Test; and
5. Citizenship Test.

Support Test

To meet this test, you must furnish over one-half of the total support of an individual during the calendar year. Support includes:

- Food and lodging;
- Clothing;
- Education;
- Medical expenses;
- Transportation;
- Child care; and
- Payments to an institution for the care of an elderly parent.

Support does not include:

- Federal, state, and local income taxes paid by persons from their own income;
- Social Security and Medicare taxes paid by persons from their own income;
- Life insurance premiums;
- Funeral expenses; or
- Scholarships received by your child if he or she is a full-time student.

You can calculate whether or not you have provided more than half of the support of a person by comparing the amount you contributed to that person's support with the entire amount of support he or she received from all sources. This amount includes the person's own funds used for support.

Example

Edward Newman contributed $4,500 toward the support of his daughter, Scout, a full-time student. Scout earned $3,500 from a part-time job, which she spent meeting her college expenses. She also received a $5,000 scholarship to attend the local university. Since Edward paid $4,500 out of total support of $8,000, or more than 50%, he may claim Scout as a dependent. The $5,000 scholarship is not included as support for purposes of this test.

You may not include as your contribution to support any part of your child's own wages, even if you pay the wages.

A person's own funds are not considered support unless they are actually spent for support.

Example

Thomas contributed $2,500 toward his mother's support during the year. His mother received $2,400 in pension income and $300 in interest. She paid $1,800 for lodging, $400 for medical expenses, $300 for life insurance premiums, and $200 for clothing. The total amount that Thomas's mother contributed toward her own support is calculated in the following manner:

Mother's Own Support	
Lodging	$1,800
Medical expenses	400
Clothing	+ 200
	$2,400

Even though Thomas's mother received a total of $2,700, she spent only $2,400 of her own income to support herself. Life insurance premiums are not support items. Since Thomas spent $2,500 for her support and she received no other support, he has provided more than half her support.

The amount you spend, not the length of time over which you spend it, determines whether you provide more than half of the support. You may still be able to claim someone as a dependent even though you provided support for less than half a year.

TaxPlanner: You should maintain adequate records for expenditures made to support anyone you intend to claim as an exemption. This is important, since the dependent exemption may be questioned by the IRS.

In figuring total income available for support, include tax-exempt income, savings, and borrowed amounts. Tax-exempt income includes certain Social Security benefits, welfare benefits, nontaxable life insurance proceeds, Armed Forces family allotments, and tax-exempt interest.

Example

Ms. Brown contributed $3,000 toward her father's support during the year. Her father received $2,800 of nontaxable Social Security benefits and $300 of dividend income. All of these amounts were used for his support during the year. Since the Social Security payments are included in the determination of total support, Ms. Brown cannot claim her father as a dependent. She did not provide more than half of his total support of $6,100.

Generally, the amount of an item of support is the amount spent in providing that item. Expenses that are not directly related to a specific member of a household must be prorated among all its members. If you are calculating the cost of lodging someone, use the fair rental value of the lodging you provide, even if you own your home. Fair rental value is the amount you could reasonably expect to receive from an unrelated party for the same kind of lodging.

Example

Mr. White's parents live with him in a household that includes his spouse, and their three children. The fair rental value of his parent's share of lodging is $4,000 a year. This includes furnishings and utilities. Mr. White's father receives a nontaxable pension of $8,400, which he spends equally to support himself and his wife. The total food expense for the household of seven people is $9,800. The utility bills for the household are $1,400. Mr. White's mother incurred medical expenses of $1,000 during the year, which Mr. White paid. The total support provided for Mr. White's parents is calculated in the following manner:

	Father	Mother
Fair rental value of lodging	$2,000	$2,000
Pension	4,200	4,200
Share of food (1/7 of $9,800)	1,400	1,400
Medical expenses	+ 0	+1,000
	$7,600	$8,600

The dependency status of each parent must be computed separately, since Mr. White provided different amounts of support to each parent. He provided only $3,400 of his father's total support of $7,600—less than half. He provided $4,400 of his mother's total support of $8,600—more than half. Mr. White can claim his mother as a dependent, but not his father.

Capital expenditures such as furniture, appliances, and automobiles may be included in total support, under certain circumstances.

Example

Frank paid $10,000 for an automobile and registered it in his own name. Frank's 16-year-old son shares the automobile equally with Frank. Since Frank did not give the automobile to his son, he cannot include the cost of the car in his son's support. However, the out-of-pocket operating expenses spent for the benefit of his son can be included in the son's support.

TaxSaver: If you contribute support to another household where more than one person may qualify as your dependent, you may designate the individual for whom your support is intended. This may enable you to claim a dependency exemption which would otherwise be lost. You should designate your dependent in writing. If there is no written documentation, the IRS will generally prorate the money contributed among all members of the household.

Example

Terry provided $8,000 of support for his parents in 1992. During the year, his parents, who live in their own condominium, spent $10,000 for their joint support. Terry established in writing that $6,000 of the support he provided was for his father and the remaining $2,000 for his mother. Terry may claim his father, but not his mother, as a dependent. If Terry had not designated $6,000 of his support to his father, he would not have been able to claim either parent as a dependent for 1992.

Multiple Support Agreement

One exception to the support test is provided by a multiple support agreement. A multiple support agreement allows one of a group of individuals who *together* provide more than 50% of a person's support to claim an exemption even though no one individual provides more than half of the support. Any individual who contributed more than 10% of the person's support may claim the exemption. However, only *one* individual may claim the exemption. Each of the others who contributed more than 10% must sign a written statement, federal Form 2120, Multiple Support Declaration, agreeing not to claim the exemption for the year. The statements must be filed with the income tax return of the individual claiming the exemption.

Support Test for Divorced or Separated Parents

A second exception to the more than 50% support requirement may occur with respect to a child of parents who are divorced or separated. The parent who has custody of the child for the greater part of the year is generally treated as the parent who provides more than half of the child's support. It does not matter whether or not that parent actually provided more than half of the support. However, under rules that went into effect after 1984, the noncustodial parent can

claim the child as a dependent if the custodial parent agrees not to claim the child.

Example

John and Mary obtained a divorce decree in 1990. Mary has custody of their three children. John provides over half of the support for each child. Unless the divorce decree or other agreement specifically states that John can claim the exemption, Mary is entitled to claim exemptions for the children in 1992.

For a noncustodial parent to claim the exemption, the custodial parent must complete federal Form 8332, Release of Claim to Exemption for Child of Divorced or Separated Parents, or a similar statement. The exemption may be released for a single year, a number of specified years, or for all future years. The noncustodial parent must attach the form or statement to his or her return. Form 8332 (or similar statement) is not required if there is a pre-1985 agreement that allows the noncustodial parent to claim the exemption and the noncustodial parent provides at least $600 of support for each child.

Member of Household or Relationship Test

A person you wish to claim as a dependent must be either related to you or live with you for the entire year as a member of your household. A spouse cannot be claimed as a dependent. For an unrelated person to qualify, he or she must live with you at your principal home. Otherwise, an unrelated person does not qualify, even if you maintained a separate house for him or her for the entire year.

You are considered to occupy the same household even if you or the other person is temporarily absent because of special circumstances. Such circumstances include:

- Illness;
- Education;
- Business;
- Vacation; or
- Military service.

You may claim the following individuals as dependents even if they are not members of your household or do not live with you:

- Child, grandchild, great grandchild (a legally adopted child is treated as a natural child);
- Stepchild;
- Brother, sister, stepbrother, stepsister;
- Parents, grandparents;
- Stepfather or stepmother;
- Uncle or aunt;
- Nephew or niece; and
- Father-in-law, mother-in-law, brother-in-law, sister-in-law, son-in-law, daughter-in-law.

The above relationships, once established by marriage, are not ended by death or divorce.

The following individuals can qualify as dependents if they live with you as a member of your household for the entire year:

- Cousin; and
- Foster child or adult.

TaxAlert: Before a child is legally adopted, he or she is considered your child if the child was a member of your household and was placed by an authorized adoption agency. If the child was not placed by an authorized agency, he or she must have been a member of your household for the entire year to meet this test.

Example

Ted and Kathy are married. Emily, a three-year-old orphan, was placed in their home by an authorized adoption agency in September of 1992. She was a member of the household for the remainder of the year. Ted and Kathy are unable to adopt Emily legally until 1993. Emily may be claimed as a dependent for 1992, since she was placed by an authorized agency.

Joint Return. If you and your spouse file a joint return, you do not need to show that a dependent is related to both of you. You also do not need to show that a dependent is related to the spouse who provides support.

Gross Income Test

Your dependent's gross income must be less than the exemption amount for you to claim him or her as a dependent. This test does not apply if the individual is your child and is under 19 or is a full-time student under the age of 24.

A child is defined as a son, daughter, stepson, stepdaughter, a legally adopted child, or a child who was placed by an authorized adoption agency for legal adoption. A foster child is also considered a child if he or she was a member of your household for the entire year.

Gross income is all income in the form of money, property, and services that is not exempt from tax. This includes gross receipts from rental property, a partner's share of gross partnership income, all unemployment compensation, gross profit from self-employment, gain from the sale of stock or real estate, and the gain on the sale of a personal residence even if deferred or partially exempt.

Example

Ellen's mother retired two years ago and receives over half her support from Ellen. Ellen's mother owns rental property and receives annual gross rental income of $4,500 before expenses. After expenses, her net rental income is $1,500. Ellen may not claim her mother as a dependent. Her mother's gross rental income exceeds the $2,150 federal exemption amount.

Gross income does not include tax-exempt income, such as Social Security payments, tax-free municipal bond interest, and gift received from others.

TAXSAVER: Since tax-free municipal bond interest is not included in gross income, a person who can possibly be claimed as a dependent may be better off holding municipal bonds rather than taxable bonds. However, saving taxes is only one of many factors to consider in making an investment decision.

The gross income test does not apply to a child who is under the age of 19 at the end of the year. If all other dependency tests are met, your child may have any amount of income and still be claimed as your dependent.

Example

Jacob, who is 18, earned $2,800 during the year. His father provided more than half his support. Jacob can be claimed as a dependent by his father. The gross income test does not apply and all other dependency tests are met.

If your child is under 24 years of age at the end of the calendar year and is a student, the gross income test does not apply. The other dependency tests must still be met.

To qualify as a student, your child must fall into one of the categories listed below, during some part of each of five months during the calendar year; the months do not have to be consecutive:

- A full-time student at a school that has a regularly enrolled body of students who attend, a regular teaching staff, and a course of study, or
- A student taking a full-time training course on a farm. The course must be given by a school or a state, county, or local government and have a regularly enrolled body of students, and a regular teaching staff.

Elementary schools, junior and senior high schools, colleges, universities, and technical, trade, and mechanical schools meet the definition of a "school." On-the-job training courses, correspondence schools, and night schools are not considered schools.

Joint Return Test

If your dependent files a joint return with his or her spouse, you generally are not allowed an exemption. This is true even if the other dependency tests are met.

Example

Mr. Walker supported his daughter, Laura, for the entire year while her husband was in the Navy. Laura and her husband file a joint return. Mr. Walker cannot claim his daughter as a dependent even though the other dependency tests are met.

Citizenship Test

To qualify as your dependent, an individual must be either a U.S. citizen, resident, or national, or a resident of Canada or Mexico for some part of the calendar year in which your tax year began. Children usually are considered citizens or residents of their parent's country.

Your child may be a U.S. citizen if you are a U.S. citizen even though your child was born in a foreign country and the other parent is a nonresident alien. You must have lived in the U.S. for at least ten years before the child's birth and for at least five years after the age 14. Assuming the other dependency tests are met, you can claim the exemption, even if the child lives abroad with the nonresident alien parent.

If you are a U.S. citizen and have legally adopted a child who is not a U.S. citizen or resident, you may still claim the exemption. Your child must be a member of your household for the entire year and your home must be the child's main home.

Foreign exchange students placed in American homes for a temporary period may generally not be claimed as dependents. They are generally not U.S. residents and do not meet the citizenship test.

How To Figure Your Dependent Exemption

As a resident or a nonresident of New York, you are entitled to a $1,000 exemption for each dependent that you claimed on your federal return. To compute your number of allowable dependent exemptions, you must subtract your personal exemptions from your total federal exemptions. Use the following worksheet to calculate your dependent exemption if you filed federal Form 1040 or 1040A. If you did not have to file a federal return, enter on lines a and b the number of exemptions that would have been allowed for federal income tax purposes.

Dependent Exemption Worksheet

a. Enter the number of exemptions claimed on federal Form 1040A or 1040, line 6e .... a. _____

b. Enter the total number of boxes checked on federal Form 1040A or 1040, line 6a and line 6b .... b. _____

c. Subtract line b from a. This is the number of your dependent exemptions. Enter this number in the white space on Form IT-200, line 14, or Form IT-201, line 49, or Form IT-203, line 49 .... c. _____

Note: If you filed federal Form 1040EZ, you cannot claim any dependent exemptions.

New York State Tax Forms

Which Forms to Use

This section contains brief descriptions of the basic forms used to file tax returns in New York State. It also describes other forms often required to be attached to the basic forms. Knowing which forms you need can be a great help at filing time.

Form IT-100. The simplest form you can file as a New York State resident is Form IT-100. This form, and the one discussed in the next section, Form IT-200, are often referred to as "short forms." They are similar to federal Form 1040EZ. Compared to the standard New York resident return, Form IT-201, they are shorter and simpler.

The biggest advantage of Form IT-100 is that you do not have to figure out the amount of tax you owe. You merely list your exemptions, income, IRA deduction, federal tax credit for child or dependent care, and any state and city taxes withheld. The Department of Taxation will figure out the amount of tax you owe or the refund you are due. If you owe any additional taxes, they will send you a statement showing how the tax liability was calculated, along with a bill for the tax. The bill must be paid within ten days of receipt or by April 15th, whichever is later. If you are due a refund, they will send you a check for the refund, along with a statement showing how the refund was determined.

While having the state do the number-crunching for you has broad appeal, you must meet certain criteria in order to be eligible to file an IT-100. Most taxpayers will be unable to file this form. You may file Form IT-100 only if *all* of the following statements are true:

1. You have income *only* from wages, salaries, tips, taxable interest, dividends, and unemployment compensation.
2. You were a New York State resident for the entire year.
3. You file your return no later than April 15th.

You *cannot file Form IT-100* if *any* of the following statements are true:

1. You have requested an extension of time to file.
2. You are married and filing separately.
3. You have pension, annuity income, Social Security benefits, or IRA distributions included in your federal adjusted gross income.
4. You itemized your deductions on your federal return and want to itemize on your New York return.

5. You were a part-year resident of New York City or Yonkers.
6. You earned wages or self-employment income in New York City or Yonkers and were *not a resident* of the city in which you worked.
7. You wish to claim the Real Property Tax Credit on Form IT-214.
8. You have made estimated tax payments to New York State, New York City, or Yonkers.
9. You are a member of the New York State or New York City retirement system (Tier III and Tier IV members) or you are an employee of the State University of New York or the City University of New York who is a member of TIAA/CREF, or a New York City uniformed force member.
10. You wish to claim any New York State tax credits *other than* the child and dependent care credit and household credit. (For an explanation of tax credits, see Chapter 3.)
11. You wish to disclaim your spouse's debt.

Example

Sally is a civil engineer who earned $28,000 last year from her job and $200 of interest from her savings account. She has no other source of income. Sally lives and works in Nassau County, Long Island. Sally is eligible to file Form IT-100 if she files her return by April 15th.

Example

Jeff is a bond broker who works on Wall Street and earns $80,000 per year. Jeff sold some of his IBM stock during the year at a substantial gain. At the advice of his accountant, Jeff made an estimated tax payment of $500 to New York State to cover the additional taxes he will owe as a result of the profit from his stock sale. Jeff *cannot* file Form IT-100 because gains and losses from sales of stock cannot be reported on Form IT-100. In addition, the estimated tax payment Jeff made precludes him from filing Form IT-100. Jeff must file Form IT-201 instead.

TAXPLANNER: Form IT-100 is simple enough for teenagers to complete themselves and will relieve you of the burden of filling out your teenager's tax forms, in addition to your own. However, even if you must fill out the forms for your children, Form IT-100 is a great timesaver.

Form IT-200. New York State provides another short form, Form IT-200, which has broader eligibility criteria than Form IT-100, but is still somewhat restricted in use. Unlike Form IT-100, this form may be filed by couples claiming *married filing separately* status. If you are ineligible, or don't wish to file Form IT-100, filing Form IT-200 may be a desirable alternative. You can file Form IT-200 if you meet *all* of the following criteria:

1. Your taxable income is less than $65,000.
2. You claimed a standard deduction for federal purposes *or* your New York itemized deductions do not exceed the New York standard deduction for your filing status.
3. You received income *only* from wages, interest, dividends, taxable refunds of state and local income taxes, or unemployment compensation.

4. Your adjustments to income are for IRA deductions, public employee 414(h) retirement contributions, interest income on United States government bonds, or taxable refunds of state and local income taxes. (Adjustments to New York State income are discussed in Chapter 3.)

5. You did not pay income taxes to any other states or localities except for New York City or Yonkers.

6. You are not a part-year resident of New York City or Yonkers.

Eligibility to File New York State Form IT-200: Figuring Which Deduction is Larger

a. Total itemized deductions from federal Schedule A, line 26....................................... a. _____

b. State, local, and foreign income taxes from federal Schedule A, lines 5 and 7................... b. _____

c. Subtract line b from line a.............................. c. _____

d. Enter the standard deduction that applies to your filing status:
   • Single and can be claimed as a dependent $2,800
   • Single and cannot be claimed as a dependent...................................... 6,000
   • Married filing joint return 9,500
   • Married filing separate return......... 4,750
   • Head of household 7,000
   • Qualifying widow(er)...................... 9,500   d. _____

If the amount on line d is larger than on line c, you will be eligible to file Form IT-200, provided that you meet the other criteria. If the amount on line c is larger than on line d, you must file Form IT-201. (See *Personal Exemptions and Dependents* earlier in this chapter for further information.)

Form IT-201. Even though you may meet the criteria listed above, you *must file Form IT-201* if you meet any of the following criteria:

1. You made estimated tax payments to New York State, New York City, or Yonkers.

2. You filed a request for extension of time to file a return on Form IT-370.

3. You do not report your income on a calendar-year basis.

4. You intend to claim New York State tax credits *other than* the child and dependent care credit, the household credit, and the real property tax credit.

5. You are subject to any of the following taxes or adjustments:
   a. minimum income tax,
   b. separate tax on lump-sum distributions,
   c. addback of investment credit on early dispositions of eligible property,
   d. addback of Economic Development Zone (EDZ) investment tax credit,
   e. addback of resident credit for taxes paid to a province of Canada.

6. You have IRA distributions, pension or annuity income, or Social Security benefits included in your federal adjusted gross income.

7. You want to apply any current year's overpayment as a credit against the succeeding year's tax.

8. You were a New York State resident for all of the year, but were a part-year resident of the City of New York or Yonkers. If you were a part-year resident of either city, you must complete Form IT-360.1 and attach it to Form IT-201.

Form IT-201 is the standard resident income tax form. It is generally filed by those who itemize or have income or adjustments that cannot be reported on a short form. For example, if you realized a capital gain during the year, you must report it on Form IT-201. The short forms, IT-100 and IT-200, cannot be used to report this type of income. The same is true for pensions or annuities. This type of income must be reported on Form IT-201. Generally, if you have sources of income other than wages and interest or dividends, excluding unemployment compensation, you will be required to file Form IT-201. If you are a resident taxpayer, you may choose to file Form IT-201 even if you meet the requirements to file the short forms. If you are not sure whether or not you should be filing as a *resident* for New York income tax purposes, refer to the section on *Determining Residency/Domicile* in an earlier section of this chapter for more information.

> **TAXPLANNER:** Knowing beforehand which form you are eligible to file will help you avoid frustration. Don't wait until you have completed part of a short form to discover that, because of certain types of income you earned, you must begin again with the long form.

Nonresident/Part-Year Resident Form IT-203. New York State nonresidents must file Form IT-203 to report income that is derived from New York sources. If you are a part-year resident, you must also file an IT-203. Computing your nonresident and part-year resident tax is discussed in Chapter 4.

Attachments

In addition to the forms discussed above, you may need to attach additional forms to the IT-200, IT-201, or IT-203. One such attachment is Form IT-214, the form used to claim the Real Property Tax Credit. (You can also file this form separately to claim a refund.) Another form that New York City commuters must attach is the New York City nonresident earnings tax return Form NYC-203. Other attachments are discussed in the section on *Attachments* included in Chapter 4.

It should be noted that, although Forms NYC-203 and Y-203 are attached to the State return, they are discrete forms representing separate filing obligations. They must be signed and dated by the taxpayer. Do not treat them the same as supplementary schedules that are attached to the State return.

S Corporations, Partnerships, Estates, and Trusts

New York does not require that a separate Schedule K-1 be prepared for each partner or shareholder. However, the partnership or S corporation is required to file an information return with New York, reporting the New York State adjustments to its partners and shareholders. You should request this information from any partnership or S corporation in which you invested.

Note: A partnership may be liable for the Unincorporated Business Tax if it conducts business in New York City. An S corporation doing business in New York City must pay tax like any other corporation. Unlike New York State or the federal government, New York City does not give S corporations any special tax treatment.

Estates and trusts that have New York taxable income file Form IT-205, Fiduciary Income Tax Return. In addition, certain estates and trusts may be required to attach Form IT-205-A, Fiduciary Allocation, to their completed IT-205. (See the *Attachments* section in Chapter 4.)

Where to File

Form Name and Number	To Send A Tax Payment	To Claim A Refund
IT-100 Resident Fast Form Income Tax Return	NYS Income Tax W.A. Harriman Campus Albany, NY 12227-0125	NYS Income Tax W.A. Harriman Campus—Refund '92 Albany, NY 12227-0125
IT-200 Resident Income Tax Return	NYS Income Tax W.A. Harriman Campus Albany, NY 12227-0125	NYS Income Tax W.A. Harriman Campus—Refund '92 Albany, NY 12227-0125
IT-201 Resident Income Tax Return	NYS Income Tax W.A. Harriman Campus Albany, NY 12227-0125	NYS Income Tax W.A. Harriman Campus—Refund '92 Albany, NY 12227-0125
IT-203 Nonresident & Part-year Resident return	NYS Income Tax W.A. Harriman Campus Albany, NY 12227-0125	NYS Income Tax W.A. Harriman Campus—Refund '92 Albany, NY 12227-0125

Due Dates—When Do I File?

Resident, Nonresident, and Part-Year Resident Individuals. The due date for filing your 1992 income tax return is April 15, 1993, if you file on a calendar year basis (a year ending on December 31). If you use a fiscal year (a year ending on the last day of any month except December, or a 52/53 week year), your income tax is due by the 15th day of the fourth month after the close of your fiscal year. (See the following section, *Extensions*, for information about requesting an extension of your return due date.)

When the due date for filing your return falls on a Saturday, Sunday, or legal holiday in New York state, it is automatically extended to the next succeeding day that is not a Saturday, Sunday, or legal holiday.

Your return is considered to be filed on time if it is properly addressed and postmarked no later than the due date. The return must have sufficient postage. If you send your return by registered mail, the date of the registration is the postmark date. If you send a return by certified mail and have your receipt postmarked by a postal employee, the date on the receipt is the postmark date. Evidence of metered, messengered, or "faxed" mailing may not qualify as proof of timely mailing.

If you file late, you may be subject to penalties and interest. Penalties may apply to late filing, late payments, and underpayments of estimated taxes. (See *Penalties* in Chapter 5 for further information.)

EXCEPTION: For Upstate New York Taxpayers (*Andover Filers Only*). If you mail your federal tax return to the Andover, Massachusetts IRS Center, special filing rules apply. If April 15 falls on a Saturday or Sunday and the following Monday is Patriots' Day, or if the 15th falls on Patriots' Day, you will have until the Tuesday immediately after April 15 to file your federal income tax return. Patriots' Day is a legal holiday in Massachusetts and Maine that falls on the third Monday in April. New York State conforms to this federal policy and gives Andover filers until the Tuesday after Patriots' Day to file their New York State tax returns.

Deceased Taxpayers

The due date for filing a personal income tax return for a taxpayer who died during the tax year is the same as if the taxpayer was alive. The executor, administrator, or spouse must file the return.

Partnerships

The partnership return is an information return showing each partner's distributive share in the various classes of partnership income, losses, deductions, and credits. The partnership return is due the 15th day of the fourth month following the close of the tax year.

If you change your partnership's tax year or accounting method for your federal tax filing purposes, do the same for your New York partnership return.

If a partnership is terminated and completely liquidated during its normal taxable year, resulting in an accounting period of less than 12 months for federal income tax purposes, the return is due the 15th day of the fourth month after the end of the accounting period.

Other Taxes

You may be subject to filing requirements for other taxes, such as Unincorporated Business Tax, Sales and Use Tax, Estate and Gift Tax. (Refer to Chapter 7 for a discussion of other taxes.)

New York City and Yonkers

The New York State due dates for personal income tax returns also apply to New York City and Yonkers nonresident returns.

Fiduciaries

Fiduciary returns are subject to the same filing requirements as state resident returns.

Extensions

There are many reasons why you may not be able to file your income tax return on time. Business pressures or not having certain information available are common reasons. If you will not be able to file your New York income tax return by the deadline, usually April 15, you may request an extension of time. Regardless of the reason, extension is a matter of right. However, you must pay any tax you still owe *when* you file your extension request. Otherwise, you may be liable not only for the unpaid tax but for interest and penalties as well. You may not extend your filing time for more than six months unless you are out of the country.

To receive an automatic four-month extension of time to file your return, you must complete an Application for Automatic Extension of Time to File for Individuals (Form IT-

370). You must file this form by the due date of your New York State income tax return. If you file a New York City nonresident earnings tax return (Form NYC-203) or City of Yonkers nonresident earnings tax return (Form Y-203), your state extension automatically applies to those returns. If you do not owe any tax, you can obtain an automatic four-month extension merely by sending a copy of your Federal Extension Request (Form 4868) to New York State by April 15. Save a copy and write "New York State Copy" across the top. You will need to attach it when you file your New York return. If you are a taxpayer traveling or residing outside the United States and are granted a federal automatic two-month extension, you don't need to request a separate New York extension or pay your tax by April 15. You must attach the federal statement authorizing the additional time to your New York return.

EXCEPTION: Partnerships or fiduciaries requesting an extension must complete an Application for Automatic Extension of Time to File for Partnerships and Fiduciaries (Form IT-370PF).

Partnerships or trusts that anticipate no tax may obtain an automatic three-month extension by filing a copy of federal Form 8736 with New York by the due date of the state return. A fiduciary of an estate must file Form IT-370-PF. A copy of federal Form 2758 is not acceptable because it covers a different time period.

Automatic extensions may be revoked or terminated by the state. However, the state must notify you by mail at least ten days before termination.

Additional Extensions of Time

If your original four-month extension is about to expire, and you still need more time to file, you can request an additional two-month extension. You must file two copies of an Application for Extension of Time to File for Individuals (Form IT-372) *before* the expiration of the four-month extension period. If the additional time is granted, you will be notified by mail. Partnerships, estates or trust can request an additional two-month extension by filing Form IT-372-PF.

To complete Forms IT-370 or IT-370-PF, you must estimate your tax liability for those jurisdictions in which you are subject to tax. Lines 1–3 ask for your state and city estimated tax liabilities. Fill in any estimated tax payments you made, credits you are due, or amounts that were withheld from your wages on Lines 5–9. Report your total credits and prepayments on Line 10 and calculate the balance due on Line 11. This amount must be paid with the Form IT-370 or IT-370-PF by the due date. Your total payments, including any payment you made with your extension, must add up to at least 90% of the tax ultimately due when you file your return. Your estimate must be accurate in order to avoid both late filing and late payment penalties. These rules apply both to individuals and to estates. Any balance due on your return will be subject to interest charges. (See, in Chapter 5, the section on *Penalties*, for further information.)

Example

After completing an extension request on Form IT-370, Julie estimates that her total tax liability for 1992 will be $3,000. The amount of taxes withheld from her wages in 1992 was $2,500. She did not make any other payments of tax during the year and is not eligible to take a credit against her tax. She must enclose a check for *at least* $500 when she files her

extension request. If the *actual* balance of the tax that Julie owes at the time she files her return is less than $334, she will still not be subject to penalties.

TaxPlanner: To avoid interest charges for underpayment of tax, it is advisable to be conservative when estimating your New York income tax due. In addition to interest, you may be liable for a penalty based on the amount of underpayment.

Mailing

You must file your request on time. The state will consider an extension request filed on time if it is sent in a properly addressed envelope with the proper postage. It must be postmarked by the United States Post Office on or before the due date. Hand-delivered, overnight delivery, or messenger delivery will be considered filed on the date the state receives the request. Forms that are sent by registered or certified mail are considered mailed on the date the Post Office stamps them.

TaxPlanner: Do not rely on a postmark from a private postal meter, such as those used in your office, as proof that you mailed your request on time. Only a postmark from the United States Post Office is acceptable proof that you mailed your extension request on time. As with any other tax form where the date of mailing is important, professional tax advisors recommend using U.S. certified or registered mail. Keep your receipts in a safe place!

If you are seeking an automatic four-month extension (Form IT-370) or three-month extension (Form IT-370-PF), the request should be mailed to:

New York State Income Tax
W.A. Harriman Campus
Albany, NY 12227-0125

If you are required to pay tax with your extension request, you must send the form and a check for the amount due to:

New York State Income Tax
Processing Center
P.O. Box 1195
Albany, NY 12201-1195

TaxPlanner: Note your Social Security number, the tax year for which you are requesting an extension, and the number of the form you will file on the face of your check. Keep a copy of your extension request and your check.

If you are filing Form IT-372 or Form IT-373-PF, mail two copies to:

New York State Income Tax
W.A. Harriman Campus
Albany, NY 12227-0125

Information Block

The top portion of your income tax return is called the "information block." It requests general information about you and your spouse, primarily for purposes of identification. This section covers the types of information you will need to complete this portion of your return. Examples are your name, address, and Social Security number.

If you received a pre-printed label from New York State when you received your income tax return forms, place it over the sections requesting your home and mailing address. The following Sections (1–5) do not apply to you. Skip to Section 6.

If the name on the label (yours or your spouse's) is incorrect, cross it out and write in the correct name. If other parts of the label are incorrect, or you do not have a label, read on.

If you file Forms: *IT-201, IT-203, IT-100, or IT-200 and do not have an address label, follow these instructions:*

1. *Name:* List your last name first, followed by your first name. Put your Social Security number next to your name in the space provided. If you and your spouse are filing jointly, both of your names and Social Security numbers must appear on the return.

Example
Last name, first and middle initial (if joint return, enter both names)
Jones, William C. and Brenda L.

TaxAlert: If you and your spouse file a joint return and have different last names, be sure to list *both* last names. The two names for husband and wife should be separated by the word "and."

Example
Jones, William C. and Smith, Brenda L.

Make sure your Social Security numbers are listed in the same order as your names.

TaxAlert: If a married woman uses her husband's last name on her income tax return without notifying the Social Security Administration of her name change, the taxing authorities will have difficulty matching the Social Security number to the proper name. This may cause a delay in processing your return.

2. *Mailing address:* Enter the current address at which you receive your mail. If you are a nonresident of New York State when you file your return, then your mailing address for tax return preparation purposes is the address at which you currently live.
3. *School District Name and Code Number:* Enter the name and code number of the public school district in which you were a resident on December 31. School districts and code numbers are listed in the instructions for each of the forms. If your school district is not listed, call 1-(800)-225-5829 (instate), the *New York Taxpayer Assistance* line, for help. Out-of-state, call 1-(518)-438-8581. The school district name and code number section must be completed even if your children do not attend the local school or you have no school-age children.

   If you were not a resident of New York State either at the end of the year or for the entire year, follow these instructions:

   • Part-year nonresident: Enter the school district name and code number of the district in which you resided before leaving the state.

• Full-year nonresident: Enter the abbreviation "NR" in the space for school district name.

TaxAlert: If you are a student attending school in New York, you should use your *home* address as your mailing address, not your address while you are at school. This will save mailing time if the state corresponds with you after you leave school and your tax return is filed. If you are due a refund, you may get it faster by remembering to use your home address.

5. *Permanent Home Address*—This section must be completed only if your mailing address is different from the last address where you lived during 1992. For example, you should complete this section if:

   • You use a post office box for your mailing address; or
   • You are in the Armed Forces; or
   • You moved after December 31 of last year.

If you use a post office box for your mailing address, enter your street address as your permanent address. The permanent address is used to verify your school district name and code number.

If you were a resident of New York when you entered in the Armed Forces, enter your New York permanent home address, regardless of where you are stationed.

If you moved into or within New York after December 31, 1992, enter your address as of December 31, 1992, as your "permanent home address." Do *not* enter your current home address in the space marked. If you moved out of New York during 1992, enter the address of your last New York residence.

6. If you are filling out an income tax return for a deceased taxpayer, enter the deceased person's first name and date of death in the appropriate sections. Even if you are using a preprinted label when filing this return, you must complete this information box.
7. *Filing Status:* You must generally use the same filing status as you did on your federal return. If you were not required to file a federal return, then use the filing status you would have used if you had filed a federal return. (See *Filing Status* earlier in this chapter, for a full discussion of how to choose the proper filing status.)
8. *Did you itemize your deductions?* If you itemized your deductions on your federal return, check the "Yes" box. If you claimed the standard deduction on your federal return, check the "No" box.

EXCEPTION: Question 8 (above) does not appear on Form IT-100.

9. *Can you be claimed as a dependent on another taxpayer's federal return?* If you can be claimed as a dependent on another taxpayer's federal return, check the "Yes" box. If not, check the "No" box. (For a full discussion of claiming dependents, see *Personal Exemptions and Dependents* earlier in this chapter.)
10. *Part-Year Residents:* (Form IT-203 only): If you were a New York State resident for part of the tax year, check the box which described your situation on the last day of the tax year. Do not check more than one box.

    • If you moved into New York State during the year, check box 1 and enter the date you moved into New York.
    • If you moved out of New York State during the year, but you continue to receive income from New York

State sources such as wages or pensions from a New York employer, check box 2 and enter the date you moved. (If you don't know whether or not you have any income that can be attributed to New York sources, see Chapter 3, *Calculating Your Taxable Income*.)

- If you moved out of New York State and no longer receive any income from New York State sources, check box 3 and enter the date you moved out of New York.

11. *Nonresidents* (Form IT-203 only): If you or your spouse had living quarters available for your use in New York State during any part of the tax year, check the "Yes" box and complete Schedule B on Form IT-203-ATT. Examples of living quarters include a house, apartment, co-op, condominium, or any other habitable space that you or your spouse maintained or paid for. Living quarters also include any New York State living space maintained for your primary use by another person, family member, or employer. Be sure to answer this question truthfully.

EXCEPTION: If you are in the Armed Services and your only living arrangement in New York State is your use of a Bachelor Officer Quarters located in New York, you will not generally be considered to maintain living quarters in New York State. Check the "No" box next to the question on Form IT-203 concerning living quarters available for your use.

12. *Were you a resident of the City of New York for all of 1992?* (Form IT-100 only): If the answer is yes, then check the "Yes" box. If you were not a resident of the City of New York for the entire year, then check the "No" box. If you were a New York City resident for only part of the year, you must use Form IT-201. You cannot use Form IT-100.

    If you were not a resident of New York City, but you earned wages there, you cannot use Form IT-100.

13. *Were you a resident of the City of Yonkers for all of 1992?* (Form IT-100 only): if the answer is yes, check the "Yes" box. If not, check the "No" box. If you were a resident of Yonkers for part of last year, you must use Form IT-201. You cannot use Form IT-100. If you were not a resident of Yonkers, but you earned wages there, you must use Form IT-200. You cannot use Form IT-100.

14. *If you used a paid preparer:* (Forms IT-200 and IT-201 only) If you do not want a tax packet sent to you next year because you do not prepare your own return, check this box. The Department of Taxation will still mail you a pre-printed label, which can be used on next year's income tax return.

15. *Number of Exemptions:* Enter the number of exemptions you claimed on your federal return (Line 6e). If you file Form 1040EZ, enter 0 in this box. (See the previous section, *Personal Exemptions and Dependents*, for further information.)

Form NYC-203, *City of New York Nonresident Earnings Tax Return.* If you were a nonresident of New York City for any part of 1992 and you earned wages or self-employment income while a nonresident, you must complete Form NYC-203. Form NYC-203 is used to determine your nonresident New York City tax. The amount of tax you owe must also be reported on Form IT-200, IT-201, or IT-203.

1. *Name:* Enter your name as it appears on page 1 of your New York State tax return. If your spouse also was a nonresident of New York City and earned wages or self-employment income there, your spouse must complete a separate NYC-203.
2. *Answer Item A, B, or C:*

    Item A: *Were you a City of New York resident for any part of the taxable year?* If the answer to this question is yes, check the "Yes" box and answer questions 1 and 2. Question 1 asks you to state the period of time in which you were a resident of the City of New York. Enter the first day of 1992 that you were a New York City resident and the last day of 1992 that you were a resident. Question 2 asks you whether or not you are reporting your New York City resident tax on your New York State return. If yes, check the "Yes" box. If not, check the "No" box and attach a statement explaining why you are not reporting the resident tax.

Example

John moved into New York City on January 1, 1992. He moved out of New York City on April 30, 1992. He worked in New York City during all of 1992. John was a resident of New York City from January 1, 1992 to April 30, 1992. John should check the "Yes" box for A. For Question 1, John should write in "January 1, 1992" next to the word "From" and "April 30, 1992" next to the word "To." Because John is a resident for some part of 1992, John should report his City of New York resident tax on his New York State return (IT-201 or IT-203) and check "Yes" for Question 2. If John does not report his New York City resident tax on his New York State return, John must check the "No" box for Question 2 and attach a written explanation. John is required to report his wages for the period May 1, 1992 to December 31, 1992 on Form NYC-203. He should report only the wages or self-employment income he earned from New York City sources while a nonresident.

Item B: *Did you or your spouse maintain an apartment or other living quarters in the City of New York during any part of the year?* If yes, check the "Yes" box and enter the number of days you spent in New York City during 1992. Also, enter your New York City address. Examples of maintaining an apartment or other living quarters include renting an apartment or owning or renting a coop, condo, or house. If you did not maintain living quarters in New York City, check the "No" box.

Item C: *If you are reporting income from self employment on Line 5 below, complete the following:*

a. *Business name:* Enter the name under which you earned your self-employment income. If you operated your business under your given name, enter your name. If you were a general partner of a partnership, enter the partnership's name. If you used an assumed name or trade name, enter that name. *Note:* A limited partner is not subject to self-employment tax on a partnership distribution.

b. *Business address:* Enter the address of your business. If you work primarily out of your home, list your home address.

c. *Employer Identification Number:* If your business has a separate federal identification number, list that number in the space provided. If not, list your own Social Security number as the employer identification number.

d. *Principal business activity:* Enter a brief description of the work you performed. If you performed a different activity outside the city, list only the work you did inside the city.

Example
If you were a general partner in a partnership, enter the business activity of the partnership. If the partnership operated a retail store for automobile accessories, write "retail—automobile accessories."

e. *Form of Business:* Check the box that applies.

Example
If you operated a business by yourself, check the box for "sole proprietorship."

If you are not conducting business in your own name or as a partner in a partnership, check the box "Other" and write a brief explanation.

Form Y-203, *City of Yonkers Nonresident Earnings Tax Return.* If you were a nonresident of Yonkers for any part of 1992 and you earned wages or self-employment income there, you must complete Form Y-203 to determine your nonresident tax. The amount of tax you owe will be entered on your Form IT-200, IT-201, or IT-203.

1. *Name:* Enter your name—last name followed by your first name and middle initial. If your spouse was also a nonresident of Yonkers and earned wages or self employment income there, he or she must complete a separate Y-203.
2. *Answer Item A, B, or C:* Refer to the preceding section on Form NYC-203. Substitute "Yonkers" for references to New York City.

3 | Calculating Your Taxable Income

Residents—Starting Point

Introduction

The preceding chapters discussed preliminary matters, such as deciding whether or not you need to file a personal income tax return, whether to file as a resident or nonresident, and which income tax form to choose. By now, you've organized your records, figured out who your dependents are for tax purposes, and made the basic decisions about how to file.

Now it's time to start actually calculating your tax. Don't be nervous. This chapter and the succeeding ones will lead you through the process, step by step and line by line. If you are a *resident*, this chapter will show you how to fill in the first few lines of your return to report your *federal adjusted gross income* to New York. If you are a *nonresident*, please skip ahead to the sections on *Nonresidents/Part-Year Residents*. If you are not sure whether you should be filing as a resident or a nonresident, review the sections on *Determining Residency/Domicile* and *Nonresidents* in Chapter 2.

To calculate your New York adjusted gross income, you must begin with your federal adjusted gross income. This is the amount you entered on Line 31 of your federal Form 1040 (Line 3 of Form 1040EZ or Line 16 of Form 1040A). You must report certain items of income in exactly the same manner on your New York return as you do on your federal return. So it is helpful to complete your federal return first and have it in front of you when you prepare your New York tax return.

> **TAXALERT:** Each line item on Form IT-100 corresponds to a particular line on the federal 1040EZ or 1040A. If you qualify to use the IT-100, you will not be required to calculate your tax. New York will do that for you. If any tax is due or you are due a refund, the state will send you a detailed explanation of how your tax liability or refund was calculated.

Wages, Salaries, Tips: *IT-100, Line 2; IT-200, Line 1; IT-201, Line 1*

Enter the total of all wages, salaries, and tips; fees, commissions; bonuses; and fringe benefits reported on your federal return (Form 1040, Line 7). The figures you report must also conform to the amounts reported on your federal Form W-2, Box 10 (wages, tips, other compensation). Remember to attach the correct copy of this form to your New York return.

Taxable Interest Income: *IT-100, Line 3; IT-200, Line 2; IT-201, Line 2*

All taxable interest you reported on your federal return must be entered on this line. Generally, this will be the same as the amount you entered on Line 8a of federal Form 1040.

Interest includes income earned from bank accounts or bonds. The amount will be reported to you on Form 1099-INT, Interest Income, Form 1099-OID, Original Issue Discount, or a similar statement. These forms show you the interest you received during the year and are for your records only. These forms should not be attached to the New York return. Any interest income you received from a partnership or S corporation will appear on your Schedule K-1. Any interest you received on a tax refund is includable in your income and must be reported on this line. Dividends paid to you on deposits or share accounts in cooperative banks, credit unions, domestic savings and loan associations, federal savings and loan associations, and mutual savings banks are "dividends" that are considered interest included on this line. Amounts you have received from mutual funds are considered dividends rather than interest and are reported as such.

Federal law provides an exemption for interest from all state and local municipal bonds and notes. New York allows an exclusion only for interest on bonds or notes of New York State or local governments. If you are a New York resident and invest in bonds from states other than New York, you must include the interest income from these bonds in your New York taxable income. This exemption is discussed in greater detail in the following section, *Residents—Additions and Subtractions*.

Example

Marla's investment portfolio includes federal bonds and bonds from New York State, New York City, New Jersey, and California. She must enter the amount of interest received on the New Jersey and California bonds on Line 20 of Form IT-201.

Dividend Income: *IT-100, Line 5; IT-200, Line 3; IT-201, Line 3*

Dividends—that is, any distributions made by a corporation to its shareholders, whether in the form of money or property—are fully taxable. You must enter the amount of dividends you reported on your federal income tax return, Form 1040, Line 9 on the appropriate line of your IT-100, IT-200, or IT-201. The amount of your taxable dividends will be reported to you on federal Form 1099-DIV, *Dividends and Distributions*, Schedule K-1 (if you are a partner in a partnership or a shareholder in an S corporation, dividends that "flow through" to you from the partnership or S corporation are included in this amount) or perhaps Form 1099-MISC, *Miscellaneous Income*. Most corporations use Form 1099-DIV, *Dividends and Distributions*. These forms are for your records and need not be attached to your New York return.

Ordinary dividends are the most common type of dividends

distributed by a corporation to its shareholders. Unless otherwise noted, assume that any dividend is an ordinary dividend taxed as ordinary income. Your ordinary dividends are reported on box 1b of the Form 1099-DIV, *Dividends and Distributions*. This entire amount is included in New York Income.

Taxable Refunds of State and Local Taxes: IT-200, Lines 4 & 10; IT-201, Line 4

If you received a taxable refund of state or local income taxes because of an overpayment of tax paid in a previous year, you may be required to include the refund in taxable income for the current year. Generally, the refund is taxable to the extent that you claimed a deduction for the tax expense in the previous year on your federal Form 1040, Schedule A. You will generally receive Form 1099-G, *Certain Government Payments*, reporting your taxable refunds. (See also the discussion of New York adjustments to *federal adjusted gross income* later in this chapter under *Additions and Subtractions* for *Nonresidents/Part-Year Residents*.)

Alimony Received: IT-201, Line 5

If you received alimony payments or separate maintenance payments during the year, report that amount on your state return. Child support payments may not be included in New York income, just as they may not be included in federal income.

Business Income: IT-201, Line 6

You must include income from a trade or business of which you were a sole proprietor on your New York return. You must enter any such income you reported to the federal government on Schedule C and attach a copy of this schedule to your New York return. If you are self-employed and carry on business in New York City, you may also be required to file an Unincorporated Business Tax Return (Form NYC-202). (See *Unincorporated Business Tax* in Chapter 7 for more information.)

Capital Gain or Loss: IT-201, Line 7

Enter the amount of capital gain or loss from the sale or exchange of property, including securities reported on federal Schedule D, *Capital Gains and Losses*, and also on Line 13 of federal Form 1040. Attach a copy of Schedule D to your New York return.

Capital Gain Distributions not reported on Line 7: IT-201, Line 8

If you reported any other capital gain distributions on your federal return, you must report them to New York on this line. The amount reported on Line 8 of your Form IT-201 should be the same as the amount you reported on Line 14 of your federal Form 1040. Use this line to report distributions included in box 1c on federal Form 1099-DIV, *Dividends and Distributions*.

Other Gains: IT-201, Line 9

If you realized a gain on the sale or exchange of any property used in your trade or business, you must report it on your New York return. This should be the same amount that you reported on Line 15 of your federal Form 1040 and also on Line 18 of federal Form 4797. Attach a copy of your federal Form 4797.

Taxable Amount of IRA Distributions: IT-201, Line 10

If you reported a distribution from an individual retirement arrangement (IRA) on your federal return, you must report the same amount on Line 10 of Form IT-201. Include the amount you reported on Line 16b of federal Form 1040. Include regular distributions, premature distributions, rollovers, and any other money or property you received from your individual retirement account. The amounts of your distributions will be reported on federal Form 1099-R *Distributions from Pensions, Annuities, Retirement or Profit-Sharing Plans, IRAs, Insurance Contracts, Etc.*

Taxable Amount of Pension or Annuities: IT-201, Line 11

If you received income from pensions or annuities, you must enter on this line the amount you reported on your federal return, Line 17b. This amount includes any disability payments received after you reached the minimum age set by your employer. Also include all payments from a profit-sharing plan, retirement plan (401-K plan), or employee savings plan. These amounts will be reported to you on Form 1099-R, *Distributions from Pensions, Annuities, Retirement or Profit-Sharing Plans, IRAs, Insurance Contracts, Etc.* from your plan administrator, showing the amount of your pension or annuity distribution.

Rents, Royalties, Partnerships, Estates, Trusts: IT-201, Line 12

Income (and in some instances, losses) from partnerships, estates or trusts or rents or royalties, that were reported on your federal return must be reported on your New York return. Attach a copy of Schedule E to Form IT-201. You should report the same amount on Line 12 of your Form IT-201 as you reported on Line 18 of federal Form 1040 and on Line 26 or Line 40 (whichever is applicable) of federal Schedule E, *Supplemental Income and Loss.*

Rents. Rents include any payments you receive for the occupation or use of property. You are entitled to deduct certain expenses from the gross amount of the rents you received. Examples of deductible expenses include advertising, cleaning, utilities, fire and liability insurance, depreciation, taxes, interest, commission for rent collection, and necessary travel costs. If you rent part of your property and reserve the other part for personal use, you must prorate your expenses. Any federal Schedule K-1s you may have received from partnerships, S corporations, estates, and trusts should be examined to see if rental income or expense has been attributed to you.

Royalties. Royalties include payments received from patents, copyrights, oil and gas, and mineral properties. Check your K-1s for any royalty income.

Partnerships and S Corporations. As a general rule, partnerships and S corporations are not subject to federal income tax. Instead, the income and expenses of these entities are "passed through" to the individual partners or shareholders. Each category of income retains its character when it is "passed through." Generally, partners will receive Schedule K-1 (Form 1065) and shareholders will receive Schedule K-1 (Form 1120S) showing their distributive or pro rata shares of income, credits, and deductions.

Example

Steve owns a 50% general partnership interest in ABC partnership. The partnership has $2,000 in interest income, $20,000 in ordinary business income, $5,000 in rents, and $1,000 in related rental expenses. Steve receives federal Schedule K-1 from the partnership indicating his share of each type of partnership income, as follows: $1,000 in interest income, $10,000 in ordinary income, $2,500 in rental income, and $500 in rental expenses. On his New York State return, Steve will include his $1,000 distributive share of partnership interest income on Line 2 with the rest of his taxable interest income. The net amount of the remaining income items, or $12,000 ($10,000 + $2,500 − $500), will be reported on Line 12.

Estates and Trust. Unlike a partnership or S corporation, an estate or trust may have to pay federal income tax. If you are a beneficiary of an estate or trust, you will be taxed on your pro rata share of its income. Much the same as partners and S corporation shareholders discussed above, beneficiaries will treat each item of income the same way the estate or trust did. In other words, if it's dividend income to the trust, it is dividend income to you. The tax is paid either by the estate or trust, or by the beneficiary. Beneficiaries will generally receive Schedule K-1 (Form 1041) or a similar statement indicating their share of income, deductions, and credits.

Farm Income: IT-201, Line 13
If you reported farm income or loss on Line 19 of your federal return, you must report the same amount to New York. Attach a copy of Schedule F, *Profit or Loss from Farming*, from your federal Form 1040.

Unemployment Compensation Income: IT-100, Line 6; IT-200, Line 5; IT-201, Line 14
Any unemployment compensation you received must be included in your income. Attach the form provided by the state that shows the amounts paid to you over the course of the year. If you received an overpayment in 1992 that you repaid in 1993, you must report the net number. Generally, you will receive Form 1099-G, *Certain Government Payments*, or a similar statement showing the total unemployment compensation paid to you during the year.

Taxable Social Security Benefits: IT-201, Line 15
If you reported taxable Social Security benefits or equivalent Railroad Retirement benefits on Line 21b of your federal Form 1040, you must report the same amount on Line 15 of your IT-201. Social Security benefits do not include any Supplemental Security Income (SSI) payments you may have received. The total amount of Social Security benefits paid to you during the year will be shown in box 3 of Form SSA-1099. You should receive these forms in the mail if they apply to you.

Other Income: IT-201, Line 16
If you reported any income as "other income" on Line 22 of your federal Form 1040, you must report the same total on your New York Form IT-201. Attach a schedule to your IT-201 identifying the components of your "other income" by type and amount. You may use the same schedule that you attached to your federal return. Other income may include items such as prizes, awards, gambling winnings, discharge of indebtedness, or bartered services.

Federal Adjusted Gross Income: IT-201, Line 19
Now you must subtract Line 18 from Line 17. Enter the difference on Line 19. This amount must be the same as the amount you entered on Line 31 of your federal Form 1040, federal adjusted gross income.

Residents—Additions and Subtractions

By now, you should have filled in all the lines of your return that comprise your federal adjusted gross income. This includes Lines 2–3 and Lines 5–7 on Form IT-100, Lines 1–8 on Form IT-200, or Lines 1–19 on Form IT-201.

This chapter will show you how to make the necessary *modifications* to your federal adjusted gross income. Each item that you already entered on your New York return was governed by federal law. In contrast, a *modification* is an addition to or a subtraction from federal adjusted gross income that is required by New York law.

Example
New York does not tax interest from U.S. Treasury savings bonds. On Line 8a of your federal Form 1040, you were required to report taxable interest income, including interest from savings bonds. You transferred this amount exactly as it appeared on your federal return to Line 2 of Form IT-200 or IT-201, or to Line 3 of Form IT-100. On your New York return, you will subtract from your federal adjusted gross income all of the savings bond interest you received, because this interest is not taxable under state law. This subtraction is called a modification.

Additions to Federal Adjusted Gross Income
New York taxes certain items of income that were excluded from your federal income tax. The New York modifications that must be added to federal adjusted gross income are discussed below.

Interest Income on State and Local Bonds of Other States: IT-201, Line 20
Enter all of the interest you received from bonds of any state or local government *except* from bonds issued by New York State or by local governments located in New York.

TAXPLANNER: If you receive a lot of interest income from bonds issued by states or localities other than those in New York, you may wish to consider buying New York bonds or U.S. obligations and selling the others. See the section below on subtractions for more information on U.S. obligations.

Example
Dennis received interest income from bonds of Michigan and New York. He must add back any interest he received from the Michigan bonds on Line 20 of Form IT-201.

Public Employee Retirement Contributions: IT-200, Line 9; IT-201, Line 21
If you are:

a. A Tier III or Tier IV member of the New York State or New York City Retirement Systems (including the New York State and New York City Teachers' Retirement Systems)

b. An employee of the State or City University of New York who belongs to the TIAA/CREF Optional Retirement System

c. A New York City uniformed force member, including police, firefighters, corrections officers, and transit, housing authority, and sanitation police.

You must add back the amount of 414(h) retirement contributions shown on Copy 2 of your wage and tax statements,

(Form IT-2102 or federal Form W-2). Do not enter contributions made to a Section 401(k) deferred arrangement, Section 403(b) annuity or Section 457 deferred compensation plan.

> **EXCEPTION:** You *cannot* use Form IT-100 if your employer made public employee 414(h) retirement contributions on your behalf.

Other Additions: *IT-201, Line 22*

Major items included in this category are listed below. Use the summary that follows to figure the *other* additions that you should enter on this line. You must attach a description of your *other* additions to your return.

Summary of *Other* Additions:

- Income taxes that were deducted from federal gross income;
- Interest expense on loans used to buy tax-exempt bonds;
- Special additional mortgage recording tax;
- Share of income or loss from an insurance business;
- Accelerated cost recovery system deductions;
- S corporation shareholder adjustments;
- Five percent of interest deduction for corporate acquisitions;
- New York City flexible benefits program (IRC §125);
- Special depreciation or research and development expenditures, waste treatment facility expenditures, air pollution control equipment expenditures, or acid deposition expenditures for tax years before 1987;
- Deductions for percentage depletion on mines, oil and gas wells, and other natural deposits;
- Solar and wind energy systems; and
- Safe harbor leases.

Taxable Interest or Dividends from U.S. Securities, A-1.

Include interest income that is exempt for federal purposes but taxable to New York. (See the chart on page NY-30.)

Income Taxes Deducted for Federal Purposes, A-2.

If you operated a business and deducted income taxes on your federal return as an expense of doing business, enter the total amount you deducted. This amount is not the same as a tax expense included in your itemized deductions. For example, if you deducted state and local taxes on Schedule A of your federal Form 1040, do not enter that amount here.

If you are a partner in a partnership, include your share of any income taxes paid by the partnership and deducted on Form 1065. If you deducted New York City unincorporated business taxes from your federal taxable income, include that deduction in the amount you add back. (The *Unincorporated Business Tax* is discussed in Chapter 7.) If you are a shareholder in an S corporation, include your share of the New York corporate franchise taxes that were deducted by the S corporation on its federal 1120S return. Do not include taxes that were paid by the S corporation to *other* states or localities.

Example

Bob is a 10% partner in Partnership ABC. ABC pays $200 in income taxes to Alabama. Bob must add back his share of the expense on his New York return. He enters $20 ($200 × 10%) on line 22.

Interest Expense on Loans Used to Buy Exempt-Interest Bonds and Securities, A-3.

If you deducted any such interest expense in calculating your federal adjusted gross income, enter that amount here. Also, enter amortization of bond premiums on exempt-interest bonds and any other expenses that relate to income that is exempt from New York tax, if you deducted it in calculating your federal adjusted gross income.

Special Additional Mortgage Recording Tax, A-4.

If you excluded or deducted the New York special additional mortgage recording tax on your federal return, you must enter that amount on this line, You only need to make this addition to the extent that you claimed a credit for this tax on your New York return Form IT-201-ATT. (See the section on *Credits* in Chapter 4 for more information.)

Special Additional Mortgage Recording Tax, A-5.

Include any special additional mortgage recording tax you paid when the property for which tax was paid is sold.

If the basis for the property was not adjusted for the special additional mortgage recording tax credit, you must enter that amount on this line.

Income or Loss from an Insurance Business, A-8.

If you operated an insurance business as a member of the New York Insurance Exchange, enter your share of any income you earned from that business on this line, to the extent that it was not included in your federal adjusted gross income. If you incurred a loss that you deducted from federal adjusted gross income, you must add it back.

Solar and Wind Energy Systems, A-10.

The category only applies if you sold a residential property on which you had previously taken a New York State solar and wind energy credit. If the basis of that property included the cost of your energy system, you must include on this line the amount of the credit you previously deducted. This addback does not apply if you sold the property at a loss.

Accelerated Cost Recovery System (ACRS) Deduction, A-14.

If you have business assets on which you took depreciation deductions in the years 1981–1984, this addback may apply. It also may apply if the property in question was purchased after 1984 and located outside New York. If you used an accelerated method of depreciation, including MACRS, you must add back all of the depreciation expense deduction claimed for these assets. You should complete and attach a copy of Form IT-399. However, you will be allowed a modified depreciation deduction, discussed in the section on *Subtractions from Federal Adjusted Gross Income*, which follows. This section also applies if you are a shareholder in an S corporation or a partner in a partnership.

Accelerated Cost Recovery Property Year of Disposition Adjustment, A-15.

If you or the entity in which you are a shareholder or partner sell or otherwise dispose of a business asset, this section may apply. If your total depreciation deductions for state purposes exceeded the deductions taken on your federal returns, you must add back the excess state deductions on this line.

S Corporation Shareholders, A-16, A-17, A-18, A-19.

If you are a shareholder of an S corporation, you may have to make additional adjustments. As mentioned earlier, you must take into consideration corporate franchise taxes paid by the S corporation to New York. Also, if the corporation had a loss for the year and it was not registered as an S corporation for New York tax purposes, you must add back your share of the loss. In addition, if all the shareholders did not make an election to be taxed as an S corporation in New York, include any distribution the corporation made to you on this line. If you reported the distribution on your federal return, you do not have to enter the amount here.

If the corporation was not a New York S corporation and sold stock or had a debt forgiven, you may have to make an adjustment for any undistributed taxable income that resulted from the transaction.

TaxAlert: Complicated books have been written about how shareholders of S corporations are taxed. It isn't our purpose to go into too much detail here. However, you will find it easier to follow the modifications for S corporation shareholders if you keep a few pointers in mind. New York does not automatically recognize federal S corporations and accord their shareholders "flow-through" treatment. The shareholders must make a special election to be taxed this way for New York purposes. They can make this election only if, in addition to having made a valid federal election, the corporation is already subject to New York tax as a general business corporation and all the shareholders consent to the election. To make the election, shareholders must file Form CT-6 within 2½ months after the end of the S corporation's taxable year.

If you are a nonresident who owns shares in an S corporation, you will not be taxed on your share of its income unless the corporation has made the New York election. Even then, you will pay tax only on the share of income that the corporation apportions to New York. If all the shareholders do not make the election, you will be treated as if you owned stock in any other corporation. The corporation will pay tax to New York, but you will not pay tax on any dividends or other distributions you receive from the corporation. If you are a part-year resident, you must include in your income your share of all income earned by the corporation if the New York S election was made, or all distributions you received if the shareholders could have made the election but did not. If the S corporation wasn't eligible to make a New York S election, you must also include your share of the corporation's income for the period during which you were a resident. New York City does not recognize S corporations at all.

Interest Related to Certain Corporate Acquisitions, A-20. If you deducted interest expense in figuring your New York adjusted gross income, you must add back five percent of this expense if you were involved in a highly leveraged transaction. If this addition applies, complete Form IT-244, *Acquisition Information Report.* Attach a separate schedule to your return showing your computation.

New York City Flexible Benefits Program, A-21. Enter the amount shown on Copy 2 of your wage and tax statement(s), Form IT-2102 or federal Form W-2. Wages deducted or deferred from an employee's salary under a flexible benefits program established for New York City and certain other New York City public employers are taxable in New York.

Note: There are other adjustments or modifications not listed here, such as safe harbor leases, new business investment deferral, depletion expenses for oil and gas, and sale of decedent's assets when the estate is small. If any of these items affect you, consult the instructions to Form IT-201 or a professional tax advisor.

Total Additions: *IT-201, Line 23*

Add Lines 19 through 22 and enter the total on Line 23.

Subtractions from Federal Adjusted Gross Income

There are also modifications or income items that you included in your federal adjusted gross income but are entitled to subtract for New York purposes. The items that may be subtracted are summarized below.

Taxable Refunds of State and Local Income Taxes: *IT-200, Line 11; IT-201, Line 24*

Enter the same amount that you entered on Line 4 of Form IT-200 or IT-201, *taxable refunds of state and local income taxes.* This amount includes refunds from New York State and City.

Example

Brian lives in New York but works in Connecticut. Brian overpaid his Connecticut taxes in 1991. In 1992, he received a refund from Connecticut. Brian reported the refund on Line 10 of his federal Form 1040. On Brian's Form IT-201, he will subtract his Connecticut refund.

Taxable Amount of Social Security Benefits: *IT-201, Line 25*

Enter the same amount that you entered on Line 15 of Form IT-201, *taxable amount of Social Security benefits.*

Interest Income on U.S. Government Bonds: *IT-100, Line 4; IT-200, Line 12*

Enter the interest income on bonds or other obligations of the United States government that you included on Form IT-100, Line 3; Form IT-200, Line 2; or Form IT-201, Line 2; *taxable interest income.* Interest income on U.S. government bonds or other direct obligations of the U.S. government is not subject to New York State income tax. See the list of U.S. government securities below to determine which securities generate exempt interest and which ones do not. You should also subtract on this line any dividends you received from a mutual fund that is a regulated investment fund with at least 50% of its assets invested in U.S. government or New York State obligations. Your mutual fund should let you know if your dividends can be subtracted from New York taxable income. If you are unsure, contact your mutual fund directly.

Pension and Annuity Income Exclusion: *IT-201, Line 27*

If you were at least age 59½ before January 1, 1992, you can deduct *up to $20,000* of the pension and annuity income you received in 1992. If you became 59½ during 1992, enter only the amount received after you became 59½, but not more than $20,000.

You cannot deduct the pension income you received from New York State, local governments within the state, and the United States on this line. This pension income must be deducted from Line 28.

Pension and annuity income that you can deduct on Line 27 includes:

* Periodic payments for services you rendered as an employee before retirement;
* Periodic and lump-sum payments from an IRA, but not payments derived from contributions made after you retired;
* Periodic payments made to you from an HR-10 (Keogh) plan, but not payments arising from post-retirement contributions; and

List of New York State Exempt and Non-Exempt Federal Securities*

Interest is Not Taxable in NY	Interest is Taxable in NY

• Banks for cooperatives
• Export-Import bank (EXIMBANK) (Series 1978-B debentures)
• Farmers Home Administration—notes (interest paid by U.S. government)
• Federal Farm Credit Banks Funding
  —Farm credit banks—interest
  —Consolidated systemwide notes
• Federal Home Loan Bank
• Federal Housing Authority debentures
 	
• General Services Administration
• Guam, Puerto Rico & Virgin Islands
• Homeowners Loan Corporation
• Housing Finance Agency-NYS
 	
• Lake Placid Housing Development Funding Corporation
• Port Authority of New York
• Housing & Urban Development project notes (issued by U.S. Territories and possessions)
• Student loan marketing association ("Sallie Mae")
• Tennessee Valley Authority
 	
• U.S. Retirement Bonds (purchases under self-employed retirement plan or IRA Plan)
 	
• U.S. Savings Bonds
• U.S. Treasury Bills
• U.S. Treasury Notes
	• Export-Import Bank (EXIMBANK) (Participation certificates)
	• Farmers Home Administration—notes (interest paid by maker)
	
	• Federal Home Loan Mortgage Corp.
	• Federal National Mortgage Association ("Fannie Mae")—interest on bonds and debentures (all years) and guaranteed participation certificates (tax years after 1976)
	• Government National Mortgage Association ("Ginnie Mae")
	• Grace Lines, SS Santa Lucia Bonds (Prud. Grace Line)
	• Inter-American Development Bank Bonds
	• International Bank for Reconstruction and Development (International Bank Bonds) (World Bank)
	• Jonathan Development Corp.
	• Niagara Hydro Housing Corp.
	• Small Business Administration
	
	• U.S. Merchant Marine ship
	• Housing and Urban Development—project notes (issued by other states)
	• Washington DC
	  —Metropolitan Area Transit
	  —Housing and Urban Development

This list is not exhaustive; it simply illustrates the wide range of taxable and nontaxable securities available.

• Lump-sum payments made to you from an HR-10 (Keogh) plan, but only if you do not have to complete federal Form 4972. Do not include that part of your payment that was derived from contributions made after retirement.

If you are married and both you and your spouse reached age 59½ in 1992, each of you can subtract up to $20,000 of pension and annuity income. However, you cannot claim any unused part of your spouse's exclusion.

If you received the pension and annuity income of a decedent, you may make this subtraction if the decedent would have qualified to make this subtraction at the time of death.

If you are also claiming a disability income exclusion, the total of your pension and annuity income exclusion and disability income exclusion cannot exceed $20,000.

Example
Brian receives a $27,000 annual pension. Brian was 64 years old in 1992. Brian can only exclude $20,000. The balance ($7,000) cannot be excluded.

Other Subtractions: IT-201, Line 28
There are many items in this category. The major *other* subtractions are listed below. Use this list to help you figure out the *other* subtractions to which you may be entitled. You must attach a description of your *other* subtractions to your return.

Summary of Other Subtractions.
• Interest or dividend income from other U.S. obligations not listed on Line 26;
• Pension from New York State, local governments in New York, federal government, possessions, and the District of Columbia;
• Tier 2 benefits and supplemental annuity payments—Railroad Retirement Act;
• Other interest or dividend income from tax exempt bonds;
• Business expenses connected with income-producing property that generated income excluded from federal adjusted gross income but taxable for state purposes;

• Difference in basis for profitable asset sales;
• Insurance business income;
• New York State depreciation;
• Accelerated cost recovery property-year of disposition adjustment; and
• S corporation shareholders stock losses/income from debt forgiveness.

Interest or Dividend Income on Bonds or Securities of any United States Authority, Commission, or Instrumentality Included in Your Adjusted Gross Income on Your Federal Return but Exempt from State Income Tax Under Federal Laws, S-1. Only include interest that you did not list on Line 26.

Example
Interest you received from bonds of Puerto Rico, the Virgin Islands, and Guam are exempt from New York State personal income tax.

Certain Pension, S-2. Enter pension income you received as an officer, employee, or beneficiary of an officer or employee of New York State or local governments, the federal government, or the District of Columbia.

Enter on this line the amount you included as taxable pension and annuity income in your federal adjusted gross income (Line 17b of your federal Form 1040).

Benefits from the Railroad Retirement Act, S-3. Enter the amount of supplemental annuity and Tier 2 benefits you received under the Railroad Retirement Act of 1974 and the amount of Railroad Unemployment Insurance Act benefits, if you included these amounts in your federal adjusted gross income.

Interest from New York State Bonds, S-4. Enter any other interest or dividend income you included in your federal adjusted gross income that is exempt from New York State income tax. This does not include amounts subtracted above.

Interest Expense of Certain Loans, S-5. Enter interest expense on loans to buy bonds or securities that generate taxable income for New York tax purposes but exempt income for federal tax purposes.

The loans must have been used for a business purpose. If you deducted this interest expense from your federal adjusted gross income, you cannot make this subtraction.

Amortization of Bond Premiums, S-7. You may subtract amortization expense of bond premiums on any bond income that is taxable for New York tax purposes but is exempt from federal income tax, S-7.

The amortization must be a business expense that was not deducted from your federal adjusted gross income.

Disposition of Certain Property, S-10. If you sold certain oil and gas properties at a gain, this category may apply to you. If the oil and gas property has a higher adjusted basis for New York tax purposes than for federal income tax purposes, you should report the difference in basis as a subtraction. The term "basis" generally means the cost of the property. "Adjusted basis" means the cost adjusted for depreciation or depletion of the property. Differences between federal and state tax laws with respect to depreciation and depletion may cause you to have a different adjusted basis for federal and New York purposes.

Income from Insurance Business, S-14. If you operated an insurance business as a member of the New York Insurance Exchange, subtract your share of the income or gain derived from that business.

New York State Depreciation, S-19. If you had business assets located in New York during 1981 through 1984, or located outside New York after 1984, this subtraction may apply. Enter your New York State depreciation expense for the current year on this line. Use Form IT-399, New York State Depreciation, to calculate this subtraction. If you are a shareholder in an S corporation that is not taxed as a regular business corporation in New York, you are entitled to subtract your share of the S corporation's New York depreciation expense. The same is true if you are a partner in a partnership.

Accelerated Cost Recovery Property—Year of Disposition Adjustment, S-20. If you or the entity in which you are a shareholder or partner sell or dispose of a business asset, this section may apply. Enter the amount by which total federal depreciation expense exceeds total New York depreciation expense. Use Form IT-399 to figure your adjustment.

S Corporation Shareholders, S-21, S-22. If you are a shareholder in a federal S corporation taxed by New York that is treated as a regular business corporation, you must make certain adjustments if you had a federal gain or loss due to a sale of stock or forgiveness of debt. Subtract any reductions in the basis of your stock or indebtedness that you were required to make by federal law. The effect of this subtraction is to make sure that dividends you received from the S corporation are not taxed twice. Also subtract any additions to income you were required to make in previous years for certain distributions that were excluded from your federal income made in prior years. Consult your K-1 statements for the proper amount.

In addition, subtract your share of any income from a federal S corporation that is subject to the New York corporate franchise tax.

Disability Income Exclusion, S-23. Subtract any disability income that you could have excluded from your federal adjusted gross income but did not. Use Form IT-221, *Disability Income Exclusion*, to figure your disability income exclusion and attach it to your return. The maximum subtraction you can make for disability, pension, and annuity benefits is $20,000.

If you claim this exclusion, you must have your physician complete the statement at the bottom of Form IT-221.

Accelerated Death Benefits, S-24. If you received accelerated amounts as part of a death benefit or special surrender value that were included in your federal adjusted gross income, subtract the amount you received here.

Add Lines 24 through 28 to complete your subtraction modifications. Enter the result on Line 29.

This completes your New York modifications to federal adjusted gross income. Now subtract Line 29 from Line 23 and enter the result on Line 30. This is your *New York Adjusted Gross Income*. Proceed to the next section, *Deductions*.

Deductions

Introduction

In addition to the subtractions permitted under New York law and discussed in this chapter, deductions also reduce your taxable income. You may wonder what the difference is between a subtraction modification and a deduction. A *subtraction* is an adjustment to your federal adjusted gross income that is required by New York law to calculate New York adjusted gross income. A *deduction*, on the other hand, represents an expense, either real or assumed, that reduces your income. The purpose of this section is to explain what deductions you are entitled to take and to help you decide between taking a standard deduction and itemizing your deductions.

Personal Exemptions and Dependents will also be reviewed briefly. This topic is discussed in detail in Chapter 2.

Choosing Between Standard and Itemized Deductions

A *standard deduction* is a set figure determined by your filing status and your status as a dependent on someone else's federal return. It is exactly the same for each taxpayer with the same filing and dependent status. *Itemized deductions* consist of certain expenses that are deductible under federal law. The expenses that you may itemize include medical and dental expenses above certain thresholds, taxes paid, interest on certain types of loans, gifts to qualified charities, losses due to thefts or casualty, moving expenses, some job expenses, and certain miscellaneous expenses. A number of restrictions and limitations apply. To learn more about itemizing deductions, consult *The Ernst & Young Tax Guide 1993* or a professional tax advisor.

If you are not required to file a federal tax return or if you filed your federal return using the federal standard deduction, you *must* take the New York standard deduction. If you itemized your deductions on your federal return, you may choose between taking the New York standard deduction or itemizing your deductions on Form IT-201. Of course, you should choose whichever deduction is greater.

If you are married and file separate New York returns, each spouse must take the standard deduction, unless each of you itemize your deductions on your federal return and both of you itemize on your New York return. Although you may apportion itemized deductions between the two of you, the total taken must not exceed the total amount of each separately itemized deduction.

The following table shows the standard deduction for each filing status:

Note: The standard deduction amounts are subject to change each year.

New York Standard Deduction Table

Filing Status	Standard Deduction (enter on Line 13)
1. Single and you can be claimed as a dependent on someone else's return	$2,800
2. Single and you cannot be claimed as a dependent on someone else's return................	6,000
3. Married filing joint return	9,500
4. Married filing separate return	4,750
5. Head of household (*with qualifying person*).......................	7,000
6. Qualifying widow(er) with dependent child..........................	9,500

Example

Alice and Mike are New York residents and married taxpayers who elect to file separate New York State tax returns. They also file separate federal tax returns and itemize their deductions on Schedule A of federal Form 1040. Their reported itemized deductions on Schedule A of their respective federal Forms 1040 are as follows:

Itemized Deduction	Alice	Mike	Total Amount
Property taxes paid	$3,500	$ 3000	$ 6,500
Interest paid	3,000	0	3,000
Gifts to charity	200	200	400
Moving expenses	300	700	1,000
Job expenses	0	100	100
Total	$7,000	$4,000	$11,000

Since Alice and Mike both itemize their deductions on their respective federal returns, they have the option to itemize on their New York returns. However, both must choose the same option. They must either *both* take the standard deduction or *both* itemize their deductions.

Since their filing status for New York is *married filing separately*, Mike and Alice are each entitled to take a standard deduction of $4,750. Between the two of them, they are allowed a total standard deduction of $9,500. The total amount of their itemized deduction on their federal return, $11,000, exceeds their total New York standard deduction.

If Mike and Alice each have the same effective tax rate, or if Alice's effective tax rate is higher, they will save on taxes by electing to itemize their deductions.

Itemized Deductions. If you are a New York resident and choose to itemize your deductions for New York tax purposes you can only do so if you file Form IT-201. Form IT-200 only allows you to take a standard deduction.

On Form IT-100, the state takes your standard deduction into account when it calculates your tax, so you need not make any election.

The following sections explain what items are deductible, any limits to the deduction, and any modifications New York may require. This section applies only to Form IT-201 filers and only to taxpayers who are itemizing their deductions. If

you are not itemizing your deductions, enter your standard deduction on Line 47 of Form IT-201 or Line 13 of Form IT-200. Skip the following discussion of itemized deductions and go directly to the section on Dependent Exemptions, Line 49.

Medical and Dental Expenses: *IT-201, Line 31*

Enter the amount from Line 4 of federal Schedule A, *Medical and Dental Expenses*. You are allowed to deduct certain medical and dental expenses that exceed 7.5% of your federal adjusted gross income. You can include qualified expenses that you paid for yourself, your spouse, or a qualified dependent, as long as you were not reimbursed for these expenses by insurance or another source.

Qualified medical and dental expenses include payments for doctors, dentists, and other medical fees, hospital or nursing care, medicines and drugs, prosthetic devices, x-rays, medical insurance premiums, and other diagnostic services by a doctor or dentist. In addition, you may also include amounts paid for transportation to medical care and insurance covering medical care.

Example

Scott and Sally are married and file jointly. Their federal adjusted gross income for 1992 is $25,000. They have two children. Scott's mother also lives with his family and is supported by Scott. She is claimed as a dependent by Scott on his 1992 federal tax return. During 1992, the family had the following medical and dental expenses reimbursements and unreimbursed expenses:

Medical and Dental Expenses	Total Fee	Amount Reimbursed	Unreimbursed Expenses
Doctor's fees	$3,000	80% or $2,400	$ 600
Prescription medicines	200	80% or $160	40
Transportation to doctors	100	0% or $0	100
Hospital fees (including lab, nursing, and therapy)	4,000	50% or $2,000	2,000
X-rays	200	80% or $160	40
Dentist's fees	500	90% or $450	50
Total	$8,000	$5,170	$2,830

Scott and Sally can deduct $955 in medical and dental expenses on their 1992 federal and New York tax returns, calculated as follows:

Federal adjusted gross income for 1992:	$25,000
Multiplied by 7.5% threshold	× 7.5%
	$ 1,875
Total unreimbursed medical expenses:	$ 2,830
7.5% threshold from above	(1,875)
Itemized deduction for medical and dental expenses:	$ 955

If, in the above example, Scott and Sally had federal adjusted gross income of $37,750 or more, they would not be able to deduct any unreimbursed medical and dental expenses. Their threshold amount ($37,750 × 7.5% = $2,831) would exceed their total unreimbursed medical expenses.

Special Rule for Decedents

If expenses for medical care are paid out of the estate of a deceased taxpayer, they may qualify as deductible medical expenses for federal purposes. Any payments made within one year, beginning with the day after death, will be treated as paid by the taxpayer in the year they were incurred if the expenses are not deducted in figuring the taxable estate for federal estate tax purposes.

Example

Bill filed his 1991 income tax return on March 1, 1992. Bill died on July 4, 1992. He had unpaid medical expenses for 1991 of $2,500 and $1,000 for 1992. Bill's executor paid his medical expenses in February 1993, within the one-year requirement period. Bill's executor can file an amended return for 1991, claiming the $2,500 medical expenses as if they were paid in 1991. When Bill's executor files Bill's 1992 tax return, he or she can claim $1,000 of medical expenses in calculating Bill's itemized deduction.

Taxes You Paid: *IT-201, Line 32*

Enter the amount from Line 8 of federal Schedule A.

You are allowed to deduct certain taxes you paid during the year if you itemize your deductions.

The taxes you are allowed to deduct on your federal tax return are state and local income taxes, real estate taxes, and other taxes. New York allows a deduction for some of these taxes, but also adjusts or disallows certain portions. See *State, Local, and Foreign Income Taxes and other Subtraction Adjustments, Line 40*, on the following page.

Real Estate Taxes. If you paid taxes during the year on real property that was not used for business you are entitled to claim an itemized deduction for them. If your mortgage payments include real estate taxes, you are not allowed to deduct the taxes until they are actually paid by the mortgage company. (If you bought or sold real estate during the tax year, you may only deduct the real estate taxes for that portion of the year during which you were the owner of the property.)

Other Taxes

Certain taxes that are ordinary and necessary expenses of your business or trade may be deductible. (See *The Ernst & Young Tax Guide 1993* for more information on taxes that you may deduct.) Taxes that are *not* deductible include sales tax, taxes on certain goods, cigarettes, gas, or liquor, and fines, such as parking or speeding tickets.

Interest You Paid: *IT-201, Line 33*

Enter the amount you reported on Line 12 of federal Schedule A.

Your itemized deductions include interest paid on certain nonbusiness items.

TaxAlert: Beginning in 1991, you may no longer include personal interest in your itemized deductions, such as interest paid on credit cards or interest on a loan you used to purchase personal property. However, interest you paid on a mortgage for your principal residence is deductible.

Investment Interest. Investment interest is interest paid on money you borrowed to buy property held for investment. Examples of property held for investment are stocks and bonds. You must complete federal Form 4952 to calculate your investment interest deduction. Interest on money you borrowed to buy tax-exempt investments is not deductible.

Gifts to Charity: *IT-201, Line 34*

Enter the amount from Line 16 of federal Schedule A.

Contributions or gifts to qualified organizations that are re-ligious, charitable, educational, scientific, or literary in purpose are deductible. Examples of qualified organizations include churches or synagogues, charitable organizations such as the Red Cross or United Way, and federal, state, or local governments if the gifts are solely for public purposes. Contributions may be in cash, property, or out-of-pocket expenses incurred in connection with volunteer work. Contributions that are not deductible include political contributions, the value of any benefit you received in connection with a contribution, dues or fees paid to county clubs or similar groups, costs of raffle tickets, the value of your time or services as a volunteer, and gifts to individuals or groups operated for personal profit. Good recordkeeping is essential to prove the value of the gift, including cash, you contributed.

Casualty and Theft Losses: *IT-201, Line 35*

Enter the amount from Line 17 of federal Schedule A.

Casualty and theft losses are deductible on certain property that is stolen, damaged, or destroyed in an accident or by an act of nature. You must complete federal Form 4864. The property must not be used in a trade or business or to produce business income, rents, or royalties. You may not take a deduction if you are compensated for the loss by insurance. You may also deduct the costs you incurred to prove that you had a property loss. These costs include appraisal fees and photographs used to establish the value of loss. Certain federal limitations apply.

Moving Expenses: *IT-201, Line 36*

Enter the amount from Line 18 of federal Schedule A.

If your move was in connection with your job or business and your new workplace is 35 miles or more from your old home, you may deduct some of your moving expenses for:

- Moving your household goods and personal effects;
- Traveling to your new home;
- Trips prior to your move to find a new home;
- Temporary living arrangements in the new location;
- Selling your old home and buying your new one; or
- The cost of moving yourself and any person who was a member of your household before the move who will continue to be a member of your household after the move.

Some limits apply to this deduction.

Job Expenses and Most other Miscellaneous Expenses: *IT-201, Line 37*

Enter the amount from Line 24 of federal Schedule A.

The expenses in this category must exceed 2% of your federal adjusted gross income to be deductible. They include certain unreimbursed employee expenses and other expenses incurred to produce or collect income. Examples include travel, meal or entertainment expenses, union dues, safety equipment and uniforms, the business use of part of your home, and educational expenses you paid for courses required by your employer or by law.

Other miscellaneous expenses include amounts you paid to manage or protect property held for investment income. Examples include safe deposit box rental and custodial fees or fees for tax preparation services.

Miscellaneous Deductions Not Subject to the 2% Limit: *IT-201, Line 38*

Certain other miscellaneous deductions are not subject to the 2% federal limit. Examples include gambling losses to the extent of gambling winnings, amortizable premiums on taxable bonds acquired before October 23, 1986, and impairment-related work expenses of persons with disabilities.

Total Itemized Deductions: *IT-201, Line 39*

Enter the total amount of your federal itemized deductions from Line 26 of federal Schedule A.

As we mentioned previously, New York does not allow all of the deductions taken on your federal Schedule A. If you are required to adjust any of your federal deductions, you must complete Lines 40 through 44, discussed below.

State, Local, and Foreign Income Taxes and other Subtraction Adjustments: *IT-201, Line 40*

State, Local and Foreign Income Tax Adjustments.

New York does not allow a deduction for any state, local or foreign *income* taxes. State and local income taxes deducted for federal purposes were entered on Line 5 of your federal Schedule A. Foreign taxes were reported on Line 7.

EXCEPTION: If you deducted New York City nonresident earnings taxes on your federal Form 1040, Schedule A, Line 5, you do not need to reduce your New York itemized tax deduction for the difference in tax between the old rate (0.25%) and the new rate (0.45%). Multiply your New York City taxable wages by the difference between the two rates (0.20%). This amount does not have to be added back on Line 40 of the IT-201. The same is true for New York City nonresident earnings tax on net earnings from self-employment. Here, the difference between the old rate (0.375%) and the current rate (0.65%) is 0.275%. Otherwise, the concept is the same.

Example

On her federal Schedule A, Line 5, Jane deducted state and local income taxes totaling $500. She included her New York City nonresident earnings in the itemized deduction. Jane's taxable New York City wages from Form NYC-203 were $15,000. She can exclude $30 from her Line 40 adjustments ($15,000 × 0.20%). When she makes the adjustment, she must enter $470 ($500 − $30) on Line 40 of her IT-201.

If your federal adjusted gross income is $100,000 or less ($50,000 if you are *married filing separately*) you must include on Line 40 the amount of state and local income taxes that you deducted on your federal 1040, Schedule A. The exception for New York City taxes is discussed above. If your federal adjusted gross income is over this limit, you may choose between the following two options.

A. Enter the amount of state, local, and foreign income taxes included on your federal Schedule A, plus any other subtraction adjustments listed below that apply; *or*

B. Complete the *Subtraction Adjustment Limitations Worksheet* below.

1. Federal itemized deductions from federal itemized deductions worksheet line 3*............................ 1. _____

2. Amount of state, local, and foreign income taxes and other subtraction adjustments included in line 1 .... 2. _____

3. Subtract line 2 from line 1 .... 3. _____

4. Enter amount from federal itemized deduction worksheet line 9*............ 4. _____

5. Multiply line 3 by 80% (.80). If line 5 is greater than or equal to line 4, transfer the amount on line 2 to Form IT-201, line 40. **Do not continue with this worksheet.** If line 5 is less than line 4, continue on line 6 .... 5. _____

6. Subtract line 5 from line 4............... 6. _____

7. **Subtract line 6 from line 2.** Enter this amount here and on Form IT-201, line 40.................................... 7. _____

*For items No. 1 and 4 above you will need to use the itemized deduction worksheet found in the instructions for Schedule A, Form 1040.

Other Subtraction Adjustments. Included in the adjustments on Line 40 are *other subtraction adjustments.* These adjustments will further reduce the amount of itemized deductions you are allowed to take on your New York tax return. There are six subtraction adjustments listed in the instructions for Form IT-201. They are:

- Interest expense on money borrowed to purchase or carry bonds or securities generating interest that is exempt from New York income tax;
- Ordinary and necessary expenses paid or incurred in connection with income or property held for the production of income. You may deduct these expenses only to the extent that they were deducted in figuring your federal taxable income;
- Amortization of bond premium if the interest income is exempt from New York income tax, but only to the extent deducted in figuring your federal taxable income;
- Your distributive or pro rata share of deductions from an insurance business operating as a member of the New York Insurance Exchange;
- If you are a shareholder of a federal S corporation that did not elect to be a New York S corporation, any S corporation deductions included in your federal itemized deductions; and
- Five percent of your deduction for interest related to corporate acquisitions, to the extent the interest was deducted in figuring the New York itemized deduction. If this subtraction applies, complete Form IT-244, *Acquisition Information Report.* Attach a separate schedule to your return showing your computation.

If you are required to make any of these adjustments to your itemized deductions, you must list each adjustment on a separate sheet of paper. This sheet of paper must be attached to your return. Your other subtraction adjustments should be combined with any adjustments for state, local, and foreign total taxes. The total amount should be entered on Line 40.

Addition Adjustments: *IT-201, Line 42*

The three addition adjustments should be listed on a separate piece of paper, which must be attached to the tax return. The adjustments are:

- Interest expense on money borrowed to purchase or carry bonds or securities whose interest is subject to New York income tax, but exempt from federal income tax. Include this expense if it was not deducted on your federal return or shown as a New York subtraction on the front page of your state return;
- Ordinary and necessary expenses paid or incurred during 1991 in connection with income, or property held for the production of income that is subject to New York income tax but exempt from federal income tax. Include these expenses if they were not deducted on your federal return or shown as a New York subtraction on the front page of your state return; and
- Amortization of bond premium if the interest income is subject to New York income tax, but exempt from federal income tax. Include this item if the amortization was not deducted on your federal return or shown as a New York subtraction on the front page of your state return.

The total of your additions should be entered on Line 42 and added to Line 41.

Itemized Deductions Adjustments: *IT-201, Line 44*

Itemized deductions may be subject to a reduction if your New York adjusted gross income is greater than $100,000. If your New York adjusted gross income is more than $100,000 but not more than $475,000, use Worksheet A below. If your New York adjusted gross income is more than $475,000 but not more than $525,000, then compute your adjustment using Worksheet B below. If your New York adjusted gross income is more than $525,000, you are only allowed to deduct one-half of your total adjusted itemized deductions on your New York tax return.

WORKSHEET A

1. New York adjusted gross income from Form IT-201, Line 30............................ 1. _____
2. Filing status (1) or (3) enter $100,000, filing status (4) enter $150,000, filing status (2) or (5) enter $200,000............ 2. _____
3. Subtract line 2 from line 1. (If line 2 is more than line 1, enter "0" on Form IT-201, Line 44. **Do not continue with this worksheet.**)................................ 3. _____
4. Enter the lesser of line 3 or $50,000..... 4. _____
5. Divide line 4 by $50,000 and carry the result to four decimal places .... 5. _____
6. Enter 25% of Form IT-201, Line 43 ...... 6. _____
7. Multiply line 5 by line 6 .... 7. _____

Transfer this amount to Form IT-201, Line 44.

WORKSHEET B

1. Enter the amount by which New York adjusted gross income exceeds $475,000 (Not more than $50,000) .... 1. _____
2. Divide line 1 by $50,000 and carry the result to four decimal places .... 2. _____
3. Enter 25% of Form IT-201, Line 43 ...... 3. _____
4. Multiply line 2 by line 3 .... 4. _____
5. Add lines 3 and 4................................. 5. _____

Transfer this amount to Form IT-201, Line 44.

Itemized Deductions: *IT-201, Line 45*

Subtract Line 44 from Line 43 and enter the difference on Line 45. Line 45 is the amount of itemized deductions that you are allowed to deduct from your New York adjusted gross income. *Line 46* Enter your New York adjusted gross income as you reported it on Line 30. *Line 47* Compare the amount on Line 45 with the amount you are entitled to take as a standard deduction. Enter the larger of the two amounts on Line 47 and check the appropriate box that corresponds with the amount you used. *Line 48* Subtract Line 47 from Line 46 and enter the result.

Dependent Exemptions: *IT-201, Line 49*

See the section on *Personal Exemptions and Dependents* in Chapter 2 for information about who qualifies for a dependent exemption.

Once you have determined the number of dependent exemptions you may take, multiply that number by $1,000. Enter the total on Line 49. (If you are filing Form IT-200, your dependent exemption is entered on Line 14. If you are using Form IT-100, the state will make this calculation for you. All you need to do is enter on Line 1 the number of exemptions you reported on Line 6e of your federal 1040 or 1040A. If you filed federal Form 1040EZ, enter "1".)

Taxable Income: *IT-201, Line 50*

Your total dependent exemption from Line 49 should be subtracted from the amount on Line 48. Enter the result on Line 50. This is your taxable income for this tax year. (Form IT-200 filers should add Lines 11 through 14 and report the total on Line 15. To complete Line 16, subtract Line 15 from the amount you reported on Line 10.) You can skip the next sections for nonresidents/part-year residents and turn to Chapter 4, *How to Figure Your Tax.*

Nonresidents/Part-Year Residents—Starting Point

If you were a nonresident for the entire year, your New York State tax is based on income you received from New York State sources. If you moved into or out of New York State during the tax year, you must pay tax on your income from New York State sources while you were a nonresident and on *all* income you received while you were a resident.

This section will show you how to complete Lines 1–19 of your nonresident income tax return. It assumes that you have obtained a copy of Form IT-203 and determined your filing status. If not, review the preceding chapter. Have your filled-out federal Form 1040 or Form 1040A in front of you. If you didn't file a federal return, you will need to figure out what you would have reported if you had calculated your federal adjusted gross income for the year.

Computing Your Tax Base

If you are a nonresident or a part-year resident, you must first compute what your tax would be if you were a New York resident for the entire year. This is the tax you would have to pay on all of your items of income, gain, loss, and deduction from *all* sources. If you are a part-year resident, this amount will include special accruals. Next, you must divide your New York source income by your federal adjusted gross income to determine an *income percentage* attributable to New York. Then multiply your "resident" tax by your income percentage to compute the amount of tax that, as a nonresident or part-year resident, you actually owe to New York. It is incorrect to compute your New York State nonresident or part-year resident tax based only on your New York source income.

> **TAXALERT:** If you are *married filing jointly*, this method of calculating your tax automatically insures that you will be in the highest possible tax bracket based on the *total* taxable income reported by you and your spouse. Even if your combined income from New York sources is considerably less than your combined taxable income from all sources, you will still pay tax to New York at the rate applicable to your total income, just as you would if you were a resident!

Overview

Use your federal adjusted gross income as the starting point for computing your New York taxable income. Enter all items of your income in the Federal Amount column on Lines 1 through 19 of Form IT-203, just as you have reported them on your federal return. If you were not required to file a federal return, you will enter the amounts that you would have reported federally, if you had been required to file. For assistance, please consult *The Ernst & Young Tax Guide 1993.*

If you are a part-year resident, you must use the accrual method of accounting. (For more information, see the section on *Attributing Income to New York—Sourcing Rules* later in this chapter.)

> **TAXALERT:** If you and your spouse file a joint federal income tax return but file separate New York State returns, you must compute your New York adjusted gross income as if your federal adjusted gross income had been determined separately.

Filling Out the "Federal Amount Column"

For Lines 1–19, the entries will be exactly the same as the entries for the corresponding line numbers on Form IT-201, *Resident Income Tax Return*. (Please refer to the sections for *Residents* at the beginning of this chapter and follow the instructions there.)

Whether you are a nonresident or a part-year resident, you must enter in the Federal Amount column, the exact amount you reported on your federal return for each item listed on Lines 1–19.

Filling Out the "New York State Amount" Column

If you are a nonresident, you must enter in the "New York State Amount" column on Lines 1–19 all of the income included in the "Federal Amount" column that you received from New York State sources. If you moved into or out of New York State during the year, this includes income you received from the New York State sources while you were a nonresident and income you received from *all* sources while you were a resident. If you are a part-year resident, use the *Part-Year Resident Income Allocation Worksheet* on page NY-46 to assist you in allocating your items of income between your resident and nonresident periods.

Wages, Salaries, Tips, etc.: IT-203, Line 1

Nonresidents. If you are a nonresident, enter that part of the "Federal Amount" column that represents compensation for services you performed in New York.

Any income you earned *partially* in New York may be allocated according to your "days in" and "days outside" New York. However, New York has very strict rules about which days can be counted as "days outside" New York. For an explanation of these rules, see the section on *Attributing Income to New York—Sourcing Rules* later in this chapter.

Part-Year Residents. If you moved into or out of the state during the year, you must also include the portion of the federal amount that represents compensation you earned while you were a resident.

Taxable Interest Income and Dividend Income: IT-203, Line 2 and Line 3

Normally, a nonresident will enter zero on this line. However, if you use stocks or bonds in a business that is carried on in New York, the dividends or interest may be subject to tax. See the section on *Special Problems in Attributing Income*, later in this chapter, for more information.

Taxable Refunds of State and Local Income Taxes: IT-203, Line 4

Nonresidents. If you are a nonresident, do *not* enter any amount in this column.

Part-Year Residents. If you are a part-year resident, enter the part of the "Federal Amount" column that you received while you were a resident.

Alimony Received: IT-203, Line 5

Nonresidents. Do *not* enter any alimony received for the period you were a nonresident.

Part-Year Residents. If you are a part-year resident, enter only that part of the "Federal Amount" column which represents the total alimony received while you were a resident.

Business Income: IT-203, Line 6

(See the sections *Attributing Income to New York—Sourcing Rules*, and *Special Problems for Attributing Income* in this chapter in order to determine the amount you should enter.)

IT-203, Lines 7–11

(Refer to *Special Problems in Attributing Income*, for a complete discussion of how to determine the amounts you should enter on these lines.)

Rents, Royalties, Partnerships, Estates, Trusts, etc.: IT-203, Line 12

Nonresidents. If you are a nonresident, enter that part of the "Federal Amount" column connected with property located in New York. As a nonresident, you must report in the "New York State Amount" column any rents or royalties you received from:

1. Real property located in New York State;
2. Tangible personal property located in New York State; and
3. Intangible personal property used in or connected with a trade or business that you carried on in New York State.

If your business is carried on both inside and outside New York, you must generally apply a business allocation percentage (Form IT-203-A) to rent or royalty income. (See the section on *Attributing Income to New York—Sourcing Rules*, for instructions on how to determine your business allocation percentage.)

> **EXCEPTION:** Income or loss you receive from real property *cannot* be allocated. You must include the entire amount of any gains, losses, or rents in the "New York State Amount" column if the real property is located in New York State. Likewise, exclude the entire amount of this income or loss if the real property is located outside of New York State.

Also, you must include in the "New York State Amount" column your share of any rent or royalty income you received from a partnership, estate, or trust. (See *Special Problems in Attributing Income* for more information.)

Part-Year Residents. If you were a part-year resident, you must add the part of the "Federal Amount" column that you received from these sources while you were a resident.

> **TAXALERT:** If you have a deduction for passive activity losses, you must recompute the deduction to determine the amounts that would be allowed if, in determining your federal adjusted gross income, you took into account only items of income, gain, loss, or deduction derived from or in connection with New York sources.

Farm Income: IT-203, Line 13

Nonresidents. Enter the part of the "Federal Amount" column that represents your income or loss from farming carried on in New York State.

Part-Year Residents. If you were a part-year resident, you must also add the part of the federal amount of your farm income, as reported on Schedule F, that represents your farm income or loss for the period you were a resident.

Unemployment Compensation: *IT-203, Line 14*

Nonresidents. Because unemployment compensation is a direct result of past employment, the rules for sourcing this income are the same as for any other type of compensation. (See *Attributing Income to New York—Sourcing Rules*.)

Part-Year Residents. Include *all* unemployment compensation you received during your resident period.

Taxable Amount of Social Security Benefits: *IT-203, Line 15*

Nonresidents. Do *not* enter any amount received for the period you were a nonresident.

Part-Year Resident. Enter that part of the "Federal Amount" column that represents any taxable amount of Social Security (and Tier 1 railroad benefits) you received while you were a New York State resident.

Other Income: *IT-203, Line 16*

Nonresidents. Enter the portion of the Federal Amount column derived from or connected with New York State sources.

If you have a net operating loss derived from New York sources (without a corresponding federal net operating loss) that you are carrying forward, enter the amount of this loss in the "New York State Amount" column on Line 16 in parentheses. Attach a statement to your state return explaining this loss.

Part-Year Residents. If you were a part-year resident, you must also add the part of the federal amount of "other income" that you received while you were a resident.

Add *Lines 1–16* and enter on *Line 17*.

Total Federal Adjustments to Income: *IT-203, Line 18*

Any adjustment item that relates to wage or salary income that you earned partly in New York State or to income you received from a business carried on partly inside and partly outside New York must be allocated to New York on the same basis as the income to which it relates. (Refer to *Attributing Income to New York—Sourcing Rules*, for details on allocation.)

Nonresidents. Enter on this line the part of the federal amount that represents your adjustments connected with New York State sourced income.

Part-Year Residents. If you were a part-year resident, you must also add the part of the federal adjustment that is deductible for the time you were a New York State resident.

> **TaxAlert:** If you have a federal adjustment for alimony paid, include in the "New York State Amount" column only the portion of your alimony adjustment that is attributable to your resident period.

Federal Adjusted Gross Income: *IT-203, Line 19*

Subtract *Line 18* from *Line 17* and enter the result on *Line 19*.

Also, enter the amount from *Line 19* in the "New York State Amount" column in the area next to the income percentage on *Line 56*, IT-203. If either the amount on *Line 19* in the "Federal Amount" column or the "New York State Amount" column is zero or less, skip *Lines 20–56*; enter 0 on *Line 57* and continue on *Line 58*.

If the amount in either column on *Line 19* is greater than zero, continue on to *Additions and Subtractions* for information on completing *Lines 20–30*.

Additional information on how to determine the "New York State Amount" for items of income not discussed in detail under this section can be found in the sections *Attributing Income to New York—Sourcing Rules* and *Special Problems in Attributing Income* later in this chapter.

Chapter 4 explains how you will use the New York State Amount as a percentage of your total income to determine your tax.

Nonresidents/Part-Year Residents— Additions and Subtractions

This section assumes that you have completed at least the *federal adjusted gross income* portions of your New York nonresident and part-year resident tax return, Form IT-203 (Lines 1 through 19, *Federal Amount* column). If you haven't done this yet, go back and review the preceding section, *Nonresidents/Part-Year Residents—Starting Point*.

Here we will show you how to make the modifications that New York requires to federal adjusted gross income. You will make additions and subtractions required by law to reflect the various differences between income taxed by the federal government and income taxed by New York. The result will be your *New York adjusted gross income*, entered on Line 30 and again on Line 46 of your return.

Now look at your return. You will see three lines for additions to your federal income, as follows:

- Interest income on state and local bonds, *Line 20;*
- Public employee 414(h) retirement contributions, *Line 21;* and
- Other additions, *Line 22.*

You will see five lines for subtractions allowing you to subtract the following items from your federal adjusted gross income as follows:

- Taxable refunds from state and local income taxes, *Line 24;*
- Taxable amount of social security benefits, *Line 25;*
- Interest income on United States government bonds, *Line 26;*
- Pension and annuity income exclusion, *Line 27;* and
- Other subtractions, *Line 28.*

All of these additions and subtractions will be discussed in detail in the following paragraphs.

Additions to Federal Adjusted Gross Income

Nonresidents with Interest Income From State and Local Bonds: *IT-203, Line 20*

Generally, if you were not a New York State resident during any part of the year, you do not have to include interest income you received from state and local bonds in your New York taxable income. However, if you acquired bonds for use in a business or occupation carried on in New York, you must report any interest income from the bonds on this line.

EXCEPTION: Interest income from bonds issued by New York State or any of its local governments is always tax-exempt in New York, no matter how you acquired these bonds. This is true whether you are a resident, nonresident, or part-year resident of New York.

Example

Peter, a New Jersey resident, commutes every weekday to his job in New York City. Peter's yearly salary is $32,000 a year. Peter also receives $300 in interest income from his Ohio bonds. The Ohio State bonds were purchased as a personal investment.

Because Peter is not a New York resident and the bonds were not purchased in connection with Peter's job in New York, he does not have to include the interest in his New York taxable income.

Part-Year Residents with Interest Income From State and Local Bonds: *IT-203, Line 20*

If you were a part-year New York State resident, you must include in your taxable income any interest you received from state and local bonds (except New York State and local bonds) while you were a resident of New York. This includes interest you had a right to collect but did not collect until you moved out of New York. This is in keeping with the general principle that part-year residents must keep track of their income on an *accrual basis*, rather than a *cash basis*.

Example

Cindy moved out of New York State on July 1, 1992. While she was a resident of New York, Cindy purchased a Texas bond. At the end of 1992, this bond will pay Cindy $120 in interest. Because Cindy lived in New York for six months and earned $10 per month in interest ($120 per year ÷ 12 months − $10 per month), she must include six months worth of interest, or $60, on Line 20 of her New York part-year resident return, even though she did not actually receive the cash until after her move.

Public Employee 414(h) Retirement Contributions: *IT-203, Line 21*

This line applies to you only if you are one of the following:

1. A Tier III or Tier IV member of the New York State or New York City retirement systems, which includes New York State and New York City teachers;
2. An employee of the State or City University of New York who belongs to the TIAA/CREF Optional Retirement System; or
3. A New York City uniformed force member (e.g., police, firefighters, corrections officers, transit, housing authority, or sanitation police).

Include on Line 21 of your New York State nonresident or part-year resident income tax return the amount of your 414(h) retirement contributions. You can find this amount on Copy 2 of your wage and tax statement, Form IT-2102, or federal Form W-2.

TAXALERT: Do not include any amount you may have contributed to your 401(k) deferred arrangement account, your qualified annuity plan, or your deferred compensation plan. New York defers the taxation of these amounts until you actually receive them.

Other Additions: *IT-203, Line 22*

Miscellaneous additions must be included on Line 22 of your New York State nonresident or part-year resident income tax return. These other additions will apply to you if you are a part-year resident, a sole proprietor, a partner in a New York partnership, a shareholder in a New York S corporation, or if you own property in New York. If you are required to make any of the following additions, write the item number(s) [e.g., A-1] and the amount(s) of each item in the white area labelled *identify* on Line 22. If you need extra room, attach a separate piece of paper. Enter the sum of your other additions in the *federal amount* column on the right-hand side of the return.

Interest or Dividend from United States Bonds and Obligations, A-1. You must include on your New York part-year resident income tax return any interest or dividend income earned during your resident period from certain United States bonds or obligations. The interest on these bonds is exempt from federal income tax but is taxable in New York. This includes any income you received or were entitled to receive (but chose to defer) while you were a New York State resident.

A list of bonds and obligations that are exempt for federal tax purposes but not for New York purposes is included in the *Residents—Additions and Subtractions* section earlier in this chapter.

New York nonresidents do not have to include any interest that would be taxable to a resident, unless the bonds or securities were acquired in connection with a business or occupation carried on in New York State. If you invest any money in a mutual fund that has at least 50 percent of its assets invested in exempt federal or U.S. territory obligations, dividends you receive as a result of these investments are exempt from New York State tax.

Income Taxes Deducted for Federal Purposes, A-2. Include any income taxes you deducted from your federal gross income. This includes income taxes deducted in figuring your share of a partnership's net income. You can find this information on your federal Schedule K-1. If you are a shareholder in a New York S corporation, you must also add back your share of New York State corporation franchise taxes paid by the S corporation. You do not have to add back any other taxes paid by the S corporation.

Interest Expense on Certain Loans, A-3. You must include any interest expense on loans that you deducted on your federal income tax return if you used the money to buy bonds and securities whose interest income is exempt from New York tax.

Mortgage Recording Tax Credit, A-4. If you are a shareholder of an electing New York S corporation, include your prorated share of the S corporation's special additional mortgage recording tax credit. You can find this amount on the S corporation's Form CT-3-S.

Special Additional Mortgage Recording Tax, A-5. Include the amount of special additional mortgage recording tax you originally paid if you sold or disposed of the property for which the tax was paid during the year. Make this addition only if the basis of the property was not adjusted for the special additional mortgage recording tax credit.

Addback of Certain Elections, A-6. Before 1987, New York taxpayers could make an election for a favorable computation of depreciation expenses for research and development expenditures, certain pollution control or acid deposition equipment, or waste treatment facilities. If you made such an election and later sold the property, you may need to add back a portion of your original deduction.

Addback of Depletion, A-7. You must also include any deduction for percentage depletion on mines, oil and gas wells, and other natural deposits from your federal adjusted gross income.

Addback of Losses from an Insurance Business, A-8. Include your share of allocated net income or loss from an insurance business operating as a member of the New York Insurance Exchange.

Gain from Property Acquired by an Estate, A-9. Include any gain that you realized for New York State tax purposes from the sale or other disposition of New York property acquired from a decedent if the estate had insufficient assets and did not file a federal estate tax return.

Solar and Wind Energy Systems, A-10. Taxpayers were allowed to claim a credit for these systems before 1987. If you sold residential property at a gain on which such a credit was taken, include the credit income if the basis of your property was not adjusted for the cost of the energy system.

New Business Investment-Deferral Recognition, A-11. Before 1988, New York taxpayers were entitled to certain deferrals of capital gains if they reinvested in a new business. If you made such deferrals, but later sold the new business investment property, you must add the deferrals back.

Safe Harbor Leases, A-12. Add back any deductions that were available to you federally solely because you made a special federal election with respect to a "safe harbor" lease agreement entered into before 1984.

Safe Harbor Leases, A-13. See A-12, above. Add back any exclusions from federal adjusted gross income resulting from the special federal election.

Accelerated Cost Recovery System (ACRS) Deduction, A-14. Add back any accelerated depreciation you deducted in figuring your federal adjusted gross income for property placed in service during 1981 through 1984 and for property placed in service *outside* New York after 1984. Use Form IT-399 to calculate this adjustment and your subtraction for New York State Depreciation (See *New York State Depreciation, S-19* under *Other Subtractions*.).

Accelerated Cost Recovery Property Year of Disposition Adjustment, A-15. If you dispose of property on which the total depreciation allowed for New York State purposes is greater than your total federal deductions, add back the difference.

S Corporation Shareholders, A-16. If you are a shareholder of a New York S corporation, include your share of federal reductions for taxes paid by the corporation on built-in gains or passive income.

S Corporation Shareholders, A-17. If you are a shareholder of a federal S corporation that could have made an election to be taxed as a New York S corporation, but did not, add back any of the S corporation's losses or deductions from your federal adjusted gross income.

S Corporation Shareholders, A-18. If you are a shareholder in an S corporation that could have made the New York election but did not, add any distributions not included in your federal adjusted gross income and not previously subject to tax in New York. Make this addition only if you are a part-year resident and received such distributions during the time you were a resident. Nonresidents do not need to make this addition unless the stock was used in a trade or business in New York.

S Corporation Shareholders, A-19. If you sold stock in an S corporation that could have made the New York election but did not, add any increases and subtract any reductions in your federal basis for all the years that a New York election was not in effect.

Interest Related to Corporate Acquisitions, A-20. Add five percent of your deduction for interest related to highly leveraged corporation acquisitions, if you deducted the interest in figuring your New York adjusted gross income. If this addition applies, complete Form IT-244, *Acquisition Information Report*. Attach a separate schedule to your return showing your computation.

New York City Flexible Benefits Program (IRC 125), A-21. You must add back the amount shown on Copy 2 of your wage and tax statement(s), Form IT-2102 or federal Form W-2, deducted or deferred from an employee's salary under a flexible benefits program established by the City of New York and certain other New York City public employers.

Total your New York Other Additions and enter them on Line 22 of your return.

Subtractions from Federal Adjusted Gross Income

Taxable Refunds of State and Local Income Taxes, *Line 24*

Enter the amount you entered on Line 4 in the Federal Amount column.

Taxable Amount of Social Security Benefits, *Line 25*

Enter the same amount you entered in the Federal Amount column of Line 15.

Interest Income on United States Government Bonds, *Line 26*

Enter any interest income you received from U.S. Government bonds or obligations included in the Federal Amount column of Line 2. This subtraction is allowed because New York does not tax interest income you receive from bonds or other obligations of the U.S. government. This income is taxable for federal purposes. *Other obligations* include qualifying dividends received from regulated investment companies (mutual funds) that invest 50% or more of the assets in United States government obligations.

Example

Samantha, a New Jersey resident, works full time as a news reporter in New York. Samantha generally invests part of her yearly salary in mutual funds. The mutual fund that Samantha invests in makes it a practice to invest more than 50% of their funds in U.S. treasury bonds. At the end of each year, the mutual fund sends Samantha a statement required by law showing how her assets are invested. For federal purposes, Samantha must include any interest income she receives from this mutual fund in her adjusted gross income. For New York State purposes Samantha can subtract this amount from her New York taxable income.

TaxAlert: Be sure not to subtract this amount more than once. Some taxpayers make this mistake because *other subtractions*, S-1 and S-4 on Line 28, are similar to Line 26.

On Line 26 you enter any interest or dividend income you receive from U.S. government bonds. On Line 28, S-1, you enter any interest or dividend income you receive from bonds or securities issued by a United States authority, commission, or instrumentality. Also, on Line 28, S-4, you enter any interest or dividend income you receive from New York bonds or securities.

Pension and Annuity Income Exclusion: IT-203, Line 27

When dealing with annuities, New York makes a distinction between residents, part-year residents, and nonresidents. Resident taxpayers may exclude $20,000 of private pension or annuity income received after the recipient attains the age of 59½. If you reach the age 59½ before January 1, 1992, you qualify for the full pension and annuity income exclusion. If you become 59½ during any part of 1992, you can exclude any amount you receive after you reach such age, up to $20,000.

Spouses can each qualify for a $20,000 pension and annuity exclusion. However, you cannot claim any unused part of your spouse's exclusion.

Nonresidents receive even more favorable treatment. Normally, a pension or retirement benefit received by a nonresident that qualifies as an annuity is not taxable in New York. (See *Special Problems in Attributing Income* for further information.)

Exception: Government employees cannot claim the $20,000 subtraction.

Other Subtractions: IT-203, Line 28

You may be able to use other subtractions to reduce your federal adjusted gross income. If any of the following subtractions apply to you, write the item number and the amount of the subtraction in the white area marked *identify* on Line 28. Put the total amount of your subtractions in the Federal Amount column on the right of the return.

Interest on United States Bonds, S-1. Subtract any interest or dividend income you receive from bonds or securities of any United States authority, commission, or instrumentality that is exempt from New York tax, if you *included* in your federal adjusted gross income. Do not include interest subtracted on Line 26. (See *Residents—Additions and Subtractions*, for a list of bonds that are taxable for federal purposes but exempt from New York tax.)

Certain Pensions, S-2. Subtract any pension you receive as an officer, employee, or as a beneficiary of an officer or employee of New York State or local governments that you included in your federal adjusted gross income. Also subtract pensions received from the United States, its territories or possessions, political subdivisions of these territories or possessions, the District of Columbia or any agency or instrumentality of any of the above (including the military) that you included in your federal adjusted gross income.

Benefits from the Railroad Retirement Act, S-3. Subtract any supplemental annuity and Tier 2 benefits you received under the Railroad Retirement Act of 1974 or Railroad Unemployment Insurance Act, included in your federal adjusted gross income.

Interest from New York State Bonds, S-4. Subtract any interest or dividend income included in your federal adjusted gross income but exempt from New York State tax.

Interest Expense of Certain Loans, S-5. Subtract interest on loans used to purchase or carry bonds or securities whose interest income is subject to New York State income tax but exempt from federal income tax. This expense must be a current business expense not deducted in figuring your federal adjusted gross income.

Certain Business Expenses, S-6. Subtract ordinary and necessary business expenses incurred in connection with income or income-producing property subject to New York State tax but exempt from federal income tax.

Amortization of Bond Premium in the 1992 Year, S-7. You may take as a deduction any amortization expense of a premium of a federally tax-exempt bond that is taxable for New York State purposes. Since the interest on these bonds is taxable in New York, the amortization of the premium is deductible.

Income Included in Prior Taxable Year, S-8. If you are a shareholder of a professional service corporation, subtract any income that was previously taxed by New York. Because of differences between federal and state tax laws, such income may have been included in your federal adjusted gross income for the year.

Federal Targeted Job Credit, S-9. You may subtract the amount of wages and salaries paid or incurred during the taxable year for which a federal salaries deduction is not allowed because a federal targeted jobs credit was claimed.

Disposition of Certain Property, S-10. Subtract the part of any gain included in your federal adjusted gross income from the sale or other disposition of:

1. Property that had a higher basis for New York State income tax purposes than for federal income tax purposes on December 31, 1959; and
2. Property held in connection with mines, oil or gas wells, and other natural deposits that has a higher adjusted basis for New York State income tax purposes.

This subtraction cannot exceed the difference in basis. When the gain on the sale or other disposition of jointly owned property is divided between you and your spouse on your separate state returns, any subtraction due to a higher New York than federal basis must also be divided.

Gain Already Reported, S-11. Any amount of income or gain included in your federal adjusted gross income that was properly reported as income or gain on a previous New York State return.

Depletion of Property, S-12. Subtract cost depletion figured according to federal tax law on property where percentage depletion was added on Line 22. See *Addback of Depletion, A-7* for more detailed information on this subtraction.

Depreciation Expenditures, S-13. Exclude special depreciation expenditures or carryover of research and development expenditures incurred in taxable years beginning before 1987 in connection with depreciable business property located in New York.

Gains from an Insurance Business, S-14. Subtract any amount included in your federal adjusted gross income that represents your share of income or gain from an insurance business operating as a member of the New York Insurance Exchange.

Losses from Property Acquired from a Decedent, S-15. Subtract any loss that would have been realized for New York State tax purposes from the sale or other disposition of property acquired from a decedent but was not because the estate had an insufficient amount of assets to require the filing of a federal estate tax return.

New Business Investment Exclusion, S-16. Subtract any gain from the sale of a New York new business investment that was included in your federal adjusted gross income.

Safe Harbor Leases, S-17. Subtract any amount that was included in your federal adjusted gross income (except for mass transit vehicles) solely because of a pre-1984 "safe harbor" election.

Safe Harbor Leases, S-18. Subtract any amount that could have been excluded from federal adjusted gross income (except for mass transit vehicles) because a pre-1984 "safe harbor" election was *not* made.

New York State Depreciation, S-19. Subtract the amount of New York depreciation allowed for property placed in service during taxable years 1981 through 1984 and for property placed in service outside New York State after 1984. Use Form IT-399 to calculate your New York State depreciation and attach is to your Form IT-203.

Accelerated Cost Recovery Property—Year of Disposition Adjustment, S-20. If you disposed of property in 1992, subtract the amount by which your total federal accelerated cost recovery deductions were greater than the total depreciation you took for New York State purposes on that property.

S Corporation Shareholders, S-21 (See preceding explanation under New Business Investment Exclusion, A-16). If you recognized any gain or loss on your federal income tax return because you disposed of stock or indebtedness of an S corporation that did *not* make the New York election, subtract any part of the gain that is due to a reduction in basis of stock or indebtedness for each taxable year that the New York election was *not* in effect.

Also, subtract any additions to federal adjusted gross income that you were required to make for certain distributions of property, cash, or benefits excluded from federal income.

S Corporation Shareholders, S-22. If you are a shareholder of an S corporation for which the election to be a New York S corporation was *not* in effect for the taxable year, any S corporation income included in federal may be subtracted from your adjusted gross income.

Disability Income Exclusion, S-23. You may subtract any amount that could have been excluded from federal adjusted gross income before January 1, 1984. However, the sum of disability income excluded and pension and annuities income excluded may *not* exceed $20,000.

> **TAXALERT:** If you claim this exclusion, you must also complete the physician's statement at the bottom of Form IT-221.

Accelerated Death Benefits, S-24. Subtract the amount received as an accelerated payment of part or all of the death benefit or special surrender value under a life insurance policy. Eligible payments may be received as a result of terminal illness or of a medical condition requiring extraordinary medical care. Any amounts included in federal adjusted gross income may be excluded for New York purposes.

Your New York adjusted gross income, entered on Line 30, equals your federal adjusted gross income plus additions and minus subtractions. To complete the next section of your nonresident tax return, see the preceding section on *Deductions*.

Attributing Income to New York— Sourcing Rules

Sourcing Income for Nonresidents

New York's tax laws require that nonresidents compute their tax as if they were full-year residents. Once you figure out what your tax would be if you were a resident, multiply it by the percentage of your New York source income to your total federal adjusted gross income.

Who May Allocate

If you are a nonresident employee who performed services partly in and partly outside the state, you may allocate your wages or salary to determine your New York source income. Your allocation will be based on the proportion of days you worked in New York to the days you worked altogether. This method is called the *days worked* method.

> **EXCEPTION:** Professional athletes, seamen, and salespeople must allocate their wages and salaries using different methods, explained later in this chapter.

Example

Jeanine, a resident of New Jersey, is an employee of Acme Corporation. The main offices of Acme are located in New York, but Acme also has other offices located in California and North Carolina. During 1992, Jeanine was sent to the North Carolina office for three months to help establish a new marketing department. She worked in the New York office for the rest of the year. Since Jeanine performed some services for her employer outside New York, she may allocate her wages.

Counting Days Outside New York

You should exercise caution when counting the number of days you worked outside the state. New York's rules are very strict. You cannot claim a day as one worked outside New York unless you were at another place because your employer required it. If you worked outside New York for your own convenience, you may not count that day as a day worked outside New York. Days you worked at home are usually not counted as days worked outside New York.

> **TAXALERT:** Although it's easy to confuse the two, a "day outside New York" for allocation purposes is different from a "day outside New York" for purposes of the residency test, discussed in Chapter 2. An *entire* day spent elsewhere may count as a day outside New York when you are deciding whether to file as a resident or a nonresident. It will *not* count as a day outside New York for allocation purposes unless your employer required you to work outside New York on that particular day.

Example

Dr. Finch, a Connecticut resident, is a tenured professor at a New York college where he teaches history. Although Dr. Finch has an office on the college campus, he prefers to conduct his research and prepare his lectures at his Connecticut home. The days Dr.

Finch works at home cannot be counted as days worked outside the state, since the work is done for his own convenience and not because his employer requires it.

Example

Ms. King, a Connecticut resident, works for XYZ Corporation, which is located in New York City. During the year, Ms. King worked several days at her Connecticut home office because her New York office did not provide adequate secretarial support. The days worked at her home office were for her own convenience and not because her New York employer required her to do so. She cannot count the days she worked at home as days worked outside New York.

Example

Jay, a New Jersey resident, works for ABC Corporation, which is located in New York. During the year, Jay was involved in a serious automobile accident in which he fractured his leg. Since his accident, Jay has been working from his New Jersey home using a computer. Even though Jay's physical condition makes it difficult for him to commute to his office, the days he works at his home cannot be counted as days worked outside of New York. He works at home for his own convenience, not to accommodate the needs of his employer.

Example

Mr. Anderson, an attorney employed by a New York City law firm, was forced to move from New York to Arizona because of his wife's illness. Mr. Anderson set up an office in his Arizona home and continued to work for his employer. Mr. Anderson may not count the days he worked from his Arizona home office as days worked outside New York. He worked in Arizona for his own convenience.

New York courts and administrative bodies have ruled in many other instances that work was performed for a taxpayer's own convenience, and thus is not allocable outside New York. Some examples include:

- A television reviewer who worked at home because her employer failed to provide an office
- A casting director at a television station who maintained personnel files at home and worked at home because the television station could not guarantee the safety of the files
- A baseball manager who worked at home during the off-season

On the other hand, a firearms expert who installed a firing range on the grounds of his out-of-state home was able to allocate the days he worked at home as days outside New York. The reason? He could not have legally tested firearms at the offices of his New York City employer!

Determining Your Allocation

When allocating the days you worked inside and outside the state, you should not count nonworking days. Nonworking days include:

- Saturdays, Sundays, and holidays;
- Sick days or days lost due to personal injury;
- Vacation days (paid or unpaid); and
- Days spent outside the state on jury duty.

Travel days for business are considered working days and should be included in your total days worked.

Example

Ms. Thatcher, a resident of New Jersey, is the sales manager for a New York corporation. During the year, she was sent to Pittsburgh to help establish a new sales office. Ms. Thatcher left on Sunday from LaGuardia Airport. She spent two weeks in Pittsburgh, holding meetings in her hotel room. All other services she performed for the New York corporation were performed within the state. Her salary allocation percentage is determined as follows:

Total days in year		365
Nonworking days:		
Saturdays and Sundays:		
Total	104	
Less: Travel day	(1)	
Holidays	10	
Sick days	4	
Vacation	10	
Total nonworking days		(127)
Working days		238
Days worked outside New York		
Travel day to Pittsburgh	1	
Regular workdays in Pittsburgh	10	
Total non-NY working days		(11)
Days worked in New York		227

$$\text{Salary Allocation Percentage} = \frac{227}{238} = 95.38\%$$

Example

Mr. Moore, a Connecticut resident, is employed as a salesman by Y Corporation, which is located in New York. During the year, Mr. Moore spent 30 days outside New York calling on customers in the Midwest. In addition, he spent five days in Connecticut on jury duty. All remaining services performed on behalf of Y Corporation were performed in New York. Mr. Moore's salary allocation percentage is calculated in the following manner:

Total days in year		365
Nonworking days:		
Saturdays and Sundays:	104	
Holidays	11	
Sick days	2	
Vacation	15	
Jury duty	5	
Total nonworking days		(137)
Working days		228
Days worked outside New York:		
Calling on customers in Midwest states	30	
Total non-NY working days		(30)
Days worked in New York		198

$$\text{Salary allocation percentage} = \frac{198}{228} = 86.84\%$$

TAXPLANNER: You should maintain adequate records to support those days you are counting as non-New York working days. These days may be challenged by New York if you are audited. Examples of supporting records include work diaries, appointment calendars, expense reports, and trip sheets. You will also need to substantiate these records through airline boarding passes, gasoline or toll receipts, credit card receipts and other such proof that you really were outside New York when you say you were.

If you are a nonresident who works solely at home because you are required to do so by a New York employer, you do not have to allocate any salary to New York. In addition, if you are a nonresident who was required to work at home because your New York office was shut down due to a strike, you do not have to allocate your salary to New York for those days.

A nonresident employee who performs services partly inside and partly outside New York for only part of the tax year may only allocate that compensation he or she received during the period services were performed both inside and outside the state.

Example

Sandy, a full-year resident of Connecticut, was employed by Z Corporation during the 1992 tax year. During the period January 1 through April 30, he worked at the company's Englewood, New Jersey office. All services performed during that period were performed in New Jersey. On May 1, Sandy was transferred to the company's New York City office where he was required to perform services partly in and partly outside New York. Sandy may only allocate the compensation he received from May 1 through December 31, the period he performed services both inside and outside. Sandy's compensation received during January 1 through April 30 would not be taxable in New York.

A nonresident employee who performs services both inside and outside New York for more than one employer must separately allocate the salaries received from the different employers.

Example

Jeffrey, a resident of New Jersey, performed services for X Corporation from January 1 through June 30. He received $30,000 for his work. He performed services for X Corporation both inside and outside the state. Of his 125 working days during this period, 75 were spent in New York. The remaining 50 were spent performing services outside the state. Jeffrey resigned from X Corporation and went to work for Y Corporation on July 6. From July 6 through December 31, he received $35,000 in salary. Of his 120 working days during this period, 60 were spent in New York, while the remaining 60 were spent performing services outside the state. Jeffrey's New York adjusted gross income is computed as follows:

$$\text{X Corp. } \frac{75}{125} \times 30,000 = \$18,000$$

$$\text{Y Corp. } \frac{60}{120} \times 35,000 = \underline{\$17,500}$$

Total New York adjusted gross income = $35,500

Forms

If you allocate your salary or wages, you are required to complete Form IT-203-ATT, Schedule A–*Allocation of Wages and*

Schedule A

Allocation of Wages and Salary Income to New York State

a	Wages, salaries, tips, etc. *(to be allocated)*	a
b	Total days in year	b
c	Nonworking days:	
	Saturdays and Sundays.. *Do not count days worked*	
	holidays	
	sick leave	
	vacation	
	other nonworking days	
	Total nonworking days	c
d	Total days worked in year *(subtract line c from line b)*	d
e	Total days worked outside New York State	e
f	Days worked in New York State *(subtract line e from line d)*	f
g	New York State amount:	

$$\frac{\text{line f:}}{\text{line d:}} \times \underline{\text{line a:}} = \boxed{g}$$

Include line g amount on Form IT-203, line 1, New York State Amount column.

h	Days worked at home included in line e	h

Form IT-203-ATT: Schedule A

Salary Income to New York State. If you are a professional athlete, seaman, or salesperson, do not use Schedule A.

Line a of Form IT-203-ATT, Schedule A includes any amount that was reported in the Federal Amount column on Line 1 of Form IT-203 that was earned partly inside and partly outside New York State. This is your income that is subject to allocation.

Complete Lines b–f and use the allocation formula on Line g to determine the amount of wages or salary that you earned within New York. The amount you computed on Line g must then be entered on Line 1 of Form IT-203 in the New York State amount column. Attach Form IT-203-ATT to your New York nonresident return (Form IT-203).

If you are a nonresident who allocates wages and salaries received from different employers, you must complete a separate Form IT-203-ATT for each job. Attach all such forms to your tax return.

If your period of employment is less than a full year, you must base the figures entered in Schedule A on your actual period of employment.

If you are married and both you and your spouse are allowed to allocate your wages and salaries, you must each separately complete a Schedule A.

TaxAlert: Your failure to complete and attach Schedule A to your Form IT-203 will result in a delay in the processing of your return.

Special Allocations

Professional Athletes. New York does not consider the method described above to be a fair and equitable method when allocating the income earned by nonresident professional athletes. If you are a nonresident professional athlete, you must allocate your salary to New York based on the number of games that you played or were obligated to play in New York to total games that you were obligated to play during the year. Pre-season exhibition games and playoff games are included in total games played.

Example

Kevin, a nonresident professional basketball player, played in all six pre-season exhibition games and 82 regular season games for his Illinois-based team during the 1992 tax year. Of the total 88 games played during the year, three were played in New York. Kevin's New York source income is calculated by multiplying his salary by 3/88, since pre-season exhibition games are included in total games played.

Seamen. If you are a nonresident seaman working on a vessel that operates exclusively within New York, you must include all your wages as New York income. If you are a nonresident seaman working on a vessel that operates exclusively between New York and foreign ports, or ports of other states, none of your wages is sourced to New York. This is true even if you work aboard the ship while it is temporarily docked at a New York port. If you are a nonresident seaman working on a vessel that operates between New York and New Jersey ports, you must allocate 50 percent of your wages to New York.

Salespeople. If you are a nonresident salesperson whose wages or commissions depend directly upon the volume of business you transact, you must allocate your income based on a ratio of your volume of business transacted in New York to your total volume of business. The location where the services or sales are performed determines where business is transacted. Any other payments received by a salesperson are allocated using the *days worked method* described above.

If you are a nonresident who allocates wages and salary using a special allocation method, you should attach a schedule to your tax return showing how you figured this allocation.

Self-Employed Individuals

If you are a nonresident who is self-employed and earning income from a business carried on partly inside and outside New York, you must determine your New York source income using one of the following methods:

- Separate accounting;
- Three-factor formula; or
- An alternative method which fairly and equitably reflects New York source income.

You are considered to be carrying on a business inside and outside New York if you occupy or maintain desk space, an office, a shop, a store, a warehouse, a factory, an agency, or other place where your business matters are systematically and regularly carried on outside New York.

Special problems faced by partners and shareholders of S corporations in determining their New York source income are discussed in the section on *Special Problems in Attributing Income*, later in this chapter.

TAXALERT: An occasional or isolated business transaction outside New York will not qualify you to allocate your income. You are not systematically and regularly carrying on business outside the state. You must also have a regular place of business outside New York in order to allocate business income.

Separate Accounting

In general, separate accounting is used to source your New York income when you can specifically identify the profits earned from your New York location. If you use this method, you must keep books and records which disclose to the sat-

isfaction of the Tax Commissioner the items of income, gain, loss, and deduction attributable to your business activities carried on inside New York. Otherwise, you must allocate your income, using the three-factor formula method.

Three-Factor Formula

You must use this method to allocate your income if you cannot determine your New York income from your books and records. Under this method, your business income is apportioned using the average of the following percentages:

- Property Percentage;
- Payroll Percentage; or
- Gross Income Percentage.

Property Percentage. The property percentage is computed by dividing the average of the beginning and ending values of real and tangible personal property located in New York by the average of the beginning and ending values of real and tangible personal property located everywhere. Real property also includes real property rented by the business. To determine the fair market value of rented real property both inside and outside New York, you must multiply the gross rents payable during the tax year by eight.

Gross rent includes:

- Any amount payable for the use or possession of real property whether paid as a fixed sum of money or as a percentage of sales, profits, or otherwise;
- Any amount payable as additional rent or instead of rent, such as interest, taxes, insurance, repairs or any other amount required to be paid by the terms of a lease; and
- A proportion of the cost of any improvement to real property made by or on behalf of the business which reverts to the owner or lessor upon termination of a lease or other arrangements; however, if a building is erected on leased land by or on behalf of the business, the value of the building is determined in the same manner as if it were owned by the business.

Payroll Percentage. The payroll percentage is computed by dividing the total compensation paid during the year to employees in connection with operations carried on in New York by the total compensation paid during the year to employees everywhere.

TAXALERT: You should not include payments made to independent contractors, independent sales agents, etc. in the payroll percentage. These individual are not considered employees of your business.

Gross Income Percentage. The gross income percentage is computed by dividing the gross sales or charges for services performed by or through an office or agency of the business located in New York by the total gross sales or charges for services performed inside and outside New York. The sales or services allocated to New York include sales made or services performed by an employee, agent, or independent contractor connected to or sent out from offices of the business or its agencies located in New York. It does not matter that an employee, agent, or independent contractor may make sales outside the state. All sales made by that individual are allocated to New York.

Example

Dane, a Connecticut resident, owns a chain of record stores. He runs his multistate business from his headquarters located in Connecticut. During 1992, his operating results were as follows:

	–(in thousands)–	
	New York	Total
Revenue	$1,000	$3,000
General Administration		650
Advertising		200
Salaries	200	600
Rent Expense	100	300
Depreciation		250
Total Expenses		2,000
Net Income		$1,000

Dane owns no real property but does own tangible personal property. The net book value of the property at the beginning of the year everywhere was $300,000 and at the end of the year $200,000. The value of the property owned at the beginning of the year in New York was $100,000 and at the end of the year was $100,000. Dane would compute his New York income using the three-factor formula in the following manner.

	–(in thousands)–	
Property Percentage	New York	Everywhere
Rent (Rent Expense × 8)	800	2,400
Average Property Value:		
[1]Beg-EW 300,000		
[1]End-EW 200,000	100	250
Total	900	2,650

Percentage = 900/2,650
= 33.96%

Payroll Percentage	New York	Everywhere
Salaries	200	600

Percentage = 200/600
= 33.33%

Gross Income Percentage	New York	Everywhere
Revenues	1,000	3,000

Percentage = 1,000/3,000
= 33.33%

Total Percentages (Property, Payroll, Gross Income)
= 100.62
Average = 100.62/3
= 33.54

Net Income Allocable to New York = 1,000,000 ×
33.54%
= $335,400

[1]EW means everywhere

If a percentage is missing, you must add the remaining percentages and divide by the number of percentages present. A percentage is missing when both your New York amount and everywhere amount are zero. For example, if you had no rent or personal property located inside or outside the state, you would not have a property percentage. In this instance, you must add your payroll percentage and gross income percentage and divide by two.

Alternative Method

If you cannot determine your New York income from your books and the three-factor formula method does not fairly reflect your New York income, you may use an alternative method to allocate income. Any alternative method used must be approved by the New York State Commissioner of Taxation and Finance.

TaxAlert: The three-factor formula or alternative method is not applied to income from the rental of real property or gains or losses from the sale of real property. The entire rental income from New York real property or gain from the sale of such property is taxed by New York. Likewise, any loss connected with such property can be deducted on your New York return.

If you are a nonresident who carried on a business both inside and outside New York, you must complete IT-203-A, *New York State Nonresident Business Allocation Schedule*. If you carried on more than one business for which an allocation is required, you must prepare a separate IT-203-A or similar statement for each business. Each schedule must be attached to your Form IT-203.

Part-Year Residents

New York requires that part-year residents compute their tax as if they were full-year residents. Once the tax is calculated, it is prorated based on a ratio of New York source income to total federal adjusted gross income.

Your New York source income is the sum of:

- Your federal adjusted gross income for the period you resided in New York, computed as if the federal taxable year were limited to that period; and
- Your New York source income for the period you were a nonresident, determined as if the federal taxable year were limited to that period.

In addition, adjustments must be made for special accruals.

Special Accruals. If you moved out of New York State during the tax year, you must accrue and report as New York source any income, gain, loss, or deduction during your resident period if you would be required to include it if you were filing a federal return on an accrual basis. This includes:

- Income or gain that you elected to report on the installment basis;
- New York lottery prizes; and
- Any lump-sum distributions subject to the separate tax on lump-sum distributions.

Example

On July 1, 1992, Fred, a New York resident, terminated his employment in the state and moved to Montana. Fred earned $40,000 in salary before he resigned. Before his move, Fred sold a tract of land in Connecticut and realized a gain of $10,000. Fred elected to report the gain on an installment basis. Fred must include in his New York source income his New York salary of $40,000, plus the $10,000 gain he realized on the sale of his Connecticut land. Fred cannot defer any of the $10,000 gain to his nonresident period, even though he is reporting the gain on a cash basis for federal purposes.

Example

Jennifer moved from New York to Florida on August 1, 1992. On July 28, 1992, her employer awarded her a guaranteed bonus of $1,000. The bonus was not paid until August 15, 1992. Although the bonus was paid after her move, Jennifer must include the $1,000 in her New York source income because this income accrued to her during her resident period.

You also must accrue to New York any items of tax preference that are subject to the minimum income tax (Form IT-220).

Accruals are not required if you post a surety bond or other acceptable security with the Department of Taxation and Finance. It must be equal to or greater than the additional tax that would be due if the accrued items were included on your part-year resident return. If the security requirements are satisfied, you must include the accrued amounts of your New York nonresident return for subsequent tax years, as if no change in residence had occurred.

If you elect to file a bond or other form of security, you must complete and file either Form IT-260, *Surety Bond Form* or Form IT-260.1, *Change of Resident Status—Special Accruals*.

If you became a New York State resident during the tax year, you may exclude in determining New York source income, New York adjusted gross income, or minimum taxable income or any item of income, gain, loss, or deduction that accrued before you changed residence. This exclusion applies to future tax years as well as the year of change.

If you moved in or out of New York State during the tax year, the following worksheet should be used to help you calculate your 1992 New York State source income.

Part-Year Resident Income Allocation Worksheet

Adjusted Gross Income Married persons filing separate New York State returns should complete separate worksheets		Federal income (all sources) Column A Income from federal return & accruals		New York State Resident Period Column B Income from Column A for this period		New York State Nonresident Period			
						Column C Income from Column A for this period		Column D Income from Column C from New York State sources	
1. Wages, salaries, tips, etc.	1.								
2. Taxable interest income	2.								
3. Dividend income	3.								
4. Taxable refunds of state and local income taxes	4.								
5. Alimony received	5.								
6. Business income or (loss) (*from federal Schedule C*)	6.								
7. Capital gain or (loss) (*from federal Schedule D*)	7.								
8. Capital gain distributions not reported on line 7	8.								
9. Other gains or (losses) (*from federal Form 4797*)	9.								
10. Taxable amount of IRA distributions	10.								
11. Taxable amount of pensions and annuities	11.								
12. Rents, royalties, partnerships, estates, trusts, etc. (*from federal Schedule E*)	12.								
13. Farm income or (loss) (*from federal Schedule F*)	13.								
14. Unemployment compensation (insurance)	14.								
15. Taxable amount of social security benefits	15.								
16. Other income	16.								
17. Add lines 1 through 16	17.								
18. Total federal adjustments to income Identify:	18.								
19. Subtract line 18 from line 17 (*see instructions above*). This is your federal adjusted gross income	19.								

The combined total of Columns B and C should equal Column A. Add the amounts in Column B and D for each line of the worksheet above and transfer the total to the corresponding line of Form IT-203 in the New York State Amount column.

Enter the amounts of income and adjustments reported on your federal return in Column A. You should also enter in this column all items you would be required to include if you were filing a federal return on an accrual basis.

The amounts from Column A that you received while a New York resident are entered in Column B.

The amounts from Column A that you received while a New York nonresident are entered in Column C.

The amounts from Column C that you received from services performed in New York, property located in New York and businesses, trades, professions, or occupations conducted in New York are entered in Column D.

The total on Line 19 of Column A of the worksheet should be transferred to the corresponding line on Form IT-203 in the Federal Amount column.

The totals from Line 19, Columns B and D of the worksheet must be added together to compute your total New York source income. This number should be entered on Line 19 of Form IT-203, in the New York State Amount column.

Special Problems in Attributing Income

It's worthwhile to spend a few moments considering the unique items of income, such as deferred compensation and other retirement benefits, income from intangible personal property, and distributions from partnerships and S corporations, that affect the computation of tax for nonresidents.

Deferred Compensation

So you're dreaming about retiring to some quiet town in a far-away state, where the sun shines almost every day and you won't have to pay a state income tax? Well, be careful, because there's an increasing possibility that the state where you formerly worked will find you and demand that you pay tax on your pension or other retirement benefit.

Deferred compensation generally includes income which will be taxed when received and not when earned. For example, contributions made by an employer to a qualified pension or retirement plan on behalf of an employee generally will not be taxed to the employee until the funds are made available or distributed to the employee upon retirement.

Annuities

If you previously worked in New York state, any pension or other retirement benefit you receive from your former employer is not taxable to New York State if you are (1) a nonresident *and* (2) the payment constitutes an annuity. To qualify as an annuity, a pension or other retirement benefit must meet the following requirements:

1. It must be paid in money only, not in securities of the employer or other property.
2. It must be payable at regular intervals, at least annually, for the life of the recipient, or for a period covering at least half of the recipient's life expectancy at the date the payments begin.
3. It must be payable at a rate that meets *one* of the following standards:
   - remains uniform during the payment period;
   - varies with the market value of the assets on which the benefits are based. The rate may also be based on a

generally recognized cost-of-living index, such as the Consumer Price Index; or
   - changes only when the recipient is eligible for Social Security benefits.
4. Your right to receive the retirement benefit must be based on a written instrument which was signed by your employer or by a plan established and maintained by your employer and distributed to employees in the form of a definite written program.

Special rules apply to a pension or similar benefit paid to a nonresident beneficiary of a deceased employee:

If the employee died after retirement and the pension or other retirement benefit he or she was receiving was considered an annuity, payments made to a beneficiary will be considered an annuity for personal income tax purposes even though they may not meet the requirements set forth above.

If an employee died before retirement, the pension or other benefit payable to a beneficiary need not be payable for the beneficiary's life or for half of his or her life expectancy. However, it must still be payable pursuant to a plan established and maintained by the employer before the employee's death, *and* all other requirements must be satisfied.

Example

Barry was employed as a custodial engineer for many years in New York by the Big Apple Corporation. Upon his retirement from the Big Apple Corporation at the age of 64, Barry moved to Florida. Based on his employer's retirement plan, Barry receives a monthly pension check for his former services in accordance with a fixed, uniform rate of return for the remainder of his life. The pension Barry receives is not taxable for New York State personal income tax purposes since it qualifies as an annuity *and* Barry is a nonresident.

Example

Joe, a nonresident working in New York, opted for early retirement. Joe's employer, ABC Corporation, had a retirement plan that gave a direct bank pension to early retirees until the employee reached the age of 65. After that, he or she would be eligible to receive a life pension from ABC Corporation's insurance company. Because Joe's early retirement pension was not payable for life, it failed to qualify as an annuity. Any payments under this plan must be included in Joe's New York source income on his nonresident return. However, his life pension, from which he received regular payments after his 65th birthday, will qualify as an annuity and will not be included in New York source income.

TaxSaver: Nonresidents contemplating retirement from a New York-based job who will be receiving a pension or other retirement benefit based on services performed in New York can avoid New York personal income tax on the pension. They can do so by restructuring the payments as an annuity. Residents, however, cannot take advantage of this TaxSaver unless they become nonresidents.

Pensions or Other Retirement Benefits

When a pension or other retirement benefit does not qualify as an annuity, it is considered compensation for personal services. If you are a nonresident receiving such benefits, they are taxable to New York to the extent that they are based on services you performed in New York State. If you have reached the age of 59½, you may take an exclusion of up to $20,000 for these benefits.

The term *compensation for personal services* generally includes the following:

• Amounts received in connection with the termination of employment (for example, severance pay);
• Amounts received upon early retirement in consideration of past services performed;
• Amounts received after retirement for consultation services;
• Amounts received upon retirement under a covenant not to compete. A *covenant not to compete* is an agreement in which an employee agrees to refrain after retiring from working in the same line of business as his or her former employer or to sever all ties with his or her employer's client or customer base; and
• Amounts received in connection with the waiver of various employee lawsuits (for example, an age discrimination claim).

Example

Jody received payments from his employer corporation under an existing agreement. The agreement provided that Jody, on leave of absence as an officer of the corporation, would receive monthly payments that would continue for several years in consideration of his waiver of an age discrimination claim. The corporation reported the payments on a Form W-2. While this factor was not controlling, it did indicate the belief by the corporation that it was paying Jody wages. The payments Jody received were taxable since they were in the nature of wages.

If a pension or other retirement benefit is based solely on services performed outside New York State, it is not taxable by New York. However, if you performed services for your employer partly within New York State, the taxable amount is determined by an allocation formula. You will need to know the percentage of time you spent working in New York for the part of the year immediately before your retirement date and the percentages that you used to allocate your salary to New York for the three preceding years. You can get these percentages for the preceding years from copies of your old tax returns. For each of the four periods, multiply the percentage for that period by your total compensation for the same period. To obtain your allocation fraction, add the results for the four periods together. Divide this amount by your *total* compensation over the entire four periods. Then, multiply the resulting allocation fraction by the payments you receive annually under your deferred compensation or retirement plan. Confusing? The following example should make it clear.

Example

Spock, a nonresident of New York State, performs services partially within New York for his corporate employer. Under his employment contract, Spock receives an annual salary of $40,000. He receives an additional $100,000, payable in ten equal annual in-stallments, after his employment terminates. Spock's employment is terminated on July 1, 1977, when he is 50 years of age. Because he is a Vulcan, his life expectancy is at least 250 years. The New York State percentages he used to allocate his salary were 50% for 1974, 60% for 1975, 75% for 1976, and 40% for the first half 1977. Spock computes the part of his annual installments that must be included in his income sourced to New York as follows:

	Percentage of Services Performed in New York	Total Compensation	New York Compensation
1974	50%	$ 40,000	$20,000
1975	60%	40,000	24,000
1976	75%	40,000	30,000
1977 (6 months)	40%	20,000	8,000
		$140,000	$82,000

New York Allocation Fraction:

$$\frac{\$82,000}{\$140,000} = 0.59 \text{ or } 59\% \text{ (approximately)}$$

Each year, Spock would report $5,900 as his income sourced to New York.

$$(\$10,000 \times 59\% = \$5,900)$$

Other Business Income From New York State Sources

In addition to pension income, the New York tax base of a nonresident may also include income, gain, loss, or deductions received from a business, trade, profession, or occupation conducted in New York State.

Business, Trade, Profession, or Occupation Conducted in New York

A business, trade, profession, or occupation is considered conducted in New York State if you occupy or maintain any one of the following business locations within the state:

• A desk;
• An office;
• A shop;
• A store;
• A warehouse;
• A factory;
• An agency; or
• Any other place for carrying on regular business activities.

Personal Services

If you are a nonresident performing personal services as an employee for a New York employer, you will be subject to New York personal income tax. However, you will be taxed only on compensation you received for services performed within New York State. Compensation for personal services performed by a nonresident outside New York is not subject to New York State personal income tax, even if payment was made from an office in New York and the employer is a resident individual or corporation. If you work only part of the time in New York, the part of your compensation that you receive for services performed in New York is subject to tax. The rules for allocating income to nonresidents were described in the preceding section.

Property Within New York

A nonresident individual is also subject to New York income tax on income, gain, loss, or deductions connected with the ownership of any interest in real estate or tangible personal property located in New York. For example, you must include in your New York tax base such income as rents from real estate located in New York. However, if the real estate you own is located outside of New York, you do not need to include the rent payments in your New York income base even if they are made from a point within New York State.

Note: If you sell your principal residence in New York, any gain will be a New York source gain. However, if you excluded the gain from your federal tax return under federal "rollover" rules, you won't have to report it to New York either. New York follows the Internal Revenue Code in excluding income from the sale of a principal residence.

Income From Intangible Property

Income that is generated by intangible personal property owned by a nonresident is generally not subject to New York taxation.

Stocks, bonds, or an intangible right, such as a copyright, are examples of intangible property you might own that could generate income. As a nonresident, you would generally not be taxed by New York on the dividends, interest, or royalties you received from these types of property. Similarly, you would not be taxed if you sold intangible property at a gain. The reason this income is not subject to New York taxation is because it is not derived from or connected with any activities in New York. However, if this income comes from intangible property used in a trade, business, profession, or occupation carried on in New York, it would be subject to tax.

Example

Joyce, a resident of New Jersey, owns 100% of the stock of X corporation, which operates a store in New York State. The corporation pays Joyce a salary of $20,000, all of which is earned in New York. In addition, Joyce receives a dividend of $2,000 from her investment. Joyce's salary of $20,000 is subject to New York State personal income tax. However, the dividend is not taxable for New York State personal income tax purposes. Even though the company paying the dividend owns property in New York, Joyce's stock is not considered "used in the business."

Example

Max, an amateur rock musician living in Massachusetts, operates a music publishing business located in New York. In connection with operating the business, he has acquired copyrights to several original scores. Any royalty income he receives from performances by other musicians of music Max publishes under his copyright must be reported on his New York nonresident return.

Flow-Through Entities

If you do business through a partnership, the entity itself will not be subject to New York State taxation. However, as a nonresident partner you will be subject to the personal income tax on your share of the partnership's income and deductions, if the partnership does business in New York. The tax will be based on your interest in the partnership, not on whatever cash you might receive from the partnership. The same is true of S corporations that have made the New York

election, except that a reduced tax is imposed on the corporation. These types of business organizations ae called "flow-through" entities because the income, deductions, gains, and losses all flow through to their individual partners or shareholders. By choosing to do business in these forms, you also become responsible for paying tax on your share of the partnership's or S corporation's income. However, you can avoid most of the double taxation that is imposed on a C corporation and its shareholders. Although a full discussion of flow-through entities is beyond the scope of this book, you may find the following information useful if you are a nonresident partner or a shareholder in an electing New York S corporation.

Note: An explanation of how S corporations are taxed in New York is contained in *Residents—Additions and Subtractions*.

Partnerships

TaxAlert: New York City has different rules dealing with partnerships. It imposes an Unincorporated Business Tax on partnerships doing business in the city. (See *Unincorporated Business Tax* in Chapter 7, for a more detailed description.)

As nonresident partner, you are required to report only your share of partnership income, gains, losses, or deductions derived from or connected with New York operations. This information can be found on the Form IT-204, *Partnership Return*, which the partnership was required to file as an information return. It is determined by the allocation rules applicable to partnerships, such as separate accounting, formulary apportionment, etc. New York's taxing authorities will ignore a partnership agreement that attempts to avoid tax on its partners by disguising or misrepresenting certain types of income. For example, if the partners agree among themselves to report payments to a nonresident partner as "salary," New York will overlook the agreement if the partner is not, in fact, performing services. Also, your salary from the partnership must be similar to what you would be paid if you performed the same services for an independent employer. The taxing authorities will not allow the partners to allocate a greater share of income or gain from sources outside New York to a nonresident partner than the partnership as a whole allocates outside New York.

Example

Robert is a nonresident partner in Anna Partnership. Robert's total distributive share of partnership income this year is $5,000. Sixty percent of this amount arises from the partnership's total income from New York operations. Robert is required to report $3,000 (60% × $5,000) on his New York State nonresident personal income tax return (IT-203, Line 12, column B). Robert will still be required to report $3,000 to New York, even though the partnership agreement specifically states that his share of the New York income of the partnership may be fixed at less than $3,000.

TaxAlert: If the share of partnership losses of a nonresident partner is 50% for federal income tax purposes, that partner is not allowed to deduct more than 50% of any particular partnership loss or deduction connected with New York activities. Any special provision in the partnership agreement which gives a larger portion of the specific loss or deduction to the nonresident partner will not apply.

S Corporations

The shareholders of a federal S corporation that is subject to tax in New York may elect to have the corporation treated as an S corporation for New York State purposes as well.

If you are a nonresident shareholder of an S corporation, you must include your share of the S corporation's income in the income you report on Line 12, Column A of your New York State nonresident return. However, unlike resident shareholders, you need only report your share of the income that the *corporation* apportioned to New York in Column B.

TaxSaver: You may be able to take a credit for any income taxes you paid *personally* to another state as a result of sharing in the S corporation's income. (See *Credits* in Chapter 4 for more information.)

4 | How to Figure Your Tax

Computation of Tax for Residents

How much tax do you owe? Once you have calculated your state taxable income and entered it on your return, the next step is to determine the amount of tax due on your taxable income. This is referred to on your New York State return as "state tax due." We will also refer to this amount as your "state tax due" to distinguish it from the amount you will actually pay with your return, called your "tax payment." So, don't start writing a check yet! Once you know what your New York State tax due is, you will subtract any amounts you have already paid through payroll withholdings, estimated payments, and overpayments of taxes credited to you from prior years. In addition, any credits due to you may be applied against your state tax due to arrive at your total tax payment. (See the section on *Credits* later in this chapter.)

If the sum of your payments and credits exceeds your state tax due, you are entitled to a refund of income taxes. If the sum of your payments and credits is less than your state tax due, however, you must make an additional tax payment. It is possible that penalties and interest may be imposed if you have not paid the full amount of your tax liability by April 15th. This chapter should help you make sure that doesn't happen. It will show you how to calculate your New York State tax due before subtracting credits.

Calculating Your State Tax Due

There are several ways to determine your state tax due. First, if you are eligible and choose to file Form IT-100, New York will calculate your tax due and any household credit to which you are entitled for you. New York will send you a statement showing their calculation, along with your refund or a bill for additional taxes owed.

Second, you can use the tax tables that accompany Forms IT-200 and IT-201. An example illustrating the use of this table is shown later in this chapter. In general, taxpayers with *taxable income not exceeding $65,000* will be able to use the New York State tax tables to calculate their tax liability. A reproduction of this schedule can be found in Chapter 10.

Third, you can use the tax worksheets provided in the instructions to Form IT-201. Although most taxpayers can use the tax tables, you **must** use one of the worksheets to figure your New York state tax due if you meet **at least one** of the following conditions:

1. Your *New York State* **taxable income** (IT-201, Line 50) is at least **$100,000**; or
2. Your *New York State* **adjusted gross income** (IT-201, Line 30) exceeds **$100,000**.

There are different worksheets provided for resident taxpayers. Which one you use depends upon your New York adjusted gross income. Use the flowchart on the next page to help you decide which worksheet you should be using to determine your New York State tax due. The worksheets themselves are reproduced later in this chapter, along with several examples that show how the calculations work at different income levels.

Once you have determined your state tax due, enter it on Line 17 of Form IT-200 or Line 51 of Form IT-201.

City of New York and Yonkers Taxes. You *must* fill out Lines 22–27 of Form IT-200 if one or more of the following statements are true:

1. You are a resident of New York City;
2. You work in New York City as a nonresident;
3. You are a resident of Yonkers; or
4. You work in Yonkers as a nonresident.

You *must* fill out Lines 59–67 of Form IT-201 if one or more of the following statements are true:

1. You are a resident of New York City;
2. You work in New York City as a nonresident;
3. You were a part-year resident of New York City;
4. You are a resident of Yonkers;
5. You work in Yonkers as a nonresident;
6. You are a part-year resident of Yonkers; or
7. You owe other New York City taxes, such as the tax on lump-sum distributions or the minimum income tax.

These taxes are discussed in the following sections on *Other Resident Taxes* and *Other Nonresident Taxes*.

New York State also provides taxpayers with an opportunity to make a donation to preserve wildlife. Line 30 of Form IT-200 and Line 68 of Form IT-201 are earmarked for donations that are put in the state fund to preserve open areas for wildlife. This donation is purely voluntary and is non-refundable. You can't file an amended return revoking your gift to wildlife!

Total Tax Due. After determining your tentative state tax, the type and amounts of any tax credits to which you are entitled, any City of New York or Yonkers taxes and your gift to wildlife (if any) enter your total tax due on Line 31 of Form IT-200 or Line 69 of Form IT-201. Next, you will figure out how much of these taxes you have already paid through payroll withholdings, estimated tax payments, payments made with an extension request, and prior year overpayments that you chose to apply to this year's taxes. Turn to the section on *Payments* to find out how much you will actually need to pay with this return.

**Figure 1
New York State—How to Calculate Your State Tax Due**

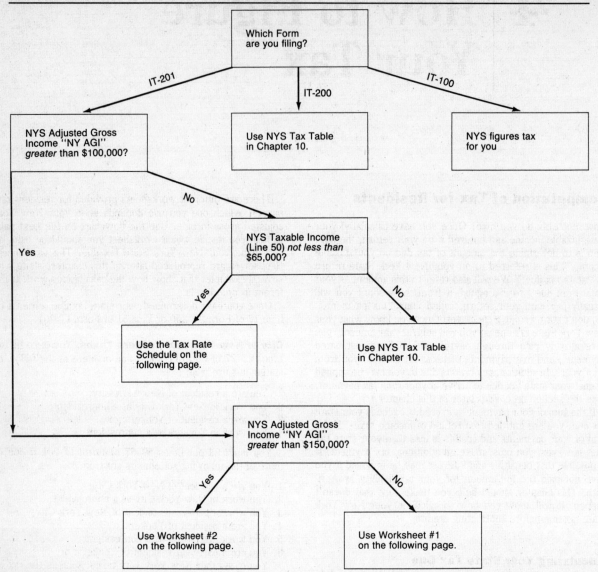

Using the Tax Table

If line 50 Form IT-201 or line 16, Form IT-200 is		And you are		
At Least	But less than	Single or Married Filing Separately	Married Filing Jointly	Head of Household
		Your New York State tax is		
$18,600	$18,650	$1,108	$848	$ 983
18,650	18,700	1,112	851	987
18,700	18,750	1,116	854	991
18,750	18,800	1,120	857	995
18,800	**18,850**	**1,124**	**860**	**999**
18,850	18,900	1,128	863	1,003
18,900	18,950	1,132	866	1,007
18,950	19,000	1,136	869	1,011

Example

Kathy's filing status is *head of household*. She has one dependent child. She is not a resident of New York City or Yonkers and has no income from those cities.

She has calculated her New York State taxable income to be $18,825. She uses the Tax Table to find her New York State tax due. Kathy claimed a federal child care credit of $500. (See *Credits* that follows.) Her allowable household credit is $75. These are the only credits she is claiming. Kathy's New York State tax due after credits is calculated as follows:

Form IT-201

Line 51	NY State tax due on $18,825 of taxable income:	$ 999
Line 52	NY State allowable child care credit $500 ×20% $100	$(100)
Line 53	NY State allowable Household credit	$ (75)
Line 55	Total Credits	$(175)
Line 56	Kathy's NY State tax due after credits	$ 824

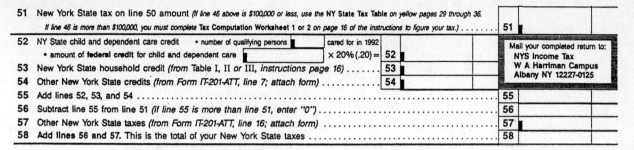

51	New York State tax on line 50 amount *(If line 46 above is $100,000 or less, use the NY State Tax Table on yellow pages 29 through 36.* *If line 46 is more than $100,000, you must complete Tax Computation Worksheet 1 or 2 on page 16 of the instructions to figure your tax.)*	**51**	
52	NY State child and dependent care credit • number of qualifying persons ▮ cared for in 1992 ▮▮ • amount of federal credit for child and dependent care ▮ × 20% (.20) =	**52**	
53	New York State household credit *(from Table I, II or III, instructions page 16)*	**53**	
54	Other New York State credits *(from Form IT-201-ATT, line 7; attach form)*	**54**	
55	Add lines 52, 53, and 54	**55**	
56	Subtract line 55 from line 51 *(if line 55 is more than line 51, enter "0")*	**56**	
57	Other New York State taxes *(from Form IT-201-ATT, line 16; attach form)*	**57**	
58	Add lines 56 and 57. This is the total of your New York State taxes	**58**	

Mail your completed return to:
NYS Income Tax
W A Harriman Campus
Albany NY 12227-0125

Form IT-201. Calculating Your State Tax Due (Line 58).

Note: Any references to tables or worksheets refer to those found in the filing instructions to the tax forms.

Using the Tax Rate Schedule

Tax Rate Schedule

If you are	Your New York State tax is
Single or married filing separately	**$4,760 plus 7.875% of amount over $65,000**
Married filing jointly	$4,401 plus 7.875% of amount over $65,000
Head of a household	$4,635 plus 7.875% of amount over $65,000

Example

Jennifer is single and has calculated that her New York State taxable income is $75,000. Using the New York tax rate schedule, her New York State tax due may be calculated as follows:

NY State taxable income		$75,000
Tax on 1st $65,000 of income		$ 4,760
	$75,000 −(65,000)	
Remaining income	$10,000	
Tax rate	× 7.875%	
Additional tax	787.50	$ 788
Total Tax Due		$ 5,548

Jennifer enters $5,548 on Line 51 of Form IT-201.

Using the Tax Computation Worksheets

Tax Computation Worksheet #1

1. Enter your New York adjusted gross income from Form IT-201, Line 46 . . . . .1. _____
2. Enter your taxable income from Form IT-201, Line 50 . . . . .2. _____
3. Multiply Line 2 by 7.875% (.07875) . . . . .3. _____
4. Enter your New York State tax on the Line 2 amount above from the New York State Tax Table, Chapter 10 . . . . .4. _____
5. Subtract Line 4 from Line 3 . . . . .5. _____
6. Enter the excess of Line 1 over $100,000 (cannot exceed $50,000) . . . . .6. _____

7. Divide Line 6 by $50,000 and carry the result to four decimal places (cannot exceed 1.0000) . . . . .7. _____
8. Multiply Line 5 by Line 7 . . . . .8. _____
9. **Add Lines 4 and 8.** Enter here and on Form IT-201, Line 51 . . . . .9. _____

Example

Ed and Corinne are married and filing a joint return. Their New York State adjusted gross income is $130,000. Their New York State *taxable income* is $110,000. After using the flowchart, they have decided that they should use Worksheet #1 to calculate their tax liability. Their New York State tax due is calculated as follows:

1.	NY State adjusted gross income	$130,000
2.	NY State taxable income	$110,000
3.	7.875% of Line 2 . . . . ($110,000 × 0.0785 = $8,662.50)	$ 8,663
4.	NYS tax as determined using NY Tax Table	$ 7,945
5.	Line 3 less Line 4	718
6.	Line 1 less $100,000	$ 30,000
7.	Line 6 divided by $50,000	.6000
8.	Amount on Line 5 multiplied by percentage on Line 7	431
9.	Add Lines 4 and 8 to get NY State tax liability	$ 8,376

Ed and Corinne enter $8,376 on Line 51 of Form IT-201.

Tax Computation Worksheet #2

1. Enter your taxable income from Form IT-201, Line 50 . . . . .1. _____
2. Multiply Line 1 by 7.875% (.07875). Enter here and on Form IT-201, Line 51 . . . . .2. _____

Example

Marc and Lisa live on Long Island and are filing a joint return. Their New York State adjusted gross income is $250,000. They have calculated their New York State taxable income to be $175,000. Marc's salary is $125,000 and is earned entirely in New York City.

After using the flowchart, they have decided to use Worksheet #2 to calculate their New York State and City taxes. Their calculation is as follows:

Line 50	New York State taxable income		$175,000
		175,000	
		× 7.875%	$ 13,781
Line 51	New York State tax due		$ 13,781
Line 62	NYC nonresident earnings tax*	125,000	
		× .45%	$ 563
Line 69	New York State and City tax liability		$ 14,344

*See *Taxes On Wages: NYC-203, Line 4* on page NY-59.

Assuming they are not entitled to any tax credits and do not make a gift to wildlife, Marc and Lisa will enter $14,344 on Line 69 of Form IT-201.

Other Resident Taxes

The last section took you through calculating the tax due (before credits) on your New York State taxable income. This section explains how to calculate and report your tax liability for other taxes on your income. The other taxes covered here are:

- New York Minimum Income Tax;
- New York Separate Tax on Lump-Sum Distributions;
- New York City Personal Income Tax;
- New York City Minimum Income Tax;
- New York City Separate Tax on Lump-Sum Distributions; and
- City of Yonkers Resident Income Tax Surcharge.

If you are a *nonresident* of New York City or Yonkers, you should also look at the section on *Other Nonresident Taxes*, which follows.

New York Minimum Income Tax

In addition to paying tax on New York State taxable income, some taxpayers may have to pay a New York State Minimum Income Tax. This tax is imposed on your New York *minimum taxable income*. New York tax law, similar to federal tax law, gives special treatment to certain kinds of income and allows special deductions and credits for some kinds of expenses. Taxpayers who benefit from these laws by reducing their taxable income must pay a minimum amount of tax on these so-called tax preference items.

To determine whether you owe the minimum income tax, you must first know your minimum taxable income. New York minimum taxable income is determined by reference to federal tax preference items. Items of federal tax preference will be listed on your federal Form 6251, Lines 6a–6g. Tax preference items consist of certain deductions and tax-exempt items that are not reported for regular federal tax purposes but must be added back to adjusted gross income to arrive at federal alternative minimum tax. If you have tax preference items, you must complete Form IT-220 to determine if you are subject to New York minimum income tax. See the following chart for a list of federal tax preference items.

Federal Tax Preference Items	Considered a preference item for New York purposes	
	Yes	**No**
1. Excess of mineral depletion deduction claimed over the taxpayer's adjusted basis of his or her interest in the entity.		X
2. Excess intangible drilling costs.	X	
3. Excess bad debt deduction for financial institutions.	X	
4. Tax-exempt interest on specified private activity bonds issued after 8/7/86.		X
5. Taxpayer's share of the appreciation in capital gain property which he or she donated (does not include donated tangible personal property).	X	
6. *Pre-1987 Property*—excess of accelerated depreciation on nonrecovery real property over the deduction that would have been allowed if the straight-line method was used.		X
Luxury Automobiles—New York State provides for the inclusion of the federal tax preference of accelerated depreciation over straight-line depreciation on luxury automobiles for *all* years.	X	
1985 & 1986 only—excess of accelerated depreciation on nonreal recovery property placed in service in 1985 & 1986 over the deduction that would have been allowed if the straight-line method was used.	X	

EXCEPTION: If you have taken cost recovery deductions on luxury automobiles or you have depreciated property placed in service in New York during 1985 and 1986, these preferences may not be separately stated on your federal Form 6251. However, they must still be included on Form IT-220. If you have these preferences, you *must* file Form IT-220.

For New York purposes, your minimum taxable income will be your total items of federal tax preference (from Form 6251) less certain exclusions discussed below. The minimum tax is imposed at a rate of 6% of the New York minimum taxable income of every individual, estate, or trust.

TaxAlert: If you filed federal Form 6251, you must attach a copy to Form IT-220.

Tax Preference Items: IT-220, Lines 1–10. When computing *minimum taxable income*, individuals, estates, and trusts must adjust their federal items of tax preference as explained below.

Subtractions

1. The federal tax preference for depletion is excluded from New York minimum taxable income (Form 6251, Line 6c).
2. The federal tax preference for accelerated cost recovery deductions is excluded from New York minimum taxable income (Form 6251, Line 6d).

EXCEPTION: Cost recovery deductions taken on luxury automobiles and property placed in service in New York in taxable years beginning after December 31, 1984 are not excluded from New York minimum taxable income.

3. Tax preference items from a federal S corporation do not pass through to the shareholders if they did not elect to have the entity treated as a New York S corporation. (See *Additions and Subtractions* in Chapter 3 for a brief discussion of New York S corporations.)
4. The federal tax preference for tax-exempt interest from private activity bonds is excluded from New York minimum taxable income (Form 6251, Line 6b).

Generally, a *private activity bond* is any debt that is issued by a municipality or state as part of a larger issuance of debt. The face of the bond will usually indicate that it is a private activity bond. If you are not sure about the status of a bond you hold, call the financial institution from which you purchased it.

Deductions Against Minimum Taxable Income. Before computing your New York minimum income tax, you may make certain deductions from the total amount of your New York items of tax preference. Your items of tax preference may be reduced (but not below zero) by the sum of the following:

1. Your applicable specific deduction. This deduction depends upon your filing status.
   Married filing jointly $5,000
   Married filing separately $2,500
   Single, head of household, or qualifying widow(er) $2,500
2. Your New York personal income tax from Line 51 of Form IT-201, minus the following credits:

   - Investment credit;
   - Dependent care credit;
   - Real property tax circuit breaker credit;
   - S corporation shareholder credit;
   - Economic development zone credit; and
   - Credit for income tax in another state.

   (See *Credits* later in this chapter for more information.)

3. Any net operating loss determined for federal purposes that you are carrying forward to the next year. The net operating loss may be deducted from your New York tax preferences only if the preference items exceed the total amount of your specific deduction and credits.

TaxAlert: Any net operating loss (NOL) currently used to reduce your New York tax preferences will be treated as a New York tax preference item in the future when it is carried forward and used to reduce federal taxable income. When the NOL is used in the future, to reduce your federal taxable income, you will add that portion of the NOL to your total federal preferences by entering the claimed deduction on Line 9 of the IT-220. All unused net operating losses remaining as carryforwards after completion of your federal return may be used to reduce your New York items of tax preference.

New York Separate Tax on Lump-Sum Distributions

Individuals who elect to receive a lump-sum distribution and file federal Form 4972 will be subject to a separate tax imposed by New York State on the ordinary income portion of a lump-sum distribution.

A lump-sum distribution is generally defined as a payment from a tax-exempt profit-sharing, pension, or stock bonus plan. For New York purposes, all of the federal rules concerning lump-sum distributions are applicable. Certain payments from various tax-exempt annuity plans may also be termed "lump-sum distributions." These plans must be administered by your employer unless you are self-employed. Self-employed individuals may also qualify for similar treatment.

To qualify as a lump-sum distribution, the payment must occur within one year of an individual's separation from the plan. Separation from the plan is deemed to occur under the following circumstances:

1. When the death of the participant occurs;
2. When the participant reaches age 59½;
3. When an employee leaves his or her job or is terminated by an employer; or
4. When a self-employed individual becomes disabled.

TaxAlert: If you receive any distribution from a qualified plan after 1990, you should receive federal Form 1099-R. Your employer is required to provide this form to you by January 31 of the year following the distribution.

Individuals who were plan participants, received plan distributions, and have filed federal Form 4972 must complete Form IT-230. When completing Form IT-230, you must make the same elections as you did on your federal Form 4972. Thus, on the IT-230 you will complete the same parts as you did on Form 4972. If you were not required to file Form 4972, then your lump-sum distribution will not be subject to the separate tax. Simply mark the box "No" in Part I of the IT-230 and attach it to Form IT-201-ATT. New York State and New York City effectively adopt the federal elections, qualifications, and guidelines relating to lump-sum distributions.

Tax Treatment. You may be entitled to deduct certain amounts from your total lump-sum distribution. In general, under federal and state laws, a deduction is permitted for:

1. Your total nondeductible contributions to the plan;
2. The total of your taxable one-year term costs of life insurance;
3. Any employer contributions that were available to you; or
4. Repayments of loans that were previously taxed.

You must reduce these costs by any amounts previously distributed to you tax-free.

Taxpayers born before 1986 may choose to treat a portion of the taxable amount as a long-term capital gain (Part II, federal Form 4972).

Exception: Lump-sum distributions received from a New York State municipal or local retirement system will be exempt from taxation under New York State law. Distributions from retirement systems of the United States (including military pension) or District of Columbia are also exempt.

TaxSaver: If you were a member of a qualified plan for a considerable amount of time before 1974, you should probably choose the capital gain election (Part

II on Form 4972). This will allow for a larger portion of your distribution to be taxed at a lower rate on your federal and New York tax returns.

For a more thorough discussion of lump-sum distributions, see *The Ernst & Young Tax Guide 1993*.

New York City Personal Income Tax

New York City imposes a personal income tax on the taxable income of any individual who is a resident of any of the five boroughs of New York. This tax is levied on the same income tax base as your New York State tax. However, a different tax rate is applied to the base. To compute the tax, use the City of New York tax tables in the instructions to Form IT-201 and report the tax on Line 59 of your Form IT-201. The tax for New York City is added to your total New York State taxes. New York City also imposes a tax on nonresidents, based on wages and income from self-employment earned within the city. See the following section on *Other Nonresident Taxes* for more information.

City taxable income is precisely the same amount determined as *taxable income* for New York State. You should already have entered this amount on Line 50 of your IT-201 or Line 16 of Form IT-200. A *resident* is any individual who is domiciled in the city or who maintains a home in the city and spends more than 183 days of the taxable year there. (See the *Determining Residency/Domicile* section in Chapter 2 for a complete discussion of residency rules for New York State. New York City follows the same rules.)

Example

Mr. and Mrs. Jones are filing a joint return. Their taxable income on Line 50 of Form IT-201 is $46,750. First, they locate the correct line on the New York State tax table. The correct line is the $46,750–46,800 income line. Next, they find the column for *Married filing jointly*. The amount shown where the income line and the filing status column meet is $1,665 (illustrated below). This is the tax amount they must write on Line 59 of Form IT-201.

If Line 50 (taxable income) is:		And you are		
At least	But less than	Single or married filing separately	Married filing jointly	Head of a household
		Your City of New York tax is:		
$46,600	$46,650	1,831	1,659	1,816
46,650	46,700	1,833	1,661	1,818
46,700	46,750	1,835	1,663	1,820
46,750	**46,800**	**1,837**	**1,665**	**1,822**

If you are married and filing a joint New York State return and only one spouse was a resident of New York City for all of 1992, you should calculate the New York City resident tax on the New York State taxable income of the city resident as it would be reported if separate federal and New York returns were filed. Attach a separate schedule showing your computations. Be sure to write the name, Social Security number, and taxable income of the New York City resident on the schedule.

TaxAlert: If you were not a New York City or Yonkers resident but you earned wages or self-employment income in either of these cities, you must also file Form NYC-203 or Form Y-203 and attach it to Form

IT-200 or IT-201 (whichever form you choose to use to report your New York State income). You may not use Form IT-100, Resident Fast Form Income Tax Return.

New York City Minimum Tax

The minimum tax base for New York City residents is computed exactly the same as it is for New York State purposes. The only difference is the rate of tax. The tax is computed on Line 25 of Form IT-220 at a rate of 2.85% of the minimum taxable income (Line 23) as determined for New York State purposes. There is no deduction for New York City resident taxes paid. The tax computed on Line 25 must also be entered onto Line 18 of Form IT-201-ATT, Summary of Other Credits and Taxes.

TaxAlert: Forms IT-220 and IT-201-ATT must be attached to your New York State return.

New York City Separate Tax on Lump-Sum Distributions

The New York City provisions for the tax on lump-sum distributions are the same as those of New York State. The tax is computed on Form IT-230 by completing the same parts in the City of New York column as you did in the New York State column. If you are only completing Part II, enter the amount on Line 2, City of New York Column, or Line 1 of Worksheet B on Form IT-201-ATT. If you are completing Part III or Part IV, enter the amount on Line 20, City of New York Column, on Line 19 of Form IT-201-ATT.

City of Yonkers Resident Income Tax Surcharge

If you were a resident of Yonkers for the entire year, you may be subject to the City of Yonkers resident income tax surcharge. The surcharge is 15% of your total New York State tax from Line 58, after subtracting your Real Property Tax Credit. Enter the amount of your Yonkers surcharge on Line 64 of Form IT-201. See worksheet below:

Yonkers Worksheet

a. Amount from Line 58, Form IT-201	a. _____
b. Amount from Form IT-214, Line 17 (real property tax credit)	b. _____
c. Subtract Line b from Line a (if Line b is larger than Line a, enter "0" on Line 64)	c. _____
d. Yonkers resident tax rate (15 percent)	d. __15%__
e. Multiply Line c by Line d. Enter this amount on Form IT-201, Line 64	e. _____

TaxAlert: If you filed Form IT-214, Claim for Real Property Tax Credit for Homeowners and Renters, you may deduct the amount of the credit (Line 17) from your total New York State taxes before applying the 15 percent rate. (See the *Credits* section later in this chapter for further information.)

Example

Maurice is single and lives in Yonkers. His total New York State taxes from Line 58 of Form IT-201 are $2,350. Maurice also qualified for a Real Property Tax Credit and filed Form IT-214. (See *Credits*, later.) The Credit amounted to $440. Maurice's City of Yonkers resident income tax surcharge will be computed as follows:

Total NYS Tax	$2,350
Real Property Tax Credit	(440)
	1,910
	x .15
Total City of Yonkers resident income tax surcharge:	$ 287

TaxAlert: If your total New York State taxes on Line 58 are "0," you will not be subject to the City of Yonkers Resident Income Tax Surcharge. If Line 58 is "0," enter "0" on Line 64.

TaxAlert: You may be subject to the Yonkers Income Tax Surcharge even if you were not a resident of Yonkers for *any* part of the year. Nonresidents who earn wages, conduct a trade or business, or are partners of partnerships conducting business in Yonkers may be subject to City of Yonkers Nonresident Earnings Tax. (See the section on *Other Nonresident Taxes* later in this chapter.)

Computation of Tax for Nonresidents

The objective of the New York State nonresident and part-year resident tax is to tax only your income from New York sources. Under the pressure of filling out your return, however, you may have reached a different conclusion since *taxable income* consists of your income from *all* sources. Until now, you have been required to make entries on your tax return as if you were a resident. In this section, you will finally see how your nonresident or part-year resident status affects your tax computation.

Tax Computation: Step-by-Step Analysis

Step One: Base Tax. When computing your base tax, remember that the starting point is your taxable income from *all* sources, not just your income from New York sources. Nonresidents, part-year residents, and full-year residents all calculate their base tax using the same method. However, nonresidents and part-year residents must complete an additional step. They must allocate their base tax to New York by using a fraction, the numerator of which is income from New York sources and the denominator of which is federal adjusted gross income. This is more easily understood by looking at the following formula:

$$\frac{\text{Income From New York Sources}}{\text{Federal Adjusted Gross Income}} \times \text{Your Base Tax}$$

$$= \text{Your Nonresident or Part-Year Resident Tax}$$

How you determine your income from New York sources is discussed in the previous chapter under the section, *Nonresidents/Part-Year Residents—Starting Point*. See especially the sections on *Attributing Income to New York—Sourcing Rules* and *Special Problems in Attributing Income* in Chapter 3.

There are two things to consider when choosing a method for computing your tax: your *taxable income* and your *New York adjusted gross income*. Both terms are discussed in Chapter 3. If your New York adjusted gross income is $100,000 or less, you will either use the tax table or the tax calculation schedule. The tax table, which is reproduced in the last chapter of this part, should be used if your taxable

income is less than $65,000. If your taxable income is $65,000 or more, you must use the tax calculation schedule, which is reproduced here with Example 2. A flat tax rate of 7.875% is applied to your taxable income if your New York adjusted gross income exceeds $150,000. The chart below should make it clear.

How Do I Calculate My Tax?

If your New York adjusted gross income was	and your taxable income is	you must use the
$100,000 or less	less than $65,000	tax table
$100,000 or less	$65,000 or more	tax calculation schedule
more than $100,000 but not more than $150,000	any amount	tax computation worksheet
more than $150,000	any amount	flat rate of 7.875%

Example 1

Daniel's filing status is *single* and his taxable income consists of the following items:

Wages—New York sources	$30,000
Wages—Other sources	$24,375
Federal Adjusted Gross Income	$54,375
Less: New York Itemized Deductions	($ 8,000)
Taxable Income	$46,375

Daniel must use the tax table to determine his base tax. According to the section of the tax table reproduced below, his base tax is $3,293.

If your taxable income is		And you are		
At least	But less than	Single or Married filing separately	Married filing jointly	Head of household
		Your New York State tax is		
46,200	46,250	3,281	2,923	3,156
46,250	46,300	3,285	2,927	3,160
46,300	46,350	3,289	2,931	3,164
*46,350	46,400	3,293	2,935	3,168

Example 2

Janet and Tom are *married filing jointly*. Their taxable income consists of the following items:

Income—New York Sources	$95,000
Losses—Other Sources	($10,000)
Federal Adjusted Gross Income	$85,000
Less: New York Itemized Deductions	($10,000)
Taxable Income	$75,000

Their base tax is computed in the following manner:

$65,000	$ 4,401

Tax on excess over $65,000
Excess over $65,000

	$75,000
	−65,000
	$10,000

$10,000 × 7.875% (.07875)	$ 788
Base Tax	$ 5,189

Tax Calculation Schedule

If your filing status is:	Your tax is:
Single or married filing separately	$4,760 plus 7.875% of the amount over $65,000
Married filing jointly	**$4,401 plus 7.875% of the amount over $65,000**
Head of a household	$4,635 plus 7.875% of the amount over $65,000

Flat Rate

Example 3

Jennifer's taxable income is $145,000. Her New York adjusted gross income is $170,000. Because her New York adjusted gross income exceeds $150,000, her base tax is computed at the flat rate of 7.875%.

$145,000 × 7.875% (.07875) equals..... $11,419

Step Two: Base Tax Allocation. The second step in calculating your tax is to multiply your base tax by a base tax allocation fraction. Your base tax allocation fraction is simply your income from New York sources from Line 19, Column B of your Form IT-203 divided by federal adjusted gross income from Line 19, Column A of your Form IT-203.

Example 1

Using the same facts as in the preceding "Example 1," Daniel's allocated base tax is $1,817, calculated as follows:

$$\left(\frac{\text{Income From New York Sources}}{\text{Federal Adjusted Gross Income}}\right) \times \text{Base Tax}$$

$$= \text{Allocated Base Tax}$$

$$\frac{\$30,000}{\$54,375} \times \$3,293$$

$$= .5517 \times \$3,293$$

$$= \underline{\$1,817}$$

Example 2

Using the same facts as in the preceding "Example 2," Janet's and Tom's allocated tax is $6,105, calculated as follows:

$$\frac{\$95,000}{\$85,000} \times \$5,189$$

$$= 1.1765 \times \$5,189$$

$$= \underline{\$6,105}$$

Note: Your base tax allocation fraction can be greater than 1, as in Example 2.

Other Nonresident Taxes

In an earlier section, *Other Resident Taxes*, we discussed taxes imposed by New York City and Yonkers on *residents* of those cities. In addition to taxing residents, both cities tax *nonres-*idents earning certain types of income within their borders—the so-called "commuter taxes."

If you live outside of New York City or Yonkers and earn income from some activity in either city, you may have to file a nonresident earnings tax return.

This section will discuss whether or not you are required to file a City of New York Nonresident Earnings Tax Return, (Form NYC-203) or a City of Yonkers Nonresident Earnings Tax Return, (Form Y-203).

City of New York Nonresident Earnings Tax Return

Only income from wages, salary, or self-employment is subject to the nonresident earnings tax. Generally, if you receive only investment income or your role in a New York City business is merely *passive*, such as a limited partnership interest, you won't be subject to this tax.

You must file a nonresident earnings tax return if you meet all of the following requirements:

- You are employed or carried on your own trade or business as either an individual or a general partner in New York City; and
- You did not live in any of the five boroughs of New York City when the above activity took place.

You do not have to file if you meet all the following requirements:

- You do not have to file a New York State resident or nonresident income tax return;
- You received income in New York City consisting entirely of wages paid to you by an employer who withheld the proper amount of taxes; and
- You received wages from more than one New York City employer totaling less than $3,000.

However, even if you meet all the requirements set forth above, you must file a return if you are requesting a tax refund.

TaxAlert: You cannot file a joint nonresident earnings tax return with your spouse. Each person subject to the tax must file a separate return, even if you and your spouse file a joint New York State return. If you and your spouse file a joint New York State return, add the amounts from Line 9 of both New York City nonresident earnings tax returns, and enter this total on Line 62 of your New York State resident return or Line 62 of your New York nonresident return. Remember to sign and attach a copy of *both* Forms NYC-203 to your New York State tax return.

Filling Out the Top of Form NYC-203

If you need assistance filling out the top portion, called the "Information Block," refer to Chapter 2, *The Income Tax Return.*

Calculating Your Nonresident Earnings Tax

Gross Wages and Other Employee Compensation: NYC-203, Line 1. Enter the total amount of wages you earned in New York City during the year. You must include all cash payments plus the value of all other items you received for services performed for an employer.

You must also include in your wages any money deducted from your salary and contributed to a retirement plan established by New York City. You can find this amount on Copy 2 of your wage and tax statement (federal Form W-2 or New York Form IT-2102). Wages also include bonuses, tips, commissions on sales or on insurance premiums, vacation allowances, and severance pay.

Do not include any payment you received from active duty as a member of the Armed Forces, National Guard, or reserves, or from an insurance business that is a member of the New York Insurance Exchange. If you earned your wages partially in New York City and partially outside of New York City, you must complete Schedule A. Schedule A is the allocation of your wages according to the ratio of the number of days you worked in New York City to the total number of days you worked everywhere. (For more detailed information on how to calculate this number, see *Attributing Income to New York—Sourcing Rules* in Chapter 3. These rules are exactly the same for New York City and New York State.) If you must complete Schedule A, enter the number from Line 21 on Line 1 of your NYC-203.

Allowable Exclusion: NYC-203, Line 2. If you earned $30,000 or less in New York City, you are allowed to exclude a certain amount of your gross wages and net earnings from self-employment. The amount you are allowed to exclude depends on your total wages, as indicated in the table below.

Total of Wages and Net Earnings From Self-Employment	Allowable Exclusion
$10,000 or less	$3,000
more than $10,000 but less than $20,000	$2,000
more than $20,001 but less than $30,000	$1,000
$30,000 or more	None

If you earned both wages and earnings from self-employment, the exclusion is divided proportionally between the two types of income. The portion of the exclusion related to your wages is entered on Line 2. The remainder is entered on Line 6.

Example

Logan lives in Westchester, New York, and commutes every weekday to his job in New York City. Logan was paid $18,000 in salary in 1992. On weekends in the summer months, Logan ran a business called "Cheap Skates." Cheap Skates rents roller skates in Central Park. In 1992 Logan earned $4,500 from his business activities in Cheap Skates. Logan's total wages and self-employment earnings equaled $22,500.

$$\$18,000 + \$4,500 = \$22,500$$

He is allowed a total exclusion of $1,000. He must divide this exclusion proportionally between Line 2 and Line 6 of his New York City nonresident earning tax return, as follows:

Percentage of earnings from wages	$\dfrac{18,000}{22,500} = 0.8 = 80\%$	
Percentage of earnings from self-employment	$\dfrac{4,500}{22,500} = 0.2 = 20\%$	
Line 2 Allowable Exclusion	80% of $1,000 = $800	
Line 6 of Allowable Exclusion	20% of $1,000 = $200	

If you were a part-year resident, you can only use the part of your allowable exclusion that reflects the number of months during which you were a resident. A period of more than two weeks counts as a whole month; a period of less than two weeks is not counted.

Taxable Amount of Wages: NYC-203, Line 3
Subtract Line 2 from Line 1

Gross Wages − Allowable Exclusion = Taxable Amount of Wages

Taxes on Wages: NYC-203, Line 4
Multiply Line 3 by .45% (.0045). Enter this number on Line 4.

Taxable Amount of Wages × .0045 = Tax on Wages

Net Earnings from Self-Employment: NYC-203, Line 5. Enter the total amount of net earnings from your self-employment activity. Your net earnings from self-employment is equal to all the income you receive from any trade, business, or general partnership interest in New York City, minus any deductions from the business allowed on your federal return.

If your net earnings from self-employment were not earned completely from a New York City business, you may have to allocate your income using Schedule C. The amount you enter on Line 5 is generally the same as the amount shown on your federal Form 1040, Schedule SE, Social Security Self-Employment Tax, minus any allowable deductions. If the total amount shown on Schedule SE represents both income earned in New York City and separate income earned wholly outside New York City, deduct the amounts earned outside New York City from the total before entering the amount on Line 5 of your return.

Allocating Net Earnings from Self-Employment
If your net earnings from self-employment were from a business that operated both in and outside of New York City, you will be taxed only on the portion of your net earnings that is attributable to your New York City operations. Figuring out what income is taxable in New York City and what income is not is called *allocation*. You can *only* allocate your net earnings from self-employment if you had a regular place of business, such as an office or warehouse, outside of New York City. Otherwise, your net earnings will be entirely taxable to New York City.

There are two methods for allocating income from self-employment:

1. Your books and records. The preferred method is to show your New York City source earnings through separate accounting on your own books and records. Your books and records must fairly and equitably show net earnings from self-employment in New York City. If your books and records don't adequately trace your New York City earnings you must use the second method.
2. Schedule C—Allocation of net earnings from self-employment.

If you cannot use the *books and records* method, described above, you must complete Schedule C of Form NYC-203. To determine how much of your net earnings from self-employment are allocated to New York under this method, you must use a three-factor formula. See the discussion in Chapter 3, in the section called *Attributing Income to New York—Sourcing Rules.* These rules are the same for both New York State and New York City.

> **TaxAlert:** If you have separate activities generating net earnings from self-employment, you must use separate allocation factors.

Example

Mitch has a loss of $10,000 from self-employment as a partner in a partnership that allocated 50% of its earnings to New York City. Mitch also has $35,000 from self-employment, all of which was earned in New York City. Mitch must report $30,000 as income from self-employment earnings.

$35,000	100% New York City
(5,000)	or 50% of ($10,000)
$30,000	Enter this amount on Line 27

Net Earnings from Self-Employment to be Allocated: NYC-203, Line 30. Put the total of your self-employment earnings on this line.

Allocated Net Earnings from Self-Employment: NYC-203, Line 31. Multiply Line 30 by the percentage of Line 29. Enter this amount on Line 31 of Schedule C and on Line 5.

Allowable Exclusion: NYC-203, Line 6. Enter your allowable exclusion amount. See discussion under Line 2.

Taxable Amount of Net Earnings from Self-Employment: NYC-203, Line 7. Subtract Line 6 from Line 5 and enter the result on Line 7.

Net Earnings − Allowable Exclusion = Taxable Earnings.

Tax on Net Earnings from Self-Employment: NYC-203, Line 8. Multiply Line 7 by *.0065.* This is your tax on earnings from self-employment. Enter this number on Line 8.

Total Nonresident Earnings Tax: NYC-203, Line 9. Add Lines 4 and 8 together. Enter the total on Line 9. You must also enter this amount on Line 25 of your Form IT-200, on Line 62 of your Form IT-201 or Form IT-203.

Don't forget to sign and attach your NYC-203 to your New York State Form IT-200, IT-201, or IT-203.

Note: Other New York State taxes may apply to nonresidents, such as the tax on minimum taxable income. For a discussion of this tax, see the section on *Other Resident Taxes.*

City of Yonkers Nonresident Earnings Tax Return

The rules for determining your City of Yonkers nonresident earnings tax are similar to those for the New York City nonresident earnings tax discussed above. The same rules determine whether or not you must file a Y-203. The same rules apply to calculating your gross wages and net earnings from self-employment. You allocate earnings using exactly the same method. There are two main differences between the New York City and Yonkers tax computations:

1. Your exclusion on Line 4 does not need to be apportioned between your gross wages and your net income from self-employment; and
2. Your nonresident tax rate is 0.5% (.005).

Credits

After you have calculated your state tax due (see the beginning of this chapter), tax credits may be used to reduce the amount of tax due. New York State provides a variety of tax credits. However, in most cases you must meet specific requirements to be eligible to claim them. In this section we'll describe the available credits, explain the requirements for each credit, and provide examples and sample calculations for the most frequently claimed credits.

New York State and New York City—List of Available Tax Credits

New York State

- Child and dependent care credit;
- Household credit;
- Claim for Real Property Tax Credit for Homeowners and Renters (NY State Residents Only);
- Resident credit for taxes paid to another state (NY State Residents Only);
- Resident credit against the separate tax on lump-sum distributions (NY State Residents Only);
- Investment credit;
- Accumulation Distribution credit; and
- Economic Development Zone credits.

The following credits are not currently available but are allowed as carryovers from previous years:

- Special additional mortgage recording tax credit;
- Solar and wind energy credit; and
- Credit for Research and Development.

New York City

- Household credit (NYC Residents Only)

Child and Dependent Care Credit

Similar to federal law, New York State provides a credit for child and dependent care expenses. You are eligible for this credit if you were able to claim the federal credit. For federal purposes, you are eligible for the credit if you are gainfully employed and maintain a household for one of the following individuals:

1. A dependent under age 13 for whom a dependency exemption may be claimed;
2. Any other person who is physically or mentally incapable of caring for himself or herself;
3. A spouse who is physically or mentally incapable of self-care; or
4. Certain dependent children of divorced parents.

The child care credit is claimed on either Line 18 of Form IT-200 or Line 52 of Form IT-201 and Form IT-203. No additional form needs to be attached. The amount of credit for New York purposes is equal to 20% of the credit you claimed on your federal return. For more information on the federal child and dependent care credit, consult *The Ernst & Young Tax Guide 1993.*

New York State Household Credit

Many New York State taxpayers are eligible for the New York State household credit. You are eligible to claim this credit if you file a New York State tax return, you have not been claimed as a dependent on another person's New York State tax return, and you meet certain income guidelines. This credit is also available to nonresident and part-year resident taxpayers.

Example

Bill and Carol's sixteen-year-old son Pat worked part-time. Pat files a resident income tax return. Bill and Carol are filing a joint return and claim Pat as a dependent. Pat will not be allowed to take the New York State household credit on his New York State resident return. However, if Bill and Carol's New York State adjusted gross income is not greater than $32,000, they will be eligible for the credit on their joint New York return.

Figure 2 contains a flowchart to help you determine your eligibility for the New York State household credit. Use Tables I–III to determine the amount of your credit. Enter your credit on Line 18 of Form IT-200 and Line 53 of Form IT-201 and Form IT-203.

New York City offers a similar credit to city residents. The income limits for eligibility for the New York City household credit are more restrictive than the state limits, so if you are ineligible for the state credit, you will automatically be ineligible for the city credit. If you are eligible for the state credit, use the flowchart (Figure 3) to determine your eligibility for the New York City household credit. Then use Tables IV through VI to calculate your allowable credit. The New York City household credit you are entitled to is entered on Line 23 of Form IT-200 and Line 60 of Form IT-201.

Figure 2
New York State—How to Determine Your Household Credit

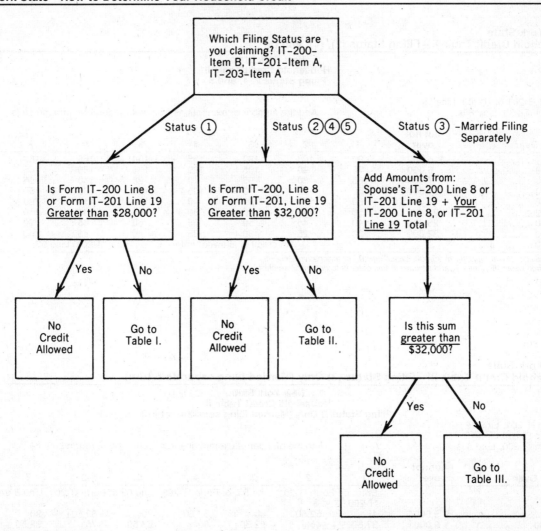

Note:
Use the filing status you checked on the front of your Form IT-200, IT-201, or IT-203. As a reminder, your filing status is one of the following:
1. Single;
2. Married Filing Jointly;
3. Married Filing Separately;
4. Head of Household; or
5. Qualifying Widow(er).

New York State
Household Credit Table I—Filing Status (1) Only (Single)

**New York State
Household Credit Table I
Filing Status (1) Only (Single)**

If Form IT-201 or IT-203, Line 19 or
Form IT-200, Line 8 is:

Over	but not over	enter on Form IT-201 or IT-203, Line 53: or enter on Form IT-201, Line 20:
$	$ 5,000*	$75
5,000	6,000	60
6,000	7,000	50
7,000	20,000	45
20,000	25,000	40
25,000	28,000	20
28,000		No credit is allowed; enter "0" on Form IT-201, Line 53

*This may be any amount up to $5,000, including "0" or a negative amount.

New York State
Household Credit Table II—Filing Status (2), (4), and (5)

**New York State
Household Credit Table II
Filing Status 2, 4, and 5**

If Form IT-201 or IT-203, Line 19
or Form IT-200, Line 8 is:

And the number of exemptions from your federal return Line 6e is:

Over	but not over	1	2	3	4	5	6	7	over 7**
$	$ 5,000*	90	105	120	135	150	165	180	15
5,000	6,000	75	90	105	120	135	150	165	15
6,000	7,000	65	80	95	110	125	140	155	15
7,000	20,000	60	75	90	105	120	135	150	15
20,000	22,000	60	70	80	90	100	110	120	10
22,000	25,000	50	60	70	80	90	100	110	10
25,000	28,000	40	45	50	55	60	65	70	5
28,000	32,000	20	25	30	35	40	45	50	5
32,000		No credit is allowed; enter "0" on Form IT-201, Line 53.							

*This may be any amount up to $5,000, including "0" or a negative amount.
**For each exemption over 7, add amount in this column to column 7 amount.

New York State
Household Credit Table III—Filing Status (3) Only (Married filing separate return)

**New York State
Household Credit Table III
Filing Status 3 Only (Married filing separate return)**

If Form IT-201, Line 19
or Form IT-203 Line 19
or Form IT-200, Line 8 is:

And the number of exemptions from your federal return Line 6e is:

Enter on Form IT-201, Line 53, or Form IT-203, Line 53 or Form IT-201, Line 8 or Forms IT-200, Line 8:

Over	but not over	1	2	3	4	5	6	7	over 7**
$	$ 5,000*	45	52.50	60	67.50	75	82.50	90	7.50
5,000	6,000	37.50	45	52.50	60	67.50	75	82.50	7.50
6,000	7,000	32.50	40	47.50	55	62.50	70	77.50	7.50
7,000	20,000	30	37.50	45	52.50	60	67.50	75	7.50
20,000	22,000	30	35	40	45	50	55	60	5
22,000	25,000	25	30	35	40	45	50	55	5
25,000	28,000	20	22.50	25	27.50	30	32.50	35	2.50
28,000	32,000	10	12.50	15	17.50	20	22.50	25	2.50
32,000		No credit is allowed; enter "0" on Form IT-201, Line 53.							

*This may be any amount up to $5,000, including "0" or a negative amount.
**For each exemption over 7, add amount in this column to column 7 amount.

Figure 3
New York City—How to Determine Your Household Credit

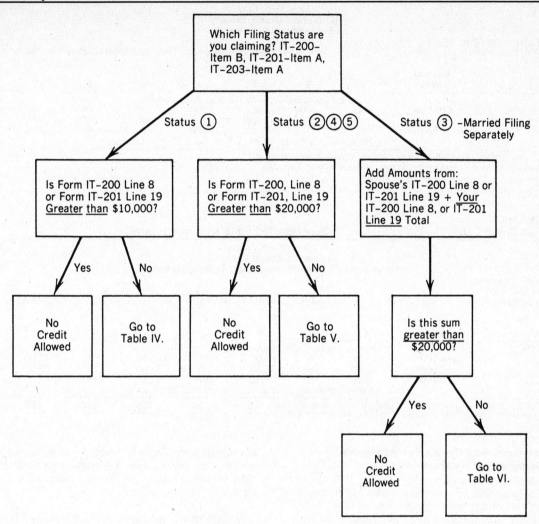

Note:
Use the filing status you checked on the front of your IT-200 or IT-201. As a reminder, your filing status is one of the following:
1. Single
2. Married Filing Jointly
3. Married Filing Separately
4. Head of Household
5. Qualifying Widow(er)

New York City
Household Credit Table IV—Filing Status (1)

New York City
Household Credit Table IV
Filing Status (1) Only (Single)

If Form IT-201, Line 19
or Form IT-200, Line 8 is:

Over	but not over	enter on Form IT-201, Line 60 or Form IT-200, Line 23:
$	$ 7,500*	.... $15
7,500	10,000	 10
10,000..		No credit is allowed; enter "0" on Form IT-201, Line 53.

This may be any amount up to $7,500, including "0" or a negative amount.

New York City
Household Credit Table V—Filing Status (2), (4), and (5)

New York City
Household Credit Table V
Filing Status 2, 4, and 5

If Form IT-201, Line 19 or
Form IT-200, Line 8 is:

And the number of exemptions from your federal return Line 6e is:

Over	but not over	1	2	3	4	5	6	7	over 7**
		Enter on Form IT-201, Line 60 or IT-200, Line 23:							
$	$15,000*	$50	100	150	200	250	300	350	50
15,000	17,500	25	50	75	100	125	150	175	25
17,500	2,000	15	30	45	60	75	90	105	15
20,000		No credit is allowed; enter "0" on Form IT-201, Line 53.							

*This may be any amount up to $15,000, including "0" or a negative amount.
**For each exemption over 7, add amount in this column to column 7 amount.

New York City
Household Credit Table VI—Filing Status (3) Only (Married filing separate return)

New York City
Household Credit Table VI
Filing Status 3 Only (Married filing separate return)

If Form IT-201, Line 19
or Form IT-200, Line 8
total from both returns is:

And the number of exemptions from your federal return Line 6e is:

Over	but not over	1	2	3	4	5	6	7	over 7**
		Enter on Form IT-201, Line 60:							
$	$15,000*	$25.00	50	75.00	100	125.00	150	175.00	25.00
15,000	17,500	12.50	25	37.50	50	62.50	75	87.50	12.50
17,500	20,000	7.50	15	22.50	30	37.50	45	52.50	7.50
20,000		No credit is allowed; enter "0" on Form IT-201, Line 53.							

*This may be any amount up to $15,000, including "0" or a negative amount.
**For each exemption over 7, add amount in this column to column 7 amount.

Real Property Tax Credit for Resident Homeowners and Renters

If your household gross income was $18,000 or less, you may be entitled to a credit on your New York State income tax return for part of the real property taxes or rent you paid during the tax year. Even if you are not required to file an income tax return, you may be eligible to receive this credit as a refund. You need not be a homeowner to claim this credit. Renters are also eligible to receive this credit if they meet certain requirements. The real property tax credit, sometimes called the *circuit breaker* credit, must be claimed by filing Form IT-214.

Homeowners. To qualify for the real property tax credit, you must meet all of these conditions for the taxable year:

1. The total adjusted gross income of all members of your household was $18,000 or less for the year;
2. You occupied the same New York residence for six months or more;
3. You were a New York State resident for the entire year;
4. You could not be claimed as a dependent on someone else's federal income tax return;
5. You or your spouse paid real property taxes on your residence;
6. The current market value of your residence was $85,000 or less; and
7. If you rented the property, any rent you received from nonresidential use was 20% or less of the total rent.

Renters. Renters may qualify to receive the real property tax credit if they meet requirements 1–4 listed above. You or your spouse must pay rent for your residence and it must not be exempt from property taxes. In addition, the average monthly rent you and other members of your household pay must be $450 or less, not counting charges for heat, gas, electricity, furnishings, or board.

EXCEPTION: You cannot file a real property tax credit claim for a taxpayer who has died.

Resident Tax Credit for Taxes Paid to Other States or Cities

If you live in New York and work in another state or receive income from out-of-state sources, other jurisdictions may require you to pay income taxes. Because a resident is taxed on income from *all* sources, including sources outside the state, the same income could be taxed twice. To avoid this, almost all states, including New York, provide residents and part-year residents with a credit for taxes paid to another state or locality (not including New York City or Yonkers) on the same income that the home state also includes in its taxable income base.

Example

Teresa lives in Nyack, New York but works in Montclair, New Jersey. Her employer in New Jersey withheld $1,000 from her pay to cover personal income taxes to New Jersey. To avoid being taxed on the same income in both New Jersey and in New York, Teresa should claim a resident tax credit on her New York State personal income tax return. Teresa must also fill out a New Jersey nonresident personal income tax return (Form NJ-1040NR).

In general, a resident credit is allowed for taxes paid to another state on salary, income from a business or profession, or rent. New York residents will generally receive a full credit for taxes paid on income earned elsewhere because in most cases, the New York tax will exceed the other state's tax on the same income. However, if the tax in the other state or city exceeds the New York tax, New York will only grant a credit to the extent of the New York tax that would be due on the same income. Sourcing rules are discussed in Chapter 3.

Although New York State generally will allow a full resident credit for the types of income listed above, **no credit is allowed** for taxes on income derived from intangible assets that are not used in a trade or business. Examples of this type of income include interest, dividends, and lottery prize winnings.

Limitations on the Resident Tax Credit. The limitations on the resident tax credit you are allowed are as follows:

1. The credit may not exceed your total income tax payable for the year to other states or cities.
2. The credit may not exceed the percentage of your New York income tax attributable to income taxed by other states or cities. The formula below illustrates this limitation:

$$\frac{\text{NY income taxed by another state}}{\text{NY adjusted gross income}} \times \frac{\text{NY tax before}}{\text{resident tax credit}}$$

$$= \text{Limitation on resident tax credit}$$

3. The credit may not reduce your tax to an amount less than the amount that would have been due if the income subject to taxation by the other state/city were excluded from the taxpayer's New York income.
4. If you paid tax in several jurisdictions, the limitations must be applied on a state-by-state basis.

The following example illustrates the application of the three limitations pertaining to taxes paid to another state and one or more of its cities:

Example

Harry and Sally, residents of New York, filed a joint return. Harry performed services as a salesman in Ithaca, New York, and Pennsylvania. Harry earned $32,000 of salary (plus $10,000 from Pennsylvania sources) and Sally received $2,000 of interest income and $2,000 of dividends. They claimed New York State exemptions for their two children. The resident tax credit is determined as follows:

Item	NY State	PA State
Salary	$32,000	$10,000
Interest	2,000	
Dividends	2,000	
Total NY Income before deductions and exemptions	$36,000	$10,000
Standard deduction	(9,500)	
NY AGI	26,500	
Exemptions	2,000	
Taxable income	$24,000	$10,000
Personal income tax	1,227	
Household credit	40	
Tax	$ 1,187	$ 200

Harry and Sally calculate their resident tax credit limitations as follows:
Limitation 1

The tax payable to other states:
Tax payable to Pennsylvania: $200
  Total Tax Payable $200

Limitation 2
  Percentage of New York tax attributable to income taxed by other states or cities:

A: Income sourced to Pennsylvania:	$10,000
B: New York Adjusted Gross Income:	$36,000
C: Line A divided by Line B	.2778
D: Pro rata portion of New York tax .2778 * 1,187 = $330	$ 330

Limitation 3
  The amount of income taxable in Pennsylvania is $10,000. Limitation 3 is calculated as follows: If the $10,000 of income from Pennsylvania is excluded and the standard deduction and exemptions ($2,000) are subtracted, the New York taxable income is $14,500. The tax is $616. Therefore, the amount by which the New York tax is reduced by the exclusion of the income subject to taxation by the state of Pennsylvania is $571 ($1,187 − $616).
  Harry and Sally are required to pick the limitation that yields the least amount of resident tax credit. Thus, Harry and Sally are entitled to a $200 resident tax credit.

Which Forms Must I File in Order to Claim the Resident Credit?

You must complete Form IT-201-ATT, *Summary of Other Credits and Taxes*, and Form IT-112-R, *Resident Tax Credit*, to claim a resident tax credit. A separate Form IT-112-R must be filled out for each state or city for which you are claiming a resident tax credit. However, if you paid taxes to a state and also to a local jurisdiction within that state, you need file only *one* Form IT-112R. Both forms must be attached to your resident income tax return, Form IT-201. You cannot claim the resident tax credit if you file Forms IT-100 or IT-200. (See *Attachments*, later in this chapter, for more information about Form IT-201-ATT.)

Part II of Form IT-112-R shows how the limitations discussed in the preceding section are applied.

Resident's Credit Against Separate Tax On Ordinary Portion of Lump-Sum Distributions

If you are a resident who filed federal Form 4972, Tax on Lump-Sum Distributions, and some or all of your lump-sum distribution was taxed in another state or city, you may be eligible for a tax credit.

New York allows a resident credit against the New York separate tax on the ordinary income portion of lump-sum distributions. (See *Other Resident Taxes*, earlier in this chapter, for a discussion of this tax.) The credit is based on the income tax imposed by another state, a political subdivision of such a state, the District of Columbia, or a province of Canada on the ordinary income portion of a lump-sum distribution. You must add back any credit previously claimed for income taxes imposed by a province of Canada if you subsequently claimed a federal foreign tax credit on the taxes.

The portion of the regular income tax attributable to the ordinary income portion of a lump-sum distribution is equal to the ratio of the ordinary income portion of the lump-sum distribution to the total gross income subject to tax by the other jurisdiction. The limitations on this credit are similar to the ones for the resident tax credit. See the preceding section.

Forms for Claiming the Resident Credit Against Separate Tax on Lump-Sum Distribution

A New York resident claiming this credit must complete Form IT-112.1, *NYS Resident Credit Against Separate Tax on Lump-Sum Distributions*, and attach it to his or her New York personal income tax return. In addition, Form IT-201-ATT— *Summary of Other Credits and Taxes*, must be attached. (See *Attachments*, later in this chapter.)

Separate Forms IT-112.1 are not required for cities within a single state that also tax a portion of the lump-sum distribution. The credit for these state taxes and local taxes paid on the lump-sum distribution is calculated jointly. You must file a separate Form IT-112.1 for each state taxing any part of the lump-sum distribution. Copies of your completed Forms IT-112.1, together with copies of your tax returns from the other taxing jurisdictions, must be attached to your New York personal income tax return.

Investment Tax Credit

New York allows both residents and nonresidents an investment tax credit if they invest in certain property, including buildings and structural components of buildings located in New York. Such property may include:

- Tangible property used in production, such as machinery and equipment;
- Certified industrial waste treatment and air pollution control facilities used in a trade or business;
- Research and development property; and
- Retail enterprise property.

The amount of the credit is 4% (or 7% for research and development property) of the cost of the property, less nonrecourse financing. Nonrecourse financing is any loan that is not secured by the property itself or personally guaranteed.

Qualifying Investment Credit Property

The credit is allowed for investment in new or used tangible personal property that:

1. Is acquired, constructed, reconstructed, or erected by the taxpayer after December 31, 1968;
2. Is depreciable under federal depreciation rules;
3. Has a useful life of four years or more;
4. Is acquired by purchase;
5. Is located in New York;
6. Is manufacturing and production property, waste treatment property, pollution control property, research and development property, or retail enterprise property.

The credit may be claimed only for the taxable year in which qualified property is placed in service. If you cannot use all of the credit in the year the property is placed in service, you may carry over the unused amount to the following seven years.

The investment credit is figured on the investment credit base. The *investment credit base* is the cost or other basis of the qualified property for federal income tax purposes. The base does not include any amount that was expensed as "Section 179(a)" expense.

What Forms Must I File in Order to Claim the Credit?

If you are claiming the investment credit, you must complete Form IT-212, *Investment Credit*, and attach it to your return. Form IT-212 *must also be filed* if you are claiming a carryover of unused investment credit, retail enterprise credit, or research and development credit from a prior period, or if you had an early disposition of property for which a credit was allowed in a prior year.

TAXALERT: For the year you originally claim the investment tax credit, you should fill out Part II of Form IT-212 and transfer the allowable credit to Part I of the Form.

If you are receiving the credit as a flow-through item from a partnership or S corporation you are invested in or from a trust that you are a beneficiary of, the following examples illustrate how to report the credit.

Example

You are invested in Green Valley Associates, a New York partnership. The partnership claimed an investment tax credit on machinery it purchased last year. Your pro rata share of this credit (based on your partnership profits ratio) can be claimed on your personal income tax return by completing Lines 4, 5, and 6 of Form IT-212. You can get information you need from the partnership's New York State information return, Form IT-204. (See Schedule B, Part III, Lines 18 and 19.)

Example

If you are a shareholder in a New York S corporation, your share of the S corporation's tax credit (based on your stock ownership percentage) should be applied to any investment tax credit on the S Corporation's New York return (Form CT-3-S, Part IV, Lines 81 and 82).

TAXPLANNER: An owner of a new business may be entitled to receive a refund of an unused investment credit (without interest) as an overpayment of personal income taxes. You qualify as an owner of a new business if you are a sole proprietor or member of a partnership and:

- You have not previously received a refund of an investment credit or a retail enterprise credit;
- The business you own is not substantially similar in operation or in ownership to a predecessor business entity that was taxable in New York. This includes "flow-through" entities, such as partnerships and S corporations, whose income was taxable on your personal return;
- You have operated the new business *for no more than four years* prior to the first day of the tax year for which the refund is being claimed.

Economic Development Zone (EDZ) Credits

New York provides a package of tax incentives to benefit businesses within designated economic development zones (EDZ). Part of the package includes credits for businesses operating within an EDZ. The authorized credits and related tax forms are:

- EDZ wage credit (Form DTF-601);
- EDZ capital corporation credit (Form DTF-602); and
- EDZ investment tax credit (Form DTF-603).

Shareholders in a New York S corporation doing business in New York are entitled to claim a share of EDZ credits taken by the corporation.

If you are a sole proprietor, you will have to decide if you qualify for these credits. Most individual taxpayers, however, will receive the benefit of these credits via pass-through entities such as partnerships, S corporations, and trusts. If you invested in the pass-through entity or are a beneficiary of a trust, you are entitled to claim a share of any EDZ credit based on your percentage interest.

Credit for Special Additional Mortgage Recording Tax

For most taxpayers, 1987 was the last year that the credit for special additional mortgage recording tax paid could be claimed. However, the credit is still allowed to individuals, estates, and trusts who are shareholders of an electing New

Payments

In the preceding sections you have calculated the tax you owe. Now it is time to figure what total payments you will need to make. This section will help you fill out the payment section of your New York State tax return.

Your total payments are comprised of amounts withheld, your estimated payments, payments you may have made with your extension (Form IT-370), and any overpayment from previous years that you have applied to this year's tax. Depending on which return you file, your payment information will be entered on either Lines 70–75 on Form IT-201, Lines 69–73 on Form IT-203, Lines 32–36 on Form IT-200, or Lines 10–12 on Form IT-100. The following sections contain a line-by-line discussion of the payment section of Form IT-201 reproduced below. Corresponding lines on Forms IT-100, IT-200, and IT-203 are noted in the following discussion.

70	Real property tax credit *(from Form IT-214, line 17; attach form)*	70	Staple your wage and tax statements at the top of the back of this return. See Step 7, page 20, for the proper assembly of your return and attachments.
71	Total New York State tax withheld *(staple wage and tax statements; see inst.)*	71	
72	Total city of New York tax withheld *(staple wage and tax statements; see instructions)*	72	
73	Total city of Yonkers tax withheld *(staple wage and tax statements; see instructions)*	73	
74	Estimated tax paid / Amount paid with Form IT-370	74	
75	Add lines 70 through 74. This is the total of your payments		75

Form IT-201—Payments (Lines 70–75).

York S corporation. The amount of the credit allowed is based on the shareholder's pro rata share of the credit taken by the corporation. Any unused credit from a previous year can be carried over to following years.

Solar and Wind Energy Credit Carryover

For years ending before 1987, a credit was available to a New York taxpayer who installed a solar or wind energy system in his or her principal residence. The credit was equal to 55 percent of the cost of purchasing and installing the system, up to a maximum of $2,750. Although the credit is no longer available, unused amounts from pre-1987 years can still be carried over.

Any credit carryover can be applied *after* deducting all the other available credits. The solar and wind energy carryover cannot be applied against the minimum income tax or the separate tax on lump-sum distributions.

Taxpayers carrying over any unused solar and wind energy credits from one year to the next must attach Form IT-218.1, Solar and Wind Energy Credit Carryover, to the return for the later year.

Credit for Research and Development

For years before 1989, a taxpayer was allowed a credit equal to 10 percent of the cost or other basis of property used in research and development. Any unused credits may be carried over, but must be used before 1994.

Credits to Trust Beneficiaries Receiving an Accumulation Distribution

Resident and nonresident trust beneficiaries whose New York adjusted gross income includes all or part of an accumulation distribution are allowed a credit for any tax paid by the trust in a preceding taxable year that would not have been payable had the trust made distributions to its beneficiaries.

Real Property Tax Credit: *IT-201, Line 70; IT-200, Line 32*

Refer to the preceding section, *Credits*, to see if you qualify to take advantage of this credit. If you qualify, enter your real property tax credit on this line. To claim this tax credit, you must have completed Form IT-214. Transfer the amount from Form IT-214, Line 17 to Form IT-201, Line 70. Remember to attach Form IT-214 to your state return.

Total New York State Tax Withheld: *IT-201, Line 71; IT-100, Line 10; IT-200, Line 33; IT-203, Line 69*

Enter the total *New York State* tax that was withheld from your employment compensation. This amount is shown on your wage and tax statement(s), Form IT-2102 or federal Form W-2. If you are filing a joint return, enter the total New York State tax withheld for both you and your spouse. Remember to attach the state copy of your wage and tax statement(s) to the area indicated on the *front* of your New York State return.

If New York State tax was withheld from annuities, pensions, retirement pay, or IRA payments that you received, include this amount on Line 71. Attach the state copy of Form IT-2102-P or federal Form 1099A to your return.

If you were lucky enough to receive New York State lottery distributions or gambling winnings from horse racing, you must include any New York State tax withheld on Line 71. Attach the state copy of Form IT-2102-G or federal Form W-2G to your return.

Also, include on Line 71 the amount of any investment credit refund for new businesses to which you are entitled. In the white space to the left of the total for this line, write "ICR" and report the amount.

Total City of New York Tax Withheld: *IT-201, Line 72; IT-100, Line 11; IT-200, Line 34; IT-203, Line 70*

Note: If you did not have New York City tax withheld, skip Line 72.

Enter the total *New York City* tax withheld from your compensation, as shown on your wage and tax statement(s). If you are filing a joint return, enter the total New York City tax withheld for both you and your spouse.

If New York City tax was withheld from annuities, pensions, retirement pay, or IRA payments you received, include this amount on Line 72.

If you received New York State lottery distributions or gambling winnings from horse racing, you must also include any New York City tax withheld from these proceeds on Line 72.

Be sure to attach copies of the appropriate forms that indicate your withholding as discussed under Line 71 above.

TaxAlert: If you are a New York City nonresident and have New York City tax withheld from your paycheck, you may need to fill out Form NYC-203 and attach it to your New York State return. (See the earlier section, *Other Nonresident Taxes*, for more information.)

Total City of Yonkers Tax Withheld: *IT-201, Line 73; IT-100, Line 12; IT-200, Line 35; IT-203, Line 71*

Note: If you did not have Yonkers tax withheld, skip Line 73.

See the preceding section on *City of New York Tax Withheld*. Exactly the same instructions apply to Yonkers residents. Just substitute the word "Yonkers" for "New York City."

TaxAlert: If you are a Yonkers nonresident and have Yonkers tax withheld from your paycheck, you may need to fill out Form Y-203 and attach it to your New York State return. (See *Other Nonresident Taxes*, earlier in this chapter, for more information.)

Estimated Tax Paid/Amount Paid with Form IT-370: *IT-201, Line 74; IT-203, Line 72*

Estimated Tax. If you were required to make estimated payments of tax, enter on this line the total of your quarterly estimated tax payments (Form IT-2105) to New York State, New York City, and Yonkers.

Don't forget to include your last installment for 1992, even if you paid it in 1993. Also, include any *overpayment* from your prior year's return (1991) that was applied to your estimated tax for this taxable year.

TaxAlert: If you and your spouse filed a joint state return but made separate estimated tax payments (Form IT-2105), you must enter the combined total estimated tax you both paid on this line.

TaxAlert: If you are a beneficiary of a trust and are claiming your share of any overpayment of estimated taxes allocated to you by the trust, you must include the amount on this line. Attach a copy of the notification issued by the trust to the front of your return. This notification must include the name and identifying number of the trust and the amount allocated to you.

TaxAlert: Do not include any amounts you paid as New York City unincorporated business tax. If you have an unincorporated business, you must pay any unincorporated business tax you owe directly to the New York City Department of Finance. Because this tax is imposed on your unincorporated business, rather than you individually, any payment you made of the unincorporated business tax does not count as a payment of your personal income tax. (See *Unincorporated Business Tax* in Chapter 7 for more information.)

TaxSaver: If you changed your name during the year because of marriage, divorce, or other reasons, and you made estimated tax payments using your former name, attach a statement to your return explaining the payments you made under different names. If you are filing a joint return, include estimated payments made by your spouse for the taxable year. For each payment, indicate the name(s) and Social Security number(s) under which you made the payment.

Amount paid with Form IT-370. If you filed Form IT-370 *Application for Automatic Extension of Time to File for Individuals*, include on this line the amount you paid when you requested an extension of time to file your state return. Attach a copy of Form IT-370 to your return.

TaxAlert: If you and your spouse are filing a joint return but filed separate Forms IT-370, you should enter the total amount that both you and your spouse paid with your separate extension requests.

Add Lines 71–74 and enter the result on Line 75 (Form IT-200, Lines 32–35 or Form IT-203, Lines 69–72). This is the total amount of tax you've already paid.

Overpayment: *IT-201, Line 76; IT-203, Line 74*

If Line 75 is more than Line 69, subtract Line 69 from Line 75 and enter the result on Line 76. This is the amount of your overpayment.

TaxPlanner: You may elect to have all or only part of your overpayment refunded to you. You may apply a portion of your overpayment to your 1993 estimated tax. (see Chapter 5, *Estimated Taxes*.)

Note: Any overpayment credited toward your estimated tax will not be refunded until after April 15, 1993.

Refund: *IT-201, Line 77; IT-200, Line 37; IT-203, Line 75*

Enter on this line the amount of overpayment from Line 76 that you want refunded to you.

TaxAlert: New York State will keep all or part of your refund if you owe a federal, New York State, New York City, or Yonkers tax liability; past due spousal or child support; or if a judgment was filed against you because you have not repaid certain student loans such as:

1. Guaranteed student loans by:
   - New York State Higher Education Services Corp.; or
   - Perkins National Defense/National Direct.

2. Health professions or nursing student loan provided to students at state-operated units of the:
   - State University of New York; or
   - City University of New York.

Any amount that exceeds your debt will be refunded.

If you have any questions about whether you owe any of the above liabilities, be sure to contact the appropriate federal, state, or city agency.

TaxAlert: If you are filing a joint return and you do not want to apply your part of the refund to your spouse's debt because you are not liable for it, complete Form IT-280, *Nonobligated Spouse Allocation,* and attach the original to your return. (See *Filing Status* in Chapter 2 for more information.)

New York State, New York City, and Yonkers Estimated Tax: IT-201, *Line 78;* IT-203, *Line 76*

Enter the amount of your overpayment from Line 76 that you want credited to your New York State, New York City, and Yonkers estimated tax for 1993. Do not include any amount you claimed as a refund on Line 77.

Amount You Owe: IT-201, *Line 79;* IT-200, *Line 38;* IT-203, *Line 77*

If Line 75 is less than Line 69, subtract Line 75 from Line 69 and enter the result on Line 79. This is the amount you owe.

Make your check or money order payable to: New York State Income Tax. Be sure to write your Social Security number and ''1992 Income Tax'' on the face of your check.

TaxAlert: If you have to pay an estimated tax penalty (Line 80 below), send one check or money order for the total amount (penalty plus tax due).

Do not include any other penalty or interest amounts on Line 79. If you include penalties or interest with your payment, identify and enter these amounts in the right margin of the back page of Form IT-201 (but not underpayment of estimated tax penalty; see Line 80 below). Attach your payment to the area indicated on the front of your return.

Estimated Tax Penalty: NYC-201, *Line 80;* IT-203, *Line 78*

If Line 79 is at least $100 and, in addition, represents more than 10% of the tax shown on your return, or you underpaid your estimated tax liability for any payment period, you may owe a penalty. (See the discussion of *Penalties* in Chapter 5, *Estimated Taxes,* to determine if you owe a penalty and to figure the amount.) If you owe a penalty, enter the amount on Line 80 and attach Form IT-2105.9 to your return.

TaxAlert: Don't forget to sign and date your return!

Note: Both husband and wife must sign a joint return.

(For filled-in examples of forms, refer to Chapter 9, *New York Sample Forms.*)

Attachments

You may be required to attach other forms or schedules to your New York income tax return (Form IT-201, Form IT-203, Form IT-200, or Form IT-100). These forms or schedules provide additional information to the New York tax authorities that will assist them in processing your return. These attachments may be forms or schedules provided by New York, federal schedules you used in preparing your federal income tax return, or tax returns for other states or localities. The following section summarizes what attachments may be required.

New York Forms and Schedules

You may need to prepare the following forms to complete your state tax return. Unless otherwise indicated, these forms should be attached in numerical order to the back of Form IT-100, *Resident Fast Form Income Tax Return,* Forms IT-200 or IT-201, *Resident Income Tax Return,* or Form IT-203, *Nonresident and Part-Year Resident Income Tax Return.*

IT-370, Application for Automatic Extension of Time to File for Individuals and Gift Tax Return Filers. This form is used for an initial extension of time to file your tax return. If you were not required to file this form because you did not expect to owe tax with your New York State tax return, you must attach a copy of your federal extension, federal Form 4868, to your state tax return. (For more information on *Extensions,* please refer to Chapter 2.)

IT-372, Application for Additional Extension of Time to File for Individuals and Gift Tax Return Filers. If you requested an additional extension of time to file, you must attach the approved copy of your extension request to your tax return. When you filed your second extension request, you should have sent two copies to New York. The approved copy is the copy that New York stamped and mailed back to you.

IT-280, Nonobligated Spouse Allocation. Attach this form if your filing status is *married filing jointly* and you do not want New York to apply your share of any refund due to you to your spouse's delinquent student loans, past-due spousal support, or other debt.

IT-2105.1, Reconciliation of Estimated Income Tax Account. This form is used to reconcile any differences between your records of estimated tax payments and those of New York. You can verify your account status by reviewing the *Statement of Estimated Income Tax Account* that you received with your estimated tax packet, Form IT-2105. If there is a discrepancy, complete a copy of this form for each error and attach the form(s) to the front of your tax return.

IT-2105.9, Underpayment of Estimated Tax by Individuals. If you underpaid your estimated tax liability for any payment period, you should complete this form to see if you owe any penalties. (Please refer to Chapter 5, *Estimated Taxes,* for additional information.)

IT-2601.1, Change of Resident Status. If you moved into or out of New York State during the year, you may need to complete this form. (Please refer to *Nonresidents* in Chapter 2 for additional information.)

IT-360.1, Change of City Resident Status. If you moved into or out of New York City or the City of Yonkers during the year, you may need to fill out this form. (Please refer to *Nonresidents* in Chapter 2 for additional information.)

IT-221, Disability Income Exclusion. Use this form to determine whether all or a part of your disability income may be excluded from taxable income.

IT-399, New York State Depreciation. This form is used to calculate your depreciation deduction for New York State.

In addition, you may need to make an adjustment for the accumulated difference between New York State depreciation and federal depreciation if you sold an asset. This form is used to calculate your adjustment. (Please see *Additions and Subtractions* in Chapter 3 for additional information.)

IT-211, Special Depreciation Schedule. If you have certain depreciable property which was acquired before 1969, you may be eligible for an additional depreciation deduction.

You may need to attach one or more of the following forms to your state tax return to reflect your liability for additional New York taxes:

NYC-203, City of New York Nonresident Earnings Tax. If you live outside of New York City and earned income from within the city, you will need to complete this form. (Refer to *Other Nonresident Taxes*, earlier in this chapter, for more information.)

IT-230, Separate Tax on Lump Sum Distributions. If you received your entire balance due from your employer's pension plan, stock bonus plan, or profit-sharing plan, you may need to complete this form. (See the earlier section *Other Resident Taxes*, for more information.)

IT-220, Minimum Income Tax. If you have any tax preference items, such as charitable contributions of appreciated property, you must complete this form. (See the earlier section, *Other Resident Taxes*, for more information.)

You may need to prepare one or more of the following forms in order to claim a tax credit. (Please refer to *Credits*, earlier in this chapter, for additional information.)

IT-201-ATT, Summary of Other Credits and Taxes.

IT-203-ATT, Summary of Other Credits and Taxes—Nonresidents. The credits included on these forms are: resident credit, accumulation distribution credit, investment credit, special additional mortgage recording tax credit, solar and wind energy credit carryover, and economic development zone credit.

IT-214, Claim for Real Property Tax Credit for Homeowners and Renters. If your household gross income was less than $18,000, you may be entitled to this credit. If you take this credit you must place this form behind all other attachments to your tax return, so that the front page of the form faces out from the back of your tax return.

IT-218.1, Solar and Wind Energy Credit Carryover. If you have a solar and wind energy credit carryover, you may use this form to claim the allowable unused credit. 1985 was the last year that this credit could be claimed. However, any unused credit may be carried forward to future years.

IT-112-R, Resident Tax Credit. You may be eligible for a credit if you paid taxes to other states. You will need to attach copies of the tax returns that you filed in other states if you are claiming a resident tax credit.

DTF-601, Claim for Economic Development Zone Wage Tax Credit.

DTF-602, Claim for Economic Development Zone Capital Corporation Tax Credit.

DTF-603, Claim for Economic Development Zone (EDZ) Tax Investment Tax Credit and Additional EDZ Investment Tax Credit. These credits are only available to taxpayers conducting business in areas that have been designated as economic development zones under Article 18-B of New York's General Municipal Law.

IT-212, Investment Credit. You may be eligible for a credit for certain property used in a trade or business.

IT-112.1, Resident Credit Against Separate Tax on Lump-Sum Distributions. You may be eligible for a credit against income taxes paid to other states on lump-sum distributions.

Federal Forms That Were Attached to Your Federal Tax Return

Many of the forms and schedules that you filled out to complete your federal Form 1040, *U.S. Individual Income Tax Return*, must be attached to your state tax return. Unless otherwise noted, they should be placed in numerical order behind your New York State forms. If you are not sure whether you should have filled out any of the following forms when preparing your federal return, please refer to *The Ernst & Young Tax Guide 1993.*

Schedule C, Profit or Loss From Business.

Schedule D, Capital Gains and Losses.

Schedule E, Supplemental Income and Loss.

Schedule F, Profit or Loss From Farming.

Form 4797, Sales of Business Property.

Other Statements. You may have attached statements to your federal tax return that describe certain types of income, such as miscellaneous income. These statements should also be attached to your state tax return.

Other Federal Forms

Form W-2 (or Form IT-2102), Wage and Tax Statement. If you received wages during the year, your employer will send you Form W-2. While it may look as though you are provided with three identical copies of the same form, the form marked *Copy 2* is designated for state use and must be stapled to the front page of your state tax return.

1099-Misc, Miscellaneous Income.

1099-R, Distributions From Pensions, Annuities, Retirement or Profit Sharing Plans, IRAs, Insurance Contracts, etc.

W-2P (or IT-2102-P), Statement for Recipients of Annuities, Pensions, Retired Pay or IRA Payments.

W-2G, Certain Gambling Winnings.

W-2P (or IT-2102-G), Statement for Recipients of Certain Gambling Winnings.

5 | Estimated Taxes

[handwritten: 1991 - 16,287.86 ?md]

[handwritten: 26,481.95 @ 90% = 23833.75]

Requirements

The airlines used to have an advertising slogan: "Fly now, pay later!" New York's slogan for paying taxes might be: "Pay as you play." New York, like the federal government, requires that taxpayers pay tax as they earn income. Thus, you must make tax payments throughout the year, in the form of estimated tax payments or withholding of tax from your salary or wages, even though your return is not due until April 15 of the following year.

This chapter discusses estimated tax payments. It explains who must pay estimated taxes, when and how much you must pay, and what forms you must file. Withholding of tax is discussed in Chapter 7.

Who Must Pay Estimated Taxes?

New York law requires that you pay estimated taxes if you expect that your total withholding and credits for 1993 will be less than the *smaller* of the following two amounts:

- 100% of your 1992 tax (assuming your return covered all twelve months); or
- 90% of your anticipated 1993 tax.

TaxALERT: If you will owe less than $100, you can skip the rest of this chapter. You won't have to pay estimated taxes.

Example

Mary has New York State and City taxes withheld from her salary. In 1992, Mary had $400 in state taxes withheld from her salary. In 1991, she paid New York State taxes of $500. When Mary files her 1992 New York tax return, she computes a total tax due of $700, or $300 more than was withheld from her salary. Mary should have paid estimated taxes for 1992. Mary's withholdings ($400) were less than the smaller of 100% of lat year's tax ($500) or 90% of this year's tax ($630). Mary will be liable for penalties on the underpayment.

TaxALERT: Many taxpayers will still be liable for estimated tax payments, even if their withholdings equal the tax they paid last year. These taxpayers will be subjected to the "90% rule," discussed below.

The "90% Rule"

Formerly, all New York taxpayers could choose to pay 100% of their previous year's tax in quarterly estimated tax payments and avoid penalties. This gave taxpayers a "safe harbor," since most people paying estimated taxes don't know what their final tax due will be until they prepare their return in the following year. Last year's tax, on the other hand, is generally a known quantity.

Effective in 1992, however, New York law has changed to conform to similar changes in federal law. Beginning this year, most New Yorkers who pay estimated taxes must have made installment payments of at least 90% of their 1992 tax by January 15, 1993, the date of the last installment payment. They can no longer base their estimated tax payments on last year's tax. For convenience, we'll call this the "90% Rule."

You are subject to the 90% rule if any of the following statements are true:

1. You earned $40,000 more in modified New York adjusted gross income this year than you did last year ($20,000 if you are *married filing separately*); ✓
2. Your New York adjusted gross income exceeds $75,000 ✓ ($37,500 if you are *married filing separately*);
3. You made estimated tax payments during any of the last ✓ three years;
4. You were penalized for failing to make estimated tax payments during any of the last three years; or
5. You are required to base your federal estimated tax payments on the "90% Rule."

A taxpayer may switch between the 90% and 100% tests on a quarterly basis if, at the end of the tax year, he or she falls within the "safe harbor" category exempting him from an estimated tax penalty.

Each quarterly installment of estimated taxes you pay must equal 25% of your total estimated tax for the year. For example, you must pay 25% of your total estimate by the end of the first quarter, 50% by the end of the second quarter, and so on. If your estimate of tax due increases during the year, you must adjust the amount of your next quarterly payment to reflect the increase. In other words, you must play "catch-up." Of course if your estimate decreases, you can decrease the amount of your payments. However, if you underestimate your liability, you will be subject to penalties. Penalties are discussed later in this chapter.

TaxALERT: Your quarterly estimated tax payments must be based on the total tax you expect to be due, not 90% of the tax you expect to be due. For example, if you expect to owe $1,000 in tax for the year, you are expected to pay $250 each quarter (assuming your estimate doesn't change during the year). Your installment payment cannot be based on 90% of your $1,000 estimate, which would work out to $225 a quarter. However, if your estimate is "off" by less than 10%, you will not be subject to penalties on the underpayment.

Example

Dennis paid New York State taxes of $6,000 in 1992. Early in 1993, he estimated that he would earn approximately the same amount of income as he did in 1992. For both his first and second quarter 1993 estimated payments, Dennis paid 25% of $6,000

($1,500). In the third quarter, he determined that his income has increased. According to his new estimate, he will owe $7,200 in taxes for 1993. Dennis must pay $2,100 with his third quarter estimate, calculated as follows:

Estimated 1993 tax (new):	$7,200
Total Paid in 1st and 2nd Quarters:	−$3,000
Balance to be Paid in 3rd & 4th Quarters:	$4,200
Divide by Remaining Number of Quarters:	÷ 2
Estimated Payment Due in 3rd Quarter	$2,100

Example

Dennis paid New York State taxes of $6,000 in 1992. Dennis files as a single taxpayer. For 1993, he estimates that he will owe $7,000. His New York adjusted gross income this year will exceed $75,000. Dennis must base his estimated tax payments on his current-year estimate. Although he prepared his estimate carefully, there is always the possibility that his income may go up unexpectedly. What if he is self-employed and a customer pays a long-disputed bill around Christmas? Dennis must make up the difference in his January 15, 1993, estimated tax payment. If he is not sure of what his final 1992 tax will be by that date, he risks penalties if he has underestimated by more than 10% (unless he uses the *annualized income method*, described in the following section on *Penalties*).

Example

Sally earned $20,000 in 1992 from a part-time job as a bookkeeper. She is an independent contractor who is paid on an hourly basis. Her customer does not withhold New York State income taxes from her contract fees. For 1992, Sally owed New York State $1,200 in taxes. If she expects no change in her income, Sally could use $1,200 as her basis for paying estimated taxes in 1993. However, Sally expects to earn more money in 1993 and estimates she will owe New York State tax of $2,000 for 1993. Sally can either use $1,200, her last year's tax, as her basis for paying estimated taxes in 1993 or use her current-year estimate of $2,000, whichever is less. Either way, Sally will be making four quarterly payments of estimated tax. She must pay at least $300 a quarter ($1,200 divided by 4) to avoid penalties for underpayment of tax.

Filing and Paying Quarterly Estimated Taxes

If you made estimated tax payments to New York last year, you will receive an estimated tax form in the mail. If you have not received one, you can request Form IT-2105, *Estimated Income Tax Payment Voucher*, by calling the New York State Department of Taxation and Finance at 1-800-462-8100. If you are calling from outside New York, call 1-518-438-1073.

On the form, you will see a space for your name, address, Social Security number (or employment identification number if you are a fiduciary) and four other lines. Three of the four lines refer to estimated tax payments for New York State, New York City, and Yonkers, respectively. Complete as many of these lines as are applicable to you. The last line is the total payment line. Make your check payable to "NYS Income Tax" and write your Social Security or other identification number and "1992 Form IT-2105" on the check. The check amount should match the total payment amount. Send the check and the completed Form IT-2105 to the following address:

New York City Area Only:	All Other Areas:
NYS Estimated Income Tax Processing Center P.O. Box 2111 New York, NY 10008-2111	NYS Estimated Income Tax Processing Center P.O. Box 1195 Albany, NY 12201-1195

Use U.S. certified mail, if possible, and retain your receipt as proof that you filed your estimated tax on time.

When to Make Estimated Payments

For calendar-year taxpayers, estimated tax payments are due on the following dates: April 15, June 15, September 15, and January 15 of the following year. The payment due on each date is 25% of the total tax you estimate will be due for the year.

Fiscal-year taxpayers pay estimated taxes by the 15th day of the fourth month, sixth month, ninth month of their taxable year and first month of the following taxable year.

However, if you will not owe estimated taxes by April 15 of this year, use the schedule below. This schedule is only for people who do *not* owe estimated taxes for the first three months of this year.

If You Meet the Requirements	Installment Due Dates	Percentage of Estimated Tax Due
After March 31 but before June 1	June 15 September 15 January 15	50 Percent 25 Percent 25 Percent
After May 31 but before September 1	September 15 January 15	75 Percent 25 Percent
After August 31	January 15	100 Percent

Penalties

Introduction

As a New York resident, you must prepay your income tax during the year. This is usually accomplished through taxes that are withheld by your employer. If you have certain income from which tax is not withheld, such as self-employment income, you are generally required to make estimated tax payments. Penalties on estimated taxes are in addition to any other penalties, such as penalties for failure to file your return or pay your actual tax due on time. They are levied on the amount by which you underpaid your estimated taxes.

TAXALERT: You can avoid penalties on underpayment of estimated taxes if you file your return and pay your tax due by February 9, 1993.

If you do not make timely estimated tax payments when you are required to do so, you will be subject to penalties based on the amount of your deficiency.

Underpayment of Estimated Tax

If you are subject to a penalty for underpayment of estimated tax, you must complete Form IT-2105.9. You will need a copy of this form, along with the accompanying instructions and worksheet. Generally, the penalty you pay is like an interest charge on the amount of each underpayment. The penalty rate is set by the Commissioner of Taxation and Finance and is specific for each payment period. It is based on the number of days that the installment was not paid. To determine if you are subject to the underpayment penalty, you should complete Part I of Form IT-2105.9—*Required Annual Payment.* You will compare 90% of the tax due on your 1992 return to your total tax due for the previous year, and will choose the lesser of the two.

Example

Jim's total tax due for 1993, before withholding and estimated payments, is $5,000. Of this amount, $3,000 was withheld during the year.

A. 1992 tax $5,000
B. 90% of 1992 tax.................................. $4,500
C. 100% of 1992 tax $4,000
D. the lesser of B or C $4,000

Since the total amount withheld ($3,000) is less than $4,000 (see D above), Jim will pay a penalty.

Calculating the Penalty

Form IT-2105.9 supplies two methods for calculating your penalty. Use Part II—*Short Method* for figuring your penalty if you:

- Paid withholding tax;
- Paid four equal installments of estimated tax on time; or,
- Made no estimated tax payments.

If you don't meet these requirements, you must complete Part III—Regular Method.

TAXSAVER: Only use the short method if you made your estimated tax payments *on* the due dates. Be sure to include total estimated payments made to New York State, New York City, and Yonkers. If you paid any installment early—before the actual due date—using the short method will cause you to pay a higher penalty. Use the regular method instead.

Part III—Regular Method. The Regular Method contains two alternative ways to figure your penalty. If you received unexpected or seasonal income after March, use the annualized income installment method. Check the appropriate box on the form and complete the *"Annualized Income Installment Worksheet"* from the instructions.

If you annualize your income: Complete the Annualized Income Installment Worksheet and enter the amounts on Line 14, Columns A–D.

If you do not annualize your income: Begin with the total amount from Part I, Line 6 (see Line E of the preceding example). Divide by four and place each amount in columns A–D on Line 14 of Part III of Schedule A.

Begin with *Schedule A—Figuring the Underpayment.* In this Schedule, you will be comparing the installment of estimated taxes due on the appropriate due date to the total estimated tax withheld or actually paid. Be sure to complete each column from top to bottom before moving to the next one. That way it will be easier to figure if you overpaid or underpaid any installment.

After you have completed Section A, turn over the form and complete Schedule B. Schedule B is where you calculate the penalty due.

Installment Calculations

The penalty calculations will be different depending on whether you made your payment of estimated taxes *before* the due date or *after* the due date. As an example, start with

April 15th, which is generally the date your first estimated tax payment is due. New York requires that you pay a penalty on any underpayment from the actual due date until the date that the payment is finally made.

You must pay a penalty for the period of time during which an underpayment existed. This calculation is used to figure the penalty for each installment:

$$\left[\frac{\text{Number of days tax was unpaid during the quarter}}{\text{Number of days in the year (365)}} \right]$$

$\times$ penalty rate

$\times$ underpayment

$=$ penalty for quarter

Example 1

Assume you had an estimated tax payment due on April 15 of $4,000. You made no payments and did not have any tax withheld from your paycheck. Thus, you owe an underpayment penalty for the whole period. Assume also that the applicable penalty rate for this period is 9%. The penalty on the underpayment of tax for your first quarter is computed as follows:

$$\left[\frac{\text{Number of days in period}}{\text{Number of days in the year}} \right] \times \text{penalty rate}$$

$\times$ underpayment $=$

$$\frac{61}{366*} \times 9\% \times 4{,}000 = \$60.00 \text{ underpayment penalty}$$

Example 2

Assume instead that you paid the $4,000 on May 10: The number of days from April 15 to May 10 is 25. Use that number to figure the penalty, as follows:

$$\left[\frac{\text{Number of days in period}}{\text{Number of days in the year}} \right] \times 9\% \times \$4{,}000 =$$

$$\frac{25}{366} \times 9\% \text{ or } 4{,}000 = \$24.59 \text{ underpayment penalty}$$

TAXALERT: Time is money, as the saying goes. The longer your payment remains outstanding, the higher your penalty will be.

Exceptions

If you fail to pay installments of estimated tax or underpay these installments, you may be charged with a penalty on the amount of tax you owe. As you learned in the previous chapter, underpayments are calculated on Form IT-2105.9 (Underpayment of Estimated Taxes by Individuals and Fiduciaries). However, even if you calculated an underpayment, you may qualify for one of New York's five exceptions to the imposition of a penalty.

In New York you will not be subject to the underpayment penalty if:

1. The tax liability you owe, after taking withholding taxes into consideration, is less than $100. If you owe taxes in two jurisdictions, for example, New York State and New York City, the amount is $200. If you owe New York State,

*1992 was a "Leap Year."

New York City, and City of Yonkers tax, the amount is $300;

2. If an installment of estimated taxes is due to New York on the date of, or after, an individual's death, penalties will not be imposed on the amount of the underpayment. However, penalties may be imposed on any amount underpaid before the individual's death;

3. If the underpayment was caused by a disaster, casualty, or other unusual circumstance, no penalty will be imposed. The state will accept causes such as natural disasters, fire, flood, or similar events as reason to excuse penalties; or

4. If you retired in the current tax year after reaching age 62, or if you became disabled and the underpayments were due to reasonable cause, penalties will be excused.

TaxAlert: If you request an excuse of penalties, you must prepare a written explanation giving the reasons why the state should not impose penalties. This written request should be attached to your Form IT-2105.9.

TaxAlert: New York amended its tax laws to reflect a repeal of the reduction of tax rates scheduled to go into effect in 1992. The legislature also extended certain supplemental tax provisions placed upon high income taxpayers. You will not owe a penalty on any underpayment of estimated taxes from the first quarter of 1992, as long as you made up the deficiency with your June payment.

6 | Refunds (Amended Returns)

At some point, you may conclude that you are owed a refund of taxes you previously paid. To obtain a refund, you will have to file an amended return. You may also be required to file an amended return with New York if there are changes to your federal income tax. This chapter will discuss refund claims and other circumstances in which the filing of an amended return may be required.

Refunds in General

If you paid more taxes on your income than you actually owe, whether through estimated tax payments or withholding, you may be entitled to receive a refund.

You may also be entitled to a refund of state taxes if the Internal Revenue Service has made changes to your federal income tax return that result in a reduction of your federal adjusted gross income. Finally, you may have made an error in New York's favor on your original tax return. You will need to file an amended New York State income tax return to obtain a refund.

When to Submit an Amended Return

There are a number of reasons why you might need to file an amended return. Here are some of the most common ones:

- You did not report some income you received;
- You overstated your income;
- You claimed deductions or tax credits for which you were not eligible;
- You were entitled to deductions or tax credits you did not take;
- The information on your federal tax return changed, requiring you to file an amended federal tax return; or
- The Internal Revenue Service made adjustments to your federal return.

There are strict time limits for seeking refunds. Generally, to claim a refund, you must file an amended return within three years from the due date of your original return, including any extension of time you received to file the return, or within two years of the date the tax was paid, *whichever is later*. If you filed your return early, it is still deemed to be filed on the due date rather than the actual date you mailed it.

If you file an amended federal return, you *must* file an amended New York return. You must also file an amended return if you receive a determination from the Internal Rev-

enue Service that changes any one of the following items on your federal return:

- Federal taxable income;
- Tax preference items;
- Total taxable amount of the ordinary income portion of a lump-sum distribution;
- Federal credit for employment-related expenses;
- Federal foreign tax credit;
- Amount of income tax withheld; or
- Amount of refund claimed.

An amended New York State tax return is due within 90 days from the date you filed an amended federal return or received a notice of final determination from the Internal Revenue Service. For more information on time limits for filing amended returns, see the *Statute of Limitations* section in Chapter 8.

TaxAlert: If you disagree with a final determination of change or credit by the Internal Revenue Service, you are still required to file an amended New York return within the 90-day period following the date you received the determination. You should clearly indicate your disagreement when you file the amended return by attaching a statement to the return. Briefly explain the reasons for your disagreement.

TaxAlert: If you are seeking a refund or credit for an overpayment on your New York return that was caused by a change or correction on your federal return, you must apply for it within two years from the time you were required to notify the state.

Which Form to Use

If you filed your original return on Form IT-100, IT-200, or IT-201, you must use Form IT-201X, *Amended Resident Income Tax Return*, for the corresponding tax year.

If you are a nonresident taxpayer and filed Form IT-203, there is no special form for amended returns. Use a blank copy of Form IT-203 and write **Amended**, on the top of the front page. Be sure to use the correct form for the year you are amending.

Interest on Overpayments

The state will pay interest on overpayments of taxes. The interest on your overpayment may be limited. The following are a few of the conditions that will limit your receipt of interest:

- If you file your return or an amended return past its due date, no interest will be allowed for any day before the return was filed;
- If you receive a refund or credit for an overpayment within three months of your claim, the state is not obligated to pay interest; and
- If your return cannot be processed because you have failed to include all the necessary information, no interest will be paid until you supply the required information.

Limits on Amounts of Refunds

Your refund will normally be limited to the tax you paid during the preceding three years. However, because estimated and withholding taxes are deemed paid on the date you file your return, refunds of these amounts may be claimed more than three years after the payment or withholding.

Example

Sonny's 1990 New York State income tax return was due on April 15, 1991. He filed it on March 31, 1991. Sonny had income tax withheld by his employer of $1,000 and paid estimated income taxes of $2,000. Even though Sonny filed his return before April 15 and had paid most of his estimated taxes long before that date, he can file an amended return at any time before April 16, 1994, three years after the original due date, to claim a refund. He can claim a refund of any amount of tax up to the total amount paid ($3,000).

If Sonny received an extension of time to file his return, he would still have three years from the date he filed the return to claim a refund of tax. If Sonny received a four-month extension and filed his return on August 15, 1991, he would have until August 15, 1994, to file an amended return.

You also have up to two years after you pay your income taxes to claim a refund. Occasionally, this will give you more time in which to claim a refund than the three-year limit discussed above.

If you file a refund claim later than three years but within two years from the time you paid the tax, your refund is limited to the amount of tax you paid within the two-year period.

Example

Melvin filed his 1990 New York State income tax return on April 15, 1991. He paid taxes in the amount of $100. On December 20, 1992, New York audited his 1990 return and determined Melvin owed an additional $500 for 1990, which Melvin paid. On June 15, 1994, Melvin discovers a tax credit he did not take on his 1990 return that would amount to $800 and files an amended return. Since the amended return is filed past three years of the original filing date of the return, April 15, 1991, Melvin would not be entitled to any amount paid prior to or with the return. Melvin will only be entitled to receive a refund up to the amount paid on December 20, 1992, or thereafter, as long as it is within the two-year time frame.

What if Your Refund Claim is Denied?

If you are denied a refund, you will generally receive an informal notice to this effect. You must then file an informal protest letter. Simply write a letter to the person and/or office that responded to your refund claim. Include any extra information you think will help the tax department understand your position. If your refund is denied again, you will be issued a formal denial letter with instructions on how to proceed.

TaxAlert: If you feel you are due a state personal income tax refund but time is running out, you should file a protective refund claim. You may file a protective refund claim on Form IT-113X. By filing this claim, you have suspended the Statute of Limitations to give you the extra time you need to try to successfully secure your claim.

Filing Your Amended Return

An amended return is prepared just like an original return. Please consult the earlier chapters of this book if you need assistance. Once your amended return is complete, attach any supporting schedules and send everything to:

New York State Income Tax
W. A. Harriman Campus
Albany, NY 12227-0125

As with every other tax return, be sure to sign and date the amended return and send it by U.S. certified mail. Keep a copy for your files.

7 | Other Taxes

Sales and Use Tax

A sales tax is a tax on the sale, exchange, or rental of goods and certain services. For the most part, it is imposed on sales that take place between a merchant or supplier and customer inside the state. As a New York consumer, you generally pay sales tax directly to the merchant or supplier of the goods or services you purchase. He or she is responsible for collecting the tax from you and paying it to the Department of Taxation and Finance. An out-of-state merchant may be required to collect sales tax from New York residents if he or she has some connection with New York.

A use tax is a complement to the sales tax and is imposed at the same rate as the sales tax. If you are a New York resident, you owe use tax on all taxable goods and services used in New York unless they were taxed at the time of purchase. For example, you may have purchased goods outside the state from a vendor not required to collect New York sales tax. You will owe use tax on those goods when you bring them into New York or have them delivered here. You must also pay use tax when you purchase items in a New York locality with a lower combined state and local sales tax rate than the locality in which they are used. Finally, when you purchase goods outside the state and pay sales tax at a lower rate than the New York rate, you are liable for the *difference* in the sales tax rates when you bring the goods into the state.

The current state sales and use tax rate is 4%. Some New York counties, cities, and school districts also impose their own sales tax. These rates vary by locality. In addition, the state imposes a 0.25% surcharge in the Metropolitan Commuter Transportation District (the counties comprising New York City and the surrounding area).

What is Taxable?

As a consumer, you pay sales tax on many goods and services used in your daily life. In general, the following goods and services are taxed by New York:

- Retail sales and rentals of tangible personal property, including items such as appliances, clothing, automobiles, household products and housewares, video rentals, cosmetics, pet foods and supplies, cigarettes, soft drinks, alcoholic beverages, bottled water, books and publications, and records and tapes;
- Gas, utilities, telephone and telegraph services, and telephone answering services;
- Information services, unless they are individual or personal in nature;
- Certain processing and printing services;
- Charges for installation, repair, and maintenance of tangible personal property;
- Charges for maintenance, service or repair of real property, unless part of a capital improvement;

- Safe deposit box rentals, storage of property that is not held for sale;
- Motor vehicle parking and garaging services;
- Interior decorating and design services;
- Protective and detective services;
- Charges for calls to a "900 number";
- Sales of food or drink in or by restaurants, taverns, or caterers;
- Temporary rental of hotel and motel rooms;
- Most admission charges to entertainment events; and
- Most dues paid to social and athletic clubs.

EXCEPTION: Some sales of tangible personal property are exempt from sales tax. Common exempt items include sales for resale, food other than candy and confections, beverages other than soft drinks and alcoholic beverages, drugs and medicines, newspapers and periodicals, eyeglasses, hearing aids, prosthetic aids, and other artificial devices used to correct a physical disability.

New York City imposes a local sales tax at the rate of 4% on certain services that are not subject to tax elsewhere in the state. These taxable services include credit rating and reporting services, beauty, barbering, hair restoring, manicuring, tanning, pedicure, electrolysis, and massage services.

Who is Required to Collect Sales Tax?

If you operate a business in New York that sells taxable goods or services to people in this state, you must collect and pay state sales and use tax. You must also collect a local sales tax on all taxable sales made or services performed in a locality that has such a tax. You are only required to collect tax on those goods and services that are specifically taxed by New York.

If your business requires you to collect New York sales tax, you must register as a vendor at least 20 days before commencing business. To register as a vendor, you must complete Form DTF-17, *Application for Registration as a Sales Tax Vendor.*

Exempt Sales. Some persons and organizations are exempt from paying sales tax. If the purchaser is exempt, he or she should provide you with a valid exemption certificate at the time of sale. If none is provided at that time, the sale may still qualify as an exempt sale if a certificate is provided within 90 days after goods are delivered or services are rendered to the purchaser.

TaxSaver: Caution should be exercised when accepting exemption certificates. If you accept an untimely and improperly completed exemption certificate, you may be personally liable for any tax, penalties, and interest that may be due.

Exempt Purchases. Some goods you purchase for use in your business may be exempt from sales and use tax. Since New York does not tax sales for resale, any purchase of tangible personal property that you intend to sell to others is exempt. This is true whether the property is sold in the same form in which you purchase it, whether it becomes a physical component of some other goods, or whether it is used in performing certain taxable services. In order to purchase resale items tax-free, you should submit a *Resale Certificate* (Form ST-120) to the vendor at the time of purchase. If no certificate is submitted at the time of purchase, your purchase may still be recognized as exempt if a certificate is provided within 90 days after the goods are delivered.

In addition, if you are in the manufacturing, processing, assembling, or refining business, you are exempt from paying tax on the following items:

- Any machinery and equipment used or consumed directly or predominantly in the production of tangible personal property for sale;
- Any fuel, utilities, and utility services used or consumed directly and *exclusively* in the production of tangible personal property for sale. (New York City does not exempt these purchases.); and
- Parts with a useful life of less than a year, as well as all tools and supplies used in connection with production machinery and equipment. (New York City does not exempt these purchases.)

You should submit an *Exempt Use Certificate* (Form ST-121) to the vendor at the time of purchase to purchase these items tax-free. If none is submitted at that time, your purchase may still be recognized as exempt if a certificate is provided within 90 days after the goods are delivered.

Unincorporated Business Tax (UBT) for New York City

This section will present an overview of the New York City unincorporated business tax, which is imposed on any individual or unincorporated entity that carries on a business within the city. For example, a law firm organized as a partnership would be subject to this tax. An architect, caterer, chiropractor, or commercial designer operating on his or her own would also be subject to the unincorporated business tax. This tax is unique to New York City.

Although a full discussion of the unincorporated business tax as it pertains to partnerships, fiduciaries, or corporations in liquidation is beyond the scope of this book, you may find the following information useful if you are doing business in an individual capacity or as part of a partnership within New York City.

What is an Unincorporated Business?

An unincorporated business is any trade, business, profession, or occupation carried on by an individual or unincorporated entity. An unincorporated entity is a business that has not been formed under the state's corporation laws. Unincorporated entities include partnerships, fiduciaries, and corporations in liquidation.

The taxing authorities, when determining whether a particular activity constitutes an unincorporated business, usually look at the frequency and regularity of the activity, to distinguish it from casual or isolated transactions that are not subject to the tax.

Example

Joey, who is not a songwriter by profession, lives within New York City. He composed a single song which was used by a well-known artist. Joey is not considered to be engaged in an unincorporated business. His royalty income will not be subject to the unincorporated business tax.

Generally, you will not be considered to be conducting an unincorporated business solely because you purchase stocks or securities for your own account. However, if you perform other services in addition to trading for your own account, *both* activities may be deemed taxable. You will also be considered to be carrying on an unincorporated business if you invest funds in an operating unincorporated business, such as a manufacturing plant, retail store, or hotel, where conducting business is necessary to realize a profit on your investment. You will still be considered to be carrying on an unincorporated business even though you may devote little of your time and energy to managing your business affairs.

Employees

Whether or not you are subject to the unincorporated business tax may depend upon whether you are acting as an employee or as an independent contractor. The term *employee* means an individual who performs services for an employer under an employer-employee relationship. Generally, such a relationship exists when the person for whom services are performed has the right to control and direct the individual performing the services. For example, an employee is usually required to work during stated days and hours and is subject to company-established standards. An *independent contractor*, by contrast, is generally an individual who is subject to the control or direction of another person only with respect to the end result, such as delivering a particular product or performing a specific service, but not with respect to the means and methods of getting the job done. For example, agents, auctioneers, brokers, and contractors who offer their services to the general public are generally considered independent contractors.

If you engage in the practice of a profession, such as law, medicine, accounting, dentistry, or architecture, you will be deemed to be carrying on an unincorporated business. The term *profession* includes any occupation in which you use knowledge gained through specialized schooling. Typically, professionals are licensed by the state.

Example

Mitchell is a salaried employee teaching at a well-known business school. In connection with his research into the effects of sunspots on the stock market, Mitchell has written several books on finance, for which he received royalty income. Mitchell is also a football fan and has written several books on the subject of football, receiving additional royalties. Mitchell will be subject to the unincorporated business tax. The royalty income from the football books is clearly subject to tax. The royalty income from the finance books is also subject to the tax unless Mitchell can show that the books were written in his capacity as an employee of the university.

TAXPLANNER: If you write any books as an employee for which you receive royalty payments, be sure you have a written agreement with your employer stating that the publishing of books is a requirement of your employment and that the writing is under the direct supervision and control of your employer. However, a written agreement, by itself, will not prove that you are not carrying on an unincorporated business. Other facts must support your position that you are merely performing services as an employee.

Purchase and Sale of Property

An individual or unincorporated entity is not considered engaged in an unincorporated business solely because he or she purchased or sold property (real or personal) for his or her own account.

EXCEPTION: A dealer who holds property primarily for sale to customers in the ordinary course of his or her business is considered to be carrying on an unincorporated business. A dealer is a person who regularly engages in the purchase of property and its resale to customers.

Holding, Leasing, or Managing Real Property

An owner, lessee, or fiduciary will not be considered engaged in an unincorporated business if he or she holds, leases, or manages real property *solely* for his or her own account.

EXCEPTION: If you hold, lease, or manage real estate in connection with your unincorporated business, any gains, profits, rents, or other income from the property must be included in your taxable income.

TaxALERT: If you earn income from an activity that is exempt from the unincorporated business tax, such as trading in stocks and bonds or managing property for your own account, be aware that any income from a *taxable* activity may subject your entire earnings to tax. For example, if you normally manage only your own investments in the stock market but decide, as a favor to a friend, to accept a commission for giving investment advice, your entire investment earnings could be "tainted" by the taxable activity.

Filing Requirements

If you are carrying on an unincorporated business or profession wholly or partially within New York City and your total gross income from the business exceeds $10,000, you must file an unincorporated business tax return.

TaxALERT: Individuals, estates, and trusts which are engaging in an unincorporated business must file Form NYC-202. Partnerships file Form NYC-204.

For calendar-year taxpayers, the unincorporated business tax return is due by April 15. For a fiscal-year taxpayer, the return is due on or before the 15th day of the fourth month following the close of the taxable year. An automatic extension of six months is available if you file an application for an extension on Form NYC-62 before the due date of your return and remit any tax due. Partnerships must use Form NYC-64 to request an extension.

Allocation and Apportionment

If an unincorporated business is carried on partly within and partly outside New York City, its net income can be allocated. However, if the unincorporated business has no regular place of business outside the city, *all* of its income will be subject to tax, without allocation.

A "regular place of business" is any office, factory, warehouse, or other place that you regularly and systematically use in carrying on your business.

EXCEPTION: An unincorporated business entity is not considered to have a regular place of business outside the city merely because it makes sales or performs services for customers located outside the city. If you use an independent contractor or agent with a regular place of business outside New York City to make sales or perform services, you cannot claim your agent's premises as your own place of business for purposes of allocation.

Note: The "regular place of business" rule discussed here applies only for purposes of allocating income outside New York City. The rules for determining whether your business is taxable by New York City are different. You may still be subject to the unincorporated business tax even if you don't have a regular place of business within the city.

Example

Sam, an accountant, has an office in New York City. Although Sam performs some of his services at his clients' places of business outside the city, he cannot allocate his income for unincorporated business tax purposes since Sam himself does not have a regular place of business outside the city.

Example

Ted, a freelance journalist, maintains an office solely within the city. Although he spends part of his working time traveling to gather materials for his articles, he cannot allocate his income for unincorporated business tax purposes.

Example

Ray, an anesthesiologist, performs all his medical services at a hospital in New York City. Although he keeps his records at, and bills his patients from, his home outside the city, his home does not constitute a regular place of business for unincorporated business tax allocation purposes.

EXCEPTION: Income from the rental, sale, or exchange of real property and from the rental of business personal property in connection with an unincorporated business is not subject to allocation. If the property is located in New York City, all income from it is included in unincorporated business taxable income.

In general, you will use separate books and records to allocate all other income, if they accurately reflect your activity in and out of the city. If they do not, you should use a three-factor apportionment formula, similar to the formula of property, payroll, and sales discussed in Chapter 3, in the section on *Attributing Income to New York—Sourcing Rules*. However, for purposes of the unincorporated business tax, separate accounting is the preferred method.

Imposition of Tax

The unincorporated business tax is imposed at the rate of 4% on the unincorporated business taxable income.

Withholding

If you are an employee, your salary or wages are probably subject to the withholding of income taxes. Also, other forms of compensation or income may be subject to withholding. This section will explain who is subject to withholding, what forms of compensation are subject, how the amount to be withheld is calculated, and how you can adjust the amount of withholding to fit your tax situation. Generally, New York follows federal rules concerning the withholding of income tax. To learn more about the federal provisions, consult *The Ernst & Young Tax Guide 1993*.

Who is Subject to Withholding?

Residents. If you are a resident of New York State and your employer is located in New York, he or she is required to withhold income tax for all services you perform, even though the services may have been performed outside the state. Also, if you are a resident of New York City or Yonkers and your employer is located in New York State, he or she is obligated to withhold income taxes regardless of where your services as an employee are performed.

If you work for an employer who is located outside New York, and he or she does not transact any business in New York, the employer *will not* be obligated to withhold any New York income tax from your wages, although he or she may be required to withhold income taxes on your wages for the state in which he or she is located. As a resident, you will still be obligated to file a New York State tax return and pay income taxes. If income taxes are withheld by your out-of-state employer, you may be entitled to a credit for taxes paid against any income tax you may owe to New York. (See *Credits* in Chapter 4.)

Nonresidents and Part-Year Residents. If you are a nonresident of either New York State, New York City, or Yonkers, your employer must withhold income taxes on wages paid to you for services performed in any one or more of these locations. If your job requires that you perform services solely within any one of these places, tax must be withheld on all wages paid to you. (See *Attributing Income to New York—Sourcing Rules* in Chapter 3.)

If you work partly within and partly outside New York State, New York City, or Yonkers, you should file a *Certificate of Nonresidence and Allocation of Withholding Tax Form* unless the portion of your wages allocable to these jurisdictions is exactly the same as it was last year. The form number for each location is as follows: New York State, Form IT-2104.1; New York City, IT-2104.2; and Yonkers, Form IT-2104.5. You must file these forms to certify your nonresident status and estimate the percentage of services you will perform within each location. If these forms are not filed and your allocation of wages has changed, your employer is obligated to withhold income taxes on all wages paid to you unless he or she keeps records to determine the amount of your wages from sources within these locations.

What Income is Subject to Withholding?

The main category of income from which taxes must be withheld is wage or salary income. Any supplemental wages you receive are also subject to withholding of tax. Supplemental wages include bonuses, commissions, overtime pay, sales awards, tips, and vacation allowances. If supplemental wages are paid to you at the same time as your regular wages, your employer should withhold tax on the entire amount at the same rate as the rate applicable to your wages. However, if the supplemental wages are paid to you separately from your regular wages, your employer may withhold income taxes at the highest rate, without allowance for withholding exemptions, discussed below. Other types of income subject to income tax withholding are taxable fringe benefits, sick pay, pensions and annuities, and certain gambling winnings.

Exemptions From Withholding

If you had no income tax liability last year and you anticipate no income tax liability this year, you may be able to claim an exemption from income tax withholding. To claim the exemption you must be:

- Less than 18 years of age;
- Less than 25 years of age and a full-time student; or
- Over 65 years of age.

If you claim this exemption and your situation changes, you must revoke your claim to the exemption within 10 days from the day you will no longer meet these requirements.

If you claim an exemption from withholding you must complete Form IT-2104-E, *Certificate of Exemption From Withholding*, for every year you wish to continue the exemption with your current employer. If you are in the Armed Forces and have changed your residence from New York to another state, you should file Form IT-2104-MS, *New York State Withholding Exemption Certificate for Military Service Personnel*, with your employer.

Determining Withholding Taxes

Your employer can determine the amount of income taxes to be withheld from your wages by using the tax tables provided by the state or by calculating the tax himself or herself. The amount of tax to be withheld depends upon the amount of income you earned for the pay period and the information you gave your employer on a withholding allowance certificate (federal Form W-4 or New York Form IT-2104). A withholding allowance certificate tells your employer the rate at which you want your income tax withheld, whether you want any additional amount withheld, and how many withholding allowances you want to claim.

If you filed federal Form W-4 with your employer and it accurately reflects how you want your taxes withheld for New York purposes, it is not necessary to file Form IT-2104. If you have not filed Form W-4 or the information on your W-4 is not accurate for New York withholding purposes, you should file a separate Form IT-2104.

You will want to calculate as accurately as possible the amount of income tax to be withheld from your earnings, so that it will cover your final tax liability at the end of the year. This may enable you to avoid penalties for underpaying your income tax. (See the section, *Penalties*, in Chapter 8.) Although you may owe interest and penalties if your employer underwithholds your income tax, you do not receive any interest or additional money if he or she overwithholds.

You can choose to have your income tax withheld at a higher tax rate for *single* taxpayers or a lower tax rate for *married* taxpayers. You can choose either tax rate, regardless of your marital status. (However, as discussed above, you may owe interest and penalties if your income tax is underwithheld.) You can also request that your employer withhold additional amounts beyond the income tax calculated at the tax rate you choose. You may want to have additional income tax withheld if you believe the calculated withholding amount may not be enough to cover your income tax liability for the year. You may wish to have additional withholdings from tax if you and your spouse both work, you have more than one job, or you have income from interest, dividends, alimony, or self-employment. If you choose to have additional withholdings from your paycheck, you must have a written agreement to this effect with your employer.

You are entitled to the same number of withholding allowances on your Form W-4 or Form IT-2104 as the number of dependent exemptions you are allowed to take on your New York tax return (Form IT-200 Line 14, Form IT-201 Line 49). Your employer uses the number of withholding allowances you request to more accurately calculate the amount of tax to be withheld from your pay for each pay period. This is so that when you file your tax return, the amount of tax that was withheld over the course of the tax year will more closely equal the amount of tax you will calculate on your tax return. If you and your spouse both work, each of you must complete a separate Form W-4 or IT-2104. You can divide the total number of withholding exemptions you and your spouse are entitled to between yourselves in any combination you wish.

TAX*SAVER:* You should review your Form W-4 and Form IT-2104 (if filed) periodically to assure their accuracy with respect to your current tax situation. For example, if you can no longer claim a child as a dependent or you or your spouse reach the age of 65, you should amend these forms to correct the appropriate information.

TAX*ALERT:* If you do not file Form W-4 or Form IT-2104 with your employer, your employer must withhold taxes from your pay at the highest rate. Your paycheck may contain less money than you are actually entitled to receive if taxes are overwithheld.

Credit for Tax Withheld

You are allowed a credit against your income tax due for any withholding of tax during the year. If you had income taxes withheld, you should apply the credit on the appropriate line of your income tax return. See the section on *Payments* in Chapter 4.

Your employer is required to supply you with a summary of all wages paid to you and all taxes withheld from your wages. Typically, you will receive several copies of federal Form W-2, *Wage and Tax Statement*. You should attach the appropriate copy of your W-2 to your federal, state, or local return. You should receive this form from your employer no later than January 31, following the close of the tax year. If you are unable to obtain it from your employer, you should file Form IT-2102.6, *Certificate of Income Tax Withheld*. You can only use Form IT-2102.6 if you have exhausted every effort to obtain federal Form W-2 from your employer.

Real Property Transfer and Gains Tax

This section will survey taxes you may have to pay if you buy or sell real property in New York State or City. It will explain how these taxes work and what forms you may need to file if you are subject to them. In some cases, you may have to pay one or more of these taxes even though you never owned the sold property directly.

New York State Real Property Transfer Tax

You may be subject to the Real Property Transfer Tax if you sell real property located in New York. You may also be subject to this tax when you lease property to another person if the leasehold interest is for 99 years or more. *Real Property* that is subject to this tax includes houses, condominiums, co-

operatives, buildings, and land. In general, this tax is imposed on the seller; however, if the seller is an exempt entity, the buyer may need to pay the tax. The tax is levied on the *full purchase price*, which includes cash, the underlying mortgage (if assumed), and the fair market value of any other consideration transferred to you. (Note: The value of any mortgage or other encumbrance is excluded if the consideration is less than $500,000 or residential property is sold.) Persons subject to this tax in New York State must complete Form TP-584. If you sell property in New York State, you may also need to pay the *Real Property Transfer Gains Tax*. This tax is discussed below.

Controlling Interest. You may be responsible for the Real Property Transfer Tax even if you do not own the transferred real estate directly. The tax applies if you transfer a controlling interest in a corporation, partnership, association, trust, or other entity that owns an interest in real property located in New York. *Controlling interest* is defined as ownership of 50% or more of the stock or beneficial interest in an entity. A transfer of a controlling interest may occur through a series of transactions or through the combined efforts of a group. Transfers made within a three-year period will be combined for this purpose.

Example

Alan and Brenda each own a 30% interest in ABC Partnership which owns a building in New York City, Together, they decide to sell their interests in the partnership. This transfer is subject to tax because their combined effort will result in a transfer of at least 50% of the interest in an entity that owns real property in New York.

Exemptions: You will not have to pay the Real Property Transfer Tax if your transaction meets one of the following requirements:

- The money or other consideration transferred to you is less than $500;
- You sell property to the United States of America, the United Nations, New York State, or any instrumentality, agency, or subdivision of these bodies. These agencies are exempt from the transfer tax. However, if you purchase realty from one of these agencies, you may need to pay the transfer tax;
- You transfer a deed to release security for a debt or obligation;
- Realty you own is transferred to a trustee for the benefit of your creditors. The transfer of the deed from your trustee to your creditor(s) or to any other person is subject to tax;
- You are correcting a deed that was previously recorded;
- Your property is seized to pay delinquent taxes;
- You divide your realty into separate shares or units but do not transfer the shares to another person;
- You grant an option to purchase real property without use or occupancy of the property;
- You grant an option to a potential buyer to purchase your residence and the consideration is less than $200,000;
- Your conveyance is merely a change of identity or form of ownership; or
- You convey property under a decree of bankruptcy.

TAX*ALERT:* Partial and successive transfers of adjacent parcels of real property may be combined in order to determine whether the consideration is $500 or more.

Calculation of Tax. If you paid tax on the creation of a lease of real property, you will be entitled to a credit on the subsequent sale of the property. This credit is limited to the amount of tax previously paid. A credit is also allowed for the tax paid upon the initial transfer of property to a cooperative housing corporation if the conveyance was a mere change of identity and not a change in the beneficial ownership of the property.

Example

Two individuals transferred a building containing five apartments to cooperative housing corporation H in exchange for the stock of H. The Real Property Transfer Tax paid as a result of this transfer was $5,000. When the H corporation shares are sold to unit purchasers, a credit up to $5,000 will be allowed.

The tax rate is $2 for each $500 or fraction of $500 of the full purchase price. An additional tax of 1% (0.01) is imposed on residential property that is sold for $1 million or more.

Example

Mary sold her one-family house in New York State for $1.5 million. Her total New York State Real Property Transfer Tax is computed as follows:

$1,500,000 ÷ 500 = 3,000 × $2	= $ 6,000
$1,500,000 × 1% (0.01)	= 15,000
Total Tax	**$21,000**

New York State Real Property Transfer Gains Tax

In addition to the real property transfer tax described above, New York State may impose another tax on the seller of real property. Unlike the transfer tax, which is levied on the total purchase price of the property, this tax is only paid if property is sold at a *gain*. New York City does not have a similar tax.

You may be responsible for the Real Property Transfer Gains tax if you transfer a controlling interest in real property located in the state. Please refer to *controlling interest*, which is covered in the discussion of the *Real Property Transfer Tax.*

Exemptions: You will not be subject to the Real Property Transfer Gains Tax if your transaction meets one of the following requirements:

- You transfer real property for less than $1 million;
- You transfer real property that was occupied and used as your residence;
- You buy real property from the United States of America, the United Nations, New York State, or any instrumentality, agency or subdivision of these bodies;
- Your conveyance is merely a change of identity or form of ownership; or
- You are merely providing an option to a potential buyer to purchase real property but are not actually selling the property. This option may not include the right to use such property.

Calculation of Tax. The Real Property Transfer Gains tax is imposed at a rate of 10% on the gain you realized on the transfer of your property. *Gain* is the amount by which the *consideration* exceeds your *original purchase price. Consideration* includes the money, underlying mortgage assumed by the purchaser, the fair market value of other consideration, less customary brokerage fees that you paid. Your *original purchase price* includes the amount you paid to acquire the real property plus the cost of capital improvements and rea-

sonable legal, engineering, and architectural fees you had to pay in order to sell your property.

Example

Mary sold her house to John for $900,000. John also assumed her underlying mortgage of $250,000. Mary paid $15,000 to a broker to sell her house. Mary's original purchase is computed as follows:

Money paid for house	$400,000
Capital Improvement	200,000
Engineering fees	5,000
Legal fees	10,000
Total	$615,000

Mary's gain is computed in the following manner:

Consideration	
Money	$ 900,000
Underlying Mortgage	250,000
less: Brokerage fees	(15,000)
	$1,135,000
Original Purchase Price	615,000
Gain	520,000
Multiply by 10% (0.1)	10%
Total Tax	$ 52,000

New York City Real Property Transfer Tax

You may be subject to pay the Real Property Transfer Tax if you sell real property located in New York City. You may also be subject to this tax when you lease property to another person if the leasehold interest is for 99 years or more. *Real property* that is subject to this tax includes houses, condominiums, cooperatives, buildings, and land. In general, this tax is imposed on the seller; however, if the seller is an exempt entity, the buyer may need to pay the tax. You will only be subject to the Real Property Transfer Tax on the sale of property located in New York City if the full purchase price of the property is at least $25,000. The *full purchase price* includes money, the underlying mortgage (even if this mortgage is not assumed by the purchaser), and the fair market value of other consideration transferred to you. Persons transferring property in New York City must complete Form NYC-RPT, *Real Property Transfer Tax Return.* Note: The rules concerning transfers of a controlling interest in real property, discussed earlier in this section, also apply to the New York City tax.

Exemptions: You will not be subject to the Real Property Transfer Tax in New York City if your transaction meets one of the following requirements:

- You transfer your realty as a bona fide gift. A gift of property with underlying debt is *not* exempt because the debt is treated as a part of the full purchase price;
- You record your deed as a confirmation or a correction of a transaction for which the tax has already been paid;
- You merely provide an option to purchase or sell real property;
- You transfer property for less than $25,000;
- You sell your property to, or buy property from, the United Nations or a charitable organization;
- You sell property to the United States of America or New York State or agencies, instrumentalities, or subdivisions of these governments;
- Property is transferred to or from your agent;
- You secure debt by transferring a deed; or

- You transfer property as part of a reorganization under bankruptcy laws.

Calculation of Tax

Type of Property Sold	Purchase Price	Tax Rate
One, Two, or Three Family House, Individual Residential Condominium Units, Individual Dwelling Unit	$500,000 or less	1% (0.01)
	Over $500,000	1.425% (0.01425)
Other Property	$500,000 or less	1.425% (0.01425)
	Over $500,000	2.625% (0.02625)

TAXALERT: Tax credits are available for certain transfers of controlling interests in various entities and for certain transfers of cooperative apartments. See the discussion in the section on New York State Real Property Transfer Tax.

New York State Mortgage Recording Tax

New York State imposes a mortgage recording tax on mortgages for real property located in the state. This tax is imposed at a rate of $1.00 on each $100 of the mortgage. However, the first $10,000 of a mortgage for a one or two family dwelling is taxed at a rate of $0.75 per $100.

New York City Mortgage Recording Tax

New York City imposes a mortgage recording tax on mortgages for real property located in the city. This tax for individual residential cooperative and condominium units and one, two, or three family homes is $1.00 per $100 if the mortgage is less than $500,000, and $1.125 per $100 on mortgages over $500,000. The tax rate for all other types of property is $1.75 per $100.

Estate and Gift Tax

This section will provide you with an overview of New York estate and gift taxation. The estate tax is imposed on the estates of residents and nonresidents who die while owning New York property exceeding a certain amount. This tax is in addition to any federal estate taxes owed. The gift tax is imposed on gifts of real or tangible personal property located in New York that exceed a set annual amount. Gifts of intangible property made by residents are also subject to tax.

An explanation of all the provisions concerning estate and gift taxation is beyond the scope of this book. However, the information below will help you determine whether or not you or your estate may be liable for one of these taxes. If you are an executor of an estate, it will help you determine your filing responsibilities.

Estate Tax

The estate of a deceased person who was a resident of New York is subject to the New York Estate Tax. The estate of a nonresident that includes real or tangible personal property located in New York is also subject to the tax.

The value of the New York gross estate is determined by making certain state modifications to the federal gross estate. The New York taxable estate is then computed by subtracting allowable deductions from the New York gross estate. After the New York taxable estate is determined, post-1982 taxable gifts that are not included in the gross estate must be

added. This results in the New York tentative tax base, against which the estate tax rates are applied to determine the tentative tax. Finally, certain credits are allowed against the tentative tax. The net estate tax is the tentative tax minus the credits.

Filing the Return

For the estates of both residents and nonresidents, Form ET-90, *New York Estate Tax Return*, must be filed by the executor of the estate within nine months of an individual's death. A request for an extension of time to file the return can be made by filing Form ET-133, *Application for Extension of Time to File and/or Pay Estate Tax*.

Estates required to file an estate tax return must also file a copy with the Surrogate's Court. The copy is due when a petition is filed with the court to begin the probate of a will or to begin the administration of the estate if there is no will. There is a fee charged to file a copy of the return with the court.

Paying the Tax

The estate tax is due before the date the estate tax return is filed. Eighty percent of the tax must be paid within 6 months of the date of death; the balance is due within 9 months. Interest begins to run 6 months from the date of death. If you need additional time to pay the tax, you must file Form ET-133, *Application for Extension of Time to File and/or Pay Estate Tax*. Extensions are granted if undue hardship would result from requiring payment to be made within nine months of the date of death.

If a large part of the estate consists of an interest in a closely held business, you can elect to defer the payment of the estate tax. Generally, this election must be made within nine months of the date of death by filing Form ET-415, *Application for Deferred Payment of Estate Tax*.

New York Gift Tax

A gift tax is imposed on all transfers of real or tangible personal property located in New York. A gift, for tax purposes, is a transfer of property for which no money, or an amount of money substantially less than the property is worth, is given in return. The giver of the gift must pay the tax, but if the tax is not paid, the person receiving the gift is liable for the tax to the extent of the value of the property. Only gifts exceeding $10,000 to a single individual in a calendar year are subject to tax.

Filing the Return

A gift tax return, Form TP-400, *New York State Annual Gift Tax Return*, must be filed on or before April 15 following the close of the calendar year in which the gift is made. If the due date falls on a Saturday, Sunday, or legal holiday, the return is due on the next business day. An estimated return, including a payment equal to 90% of the tax due, must be filed by January 15 of the following year if no gift tax return has been filed. If the giver of the gift dies during the calendar year, the gift tax return must be filed, and the gift tax paid, by the date the estate tax return is due, but not later than April 15.

EXCEPTION: The gift tax does not apply to:

- Transfers for payment of an individual's tuition made to an educational institution;
- Transfers for a person's medical care made to a health care provider or a medical facility;
- Transfers to qualifying charitable organizations; and
- Transfers to a spouse that qualify for the marital deduction.

8 | What to Do If Your Return is Examined

Audits

The word "audit" strikes fear into the hearts of taxpayers. The thought of a tax official knocking at your door is a nightmare many begin to have soon after April 15th. This chapter will explain what an audit is, how an audit is triggered, and how to survive an audit with the least amount of pain and suffering.

What is an Audit?

An audit is, simply, a review of your tax return by the taxing authorities. New York conducts audits through the mail, in district offices around the state, and at the homes or places of business of its taxpayers. Simple computational errors on your return are corrected by computers. You are notified by mail of any resulting correction in the tax due (or refund).

The most common type of audit is the desk audit. The desk audit is conducted through the mail. Typically these audits revolve around simple issues, such as substantiation of deductions, that are easily handled by mail.

A field audit is typically a much more thorough review than a desk audit. These audits are usually conducted by agents of the district office in your area of the state. Information is requested, and you may be asked to appear at the auditor's office to discuss the issues under examination. Agents may also ask to visit your home or place of business as part of a field audit. They may request access to your books and records, or may examine your property.

Whose Return is Audited?

Many taxpayers wonder how New York determines who will be audited. Tax returns are selected for audit in a variety of ways. Sometimes a random selection by computer triggers an audit. At other times, a tax return is picked for audit because it involves certain types of income or deductions that New York has decided to examine. The most common reasons for examining taxpayers' returns are listed below.

Issues That May Trigger an Audit:

1. Errors made in filling out a return that require a taxpayer's explanation before a computational correction can be made.
2. Audits made as a result of a federal audit. For example, changes made on your federal Form 1040 are reported to New York under an information exchange agreement aimed at consistency between federal and state reporting. New York requires you to notify them of any changes you may have made on your federal return or changes the IRS may have made. These changes must be reported to New York within 90 days of the IRS's final determination or the filing of an amended federal return.
3. Other exchange-of-information programs with the Internal Revenue Service and other states. For example, information reported to the IRS on Schedule K-1 of Form 1065, *Partnership Return*, is available to New York taxing authorities. New York has also recently joined some other states in exchanging certain types of tax information with respect to individuals, estates, and trusts. Member states can check whether a taxpayer has established residency in another state, filed as a non-resident in two or more states, or improperly claimed income in another state in order to reduce his or her resident taxes.
4. State issues. These are specific New York State issues more likely to be audited by the state than items of income and deductions that are also reported on federal Form 1040. Such items may include nonresident allocation of pension income and income from stock options.
5. Residency issues. The New York taxing authorities may look carefully at whether a taxpayer filing as a nonresident or part-year resident should have filed a resident return. For part-year residents, they look at whether the taxpayer properly reported income attributable to his or her resident period. Because of the potential loss of revenue from improper filing, residency is a major audit issue. For more information about filing as a resident or nonresident, consult Chapter 2.
6. Federal issues. These issues typically include federal deductions, such as travel and entertainment, or interest expense. Although not often the subject of state audits in the past, these issues are getting increased attention as a potential source of state revenue.
7. Special audit projects of the Department of Taxation and Finance. State audit projects involve auditing certain preselected groups of taxpayers whose returns are especially complex. Examples include limited partners or persons with exceptionally high amounts of income.
8. Multi-audit. Multi-audits are combined, simultaneous audits of a taxpayer and his or her business. Typically, they may involve an individual income tax and sales tax audit, in the case of an unincorporated business, or an income tax, sales tax, and corporate franchise tax audit, in the case of an incorporated business. Other taxes may also be involved, such as the Real Property Transfer and Gains Taxes.

9. Special requests by district office agents based on their personal knowledge of particular taxpayers. If you have been audited before, chances are that you will be audited again.

How to Survive an Audit

If your return is selected for an audit, you will generally be notified by mail. The notice will inform you that your return has been selected for examination. It will also tell you which years New York wishes to examine. Generally, the taxing authorities may examine your return within three years after it was filed. However, many exceptions apply. (See the following section, *Statute of Limitations*, for a full discussion.)

TaxPlanner: Although many people believe that saving taxpayers' records for three years is sufficient, professional tax advisors are increasingly advising clients to keep all records relating to their tax returns for eight to ten years, or longer. Save copies of your filed returns, checks for deductions, receipts, income and wage statements, as well as any substantiation for deductions or income items not covered by checks or receipts you may have. If you change your residence for tax purposes, save adequate documentation of the change. See the *Abandoning Your Domicile Checklist* in Chapter 2. If you allocate your income based on days in and days out of New York, save the documents showing where you were on any particular day. See Chapter 3 for more information on attributing income to New York. Get into the habit of keeping your tax information in a safe place.

An agent prepares for an audit by examining a taxpayer's file, particularly for unusual or unexplained items. These include the items mentioned earlier, such as unusual deductions or unexplained changes in income. The pre-audit preparation by the auditor may determine the thoroughness with which your records will be examined.

What is Examined? If your return is selected for examination on a preliminary basis, the agent will look for unusual or unexplained items. The agent may use a preset numeric guideline to determine whether an item is "unusual."

TaxAlert: Save all receipts that support deductions and expenses. If audited, you will have the burden of proving the propriety of each challenged item. The better your documentation, the easier it will be to prove your case.

The agent may also ask you to explain certain items that are only broadly described on the return, such as:

- Deductions or expenses classified as miscellaneous or general;
- Professional fees;
- Business expenses not adequately explained;
- Sales of assets not fully described; or
- Unexplained or apparently unreasonable deductions from gross rents or royalties.

TaxAlert: Take the time to prepare detailed schedules explaining your deductions. Be sure to attach any such schedules to your return. Save all documents related to the schedules so you can explain them to the agent.

Some items are singled out for further investigation because they have historically been prone to taxpayer abuse. These items might include:

- Casualty losses;
- Losses that may result from a hobby rather than a business;
- Expenses for an office in your home;
- Deductions taken for dependents who are not members of your immediate family or who do not live with you; or
- Educational expenses.

Items that are not consistent with other items on your return may also be questioned. Examples of such inconsistent items are:

- Deducting rent for business property if your depreciation deductions show that you own the property; and
- Deducting automobile expenses, if you took a separate mileage deduction for the use of your automobile.

Finally, some items are conspicuous by their absence. If you do not report certain items, the agent may question whether they should have been reported. Such items include:

- Not reporting insurance reimbursement offsets to your medical expense deductions if you also deducted medical insurance premiums;
- Not reporting interest deductions if your return shows a large asset purchase; and
- Reporting little or no interest or dividend income if you have a large amount of adjusted gross income.

The Audit Itself. The agent will first contact you by mail for an appointment. A letter will advise you as to what books, records, and other documents the agent wishes to examine. In a field audit, the agent will usually visit your place of business or your home.

TaxAlert: At this stage, it may be advisable to contact your accountant or retain competent legal advice and representation. If you determine that representation is warranted, you must assign your representative the right to speak on your behalf by executing a Power of Attorney. The Power of Attorney must be given to your representative before the meeting.

Your first meeting with the agent will be a preliminary conference. This conference is designed to acquaint the auditor with you and your particular situation. If you have retained representation, be sure that your representative is present at any meeting with the agent and that he or she sees the auditor's information request before you hand over any documents or sign any papers.

Generally, during the full audit, documents associated with reported items of income and loss, deductions, and interest expenses will be examined in some detail. The agent may request additional information by sending you further notices. Depending upon the complexity of your return, the auditor might issue more than one document request or schedule more than one meeting. It is important to consult your representative, if you choose to use one, before releasing any documents to the auditor.

If you report income or loss from a partnership, the agent may request copies of partnership documents, such as the partnership agreement, and tax returns.

The Closing Conference. Once the agent has concluded the examination, you will be asked to attend a closing conference. At this conference, the agent will explain to you or your representative any adjustments made to your return and may give you work papers for your review. You may be asked to sign a statement agreeing to the audit findings and any assessment. If you sign *this* statement called a *Consent to Audit Adjustment*, you agree to pay any deficiency of tax shown on the consent, plus interest and penalty, if applicable. If you do not agree with the audit findings, the agent will advise you of your right to appeal. You may request an informal meeting with the agent and his or her supervisor to discuss your reasons for disputing the agent's adjustments. If, after that meeting, you and the agent still disagree, you will receive a formal assessment, or a *Notice of Tax Deficiency*, from which a formal appeal may be made. If the audit resulted from a refund request and the agent denied the refund, you will receive a letter to this effect. You may also formally appeal the denial of a refund.

For information on protesting the *Notice of Tax Deficiency*, please consult the following section. As explained filing the right documents *on time* is critical to the outcome of your protest. Don't delay!

Protesting the Audit

In the preceding section, we discussed the personal income tax audit. We discussed the examination process, the Audit Division's policies and procedures, and *your* rights as a taxpayer. We explained that your auditor will prepare a proposed audit adjustment that may increase your taxes for the year or years under examination or, in some cases, reduce them, resulting in a refund. At this point, you can sign a formal consent to the audit adjustments, pay any additional taxes due, and your audit will be finished. What if you don't agree? Suppose you've tried negotiating with your auditor but neither you nor the auditor can reach a mutually acceptable position?

This section discusses how to protest a personal income tax audit and explains your legal remedies as a taxpayer. The same remedies apply to protesting a New York City income tax audit as well, since the state administers the city income tax.

Notice of Tax Deficiency
If you don't consent to the income tax adjustments proposed by the Audit Division, the next step in the process is the issuance of a formal *Notice of Tax Deficiency*.

TaxAlert: It is of the *utmost* importance, from here on, that you pay strict attention to time limits and proper filing requirements. Your right to protest a *Notice of Tax Deficiency* can be lost if you are late in filing a required petition by even one day! There are requirements that the state must fulfill, too. For example, the *Notice of Tax Deficiency* must be mailed by certified or registered mail to your *last known address*. This is usually the address on your last tax return, unless you've since notified the Department of Taxation and Finance that you've moved.

Conciliation Conference
If you decide to protest a *Notice of Tax Deficiency* or a denial of a refund claim, your first recourse is to request a conciliation conference.

A conciliation conference provides you with a rapid, inexpensive, and relatively informal way of resolving your dispute with the taxing authorities. In this type of proceeding, you or your representatives will meet with the Audit Division's agents in an attempt to resolve the controversy. A mediator,

called a conferee, will oversee the conciliation conference. The conferee is an employee of the Department of Taxation and Finance but works in a separate bureau from the Audit Division, called the Bureau of Conciliation and Mediation Services. The conferee may request additional information from you if he or she thinks it would be helpful in clarifying the issues or resolving the dispute. If you are unable to resolve your dispute with the Audit Division at the conciliation conference, the conferee will issue a conciliation order. This order is binding upon both parties unless you or the Audit Division request a formal hearing within 90 days after the order is issued.

TaxAlert: If you are requesting a conciliation conference, you must file Form CMS-1 *Request for Conciliation Conference*. You must state, in writing, the reasons why you are protesting the *Notice of Tax Deficiency*. If Form CMS-1 does not contain enough space, attach a separate statement to the form. Form CMS-1 must be filed in duplicate, with a copy of the *Notice of Tax Deficiency* attached. If you will be represented at the Conciliation Conference by another person, you must also attach a properly completed Power of Attorney to Form CMS-1; this Power of Attorney formally grants someone else the power to act on your behalf with respect to a particular matter.

TaxSaver: You must file a request for a conciliation conference within 90 days from the date your *Notice of Tax Deficiency* was issued. If you fail to file this request on time, you will lose your opportunity to appeal before you pay the tax deficiency. However, if you fail to file the request within 90 days (150 days if you are living outside the U.S.), you can still pay the tax deficiency and file a claim for a refund. Assuming your claim for a refund is denied, you will then have another 90 days in which to file a request for a conciliation conference.

You will receive notification of your hearing date, generally within 6 to 9 months from the state's acknowledgement. You will be given at least 30 days prior notice of your scheduled hearing date.

TaxPlanner: You have the option of bypassing the informal conciliation conference and taking your protest directly to the Division of Tax Appeals, as long as you file a timely petition within the 90-day period. We recommend that you confer with a professional tax advisor before making this decision.

Division of Tax Appeals
The Division of Tax Appeals is an autonomous unit within the Department of Taxation and Finance. Its function is to provide an independent forum for disputes between taxpayers and the Department and to render independent decisions on tax issues.

Administrative Law Judge. You (or the Department of Taxation) have 90 days from the date of conciliation order to appeal the decision. If you or the Department of Taxation files a formal protest from a conciliation order, the next step in the appeal process is a formal hearing conducted by an administrative law judge. The administrative law judge may hear evidence from witnesses, who will testify under penalties of perjury, as well as review documentary evidence. The Department of Taxation will be represented by an attorney employed by New York. At this formal level, a transcribed record is created that will be binding in any subsequent review proceedings.

TaxSaver: It is recommended that you obtain expert representation at this level, such as a tax accountant or lawyer experienced in handling tax appeals. The reason is that formal courtroom procedures will be followed. Also, a transcribed record of the proceeding will be created that will affect *all* subsequent administrative and judicial review of your case. Many taxpayers have lost cases on appeal, merely because they failed to enter a critical fact into the record created at a hearing before an administrative law judge.

The state will acknowledge your timely filed petition generally within 30 days from its receipt. You will be notified of your court date generally within 6 to 9 months from the state's acknowledgement. You will be given at least 30 days prior notice of your scheduled court appearance.

The administrative law judge will generally issue a determination within six months after the completion of the formal hearing or the submission of briefs, whichever is later. If either party is dissatisfied with the determination, an appeal can be made to the Tax Appeals Tribunal. You must request a hearing before the tribunal within 30 days after you are notified of the administrative law judge's decision.

TaxAlert: If you are requesting a hearing by the Division of Tax Appeals, you must file a Petition for Hearing (Form TA-10). The requirements for filing this form are similar to those for filing a request for a conciliation conference.

Tax Appeals Tribunal. The Tax Appeals Tribunal is comprised of three commissioners appointed by the Governor of New York. Together, they decide all appeals of decisions by administrative law judges.

As a taxpayer, this is your final administrative level of review. You must file a *Notice of Exception* to an administrative law judge's determination within 30 days. The Tax Appeals Tribunal will review the record of the hearing before the administrative law judge. It will set dates for presenting oral and written arguments based on the previous record. The Tribunal will generally issue a decision within six months from the oral arguments or submissions of briefs, whichever is later. It may affirm, reverse, or modify the administrative law judge's determination. The Tribunal's decision is binding upon the state taxing authorities. They cannot request judicial review of an adverse ruling.

TaxAlert: The administrative review process, from conciliation through a hearing before the Tax Appeals Tribunal, can take as much as 2 years or longer until a final administrative resolution is achieved.

Beyond the Tax Appeal Tribunal

You may seek judicial review if you are not satisfied with the decision of the Tax Appeals Tribunal. You must begin a formal proceeding in the Appellate Division of the State Supreme Court.

Small Claims Hearings

You may elect to have a hearing held in the Small Claims Unit of the Division of Tax Appeals if the amount in dispute does not exceed $10,000 a year ($20,000 for sales and use tax) not including penalties and interest. This is an informal hearing conducted by a hearing officer whose determination is final and not subject to review. At any time before the small claims hearing is concluded, you can make a written request to transfer the matter to a formal hearing.

Penalties

Introduction

By law, you are required to file a New York tax return and pay your fair share of taxes. If you do not file and pay the correct amount of tax by the due date, you can incur substantial penalties and interest. This section will describe the penalties New York imposes on delinquent taxpayers.

Penalties and Interest

A tax "penalty" is an addition to the tax you owe if you fail to file a New York State tax return on time or fail to pay a tax that is due. Interest, on the other hand, is an amount you owe because you had the use of money that properly belonged to New York. Some people confuse interest and penalties, but the interest you owe New York for a late payment of tax is no different from the interest you owe your credit card company if you fail to pay your monthly balance. Both represent a charge for extending credit. If you extend "credit" to New York by overpaying your tax, the state must refund your tax with interest (subject to certain limitations and differences in rate). New York may waive a penalty if you show "reasonable cause" for your failure to pay the tax. Interest, however, cannot be waived under any circumstances.

Late Filing Penalty. The penalty for failure to file a return is 5% per month of the tax due, up to a total amount of 25%. A fraction of a month is counted as a whole month. This penalty may apply if you have an invalid extension. See the section on *Extensions* in Chapter 2 for more information.

Late Payment Penalty. You will also have to pay a penalty of 0.5% of the tax due per month (or fraction of a month), up to a maximum of 25%, if you fail to *pay* the tax shown on your return. Both penalties are imposed on the actual amount of tax due on the return, less any withholding, estimated payments, partial payments, and other credits. They are in addition to any interest charged for late payments.

TaxSaver: You may be able to have this penalty waived if you attach an explanation to your return showing that you have a reasonable cause for the delay.

TaxAlert: Both the late filing penalty and late payment penalty are applied from the *original* (April 15) due date of your return, *regardless* of any extensions. Remember that the state allows only an extension of time to file your return, not an extension of time to pay your tax. If you do not pay *all* of the tax you owe by April 15, your extension will be invalidated and a late filing penalty, as well as a late payment penalty, will be applied. (If both penalties are applied, the late filing penalty is *reduced* by the late payment penalty.) If your return is more than 60 days late, you will have to pay a minimum penalty of $100 or 100% of the tax due, whichever is less.

Substantial Understatement of Liability

If you substantially understate the tax you owe, a penalty of 10% of the tax will be added to your bill. A substantial understatement means that you underreported your tax due by

10% or more of what you owe, or at least $2,000, and there is neither substantial legal authority for the reporting position nor adequate disclosure of the position on the return. Since substantial understatement of tax can occur even if you made a good faith effort to report your tax correctly, the Commissioner may waive all or part of this penalty if you show reasonable cause for the understatement.

Additional Rules

New York has a number of additional rules that apply to penalties and interest. Generally, the punishment that New York applies to a tax transgression fits the severity of the offense. You could be held liable for criminal prosecution if you commit tax fraud.

Some special rules may apply to you:

1. If you had a Net Operating Loss Carryback—Net Operating Loss carrybacks *do not* affect the accrual of interest charges for tax that should have been paid in a previous year. Therefore, if you have losses in the current tax year that you carry back to a previous year in which you have unpaid taxes, you are still going to owe any interest that has accrued on your debt to New York.
2. If you must pay a penalty—Interest will accrue on penalties and other additions to tax unless you pay them within ten days after you receive a notice demanding payment. Interest will accrue from the date of the notice until you make payment.
3. If your return is more than 60 days late—You will be subject to a minimum *non-filing penalty* equal to $100, or 100% of the tax due, whichever is less.

Limits on Tax and Penalties

1. If you have mathematical errors on your return—You will not be charged interest if your return contains unintentional mathematical errors. However, this is true only if you filed your return and paid your tax on time.
2. If you fail to file *and* fail to pay tax that you owe—The penalty for not filing your return on time may be *reduced* by any late payment penalty you owe. Thus, the *total* penalty for both offenses will not exceed 25% of the tax due.

EXCEPTION: This reduction does not apply to any minimum non-filing penalty for which you are liable because your return is more than 60 days later (see item 3, above).

3. Reasonable cause—Penalties for failure to file and pay your tax can be reduced or eliminated if you can demonstrate ''reasonable cause,'' and were not willfully negligent. Events that may be considered ''reasonable cause'' are death, a serious illness, or the destruction of your home or place of business. Reasonable cause is *not* established by your ignorance of the law or the ignorance of your tax return preparer (although, in some cases, good faith reliance on the advice of a professional tax advisor may be considered ''reasonable cause''). In any case, it is better to file on time and pay the tax due than to worry about whether the state will accept your excuse in the future.

Negligence and Fraud

Negligence. Negligence implies that you intentionally disregarded the law or acted carelessly with respect to the records you kept or the returns you prepared. If the state determines that any or all of an underpayment of tax was due to negligence, a two-part penalty may be imposed:

- An addition to tax of 5% of the *total* underpayment; plus
- An addition of 50% of the interest due on the part of the underpayment caused by negligence.

Fraud. A criminal intent to evade tax constitutes fraud. A two-part penalty may be imposed:

- A penalty of 50% of the deficiency. This includes the *entire* underpayment, and not just the items determined to be fraudulent; plus
- A penalty of 50% of the interest due on the part of the underpayment caused by fraud.

Assessments of Penalties and Interest

Taxpayers who are liable for penalties will generally receive a bill from New York in the form of a *Notice of Tax Due.* The Notice will state the amount of the tax underpayment, if applicable, any interest due on the underpayment through the date of the notice, and the amount of any penalty that was assessed. If you don't pay the bill promptly, it will be followed by a *Notice of Tax Deficiency.* You *must* pay this bill *or* file a formal protest within 90 days of the date of the Notice of Tax Deficiency. Otherwise, your right to protest will be lost and the matter will be turned over to the state's collections unit for further proceedings.

TAXALERT: Don't ignore a Notice from New York's taxing authorities, even if you think it's wrong. The two most important pieces of advice in dealing with a penalty assessment are (1) respond *in writing* to any formal Notice, preferably by U.S. certified mail, and (2) keep a copy of all correspondence with the tax authorities, including logs of telephone calls you made to resolve the disagreement. Be sure to respond by the due date given on the Notice. If you're confused about how best to assert your rights, consult a professional tax advisor.

For additional information on protesting a Notice of Tax Deficiency, see the preceding section on *Protesting the Audit.*

Criminal Penalties

If you grossly violate the rules set forth by New York, you may be liable for criminal penalties. Most criminal tax offense actions are classifiable as misdemeanors or felonies, and can result in more severe punishments including fines, imprisonment, or both.

Statute of Limitations

General Rule

The period of time during which the New York Department of Taxation can assess a tax deficiency is limited by statute. As a general rule, the *statute of limitations* allows New York's taxing authorities to make an assessment of additional taxes at any time within three years after the date you actually filed your return. This section will discuss the statute of limitations and exceptions.

The Three-Year Rule

Except as otherwise discussed in this section, you may be assessed a deficiency anytime within three years after filing your income tax return. If you file your return before April

15 (or August 15 if you filed an extension), the three-year statute of limitations period does not start running until the last day you could have filed. If you file your income tax return late (after the April 15 or August 15 due date) the three-year statute of limitations does not start to run until the date you actually file your return.

No Income Tax Return Filed or Fraudulent Return Filed

The general three-year rule does not apply if you fail to file your New York income tax return or if you file a state tax return with information that you know to be false or fraudulent. In these instances, the state can assess you additional taxes, penalties, and interest at any time. However, the taxing authorities must have reason to believe that you *intentionally* withheld information in the interest of avoiding or evading your fair share of income taxes.

Extension by Agreement

New York can extend the time to assess additional taxes beyond the statutory three years if you agree in writing to the extension. This written agreement to extend the statute of limitations must be signed by you and the taxing officials before the expiration of the statutory three-year period. An agreement to extend the statute of limitations is always limited to a particular tax and specific filing year(s). It extends the time during which the state can assess you only for a specific period—usually, one year.

You may wonder why anyone would willingly consent to let the taxing authorities have more time in which to make an assessment. Usually, such agreements are made in connection with an audit or a review of a refund request. It may well be in the interest of *both* parties to allow the state more time to complete its examination. The extra time may enable a taxpayer to present new facts that support a refund claim or reduce a proposed assessment. If your extension agreement is about to expire and the state requires still more time to complete its examination, you may sign a new agreement before the expiration of the old agreement.

Report of Federal Change

The statute of limitations can also be extended if you amend your federal income tax return or consent to a federal income tax adjustment. If you report a change in your federal income tax, the New York taxing authorities are deemed to have made a valid assessment of any additional taxes owing on the date you reported the changes to New York. Amended federal returns, whether filed by choice or because you conceded to an adjustment, automatically extend New York's normal three-year statute of limitations. If you file an amended federal return showing any change in your taxable income, you must file an amended New York return within 90 days from the date you amend your federal return.

TaxAlert: If you fail to report a federal change or file an amended state return within the required 90-day period, New York may assess additional income tax (plus penalties and interest) resulting from the federal change at any time. The statute of limitations does not run in such cases.

If you file an amended state return as a result of filing a federal amended return, or reporting a federal audit adjustment, New York can assess additional taxes within two years from the date you filed your amended state return.

However, if the extended two-year period runs beyond the general three-year limitation on assessments, the state can-

not review or assess more tax that the amount attributable to the federal changes on your amended return. If, however, an assessment is made during the normal three year period, any amount can be assessed.

Omission of Income

New York law provides for an extension of the statute of limitations if you fail to include certain items in your New York adjusted gross income. The period in which New York can assess you additional tax is extended to six years if the sum of the omitted items exceeds 25% of your New York adjusted gross income. The assessment period will not be extended if you fully disclose the omitted items on your return.

Deficiency Attributable to Net Operating Loss Carryback

If you carry back a net operating loss to a previous year's income tax return, the time for assessing any additional tax for the carryback year is extended until the limitation period for the loss year expires. Thus, the extended period runs for three years beginning with the date you filed the return on which you reported the original net operating loss.

TaxAlert: If you claim a refund because of a net operating loss carryback and the general three-year assessment period has expired for the year in which you are claiming the refund, New York cannot assess more tax than the amount you have claimed as a refund. However, New York can reduce your refund to zero by assessing you additional tax up to the amount you are claiming as a refund. In making this reduction, the state may look at *any* items on your return, not just those having to do with the net operating loss.

Erroneous Refund

If you receive an erroneous refund of tax, it is treated as an underpayment of tax on the date you received the payment. The tax deficiency created by this erroneous refund may be assessed within two years after the refund is made. However, if the refund was a result of fraud or misrepresentation of important facts, then New York has five years in which to make an assessment. An *erroneous refund* is a refund given because of a mistake made by an employee of the New York State Department of Taxation and Finance, including an error made during an audit of your tax return. If you make a mistake on a claim for refund, it does not count as an erroneous refund.

Prompt Assessments

In the case of a decedent or his or her estate, you can request a prompt assessment of tax. The assessment period will be shortened to 18 months upon the written request of the executor or administrator. This request must be made within three years after a return was filed on behalf of the decedent or his estate.

Suspension of Running of Statute of Limitations

The three-year period during which the Department of Taxation and Finance is allowed to assess a deficiency is temporarily suspended in certain cases.

If you receive a *Notice of Tax Deficiency*, the three-year statute of limitations is suspended for 90 days. The Department of Taxation cannot make an additional assessment of tax during this time. If you file a petition for redetermination of the deficiency, the statute of limitations is suspended from the date of mailing of the Notice of Tax Deficiency until your appeal is resolved.

9 | New York Sample Forms

This chapter provides filled-in examples of the principal personal income tax forms used by New York residents and nonresidents for you to refer to when preparing your own return. The New York forms in this chapter are applicable for the 1992 tax year and include the following:

Form IT-100: Resident Fast Form Income Tax Return*
Form IT-200: Resident Income Tax Return*
Form IT-201: Resident Income Tax Return*

*See Chapter 2, *The Income Tax Return*, for information on which resident income tax form to use.

Form IT-201-ATT: Summary of Other Credits and Taxes, Attachment to IT-201
Form IT-203: Nonresident and Part-Year Resident Income Tax Return
Form IT-203-ATT: Summary of Other Credits and Taxes, Attachment to IT-203
Form NYC-203: City of New York Nonresident Earnings Tax Return
Form Y-203: City of Yonkers Nonresident Earnings Tax Return

New York State Department of Taxation and Finance

1992 **Resident Fast Form Income Tax Return** **IT-100**

New York State • City of New York • City of Yonkers

FINAL

For office use only

Attach label, or print or type

Last name	First name and middle initial (if joint return, enter both names)	Your social security number
Jetson	George	100 10 1000

Mailing address (number and street or rural route)   Apartment number | Spouse's social security number
10 Smith Road

City, village or post office	State	ZIP code	NY State county of residence
Queens	NY	10000	New York City

In the space below, print or type your permanent home address within New York State if it is not the same as your mailing address above (see instructions). | School district name: **Queens**

Permanent home address (number and street or rural route)   Apartment number | School district code number: **519**

City, village or post office	State	ZIP code	If taxpayer is deceased, enter first name and date of death
	NY		/ /

(A) Filing status — check one box:
- ① ✓ Single
- ② ☐ Married filing joint return
- ③ ☐ Head of household (with qualifying person)
- ④ ☐ Qualifying widow(er) with dependent child

(B) Can you be claimed as a dependent on another taxpayer's federal return?.... Yes ☐ No ✓

(C) Were you a resident of the city of New York for all of 1992?............. Yes ✓ No ☐

(D) Were you a resident of the city of Yonkers for all of 1992?.............. Yes ☐ No ✓

1. Number of federal exemptions (1040EZ filers — enter "1"; 1040A filers — copy from line 6e. We will figure your New York State dependent exemptions for you.)................ **1** | **1**

2. Wages, salaries, tips, etc. (1040EZ filers - copy from line 1; 1040A filers - copy from line 7) . **2** | **30,000**

3. Taxable interest income (1040EZ filers - copy from line 2; 1040A filers - copy from line 8a) . **3** | **500**

4. Interest income on US government bonds included on line 3 above **4**

5. Dividends (1040EZ filers - enter "0"; 1040A filers - copy from line 9) **5**

6. Unemployment compensation (1040EZ filers - enter "0"; 1040A filers - copy from line 12) . **6**

7. Individual retirement arrangement (IRA) deduction (1040EZ filers - enter "0"; 1040A filers - copy from line 15c) **7**

8. Federal credit for child and dependent care:

   Number of qualifying persons cared for in 1992 ....☐

   Amount of federal credit for child and dependent care (1040EZ filers - enter "0"; 1040A filers - copy from line 24a) **8**

9. If you want to Return a Gift to Wildlife, enter amount ($5, $10, $20, other) .... **9** | | **00**

Information from your wage and tax statements:

10. New York State tax withheld .... **10** | **2,400**

11. City of New York tax withheld .... **11** | **1,100**

12. City of Yonkers tax withheld .... **12** | **0**

Sign Your Return	Your signature	Date	Spouse's signature (If joint return)
	George Jetson	4/14/93	

Mail to: NYS Income Tax, W A Harriman Campus, Albany NY 12227-0125

NY-91

New York State Department of Taxation and Finance

1992 **Resident Income Tax Return** **IT-200**

New York State • City of New York • City of Yonkers

For office use only

FINAL

Last name	First name and middle initial *(if joint return, enter both names)*	Your social security number
Lauffer	William C. and Laurie N.	200 20 2000

Mailing address *(number and street or rural route)*	Apartment number	Spouse's social security number
One Oak Lane		400 40 4000

City, village or post office	State	ZIP code	New York State county of residence
	NY	00000	New York City

Permanent home address *(number and street or rural route)*	Apartment number	School district name
		Manhattan

City, village or post office	State	ZIP code	School district code number
	NY		

(A) If taxpayer is deceased, enter first name and date of death. ___/___/___

(B) Filing status — check one box:
① Single
② ✓ Married filing joint return
③ Married filing separate return
④ Head of household (with qualifying person)
⑤ Qualifying widow(er) with dependent child

For filing status ② and ③, enter both spouses' social security numbers above.

Attach check or money order here.

(C) Did you itemize your deductions on your 1992 federal income tax return? ..... Yes ✓ No ☐

(D) Can you be claimed as a dependent on another taxpayer's federal return? ..... Yes ☐ No ✓

(E) If you do not need forms mailed to you next year, check box *(see instructions)* ..... ☐

(F) If you filed federal Form 1040A or 1040, enter number of exemptions from line 6e; 1040EZ filers enter "0" **2**

1	Wages, salaries, tips, etc.	1	45,000
2	Taxable interest income	2	3,000
3	Dividends	3	
4	Taxable refunds, credits or offsets of state and local income taxes *(also enter on line 12 below)*	4	2,000
5	Unemployment compensation	5	
6	Add lines 1 through 5	6	50,000
7	Individual retirement arrangement (IRA) deduction *(see instructions, page 8)*	7	
8	Subtract line 7 from line 6. This is your federal adjusted gross income	8	50,000
9	Public employee 414(h) retirement contributions *(see instructions, page 8)*	9	
10	New York City flexible benefits program (IRC 125 amount) *(see instructions, page 8)*	10	
11	Add lines 8, 9 and 10	11	50,000
12	Taxable refunds, credits or offsets of state and local income taxes from line 4 above 12	2,000	
13	Interest income on US government bonds *(see instructions, page 8)* 13		
14	New York standard deduction *(from table on back)* 14	9,500	
15	New York dependent exemptions *(from line c of worksheet on back; 1040EZ filers, enter "0")* 15	,000 00	
16	Add lines 12 through 15 *(if line 16 is more than or equal to line 11, see instructions for line 17)*	16	11,500
17	Subtract line 16 from line 11. This is your taxable income *(If $65,000 or more, stop; you must file Form IT-201)*	17	38,500
18	New York State tax on line 17 amount. *(Use the State Tax Table, blue pages 21 - 28)*	18	2,316
19	New York State child and dependent care credit: number of qualifying persons ☐ cared for in 1992 Amount of federal credit for child and dependent care ☐ x 20% (.20) =	19	
20	Subtract line 19 from line 18 *(if line 19 is more than line 18, enter "0")*	20	2,316
21	New York State household credit *(from table on back)*	21	0
22	Subtract line 21 from line 20 *(if line 21 is more than line 20, enter "0")*. This is the total of your New York State taxes.	22	2,316
23	City of New York resident tax on line 17 amount. *(Use City Tax Table, pages 29 - 36)* 23	1,309	
24	City of New York household credit *(see instructions, page 9)* 24	0	
25	Subtract line 24 from line 23 *(if line 24 is more than line 23, enter "0")* 25	1,309	
26	City of New York nonresident earnings tax *(attach Form NYC-203)* 26		
27	City of Yonkers resident income tax surcharge *(from Yonkers Worksheet, page 9)* 27		
28	City of Yonkers nonresident earnings tax *(attach Form Y-203)* 28		
29	Add lines 25 through 28. This is the total of your city of New York and city of Yonkers taxes	29	1,309
30	If you want to Return a Gift to Wildlife, enter amount - $5, $10, $20, other *(see instructions, page 9)*	30	00
31	Add lines 22, 29 and 30. This is the total of your New York State, city of New York and city of Yonkers taxes and Gift to Wildlife	31	3,625
32	Real property tax credit *(from Form IT-214, line 17; attach form)* 32		
33	Total New York State tax withheld *(staple wage and tax statements; see instructions)* 33	2,300	
34	Total city of New York tax withheld *(staple wage and tax statements; see instructions)* 34	1,400	
35	Total city of Yonkers tax withheld *(staple wage and tax statements; see instructions)* 35		
36	Total payments (add lines 32 through 35)	36	3,700
37	If line 36 is more than line 31, subtract line 31 from line 36. This is the amount to be refunded to you	37	75
38	If line 36 is less than line 31, subtract line 36 from line 31. This is the amount you owe	38	

• Make your check or money order payable to *New York State Income Tax;* write your social security number and *1992 Income Tax* on it.

• See Step 7, page 11, of the Instructions for the proper assembly of your return and attachments.

Sign Your Return — Paid preparers must complete the *Paid Preparer's Use Only* section on the back of this return.

Your signature: *William C. Lauffer*
Spouse's signature *(if joint return)*: *Laurie N. Lauffer*
Date: 4/14/93

NY-92

New York State Department of Taxation and Finance

Resident Income Tax Return

IT-201

1992

New York State • City of New York • City of Yonkers

For the year Jan. 1 — Dec. 31, 1992, or fiscal tax year beginning   1992, ending   ,19

For office use only

Attach label, or print or type

Last name	First name and middle initial (if joint return, enter both names)	Your social security number
King	Dennis B. and Helen R.	300 30 3000

Mailing address (number and street or rural route)	Apartment number	Spouse's social security number
3 Thorn Street	#5	400 40 4000

City, village or post office	State	ZIP code	New York State county of residence
New York	NY	00000	NY County

In the space below, print or type your permanent home address within New York State if it is not the same as your mailing address above (see instructions, page 20).

School district name: Manhattan

Permanent home address (number and street or rural route)	Apartment number	School district code number
		369

City, village or post office	State	ZIP code	If taxpayer is deceased, enter first name and date of death.
	NY		/ /

Clip check or money order here.

(A) Filing status — check one box:

① ☐ Single

② ☑ Married filing joint return (enter spouse's social security number above)

③ ☐ Married filing separate return (enter spouse's social security number above)

④ ☐ Head of household (with qualifying person)

⑤ ☐ Qualifying widow(er) with dependent child

(B) Did you Itemize your deductions on your 1992 federal income tax return? .. Yes ☑ No ☐

(C) Can you be claimed as a dependent on another taxpayer's federal return? .. Yes ☐ No ☑

(D) If you do not need forms mailed to you next year, check box (see instructions) . . . . ☐

(E) Enter the number of exemptions claimed from your federal return, line 6e **3**

Enter your income items and total adjustments exactly as they appear on your federal return (see instructions, page 10).

Federal Income and Adjustments

1 Wages, salaries, tips, etc.	1	60,000
2 Taxable interest income	2	5,000
3 Dividend income	3	4,050
4 Taxable refunds, credits, or offsets of state and local income taxes (also enter on line 24 below)	4	500
5 Alimony received	5	
6 Business income or (loss) (attach copy of federal Schedule C or C-EZ, Form 1040)	6	2,600
7 Capital gain or (loss) (attach copy of federal Schedule D, Form 1040)	7	2,800
8 Capital gain distributions not reported on line 7	8	
9 Other gains or (losses) (attach copy of federal Form 4797)	9	
10 Taxable amount of IRA distributions	10	
11 Taxable amount of pensions and annuities	11	1,200
12 Rents, royalties, partnerships, estates, trusts, etc. (attach copy of federal Schedule E, Form 1040) .	12	4,600
13 Farm income or (loss) (attach copy of federal Schedule F, Form 1040)	13	
14 Unemployment compensation	14	
15 Taxable amount of social security benefits (also enter on line 25 below)	15	
16 Other income (see instructions, page 10) Identify:	16	
17 Add lines 1 through 16	17	80,750
18 Total federal adjustments to income (see instructions, page 10) Identify: **IRA Deductions**	18	4,000
19 Subtract line 18 from line 17. This is your federal adjusted gross income	19	76,750

New York Adjusted Gross Income

New York Additions: (see instructions, page 11)

20 Interest income on state and local bonds (but not those of New York State and local governments within the state). .	20	
21 Public employee 414(h) retirement contributions (see instructions, page 11)	21	
22 Other (see instructions, page 11) Identify: **Federal Depreciation Adjustment**	22	500
23 Add lines 19 through 22	23	76,250

New York Subtractions: (see instructions, page 12)

24 Taxable refunds, credits, or offsets of state and local income taxes (from line 4 above)	24	500	
25 Taxable amount of social security benefits (from line 15 above)	25		
26 Interest income on US government bonds	26	1,000	
27 Pension and annuity income exclusion	27	1,200	
28 Other (see instructions, page 13) Identify: **NY Depreciation Adjustment**	28	80	
29 Add lines 24 through 28	29		2,780
30 Subtract line 29 from line 23. This is your New York adjusted gross income (If you claimed the standard deduction on your federal return, skip lines 31 through 45 and enter the line 30 amount on line 46 on the back page.)	30		73,470

If you itemized your deductions on federal Form 1040, fill in lines 31 through 45 and continue on line 46.

31	Medical and dental expenses (from federal Schedule A, line 4)	31	500	
32	Taxes you paid (from federal Schedule A, line 8)	32	13,200	
33	Interest you paid (from federal Schedule A, line 12)	33	13,400	
34	Gifts to charity (from federal Schedule A, line 16)	34	800	
35	Casualty and theft losses (from federal Schedule A, line 17)	35		
36	Moving expenses (from federal Schedule A, line 18)	36		
37	Job expenses and most other miscellaneous deductions (from federal Schedule A, line 24)	37		
38	Other miscellaneous deductions (from federal Schedule A, line 25)	38		
39	Total itemized deductions (from federal Schedule A, line 26)	39	27,900	
40	State, local and foreign income taxes and other subtraction adjustments (see inst., page 14)	40	7,200	
41	Subtract line 40 from line 39	41	20,700	
42	Addition adjustments (see instructions, page 15)	42		
43	Add lines 41 and 42	43	20,700	
44	Itemized deduction adjustment (if line 30 is more than $100,000, see instructions, page 15; all others enter "0" on line 44)	44	0	
45	Subtract line 44 from line 43. This is your itemized deduction	45	20,700	

(Left margin label: Tax Computation)

46	Enter the amount from line 30 on the front page (this is your New York adjusted gross income)	46	73,470	
47	Check appropriate box and enter the larger of: ☐ your standard deduction from instructions, page 15, or ☐ your itemized deduction from line 45	47	20,700	
48	Subtract line 47 from line 46	48	52,770	
49	Dependent exemptions (from line c of Dependent Exemption Worksheet, instructions page 15)	49	1,000 00	
50	Subtract line 49 from line 48. This is your taxable income	50	51,770	
51	New York State tax on line 50 amount (If line 46 above is $100,000 or less, use the NY State Tax Table on yellow pages 29 through 36. If line 46 is more than $100,000, you must complete Tax Computation Worksheet 1 or 2 on page 16 of the instructions to figure your tax.)	51	3,360	

(Left margin label: Credits/Other Taxes/Gift/Totals)

52	NY State child and dependent care credit • number of qualifying persons ☐ cared for in 1992 • amount of federal credit for child and dependent care ☐ × 20% (.20) =	52		
53	New York State household credit (from Table I, II or III, instructions page 16)	53		
54	Other New York State credits (from Form IT-201-ATT, line 7; attach form)	54	100	
55	Add lines 52, 53, and 54	55	100	
56	Subtract line 55 from line 51 (if line 55 is more than line 51, enter "0")	56	3,260	
57	Other New York State taxes (from Form IT-201-ATT, line 16; attach form)	57		
58	Add lines 56 and 57. This is the total of your New York State taxes	58	3,260	
59	City of New York resident tax (use City of NY Tax Table on white pages 37 — 44)	59	1,885	
60	City of NY household credit (from Table IV, V or VI, page 17)	60		
61	Subtract line 60 from line 59 (if line 60 is more than line 59, enter "0")	61	1,885	
62	City of New York nonresident earnings tax (attach Form NYC-203)	62		
63	Other city of New York taxes (from Form IT-201-ATT, line 21; attach form)	63		
64	City of Yonkers resident income tax surcharge (from Yonkers worksheet, page 18)	64		
65	City of Yonkers nonresident earnings tax (attach Form Y-203)	65		
66	Part-year city of Yonkers resident income tax surcharge (attach Form IT-360.1)	66		
67	Add lines 61 through 66. This is the total of your city of New York and city of Yonkers taxes	67	1,885	
68	If you want to Return a Gift to Wildlife, enter amount: $5, $10, $20, other (see instructions, pages 8 and 18)	68	00	
69	Add lines 58, 67 and 68. This is the total of your New York State, city of New York and city of Yonkers taxes, and Gift to Wildlife	69	5,145	

Mail your completed return to:
NYS Income Tax
W A Harriman Campus
Albany NY 12227-0125

See instructions for figuring city of New York taxes and city of Yonkers taxes.

(Left margin label: Payments)

70	Real property tax credit (from Form IT-214, line 17; attach form)	70		
71	Total New York State tax withheld (staple wage and tax statements; see inst.)	71	4,700	
72	Total city of New York tax withheld (staple wage and tax statements; see instructions)	72	2,400	
73	Total city of Yonkers tax withheld (staple wage and tax statements; see instructions)	73		
74	Estimated tax paid / Amount paid with Form IT-370	74		
75	Add lines 70 through 74. This is the total of your payments	75	7,100	

Staple your wage and tax statements at the top of the back of this return. See Step 7, page 20, for the proper assembly of your return and attachments.

(Left margin label: Refund/Owe)

76	If line 75 is more than line 69, subtract line 69 from line 75 and enter the amount overpaid (also complete line 77 or 78, or both)	76	1,955	
77	Amount of line 76 to be refunded to you	77	55	
78	Amount of line 76 to be applied to your 1993 estimated tax	78	1,900	
79	If line 75 is less than line 69, subtract line 75 from line 69 and enter the amount you owe (do not send cash; make check or money order payable to NY State Income Tax; write your social security number and 1992 income tax on it)	79		
80	Estimated tax penalty (will reduce line 76 or increase line 79; see instructions, page 20)	80		

Sign your return below

Paid Preparer's Use Only	Preparer's signature	Date	Check if self-employed ☐
	Firm's name (or yours, if self-employed)		Preparer's social security number
Address			Employer identification number

Sign Your Return

Your signature: *Dennis R. King*   Date: 4/14/93

Spouse's signature (if joint return): *Helen B. King*   Date: 4/14/93

NY-94

Summary of Other Credits and Taxes

Attachment to Form IT-201

IT-201-ATT

Name(s) as shown on Form IT-201	Your social security number
Dennis B. and Helen R. King	300 30 3000

- Complete all parts that apply. Attach this and any other forms that apply to your Form IT-201.
- Complete *Worksheet A* if you are subject to the New York State tax on capital gain portion of lump-sum distribution, Form IT-230, Part II.
- Complete *Worksheet B* if you are subject to the city of New York tax on capital gain portion of lump-sum distribution, Form IT-230, Part II.

Part I — Other New York State Credits *(see instructions, page 21)*

1 Resident credit *(from Form IT-112-R; attach form and copy of return filed with other state or province of Canada)*	1	100	00
2 Accumulation distribution credit *(attach computation)*	2		
3 Investment credit *(from Form IT-212; attach form)*	3		
4 Special additional mortgage recording tax credit *(see instructions)*	4		
5 Solar and wind energy credit carryover from 1991 *(from Form IT-218.1; attach form)*	5		
6 Economic development zone credit *(total from Forms DTF-601, DTF-602, and DTF-603; attach forms that apply)*	6		
7 **Total** *(add lines 1 through 6; enter here and on Form IT-201, line 54)*	7	100	00

FINAL COPY

Part II — Other New York State Taxes *(see instructions, page 22)*

8 New York State separate tax on lump-sum distributions *(from Form IT-230; attach form)*	8		
9 Resident credit against separate tax on lump-sum distributions *(from Form IT-112.1; attach form and copy of return filed with other state or province of Canada)*	9		
10 Subtract line 9 from line 8	10		
11 New York State minimum income tax *(from Form IT-220; attach form)*	11		
12 Add-back of investment credit on early dispositions *(from Form IT-212; attach form)*	12		
13 Add-back of economic development zone investment tax credit on early dispositions *(from Form DTF-603; attach form)*	13		
14 Add-back of resident credit for taxes paid to a province of Canada *(from Form IT-112-R; attach form)*	14		
15 New York State tax on capital gain portion of lump-sum distribution *(from Worksheet A on the back)*	15		
16 **Total** *(add lines 10 through 15; enter here and on Form IT-201, line 57)*	16		

Part III — Other City of New York Taxes *(see instructions, page 22)*

17 Part-year city of New York resident tax *(from Form IT-360.1; attach form)*	17		
18 City of New York minimum income tax *(from Form IT-220; attach form)*	18		
19 City of New York separate tax on lump-sum distributions *(from Form IT-230; attach form)*	19		
20 City of New York tax on capital gain portion of lump-sum distribution *(from Worksheet B on the back)*	20		
21 **Total** *(add lines 17 through 20; enter here and on Form IT-201, line 63)*	21		

22 Investment credit refund for new businesses *(enter here and include on Form IT-201, line 71; see instructions)*	22		
23 Net investment credit available for carryover to 1993 *(from Form IT-212; attach form)*	23		
24 Net economic development zone credit available for carryover to 1993 *(from Form DTF-601 or DTF-603, or both; attach forms that apply)*	24		

NY-95

Worksheet A — New York State Tax on Capital Gain Portion
of Lump-Sum Distribution (for front page, line 15)

1 New York State tax on capital gain portion of lump-sum distribution
   (from Form IT-230, Part II, line 2, New York State column) **1**

2 Enter amount from Form IT-201, line 55 .... **2**

3 Enter amount from Form IT-201, line 51 .... **3**
   • If line 3 is equal to or more than line 2, transfer the above line 1 amount to the front page, line 15.
   Do not continue with this worksheet.
   • If line 3 is less than line 2, continue on line 4 below.

4 Subtract line 3 from line 2 .... **4**

5 Subtract line 4 from line 1. **Enter here and on the front page, line 15** **5**

Worksheet B — City of New York Tax on Capital Gain Portion
of Lump-Sum Distribution (for front page, line 20)

1 City of New York tax on capital gain portion of lump-sum distribution
   (from Form IT-230, Part II, line 2, City of New York column) **1**

2 Enter amount from Form IT-201, line 60 .... **2**

3 Enter amount from Form IT-201, line 59 .... **3**
   • If line 3 is equal to or more than line 2, transfer the above line 1 amount to the front page, line 20.
   Do not continue with this worksheet.
   • If line 3 is less than line 2, continue on line 4 below.

4 Subtract line 3 from line 2 .... **4**

5 Subtract line 4 from line 1. **Enter here and on the front page, line 20** **5**

Telephone Assistance

For forms and publications, call toll free (from New York State only) 1 800 462-8100.
From areas outside New York State, call (518) 438-1073.

For information, call toll free (from New York State only) 1 800 CALL TAX (1 800 225-5829).
From areas outside New York State, call (518) 438-8581.

For refund information only, please wait until after April 15 to call toll free (from New York State only) 1 800 443-3200.
From areas outside New York State, call (518) 438-6777.

Telephone assistance is available 8:30 a.m. to 4:25 p.m. Monday through Friday.

If you need to write, please address your letter to:

NYS Tax Department
Taxpayer Assistance Bureau
W. A. Harriman Campus
Albany, NY 12227

Mail Your Return

Mail your return and attachments in the preaddressed envelope that came with your tax packet. If you do not have one, address your envelope —

For refund returns:
NYS Income Tax
W. A. Harriman Campus
REFUND '92
Albany, NY 12227-0125

For all other returns:
NYS Income Tax
W. A. Harriman Campus
Albany, NY 12227-0125

New York State Department of Taxation and Finance

1992

New York State
City of New York
City of Yonkers

Nonresident and Part-Year Resident

Income Tax Return

IT-203

For Jan. 1 - Dec. 31, 1992, or fiscal tax year beginning _____ ,1992, ending _____ ,19 ___ .

For office use only

Attach label, or print or type

Last name	First name and middle initial (if joint return, enter both names)	Your social security number
Myers, David F. and Kennedy, Mary T.		500 50 5000

Mailing address (number and street or rural route)	Apartment number	Spouse's social security number
One Trenton Way		600 60 6000

City, village or post office	State	ZIP code	New York State county of residence
Trenton	NJ	00000	

If you are a part-year resident, print or type in the space below your permanent home address for the part of the year you were a resident of New York State if it is not the same as your mailing address above (see instructions, page 23).

School district name

Permanent home address (number and street or rural route) | Apartment number | School district code number

City, village or post office	State	ZIP code	If taxpayer is deceased, enter first name and date of death.
	NY		/ /

(A) Filing status — check one box:
1. ☐ Single
2. ☑ Married filing joint return
3. ☐ Married filing separate return
4. ☐ Head of household (with qualifying person)
5. ☐ Qualifying widow(er) with dependent child

For filing status ② and ③, enter both spouses' social security numbers above.

Clip check or money order here

(B) Did you itemize your deductions on your 1992 federal income tax return?............Yes ☑ No ☐

(C) Can you be claimed as a dependent on another taxpayer's federal return?............Yes ☐ No ☑

(D) If you do not need forms mailed to you next year, check box (see instructions, page 10)...... ☐

(E) If you filed federal Form 1040A or 1040, enter the number of exemptions from line 6e; 1040EZ filers enter "0"................... 2

(F) Part-year residents: If you were a New York State resident for only part of the year, check the box which describes your situation on the last day of the tax year:
(1) moved into New York State. Enter date of move: ___/___/___ .... ☐
(2) moved out of New York State and received income from New York State sources during your nonresident period.
Enter date of move:___/___/___ ☐
(3) moved out of New York State and received no income from New York State sources during your nonresident period. Enter date of move: ___/___/___ .... ☐

(G) Nonresidents: Did you or your spouse maintain living quarters in New York State in 1992? (If Yes, complete Form IT-203-ATT, Schedule B.)..........Yes ☐ No ☑

Enter on lines 1 through 19 in the *Federal Amount* column the amounts entered on your federal return. Enter in the *New York State Amount* column the amounts from New York State sources (see instructions, page 10).

Federal Income and Adjustments

			Federal Amount	New York State Amount
1	Wages, salaries, tips, etc.	1	50,000	25,000
2	Taxable interest income	2	5,000	
3	Dividend income	3	1,000	
4	Taxable refunds, credits, or offsets of state and local income taxes (also enter Federal Amount on line 24)	4	1,000	
5	Alimony received	5		
6	Business income or (loss) (attach copy of federal Schedule C or C-EZ, Form 1040)	6		
7	Capital gain or (loss) (attach copy of federal Schedule D, Form 1040)	7		
8	Capital gain distributions not reported on line 7.........................	8		
9	Other gains or (losses) (attach copy of federal Form 4797)	9		
10	Taxable amount of IRA distributions	10		
11	Taxable amount of pensions and annuities	11	5,000	5,000
12	Rents, royalties, partnerships, estates, trusts, etc. (attach copy of federal Schedule E, Form 1040)	12	10,000	10,000
13	Farm income or (loss) (attach copy of federal Schedule F, Form 1040)	13		
14	Unemployment compensation	14		
15	Taxable amount of social security benefits (also enter Federal Amount on line 25)....	15		
16	Other income (see instructions, page 13) Identify:	16		
17	Add lines 1 through 16..	17	72,000	40,000
18	Total federal adjustments to income (see instructions, page 13) Identify:	18		
19	Subtract line 18 from line 17. Enter here and next to line 56, Income percentage. (If zero or less, see instructions, page 13.) This is your federal adjusted gross income. .	19	72,000	40,000

New York Adjusted Gross Income

New York Additions: (see instructions, page 14)

20	Interest income on state and local bonds (but not those of New York State or its localities) .	20		
21	Public employee 414(h) retirement contributions (see instructions, page 14)	21		
22	Other (see instructions, page 15) Identify:	22		
23	Add lines 19 through 22 in the *Federal Amount* column	23	72,000	

New York Subtractions: (see instructions, page 16)

24	Taxable refunds, credits, or offsets of state and local income taxes (from line 4, Federal Amount column) .	24	1,000	Subtract line 29 from line 23 and enter the result on line 30.
25	Taxable amount of social security benefits (from line 15, Federal Amount column) ...	25		
26	Interest income on US government bonds	26		
27	Pension and annuity income exclusion	27		
28	Other (see instructions, page 16) Identify:	28		
29	Add lines 24 through 28	29	1,000	
30	Subtract line 29 from line 23. This is your New York adjusted gross income. (If you claimed the standard deduction on your federal return, skip lines 31 through 45 and enter this amount on line 46 on the back page.)	30	71,000	

NY-97

If you itemized your deductions on federal Form 1040, fill in lines 31 through 45 and continue on line 48.

31	Medical and dental expenses *(from federal Schedule A, line 4)*	31	
32	Taxes you paid *(from federal Schedule A, line 8)*	32	5,000
33	Interest you paid *(from federal Schedule A, line 12)*	33	15,000
34	Gifts to charity *(from federal Schedule A, line 16)*	34	500
35	Casualty and theft losses *(from federal Schedule A, line 17)*	35	
36	Moving expenses *(from federal Schedule A, line 18)*	36	
37	Job expenses and most other miscellaneous deductions *(from federal Schedule A, line 24)* .	37	
38	Other miscellaneous deductions *(from federal Schedule A, line 25)*	38	
39	Total itemized deductions *(from federal Schedule A, line 26)*	39	20,500
40	State, local and foreign income taxes and other subtraction adjustments *(see instructions)* .	40	2,500
41	Subtract line 40 from line 39	41	18,000
42	Addition adjustments *(see instructions, page 18)*	42	
43	Add lines 41 and 42	43	18,000
44	Itemized deduction adjustment *(if line 30 is more than $100,000, see instructions, page 18; all others enter "0" on line 44)*	44	
45	Subtract line 44 from line 43. This is your itemized deduction	45	18,000

46	Enter the amount from line 30 on the front page. *(This is your New York adjusted gross income)*	46	71,000
47	Check appropriate box and [ ] your standard deduction from instructions, page 18, enter the larger of: or [ ] your itemized deduction from line 45	47	18,000
48	Subtract line 47 from line 46	48	53,000
49	Dependent exemptions *(from line c of Dependent Exemption Worksheet, instructions page 19)*	49	000 00
50	Subtract line 49 from line 48. This is your taxable income	50	53,000
51	New York State tax on line 50 amount *(If line 46 above is $100,000 or less, use the NY State Tax Table on green pages 26 through 33. If line 46 is more than $100,000, you must complete Tax Computation Worksheet I or II on page 19 of the instructions to figure your tax.)*	51	3,458

52	NY State child and dependent care credit • number of qualifying persons [ ] cared for in 1992 • amount of federal credit for child and dependent care [ ] ×20% (.20) =	52	
53	New York State household credit *(from Table I, II, or III, instructions page 20)* . .	53	
54	Add lines 52 and 53. This is the total of your credits allowed before base tax	54	
55	Subtract line 54 from line 51 *(if line 54 is more than line 51, enter "0")*. This is your base tax	55	3,458
56	Income percentage *(see instructions, page 20)* New York State Amount (line 19): 40,000 / Federal Amount (line 19): 72,000 =	56	0.5556
57	Multiply line 55 by the decimal on line 56. This is your allocated New York State tax	57	1,921
58	Other New York State credits *(from Form IT-203-ATT, line 7; attach form)*	58	
59	Subtract line 58 from line 57 *(if line 58 is more than line 57, enter "0")*	59	1,921
60	Other New York State taxes *(from Form IT-203-ATT, line 16; attach form)*	60	
61	Add lines 59 and 60. This is the total of your New York State taxes	61	1,921
62	City of New York nonresident earnings tax *(attach Form NYC-203)*	62	108
63	Other city of New York taxes *(from Form IT-203-ATT, line 21; attach form)*	63	
64	City of Yonkers nonresident earnings tax *(attach Form Y-203)*	64	
65	Part-year city of Yonkers resident income tax surcharge *(attach Form IT-360.1)* . .	65	
66	Add lines 62 through 65. This is the total of your city of New York and city of Yonkers taxes	66	108

See instructions for figuring city of New York taxes and city of Yonkers taxes.

67	If you want to Return a Gift to Wildlife, enter amount: $5, $10, $20, other *(see instructions, pages 9 and 21)* . . .	67	00
68	Add lines 61, 66 and 67. This is the total of your New York State, city of New York and city of Yonkers taxes, and Gift to Wildlife	68	2,029
69	Total New York State tax withheld *(attach wage and tax statements; see instructions)*	69	2,200
70	Total city of New York tax withheld *(attach wage and tax statements; see instructions)* . . .	70	250
71	Total city of Yonkers tax withheld *(attach wage and tax statements; see instructions)*	71	
72	Estimated tax paid/Amount paid with Form IT-370	72	1,000
73	Add lines 69 through 72. This is the total of your payments	73	3,450
74	If line 73 is more than line 68, enter amount overpaid *(also see lines 75 and 76 below)*	74	1,421
75	Amount of line 74 to be refunded to you	75	1,421
76	Amount of line 74 to be applied to your 1993 estimated tax	76	
77	If line 73 is less than line 68, enter amount you owe *(do not send cash; make check or money order payable to NY State Income Tax; write your social security number and 1992 income tax on it)*	77	
78	Estimated tax penalty *(may reduce line 74 or increase line 77 - see instructions, page 22)*	78	

Staple your wage and tax statements at the top of the back of this return. See Step 7, page 23, for the proper assembly of your return and attachments.

Paid Preparer's Use Only	Preparer's signature	Date	Check if self-employed [ ]
	Firm's name *(or yours, if self-employed)*	Preparer's social security number	
Address		Employer identification number	

Sign Your Return

	Date
Your signature *David J. Myers*	4/14/93
Spouse's signature *(if joint return)* *Mary J. Kennedy*	4/14/93

76 Sign your return below.

Summary of Other Credits and Taxes

Attachment to Form IT-203

IT-203-ATT

Name(s) as shown on Form IT-203	Your social security number	Occupation
David F. Myers and Mary T. Kennedy	500 50 5000	Electrician

— Complete all parts that apply. Attach this form to your Form IT-203.

— Complete the *Worksheet for Front Page, Part II, Line 15* on the back if you are subject to the New York State tax on capital gain portion of lump-sum distribution, Form IT-230, Part II.

— Complete the *Worksheet for Front Page, Part III, Line 20* on the back if you are subject to the city of New York tax on capital gain portion of lump-sum distribution, Form IT-230, Part II.

— Complete *Schedule A* on the back if your wage and salary income is subject to allocation.

— Complete *Schedule B* on the back if you were a nonresident and maintained living quarters in New York State.

Part I — Other New York State Credits (see instructions, page 24)

1 Resident credit *(from Form IT-112-R; attach form and copy of return filed with other state or province of Canada)*	1	
2 Accumulation distribution credit *(attach computation)*	2	
3 Investment credit *(from Form IT-212; attach form)*	3	
4 Special additional mortgage recording tax credit *(see instructions)*	4	
5 Solar and wind energy credit carryover from 1991 *(from Form IT-218.1; attach form)*	5	
6 Economic development zone credit *(total from Forms DTF-601, DTF-602, and DTF-603; attach forms that apply)*	6	
7 **Total** *(add lines 1 through 6; enter here and on Form IT-203, line 58)*	7	

Part II — Other New York State Taxes (see instructions, page 24)

8 New York State separate tax on lump-sum distributions *(from Form IT-230; attach form)*	8	
9 Resident credit against separate tax on lump-sum distributions *(from Form IT-112.1; attach form and copy of return filed with other state or province of Canada)*	9	
10 Subtract line 9 from line 8	10	
11 New York State minimum income tax *(from Form IT-220; attach form)*	11	
12 Add-back of investment credit on early dispositions *(from Form IT-212; attach form)*	12	
13 Add-back of economic development zone investment tax credit on early dispositions *(from Form DTF-603; attach form)*	13	
14 Add-back of resident credit for taxes paid to a province of Canada *(from Form IT-112-R; attach form)*	14	
15 New York State tax on capital gain portion of lump-sum distribution from worksheet on back	15	
16 **Total** *(add lines 10 through 15; enter here and on Form IT-203, line 60)*	16	

Part III — Other City of New York Taxes (see instructions, page 25)

17 Part-year city of New York resident tax *(from Form IT-360.1; attach form)*	17	
18 City of New York minimum income tax *(from Form IT-220; attach form)*	18	
19 City of New York separate tax on lump-sum distributions *(from Form IT-230; attach form)*	19	
20 Part-year city of New York resident tax on capital gain portion of lump-sum distribution from worksheet on back	20	
21 **Total** *(add lines 17 through 20; enter here and on Form IT-203, line 63)*	21	
22 Investment credit refund for new businesses *(enter here and include on Form IT-203, line 69; see instructions)*	22	
23 Net investment credit available for carryover to 1993 *(from Form IT-212; attach form)*	23	
24 Net economic development zone credit available for carryover to 1993 *(from Form DTF-601 or DTF-603, or both; attach forms that apply)*	24	

Worksheet for Front Page, Part II, Line 15

1 New York State tax on capital gain portion of lump-sum distribution
   (from Form IT-230, Part II, line 2, New York State column) **1**
2 Enter amount from Form IT-203, line 54 **2**
3 Enter amount from Form IT-203, line 51 **3**
4 Subtract line 3 from line 2 *(if line 3 is more than line 2, enter "0")* .. **4**
5 Subtract line 4 from line 1 .... **5**
6 Enter *Income Percentage* from Form IT-203, line 56 .... **6**
7 Multiply the amount on line 5 by the percentage on line 6 ...... **7**

   • If the amount on Form IT-203, line 58 is "0," transfer the above line 7 amount to the front page, line 15. Do not continue with this worksheet.

   • If you have an amount on Form IT-203, line 58, continue on line 8 below.

8 Enter amount from Form IT-203, line 58 .... **8**
9 Enter amount from Form IT-203, line 57 .... **9**

   • If line 9 is equal to or more than line 8, transfer the above line 7 amount to the front page, line 15. Do not continue with this worksheet.

   • If line 9 is less than line 8, continue on line 10 below.

10 Subtract line 9 from line 8 .... **10**
11 Subtract line 10 from line 7 *(if line 10 is more than line 7, enter "0")* . **11**
   Enter here and on the front page, line 15.

Worksheet for Front Page, Part III, Line 20

1 City of New York tax on capital gain portion of lump-sum distribution
   (from Form IT-230, Part II, line 2, City of New York column) **1**
2 Enter amount from Form IT-360.1, line 51 **2**
3 Enter amount from Form IT-360.1, line 50 **3**

   • If line 3 is equal to or more than line 2, transfer the above line 1 amount to the front page, line 20. Do not continue with this worksheet.

   • If line 3 is less than line 2, continue on line 4 below.

4 Subtract line 3 from line 2 .... **4**
5 Subtract line 4 from line 1. Enter here and on
   the front page, line 20 .... **5**

Telephone Assistance

For forms and publications,
call toll free (from New York State only)
1 800 462-8100
From areas outside New York State,
call (518) 438-1073.

For information,
call toll free (from New York State only)
1 800 CALL TAX (1 800 225-5829)
From areas outside New York State,
call (518) 438-8581.

For refund information only,
please wait until after April 15 to call
toll free (from New York State only)
1 800 443-3200.
From areas outside New York State,
call (518) 438-6777.

Telephone assistance is available from
8:30 a.m. to 4:25 p.m. Monday
through Friday.

Mail Your Return

Mail your return and attachments in
the preaddressed envelope that
came with your tax packet. If you
do not have one, address your
envelope —

For refund returns:
NYS Income Tax
W A Harriman Campus
REFUND '92
Albany N   12227-0125

For all other returns:
NYS Income Tax
W A Harriman Campus
Albany NY   12227-0125

Schedule A

Allocation of Wage and Salary Income to New York State

a Wages, salaries, tips, etc. *(to be allocated)* ..... a 50,000
b Total days in year .... b 366
c Nonworking days:
   Saturdays and Sundays.. *Do not count* 104
   holidays .... *days worked* 12
   sick leave ....
   vacation..................... 10
   other nonworking days ....
   Total nonworking days................... c 126
d Total days worked in year *(subtract line c from line b)* .... d 240
e Total days worked outside New York State .... e 120
f Days worked in New York State *(subtract line e from line d)* ... f 120
g New York State amount:

line f: 120
———— x line a: 50,000 = g 25,000
line d: 240

Include line g amount on Form IT-203, line 1, New York State Amount column.

h Days worked at home included in line e........... h 0

Schedule B

Living Quarters Maintained in New York State by a Nonresident

If you or your spouse maintained living quarters in New York State during any part of the year, give address(es) below.

Address(es)

☐ _____
  _____

☐ _____
  _____

☐ _____
  _____

☐ _____
  _____

Check the box next to any living quarters still maintained for or by you.

Enter the number of days spent in New York State in 1992: _____ days

New York State Department of Taxation and Finance

City of New York **FINAL** **NYC-203**

Nonresident Earnings Tax Return

1992

For Jan. 1 — Dec. 31, 1992, or fiscal tax year beginning _____ , 1992 ending _____ , 19 ___ .

Name as shown on Form IT-200, IT-201 or IT-203

David F. Myers

Your social security number

500 50 5000

A Were you a city of New York resident for any part of the taxable year? ☐ Yes ☑ No
(See the Form IT-201 or IT-203 instructions for the definition of resident)

If **Yes**: 1. Give period of city of New York residence. From (month, day, year) _____ to (month, day, year) _____

2. Are you reporting the city of New York resident tax
on your New York State return? ☐ Yes ☐ No *(If No, attach explanation.)*

B Did you or your spouse maintain an apartment or other living quarters
in the city of New York during any part of the year? ☐ Yes ☑ No

If **Yes**, give address below and enter the number of days spent in the city of New York during 1992: Days _____

Address _____

C If you are reporting income from self-employment on line 5 below, complete the following:

Business name _____ Business address _____

Employer identification number _____ Principal business activity _____

Form of business ☐ Sole proprietorship ☐ Partnership ☐ Other (explain) _____

Calculation of Nonresident Earnings Tax

1	Gross wages and other employee compensation *(see instructions; if allocation is claimed, enter from line 21)*	**1** 25,000	
2	Allowable exclusion *(see instructions; use Exclusion Table below)*	**2** 1,000	
3	Taxable amount of wages *(subtract line 2 from line 1)*	**3** 24,000	
4	Tax on wages *(multiply line 3 by .45% (.0045))*		**4** 108
5	Net earnings from self-employment *(see instructions; if allocation is claimed, enter from line 31; if a loss, write **Loss** on line 5)*	**5**	
6	Allowable exclusion *(see instructions; use Exclusion Table below)*	**6**	
7	Taxable amount of net earnings from self-employment *(subtract line 6 from line 5)* .	**7**	
8	Tax on net earnings from self-employment *(multiply line 7 by .65% (.0065))*		**8**
9	Total nonresident earnings tax *(add lines 4 and 8. Enter here and transfer the line 9 amount to your New York State return as follows: Form IT-200, line 26; Form IT-201, line 62; Form IT-203, line 62)*		**9** 108

Paid Preparer's Use Only	Preparer's signature	Date	Check if self-employed ☐	**Sign Your Return**	Your signature	Date
	Firm's name *(or yours, if self-employed)*	Preparer's social security number			David F. Myers	4/14/93
	Address	Employer identification number				

Reminders:

- Sign your return.

- Enter your total nonresident earnings tax
on Form IT-200, IT-201 or IT-203.

- Attach this form to your New York State
return: Form IT-200, IT-201 or IT-203.

Exclusion Table

Total of Wages and Net Earnings		Exclusion*
over	but not over	
$ 0	$10,000	$3,000
10,000	20,000	2,000
20,000	30,000	1,000
30,000		None

*If you have an entry on line 1 and line 5, you must prorate the exclusion *(see line 2 instructions)*.

Schedule A — Allocation of wage and salary income (Use only if you worked both in and out of the city of New York. If you worked for more than one employer, complete separate schedules.)

10 Gross wages and other employee compensation	10	50,000
11 Total days in year (see instructions if employment is for period of less than entire year)	11	366

Nonworking days:

12 Saturdays and Sundays (do not count days worked).........................	12	104	
13 Holidays (do not count days worked)	13	12	
14 Sick leave	14		
15 Vacation	15	10	
16 Other nonworking days....................................	16		

17 Total nonworking days (add lines 12 through 16)	17	126
18 Total days worked in year (subtract line 17 from line 11)	18	240
19 Total days worked outside the city of New York (attach schedule or explanation)	19	120
20 Days worked in the city of New York (subtract line 19 from line 18)	20	120

21 City of New York amount: $\dfrac{\text{line 20} \quad 120}{\text{line 18} \quad 240}$ × line 10 = 25,000 (transfer this amount to line 1)

Schedule B — List all places, both in and out of the city of New York, where you carry on business (use only if your net earnings from self-employment are from a business carried on both in and out of the city of New York).

(1) Street address	(2) City and state	(3) Description (see instructions)

Schedule C — Allocation of net earnings from self-employment to the city of New York

(Use only if your business is carried on both in and out of the city of New York. If the net earnings are from a partnership, the factors must be the partnership amounts.)

If you filed Form NYC-202, City of New York Unincorporated Business Tax Return, or Form NYC-204, City of New York Partnership Return, you may use the business allocation percentage determined by the formula on either of those returns instead of figuring the percentage in Schedule C. If you use the percentage from one of those returns, check this box ☐ ; then skip lines 22 through 28 and enter the allocation percentage from either of those returns on line 29 below. Attach a copy of Form NYC-202 or NYC-204.

Items used as factors		(1) Totals — in and out of the city of New York	(2) City of New York amount	(3) Percent column (2) is of column (1)
Property percentage (see instructions):				
22 Real property owned	22			
23 Real property rented from others.................	23			
24 Tangible personal property owned..................	24			
25 Property percentage (add lines 22, 23 and 24; see instructions)	25			%
26 Payroll percentage (see instructions)	26			%
27 Gross income percentage (see instructions)	27			%
28 Total of percentages (add lines 25, 26 and 27, column (3))			28	%
29 Business allocation percentage (divide total percentages on line 28 by three or by actual number of percentages if less than three)			29	%
30 Net earnings from self-employment to be allocated (see instructions)			30	
31 Allocated net earnings from self-employment (multiply line 30 by line 29; enter result here and on line 5)			31	

City of Yonkers Nonresident Earnings Tax Return

FINAL

For Jan. 1 — Dec. 31, 1992, or fiscal tax year beginning , 1992, ending , 19 .

Name as shown on Form IT-200, IT-201 or IT-203	Your social security number
Wendy S. Jones	500 50 5000

A Were you a city of Yonkers resident for any part of the taxable year? ☐ Yes ☑ No
(See the Form IT-201 or IT-203 instructions for the definition of resident.)

If *Yes*: 1. Give period of city of Yonkers residence. From (month, day, year) _____ to (month, day, year) _____

2. Are you reporting the city of Yonkers resident income tax
surcharge on your New York State return? ☐ Yes ☐ No *(If No, attach explanation.)*

B Did you or your spouse maintain an apartment or other living quarters
in the city of Yonkers during any part of the year? ☐ Yes ☑ No

If *Yes*, give address below and enter the number of days spent in the city of Yonkers during 1992: Days _____
Address _____

C If you are reporting income from self-employment on line 2 below, complete the following:

Business name _____ Business address _____
Employer identification number_____ Principal business activity _____
Form of business ☐ Sole proprietorship ☐ Partnership ☐ Other (explain) _____

Calculation of Nonresident Earnings Tax

1 Gross wages and other employee compensation *(see instructions; if allocation is claimed, enter from line 18)* .	1	30,000
2 Net earnings from self-employment *(see instructions; if allocation is claimed, enter from line 28; if a loss, write **Loss** on line 2)*	2	0
3 Add lines 1 and 2	3	30,000
4 Exclusion *(see instructions; use Exclusion Table below)*	4	0
5 Taxable amount *(subtract line 4 from line 3)*	5	30,000
6 Total nonresident earnings tax *(multiply line 5 by .5% (.005). Enter here and transfer line 6 amount to your New York State return as follows: Form IT-200, line 28; Form IT-201, line 65; Form IT-203, line 64)*	6	150

Paid Preparer's Use Only	Preparer's signature	Date	Check if self-employed ☐	**Sign Your Return**	Your signature	Date
	Firm's name *(or yours, if self-employed)*		Preparer's social security number		Wendy S. Jones	4/1/93
	Address		Employer identification number			

Reminders:

- Sign your return.

- Enter your total nonresident earnings tax
  on Form IT-200, IT-201 or IT-203.

- Attach this form to your New York State
  return: Form IT-200, IT-201 or IT-203.

Exclusion Table

If line 3 is:		Exclusion
over	but not over	
$ 0	$10,000	$3,000
10,000	20,000	2,000
20,000	30,000	1,000
30,000		None

10 | New York Tax Tables (1992)

This chapter includes the official 1992 New York State and New York City Tax Tables. These tax tables are used to determine tax on taxable income of less than $65,000. To read your tax from the tax table, you must know your taxable income and your filing status. For an example of how to use the tax tables, see Chapter 4, *How to Figure Your Tax*.

1992 New York State Tax Table

Based on Taxable Income

For persons with taxable income of less than $65,000.

Example: Mr. and Mrs. Allen are filing a joint return. Their taxable income on line 17 of Form IT-200 is $36,275. First, they find the 36,250 - 36,300 income line. Next, they find the column for married filing jointly and read down the column. The amount shown where the income line and filing status column meet is $2,139. This is the tax amount they must write on line 18 of Form IT-200.

At least	But less than	Single or Married filing separately	Married filing jointly*	Head of a house-hold
		Your New York State tax is -		
36,200	36,250	2,494	2,135	2,369
36,250	36,300	2,498	(2,139)	2,373
36,300	36,350	2,502	2,143	2,377
36,350	36,400	2,506	2,147	2,381

If line 17 (taxable income) is - At least	But less than	Single or Married filing separately	Married filing jointly*	Head of a house-hold
		Your New York State tax is -		
$0	$10	$0	$0	$0
10	25	1	1	1
25	50	2	2	2
50	100	3	3	3
100	150	5	5	5
150	200	7	7	7
200	250	9	9	9
250	300	11	11	11
300	350	13	13	13
350	400	15	15	15
400	450	17	17	17
450	500	19	19	19
500	550	21	21	21
550	600	23	23	23
600	650	25	25	25
650	700	27	27	27
700	750	29	29	29
750	800	31	31	31
800	850	33	33	33
850	900	35	35	35
900	950	37	37	37
950	1,000	39	39	39
1,000				
1,000	1,050	41	41	41
1,050	1,100	43	43	43
1,100	1,150	45	45	45
1,150	1,200	47	47	47
1,200	1,250	49	49	49
1,250	1,300	51	51	51
1,300	1,350	53	53	53
1,350	1,400	55	55	55
1,400	1,450	57	57	57
1,450	1,500	59	59	59
1,500	1,550	61	61	61
1,550	1,600	63	63	63
1,600	1,650	65	65	65
1,650	1,700	67	67	67
1,700	1,750	69	69	69
1,750	1,800	71	71	71
1,800	1,850	73	73	73
1,850	1,900	75	75	75
1,900	1,950	77	77	77
1,950	2,000	79	79	79

If line 17 (taxable income) is - At least	But less than	Single or Married filing separately	Married filing jointly*	Head of a house-hold
		Your New York State tax is -		
2,000				
2,000	2,050	81	81	81
2,050	2,100	83	83	83
2,100	2,150	85	85	85
2,150	2,200	87	87	87
2,200	2,250	89	89	89
2,250	2,300	91	91	91
2,300	2,350	93	93	93
2,350	2,400	95	95	95
2,400	2,450	97	97	97
2,450	2,500	99	99	99
2,500	2,550	101	101	101
2,550	2,600	103	103	103
2,600	2,650	105	105	105
2,650	2,700	107	107	107
2,700	2,750	109	109	109
2,750	2,800	111	111	111
2,800	2,850	113	113	113
2,850	2,900	115	115	115
2,900	2,950	117	117	117
2,950	3,000	119	119	119
3,000				
3,000	3,050	121	121	121
3,050	3,100	123	123	123
3,100	3,150	125	125	125
3,150	3,200	127	127	127
3,200	3,250	129	129	129
3,250	3,300	131	131	131
3,300	3,350	133	133	133
3,350	3,400	135	135	135
3,400	3,450	137	137	137
3,450	3,500	139	139	139
3,500	3,550	141	141	141
3,550	3,600	143	143	143
3,600	3,650	145	145	145
3,650	3,700	147	147	147
3,700	3,750	149	149	149
3,750	3,800	151	151	151
3,800	3,850	153	153	153
3,850	3,900	155	155	155
3,900	3,950	157	157	157
3,950	4,000	159	159	159

If line 17 (taxable income) is - At least	But less than	Single or Married filing separately	Married filing jointly*	Head of a house-hold
		Your New York State tax is -		
4,000				
4,000	4,050	161	161	161
4,050	4,100	163	163	163
4,100	4,150	165	165	165
4,150	4,200	167	167	167
4,200	4,250	169	169	169
4,250	4,300	171	171	171
4,300	4,350	173	173	173
4,350	4,400	175	175	175
4,400	4,450	177	177	177
4,450	4,500	179	179	179
4,500	4,550	181	181	181
4,550	4,600	183	183	183
4,600	4,650	185	185	185
4,650	4,700	187	187	187
4,700	4,750	189	189	189
4,750	4,800	191	191	191
4,800	4,850	193	193	193
4,850	4,900	195	195	195
4,900	4,950	197	197	197
4,950	5,000	199	199	199
5,000				
5,000	5,050	201	201	201
5,050	5,100	203	203	203
5,100	5,150	205	205	205
5,150	5,200	207	207	207
5,200	5,250	209	209	209
5,250	5,300	211	211	211
5,300	5,350	213	213	213
5,350	5,400	215	215	215
5,400	5,450	217	217	217
5,450	5,500	219	219	219
5,500	5,550	221	221	221
5,550	5,600	224	223	223
5,600	5,650	226	225	225
5,650	5,700	229	227	227
5,700	5,750	231	229	229
5,750	5,800	234	231	231
5,800	5,850	236	233	233
5,850	5,900	239	235	235
5,900	5,950	241	237	237
5,950	6,000	244	239	239

* This column must also be used by a qualifying widow(er)

Continued on next page

New York State Tax Table

If line 17 (taxable income) is -		And you are -			If line 17 (taxable income) is -		And you are -			If line 17 (taxable income) is -		And you are -		
At least	But less than	Single or Married filing separately	Married filing jointly *	Head of a house-hold	At least	But less than	Single or Married filing separately	Married filing jointly *	Head of a house-hold	At least	But less than	Single or Married filing separately	Married filing jointly *	Head of a house-hold
		Your New York State tax is -					Your New York State tax is -					Your New York State tax is -		
6,000					**9,000**					**12,000**				
6,000	6,050	246	241	241	9,000	9,050	407	361	376	12,000	12,050	597	491	537
6,050	6,100	249	243	243	9,050	9,100	410	363	379	12,050	12,100	600	494	540
6,100	6,150	251	245	245	9,100	9,150	413	365	381	12,100	12,150	604	496	543
6,150	6,200	254	247	247	9,150	9,200	416	367	384	12,150	12,200	607	499	546
6,200	6,250	256	249	249	9,200	9,250	419	369	386	12,200	12,250	611	501	549
6,250	6,300	259	251	251	9,250	9,300	422	371	389	12,250	12,300	614	504	552
6,300	6,350	261	253	253	9,300	9,350	425	373	391	12,300	12,350	618	506	555
6,350	6,400	264	255	255	9,350	9,400	428	375	394	12,350	12,400	621	509	558
6,400	6,450	266	257	257	9,400	9,450	431	377	396	12,400	12,450	625	511	561
6,450	6,500	269	259	259	9,450	9,500	434	379	399	12,450	12,500	628	514	564
6,500	6,550	271	261	261	9,500	9,550	437	381	401	12,500	12,550	632	516	567
6,550	6,600	274	263	263	9,550	9,600	440	383	404	12,550	12,600	635	519	570
6,600	6,650	276	265	265	9,600	9,650	443	385	406	12,600	12,650	639	521	573
6,650	6,700	279	267	267	9,650	9,700	446	387	409	12,650	12,700	642	524	576
6,700	6,750	281	269	269	9,700	9,750	449	389	411	12,700	12,750	646	526	579
6,750	6,800	284	271	271	9,750	9,800	452	391	414	12,750	12,800	649	529	582
6,800	6,850	286	273	273	9,800	9,850	455	393	416	12,800	12,850	653	531	585
6,850	6,900	289	275	275	9,850	9,900	458	395	419	12,850	12,900	656	534	588
6,900	6,950	291	277	277	9,900	9,950	461	397	421	12,900	12,950	660	536	591
6,950	7,000	294	279	279	9,950	10,000	464	399	424	12,950	13,000	663	539	594
7,000					**10,000**					**13,000**				
7,000	7,050	296	281	281	10,000	10,050	467	401	426	13,000	13,050	667	541	597
7,050	7,100	299	283	283	10,050	10,100	470	403	429	13,050	13,100	671	544	600
7,100	7,150	301	285	285	10,100	10,150	473	405	431	13,100	13,150	675	545	603
7,150	7,200	304	287	287	10,150	10,200	476	407	434	13,150	13,200	679	549	606
7,200	7,250	306	289	289	10,200	10,250	479	409	436	13,200	13,250	683	551	609
7,250	7,300	309	291	291	10,250	10,300	482	411	439	13,250	13,300	687	554	612
7,300	7,350	311	293	293	10,300	10,350	485	413	441	13,300	13,350	691	556	615
7,350	7,400	314	295	295	10,350	10,400	488	415	444	13,350	13,400	695	559	618
7,400	7,450	316	297	297	10,400	10,450	491	417	446	13,400	13,450	698	561	621
7,450	7,500	319	299	299	10,450	10,500	494	419	449	13,450	13,500	702	564	624
7,500	7,550	321	301	301	10,500	10,550	497	421	451	13,500	13,550	706	566	627
7,550	7,600	324	303	304	10,550	10,600	500	423	454	13,550	13,600	710	569	630
7,600	7,650	326	305	306	10,600	10,650	503	425	456	13,600	13,650	714	571	633
7,650	7,700	329	307	309	10,650	10,700	506	427	459	13,650	13,700	718	574	636
7,700	7,750	331	309	311	10,700	10,750	509	429	461	13,700	13,750	722	576	639
7,750	7,800	334	311	314	10,750	10,800	512	431	464	13,750	13,800	726	579	642
7,800	7,850	336	313	316	10,800	10,850	515	433	466	13,800	13,850	730	581	645
7,850	7,900	339	315	319	10,850	10,900	518	435	469	13,850	13,900	734	584	648
7,900	7,950	341	317	321	10,900	10,950	521	437	471	13,900	13,950	738	586	651
7,950	8,000	344	319	324	10,950	11,000	524	439	474	13,950	14,000	742	589	654
8,000					**11,000**					**14,000**				
8,000	8,050	347	321	326	11,000	11,050	527	441	477	14,000	14,050	746	591	657
8,050	8,100	350	323	329	11,050	11,100	530	444	480	14,050	14,100	750	594	660
8,100	8,150	353	325	331	11,100	11,150	534	446	483	14,100	14,150	754	596	663
8,150	8,200	356	327	334	11,150	11,200	537	449	486	14,150	14,200	758	599	666
8,200	8,250	359	329	336	11,200	11,250	541	451	489	14,200	14,250	761	601	669
8,250	8,300	362	331	339	11,250	11,300	544	454	492	14,250	14,300	765	604	672
8,300	8,350	365	333	341	11,300	11,350	548	456	495	14,300	14,350	769	606	675
8,350	8,400	368	335	344	11,350	11,400	551	459	498	14,350	14,400	773	609	678
8,400	8,450	371	337	346	11,400	11,450	555	461	501	14,400	14,450	777	611	681
8,450	8,500	374	339	349	11,450	11,500	558	464	504	14,450	14,500	781	614	684
8,500	8,550	377	341	351	11,500	11,550	562	466	507	14,500	14,550	785	616	687
8,550	8,600	380	343	354	11,550	11,600	565	469	510	14,550	14,600	789	619	690
8,600	8,650	383	345	356	11,600	11,650	569	471	513	14,600	14,650	793	621	693
8,650	8,700	385	347	359	11,650	11,700	572	474	516	14,650	14,700	797	624	696
8,700	8,750	389	349	361	11,700	11,750	576	476	519	14,700	14,750	801	626	699
8,750	8,800	392	351	364	11,750	11,800	579	479	522	14,750	14,800	805	629	702
8,800	8,850	395	353	366	11,800	11,850	583	481	525	14,800	14,850	809	631	705
8,850	8,900	398	355	369	11,850	11,900	586	484	528	14,850	14,900	813	634	708
8,900	8,950	401	357	371	11,900	11,950	590	486	531	14,900	14,950	817	635	711
8,950	9,000	404	359	374	11,950	12,000	593	489	534	14,950	15,000	821	639	714

* This column must also be used by a qualifying widow(er)

Continued on next page

New York State Tax Table

If line 17 (taxable income) is — At least	But less than	Single or Married filing separately	Married filing jointly	Head of a household
15,000				
15,000	15,050	824	641	717
15,050	15,100	828	644	720
15,100	15,150	832	646	724
15,150	15,200	836	649	727
15,200	15,250	840	651	731
15,250	15,300	844	654	734
15,300	15,350	848	656	738
15,350	15,400	852	659	741
15,400	15,450	856	661	745
15,450	15,500	860	664	748
15,500	15,550	864	666	752
15,550	15,600	868	669	755
15,600	15,650	872	671	759
15,650	15,700	876	674	762
15,700	15,750	880	676	766
15,750	15,800	884	679	769
15,800	15,850	887	681	773
15,850	15,900	891	684	776
15,900	15,950	895	686	780
15,950	16,000	899	689	783
16,000				
16,000	16,050	903	692	787
16,050	16,100	907	695	790
16,100	16,150	911	698	794
16,150	16,200	915	701	797
16,200	16,250	919	704	801
16,250	16,300	923	707	804
16,300	16,350	927	710	808
16,350	16,400	931	713	811
16,400	16,450	935	716	815
16,450	16,500	939	719	818
16,500	16,550	943	722	822
16,550	16,600	947	725	825
16,600	16,650	950	728	829
16,650	16,700	954	731	832
16,700	16,750	958	734	836
16,750	16,800	962	737	839
16,800	16,850	966	740	843
16,850	16,900	970	743	846
16,900	16,950	974	746	850
16,950	17,000	978	749	853
17,000				
17,000	17,050	982	752	857
17,050	17,100	986	755	861
17,100	17,150	990	758	865
17,150	17,200	994	761	869
17,200	17,250	998	764	873
17,250	17,300	1,002	767	877
17,300	17,350	1,006	770	881
17,350	17,400	1,010	773	885
17,400	17,450	1,013	776	888
17,450	17,500	1,017	779	892
17,500	17,550	1,021	782	896
17,550	17,600	1,025	785	900
17,600	17,650	1,029	788	904
17,650	17,700	1,033	791	908
17,700	17,750	1,037	794	912
17,750	17,800	1,041	797	916
17,800	17,850	1,045	800	920
17,850	17,900	1,049	803	924
17,900	17,950	1,053	806	928
17,950	18,000	1,057	809	932
18,000				
18,000	18,050	1,061	812	936
18,050	18,100	1,065	815	940
18,100	18,150	1,069	818	944
18,150	18,200	1,073	821	948
18,200	18,250	1,076	824	951
18,250	18,300	1,080	827	955
18,300	18,350	1,084	830	959
18,350	18,400	1,088	833	963
18,400	18,450	1,092	836	967
18,450	18,500	1,096	839	971
18,500	18,550	1,100	842	975
18,550	18,600	1,104	845	979
18,600	18,650	1,108	848	983
18,650	18,700	1,112	851	987
18,700	18,750	1,116	854	991
18,750	18,800	1,120	857	995
18,800	18,850	1,124	860	999
18,850	18,900	1,128	863	1,003
18,900	18,950	1,132	866	1,007
18,950	19,000	1,136	869	1,011
19,000				
19,000	19,050	1,139	872	1,014
19,050	19,100	1,143	875	1,018
19,100	19,150	1,147	878	1,022
19,150	19,200	1,151	881	1,026
19,200	19,250	1,155	884	1,030
19,250	19,300	1,159	887	1,034
19,300	19,350	1,163	890	1,038
19,350	19,400	1,167	893	1,042
19,400	19,450	1,171	896	1,046
19,450	19,500	1,175	899	1,050
19,500	19,550	1,179	902	1,054
19,550	19,600	1,183	905	1,058
19,600	19,650	1,187	908	1,062
19,650	19,700	1,191	911	1,066
19,700	19,750	1,195	914	1,070
19,750	19,800	1,199	917	1,074
19,800	19,850	1,202	920	1,077
19,850	19,900	1,206	923	1,081
19,900	19,950	1,210	926	1,085
19,950	20,000	1,214	929	1,089
20,000				
20,000	20,050	1,218	932	1,093
20,050	20,100	1,222	935	1,097
20,100	20,150	1,226	938	1,101
20,150	20,200	1,230	941	1,105
20,200	20,250	1,234	944	1,109
20,250	20,300	1,238	947	1,113
20,300	20,350	1,242	950	1,117
20,350	20,400	1,246	953	1,121
20,400	20,450	1,250	956	1,125
20,450	20,500	1,254	959	1,129
20,500	20,550	1,258	962	1,133
20,550	20,600	1,262	965	1,137
20,600	20,650	1,265	968	1,140
20,650	20,700	1,269	971	1,144
20,700	20,750	1,273	974	1,148
20,750	20,800	1,277	977	1,152
20,800	20,850	1,281	980	1,156
20,850	20,900	1,285	983	1,160
20,900	20,950	1,289	985	1,164
20,950	21,000	1,293	989	1,168
21,000				
21,000	21,050	1,297	992	1,172
21,050	21,100	1,301	995	1,176
21,100	21,150	1,305	998	1,180
21,150	21,200	1,309	1,001	1,184
21,200	21,250	1,313	1,004	1,188
21,250	21,300	1,317	1,007	1,192
21,300	21,350	1,321	1,010	1,196
21,350	21,400	1,325	1,013	1,200
21,400	21,450	1,328	1,016	1,203
21,450	21,500	1,332	1,019	1,207
21,500	21,550	1,336	1,022	1,211
21,550	21,600	1,340	1,025	1,215
21,600	21,650	1,344	1,028	1,219
21,650	21,700	1,348	1,031	1,223
21,700	21,750	1,352	1,034	1,227
21,750	21,800	1,356	1,037	1,231
21,800	21,850	1,360	1,040	1,235
21,850	21,900	1,364	1,043	1,239
21,900	21,950	1,368	1,046	1,243
21,950	22,000	1,372	1,049	1,247
22,000				
22,000	22,050	1,376	1,052	1,251
22,050	22,100	1,380	1,055	1,255
22,100	22,150	1,384	1,059	1,259
22,150	22,200	1,388	1,062	1,263
22,200	22,250	1,391	1,066	1,266
22,250	22,300	1,395	1,069	1,270
22,300	22,350	1,399	1,073	1,274
22,350	22,400	1,403	1,076	1,278
22,400	22,450	1,407	1,080	1,282
22,450	22,500	1,411	1,083	1,286
22,500	22,550	1,415	1,087	1,290
22,550	22,600	1,419	1,090	1,294
22,600	22,650	1,423	1,094	1,298
22,650	22,700	1,427	1,097	1,302
22,700	22,750	1,431	1,101	1,306
22,750	22,800	1,435	1,104	1,310
22,800	22,850	1,439	1,108	1,314
22,850	22,900	1,443	1,111	1,318
22,900	22,950	1,447	1,115	1,322
22,950	23,000	1,451	1,118	1,326
23,000				
23,000	23,050	1,454	1,122	1,329
23,050	23,100	1,458	1,125	1,333
23,100	23,150	1,462	1,129	1,337
23,150	23,200	1,466	1,132	1,341
23,200	23,250	1,470	1,136	1,345
23,250	23,300	1,474	1,139	1,349
23,300	23,350	1,478	1,143	1,353
23,350	23,400	1,482	1,146	1,357
23,400	23,450	1,486	1,150	1,361
23,450	23,500	1,490	1,153	1,365
23,500	23,550	1,494	1,157	1,369
23,550	23,600	1,498	1,160	1,373
23,600	23,650	1,502	1,164	1,377
23,650	23,700	1,506	1,167	1,381
23,700	23,750	1,510	1,171	1,385
23,750	23,800	1,514	1,174	1,389
23,800	23,850	1,517	1,178	1,392
23,850	23,900	1,521	1,181	1,396
23,900	23,950	1,525	1,185	1,400
23,950	24,000	1,529	1,188	1,404

* This column must also be used by a qualifying widow(er)

Continued on next page

New York State Tax Table

If line 17 (taxable income) is -		And you are -		
At least	But less than	Single or Married filing separately	Married filing jointly *	Head of a house-hold
		Your New York State tax is -		

24,000

At least	But less than	Single or Married filing separately	Married filing jointly	Head of a household
24,000	24,050	1,533	1,192	1,408
24,050	24,100	1,537	1,195	1,412
24,100	24,150	1,541	1,199	1,416
24,150	24,200	1,545	1,202	1,420
24,200	24,250	1,549	1,206	1,424
24,250	24,300	1,553	1,209	1,428
24,300	24,350	1,557	1,213	1,432
24,350	24,400	1,561	1,216	1,436
24,400	24,450	1,565	1,220	1,440
24,450	24,500	1,569	1,223	1,444
24,500	24,550	1,573	1,227	1,448
24,550	24,600	1,577	1,230	1,452
24,600	24,650	1,580	1,234	1,455
24,650	24,700	1,584	1,237	1,459
24,700	24,750	1,588	1,241	1,463
24,750	24,800	1,592	1,244	1,467
24,800	24,850	1,596	1,248	1,471
24,850	24,900	1,600	1,251	1,475
24,900	24,950	1,604	1,255	1,479
24,950	25,000	1,608	1,258	1,483

25,000

At least	But less than	Single or Married filing separately	Married filing jointly	Head of a household
25,000	25,050	1,612	1,262	1,487
25,050	25,100	1,616	1,265	1,491
25,100	25,150	1,620	1,269	1,495
25,150	25,200	1,624	1,272	1,499
25,200	25,250	1,628	1,276	1,503
25,250	25,300	1,632	1,279	1,507
25,300	25,350	1,636	1,283	1,511
25,350	25,400	1,640	1,286	1,515
25,400	25,450	1,643	1,290	1,518
25,450	25,500	1,647	1,293	1,522
25,500	25,550	1,651	1,297	1,526
25,550	25,600	1,655	1,300	1,530
25,600	25,650	1,659	1,304	1,534
25,650	25,700	1,663	1,307	1,538
25,700	25,750	1,667	1,311	1,542
25,750	25,800	1,671	1,314	1,546
25,800	25,850	1,675	1,318	1,550
25,850	25,900	1,679	1,321	1,554
25,900	25,950	1,683	1,325	1,558
25,950	26,000	1,687	1,328	1,562

26,000

At least	But less than	Single or Married filing separately	Married filing jointly	Head of a household
26,000	26,050	1,691	1,332	1,566
26,050	26,100	1,695	1,336	1,570
26,100	26,150	1,699	1,340	1,574
26,150	26,200	1,703	1,344	1,578
26,200	26,250	1,706	1,348	1,581
26,250	26,300	1,710	1,352	1,585
26,300	26,350	1,714	1,356	1,589
26,350	26,400	1,718	1,360	1,593
26,400	26,450	1,722	1,363	1,597
26,450	26,500	1,726	1,367	1,601
26,500	26,550	1,730	1,371	1,605
26,550	26,600	1,734	1,375	1,609
26,600	26,650	1,738	1,379	1,613
26,650	26,700	1,742	1,383	1,617
26,700	26,750	1,746	1,387	1,621
26,750	26,800	1,750	1,391	1,625
26,800	26,850	1,754	1,395	1,629
26,850	26,900	1,758	1,399	1,633
26,900	26,950	1,762	1,403	1,637
26,950	27,000	1,766	1,407	1,641

27,000

At least	But less than	Single or Married filing separately	Married filing jointly	Head of a household
27,000	27,050	1,769	1,411	1,644
27,050	27,100	1,773	1,415	1,648
27,100	27,150	1,777	1,419	1,652
27,150	27,200	1,781	1,423	1,656
27,200	27,250	1,785	1,426	1,660
27,250	27,300	1,789	1,430	1,664
27,300	27,350	1,793	1,434	1,668
27,350	27,400	1,797	1,438	1,672
27,400	27,450	1,801	1,442	1,676
27,450	27,500	1,805	1,446	1,680
27,500	27,550	1,809	1,450	1,684
27,550	27,600	1,813	1,454	1,688
27,600	27,650	1,817	1,458	1,692
27,650	27,700	1,821	1,462	1,696
27,700	27,750	1,825	1,466	1,700
27,750	27,800	1,829	1,470	1,704
27,800	27,850	1,832	1,474	1,707
27,850	27,900	1,836	1,478	1,711
27,900	27,950	1,840	1,482	1,715
27,950	28,000	1,844	1,486	1,719

28,000

At least	But less than	Single or Married filing separately	Married filing jointly	Head of a household
28,000	28,050	1,848	1,489	1,723
28,050	28,100	1,852	1,493	1,727
28,100	28,150	1,856	1,497	1,731
28,150	28,200	1,860	1,501	1,735
28,200	28,250	1,864	1,505	1,739
28,250	28,300	1,868	1,509	1,743
28,300	28,350	1,872	1,513	1,747
28,350	28,400	1,876	1,517	1,751
28,400	28,450	1,880	1,521	1,755
28,450	28,500	1,884	1,525	1,759
28,500	28,550	1,888	1,529	1,763
28,550	28,600	1,892	1,533	1,767
28,600	28,650	1,895	1,537	1,770
28,650	28,700	1,899	1,541	1,774
28,700	28,750	1,903	1,545	1,778
28,750	28,800	1,907	1,549	1,782
28,800	28,850	1,911	1,552	1,786
28,850	28,900	1,915	1,556	1,790
28,900	28,950	1,919	1,560	1,794
28,950	29,000	1,923	1,564	1,798

29,000

At least	But less than	Single or Married filing separately	Married filing jointly	Head of a household
29,000	29,050	1,927	1,568	1,802
29,050	29,100	1,931	1,572	1,806
29,100	29,150	1,935	1,576	1,810
29,150	29,200	1,939	1,580	1,814
29,200	29,250	1,943	1,584	1,818
29,250	29,300	1,947	1,588	1,822
29,300	29,350	1,951	1,592	1,826
29,350	29,400	1,955	1,596	1,830
29,400	29,450	1,958	1,600	1,833
29,450	29,500	1,962	1,604	1,837
29,500	29,550	1,966	1,608	1,841
29,550	29,600	1,970	1,612	1,845
29,600	29,650	1,974	1,615	1,849
29,650	29,700	1,978	1,619	1,853
29,700	29,750	1,982	1,623	1,857
29,750	29,800	1,986	1,627	1,861
29,800	29,850	1,990	1,631	1,865
29,850	29,900	1,994	1,635	1,869
29,900	29,950	1,998	1,639	1,873
29,950	30,000	2,002	1,643	1,877

30,000

At least	But less than	Single or Married filing separately	Married filing jointly	Head of a household
30,000	30,050	2,006	1,647	1,881
30,050	30,100	2,010	1,651	1,885
30,100	30,150	2,014	1,655	1,889
30,150	30,200	2,018	1,659	1,893
30,200	30,250	2,021	1,663	1,896
30,250	30,300	2,025	1,667	1,900
30,300	30,350	2,029	1,671	1,904
30,350	30,400	2,033	1,675	1,908
30,400	30,450	2,037	1,678	1,912
30,450	30,500	2,041	1,682	1,916
30,500	30,550	2,045	1,686	1,920
30,550	30,600	2,049	1,690	1,924
30,600	30,650	2,053	1,694	1,928
30,650	30,700	2,057	1,698	1,932
30,700	30,750	2,061	1,702	1,936
30,750	30,800	2,065	1,706	1,940
30,800	30,850	2,069	1,710	1,944
30,850	30,900	2,073	1,714	1,948
30,900	30,950	2,077	1,718	1,952
30,950	31,000	2,081	1,722	1,956

31,000

At least	But less than	Single or Married filing separately	Married filing jointly	Head of a household
31,000	31,050	2,084	1,726	1,959
31,050	31,100	2,088	1,730	1,963
31,100	31,150	2,092	1,734	1,967
31,150	31,200	2,096	1,738	1,971
31,200	31,250	2,100	1,741	1,975
31,250	31,300	2,104	1,745	1,979
31,300	31,350	2,108	1,749	1,983
31,350	31,400	2,112	1,753	1,987
31,400	31,450	2,116	1,757	1,991
31,450	31,500	2,120	1,761	1,995
31,500	31,550	2,124	1,765	1,999
31,550	31,600	2,128	1,769	2,003
31,600	31,650	2,132	1,773	2,007
31,650	31,700	2,136	1,777	2,011
31,700	31,750	2,140	1,781	2,015
31,750	31,800	2,144	1,785	2,019
31,800	31,850	2,147	1,789	2,022
31,850	31,900	2,151	1,793	2,026
31,900	31,950	2,155	1,797	2,030
31,950	32,000	2,159	1,801	2,034

32,000

At least	But less than	Single or Married filing separately	Married filing jointly	Head of a household
32,000	32,050	2,163	1,804	2,038
32,050	32,100	2,167	1,808	2,042
32,100	32,150	2,171	1,812	2,046
32,150	32,200	2,175	1,816	2,050
32,200	32,250	2,179	1,820	2,054
32,250	32,300	2,183	1,824	2,058
32,300	32,350	2,187	1,828	2,062
32,350	32,400	2,191	1,832	2,066
32,400	32,450	2,195	1,836	2,070
32,450	32,500	2,199	1,840	2,074
32,500	32,550	2,203	1,844	2,078
32,550	32,600	2,207	1,848	2,082
32,600	32,650	2,210	1,852	2,085
32,650	32,700	2,214	1,856	2,089
32,700	32,750	2,218	1,860	2,093
32,750	32,800	2,222	1,864	2,097
32,800	32,850	2,226	1,867	2,101
32,850	32,900	2,230	1,871	2,105
32,900	32,950	2,234	1,875	2,109
32,950	33,000	2,238	1,879	2,113

* This column must also be used by a qualifying widow(er)

Continued on next page

New York State Tax Table

If line 17 (taxable income) is - At least	But less than	Single or Married filing separately	Married filing jointly *	Head of a house-hold
		Your New York State tax is -		
33,000				
33,000	33,050	2,242	1,883	2,117
33,050	33,100	2,246	1,887	2,121
33,100	33,150	2,250	1,891	2,125
33,150	33,200	2,254	1,895	2,129
33,200	33,250	2,258	1,899	2,133
33,250	33,300	2,262	1,903	2,137
33,300	33,350	2,266	1,907	2,141
33,350	33,400	2,270	1,911	2,145
33,400	33,450	2,273	1,915	2,148
33,450	33,500	2,277	1,919	2,152
33,500	33,550	2,281	1,923	2,156
33,550	33,600	2,285	1,927	2,160
33,600	33,650	2,289	1,930	2,164
33,650	33,700	2,293	1,934	2,168
33,700	33,750	2,297	1,938	2,172
33,750	33,800	2,301	1,942	2,176
33,800	33,850	2,305	1,946	2,180
33,850	33,900	2,309	1,950	2,184
33,900	33,950	2,313	1,954	2,188
33,950	34,000	2,317	1,958	2,192
34,000				
34,000	34,050	2,321	1,962	2,196
34,050	34,100	2,325	1,966	2,200
34,100	34,150	2,329	1,970	2,204
34,150	34,200	2,333	1,974	2,208
34,200	34,250	2,336	1,978	2,211
34,250	34,300	2,340	1,982	2,215
34,300	34,350	2,344	1,986	2,219
34,350	34,400	2,348	1,990	2,223
34,400	34,450	2,352	1,993	2,227
34,450	34,500	2,356	1,997	2,231
34,500	34,550	2,360	2,001	2,235
34,550	34,600	2,364	2,005	2,239
34,600	34,650	2,368	2,009	2,243
34,650	34,700	2,372	2,013	2,247
34,700	34,750	2,376	2,017	2,251
34,750	34,800	2,380	2,021	2,255
34,800	34,850	2,384	2,025	2,259
34,850	34,900	2,388	2,029	2,263
34,900	34,950	2,392	2,033	2,267
34,950	35,000	2,395	2,037	2,271
35,000				
35,000	35,050	2,399	2,041	2,274
35,050	35,100	2,403	2,045	2,278
35,100	35,150	2,407	2,049	2,282
35,150	35,200	2,411	2,053	2,286
35,200	35,250	2,415	2,056	2,290
35,250	35,300	2,419	2,060	2,294
35,300	35,350	2,423	2,064	2,298
35,350	35,400	2,427	2,068	2,302
35,400	35,450	2,431	2,072	2,306
35,450	35,500	2,435	2,076	2,310
35,500	35,550	2,439	2,080	2,314
35,550	35,600	2,443	2,084	2,318
35,600	35,650	2,447	2,088	2,322
35,650	35,700	2,451	2,092	2,326
35,700	35,750	2,455	2,095	2,330
35,750	35,800	2,459	2,100	2,334
35,800	35,850	2,462	2,104	2,337
35,850	35,900	2,465	2,108	2,341
35,900	35,950	2,470	2,112	2,345
35,950	36,000	2,474	2,116	2,349

If line 17 (taxable income) is - At least	But less than	Single or Married filing separately	Married filing jointly *	Head of a house-hold
		Your New York State tax is -		
36,000				
36,000	36,050	2,478	2,119	2,353
36,050	36,100	2,482	2,123	2,357
36,100	36,150	2,486	2,127	2,361
36,150	36,200	2,490	2,131	2,365
36,200	36,250	2,494	2,135	2,369
36,250	36,300	2,498	2,139	2,373
36,300	36,350	2,502	2,143	2,377
36,350	36,400	2,506	2,147	2,381
36,400	36,450	2,510	2,151	2,385
36,450	36,500	2,514	2,155	2,389
36,500	36,550	2,518	2,159	2,393
36,550	36,600	2,522	2,163	2,397
36,600	36,650	2,525	2,167	2,400
36,650	36,700	2,529	2,171	2,404
36,700	36,750	2,533	2,175	2,408
36,750	36,800	2,537	2,179	2,412
36,800	36,850	2,541	2,182	2,416
36,850	36,900	2,545	2,186	2,420
36,900	36,950	2,549	2,190	2,424
36,950	37,000	2,553	2,194	2,428
37,000				
37,000	37,050	2,557	2,198	2,432
37,050	37,100	2,561	2,202	2,436
37,100	37,150	2,565	2,206	2,440
37,150	37,200	2,569	2,210	2,444
37,200	37,250	2,573	2,214	2,448
37,250	37,300	2,577	2,218	2,452
37,300	37,350	2,581	2,222	2,456
37,350	37,400	2,585	2,226	2,460
37,400	37,450	2,588	2,230	2,463
37,450	37,500	2,592	2,234	2,467
37,500	37,550	2,596	2,238	2,471
37,550	37,600	2,600	2,242	2,475
37,600	37,650	2,604	2,245	2,479
37,650	37,700	2,608	2,249	2,483
37,700	37,750	2,612	2,253	2,487
37,750	37,800	2,616	2,257	2,491
37,800	37,850	2,620	2,261	2,495
37,850	37,900	2,624	2,265	2,499
37,900	37,950	2,628	2,269	2,503
37,950	38,000	2,632	2,273	2,507
38,000				
38,000	38,050	2,636	2,277	2,511
38,050	38,100	2,640	2,281	2,515
38,100	38,150	2,644	2,285	2,519
38,150	38,200	2,648	2,289	2,523
38,200	38,250	2,651	2,293	2,526
38,250	38,300	2,655	2,297	2,530
38,300	38,350	2,659	2,301	2,534
38,350	38,400	2,663	2,305	2,538
38,400	38,450	2,667	2,308	2,542
38,450	38,500	2,671	2,312	2,546
38,500	38,550	2,675	2,316	2,550
38,550	38,600	2,679	2,320	2,554
38,600	38,650	2,683	2,324	2,558
38,650	38,700	2,687	2,328	2,562
38,700	38,750	2,691	2,332	2,566
38,750	38,800	2,695	2,336	2,570
38,800	38,850	2,699	2,340	2,574
38,850	38,900	2,703	2,344	2,578
38,900	38,950	2,707	2,348	2,582
38,950	39,000	2,711	2,352	2,586

If line 17 (taxable income) is - At least	But less than	Single or Married filing separately	Married filing jointly *	Head of a house-hold
		Your New York State tax is -		
39,000				
39,000	39,050	2,714	2,356	2,589
39,050	39,100	2,718	2,360	2,593
39,100	39,150	2,722	2,364	2,597
39,150	39,200	2,726	2,368	2,601
39,200	39,250	2,730	2,371	2,605
39,250	39,300	2,734	2,375	2,609
39,300	39,350	2,738	2,379	2,613
39,350	39,400	2,742	2,383	2,617
39,400	39,450	2,746	2,387	2,621
39,450	39,500	2,750	2,391	2,625
39,500	39,550	2,754	2,395	2,629
39,550	39,600	2,758	2,399	2,633
39,600	39,650	2,762	2,403	2,637
39,650	39,700	2,766	2,407	2,641
39,700	39,750	2,770	2,411	2,645
39,750	39,800	2,774	2,415	2,649
39,800	39,850	2,777	2,419	2,652
39,850	39,900	2,781	2,423	2,656
39,900	39,950	2,785	2,427	2,660
39,950	40,000	2,789	2,431	2,664
40,000				
40,000	40,050	2,793	2,434	2,668
40,050	40,100	2,797	2,438	2,672
40,100	40,150	2,801	2,442	2,676
40,150	40,200	2,805	2,446	2,680
40,200	40,250	2,809	2,450	2,684
40,250	40,300	2,813	2,454	2,688
40,300	40,350	2,817	2,458	2,692
40,350	40,400	2,821	2,462	2,696
40,400	40,450	2,825	2,466	2,700
40,450	40,500	2,829	2,470	2,704
40,500	40,550	2,833	2,474	2,708
40,550	40,600	2,837	2,478	2,712
40,600	40,650	2,840	2,482	2,715
40,650	40,700	2,844	2,486	2,719
40,700	40,750	2,848	2,490	2,723
40,750	40,800	2,852	2,494	2,727
40,800	40,850	2,856	2,497	2,731
40,850	40,900	2,860	2,501	2,735
40,900	40,950	2,864	2,505	2,739
40,950	41,000	2,868	2,509	2,743
41,000				
41,000	41,050	2,872	2,513	2,747
41,050	41,100	2,876	2,517	2,751
41,100	41,150	2,880	2,521	2,755
41,150	41,200	2,884	2,525	2,759
41,200	41,250	2,888	2,529	2,763
41,250	41,300	2,892	2,533	2,767
41,300	41,350	2,896	2,537	2,771
41,350	41,400	2,900	2,541	2,775
41,400	41,450	2,903	2,545	2,778
41,450	41,500	2,907	2,549	2,782
41,500	41,550	2,911	2,553	2,786
41,550	41,600	2,915	2,557	2,790
41,600	41,650	2,919	2,560	2,794
41,650	41,700	2,923	2,564	2,798
41,700	41,750	2,927	2,568	2,802
41,750	41,800	2,931	2,572	2,806
41,800	41,850	2,935	2,576	2,810
41,850	41,900	2,939	2,580	2,814
41,900	41,950	2,943	2,584	2,818
41,950	42,000	2,947	2,588	2,822

* This column must also be used by a qualifying widow(er)

Continued on next page

New York State Tax Table

If line 17 (taxable income) is - At least	But less than	Single or Married filing separately	Married filing jointly *	Head of a household	At least	But less than	Single or Married filing separately	Married filing jointly *	Head of a household	At least	But less than	Single or Married filing separately	Married filing jointly *	Head of a household
42,000					**45,000**					**48,000**				
42,000	42,050	2,951	2,592	2,826	45,000	45,050	3,187	2,828	3,062	48,000	48,050	3,423	3,064	3,298
42,050	42,100	2,955	2,596	2,830	45,050	45,100	3,191	2,832	3,066	48,050	48,100	3,427	3,068	3,302
42,100	42,150	2,959	2,600	2,834	45,100	45,150	3,195	2,836	3,070	48,100	48,150	3,431	3,072	3,306
42,150	42,200	2,963	2,604	2,838	45,150	45,200	3,199	2,840	3,074	48,150	48,200	3,435	3,076	3,310
42,200	42,250	2,966	2,608	2,841	45,200	45,250	3,203	2,844	3,078	48,200	48,250	3,439	3,080	3,314
42,250	42,300	2,970	2,612	2,845	45,250	45,300	3,207	2,848	3,082	48,250	48,300	3,443	3,084	3,318
42,300	42,350	2,974	2,616	2,849	45,300	45,350	3,211	2,852	3,086	48,300	48,350	3,447	3,088	3,322
42,350	42,400	2,978	2,620	2,853	45,350	45,400	3,215	2,856	3,090	48,350	48,400	3,451	3,092	3,326
42,400	42,450	2,982	2,623	2,857	45,400	45,450	3,218	2,860	3,093	48,400	48,450	3,455	3,096	3,330
42,450	42,500	2,986	2,627	2,861	45,450	45,500	3,222	2,864	3,097	48,450	48,500	3,459	3,100	3,334
42,500	42,550	2,990	2,631	2,865	45,500	45,550	3,226	2,868	3,101	48,500	48,550	3,463	3,104	3,338
42,550	42,600	2,994	2,635	2,869	45,550	45,600	3,230	2,872	3,105	48,550	48,600	3,467	3,108	3,342
42,600	42,650	2,998	2,639	2,873	45,600	45,650	3,234	2,875	3,109	48,600	48,650	3,470	3,112	3,345
42,650	42,700	3,002	2,643	2,877	45,650	45,700	3,238	2,879	3,113	48,650	48,700	3,474	3,116	3,349
42,700	42,750	3,006	2,647	2,881	45,700	45,750	3,242	2,883	3,117	48,700	48,750	3,478	3,120	3,353
42,750	42,800	3,010	2,651	2,885	45,750	45,800	3,246	2,887	3,121	48,750	48,800	3,482	3,124	3,357
42,800	42,850	3,014	2,655	2,889	45,800	45,850	3,250	2,891	3,125	48,800	48,850	3,486	3,127	3,361
42,850	42,900	3,018	2,659	2,893	45,850	45,900	3,254	2,895	3,129	48,850	48,900	3,490	3,131	3,365
42,900	42,950	3,022	2,663	2,897	45,900	45,950	3,258	2,899	3,133	48,900	48,950	3,494	3,135	3,369
42,950	43,000	3,026	2,667	2,901	45,950	46,000	3,262	2,903	3,137	48,950	49,000	3,498	3,139	3,373
43,000					**46,000**					**49,000**				
43,000	43,050	3,029	2,671	2,904	46,000	46,050	3,266	2,907	3,141	49,000	49,050	3,502	3,143	3,377
43,050	43,100	3,033	2,675	2,908	46,050	46,100	3,270	2,911	3,145	49,050	49,100	3,506	3,147	3,381
43,100	43,150	3,037	2,679	2,912	46,100	46,150	3,274	2,915	3,149	49,100	49,150	3,510	3,151	3,385
43,150	43,200	3,041	2,683	2,916	46,150	46,200	3,278	2,919	3,153	49,150	49,200	3,514	3,155	3,389
43,200	43,250	3,045	2,686	2,920	46,200	46,250	3,281	2,923	3,156	49,200	49,250	3,518	3,159	3,393
43,250	43,300	3,049	2,690	2,924	46,250	46,300	3,285	2,927	3,160	49,250	49,300	3,522	3,163	3,397
43,300	43,350	3,053	2,694	2,928	46,300	46,350	3,289	2,931	3,164	49,300	49,350	3,526	3,167	3,401
43,350	43,400	3,057	2,698	2,932	46,350	46,400	3,293	2,935	3,168	49,350	49,400	3,530	3,171	3,405
43,400	43,450	3,061	2,702	2,936	46,400	46,450	3,297	2,938	3,172	49,400	49,450	3,533	3,175	3,408
43,450	43,500	3,065	2,706	2,940	46,450	46,500	3,301	2,942	3,176	49,450	49,500	3,537	3,179	3,412
43,500	43,550	3,069	2,710	2,944	46,500	46,550	3,305	2,946	3,180	49,500	49,550	3,541	3,183	3,416
43,550	43,600	3,073	2,714	2,948	46,550	46,600	3,309	2,950	3,184	49,550	49,600	3,545	3,187	3,420
43,600	43,650	3,077	2,718	2,952	46,600	46,650	3,313	2,954	3,188	49,600	49,650	3,549	3,190	3,424
43,650	43,700	3,081	2,722	2,956	46,650	46,700	3,317	2,958	3,192	49,650	49,700	3,553	3,194	3,428
43,700	43,750	3,085	2,726	2,960	46,700	46,750	3,321	2,962	3,196	49,700	49,750	3,557	3,198	3,432
43,750	43,800	3,089	2,730	2,964	46,750	46,800	3,325	2,966	3,200	49,750	49,800	3,561	3,202	3,436
43,800	43,850	3,092	2,734	2,967	46,800	46,850	3,329	2,970	3,204	49,800	49,850	3,565	3,206	3,440
43,850	43,900	3,096	2,738	2,971	46,850	46,900	3,333	2,974	3,208	49,850	49,900	3,569	3,210	3,444
43,900	43,950	3,100	2,742	2,975	46,900	46,950	3,337	2,978	3,212	49,900	49,950	3,573	3,214	3,448
43,950	44,000	3,104	2,746	2,979	46,950	47,000	3,341	2,982	3,216	49,950	50,000	3,577	3,218	3,452
44,000					**47,000**					**50,000**				
44,000	44,050	3,108	2,749	2,983	47,000	47,050	3,344	2,986	3,219	50,000	50,050	3,581	3,222	3,456
44,050	44,100	3,112	2,753	2,987	47,050	47,100	3,348	2,990	3,223	50,050	50,100	3,585	3,226	3,460
44,100	44,150	3,116	2,757	2,991	47,100	47,150	3,352	2,994	3,227	50,100	50,150	3,589	3,230	3,464
44,150	44,200	3,120	2,761	2,995	47,150	47,200	3,356	2,998	3,231	50,150	50,200	3,593	3,234	3,468
44,200	44,250	3,124	2,765	2,999	47,200	47,250	3,360	3,001	3,235	50,200	50,250	3,596	3,238	3,471
44,250	44,300	3,128	2,769	3,003	47,250	47,300	3,364	3,005	3,239	50,250	50,300	3,600	3,242	3,475
44,300	44,350	3,132	2,773	3,007	47,300	47,350	3,368	3,009	3,243	50,300	50,350	3,604	3,246	3,479
44,350	44,400	3,136	2,777	3,011	47,350	47,400	3,372	3,013	3,247	50,350	50,400	3,608	3,250	3,483
44,400	44,450	3,140	2,781	3,015	47,400	47,450	3,376	3,017	3,251	50,400	50,450	3,612	3,253	3,487
44,450	44,500	3,144	2,785	3,019	47,450	47,500	3,380	3,021	3,255	50,450	50,500	3,616	3,257	3,491
44,500	44,550	3,148	2,789	3,023	47,500	47,550	3,384	3,025	3,259	50,500	50,550	3,620	3,261	3,495
44,550	44,600	3,152	2,793	3,027	47,550	47,600	3,388	3,029	3,263	50,550	50,600	3,624	3,265	3,499
44,600	44,650	3,155	2,797	3,030	47,600	47,650	3,392	3,033	3,267	50,600	50,650	3,628	3,269	3,503
44,650	44,700	3,159	2,801	3,034	47,650	47,700	3,396	3,037	3,271	50,650	50,700	3,632	3,273	3,507
44,700	44,750	3,163	2,805	3,038	47,700	47,750	3,400	3,041	3,275	50,700	50,750	3,636	3,277	3,511
44,750	44,800	3,167	2,809	3,042	47,750	47,800	3,404	3,045	3,279	50,750	50,800	3,640	3,281	3,515
44,800	44,850	3,171	2,812	3,046	47,800	47,850	3,407	3,049	3,282	50,800	50,850	3,644	3,285	3,519
44,850	44,900	3,175	2,816	3,050	47,850	47,900	3,411	3,053	3,286	50,850	50,900	3,648	3,289	3,523
44,900	44,950	3,179	2,820	3,054	47,900	47,950	3,415	3,057	3,290	50,900	50,950	3,652	3,293	3,527
44,950	45,000	3,183	2,824	3,058	47,950	48,000	3,419	3,061	3,294	50,950	51,000	3,656	3,297	3,531

* This column must also be used by a qualifying widow(er)

Continued on next page

New York State Tax Table

If line 17 (taxable income) is -		And you are -		
At least	But less than	Single or Married filing separately	Married filing jointly *	Head of a household
		Your New York State tax is -		

51,000

At least	But less than	Single or MFS	MFJ	HoH
51,000	51,050	3,659	3,301	3,534
51,050	51,100	3,663	3,305	3,538
51,100	51,150	3,667	3,309	3,542
51,150	51,200	3,671	3,313	3,546
51,200	51,250	3,675	3,316	3,550
51,250	51,300	3,679	3,320	3,554
51,300	51,350	3,683	3,324	3,558
51,350	51,400	3,687	3,328	3,562
51,400	51,450	3,691	3,332	3,566
51,450	51,500	3,695	3,336	3,570
51,500	51,550	3,699	3,340	3,574
51,550	51,600	3,703	3,344	3,578
51,600	51,650	3,707	3,348	3,582
51,650	51,700	3,711	3,352	3,586
51,700	51,750	3,715	3,356	3,590
51,750	51,800	3,719	3,360	3,594
51,800	51,850	3,722	3,364	3,597
51,850	51,900	3,726	3,368	3,601
51,900	51,950	3,730	3,372	3,605
51,950	52,000	3,734	3,376	3,609

52,000

At least	But less than	Single or MFS	MFJ	HoH
52,000	52,050	3,738	3,379	3,613
52,050	52,100	3,742	3,383	3,617
52,100	52,150	3,746	3,387	3,621
52,150	52,200	3,750	3,391	3,625
52,200	52,250	3,754	3,395	3,629
52,250	52,300	3,758	3,399	3,633
52,300	52,350	3,762	3,403	3,637
52,350	52,400	3,766	3,407	3,641
52,400	52,450	3,770	3,411	3,645
52,450	52,500	3,774	3,415	3,649
52,500	52,550	3,778	3,419	3,653
52,550	52,600	3,782	3,423	3,657
52,600	52,650	3,785	3,427	3,660
52,650	52,700	3,789	3,431	3,664
52,700	52,750	3,793	3,435	3,668
52,750	52,800	3,797	3,439	3,672
52,800	52,850	3,801	3,442	3,676
52,850	52,900	3,805	3,446	3,680
52,900	52,950	3,809	3,450	3,684
52,950	53,000	3,813	3,454	3,688

53,000

At least	But less than	Single or MFS	MFJ	HoH
53,000	53,050	3,817	3,458	3,692
53,050	53,100	3,821	3,462	3,696
53,100	53,150	3,825	3,466	3,700
53,150	53,200	3,829	3,470	3,704
53,200	53,250	3,833	3,474	3,708
53,250	53,300	3,837	3,478	3,712
53,300	53,350	3,841	3,482	3,716
53,350	53,400	3,845	3,486	3,720
53,400	53,450	3,848	3,490	3,723
53,450	53,500	3,852	3,494	3,727
53,500	53,550	3,856	3,498	3,731
53,550	53,600	3,860	3,502	3,735
53,600	53,650	3,864	3,505	3,739
53,650	53,700	3,868	3,509	3,743
53,700	53,750	3,872	3,513	3,747
53,750	53,800	3,876	3,517	3,751
53,800	53,850	3,880	3,521	3,755
53,850	53,900	3,884	3,525	3,759
53,900	53,950	3,888	3,529	3,763
53,950	54,000	3,892	3,533	3,767

54,000

At least	But less than	Single or MFS	MFJ	HoH
54,000	54,050	3,896	3,537	3,771
54,050	54,100	3,900	3,541	3,775
54,100	54,150	3,904	3,545	3,779
54,150	54,200	3,908	3,549	3,783
54,200	54,250	3,911	3,553	3,786
54,250	54,300	3,915	3,557	3,790
54,300	54,350	3,919	3,561	3,794
54,350	54,400	3,923	3,565	3,798
54,400	54,450	3,927	3,568	3,802
54,450	54,500	3,931	3,572	3,806
54,500	54,550	3,935	3,576	3,810
54,550	54,600	3,939	3,580	3,814
54,600	54,650	3,943	3,584	3,818
54,650	54,700	3,947	3,588	3,822
54,700	54,750	3,951	3,592	3,826
54,750	54,800	3,955	3,596	3,830
54,800	54,850	3,959	3,600	3,834
54,850	54,900	3,963	3,604	3,838
54,900	54,950	3,967	3,608	3,842
54,950	55,000	3,971	3,612	3,846

55,000

At least	But less than	Single or MFS	MFJ	HoH
55,000	55,050	3,974	3,616	3,849
55,050	55,100	3,978	3,620	3,853
55,100	55,150	3,982	3,624	3,857
55,150	55,200	3,986	3,628	3,861
55,200	55,250	3,990	3,631	3,865
55,250	55,300	3,994	3,635	3,869
55,300	55,350	3,998	3,639	3,873
55,350	55,400	4,002	3,643	3,877
55,400	55,450	4,006	3,647	3,881
55,450	55,500	4,010	3,651	3,885
55,500	55,550	4,014	3,655	3,889
55,550	55,600	4,018	3,659	3,893
55,600	55,650	4,022	3,663	3,897
55,650	55,700	4,026	3,667	3,901
55,700	55,750	4,030	3,671	3,905
55,750	55,800	4,034	3,675	3,909
55,800	55,850	4,037	3,679	3,912
55,850	55,900	4,041	3,683	3,916
55,900	55,950	4,045	3,687	3,920
55,950	56,000	4,049	3,691	3,924

56,000

At least	But less than	Single or MFS	MFJ	HoH
56,000	56,050	4,053	3,694	3,928
56,050	56,100	4,057	3,698	3,932
56,100	56,150	4,061	3,702	3,936
56,150	56,200	4,065	3,706	3,940
56,200	56,250	4,069	3,710	3,944
56,250	56,300	4,073	3,714	3,948
56,300	56,350	4,077	3,718	3,952
56,350	56,400	4,081	3,722	3,956
56,400	56,450	4,085	3,726	3,960
56,450	56,500	4,089	3,730	3,964
56,500	56,550	4,093	3,734	3,968
56,550	56,600	4,097	3,738	3,972
56,600	56,650	4,100	3,742	3,975
56,650	56,700	4,104	3,746	3,979
56,700	56,750	4,108	3,750	3,983
56,750	56,800	4,112	3,754	3,987
56,800	56,850	4,116	3,757	3,991
56,850	56,900	4,120	3,761	3,995
56,900	56,950	4,124	3,765	3,999
56,950	57,000	4,128	3,769	4,003

57,000

At least	But less than	Single or MFS	MFJ	HoH
57,000	57,050	4,132	3,773	4,007
57,050	57,100	4,136	3,777	4,011
57,100	57,150	4,140	3,781	4,015
57,150	57,200	4,144	3,785	4,019
57,200	57,250	4,148	3,789	4,023
57,250	57,300	4,152	3,793	4,027
57,300	57,350	4,156	3,797	4,031
57,350	57,400	4,160	3,801	4,035
57,400	57,450	4,163	3,805	4,038
57,450	57,500	4,167	3,809	4,042
57,500	57,550	4,171	3,813	4,046
57,550	57,600	4,175	3,817	4,050
57,600	57,650	4,179	3,820	4,054
57,650	57,700	4,183	3,824	4,058
57,700	57,750	4,187	3,828	4,062
57,750	57,800	4,191	3,832	4,066
57,800	57,850	4,195	3,836	4,070
57,850	57,900	4,199	3,840	4,074
57,900	57,950	4,203	3,844	4,078
57,950	58,000	4,207	3,848	4,082

58,000

At least	But less than	Single or MFS	MFJ	HoH
58,000	58,050	4,211	3,852	4,086
58,050	58,100	4,215	3,856	4,090
58,100	58,150	4,219	3,860	4,094
58,150	58,200	4,223	3,864	4,098
58,200	58,250	4,226	3,868	4,101
58,250	58,300	4,230	3,872	4,105
58,300	58,350	4,234	3,876	4,109
58,350	58,400	4,238	3,880	4,113
58,400	58,450	4,242	3,883	4,117
58,450	58,500	4,246	3,887	4,121
58,500	58,550	4,250	3,891	4,125
58,550	58,600	4,254	3,895	4,129
58,600	58,650	4,258	3,899	4,133
58,650	58,700	4,262	3,903	4,137
58,700	58,750	4,266	3,907	4,141
58,750	58,800	4,270	3,911	4,145
58,800	58,850	4,274	3,915	4,149
58,850	58,900	4,278	3,919	4,153
58,900	58,950	4,282	3,923	4,157
58,950	59,000	4,286	3,927	4,161

59,000

At least	But less than	Single or MFS	MFJ	HoH
59,000	59,050	4,289	3,931	4,164
59,050	59,100	4,293	3,935	4,168
59,100	59,150	4,297	3,939	4,172
59,150	59,200	4,301	3,943	4,176
59,200	59,250	4,305	3,946	4,180
59,250	59,300	4,309	3,950	4,184
59,300	59,350	4,313	3,954	4,188
59,350	59,400	4,317	3,958	4,192
59,400	59,450	4,321	3,962	4,196
59,450	59,500	4,325	3,966	4,200
59,500	59,550	4,329	3,970	4,204
59,550	59,600	4,333	3,974	4,208
59,600	59,650	4,337	3,978	4,212
59,650	59,700	4,341	3,982	4,216
59,700	59,750	4,345	3,986	4,220
59,750	59,800	4,349	3,990	4,224
59,800	59,850	4,352	3,994	4,227
59,850	59,900	4,356	3,998	4,231
59,900	59,950	4,360	4,002	4,235
59,950	60,000	4,364	4,005	4,239

* This column must also be used by a qualifying widow(er)

Continued on next page

New York State Tax Table

If line 17 (taxable income) is - At least	But less than	And you are - Single or Married filing separately	Married filing jointly *	Head of a household
		Your New York State tax is -		

60,000

At least	But less than	Single or Married filing separately	Married filing jointly *	Head of a household
60,000	60,050	4,368	4,009	4,243
60,050	60,100	4,372	4,013	4,247
60,100	60,150	4,376	4,017	4,251
60,150	60,200	4,380	4,021	4,255
60,200	60,250	4,384	4,025	4,259
60,250	60,300	4,388	4,029	4,263
60,300	60,350	4,392	4,033	4,267
60,350	60,400	4,396	4,037	4,271
60,400	60,450	4,400	4,041	4,275
60,450	60,500	4,404	4,045	4,279
60,500	60,550	4,408	4,049	4,283
60,550	60,600	4,412	4,053	4,287
60,600	60,650	4,415	4,057	4,290
60,650	60,700	4,419	4,061	4,294
60,700	60,750	4,423	4,065	4,298
60,750	60,800	4,427	4,069	4,302
60,800	60,850	4,431	4,072	4,306
60,850	60,900	4,435	4,076	4,310
60,900	60,950	4,439	4,080	4,314
60,950	61,000	4,443	4,084	4,318

61,000

At least	But less than	Single or Married filing separately	Married filing jointly *	Head of a household
61,000	61,050	4,447	4,088	4,322
61,050	61,100	4,451	4,092	4,326
61,100	61,150	4,455	4,096	4,330
61,150	61,200	4,459	4,100	4,334
61,200	61,250	4,463	4,104	4,338
61,250	61,300	4,467	4,108	4,342
61,300	61,350	4,471	4,112	4,346
61,350	61,400	4,475	4,116	4,350
61,400	61,450	4,478	4,120	4,353
61,450	61,500	4,482	4,124	4,357
61,500	61,550	4,486	4,128	4,361
61,550	61,600	4,490	4,132	4,365
61,600	61,650	4,494	4,135	4,369
61,650	61,700	4,498	4,139	4,373
61,700	61,750	4,502	4,143	4,377
61,750	61,800	4,506	4,147	4,381
61,800	61,850	4,510	4,151	4,385
61,850	61,900	4,514	4,155	4,389
61,900	61,950	4,518	4,159	4,393
61,950	62,000	4,522	4,163	4,397

62,000

At least	But less than	Single or Married filing separately	Married filing jointly *	Head of a household
62,000	62,050	4,526	4,167	4,401
62,050	62,100	4,530	4,171	4,405
62,100	62,150	4,534	4,175	4,409
62,150	62,200	4,538	4,179	4,413
62,200	62,250	4,541	4,183	4,416
62,250	62,300	4,545	4,187	4,420
62,300	62,350	4,549	4,191	4,424
62,350	62,400	4,553	4,195	4,428
62,400	62,450	4,557	4,198	4,432
62,450	62,500	4,561	4,202	4,436
62,500	62,550	4,565	4,206	4,440
62,550	62,600	4,569	4,210	4,444
62,600	62,650	4,573	4,214	4,448
62,650	62,700	4,577	4,218	4,452
62,700	62,750	4,581	4,222	4,456
62,750	62,800	4,585	4,226	4,460
62,800	62,850	4,589	4,230	4,464
62,850	62,900	4,593	4,234	4,468
62,900	62,950	4,597	4,238	4,472
62,950	63,000	4,601	4,242	4,476

63,000

At least	But less than	Single or Married filing separately	Married filing jointly *	Head of a household
63,000	63,050	4,604	4,246	4,479
63,050	63,100	4,608	4,250	4,483
63,100	63,150	4,612	4,254	4,487
63,150	63,200	4,616	4,258	4,491
63,200	63,250	4,620	4,261	4,495
63,250	63,300	4,624	4,265	4,499
63,300	63,350	4,628	4,269	4,503
63,350	63,400	4,632	4,273	4,507
63,400	63,450	4,636	4,277	4,511
63,450	63,500	4,640	4,281	4,515
63,500	63,550	4,644	4,285	4,519
63,550	63,600	4,648	4,289	4,523
63,600	63,650	4,652	4,293	4,527
63,650	63,700	4,656	4,297	4,531
63,700	63,750	4,660	4,301	4,535
63,750	63,800	4,664	4,305	4,539
63,800	63,850	4,667	4,309	4,542
63,850	63,900	4,671	4,313	4,546
63,900	63,950	4,675	4,317	4,550
63,950	64,000	4,679	4,321	4,554

64,000

At least	But less than	Single or Married filing separately	Married filing jointly *	Head of a household
64,000	64,050	4,683	4,324	4,558
64,050	64,100	4,687	4,328	4,562
64,100	64,150	4,691	4,332	4,566
64,150	64,200	4,695	4,336	4,570
64,200	64,250	4,699	4,340	4,574
64,250	64,300	4,703	4,344	4,578
64,300	64,350	4,707	4,348	4,582
64,350	64,400	4,711	4,352	4,586
64,400	64,450	4,715	4,356	4,590
64,450	64,500	4,719	4,360	4,594
64,500	64,550	4,723	4,364	4,598
64,550	64,600	4,727	4,368	4,602
64,600	64,650	4,730	4,372	4,605
64,650	64,700	4,734	4,376	4,609
64,700	64,750	4,738	4,380	4,613
64,750	64,800	4,742	4,384	4,617
64,800	64,850	4,746	4,387	4,621
64,850	64,900	4,750	4,391	4,625
64,900	64,950	4,754	4,395	4,629
64,950	65,000	4,758	4,399	4,633

65,000 or more use Form IT-201

* This column must also be used by a qualifying widow(er)

Look For This Line

Return a Gift to Wildlife

MARIO M. CUOMO, Governor
THOMAS C. JORLING, Commissioner

If you want to Return a Gift to Wildlife, enter amount: $5, $10, $20, other

1992 City of New York Tax Table

For persons with taxable income of less than $65,000.

Example: Mr. and Mrs. Allen are filing a joint return. Their taxable income on line 17 of Form IT-200 is $36,275. First, they find the 36,250 - 36,300 income line. Next, they find the column for married filing jointly and read down the column. The amount shown where the income line and filing status column meet is $1,213. This is the tax amount they must write on line 23 of Form IT-200.

At least	But less than	Single or Married filing separately	Married filing jointly *	Head of a house-hold
		Your City of New York tax is -		
36,200	36,250	1,373	1,211	1,358
36,250	36,300	1,375	1,213	1,360
36,300	36,350	1,377	1,215	1,362
36,350	36,400	1,380	1,217	1,365

If line 17 (taxable income) is - At least	But less than	And you are - Single or Married filing separately	Married filing jointly *	Head of a house-hold	If line 17 (taxable income) is - At least	But less than	And you are - Single or Married filing separately	Married filing jointly *	Head of a house-hold	If line 17 (taxable income) is - At least	But less than	And you are - Single or Married filing separately	Married filing jointly *	Head of a house-hold
		Your City of New York tax is -					Your City of New York tax is -					Your City of New York tax is -		
$ 0	$ 25	$ 0	$ 0	$ 0	**2,000**					**4,000**				
25	50	1	1	1	2,000	2,050	51	51	51	4,000	4,050	101	101	101
50	100	2	2	2	2,050	2,100	52	52	52	4,050	4,100	102	102	102
100	150	3	3	3	2,100	2,150	53	53	53	4,100	4,150	104	104	104
150	200	4	4	4	2,150	2,200	55	55	55	4,150	4,200	105	105	105
200	250	6	6	6	2,200	2,250	56	56	56	4,200	4,250	106	106	106
250	300	7	7	7	2,250	2,300	57	57	57	4,250	4,300	107	107	107
300	350	8	8	8	2,300	2,350	58	58	58	4,300	4,350	109	109	109
350	400	9	9	9	2,350	2,400	60	60	60	4,350	4,400	110	110	110
400	450	11	11	11	2,400	2,450	61	61	61	4,400	4,450	111	111	111
450	500	12	12	12	2,450	2,500	62	62	62	4,450	4,500	112	112	112
500	550	13	13	13	2,500	2,550	63	63	63	4,500	4,550	114	114	114
550	600	14	14	14	2,550	2,600	65	65	65	4,550	4,600	115	115	115
600	650	16	16	16	2,600	2,650	66	66	66	4,600	4,650	116	116	116
650	700	17	17	17	2,650	2,700	67	67	67	4,650	4,700	117	117	117
700	750	18	18	18	2,700	2,750	68	68	68	4,700	4,750	119	119	119
750	800	19	19	19	2,750	2,800	70	70	70	4,750	4,800	120	120	120
800	850	21	21	21	2,800	2,850	71	71	71	4,800	4,850	121	121	121
850	900	22	22	22	2,850	2,900	72	72	72	4,850	4,900	122	122	122
900	950	23	23	23	2,900	2,950	73	73	73	4,900	4,950	124	124	124
950	1,000	24	24	24	2,950	3,000	75	75	75	4,950	5,000	125	125	125
1,000					**3,000**					**5,000**				
1,000	1,050	26	26	26	3,000	3,050	76	76	76	5,000	5,050	126	126	126
1,050	1,100	27	27	27	3,050	3,100	77	77	77	5,050	5,100	127	127	127
1,100	1,150	28	28	28	3,100	3,150	78	78	78	5,100	5,150	129	129	129
1,150	1,200	29	29	29	3,150	3,200	80	80	80	5,150	5,200	130	130	130
1,200	1,250	31	31	31	3,200	3,250	81	81	81	5,200	5,250	131	131	131
1,250	1,300	32	32	32	3,250	3,300	82	82	82	5,250	5,300	132	132	132
1,300	1,350	33	33	33	3,300	3,350	83	83	83	5,300	5,350	134	134	134
1,350	1,400	35	35	35	3,350	3,400	85	85	85	5,350	5,400	135	135	135
1,400	1,450	36	36	36	3,400	3,450	86	86	86	5,400	5,450	136	136	136
1,450	1,500	37	37	37	3,450	3,500	87	87	87	5,450	5,500	137	137	137
1,500	1,550	38	38	38	3,500	3,550	88	88	88	5,500	5,550	139	139	139
1,550	1,600	40	40	40	3,550	3,600	90	90	90	5,550	5,600	140	140	140
1,600	1,650	41	41	41	3,600	3,650	91	91	91	5,600	5,650	141	141	141
1,650	1,700	42	42	42	3,650	3,700	92	92	92	5,650	5,700	142	142	142
1,700	1,750	43	43	43	3,700	3,750	93	93	93	5,700	5,750	144	144	144
1,750	1,800	45	45	45	3,750	3,800	95	95	95	5,750	5,800	145	145	145
1,800	1,850	46	46	46	3,800	3,850	96	96	96	5,800	5,850	146	146	146
1,850	1,900	47	47	47	3,850	3,900	97	97	97	5,850	5,900	147	147	147
1,900	1,950	48	48	48	3,900	3,950	99	99	99	5,900	5,950	149	149	149
1,950	2,000	50	50	50	3,950	4,000	100	100	100	5,950	6,000	150	150	150

* This column must also be used by a qualifying widow(er)

Continued on next page

City of New York Tax Table

If line 17 (taxable income) is — At least	But less than	Single or Married filing separately	Married filing jointly *	Head of a household
6,000				
6,000	6,050	151	151	151
6,050	6,100	152	152	152
6,100	6,150	154	154	154
6,150	6,200	155	155	155
6,200	6,250	156	156	156
6,250	6,300	158	158	158
6,300	6,350	159	159	159
6,350	6,400	160	160	160
6,400	6,450	161	161	161
6,450	6,500	163	163	163
6,500	6,550	164	164	164
6,550	6,600	165	165	165
6,600	6,650	166	166	166
6,650	6,700	168	168	168
6,700	6,750	169	169	169
6,750	6,800	170	170	170
6,800	6,850	171	171	171
6,850	6,900	173	173	173
6,900	6,950	174	174	174
6,950	7,000	175	175	175
7,000				
7,000	7,050	176	176	176
7,050	7,100	178	178	178
7,100	7,150	179	179	179
7,150	7,200	180	180	180
7,200	7,250	181	181	181
7,250	7,300	183	183	183
7,300	7,350	184	184	184
7,350	7,400	185	185	185
7,400	7,450	186	186	186
7,450	7,500	188	188	188
7,500	7,550	189	189	189
7,550	7,600	190	190	190
7,600	7,650	191	191	191
7,650	7,700	193	193	193
7,700	7,750	194	194	194
7,750	7,800	195	195	195
7,800	7,850	196	195	196
7,850	7,900	198	198	198
7,900	7,950	199	199	199
7,950	8,000	200	200	200
8,000				
8,000	8,050	202	201	201
8,050	8,100	203	203	203
8,100	8,150	205	204	204
8,150	8,200	206	205	205
8,200	8,250	208	206	206
8,250	8,300	209	208	208
8,300	8,350	211	209	209
8,350	8,400	213	210	210
8,400	8,450	214	211	211
8,450	8,500	216	213	213
8,500	8,550	217	214	214
8,550	8,600	219	215	215
8,600	8,650	220	216	216
8,650	8,700	222	218	218
8,700	8,750	223	219	219
8,750	8,800	225	220	220
8,800	8,850	226	222	222
8,850	8,900	228	223	224
8,900	8,950	229	224	226
8,950	9,000	231	225	227

If line 17 (taxable income) is — At least	But less than	Single or Married filing separately	Married filing jointly *	Head of a household
9,000				
9,000	9,050	233	227	229
9,050	9,100	235	228	231
9,100	9,150	237	229	233
9,150	9,200	238	230	235
9,200	9,250	240	232	237
9,250	9,300	242	233	238
9,300	9,350	244	234	240
9,350	9,400	246	235	242
9,400	9,450	248	237	244
9,450	9,500	249	238	246
9,500	9,550	251	239	248
9,550	9,600	253	240	249
9,600	9,650	255	242	251
9,650	9,700	257	243	253
9,700	9,750	259	244	255
9,750	9,800	260	245	257
9,800	9,850	262	247	259
9,850	9,900	264	248	260
9,900	9,950	266	249	262
9,950	10,000	268	250	264
10,000				
10,000	10,050	270	252	266
10,050	10,100	271	253	268
10,100	10,150	273	254	269
10,150	10,200	275	255	271
10,200	10,250	277	257	273
10,250	10,300	279	258	275
10,300	10,350	280	259	277
10,350	10,400	282	260	279
10,400	10,450	284	262	280
10,450	10,500	286	263	282
10,500	10,550	288	264	284
10,550	10,600	290	265	286
10,600	10,650	291	267	288
10,650	10,700	293	268	290
10,700	10,750	295	269	291
10,750	10,800	297	270	293
10,800	10,850	299	272	295
10,850	10,900	301	273	297
10,900	10,950	302	274	299
10,950	11,000	304	275	301
11,000				
11,000	11,050	306	277	302
11,050	11,100	308	278	304
11,100	11,150	310	279	306
11,150	11,200	312	280	308
11,200	11,250	313	282	310
11,250	11,300	315	283	312
11,300	11,350	317	284	313
11,350	11,400	319	286	315
11,400	11,450	321	287	317
11,450	11,500	323	288	319
11,500	11,550	324	289	321
11,550	11,600	326	291	323
11,600	11,650	328	292	324
11,650	11,700	330	293	326
11,700	11,750	332	294	328
11,750	11,800	334	296	330
11,800	11,850	335	297	332
11,850	11,900	337	298	334
11,900	11,950	339	299	335
11,950	12,000	341	301	337

If line 17 (taxable income) is — At least	But less than	Single or Married filing separately	Married filing jointly *	Head of a household
12,000				
12,000	12,050	343	302	339
12,050	12,100	345	303	341
12,100	12,150	346	304	343
12,150	12,200	348	306	345
12,200	12,250	350	307	346
12,250	12,300	352	308	348
12,300	12,350	354	309	350
12,350	12,400	356	311	352
12,400	12,450	357	312	354
12,450	12,500	359	313	356
12,500	12,550	361	314	357
12,550	12,600	363	316	359
12,600	12,650	365	317	361
12,650	12,700	367	318	363
12,700	12,750	368	319	365
12,750	12,800	370	321	366
12,800	12,850	372	322	368
12,850	12,900	374	323	370
12,900	12,950	376	324	372
12,950	13,000	377	326	374
13,000				
13,000	13,050	379	327	376
13,050	13,100	381	328	377
13,100	13,150	383	329	379
13,150	13,200	385	331	381
13,200	13,250	387	332	383
13,250	13,300	388	333	385
13,300	13,350	390	334	387
13,350	13,400	392	336	388
13,400	13,450	394	337	390
13,450	13,500	396	338	392
13,500	13,550	398	339	394
13,550	13,600	399	341	396
13,600	13,650	401	342	398
13,650	13,700	403	343	399
13,700	13,750	405	344	401
13,750	13,800	407	346	403
13,800	13,850	409	347	405
13,850	13,900	410	348	407
13,900	13,950	412	350	409
13,950	14,000	414	351	410
14,000				
14,000	14,050	416	352	412
14,050	14,100	418	353	414
14,100	14,150	420	355	416
14,150	14,200	421	356	418
14,200	14,250	423	357	420
14,250	14,300	425	358	421
14,300	14,350	427	360	423
14,350	14,400	429	361	425
14,400	14,450	431	362	427
14,450	14,500	432	363	429
14,500	14,550	434	365	431
14,550	14,600	436	366	432
14,600	14,650	438	368	434
14,650	14,700	440	369	436
14,700	14,750	442	371	438
14,750	14,800	443	373	440
14,800	14,850	445	374	442
14,850	14,900	447	376	443
14,900	14,950	449	377	445
14,950	15,000	451	379	447

City of New York Tax Table

If line 17 (taxable income) is -		And you are -			If line 17 (taxable income) is -		And you are -			If line 17 (taxable income) is -		And you are -		
At least	But less than	Single or Married filing separately	Married filing jointly *	Head of a household	At least	But less than	Single or Married filing separately	Married filing jointly *	Head of a household	At least	But less than	Single or Married filing separately	Married filing jointly *	Head of a household
		Your City of New York tax is -					Your City of New York tax is -					Your City of New York tax is -		
15,000					18,000					21,000				
15,000	15,050	452	380	449	18,000	18,050	580	487	568	21,000	21,050	709	597	697
15,050	15,100	454	382	451	18,050	18,100	583	489	570	21,050	21,100	711	599	699
15,100	15,150	456	383	452	18,100	18,150	585	491	573	21,100	21,150	713	601	701
15,150	15,200	458	385	454	18,150	18,200	587	493	575	21,150	21,200	715	603	703
15,200	15,250	461	386	456	18,200	18,250	589	495	577	21,200	21,250	717	605	705
15,250	15,300	463	388	458	18,250	18,300	591	497	579	21,250	21,300	720	606	707
15,300	15,350	465	389	460	18,300	18,350	593	498	581	21,300	21,350	722	608	710
15,350	15,400	467	391	462	18,350	18,400	595	500	583	21,350	21,400	724	610	712
15,400	15,450	469	393	463	18,400	18,450	598	502	585	21,400	21,450	726	612	714
15,450	15,500	471	394	465	18,450	18,500	600	504	588	21,450	21,500	728	614	716
15,500	15,550	473	396	467	18,500	18,550	602	506	590	21,500	21,550	730	616	718
15,550	15,600	476	398	469	18,550	18,600	604	508	592	21,550	21,600	732	617	720
15,600	15,650	478	400	471	18,600	18,650	606	509	594	21,600	21,650	735	619	722
15,650	15,700	480	401	473	18,650	18,700	608	511	596	21,650	21,700	737	621	724
15,700	15,750	482	403	474	18,700	18,750	610	513	598	21,700	21,750	739	623	727
15,750	15,800	484	405	476	18,750	18,800	613	515	600	21,750	21,800	741	625	729
15,800	15,850	486	407	478	18,800	18,850	615	517	603	21,800	21,850	743	626	731
15,850	15,900	488	409	480	18,850	18,900	617	519	605	21,850	21,900	745	628	733
15,900	15,950	491	411	482	18,900	18,950	619	520	607	21,900	21,950	747	630	735
15,950	16,000	493	412	484	18,950	19,000	621	522	609	21,950	22,000	750	632	737
16,000					19,000					22,000				
16,000	16,050	495	414	485	19,000	19,050	623	524	611	22,000	22,050	752	634	739
16,050	16,100	497	416	487	19,050	19,100	625	526	613	22,050	22,100	754	636	742
16,100	16,150	499	418	489	19,100	19,150	628	528	615	22,100	22,150	756	637	744
16,150	16,200	501	420	491	19,150	19,200	630	530	617	22,150	22,200	758	639	746
16,200	16,250	503	422	493	19,200	19,250	632	531	620	22,200	22,250	760	641	748
16,250	16,300	506	423	495	19,250	19,300	634	533	622	22,250	22,300	762	643	750
16,300	16,350	508	425	496	19,300	19,350	636	535	624	22,300	22,350	765	645	752
16,350	16,400	510	427	498	19,350	19,400	638	537	626	22,350	22,400	767	647	754
16,400	16,450	512	429	500	19,400	19,450	640	539	628	22,400	22,450	769	648	757
16,450	16,500	514	431	502	19,450	19,500	643	540	630	22,450	22,500	771	650	759
16,500	16,550	516	433	504	19,500	19,550	645	542	632	22,500	22,550	773	652	761
16,550	16,600	518	434	506	19,550	19,600	647	544	635	22,550	22,600	775	654	763
16,600	16,650	521	436	508	19,600	19,650	649	546	637	22,600	22,650	777	656	765
16,650	16,700	523	438	510	19,650	19,700	651	548	639	22,650	22,700	779	658	767
16,700	16,750	525	440	513	19,700	19,750	653	550	641	22,700	22,750	782	659	769
16,750	16,800	527	442	515	19,750	19,800	655	551	643	22,750	22,800	784	661	772
16,800	16,850	529	443	517	19,800	19,850	658	553	645	22,800	22,850	786	663	774
16,850	16,900	531	445	519	19,850	19,900	660	555	647	22,850	22,900	788	665	776
16,900	16,950	533	447	521	19,900	19,950	662	557	650	22,900	22,950	790	667	778
16,950	17,000	536	449	523	19,950	20,000	664	559	652	22,950	23,000	792	669	780
17,000					20,000					23,000				
17,000	17,050	538	451	525	20,000	20,050	666	561	654	23,000	23,050	794	670	782
17,050	17,100	540	453	528	20,050	20,100	668	562	656	23,050	23,100	797	672	784
17,100	17,150	542	454	530	20,100	20,150	670	564	658	23,100	23,150	799	674	787
17,150	17,200	544	456	532	20,150	20,200	672	566	660	23,150	23,200	801	676	789
17,200	17,250	546	458	534	20,200	20,250	675	568	662	23,200	23,250	803	678	791
17,250	17,300	548	460	536	20,250	20,300	677	570	665	23,250	23,300	805	680	793
17,300	17,350	551	462	538	20,300	20,350	679	572	667	23,300	23,350	807	681	795
17,350	17,400	553	464	540	20,350	20,400	681	573	669	23,350	23,400	809	683	797
17,400	17,450	555	465	543	20,400	20,450	683	575	671	23,400	23,450	812	685	799
17,450	17,500	557	467	545	20,450	20,500	685	577	673	23,450	23,500	814	687	802
17,500	17,550	559	469	547	20,500	20,550	687	579	675	23,500	23,550	816	689	804
17,550	17,600	561	471	549	20,550	20,600	690	581	677	23,550	23,600	818	691	806
17,600	17,650	563	473	551	20,600	20,650	692	583	680	23,600	23,650	820	692	808
17,650	17,700	565	475	553	20,650	20,700	694	584	682	23,650	23,700	822	694	810
17,700	17,750	568	476	555	20,700	20,750	696	586	684	23,700	23,750	824	696	812
17,750	17,800	570	478	558	20,750	20,800	698	588	686	23,750	23,800	827	698	814
17,800	17,850	572	480	560	20,800	20,850	700	590	688	23,800	23,850	829	700	817
17,850	17,900	574	482	562	20,850	20,900	702	592	690	23,850	23,900	831	702	819
17,900	17,950	576	484	564	20,900	20,950	705	594	692	23,900	23,950	833	703	821
17,950	18,000	578	486	566	20,950	21,000	707	595	695	23,950	24,000	835	705	823

* This column must also be used by a qualifying widow(er)

Continued on next page

City of New York Tax Table

Continued on next page

If line 17 (taxable income) is —		And you are —		
At least	But less than	Single or Married filing separately	Married filing jointly *	Head of a household
		Your City of New York tax is —		

24,000

At least	But less than	Single/Married sep	Married jointly	Head of household
24,000	24,050	837	707	825
24,050	24,100	839	709	827
24,100	24,150	842	711	829
24,150	24,200	844	713	831
24,200	24,250	846	714	834
24,250	24,300	848	716	836
24,300	24,350	850	718	838
24,350	24,400	852	720	840
24,400	24,450	854	722	842
24,450	24,500	857	723	844
24,500	24,550	859	725	846
24,550	24,600	861	727	849
24,600	24,650	863	729	851
24,650	24,700	865	731	853
24,700	24,750	867	733	855
24,750	24,800	869	734	857
24,800	24,850	872	736	859
24,850	24,900	874	738	861
24,900	24,950	876	740	864
24,950	25,000	878	742	866

25,000

At least	But less than	Single/Married sep	Married jointly	Head of household
25,000	25,050	880	744	868
25,050	25,100	882	745	870
25,100	25,150	885	747	872
25,150	25,200	887	749	874
25,200	25,250	889	751	876
25,250	25,300	891	753	879
25,300	25,350	893	755	881
25,350	25,400	896	756	883
25,400	25,450	898	758	885
25,450	25,500	900	760	887
25,500	25,550	902	762	889
25,550	25,600	904	764	891
25,600	25,650	907	766	894
25,650	25,700	909	767	896
25,700	25,750	911	769	898
25,750	25,800	913	771	900
25,800	25,850	915	773	902
25,850	25,900	918	775	904
25,900	25,950	920	777	906
25,950	26,000	922	778	909

26,000

At least	But less than	Single/Married sep	Married jointly	Head of household
26,000	26,050	924	780	911
26,050	26,100	926	782	913
26,100	26,150	929	784	915
26,150	26,200	931	786	917
26,200	26,250	933	788	919
26,250	26,300	935	789	921
26,300	26,350	937	791	924
26,350	26,400	940	793	926
26,400	26,450	942	795	928
26,450	26,500	944	797	930
26,500	26,550	946	799	932
26,550	26,600	948	800	934
26,600	26,650	951	802	936
26,650	26,700	953	804	938
26,700	26,750	955	806	941
26,750	26,800	957	808	943
26,800	26,850	959	809	945
26,850	26,900	962	811	947
26,900	26,950	964	813	949
26,950	27,000	966	815	951

27,000

At least	But less than	Single/Married sep	Married jointly	Head of household
27,000	27,050	968	817	953
27,050	27,100	970	819	956
27,100	27,150	973	821	958
27,150	27,200	975	823	960
27,200	27,250	977	826	962
27,250	27,300	979	828	964
27,300	27,350	981	830	966
27,350	27,400	984	832	968
27,400	27,450	986	834	971
27,450	27,500	988	836	973
27,500	27,550	990	838	975
27,550	27,600	992	841	977
27,600	27,650	995	843	980
27,650	27,700	997	845	982
27,700	27,750	999	847	984
27,750	27,800	1,001	849	986
27,800	27,850	1,003	851	988
27,850	27,900	1,006	853	991
27,900	27,950	1,008	856	993
27,950	28,000	1,010	858	995

28,000

At least	But less than	Single/Married sep	Married jointly	Head of household
28,000	28,050	1,012	860	997
28,050	28,100	1,014	862	999
28,100	28,150	1,017	864	1,002
28,150	28,200	1,019	866	1,004
28,200	28,250	1,021	868	1,006
28,250	28,300	1,023	871	1,008
28,300	28,350	1,025	873	1,010
28,350	28,400	1,028	875	1,013
28,400	28,450	1,030	877	1,015
28,450	28,500	1,032	879	1,017
28,500	28,550	1,034	881	1,019
28,550	28,600	1,036	883	1,021
28,600	28,650	1,039	886	1,024
28,650	28,700	1,041	888	1,026
28,700	28,750	1,043	890	1,028
28,750	28,800	1,045	892	1,030
28,800	28,850	1,047	894	1,032
28,850	28,900	1,050	896	1,035
28,900	28,950	1,052	898	1,037
28,950	29,000	1,054	901	1,039

29,000

At least	But less than	Single/Married sep	Married jointly	Head of household
29,000	29,050	1,056	903	1,041
29,050	29,100	1,058	905	1,043
29,100	29,150	1,061	907	1,046
29,150	29,200	1,063	909	1,048
29,200	29,250	1,065	911	1,050
29,250	29,300	1,067	913	1,052
29,300	29,350	1,069	916	1,054
29,350	29,400	1,072	918	1,057
29,400	29,450	1,074	920	1,059
29,450	29,500	1,076	922	1,061
29,500	29,550	1,078	924	1,063
29,550	29,600	1,080	926	1,065
29,600	29,650	1,083	928	1,068
29,650	29,700	1,085	930	1,070
29,700	29,750	1,087	933	1,072
29,750	29,800	1,089	935	1,074
29,800	29,850	1,091	937	1,076
29,850	29,900	1,094	939	1,079
29,900	29,950	1,096	941	1,081
29,950	30,000	1,098	943	1,083

30,000

At least	But less than	Single/Married sep	Married jointly	Head of household
30,000	30,050	1,100	945	1,085
30,050	30,100	1,102	948	1,087
30,100	30,150	1,105	950	1,090
30,150	30,200	1,107	952	1,092
30,200	30,250	1,109	954	1,094
30,250	30,300	1,111	956	1,096
30,300	30,350	1,113	958	1,098
30,350	30,400	1,116	960	1,101
30,400	30,450	1,118	963	1,103
30,450	30,500	1,120	965	1,105
30,500	30,550	1,122	967	1,107
30,550	30,600	1,124	969	1,109
30,600	30,650	1,127	971	1,112
30,650	30,700	1,129	973	1,114
30,700	30,750	1,131	975	1,116
30,750	30,800	1,133	978	1,118
30,800	30,850	1,135	980	1,120
30,850	30,900	1,138	982	1,123
30,900	30,950	1,140	984	1,125
30,950	31,000	1,142	986	1,127

31,000

At least	But less than	Single/Married sep	Married jointly	Head of household
31,000	31,050	1,144	988	1,129
31,050	31,100	1,146	990	1,131
31,100	31,150	1,149	993	1,134
31,150	31,200	1,151	995	1,136
31,200	31,250	1,153	997	1,138
31,250	31,300	1,155	999	1,140
31,300	31,350	1,157	1,001	1,142
31,350	31,400	1,160	1,003	1,145
31,400	31,450	1,162	1,005	1,147
31,450	31,500	1,164	1,008	1,149
31,500	31,550	1,166	1,010	1,151
31,550	31,600	1,168	1,012	1,153
31,600	31,650	1,171	1,014	1,156
31,650	31,700	1,173	1,016	1,158
31,700	31,750	1,175	1,018	1,160
31,750	31,800	1,177	1,020	1,162
31,800	31,850	1,179	1,023	1,164
31,850	31,900	1,182	1,025	1,167
31,900	31,950	1,184	1,027	1,169
31,950	32,000	1,186	1,029	1,171

32,000

At least	But less than	Single/Married sep	Married jointly	Head of household
32,000	32,050	1,188	1,031	1,173
32,050	32,100	1,190	1,033	1,175
32,100	32,150	1,193	1,035	1,178
32,150	32,200	1,195	1,037	1,180
32,200	32,250	1,197	1,040	1,182
32,250	32,300	1,199	1,042	1,184
32,300	32,350	1,201	1,044	1,186
32,350	32,400	1,204	1,046	1,189
32,400	32,450	1,206	1,048	1,191
32,450	32,500	1,208	1,050	1,193
32,500	32,550	1,210	1,052	1,195
32,550	32,600	1,212	1,055	1,197
32,600	32,650	1,215	1,057	1,200
32,650	32,700	1,217	1,059	1,202
32,700	32,750	1,219	1,061	1,204
32,750	32,800	1,221	1,063	1,206
32,800	32,850	1,223	1,065	1,208
32,850	32,900	1,226	1,067	1,211
32,900	32,950	1,228	1,070	1,213
32,950	33,000	1,230	1,072	1,215

* This column must also be used by a qualifying widow(er)

City of New York Tax Table

If line 17 (taxable income) is -		And you are -		
At least	But less than	Single or Married filing separately	Married filing jointly *	Head of a household
		Your City of New York tax is -		

33,000

At least	But less than	Single or Married filing separately	Married filing jointly	Head of a household
33,000	33,050	1,232	1,074	1,217
33,050	33,100	1,234	1,076	1,219
33,100	33,150	1,237	1,078	1,222
33,150	33,200	1,239	1,080	1,224
33,200	33,250	1,241	1,082	1,226
33,250	33,300	1,243	1,085	1,228
33,300	33,350	1,245	1,087	1,230
33,350	33,400	1,248	1,089	1,233
33,400	33,450	1,250	1,091	1,235
33,450	33,500	1,252	1,093	1,237
33,500	33,550	1,254	1,095	1,239
33,550	33,600	1,256	1,097	1,241
33,600	33,650	1,259	1,100	1,244
33,650	33,700	1,261	1,102	1,246
33,700	33,750	1,263	1,104	1,248
33,750	33,800	1,265	1,106	1,250
33,800	33,850	1,267	1,108	1,252
33,850	33,900	1,270	1,110	1,255
33,900	33,950	1,272	1,112	1,257
33,950	34,000	1,274	1,115	1,259

34,000

At least	But less than	Single or Married filing separately	Married filing jointly	Head of a household
34,000	34,050	1,276	1,117	1,261
34,050	34,100	1,278	1,119	1,263
34,100	34,150	1,281	1,121	1,266
34,150	34,200	1,283	1,123	1,268
34,200	34,250	1,285	1,125	1,270
34,250	34,300	1,287	1,127	1,272
34,300	34,350	1,289	1,130	1,274
34,350	34,400	1,292	1,132	1,277
34,400	34,450	1,294	1,134	1,279
34,450	34,500	1,296	1,136	1,281
34,500	34,550	1,298	1,138	1,283
34,550	34,600	1,300	1,140	1,285
34,600	34,650	1,303	1,142	1,288
34,650	34,700	1,305	1,144	1,290
34,700	34,750	1,307	1,147	1,292
34,750	34,800	1,309	1,149	1,294
34,800	34,850	1,311	1,151	1,296
34,850	34,900	1,314	1,153	1,299
34,900	34,950	1,316	1,155	1,301
34,950	35,000	1,318	1,157	1,303

35,000

At least	But less than	Single or Married filing separately	Married filing jointly	Head of a household
35,000	35,050	1,320	1,159	1,305
35,050	35,100	1,322	1,162	1,307
35,100	35,150	1,325	1,164	1,310
35,150	35,200	1,327	1,166	1,312
35,200	35,250	1,329	1,168	1,314
35,250	35,300	1,331	1,170	1,316
35,300	35,350	1,333	1,172	1,318
35,350	35,400	1,336	1,174	1,321
35,400	35,450	1,338	1,177	1,323
35,450	35,500	1,340	1,179	1,325
35,500	35,550	1,342	1,181	1,327
35,550	35,600	1,344	1,183	1,329
35,600	35,650	1,347	1,185	1,332
35,650	35,700	1,349	1,187	1,334
35,700	35,750	1,351	1,189	1,336
35,750	35,800	1,353	1,192	1,338
35,800	35,850	1,355	1,194	1,340
35,850	35,900	1,358	1,196	1,343
35,900	35,950	1,360	1,198	1,345
35,950	36,000	1,362	1,200	1,347

36,000

At least	But less than	Single or Married filing separately	Married filing jointly	Head of a household
36,000	36,050	1,364	1,202	1,349
36,050	36,100	1,366	1,204	1,351
36,100	36,150	1,369	1,207	1,354
36,150	36,200	1,371	1,209	1,356
36,200	36,250	1,373	1,211	1,358
36,250	36,300	1,375	1,213	1,360
36,300	36,350	1,377	1,215	1,362
36,350	36,400	1,380	1,217	1,365
36,400	36,450	1,382	1,219	1,367
36,450	36,500	1,384	1,222	1,369
36,500	36,550	1,386	1,224	1,371
36,550	36,600	1,388	1,226	1,373
36,600	36,650	1,391	1,228	1,376
36,650	36,700	1,393	1,230	1,378
36,700	36,750	1,395	1,232	1,380
36,750	36,800	1,397	1,234	1,382
36,800	36,850	1,399	1,237	1,384
36,850	36,900	1,402	1,239	1,387
36,900	36,950	1,404	1,241	1,389
36,950	37,000	1,406	1,243	1,391

37,000

At least	But less than	Single or Married filing separately	Married filing jointly	Head of a household
37,000	37,050	1,408	1,245	1,393
37,050	37,100	1,410	1,247	1,395
37,100	37,150	1,413	1,249	1,398
37,150	37,200	1,415	1,251	1,400
37,200	37,250	1,417	1,254	1,402
37,250	37,300	1,419	1,256	1,404
37,300	37,350	1,421	1,258	1,406
37,350	37,400	1,424	1,260	1,409
37,400	37,450	1,426	1,262	1,411
37,450	37,500	1,428	1,264	1,413
37,500	37,550	1,430	1,266	1,415
37,550	37,600	1,432	1,269	1,417
37,600	37,650	1,435	1,271	1,420
37,650	37,700	1,437	1,273	1,422
37,700	37,750	1,439	1,275	1,424
37,750	37,800	1,441	1,277	1,426
37,800	37,850	1,443	1,279	1,428
37,850	37,900	1,446	1,281	1,431
37,900	37,950	1,448	1,284	1,433
37,950	38,000	1,450	1,286	1,435

38,000

At least	But less than	Single or Married filing separately	Married filing jointly	Head of a household
38,000	38,050	1,452	1,288	1,437
38,050	38,100	1,454	1,290	1,439
38,100	38,150	1,457	1,292	1,442
38,150	38,200	1,459	1,294	1,444
38,200	38,250	1,461	1,296	1,446
38,250	38,300	1,463	1,299	1,448
38,300	38,350	1,465	1,301	1,450
38,350	38,400	1,468	1,303	1,453
38,400	38,450	1,470	1,305	1,455
38,450	38,500	1,472	1,307	1,457
38,500	38,550	1,474	1,309	1,459
38,550	38,600	1,476	1,311	1,461
38,600	38,650	1,479	1,314	1,464
38,650	38,700	1,481	1,316	1,466
38,700	38,750	1,483	1,318	1,468
38,750	38,800	1,485	1,320	1,470
38,800	38,850	1,487	1,322	1,472
38,850	38,900	1,490	1,324	1,475
38,900	38,950	1,492	1,326	1,477
38,950	39,000	1,494	1,329	1,479

39,000

At least	But less than	Single or Married filing separately	Married filing jointly	Head of a household
39,000	39,050	1,496	1,331	1,481
39,050	39,100	1,498	1,333	1,483
39,100	39,150	1,501	1,335	1,486
39,150	39,200	1,503	1,337	1,488
39,200	39,250	1,505	1,339	1,490
39,250	39,300	1,507	1,341	1,492
39,300	39,350	1,509	1,344	1,494
39,350	39,400	1,512	1,346	1,497
39,400	39,450	1,514	1,348	1,499
39,450	39,500	1,516	1,350	1,501
39,500	39,550	1,518	1,352	1,503
39,550	39,600	1,520	1,354	1,505
39,600	39,650	1,523	1,356	1,508
39,650	39,700	1,525	1,358	1,510
39,700	39,750	1,527	1,361	1,512
39,750	39,800	1,529	1,363	1,514
39,800	39,850	1,531	1,365	1,516
39,850	39,900	1,534	1,367	1,519
39,900	39,950	1,536	1,369	1,521
39,950	40,000	1,538	1,371	1,523

40,000

At least	But less than	Single or Married filing separately	Married filing jointly	Head of a household
40,000	40,050	1,540	1,373	1,525
40,050	40,100	1,542	1,376	1,527
40,100	40,150	1,545	1,378	1,530
40,150	40,200	1,547	1,380	1,532
40,200	40,250	1,549	1,382	1,534
40,250	40,300	1,551	1,384	1,536
40,300	40,350	1,553	1,386	1,538
40,350	40,400	1,556	1,388	1,541
40,400	40,450	1,558	1,391	1,543
40,450	40,500	1,560	1,393	1,545
40,500	40,550	1,562	1,395	1,547
40,550	40,600	1,564	1,397	1,549
40,600	40,650	1,567	1,399	1,552
40,650	40,700	1,569	1,401	1,554
40,700	40,750	1,571	1,403	1,556
40,750	40,800	1,573	1,406	1,558
40,800	40,850	1,575	1,408	1,560
40,850	40,900	1,578	1,410	1,563
40,900	40,950	1,580	1,412	1,565
40,950	41,000	1,582	1,414	1,567

41,000

At least	But less than	Single or Married filing separately	Married filing jointly	Head of a household
41,000	41,050	1,584	1,416	1,569
41,050	41,100	1,586	1,418	1,571
41,100	41,150	1,589	1,421	1,574
41,150	41,200	1,591	1,423	1,576
41,200	41,250	1,593	1,425	1,578
41,250	41,300	1,595	1,427	1,580
41,300	41,350	1,597	1,429	1,582
41,350	41,400	1,600	1,431	1,585
41,400	41,450	1,602	1,433	1,587
41,450	41,500	1,604	1,436	1,589
41,500	41,550	1,606	1,438	1,591
41,550	41,600	1,608	1,440	1,593
41,600	41,650	1,611	1,442	1,596
41,650	41,700	1,613	1,444	1,598
41,700	41,750	1,615	1,446	1,600
41,750	41,800	1,617	1,448	1,602
41,800	41,850	1,619	1,451	1,604
41,850	41,900	1,622	1,453	1,607
41,900	41,950	1,624	1,455	1,609
41,950	42,000	1,626	1,457	1,611

* This column must also be used by a qualifying widow(er)

Continued on next page

City of New York Tax Table

If line 17 (taxable income) is — At least	But less than	Single or Married filing separately	Married filing jointly *	Head of a household
42,000				
42,000	42,050	1,628	1,459	1,613
42,050	42,100	1,630	1,461	1,615
42,100	42,150	1,633	1,463	1,618
42,150	42,200	1,635	1,465	1,620
42,200	42,250	1,637	1,468	1,622
42,250	42,300	1,639	1,470	1,624
42,300	42,350	1,641	1,472	1,626
42,350	42,400	1,644	1,474	1,629
42,400	42,450	1,646	1,476	1,631
42,450	42,500	1,648	1,478	1,633
42,500	42,550	1,650	1,480	1,635
42,550	42,600	1,652	1,483	1,637
42,600	42,650	1,655	1,485	1,640
42,650	42,700	1,657	1,487	1,642
42,700	42,750	1,659	1,489	1,644
42,750	42,800	1,661	1,491	1,646
42,800	42,850	1,663	1,493	1,648
42,850	42,900	1,666	1,495	1,651
42,900	42,950	1,668	1,498	1,653
42,950	43,000	1,670	1,500	1,655
43,000				
43,000	43,050	1,672	1,502	1,657
43,050	43,100	1,674	1,504	1,659
43,100	43,150	1,677	1,506	1,662
43,150	43,200	1,679	1,508	1,664
43,200	43,250	1,681	1,510	1,666
43,250	43,300	1,683	1,513	1,668
43,300	43,350	1,685	1,515	1,670
43,350	43,400	1,688	1,517	1,673
43,400	43,450	1,690	1,519	1,675
43,450	43,500	1,692	1,521	1,677
43,500	43,550	1,694	1,523	1,679
43,550	43,600	1,696	1,525	1,681
43,600	43,650	1,699	1,528	1,684
43,650	43,700	1,701	1,530	1,686
43,700	43,750	1,703	1,532	1,688
43,750	43,800	1,705	1,534	1,690
43,800	43,850	1,707	1,536	1,692
43,850	43,900	1,710	1,538	1,695
43,900	43,950	1,712	1,540	1,697
43,950	44,000	1,714	1,543	1,699
44,000				
44,000	44,050	1,716	1,545	1,701
44,050	44,100	1,718	1,547	1,703
44,100	44,150	1,721	1,549	1,706
44,150	44,200	1,723	1,551	1,708
44,200	44,250	1,725	1,553	1,710
44,250	44,300	1,727	1,555	1,712
44,300	44,350	1,729	1,558	1,714
44,350	44,400	1,732	1,560	1,717
44,400	44,450	1,734	1,562	1,719
44,450	44,500	1,736	1,564	1,721
44,500	44,550	1,738	1,566	1,723
44,550	44,600	1,740	1,568	1,725
44,600	44,650	1,743	1,570	1,728
44,650	44,700	1,745	1,572	1,730
44,700	44,750	1,747	1,575	1,732
44,750	44,800	1,749	1,577	1,734
44,800	44,850	1,751	1,579	1,736
44,850	44,900	1,754	1,581	1,739
44,900	44,950	1,756	1,583	1,741
44,950	45,000	1,758	1,585	1,743
45,000				
45,000	45,050	1,760	1,588	1,745
45,050	45,100	1,762	1,590	1,747
45,100	45,150	1,765	1,593	1,750
45,150	45,200	1,767	1,595	1,752
45,200	45,250	1,769	1,597	1,754
45,250	45,300	1,771	1,599	1,756
45,300	45,350	1,773	1,601	1,758
45,350	45,400	1,776	1,604	1,761
45,400	45,450	1,778	1,606	1,763
45,450	45,500	1,780	1,608	1,765
45,500	45,550	1,782	1,610	1,767
45,550	45,600	1,784	1,612	1,769
45,600	45,650	1,787	1,615	1,772
45,650	45,700	1,789	1,617	1,774
45,700	45,750	1,791	1,619	1,776
45,750	45,800	1,793	1,621	1,778
45,800	45,850	1,795	1,623	1,780
45,850	45,900	1,798	1,626	1,783
45,900	45,950	1,800	1,628	1,785
45,950	46,000	1,802	1,630	1,787
46,000				
46,000	46,050	1,804	1,632	1,789
46,050	46,100	1,806	1,634	1,791
46,100	46,150	1,809	1,637	1,794
46,150	46,200	1,811	1,639	1,796
46,200	46,250	1,813	1,641	1,798
46,250	46,300	1,815	1,643	1,800
46,300	46,350	1,817	1,645	1,802
46,350	46,400	1,820	1,648	1,805
46,400	46,450	1,822	1,650	1,807
46,450	46,500	1,824	1,652	1,809
46,500	46,550	1,826	1,654	1,811
46,550	46,600	1,828	1,656	1,813
46,600	46,650	1,831	1,659	1,816
46,650	46,700	1,833	1,661	1,818
46,700	46,750	1,835	1,663	1,820
46,750	46,800	1,837	1,665	1,822
46,800	46,850	1,839	1,667	1,824
46,850	46,900	1,842	1,670	1,827
46,900	46,950	1,844	1,672	1,829
46,950	47,000	1,846	1,674	1,831
47,000				
47,000	47,050	1,848	1,676	1,833
47,050	47,100	1,850	1,678	1,835
47,100	47,150	1,853	1,681	1,838
47,150	47,200	1,855	1,683	1,840
47,200	47,250	1,857	1,685	1,842
47,250	47,300	1,859	1,687	1,844
47,300	47,350	1,861	1,689	1,846
47,350	47,400	1,864	1,692	1,849
47,400	47,450	1,866	1,694	1,851
47,450	47,500	1,868	1,696	1,853
47,500	47,550	1,870	1,698	1,855
47,550	47,600	1,872	1,700	1,857
47,600	47,650	1,875	1,703	1,860
47,650	47,700	1,877	1,705	1,862
47,700	47,750	1,879	1,707	1,864
47,750	47,800	1,881	1,709	1,866
47,800	47,850	1,883	1,711	1,868
47,850	47,900	1,886	1,714	1,871
47,900	47,950	1,888	1,716	1,873
47,950	48,000	1,890	1,718	1,875
48,000				
48,000	48,050	1,892	1,720	1,877
48,050	48,100	1,894	1,722	1,879
48,100	48,150	1,897	1,725	1,882
48,150	48,200	1,899	1,727	1,884
48,200	48,250	1,901	1,729	1,886
48,250	48,300	1,903	1,731	1,888
48,300	48,350	1,905	1,733	1,890
48,350	48,400	1,908	1,736	1,893
48,400	48,450	1,910	1,738	1,895
48,450	48,500	1,912	1,740	1,897
48,500	48,550	1,914	1,742	1,899
48,550	48,600	1,916	1,744	1,901
48,600	48,650	1,919	1,747	1,904
48,650	48,700	1,921	1,749	1,906
48,700	48,750	1,923	1,751	1,908
48,750	48,800	1,925	1,753	1,910
48,800	48,850	1,927	1,755	1,912
48,850	48,900	1,930	1,758	1,915
48,900	48,950	1,932	1,760	1,917
48,950	49,000	1,934	1,762	1,919
49,000				
49,000	49,050	1,936	1,764	1,921
49,050	49,100	1,938	1,766	1,923
49,100	49,150	1,941	1,769	1,926
49,150	49,200	1,943	1,771	1,928
49,200	49,250	1,945	1,773	1,930
49,250	49,300	1,947	1,775	1,932
49,300	49,350	1,949	1,777	1,934
49,350	49,400	1,952	1,780	1,937
49,400	49,450	1,954	1,782	1,939
49,450	49,500	1,956	1,784	1,941
49,500	49,550	1,958	1,786	1,943
49,550	49,600	1,960	1,788	1,945
49,600	49,650	1,963	1,791	1,948
49,650	49,700	1,965	1,793	1,950
49,700	49,750	1,967	1,795	1,952
49,750	49,800	1,969	1,797	1,954
49,800	49,850	1,971	1,799	1,956
49,850	49,900	1,974	1,802	1,959
49,900	49,950	1,976	1,804	1,961
49,950	50,000	1,978	1,806	1,963
50,000				
50,000	50,050	1,980	1,808	1,965
50,050	50,100	1,982	1,810	1,967
50,100	50,150	1,985	1,813	1,970
50,150	50,200	1,987	1,815	1,972
50,200	50,250	1,989	1,817	1,974
50,250	50,300	1,991	1,819	1,976
50,300	50,350	1,993	1,821	1,978
50,350	50,400	1,996	1,824	1,981
50,400	50,450	1,998	1,826	1,983
50,450	50,500	2,000	1,828	1,985
50,500	50,550	2,002	1,830	1,987
50,550	50,600	2,004	1,832	1,989
50,600	50,650	2,007	1,835	1,992
50,650	50,700	2,009	1,837	1,994
50,700	50,750	2,011	1,839	1,996
50,750	50,800	2,013	1,841	1,998
50,800	50,850	2,015	1,843	2,000
50,850	50,900	2,018	1,846	2,003
50,900	50,950	2,020	1,848	2,005
50,950	51,000	2,022	1,850	2,007

City of New York Tax Table

If line 17 (taxable income) is - At least	But less than	And you are - Single or Married filing separately	Married filing jointly *	Head of a household
		Your City of New York tax is -		
51,000				
51,000	51,050	2,024	1,852	2,009
51,050	51,100	2,026	1,854	2,011
51,100	51,150	2,029	1,857	2,014
51,150	51,200	2,031	1,859	2,016
51,200	51,250	2,033	1,861	2,018
51,250	51,300	2,035	1,863	2,020
51,300	51,350	2,037	1,865	2,022
51,350	51,400	2,040	1,868	2,025
51,400	51,450	2,042	1,870	2,027
51,450	51,500	2,044	1,872	2,029
51,500	51,550	2,046	1,874	2,031
51,550	51,600	2,048	1,876	2,033
51,600	51,650	2,051	1,879	2,036
51,650	51,700	2,053	1,881	2,038
51,700	51,750	2,055	1,883	2,040
51,750	51,800	2,057	1,885	2,042
51,800	51,850	2,059	1,887	2,044
51,850	51,900	2,062	1,890	2,047
51,900	51,950	2,064	1,892	2,049
51,950	52,000	2,066	1,894	2,051
52,000				
52,000	52,050	2,068	1,896	2,053
52,050	52,100	2,070	1,898	2,055
52,100	52,150	2,073	1,901	2,058
52,150	52,200	2,075	1,903	2,060
52,200	52,250	2,077	1,905	2,062
52,250	52,300	2,079	1,907	2,064
52,300	52,350	2,081	1,909	2,066
52,350	52,400	2,084	1,912	2,069
52,400	52,450	2,086	1,914	2,071
52,450	52,500	2,088	1,916	2,073
52,500	52,550	2,090	1,918	2,075
52,550	52,600	2,092	1,920	2,077
52,600	52,650	2,095	1,923	2,080
52,650	52,700	2,097	1,925	2,082
52,700	52,750	2,099	1,927	2,084
52,750	52,800	2,101	1,929	2,086
52,800	52,850	2,103	1,931	2,088
52,850	52,900	2,106	1,934	2,091
52,900	52,950	2,108	1,936	2,093
52,950	53,000	2,110	1,938	2,095
53,000				
53,000	53,050	2,112	1,940	2,097
53,050	53,100	2,114	1,942	2,099
53,100	53,150	2,117	1,945	2,102
53,150	53,200	2,119	1,947	2,104
53,200	53,250	2,121	1,949	2,106
53,250	53,300	2,123	1,951	2,108
53,300	53,350	2,125	1,953	2,110
53,350	53,400	2,128	1,956	2,113
53,400	53,450	2,130	1,958	2,115
53,450	53,500	2,132	1,960	2,117
53,500	53,550	2,134	1,962	2,119
53,550	53,600	2,136	1,964	2,121
53,600	53,650	2,139	1,967	2,124
53,650	53,700	2,141	1,969	2,126
53,700	53,750	2,143	1,971	2,128
53,750	53,800	2,145	1,973	2,130
53,800	53,850	2,147	1,975	2,132
53,850	53,900	2,150	1,978	2,135
53,900	53,950	2,152	1,980	2,137
53,950	54,000	2,154	1,982	2,139

If line 17 (taxable income) is - At least	But less than	And you are - Single or Married filing separately	Married filing jointly *	Head of a household
		Your City of New York tax is -		
54,000				
54,000	54,050	2,156	1,984	2,141
54,050	54,100	2,158	1,986	2,143
54,100	54,150	2,161	1,989	2,146
54,150	54,200	2,163	1,991	2,148
54,200	54,250	2,165	1,993	2,150
54,250	54,300	2,167	1,995	2,152
54,300	54,350	2,169	1,997	2,154
54,350	54,400	2,172	2,000	2,157
54,400	54,450	2,174	2,002	2,159
54,450	54,500	2,176	2,004	2,161
54,500	54,550	2,178	2,006	2,163
54,550	54,600	2,180	2,008	2,165
54,600	54,650	2,183	2,011	2,168
54,650	54,700	2,185	2,013	2,170
54,700	54,750	2,187	2,015	2,172
54,750	54,800	2,189	2,017	2,174
54,800	54,850	2,191	2,019	2,176
54,850	54,900	2,194	2,022	2,179
54,900	54,950	2,196	2,024	2,181
54,950	55,000	2,198	2,026	2,183
55,000				
55,000	55,050	2,200	2,028	2,185
55,050	55,100	2,202	2,030	2,187
55,100	55,150	2,205	2,033	2,190
55,150	55,200	2,207	2,035	2,192
55,200	55,250	2,209	2,037	2,194
55,250	55,300	2,211	2,039	2,196
55,300	55,350	2,213	2,041	2,198
55,350	55,400	2,216	2,044	2,201
55,400	55,450	2,218	2,046	2,203
55,450	55,500	2,220	2,048	2,205
55,500	55,550	2,222	2,050	2,207
55,550	55,600	2,224	2,052	2,209
55,600	55,650	2,227	2,055	2,212
55,650	55,700	2,229	2,057	2,214
55,700	55,750	2,231	2,059	2,216
55,750	55,800	2,233	2,061	2,218
55,800	55,850	2,235	2,063	2,220
55,850	55,900	2,238	2,066	2,223
55,900	55,950	2,240	2,068	2,225
55,950	56,000	2,242	2,070	2,227
56,000				
56,000	56,050	2,244	2,072	2,229
56,050	56,100	2,246	2,074	2,231
56,100	56,150	2,249	2,077	2,234
56,150	56,200	2,251	2,079	2,236
56,200	56,250	2,253	2,081	2,238
56,250	56,300	2,255	2,083	2,240
56,300	56,350	2,257	2,085	2,242
56,350	56,400	2,260	2,088	2,245
56,400	56,450	2,262	2,090	2,247
56,450	56,500	2,264	2,092	2,249
56,500	56,550	2,266	2,094	2,251
56,550	56,600	2,268	2,096	2,253
56,600	56,650	2,271	2,099	2,256
56,650	56,700	2,273	2,101	2,258
56,700	56,750	2,275	2,103	2,260
56,750	56,800	2,277	2,105	2,262
56,800	56,850	2,279	2,107	2,264
56,850	56,900	2,282	2,110	2,267
56,900	56,950	2,284	2,112	2,269
56,950	57,000	2,286	2,114	2,271

If line 17 (taxable income) is - At least	But less than	And you are - Single or Married filing separately	Married filing jointly *	Head of a household
		Your City of New York tax is -		
57,000				
57,000	57,050	2,288	2,116	2,273
57,050	57,100	2,290	2,118	2,275
57,100	57,150	2,293	2,121	2,278
57,150	57,200	2,295	2,123	2,280
57,200	57,250	2,297	2,125	2,282
57,250	57,300	2,299	2,127	2,284
57,300	57,350	2,301	2,129	2,286
57,350	57,400	2,304	2,132	2,289
57,400	57,450	2,306	2,134	2,291
57,450	57,500	2,308	2,136	2,293
57,500	57,550	2,310	2,138	2,295
57,550	57,600	2,312	2,140	2,297
57,600	57,650	2,315	2,143	2,300
57,650	57,700	2,317	2,145	2,302
57,700	57,750	2,319	2,147	2,304
57,750	57,800	2,321	2,149	2,306
57,800	57,850	2,323	2,151	2,308
57,850	57,900	2,326	2,154	2,311
57,900	57,950	2,328	2,156	2,313
57,950	58,000	2,330	2,158	2,315
58,000				
58,000	58,050	2,332	2,160	2,317
58,050	58,100	2,334	2,162	2,319
58,100	58,150	2,337	2,165	2,322
58,150	58,200	2,339	2,167	2,324
58,200	58,250	2,341	2,169	2,326
58,250	58,300	2,343	2,171	2,328
58,300	58,350	2,345	2,173	2,330
58,350	58,400	2,348	2,176	2,333
58,400	58,450	2,350	2,178	2,335
58,450	58,500	2,352	2,180	2,337
58,500	58,550	2,354	2,182	2,339
58,550	58,600	2,356	2,184	2,341
58,600	58,650	2,359	2,187	2,344
58,650	58,700	2,361	2,189	2,346
58,700	58,750	2,363	2,191	2,348
58,750	58,800	2,365	2,193	2,350
58,800	58,850	2,367	2,195	2,352
58,850	58,900	2,370	2,198	2,355
58,900	58,950	2,372	2,200	2,357
58,950	59,000	2,374	2,202	2,359
59,000				
59,000	59,050	2,376	2,204	2,361
59,050	59,100	2,378	2,206	2,363
59,100	59,150	2,381	2,209	2,366
59,150	59,200	2,383	2,211	2,368
59,200	59,250	2,385	2,213	2,370
59,250	59,300	2,387	2,215	2,372
59,300	59,350	2,389	2,217	2,374
59,350	59,400	2,392	2,220	2,377
59,400	59,450	2,394	2,222	2,379
59,450	59,500	2,396	2,224	2,381
59,500	59,550	2,398	2,226	2,383
59,550	59,600	2,400	2,228	2,385
59,600	59,650	2,403	2,231	2,388
59,650	59,700	2,405	2,233	2,390
59,700	59,750	2,407	2,235	2,392
59,750	59,800	2,409	2,237	2,394
59,800	59,850	2,411	2,239	2,396
59,850	59,900	2,414	2,242	2,399
59,900	59,950	2,416	2,244	2,401
59,950	60,000	2,418	2,246	2,403

* This column must also be used by a qualifying widow(er)

Continued on next page

City of New York Tax Table

If line 17 (taxable income) is -		And you are -			If line 17 (taxable income) is -		And you are -			If line 17 (taxable income) is -		And you are -		
At least	But less than	Single or Married filing separately	Married filing jointly *	Head of a house-hold	At least	But less than	Single or Married filing separately	Married filing jointly *	Head of a house-hold	At least	But less than	Single or Married filing separately	Married filing jointly *	Head of a house-hold
		Your City of New York tax is -					Your City of New York tax is -					Your City of New York tax is -		
60,000					**62,000**					**64,000**				
60,000	60,050	2,420	2,248	2,405	62,000	62,050	2,509	2,336	2,493	64,000	64,050	2,599	2,424	2,581
60,050	60,100	2,422	2,250	2,407	62,050	62,100	2,512	2,338	2,495	64,050	64,100	2,601	2,426	2,583
60,100	60,150	2,425	2,253	2,410	62,100	62,150	2,514	2,341	2,498	64,100	64,150	2,603	2,429	2,586
60,150	60,200	2,427	2,255	2,412	62,150	62,200	2,516	2,343	2,500	64,150	64,200	2,605	2,431	2,588
60,200	60,250	2,429	2,257	2,414	62,200	62,250	2,518	2,345	2,502	64,200	64,250	2,607	2,433	2,590
60,250	60,300	2,431	2,259	2,416	62,250	62,300	2,520	2,347	2,504	64,250	64,300	2,610	2,435	2,592
60,300	60,350	2,433	2,261	2,418	62,300	62,350	2,523	2,349	2,506	64,300	64,350	2,612	2,437	2,594
60,350	60,400	2,436	2,264	2,421	62,350	62,400	2,525	2,352	2,509	64,350	64,400	2,614	2,440	2,597
60,400	60,450	2,438	2,266	2,423	62,400	62,450	2,527	2,354	2,511	64,400	64,450	2,616	2,442	2,599
60,450	60,500	2,440	2,268	2,425	62,450	62,500	2,529	2,356	2,513	64,450	64,500	2,619	2,444	2,601
60,500	60,550	2,442	2,270	2,427	62,500	62,550	2,532	2,358	2,515	64,500	64,550	2,621	2,446	2,603
60,550	60,600	2,445	2,272	2,429	62,550	62,600	2,534	2,360	2,517	64,550	64,600	2,623	2,448	2,605
60,600	60,650	2,447	2,275	2,432	62,600	62,650	2,536	2,363	2,520	64,600	64,650	2,625	2,451	2,608
60,650	60,700	2,449	2,277	2,434	62,650	62,700	2,538	2,365	2,522	64,650	64,700	2,628	2,453	2,610
60,700	60,750	2,451	2,279	2,436	62,700	62,750	2,541	2,367	2,524	64,700	64,750	2,630	2,455	2,612
60,750	60,800	2,454	2,281	2,438	62,750	62,800	2,543	2,369	2,526	64,750	64,800	2,632	2,457	2,614
60,800	60,850	2,456	2,283	2,440	62,800	62,850	2,545	2,371	2,528	64,800	64,850	2,634	2,459	2,616
60,850	60,900	2,458	2,286	2,443	62,850	62,900	2,547	2,374	2,531	64,850	64,900	2,636	2,462	2,619
60,900	60,950	2,460	2,288	2,445	62,900	62,950	2,549	2,376	2,533	64,900	64,950	2,639	2,464	2,621
60,950	61,000	2,462	2,290	2,447	62,950	63,000	2,552	2,378	2,535	64,950	65,000	2,641	2,466	2,623
61,000					**63,000**					**65,000 or more use Form IT-201**				
61,000	61,050	2,465	2,292	2,449	63,000	63,050	2,554	2,380	2,537					
61,050	61,100	2,467	2,294	2,451	63,050	63,100	2,556	2,382	2,539					
61,100	61,150	2,469	2,297	2,454	63,100	63,150	2,558	2,385	2,542					
61,150	61,200	2,471	2,299	2,456	63,150	63,200	2,561	2,387	2,544					
61,200	61,250	2,474	2,301	2,458	63,200	63,250	2,563	2,389	2,546					
61,250	61,300	2,476	2,303	2,460	63,250	63,300	2,565	2,391	2,548					
61,300	61,350	2,478	2,305	2,462	63,300	63,350	2,567	2,393	2,550					
61,350	61,400	2,480	2,308	2,465	63,350	63,400	2,570	2,396	2,553					
61,400	61,450	2,483	2,310	2,467	63,400	63,450	2,572	2,398	2,555					
61,450	61,500	2,485	2,312	2,469	63,450	63,500	2,574	2,400	2,557					
61,500	61,550	2,487	2,314	2,471	63,500	63,550	2,576	2,402	2,559					
61,550	61,600	2,489	2,316	2,473	63,550	63,600	2,578	2,404	2,561					
61,600	61,650	2,491	2,319	2,476	63,600	63,650	2,581	2,407	2,564					
61,650	61,700	2,494	2,321	2,478	63,650	63,700	2,583	2,409	2,566					
61,700	61,750	2,496	2,323	2,480	63,700	63,750	2,585	2,411	2,568					
61,750	61,800	2,498	2,325	2,482	63,750	63,800	2,587	2,413	2,570					
61,800	61,850	2,500	2,327	2,484	63,800	63,850	2,590	2,415	2,572					
61,850	61,900	2,503	2,330	2,487	63,850	63,900	2,592	2,418	2,575					
61,900	61,950	2,505	2,332	2,489	63,900	63,950	2,594	2,420	2,577					
61,950	62,000	2,507	2,334	2,491	63,950	64,000	2,596	2,422	2,579					

* This column must also be used by a qualifying widow(er)

II | New Jersey

1 | Changes in the Tax Law

This chapter summarizes and highlights recent personal income tax developments in New Jersey.

Reporting Requirements

Effective for tax year 1991, New Jersey requires every resident to report, for information and audit purposes only, the amount of exempt interest received from investments in federal and New Jersey obligations. This information must be reported on your resident New Jersey gross income tax return (Form NJ-1040). Dividends received from New Jersey qualified investment funds which are excluded from gross income must also be reported on Form NJ-1040. A New Jersey qualified investment fund is a regulated investment company in which at least 80% of the underlying investments are either federal or New Jersey obligations. Before 1991, New Jersey did not require resident taxpayers to report this information on their New Jersey returns.

2 | The Income Tax Return

Who Must File

The following individuals or groups may be required to file a New Jersey income tax return:

- Resident individuals;
- Nonresident individuals with income from New Jersey sources;
- Part-year resident individuals;
- Partners with income from a partnership that does business in New Jersey;
- A fiduciary of a trust or estate with New Jersey income; and
- A beneficiary of an estate or trust with New Jersey income.

Residents

New Jersey requires every person who is a resident of the state and has annual New Jersey gross income of more than $3,000 to file a New Jersey Gross Income Tax Return (Form NJ-1040). (For a discussion of who is a "resident," see the *Determining Residency/Domicile* section later in this chapter. For a discussion of what constitutes New Jersey gross income, see *Residents—Starting Point* in Chapter 3.)

If you are married but filing separately, you are required to file if you have annual New Jersey gross income of $1,500 or more.

Even if your New Jersey gross income is less than $3,000, you may need to file a New Jersey income tax return to obtain a refund of any taxes withheld from your wages or paid as estimated taxes. You may also need to file a return to claim a Homestead Property Tax Rebate.

Example

Joan, a student, is a New Jersey resident. Joan decided to look for a part-time job that would enable her to work between classes. After a few weeks of searching, she found a job in the corner bookstore. Joan's weekly salary in 1992 was $255. Because she started this job in late November, her total earnings in 1992 were only $1,530. Joan's employer withheld payroll taxes from her salary. Joan also had $750 of taxable interest income and a $250 stock dividend. Joan's total New Jersey gross income is $2,530. Although her New Jersey gross income is less than $3,000, Joan must file a New Jersey income tax return to receive a refund of New Jersey taxes withheld from her paycheck.

Nonresidents

If you did not make your permanent home in New Jersey but you derived any income from work performed in New Jersey,

you are required to file a New Jersey Gross Income Tax Nonresident Return (Form NJ-1040NR).

EXCEPTION: New Jersey does not require nonresident shareholders in a federal S corporation that does business in the state to file a tax return if they have no other income from New Jersey sources.

Part-Year Residents

If you were a New Jersey resident for only part of the year, you must file a New Jersey resident income tax return for that part of the year if your New Jersey gross income for the *entire* year exceeds $3,000 ($1,500 for married persons filing separately). If you had New Jersey source income as a nonresident, you would file a nonresident return for the part of the year during which you were no longer a resident.

Partnerships

Partnerships are not subject to New Jersey personal income tax. However, individual partners may be subject to state income tax on their shares of the partnership's income. If you are a partner in a partnership and a New Jersey resident, your share of the partnership's income is included in your New Jersey gross income, regardless of where your partnership does business. If you are a nonresident partner in a partnership that has business activity in New Jersey, New Jersey can tax you on the partnership's income derived from New Jersey sources. If the partnership earns any income connected with a New Jersey activity or has a resident partner, it is required to file a copy of its federal partnership return (federal Form 1065) with New Jersey. The items of income, loss, deduction, or adjustment shown by the partnership on its Form 1065 are transferred to each partner's individual resident or nonresident return, based on his or her pro rata share of the partnership's income.

Estates and Trusts

New Jersey imposes an estate tax on the estates of resident decedents. All New Jersey estates or trusts must file a New Jersey fiduciary return, Form NJ-1041. The fiduciary must provide each beneficiary with a copy of the schedule that shows the beneficiary's share of the estate or trust income. This income must then be shown on each beneficiary's individual return.

When an Individual Dies

An executor, administrator, or spouse must file a New Jersey income tax return for a taxpayer who died before filing a 1992 return. If the deceased person and his or her surviving spouse filed a joint federal income tax return, a joint New Jersey return must be filed unless one spouse was a resident and the other was a nonresident. In addition, for the two years following the deceased taxpayer's death, the surviving spouse is allowed the filing status of "surviving spouse."

> **TaxAlert:** If a taxpayer dies while on active duty in one of the Armed Forces of the United States, and the death occurred while the person was serving in a combat zone or as a result of wounds, disease, or injury incurred while serving there, New Jersey will waive all income taxes for the year of his or her death and for any prior taxable years ending after the person began serving in the combat zone.

> **TaxAlert:** The decedent's name should be entered in the name block of the return, with the word "deceased," followed by the date of death.

Members of the Armed Forces

If you are a member of the Armed Forces and a New Jersey resident, the amount of your military pay that is subject to federal income tax is also subject to New Jersey gross income tax. This is true if you are based outside New Jersey. However, if your permanent home was outside New Jersey when you entered the military, you will not be treated as a New Jersey resident for tax purposes merely because you were assigned to duty in New Jersey and established a place to live there. If you are a New Jersey nonresident, your military pay is not subject to New Jersey income tax.

> **TaxAlert:** If you are a New Jersey nonresident on assigned military duty, any income you earn in New Jersey, other than your military pay, may be subject to tax. This includes your spouse's income and any money you earn from an off-duty civilian job.

Determining Residency/Domicile

New Jersey's rules concerning residency and domicile are generally comparable to those of New York State. Please refer to *Determining Residency/Domicile* under New York State for a more detailed discussion.

For New Jersey purposes, a resident individual is an individual who is *domiciled* in the State unless he or she:

1. Does not maintain a permanent home within the State; and
2. Maintains a permanent home outside the State; and
3. Spends not more than 30 days of the taxable year in New Jersey.

A resident individual is also an individual who is *not domiciled* in the state but who maintains a permanent home in New Jersey and spends more than 183 days of the taxable year there, unless such an individual is in the Armed Forces. New Jersey defines domicile as any place that an individual regards as his or her permanent home. One's permanent home is the place to which one intends to return after a period of absence. You should be aware that New Jersey does not define the term "permanent home" or have such extensive rules on domicile and residence as New York does. It is generally New Jersey's policy to follow the New York rules and definitions in the residency and domicile areas. Therefore, you may wish to refer to the section on residency in Chapter 2 of Part I, New York, for additional guidance. See *Abandoning Your Domicile Checklist* in Part I, New York, for guidance on abandoning a New Jersey domicile and determining your residency status.

> **Exception:** Students are not usually considered residents of the state in which they attend school, as long as they have a permanent home somewhere else.

Nonresidents

If you are not a resident of New Jersey but you earned income from New Jersey sources, you are required to file a New Jersey nonresident income tax return. If you moved into or out of New Jersey during the year, you may be required to file *two* tax returns for the year. As a part-year resident, you will be required to prorate all exemptions, deductions, and credits to reflect the period covered by each return. These rules are in contrast to those of New York and Connecticut, which require that only one form be filed by a nonresident or part-year resident taxpayer.

If you were a New Jersey resident for only part of the year, you are subject to tax if your income for the entire year is greater than $3,000 ($1,500 for a married person filing separately). This is true even if your total income for the residency period is $3,000 or less. New Jersey requires nonresidents who derived income from New Jersey sources to file a New Jersey gross income tax nonresident return, regardless of how little income from New Jersey sources they receive.

New Jersey Source Income

New Jersey source income for a nonresident is any income received from the following activities:

1. Performing personal services for compensation in New Jersey;
2. Renting, leasing, or selling real or tangible personal property in New Jersey;
3. Carrying on a trade, profession, or occupation in New Jersey;
4. Receiving a distributive share of income from an unincorporated business or profession, such as a partnership, that does business in New Jersey. (If the business is conducted in more than one state, you only need to report income generated by its New Jersey activities); or
5. Receiving earnings from intangible property employed in a business or profession carried on in New Jersey.

Example

Terese is a resident of Ohio. She is an attorney for a law firm there. During 1992, Terese had income from sources within both Ohio and New Jersey. The following is a list of the income she derived from each source for the tax year 1992:

Income Source	Income	Reportable to N.J.
Salary as attorney in Ohio	$100,000	No
Income as a partner in a New Jersey partnership	$ 5,000	Yes
Rent from building located in New Jersey	$ 50,000	Yes
Her share of income from a partnership that does business only in New Jersey	$ 1,000	Yes

Terese will be required to file a New Jersey nonresident tax return and report as $56,000 income she earned from New Jersey sources.

Nonresident and Part-Year Resident—Election of Filing Status for Married Taxpayers

If a husband and wife who are both taxable nonresidents file separate federal returns, their income from New Jersey sources must be separately determined. If one spouse is a resident and the other a nonresident, taxes must be computed on their separate incomes unless they elect to file a joint return as though they were both residents.

Special Rules for Members of the Armed Forces

Your residency status for tax filing purposes as a member of the United States Armed Forces depends upon where your permanent home or domicile is located. Generally, your domicile does not change if you are serving temporarily in the Armed Forces

If your domicile was in New Jersey when you entered the military, you are still considered a New Jersey resident, even if you are stationed in another country or state. You must file your return as a New Jersey resident. However, if you did not maintain a permanent home in New Jersey during any part of the year, but maintained your home outside the state and spent fewer than 30 days during the year in New Jersey, you may file as a nonresident. (See *Determining Residency/Domicile* earlier in this chapter.)

Generally, if your permanent home was outside New Jersey when you entered the Armed Forces and you still retain your home, you will not be considered a New Jersey resident for tax purposes. This is true even if you are assigned to duty in New Jersey and own or rent lodgings there. Income you receive from military service is not sourced to New Jersey. However, if you receive any income from other New Jersey sources, including your spouse's income, you may be subject to tax as a nonresident.

Example

Corporal Tim of the U.S. Army and his wife, Sue, are stationed at Fort Dix, New Jersey. They live on the base. Tim and Sue are residents of Florida. To supplement his military pay, Tim plays the saxophone with a local band. Sue has her own business making jewelry. She sells her creations to local jewelers. Tim's military income is not taxable by New Jersey. However, his income from the band and Sue's income from her business will be taxable by New Jersey. They must file a New Jersey nonresident return.

EXCEPTIONS:

1. New Jersey does not have the Foreign Country Domicile Exemption as discussed in Group B of the New York residency section, but it does follow the Group A Domicile Exemption discussed on *page NY-6* under *Determining Residency*.
2. A spouse of a member of the Armed Forces may be deemed to be a New Jersey resident even if the spouse is not domiciled in this state. If the nonmilitary spouse maintains a home in New Jersey and spends more than 183 days there, he or she must file a resident return.

Deceased Taxpayers

The executor, administrator, or spouse of a deceased nonresident or part-year resident of New Jersey must file a New Jersey nonresident and part-year resident return if the taxpayer died before filing his or her tax return and would have been required to file a return.

If an individual dies while on active duty in a "combat zone" or as a result of injuries received in a "combat zone," no income tax or return is due for the year of death. A refund of any taxes paid for taxable years ending on or after the day the decedent first served in the combat zone may be sought. The legal representative of the estate or surviving spouse has a right to receive such a refund upon request.

Filing Status

Note: The general rules determining filing status discussed in greater detail under New York also apply to New Jersey unless otherwise indicated.

The following summarizes the rules governing the selection of your New Jersey filing status. Generally, all taxpayers must use the same filing status on their New Jersey return as they did on their federal return. (See *Joint vs. Separate Return for Married Taxpayers*, which follows.) The five possible filing statuses for federal and New Jersey purposes are:

1. Single;
2. Married filing jointly;
3. Married filing separately;
4. Head of household (with qualifying person); or
5. Qualifying widow(er) with dependent child.

Your choice of filing status determines the effective, or true, rate of tax you will pay on your income. It also determines whether you are entitled to certain *exemptions, credits,* and *deductions;* and how much income you can earn before you are taxed at all.

Your filing status for the *entire* year is determined by your marital and family situation on the last day of the tax year. For individuals, that day is almost always December 31.

Single

Your filing status is *single* if you are unmarried, divorced under a final decree, or legally separated under a separate maintenance decree as of the last day of the taxable year, provided you do not qualify to file as either *Head of Household* or *Qualifying Widow(er) with Dependent Child* (see following discussion of these categories).

Married Filing Jointly

You may choose *married filing jointly* as your filing status if you are married and both you and your spouse agree to file a joint return.

You are considered married for the whole year if on the last day of the tax year you are *either*:

1. Married and living together as husband and wife;
2. Married living apart, but not under a court-ordered decree of divorce or separate maintenance;
3. Separated under an interlocutory (not final) decree of divorce; *or*
4. Your spouse died during the year and you did not remarry before the end of the tax year. If you remarried during the year, you are considered married if you fall under one of the categories listed in 1, 2, or 3 above.

EXCEPTION: Certain married individuals may be *considered unmarried* and eligible for *head of household* status. You will not be eligible unless your spouse was not a member of your household during the last six months of the tax year. Also, your household must be the principal home of a dependent child. (See *Head of Household* for more information.) If you qualify to file as *head of household* instead of *married filing separately*, you will be entitled to use the more favorable tax rates that apply to head of household. In addition, you may benefit from certain exemptions, deductions, and credits not otherwise available.

When you file a joint return, all items of income and expense for you and your spouse are combined. Generally, married taxpayers who file joint returns enjoy more favorable tax rates than married taxpayers who file separately.

Married Filing Separately

You may prefer *married filing separately* for your filing status if you want to be responsible for your own tax or wish to avoid interest and penalties that your spouse may incur. You may be required to use this filing status if your spouse does not agree to file a joint return. Unless you are required to file separately, you should figure your tax under both methods to make sure you are using the method that results in the lower combined tax. Generally, you will pay a greater total combined tax by filing separate returns. This is because there is a higher effective tax rate for married persons filing separately.

If you live apart and meet certain tests, you may be *considered unmarried* for federal and state purposes and file as *head of household* even though you are not divorced or legally separated. (See *Head of Household* for more information.)

If you file as *married filing separately*, you must write your spouse's full name and Social Security number in the spaces provided.

Joint vs. Separate Return for Married Taxpayers

Separate Federal Returns. If you and your spouse file separate federal returns, you must also file separate New Jersey returns. Be sure to enter the name and Social Security number of your spouse on your return.

Joint Federal Returns. If you and your spouse file a joint federal return, you must also file a joint New Jersey return.

EXCEPTION: Separate New Jersey returns should be filed if one spouse is a resident and the other is a non-resident during the tax year, *unless* both of you elect to file a joint New Jersey resident return. If the resident spouse files separately in New Jersey but files a joint federal return, that spouse must compute income and exemptions as if he or she had filed a separate federal return.

If you and your spouse file a joint New Jersey gross income tax return, you will both be jointly and severally liable for the entire tax owed plus any interest or penalty due on your joint return.

Head of Household

In order to qualify as *head of household*, you must not be married or a surviving spouse at the close of the tax year. If you are a widow or widower, you may not use the *head of household* rates for tax years in which you are eligible to use the joint tax rates under *qualifying widow(er)*. In addition, you must maintain as your home a household which, for more than one-half of the tax year, is the principal home of one or more of the following:

1. A son or daughter, a stepchild, a grandchild, an adopted child, or a foster child. If any of the foregoing is married on the last day of the tax year, you must qualify to claim him or her as a dependent. (See the section on *Personal Exemptions and Dependents*, which follows.) If the person is unmarried, then it is not necessary that he or she qualify as your dependent in order for you to qualify for head of household status; or
2. Any other relative eligible to be claimed as a dependent, except those eligible to be claimed by virtue of a multiple support agreement.

EXCEPTION: It is still possible for you to qualify as *head of household* if your dependent parent lives elsewhere, such as in a rest home or home for the aged, provided you maintain your parent's household.

You are considered to "maintain a household" only if you furnish, with funds that can be traced to you, more than one-half of the cost of maintaining a home during the year. Costs of maintaining a household include property taxes, mortgage interest, rent, utility charges, upkeep and repairs, property insurance, domestic help, and food consumed on the premises. They do not include the cost of clothing, education, medical treatment, vacations, life insurance, or transportation.

A married taxpayer will be *considered unmarried* and eligible for *head of household* status if his or her spouse was not a member of the household for the last six months of the tax year and if the household is the principal home of a dependent child.

Qualifying Widow(er) with Dependent Child

If you are a surviving spouse with a dependent child, you may be able to use *qualifying widow(er) with dependent child* as your filing status, provided you have not remarried. This filing status entitles you to use joint return tax rates and other deductions for two years following the death of your spouse.

In order to qualify for this filing status, you must have a child, stepchild, adopted child, or foster child who qualifies as your dependent for the tax year and you must have paid more than half the cost of maintaining a home in which both you and the child resided for the *entire* year, except for temporary absences.

Death or Birth. If the dependent who qualifies you to file using *qualifying widow(er) with dependent child* is born or dies during the year, you may still be able to claim that filing status. You must, however, have provided for more than half of the costs of maintaining a home that was the dependent's main home during the entire part of the year he or she was alive.

Indicate your filing status by checking the appropriate box (1 through 5) on either Form NJ-1040 or NJ-1040NR. Also, be sure to use the proper table in the tax rate schedules when computing your tax: Table A should be used by *single* and *married filing separately* taxpayers and Table B should be used if your filing status is *married filing jointly, head of household,* or *qualifying widow(er)*.

Personal Exemptions and Dependents

New Jersey allows resident and nonresident filers to claim personal and dependent exemptions. However, a nonresident filer is not entitled to the full exemption amount if his or her gross income from all sources exceeds the amount of income from New Jersey sources by more than $100.

How to Calculate Your Exemptions—Residents/Part-Year Residents

Personal Exemption(s). You may claim an exemption for yourself and your spouse if both of you file a joint return. If you are a minor, you may claim a personal exemption even if your parents claim you as a dependent. These exemptions are your regular exemptions. The total number of regular exemptions you claim should be entered in the box on Line 6 of the New Jersey resident return Form NJ-1040.

If you are 65 years of age or older at the end of the year, you may claim an additional exemption. If your spouse is 65 years or older at the close of the year, he or she may also claim an additional exemption. The total number of additional exemptions you claim should be entered in the box on Line 7 of Form NJ-1040.

New Jersey also allows an additional exemption for you or your spouse if you are blind or disabled. To qualify as disabled, you must have a total and permanent inability to engage in any substantial activity by reason of medically determinable physical or mental impairment. This includes blindness. You must attach a medical certificate attesting to your condition to your return. If there is no change in your condition, you do not need to resubmit this information each year. The total number of exemptions you claim because of a disability should be entered in the box on Line 8 of your NJ-1040.

Dependent Exemption(s). You may claim an exemption for each dependent child who qualifies as a dependent for federal income tax purposes. Refer to the New York section for information on federal rules regarding dependents. The number of qualified dependent children you claim as exemptions should be entered in the block on Line 9 of your NJ-1040.

You may also claim exemptions for other dependents who qualify as such for federal income tax purposes. These may include elderly parents for whom you provide support, other relatives or even unrelated individuals, such as foster children, who live with you in your household. The number of other qualifying dependents is entered in the box on Line 10 of your NJ-1040.

Additional exemptions may be claimed for each dependent under 22 years of age who is a full-time student at a college or post-secondary institution. You must have paid 50% or more of the dependent's tuition costs and living expenses. Financial aid received by the student is not taken into account. However, grants from a College Work Study Program are considered income to the student.

To qualify as a student, the dependent must be a full-time student during some part of each of five months during the calendar year at an educational institution that maintains a regular faculty and curriculum and has other students in attendance. A student qualifies as full-time if the educational institution considers him or her to be enrolled full-time.

The number of your dependents who attend college should be entered in the box on Line 11 of your NJ-1040. You can claim the exemption for dependents attending college in addition to the regular exemption for dependents. However, you can only claim the exemption for dependents attending college if the student(s) qualifies as a dependent on Line 9 or 10.

Example

Mrs. Black's two children, Debbie, age 21, and Joe, age 20, are full-time students at the local university. Both Debbie and Joe qualify as Mrs. Black's dependents for federal income tax purposes for tax year 1992. Mrs. Black is entitled to claim two regular dependent exemptions as well as two additional dependent exemptions on her 1992 New Jersey income tax return. Mrs. Black is entitled to the additional exemptions on Line 9 of her NJ-1040 since each child qualifies as a dependent and both are under age 22 and attend college full-time.

The *total* amount of your regular exemptions from Line 6, your age 65 or older exemptions from Line 7, your blind or disabled exemptions from Line 8, and your dependent attending college exemptions from Line 11 is entered on Line 12a of your NJ-1040.

The total amount of your qualified dependent children exemptions from Line 9 and your other dependent exemptions from Line 10 is entered on Line 12b of your NJ-1040.

To compute your total exemption amount, multiply your Line 12a exemptions by $1,000 and your Line 12b exemptions by $1,500. Enter the sum on Line 27c of your NJ-1040.

How to Calculate Your Exemptions—Nonresidents

Personal Exemption(s). You may claim an exemption both for yourself and your spouse if you file a joint return. If you are a minor you may claim a personal exemption for yourself even if your parents claim you as a dependent. These exemptions are your regular exemptions. The total numbers should be entered in the box on Line 6 of your Form NJ-1040NR.

If you are 65 years of age or older at the end of the year, you may claim an additional exemption. If your spouse is 65 years or older at the close of the year, he or she may also claim an additional exemption. The total number claimed should be entered in the box on Line 7 of your Form NJ-1040NR.

New Jersey allows an additional exemption for you or your spouse if you are blind or disabled. You are disabled if you have a total and permanent inability to engage in any substantial activity by reason of any medically determinable physical or mental impairment. This includes blindness. Initially, you must attach a medical certificate to your return attesting to your condition. If there is no change in your condition, you do not need to submit this information each year. The total number of exemptions should be entered in the box on Line 8 of your NJ-1040NR.

Dependent Exemption(s). You may claim an exemption for each child who qualifies as a dependent for federal income tax purposes. Refer to the New York section for a discussion of federal rules concerning dependents. The number of qualified dependent children you claim should be entered in the block on Line 9 of your NJ-1040NR.

You may also claim exemptions for other dependents who qualify as such for federal income tax purposes, such as an elderly parent whom you support. The number of other qualifying dependents is entered in the box on Line 10 of your NJ-1040NR.

Additional exemptions may be claimed for each dependent under 22 years of age who is a full-time student at a college or post-secondary institution. However, you must have paid 50% or more of the dependent's tuition costs and living expenses. Financial aid received by the student may not be taken into account, except for College Work Study Program grants, which are considered income to the student.

To qualify as a student, the dependent must be a full-time student during some part of each of five months during the calendar year at an educational institution that maintains a regular faculty and curriculum and has a body of students in attendance. A student is full-time if the educational institution considers him or her to be in full-time attendance.

Enter the number of your dependents attending college in the box on Line 11 of your NJ-1040NR. You can claim the exemption for dependents attending college in addition to the regular exemption for dependents. It can only be claimed if the student(s) qualifies as a dependent on Line 9 or 10.

The *total* amount of your regular exemptions from Line 6, your age 65 or older exemptions from Line 7, your blind or disabled exemptions from Line 8, and your dependent attending college exemptions from Line 11 is entered on Line 12a of your NJ-1040NR.

The total amount of your qualified dependent children exemptions from Line 9 and your other dependents from Line 10 is entered on Line 12b of your NJ-1040NR.

To compute your total exemption amount, multiply your Line 12a exemptions by $1,000 and your Line 12b exemptions by $1,500. Enter the total amount on Line 16c of your NJ-1040NR.

If you are a nonresident whose gross income from all sources exceeds your New Jersey gross income by more than $100, you are not entitled to the full exemption amount. You must compute your limitation percentage on Line 15. Multiply this percentage by your total exemption and deduction amount. The total exemption and deduction amount includes your medical expenses, alimony, and separate maintenance payments as well as your exemption amount. Your limitation percentage is calculated by dividing your New Jersey gross income by your gross income from all sources. The resulting quotient should be carried out three decimal places and then converted into a percentage by multiplying the quotient by 100.

Example

Mr. Smith has gross income from all sources totalling $30,000. His New Jersey gross income totals $15,000. Since Mr. Smith's gross income from all sources exceeds his New Jersey gross income by more than $100, he is not entitled to the full exemption amount. Mr. Smith should calculate his limitation percentage in the following manner:

$$\frac{\text{New Jersey Gross Income}}{\text{Gross Income from All Sources}}$$

$$= \frac{\$15,000}{\$30,000} = .500 \text{ or } 50.0\%$$

Mr. Smith must multiply the total number of his personal and dependent exemptions, his medical expenses, and his alimony and separate maintenance payments by 50% and enter the result on Line 20 of his Form 1040NR.

New Jersey State Tax Forms

Which Forms to Use

If you are a resident of New Jersey, you must file a New Jersey resident return (Form NJ-1040). If you are a nonresident with income from New Jersey sources, you must file a New Jersey nonresident return (Form NJ-1040NR). If you are a part-year resident, and your income is above a certain level, you are required to file a resident return that prorates all income, deductions, exemptions, and credits to reflect that portion of the year you resided in New Jersey. (See *Who Must File* at the beginning of this chapter.) A single person who

lived in New Jersey for half the year would submit a completed NJ-1040 with amounts that reflect one-half of all income earned during the resident period and would take a $500 exemption (one-half of the standard exemption). A part-year resident may also be required to file a nonresident return, in addition to his or her resident return. For example, if you gave up your residence in New Jersey during the year, but you continued to work in New Jersey or received income from New Jersey sources, you must file a nonresident return and prorate your income and deductions for your nonresident period.

Example

Ms. Smith lived in New York City from January 1 to June 30. On July 1, she moved to Hoboken, New Jersey, and lived there for the rest of the year. Ms. Smith was employed by Jane's Medical Supplies in Newark, New Jersey, for the entire year. Her salary is the only income she receives. Ms. Smith is required to file a resident return on Form NJ-1040, but she will report only half her salary, since she was a New Jersey resident for only six months of the year. She is allowed to take only one-half of any exemptions, deductions, or tax credits to which she would otherwise be entitled. In addition, Ms. Smith must file a nonresident return on Form NJ-1040NR to report her income from Jane's Medical Supplies. Her salary for her period of nonresidence is considered sourced to New Jersey.

In addition to the standard forms, the following forms may have to be attached to your 1040 or 1040NR:

NJ-1040-SCH	**Schedules, A, B, & C** Use to detail amounts for state tax credits claimed, net gains from sales of property, or gains or income from rental properties, royalties, patents, or copyrights. (See Chapter 3 for a further discussion of income and what is included in gross income.)
NJ-1040-NR-A	**Business Apportionment Schedule** Use this form to allocate business income if you have a trade or business carried on both in and out of New Jersey.
NJ-2440	**Statement in Support of Exclusion for Amounts Received Under Accident and Health Insurance Plan for Personal Injuries or Sickness** Use this form to report amount of income received from your accident/health insurance plan for personal injuries or sickness. Under New Jersey rules, you are allowed to deduct these amounts from federal adjusted gross income to arrive at New Jersey taxable income. (See Chapter 3, which discusses adjustments to income.)
NJ-2210	**Underpayment of Estimated Tax by Individuals** Use this form to calculate the penalty for underpayment of estimated taxes. If you owe penalties, NJ-2210 must be attached to your tax return.
NJ-630	**Application for Extension to File New Jersey Gross Income Tax Return** Use to apply for extension of time to file a New Jersey gross income tax return. (See *Extensions* later in this chapter.)

The New Jersey resident income tax return includes a Homestead Rebate Application. This rebate is covered in the section on *Credits* in Chapter 4. Therefore, New Jersey residents who file a gross income tax return and fill out page two will have their Homestead Rebate Application automatically processed.

New Jersey does not have a separate form for partnerships to file. Therefore no separate state Schedule K-1s need to be filed either. You should use the information provided on your federal Schedule K-1 to prepare your NJ-1040 or NJ-1040NR. In addition, New Jersey does not recognize S corporation status and treats these entities as regular corporations for purposes of income taxation.

Where to File

Form Name and Number	To Send a Tax Payment	To Claim a Refund
NJ-1040 State of New Jersey Income Tax-Resident Return-Homestead Property Tax Rebate Application	State of New Jersey Division of Taxation Income Tax-CN-111 Trenton, NJ 08645-0111	State of New Jersey Division of Taxation Lakewood Processing Center 895 Towbin Rd. Suite A Lakewood, NJ 08701-5991
NJ-1040NR State of New Jersey Income Tax—Nonresident Return	Division of Taxation Gross Income Tax-CN-244 Trenton, NJ 08646-0244	Division of Taxation Gross Income Tax-CN-244 Trenton, NJ 08646-0244

Due Dates—When Do I File?

Resident, Nonresident, and Part-Year Resident Individuals. If your federal income tax return is based on a calendar year, your New Jersey income tax return must be filed no later than April 15, 1993. If you file your federal income tax return on a fiscal year basis (a year ending on the last day of any month except December, or a 52/53 week year), your New Jersey income tax return must be filed on or before the 15th day of the fourth month following the close of your fiscal year. (See the following section, *Extensions*, for information about requesting an extension of your return due date.)

When a due date falls on a Saturday, Sunday, or legal holiday, it is extended to the next business day.

Deceased Taxpayers. The due date for filing on behalf of a taxpayer who died during the year is the same as for any other taxpayer. The return should be filed for the decedent by the executor, administrator, or surviving spouse. If a member of the Armed Forces of the United States dies while serving in a combat zone or as a result of wounds or injury incurred in combat, he or she is not subject to tax in the year in which he or she died and for any prior taxable years ending on or after the day he or she began serving in a combat zone.

Partnerships. A partnership is required to file a copy of federal Form 1065, Partnership Return, with New Jersey. This return shows the distributive share of each partner in the various classes of partnership income, losses, deductions, and credits. Federal Form 1065 is due to New Jersey on the 15th day of the fourth month following the close of the tax year.

If a partnership is terminated and completely liquidated during its normal taxable year, resulting in an accounting period of less than 12 months for federal income tax purposes, the return is due the 15th day of the fourth month after the end of the accounting period.

Other Taxes. You may be subject to filing requirements for other taxes, such as Sales and Use Tax, Estate and Gift Tax. (Refer to Chapter 7, *Other Taxes*, for a discussion of these taxes.)

Fiduciaries. Persons filing as fiduciaries must follow the same filing requirements as apply to resident returns.

Extensions

New Jersey allows an extension for filing your gross income tax returns, whether you are a resident or a nonresident. You are entitled to an automatic four-month extension of time if you have been granted an extension to file your federal tax return. To receive a New Jersey extension, you must attach your federal extension request (Form 4868) to your gross income tax return. Unlike New York, New Jersey does not require an application for your initial extension. However, you must have paid at least 80% of the tax actually due for the year by the April 15th due date. Otherwise, interest charges and a penalty for late filing may be assessed against you. If you think you have underpaid, file Form NJ-630 and remit the outstanding balance by April 15th.

TAXPLANNER: An extension does not extend the time you have to pay the tax. It merely extends the time to file your return. To avoid interest and penalties, be conservative when estimating your New Jersey income tax liability.

Trusts and estates also qualify for the New Jersey four-month automatic extension. Like individuals, the estate or trust must have paid at least 80% of its actual tax liability for the year by the due date of the original return. Partnerships need not be concerned about extensions in New Jersey. Their filing obligations are informational only. (See *Who Must File* at the beginning of this chapter.)

Active military personnel unable to file on time due to injury, hospitalization, or distance are granted automatic three-month extensions. If you are in active service, attach a note to your return stating why you needed additional time to file. Remember, though, that the 80% of payment rule applies to military personnel as well as civilians.

Additional Extensions of Time

If you are not requesting a federal extension, you are requesting additional time beyond the automatic four-month period, or you are paying some or all of the remaining balance of your tax, you must file Form NJ-630, Application for Extension of Time to file New Jersey Gross Income Tax Return. Send this form to the following address:

New Jersey Division of Taxation
CN-046
Trenton, NJ 08646-0046

You must state the reason you are requesting an extension on Form NJ-630. You will *not* be notified if it is accepted.

TaxAlert: New Jersey will only notify you if your request for an extension has been denied. Generally, you cannot request an extension in New Jersey for more than six months. Once you have received the automatic four-month extension and the additional two-month extension granted by filing Form NJ-630, no further extensions will be granted except under exceptional circumstances.

Exception: New Jersey granted an additional 180 days in which to file gross income tax returns for military and civilian personnel stationed in the Persian Gulf during Operation Desert Shield and Desert Storm. The Gulf War was considered an "exceptional circumstance."

Mailing

New Jersey's mailing rules must be followed carefully. An extension request will be considered filed on time if the United States Post Office postmarks the envelope no later than the due date of the return for which you are making the request. If you send the request by certified or registered mail, the U.S. postmark or registration stamp date is considered the date of filing. An extension request that is hand-delivered or sent by overnight or messenger delivery will be considered filed on time only if the New Jersey Division of Taxation *receives* it by the date the request is due. If the last day for filing falls on a Saturday, Sunday, or legal holiday, the due date is extended to the next regular business day.

Example

If you send Form NJ-630 by U.S. certified mail on August 14, the day before your automatic extension is due to expire, it will be considered filed on time, even if the Division of Taxation does not receive it until August 17. The date of the postmark on the certified letter is considered the date you filed your request.

TaxPlanner: Save your post office receipt and return receipt. If you are ever challenged by the taxing authorities, they are proof that you mailed your request on time and that it was received.

Information Block

The top portion of your income tax return is called the "information block." It requests general information about you and your spouse primarily for purposes of identification. This section explains what information you will need to fill out this portion of your return.

If you received a pre-printed label from New Jersey, use it. Sections 1–3 do not apply to you. However, if the pre-printed label has incorrect information, cross out the incorrect information. Then just write in the correct information. If you do not have a label, read on.

Tax Year

If you are filing a return for a period *other than* calendar year 1992, you must indicate that on the top of any New Jersey return. The line to be filled in at the top of the form starts with the phrase, "For Tax Year January 1–December 31, 1992 or Other Tax Year Beginning . . . ."

Check box if application for federal extension is attached: If you asked for and were granted a federal extension to file your federal Form 1040, check the box and attach a copy of your application for federal extension, federal Form 4868.

1. *Name:* Enter your last name first, followed by your first name and middle initial, if you have one. If you are filing jointly with your spouse, list your spouse's first name and middle initial. If your spouse has a different last name, be sure to enter it, too.
2. *Address:* Enter your current home address. If this address differs from your residence during the year, attach a statement explaining why it is different.

Example

Bob moved to Connecticut on February 1, 1993, after living in New Jersey for all of 1992. Bob will attach a brief explanation to his New Jersey resident return stating that he left New Jersey on February 1, 1993. Bob will enter his Connecticut address as his current home address on Form NJ-1040.

3. *Social Security Number:* If you are filing a joint return, enter both your own Social Security number and that of your spouse. Enter each Social Security number next to the name of the spouse to whom it applies. If you are filing separately, you need enter only your own Social Security number.
4. *County/Municipality Code:* (on Form NJ-1040 only): Enter the four-digit county or municipality code for the county or municipality in which you currently reside. See the instructions to Form NJ-1040 for the list of codes. If your county or municipality does not appear on the list, call the New Jersey Taxpayer Information Services at 1-(800)-323-4400 or 1-(609)-292-6400.
5. *State of Residency* (Form NJ-1040 NR only): Enter the state of which you are currently a resident.
6. *Filing Status:* Check the appropriate box. (See *Filing Status* earlier in this chapter.)
7. *Exemptions:* Check the applicable boxes. The box for your regular personal exemption is already checked off. (For information on exemptions, see *Personal Exemptions and Dependents*.)
8. *If you were a New Jersey resident for only part of the taxable year, give the period of New Jersey residency:* If you lived in New Jersey during only part of the year, list the dates during which you were a resident.

Example

Jason moved to New Jersey on January 1, 1982 and established a residence there. On August 31, 1992, he sold his home and moved to Vermont. Jason was a resident of New Jersey from January 1, 1982 to August 31, 1992. He should fill out his residency status (Question 13) as follows:

"From January 1, 1982 to August 31, 1992."

9. *Gubernatorial Elections Fund:* If you and/or your spouse wish to have $1 of your taxes sent to the Gubernatorial Elections Fund, check the "Yes" box. Otherwise, check the "No" box. Checking the "Yes" box does not decrease your refund or increase your tax liability.

3 | Calculating Your Taxable Income

Residents—Starting Point

Introduction

The preceding chapters discussed preliminary matters, such as deciding whether or not you need to file a personal income tax return and whether to file as a resident or a nonresident. By now, you've organized your records, figured out who your dependents are for tax purposes, and made the basic decisions about how to file.

Now it's time to start actually calculating your tax. Don't be nervous. This chapter and the succeeding ones will lead you through the process, step by step and line by line. If you are a *resident*, this chapter will show you how to fill in the first few lines of your return and to report your gross income to New Jersey. If you are a *nonresident*, please skip ahead to the section titled *Nonresidents/Part-Year Residents—Starting Point*.

If you looked at the sections for New York and Connecticut, you may have noticed that the term *federal adjusted gross income* was used to describe these initial entries on your return.

Unlike New York and Connecticut, New Jersey does not require you to report your federal adjusted gross income. Rather, New Jersey requires that you report your *gross income*. Your New Jersey *gross income* consists of certain enumerated "baskets" or categories of income. If an item of income is not included in one of these baskets, that item is considered excluded from the gross income calculation, even though you may have reported it on your federal Form 1040, 1040A, or 1040EZ.

New Jersey's gross income base is the sum of several categories of income. Each category is calculated and reported separately. Each category is determined independently of the other. You cannot net losses from one category of income against gains from another category.

> **TaxAlert:** Because New Jersey requires that you calculate your income categories separately, you cannot offset capital gains or losses against profits or losses from conducting a trade or business. For the treatment of partnership gains or losses, see New Jersey's Gross Income Category #7, *Distributive Share of Partnership Income* on page NJ-13.

New Jersey's Gross Income Categories: NJ-1040, *Lines 14-26*

1. Renumeration for Services: *NJ-1040, Line 14*.
    You must report all of your wages, salaries, tips, fees, commissions, bonuses, and fringe benefits as the first category of income on Line 14 of your NJ-1040. The amounts you report must be the same as the amounts reported on Line 25, *state wage tips, etc.* of your form W-2. A copy of each W-2 you received must be attached to your NJ-1040. Because you must report your gross wages, any business expenses you incurred as an employee are not deductible. It is important to note New Jersey wages may be greater than federal wages, since no deductions are permitted for items such as moving expenses, compensation for injury, meals and lodging, etc.

2. Interest Income: *NJ-1040, Lines 15a and 15b*.
    All interest income is included in New Jersey gross income except those items specifically exempt under federal and state law. Interest from direct obligations of the U.S. government and from New Jersey obligations is exempt. However, interest income from obligations of other states is included in gross income. Enter on Line 15a only the amount of taxable interest income you received.

    Enter the amount of tax-free interest you received on Line 15b. No tax is imposed on this amount. It is requested for informational purposes only.

Example

Steven's investment portfolio includes New York State bonds, New York City bonds, federal bonds, New Jersey and California State bonds. On line 15a, he must enter the amount of interest received or accrued on his non-New Jersey state bonds. If Steven received interest income of $1,000 from New York State bonds, $1,000 from New York City bonds, $2,000 from interest on federal treasury bonds, $2,000 from New Jersey State or municipal bonds and $1,000 from California State or municipal bonds, he must include the amounts received from New York and California, ($3,000). On Line 15b he must enter his interest received from federal and New Jersey bonds for informational purposes only.

3. Dividends: *NJ-1040, Line 16*.
    Dividends are defined as any distributions made by a corporation to its shareholders, whether in the form of money or property. You need not include distributions from a New Jersey qualified investment fund. However, distributions from all other mutual funds must be included.

    For New Jersey purposes, a qualified investment fund is a fund whose portfolio assets are at least 80% invested in obligations issued by the State of New Jersey or local municipal governments. The 80% minimum must be satisfied at the close of each quarter of the tax year.

    If you received income in the form of dividends, as a shareholder from a federal S corporation, you are required to include this distribution in your gross income in the year received, regardless of the federal treatment. New Jersey does not recognize federal S corporations and does not provide for any special treatment of their shareholders. Therefore undistributed income from an S corporation is not included in gross income until it is received.

Ordinary dividends are the most common type of distribution paid out by a corporation to its shareholders. Unless otherwise noted, you should assume that any dividend you receive is an ordinary dividend and is includible in your gross income. Box 1b of Form 1099-DIV shows your ordinary dividends. This entire amount is generally included in Line 35 of Column A, Part 1.

4. Net Profits from Business: *NJ-1040, Line 17.*
New Jersey gross income includes the net profits from any business or profession you conduct. You are permitted to group net profits with business expenses in this category of income. You may not claim a deduction for taxes that were based upon the business's income. Whether you use the cash or accrual method of accounting, it must be the same method that you used for federal income tax purposes. You must attach a copy of your federal Schedule C (Form 1040), *Profit or Loss from Business*, to your NJ-1040.

Example
Laura invests in stock for her own personal gain. She does not offer her investment services to anyone else in exchange for a fee. She derives substantial income from these investment activities and incurs certain related expenses in the process. Laura's investment income is not considered net profits from a business or profession. She is required to report her gross earnings from the stock market as income from dividends.

5. Net Gains or Income from Disposition of Property: *NJ-1040, Line 18 and Schedule B, Line 14.*
Net gains or income, less net loss, from the sale, exchange, or any other disposition of tangible or intangible property is included in New Jersey gross income. To report this type of income, complete Schedule B, *Net Gains or Income from Disposition of Property*. Enter the amount you reported on Line 4 of Schedule B, *Net Gains*, on Line 18 of your NJ-1040.

You need not report capital gain distributions from qualified mutual funds if the gains are from direct obligations of the federal government or New Jersey.

6. Pension, Annuities, and Individual Retirement Arrangement withdrawals: *NJ-1040, Line 19.*
You must include all distributions from fully taxable pensions or annuities in your New Jersey gross income. A fully taxable pension or annuity is, in general, one for which your employer contributed the full cost. Because those contributions were not taxed to you as income when your employer made them, the distributions are taxable. Finally, certain withdrawals from an Individual Retirement Arrangement may be taxable gross income. In general, this includes withdrawals from accumulated earnings in your IRA that exceed the value of contributions that were taxed to you when you made them.

TAXALERT: Contributions to an Individual Retirement Arrangement are not deductible.

Enter the amount of *taxable* distributions you received from pensions or annuities, plus any taxable Individual Retirement Arrangement withdrawals you received, on Line 19a.

TAXALERT: Certain distributions from pensions or annuities may be partially taxable. Call your employer's Benefit Office or plan administrator for more information.

If you are 62 or older, or disabled, you may exclude some or all of the pension or annuity distributions you included on Line 19a. If you qualify, enter on Line 19b the lesser of (a) the amount you entered on Line 19a or (b) an amount taken from the following chart:

Filing Status	Exclusion
Married filing jointly	$10,000
Single, head of household or qualifying widow(er)	$ 7,500
Married filing separately	$ 5,000

Taxable pension and annuity income does not include:

- Social Security and Railroad Retirement Act benefits (Tier I or Tier II);
- Disability pension benefits for total or partial disability;
- Payment in the form of annuity, endowment, or life insurance contract;
- Rollovers of amounts into another federally qualified investment plan;
- 401(k) contributions made by an employer on behalf of an employee; or
- Voluntary withholding of tax from a pension or annuity.

Subtract Line 19b from Line 19a. Enter the result on Line 19c.

7. Distributive Share of Partnership Income: *NJ-1040, Line 20.*
Your share of income from a partnership of which you are a partner must be included in gross income whether or not the income was actually distributed to you. Enter the total amount of your income from all partnerships, as reported on federal Schedule K-1, on Line 20. A net loss is limited to zero. Attach a copy of your federal Schedule K-1 to your New Jersey return.

TAXSAVER: If you are a partner in more than one partnership, you may offset your share of income from a partnership with losses from another partnership in calculating your New Jersey gross income.

8. Net Gain or Income from Rents, Royalties, Patents, and Copyrights: *NJ-1040, Line 21, Schedule C, Line 3.*
You must report your net gains or income from rents or royalties from the licensing or sale of patents or copyrights on Schedule C of your New Jersey return on Line 21. In general, you must report the same amounts that you reported on your federal Schedule E for these categories of income. However, you cannot carry back or carry forward a loss. New Jersey has no special rules regarding passive losses. Therefore, treatment of these losses for New Jersey purposes may differ from federal treatment.

9. Net Gambling Winnings: *NJ-1040, Line 22.*
All winnings from gambling must be reported as gross income after netting out losses. You may exclude any winnings or losses from the New Jersey State lottery.

Lottery winnings from other states, however, are includible.

10. Alimony and Separate Maintenance Payments: *NJ-1040, Line 23.*

If you received alimony payments or separate maintenance payments during the year, pursuant to a decree of divorce or separate maintenance, you must report those amounts as gross income. Child support payments are excluded from New Jersey gross income.

11. Other Income: *NJ-1040, Line 24.*

The following list gives examples of the types of gross income that must be reported as *Other Income* on Line 24.

- Any prizes or awards you received, but not scholarships or expenses paid under a grant, fellowship, or endowment from an educational institution;
- Income in respect of a decedent: All income to which a decedent would have been entitled if death had not occurred. The income must be included in New Jersey gross income if it is included in the federal adjusted gross income;
- Net Gains or Income from Estates or Trusts: This includes any taxable distributions of trust income, as reflected on Schedule K-1 of federal Form 1041. You should have received this form from the Trustee or Fiduciary. (Note: No deduction is allowed for federal and state inheritance taxes.); and
- Rental Value of Residence Furnished by an Employer: If your employer furnishes you with a residence, the fair rental value of the residence must be included in gross income if it is reportable for federal purposes. If your employer supplements your rent by a rental allowance, the amount of the allowance must be included in gross income. Also report on Line 24 any other taxable income you received that you have not previously included on another line. If you have questions about a particular item of income, consult a professional tax advisor.

12. Total Other Income; NJ-1040, Line 25

Enter the total of Lines 21 through 24 on Line 25.

13. New Jersey Gross Income; NJ-1040, Line 26(c) to calculate your total New Jersey gross income, to which you will apply your allowable deductions, subtract Line 26(b) from Line 26(a) and enter the difference on Line 26(c).

Residents—Additions and Subtractions

Completing the last section was hard work. You may even think you've earned a break by now. Guess what? This section will be very short. Unlike New York and Connecticut, New Jersey has no modifications.

This is because New Jersey bases its tax solely on separately itemized New Jersey gross income, instead of "piggybacking" federal adjusted gross income. So there are no modifications, additions, or subtractions to federal gross income required or permitted by state law to be made.

Have a cup of coffee. Watch some television. Or proceed to the next section, *Deductions*.

Deductions

New Jersey allows resident individuals only three deductions. These deductions are:

- Personal and dependent exemptions;
- Medical expenses; and
- Alimony or separate maintenance payments.

Here we will present an overview of the three deductions mentioned above. Note that these are not really "deductions" in the federal sense. As explained earlier, New Jersey uses a different tax base, based on gross income instead. However, the deductions discussed below serve to reduce your New Jersey taxable income and, ultimately, decrease your tax.

Exemptions: NJ-1040, *Line 27*

A full discussion of personal and dependent exemptions is contained in *Personal Exemptions and Dependents* in Chapter 2. Please review that section for instructions on completing Line 27.

Medical Expenses: NJ-1040, *Line 28*

Note to Nonresidents Filing Form NJ-1040NR: The rules for completing Part IV of your nonresident return, *Medical Expenses*, are exactly the same as the rules discussed below.

You are allowed to deduct medical expenses that you paid for yourself, your spouse, or a qualified dependent, if you were not reimbursed for these expenses. Generally, the same rules apply for New Jersey purposes as for federal purposes. To be deductible, your medical expenses must exceed 2% of your New Jersey gross income as reported on Line 26c.

Medical expenses are defined as nonreimbursed payments for doctors or dentists, other medical fees, hospital or nursing care, medicines and drugs, prosthetic devices, x-rays, and other diagnostic services conducted by or directed by a doctor or dentist. In addition, you may also include amounts paid for transportation that was essential to medical care and insurance covering medical care.

Example

Scott and Sally are married and file jointly. They have New Jersey gross income of $25,000 for 1992. They have 2 children. Scott's mother lives with his family. She is supported by Scott and claimed as a dependent by Scott on his 1992 tax return. During 1992, the family had the following medical expenses:

Medical Expenses	Total Fee	Amount Reimbursed	Unreimbursed Expenses
Doctor's fees	$3,000	80% or $2,400	$ 600
Prescription medicines	200	80% or $160	40
Transportation to doctors	100	0% or $0	100
Hospital fees (including lab, nursing and therapy)	4,000	50% or $2,000	2,000
X-rays	200	80% or $160	40
Dentist's fees	500	100% or $500	0
Total	$8,000	$5,220	$2,780

Scott and Sally can only deduct the amount of unreimbursed medical expenses that are greater than 2% of their gross income.

Scott and Sally can deduct the following amount of medical expenses on their 1992 tax return:

Gross income for 1992:	$ 25,000
Multiplied by 2% threshold	× 2%
	$ 500

Total unreimbursed medical expenses:	$ 2,780
2% threshold from above	(500)
Amount deductible on Line 28.	$ 2,280

If Scott and Sally had gross income of $150,000, they would not be able to deduct any medical expenses.

Gross income for 1992	$150,000
Multiplied by 2% threshold	× 2%
	$ 3,000

Total unreimbursed medical expenses	$ 2,780
2% threshold from above	(3,000)
Amount deductible on tax return	$ -0-

TaxAlert: If you are audited by New Jersey and have taken a deduction for medical expenses, it is likely that you will be asked to support your deduction. Therefore, you should keep records, such as medical bills, that prove your expenses.

Special Rule for Decedents

If a taxpayer dies and expenses for his or her medical care are paid out of his estate that qualify as allowable medical expenses for federal purposes, any payments made within one year beginning with the day after death will be deductible in the year they are incurred.

TaxAlert: Medical expenses for decedents are not deductible for New Jersey purposes if they are not deductible for federal income tax purposes.

Example

Bill filed his 1991 income tax return on March 1, 1992. Bill died on July 4, 1992. He had unpaid medical expenses for 1991 of $2,500 and $1,000 for 1992. Bill's executor paid the medical expenses in February of 1993, within the one year requirement period. Therefore, Bill's executor can file an amended return for 1991, claiming the $2,500 medical expenses as if they were paid in 1991. When Bill's executor files Bill's 1992 tax return the executor can claim the $1,000 of medical expenses as if these expenses were paid in 1992.

Alimony and Separate Maintenance Payments: NJ-1040, *Line 29*

While a qualified deduction for alimony is treated as an adjustment to gross income before deductions or credits for federal tax purposes, New Jersey treats the deduction as if it were similar to a federal itemized deduction. Although the treatment is different, the results are the same. If your payment of alimony qualifies as outlined below, you will be allowed to deduct it from your New Jersey gross income to arrive at your New Jersey taxable income.

You may deduct any alimony and separate maintenance payments made to a spouse or former spouse if the payment meet *both* of the following rules:

- The payments are made pursuant to a court decree or order; and
- The payments are includable as income to the spouse or former spouse.

Add Lines 27c, 28, and 29. Enter the total on *Line 30*, Total Exemptions and Deductions. You have now completed Form NJ-1040 through the section on exemptions and deductions. Please turn to Chapter 4, *How to Figure Your Tax.*

Nonresidents/Part-Year Residents—Starting Point

As a nonresident you must begin preparing your tax returns by computing your New Jersey gross income from all sources as if you were a resident. Next you must determine the amount of gross income you received from New Jersey sources during the year. If you are a nonresident, income from sources within New Jersey means those items of income, gains, and losses that you earned, received, or acquired from:

1. Personal services (i.e., salaries, wages, tips, commissions, *etc.*) performed in New Jersey;
2. The ownership or sale of any interest in real or tangible personal property located in New Jersey;
3. A trade, profession, or occupation carried on in New Jersey;
4. A distributive share of an unincorporated business, profession, enterprise, undertaking, or other activity as the result of work done, services rendered, or other business activity conducted in New Jersey; or
5. Intangible personal property used in a trade, business, profession, occupation, or business carried on in New Jersey.

The ratio of your gross income from New Jersey sources over your gross income from all sources will later be used to prorate the amount of New Jersey exemptions and deductions you will be entitled to subtract from your gross income from New Jersey sources in the computation of your New Jersey taxable income. (See *Computation of Tax for Nonresidents* in Chapter 4, for more information.)

Part-Year Residents

If you moved to or from New Jersey during the year, you will be taxed as a part-year resident. If you received *no* income from New Jersey while you were a nonresident, you are subject to tax for only the portion of the year during which you were a resident. Part-year residents must prorate all exemptions, deductions, and credits, including the pension exclusion to reflect the period covered by the return. If you received income from New Jersey sources while a nonresident, you may also be subject to tax for the period of nonresidence. In this case, you must file both resident (Form NJ-1040) and nonresident (NJ-1040NR) returns. (See the section for *Residents* at the beginning of this chapter for more information regarding the resident return.)

Nonresidents

New Jersey uses "gross income" as its tax base. New Jersey gross income consists of specified categories of income that you may have received during the year. To begin calculating your New Jersey gross income as if you were a resident, you must start with the computation of total income everywhere and from New Jersey sources. Use Part I on Form NJ-1040NR for this purpose.

PART I—TOTAL INCOME (Lines 33–44)

Part I, Form NJ-1040NR is reproduced below:

PART I	TOTAL INCOME	Net losses in one category cannot be applied against income in another. In case of a net loss in any category, enter "zero" for that category		(Column A) AMOUNT OF GROSS INCOME (EVERYWHERE)	(Column B) AMOUNT FROM NEW JERSEY SOURCES
33.	Wages, salaries, tips, and other employee compensation		33		
34.	Interest		34		
35.	Dividends		35		
36.	Net profits from business (Attach copy of Federal Schedule C, Form 1040)		36		
37.	Net gains or income from disposition of property (From line 48)		37		
38.	Net gains or income from rents, royalties, patents, and copyrights (From Line 51)		38		
39.	Net Gambling winnings		39		
40.	Pensions, Annuities and IRA Withdrawals, Less New Jersey Exclusion		40		
41.	Distributive Share of Partnership Income		41		
42.	Alimony and separate maintenance payments received		42		
43.	Other—State Nature and Source _____		43		
44.	TOTAL INCOME (Add Line 33 thru 43) (Enter here and on Line 14a, Page 1)		44		

You must report your gross income from all sources in Column A of Part I. Gross income from New Jersey sources is reported in Column B. The section that follows on *page NJ-19, Attributing Income to New Jersey—Sourcing Rules*, provides information on how to allocate your wages, salary, or other employment compensation if you work outside New Jersey part of the time. *Special Problems in Attributing Income*, beginning on *page NJ-23*, discusses sourcing your income from deferred compensation and partnerships to New Jersey. Other New Jersey source income needed for Part I, Column B is discussed below. Lines 33 through 44 of Part I list the following categories of income:

Wages, Salaries, Tips, and Other Employee Compensation: NJ-1040NR, *Line 33*

Enter in Column A the total amount of your gross income from wages, salaries, fees, commissions, bonuses, tips, unemployment compensation, fringe benefits, and any other compensation you received for services as an employee. Income from employee compensation includes amounts found in Box 10 or 25 (*Wages, tips, other compensation*) of Form W-2. Remember to attach the state copies of these forms to your return. Employee business expenses and moving expenses are not deductible. However, to the extent that payments received from your employer represent reimbursements for these expenses, you are not required to include them as income.

See *Attributing Income to New Jersey—Sourcing Rules* later in this chapter, to determine your entry to Column B.

TaxAlert: If you receive excludable reimbursements for employee business expenses or moving expenses that are reflected in your W-2 form, be sure to attach a rider to your return which clearly states the amount you are excluding. Also, state the reason why you are excluding this amount. Attach a copy of your federal Form 2106, *Employee Business Expenses*, and/or federal Form 3903, *Moving Expense*, to your return as well.

Interest: NJ-1040NR, *Line 34*

Enter in Column A all your interest income, other than income from New Jersey obligations and obligations that are free from state and local taxation under state or federal laws,

such as U.S. Savings Bonds, Treasury Notes, *etc.* Interest from certain federal securities, such as "Ginnie Maes," "Fannie Maes," and "Freddie Macs," is taxable because these securities are not considered direct obligations of the federal government.

Generally, any remaining interest that you receive or that is credited to your account and can be withdrawn will be included in your gross income. Banks, savings and loans, and other payers of interest usually report your interest income to you in Box 1 on Form 1099-INT, *Interest Income*, Form 1099-OID, *Original Issue Discount*, or a similar statement. These forms show the interest you earned during the year and are for your records only. You do not have to attach them to your return.

Any interest income that you earned through a partnership, S corporation, estate, or trust will appear on your Schedule K-1. If this interest income is passive income to you, and was not earned in the ordinary course of business, it must still be reported here.

Amounts you receive from a mutual fund or other regulated investment company are includible in gross income unless the fund is a qualified investment fund as defined by New Jersey law. A New Jersey *qualified investment fund* is a regulated investment company in which at least 80% of the underlying investments are obligations issued either directly by the federal government or by the State of New Jersey or any of its political subdivisions. If you are not sure whether your mutual fund qualifies, contact your broker or mutual fund sponsor.

As a nonresident, most interest income you receive will not be taxable to New Jersey. However, "flow-through" interest you may have received from a partnership that does business in New Jersey, interest received from loans used in a New Jersey business, etc., may be considered taxable for New Jersey purposes. See the section on *Special Problems in Attributing Income*, later in this chapter, for more information.

TaxAlert: If you received a distribution from a qualified investment fund, you may only exclude from gross income the portion that is attributable to qualified exempt obligations. If you are a shareholder in a fund that is a qualified investment fund for New Jersey purposes, you should generally receive notification from the fund by February 15 telling you what portion of each distribution may be excluded from your gross income.

EXCEPTION: If you were subject to a forfeiture penalty resulting from a premature withdrawal of a time deposit account, such as a certificate of deposit, you may treat this as a loss and apply it against your interest income.

Dividends: NJ-1040NR, *Line 35*

Enter in Column A the amount of dividends you received during the year. Dividends are distributions of money, stock, or other property that you receive from a corporation. The amount of your taxable dividends will generally be reported to you on either Form 1099-DIV, *Dividends and Distributions*, or Schedule K-1. In some instances, such as substitute payments in lieu of dividends, your dividends will be reported to you on Form 1099-MISC, *Miscellaneous Income*.

Most corporations use Form 1099-DIV, *Dividends and Distributions*, to show you the types of distributions you received from them during the year. This form is for your records. You do not have to attach it to your return.

If you received income as a shareholder from a federal S corporation, you are required to include this distribution in your gross income in the year received, regardless of the federal treatment. New Jersey does not recognize federal S corporations and does not provide for any special treatment of their shareholders. Therefore undistributed income from an S corporation is not included in gross income until it is received.

Ordinary dividends are the most common type of distribution paid out by a corporation to its shareholders. Unless otherwise noted, you should assume that any dividend you receive is an ordinary dividend and is includible in your gross income. Box 1b of Form 1099-DIV shows your ordinary dividends. This entire amount is generally included in line 35 of Column A, Part 1.

As a nonresident, you do not have to include dividends in your gross income from New Jersey sources, unless the stock that gave rise to the dividends is used in a trade or business in New Jersey.

Net Profits From a Business: NJ-1040NR, *Line 36*

Enter in Column A the amount of your net income or loss from the operation of a business or the practice of your profession as a sole proprietor determined in accordance with federal provisions. All costs and expenses, other than taxes based on income, should be taken into consideration. However, similar adjustments must be made for capital gains and interest on federal, state, and local obligations as discussed under these income categories. You must attach a copy of federal Schedule C, *Profit or Loss From a Business*, to your New Jersey return.

You must enter in Column B your net income or loss from a business or profession conducted in New Jersey. (If you conducted a business both inside and outside the state, see *Attributing Income to New Jersey—Sourcing Rules*, for a discussion of business allocation.)

TAXALERT: New Jersey does not permit a carryback or carryover of net operating losses.

TAXPLANNER: When reporting business income to New Jersey, use the same method of accounting, whether cash or accrual basis, that you used for federal purposes.

TAXALERT: New Jersey does not allow a deduction for any civil, administrative, or criminal penalty or fine imposed for violation of state or federal environmental laws.

In order for an activity to be considered a business or profession, it should be entered into for a profit and must be a commercial operation; that is, goods or services must be offered to the public.

Net Gains or Income From Disposition of Property: NJ-1040NR, *Line 37*

Enter in Column A the amount of any net gains from Line 48, Part II (See Appendix I at the end of this chapter).

Enter in Column B *only* your net gains from the disposition of tangible or intangible property located in New Jersey. Net gains from installment sales should be reported in the same year in which they are reported for federal purposes.

Net Gains or Income from Rents, Royalties, Patents, and Copyrights: NJ-1040NR, *Line 38*

Enter in Column A the amount of your net income from Line 51, Part III. (See Appendix II at the end of this chapter.)

Enter in Column B all rents, etc., you received from tangible or intangible property located in New Jersey.

Net Gambling Winnings: NJ-1040NR, *Line 39*

Enter in Column A the net amount of your gambling winnings. You may use your gambling losses to offset your winnings if they are in the same year. You do not have to include gambling winnings from the New Jersey State lottery. If the net result is less than zero, enter zero. Even if you are a nonresident of New Jersey, you still have to report your gambling winnings from New Jersey sources in Column B.

Pensions, Annuities, and IRA Withdrawals: NJ-1040NR, *Line 40*

Enter in Column A the amount of pension and annuity payments you received in the year. Also include any payments or distributions you received from your individual retirement arrangement (IRA), profit-sharing plans, retirement plans (such as 401-K plan), or employee savings plans. If you have such income, you should have received Form 1099-R, *Distributions From Pensions, Annuities, Retirement or Profit-Sharing Plans, IRAs, Insurance Contracts, etc.* showing the amount of your pension or annuity distribution. If your IRA distribution is only partly taxable, only include the taxable portion on this line.

TAXALERT: Certain distributions from pensions or annuities may be partially taxable. Call your employer's Benefit Office or plan administrator for more information.

If you received a lump-sum payment, you must report the entire amount of accumulated earnings (any amount in excess of previously taxed contributions) in the year of withdrawal. There are no special provisions in New Jersey for income averaging of a lump-sum distribution. As under federal law, rollovers of cash or other assets from a qualified plan made within the 60-day grace period are generally considered tax-free distribution if you transfer the assets to another qualified plan.

EXCEPTION: If you are 62 or older, or disabled, you may exclude some or all of the pension or annuity distributions you included on Line 40, Column A. If you qualify, reduce the amount of your taxable pension income by the *lesser* of your actual taxable pension income or an amount taken from the following chart:

Filing Status	Exclusion
Married filing jointly	$10,000
Single, head of household or qualifying widow(er)	$ 7,500
Married filing separately	$ 5,000

Subtract the applicable pension exclusion from your taxable pension income and enter the result on Line 40, Column A. Exclusions from Taxable Pension and Annuity Income:

- Social Security and Railroad Retirement Act benefits;
- Disability payments for total or partial disability;
- Payment in the form of annuity, endowment, or life insurance contract;
- Rollovers of amounts into another federally qualified investment plan;
- 401(k) contributions made by an employer on behalf of the employee; and
- Voluntary withholding of tax from a pension or annuity.

Example
Kathy and Gary both qualify for the pension exclusion. They have total taxable pension income of $15,000.

Taxable pension income	$15,000
Less: Applicable pension exclusion	10,000
Amount entered on Line 40, Column A	$ 5,000

TAXSAVER: Where the maximum pension exclusion is not used, you *may* be entitled to use the unused balance on *Line 14b*, Other Retirement Income Exclusion. Be sure to complete Worksheet I which follows (under the instructions for *Line 14b*) to see if you are eligible.

Pension and annuity payments received by nonresidents are not considered income sourced to New Jersey even if you were formerly employed in the state.

Distributive Share of Partnership Income: NJ-1040NR, *Line 41*
Enter in Column A your share of any income derived from a partnership whether or not the income was actually distributed to you. Do not include undistributed gains or losses from federal S corporations. Generally, if you are a partner or shareholder in an S corporation, you will receive a federal Schedule K-1 that shows your distributive share of income, credits, and deductions. Attach copies of all your Schedule K-1s to your New Jersey return.

Enter in Column B the amount of your share of partnership income apportioned to New Jersey in accordance with the partnership's business allocation percentage. (See the section on *Special Problems in Attributing Income* for more information.)

EXCEPTION: New Jersey does not recognize federal S corporations and does not provide for any special treatment of federal S shareholders. As such, any income distributed to you as a shareholder in a federal S corporation is required to be reported in the year you received it, regardless of how the distribution was treated for federal tax purposes. Therefore, *undistributed* income from a federal S corporation is not included in your gross income until it is received.

Alimony and Separate Maintenance Payments Received: NJ-1040NR, *Line 42*
Enter in Column A the total amount of any alimony that you received in the current year, as reported on your federal return. Taxable alimony is cash payments that you received from your former spouse under a divorce or separation agreement. It includes separate maintenance payments. However, it does not include child support or payments not specifically required by a divorce or separation instrument. You do not need to report such payments as New Jersey source income if you are a nonresident. Enter zero in Column B.

Other: NJ-1040NR, *Line 43*
Line 43 is the total of any other taxable income you receive that you haven't reported elsewhere. Enter in Column A on this line the amount of any such taxable income you received. Enter in Column B the part of this amount that you received from New Jersey sources. Some categories of income that should be reported on this line are:

Prizes and Awards. Enter in Column A the cash amount or value of any prizes or awards you received during the year. Amounts you received as scholarship or fellowship grants may still be excludable for New Jersey purposes.

Enter in Column B the cash amount or value of any prizes or awards you received from New Jersey sources during the year. You do not have to include gambling winnings from the New Jersey State lottery.

Net Income from Estates or Trusts. If you are a beneficiary, include in Column A that portion of estate or trust income which was distributable or distributed to you during the year and for which no New Jersey income tax has been paid by the trust's fiduciary. Attach a copy of your Schedule K-1 (Form 1041) or similar statement, showing your share of the estate or trust's income, deduction, and credits. (Refer to *Special Problems in Attributing Income* to determine the amount to include in Column B.)

Income in Respect of a Decedent. Enter in Column A the amount of any income you received in respect of a decedent which is not reported in any other categories of income.

Residential Rental Value or Allowance Paid by Employer. Enter in Column A the rental value of a residence furnished by your employer or the rental allowance paid by your employer to provide you with a home.

EXCEPTION: You can exclude the value of a residence furnished by your employer if all three of the following statements are true:

1. The lodging is provided on your employer's business premises;
2. The lodging is furnished for the convenience of your employer; *and*
3. You are required to accept such lodging as a condition of your employment.

Any part of this amount that is connected to services performed in New Jersey should be included in Column B on this line.

Nontaxable Income. The following items of income are not taxable in New Jersey. They should not be included in income reported in either Column A or Column B:

1. Federal Social Security benefits;
2. Railroad retirement benefits (Tier I and Tier II);
3. Life insurance proceeds payable by reason of death;
4. Employee's death benefits;

5. Permanent and total disability benefits under a public or private plan and certain accident and health insurance benefits including VA disability benefits;
6. Gifts and inheritances (but not the income from property which is subject to a gift or inheritance);
7. Qualifying scholarships or fellowship grants;
8. New Jersey lottery winnings;
9. Unemployment insurance benefits;
10. New Jersey Gross Income Tax Refund;
11. Employer and employee contributions to 401(k) Salary Reduction Plans only;[1]
12. Certain distributions from New Jersey qualified investment funds;[2] and
13. Direct payments and benefits received under homeless persons assistance programs.

Total Income: NJ-1040NR, *Line 44 and Line 14a*

For both Column A and Column B, enter on Line 44 the totals of Lines 33 through 43.

Now, turn back to Page 1 of your Form NJ-1040NR. The amounts you entered on Line 44, Part I should be entered also on *Line 14a*, Column A and Column B. You are ready to continue the first page of your New Jersey nonresident return.

Other Retirement Income Exclusion: NJ-1040NR, *Line 14b*

If you are 62 years of age or over and you used less than the maximum allowable New Jersey exclusion on Line 40, Column A of Part I, Pension, Annuities, and IRA Withdrawals, you may be entitled to exclude other retirement income from your New Jersey gross income. This may include any income you receive, other than pensions or annuities.

You will not be eligible for the *Other Retirement Income Exclusion* unless your total income from wages, net business profits, and partnerships is $3,000 or less. You must also be at least 62 years old to claim this exclusion. If you file a joint return with your spouse, your *joint* income may not exceed this threshold. If you are in doubt, use the Worksheet which follows to see if you qualify.

Worksheet I—Eligibility for Other Retirement Income Exclusion

From Form NJ-1040NR:
(A) Enter amount from Line 33, Column A $ _____
(B) Enter amount from Line 36, Column A $ _____
(C) Enter amount from Line 41, Column A $ _____
(D) TOTAL Lines A through C $ _____

If the total on Line D is:
(A) Greater than $3,000, you are not eligible for this exclusion. Enter zero on Line 14b of Form NJ-1040NR.
(B) $3,000 or less, complete Worksheet II to determine your Other Retirement Income Exclusion.

Worksheet II—Other Retirement Income Exclusion

1. If you checked Form NJ-1040NR Filing Status box:
   2—Enter $10,000 on Line 2
   1, 4, or 5—Enter $7,500 on Line 2
   3—Enter $5,000 on Line 2
2. Maximum New Jersey Exclusion $ _____
3. New Jersey Exclusion Used Line 40, Part I, Column A, NJ-1040NR $ _____
4. Other Retirement Income (Subtract Line 3 from Line 2 and enter on Line 14b of Form NJ-1040NR) $ _____

[1] Employee contributions to Federal Thrift Savings Plans, 403(b), 457, SEP or any other type of retirement plan must be included in gross income.

[2] (See discussion under *Interest: NJ-1040NR, Line 34.*)

TaxAlert: When one spouse is over 62 and the other is under 62, any unused portion of the New Jersey pension exclusion for which the couple is eligible, can *only* be applied to the other retirement income attributable to the spouse who is over 62.

Exception: If you are 62 or older and are not receiving Social Security or Railroad Retirement benefits, you may be eligible to receive a Special Retirement Income Exclusion. If you think you may be eligible for this special exclusion, complete Worksheet III which follows.

Worksheet III—Special Retirement Income Exclusion

1. Circle ''Yes'' or ''No.''
   (A) Do you or your spouse (if applicable) currently receive Social Security benefits?   Yes   No
   (B) Do you or your spouse (if applicable) currently receive Railroad Retirement benefits?   Yes   No
   (C) Have you or your spouse (if applicable) ever contributed to the Social Security Fund to make you eligible to receive benefits?   Yes   No
2. Complete only if your answers to Lines 1A through 1C were *all* marked ''No.''
   (A) Enter $6,000 on line 2C if Filing Status Box 2, 4, or 5 was checked.
   (B) Enter $3,000 on line 2C if Filing Status Box 1 or 3 was checked.
   (C) Special Retirement Income Exclusion $ _____
3. Total Other Retirement Income Exclusion (Add Line 4 from Worksheet II and Line 2c, above). Enter here and on Line 14b, Column A and Column B (of Form NJ-1040NR) $ _____

Note: You should retain these worksheets for substantiation of the exclusion claimed.

Nonresidents/Part-Year Residents— Additions and Subtractions

As you've probably concluded by now, New Jersey's system of taxation is quite different from that of the federal government or its neighboring states, New York and Connecticut. New Jersey imposes its tax on gross income. This is different in some ways from an income tax. An income tax has as its basis *federal adjusted gross income* to which some state modifications are made. State modifications are income items which are added or subtracted from federal adjusted gross income.

A gross income tax, on the other hand, taxes certain income and excludes other income. For example, gross income for New Jersey tax purposes does not include interest received from obligations of New Jersey or any of its political subdivisions and U.S. obligations. If New Jersey based its tax on federal adjusted gross income, interest on U.S. government obligations would be included in that amount. By federal and state law, this interest has to be removed from federal adjusted gross income through a subtraction modification. Under the gross income method, these exempt items never entered into the income base in the first place, so they don't have to be subtracted. For this reason, this is a very short section. Under the New Jersey gross income method of taxation there are no modifications.

Attributing Income to New Jersey— Sourcing Rules

New Jersey's tax laws require nonresidents to compute their tax only on income derived from New Jersey sources. If you are a nonresident employee who earned wage and salary income both inside and outside the state and you do not know the actual amount of income earned in New Jersey, you must allocate part of your income to New Jersey.

Example

Karen, a resident of New York, is employed by Y Corporation, a New Jersey-based company. During 1992, Karen was sent to Florida for five months in order to help establish a new sales office. All other services that she performed for Y Corporation were performed in New Jersey. Since Karen performed services for her employer partly in and partly outside of New Jersey and does not know the actual amount of income she earned in New Jersey, she must allocate her wages.

In general, New Jersey requires that your allocation be based on the percentage of days you worked in New Jersey out of the total days you worked during the year. You cannot include the following days among the total days you worked:

- Saturdays, Sundays, and holidays;
- Sick days or days lost to personal injury; and
- Vacation days.

Example

Alex, a resident of Connecticut, is employed by a law firm in New Jersey at an annual salary of $80,000. During 1992, he spent 30 days in New York representing a client in a medical malpractice lawsuit. Otherwise, he worked entirely in New Jersey. Alex's income allocation percentage is determined as follows:

Total days in year		365
Nonworking days:		
Saturdays and Sundays	104	
Holidays	13	
Sick days	2	
Vacation	10	
(Total nonworking days)		(129)
Working days		236
Days worked outside New Jersey		
Days in New York	30	
(Total non—NJ working days)		(30)
Days worked in New Jersey		206

Income Allocation Percentage = 206/236 = 87.29%

TaxAlert: You should exercise caution when counting the number of days you worked outside New Jersey. Although New Jersey law and regulations do not specifically say so, it is the Division of Taxation's position that you cannot claim a day as one worked outside the state unless you were at another place because your employer required it.

TaxPlanner: Maintain adequate records to support those days you are counting as working days outside New Jersey. This is important, since these days may be questioned by New Jersey if you are ever audited. Examples of supporting records include work diaries, appointment calendars, expense reports, and trip sheets.

NJ-1040NR, Lines 55–61

If you allocate your wages or salaries, you are required to complete Part V of the NJ-1040 NR, *Allocation of Wage and Salary Income Earned Partly Inside and Outside New Jersey* (see below).

Line 55 shows your total gross income subject to allocation. This is the amount you reported on Line 33, Column A, Part I.

Complete Lines 56–60 and use the allocation formula on Line 61 to determine the amount of wages and salaries that you earned within the state. The amount included on Line 61 must be entered on Line 33, Column B, Part I.

Different rules apply if your compensation depends upon the volume of business you transact, typically if you are a salesperson on commission. Do not use Part V to calculate your New Jersey source income. You must allocate your compensation based on the percentage of business you transacted inside New Jersey out of the total business you transacted everywhere. Business is considered transacted wherever the services or sales activities involved were actually performed.

Example

Gabriel, a resident of New York, is a traveling salesman for a New York publishing company. He is paid on the basis of the volume of business he transacts. During 1992, his total volume of business transacted totalled $2,000,000. He received a 25% commission, resulting in gross income of $500,000. Only $50,000 of his total sales volume was based on sales to New Jersey customers. Gabriel must compute his New Jersey gross income in the following manner:

$$\frac{\text{Sales Volume from NJ}}{\text{Sales Volume Everywhere}} \times \frac{\text{Total}}{\text{Compensation}}$$

$$= \text{NJ Source Income}$$

$$= \frac{\$50,000}{\$2,000,000} \times \$500,000$$

$$= \$12,500$$

PART V—ALLOCATION OF WAGE AND SALARY INCOME EARNED PARTLY INSIDE AND OUTSIDE NEW JERSEY (Lines 55–61), FORM NJ-1040NR

PART V	ALLOCATION OF WAGE AND SALARY INCOME EARNED PARTLY INSIDE AND OUTSIDE NEW JERSEY	(See instructions if compensation depends entirely on volume of business transacted or if other basis of allocation is used.)		
55.	Amount reported on Line 33 in Column A of Part I required to be allocated		55	
56.	Total days in taxable year		56	
57.	Deduct non-working days (Sundays, Saturdays, holidays, sick leave, vacation, etc.)		57	
58.	Total days worked in taxable year (Line 56 minus Line 57)		58	
59.	Deduct days worked outside New Jersey		59	
60.	Days worked in New Jersey (Line 58 less Line 59)		60	
61.	ALLOCATION FORMULA $\dfrac{\text{(Line 60)}}{\text{(Line 58)}}$ x (Enter amount from Line 55) = (Salary earned inside N.J.)		(Include this amount on Line 33, Col. B, Part I)	

TaxAlert: A nonresident who allocates income based on the volume of business transacted should prepare and attach a schedule showing how the computation was made. If you use any other basis for allocating income, attach a separate schedule showing the calculation.

Self-Employed Individuals

If you are a nonresident individual who is self-employed and you earn income from a business which is carried on partly inside and outside New Jersey, you must determine your New Jersey source income using one of the following methods:

- Separate accounting;
- Formula basis apportionment of income; or
- An alternative method which fairly and equitably reflects New Jersey source income.

You are considered to be carrying on a business partly outside New Jersey if you occupy, have, maintain, or operate desk space, an office, a shop, a store, a warehouse, a factory, an agency, or other place where your business matters are systematically and regularly carried on outside New Jersey.

TaxAlert: An occasional or isolated business transaction outside New Jersey will not permit an allocation of income. You are not systematically and regularly carrying on business outside the state. You must have a regular place of business outside New Jersey in order to allocate income for business carried on outside the state.

Separate Accounting

In general, separate accounting is used to source your New Jersey income when you can specifically identify the profits earned there. If you use this method, you must keep books and records which disclose to the satisfaction of the Director of Taxation the items of income, gain, loss, and deduction attributable to your business activities carried on inside New Jersey. Otherwise, you must allocate your items of income, gain, loss, and deduction using the formula basis apportionment of income.

Formula Basis Apportionment of Income

You must use this method to allocate your income if you cannot determine your New Jersey income from your books and records. Under this method, your income is apportioned using the average of the following percentages:

- Property Percentage;
- Payroll Percentage; and
- Gross Income Percentage.

Property Percentage. The property percentage is computed by dividing the average of the beginning and ending values of real and tangible personal property located in New Jersey by the average of the beginning and ending values of real and tangible personal property located everywhere. Real property also includes real property rented by the business. To determine the fair market value of rented real property both inside and outside New Jersey, you must multiply the gross rents payable during the tax year by eight.

Gross rent includes:

- Any amount payable for the use or possession of real property whether paid as a fixed sum of money or as a percentage of sales, profits, or otherwise;
- Any amount payable as additional rent or instead of rent, such as interest, taxes, insurance, repairs, or any other amount required to be paid by the terms of a lease; and

- A proportion of the cost of any improvement to real property made by or on behalf of the business which reverts to the owner or lessor upon termination of a lease or other arrangement; however, if a building is erected on leased land by or on behalf of the business, the value of the building is determined in the same manner as if it were owned by the business.

Payroll Percentage. The payroll percentage is computed by dividing the total compensation paid during the year to employees in connection with operations carried on in New Jersey by the total compensation paid during the year to employees everywhere.

TaxAlert: You should not include payments made to independent contractors or independent sales agents in the payroll percentage. These individuals are not considered employees of your business.

Gross Income Percentage. The gross income percentage is computed by dividing the gross sales or charges for services performed by or through an office or agency of the business located in New Jersey by the total gross sales or charges for services performed inside and outside New Jersey. The sales or services allocated to New Jersey include sales made or services performed by an employee, agent, agency, or independent contractor connected to or sent out from offices of the business or its agencies located in New Jersey. It does no matter than an employee, agent, or independent contractor may make sales outside the state. All sales made by that individual are allocated to New Jersey.

Example

Aleta, a New York resident, owns a chain of book stores inside and outside New Jersey. She runs her multistate business from her headquarters located in New York. During 1992, her operating results were as follows:

	-(in thousands)-	
	New Jersey	Total
Revenues	$2,000	$4,000
General Administration		950
Advertising		400
Salaries	300	900
Rent Expense	100	300
Depreciation		250
Total Expenses		(2,800)
Net Income		$1,200

Aleta owns no real property but does own tangible personal property. The value of the property at the beginning of the year everywhere was $400,000 and at the end of the year was $300,000. The value of the property owned at the beginning of the year in New Jersey was $150,000 and at the end of the year $150,000. Aleta would compute her New Jersey income using the formula basis of apportionment in the following manner:

Property Percentage	-(in thousands)-	
	New Jersey	Everywhere
Rent (Rent Expense × 8)	$ 800	$2,400
Average Property Value:		
¹Beg-EW 400,000		
¹End-EW 300,000	150	350
Total	950	2,750

$$\text{Percentage} = 950/2{,}750$$
$$= 34.55\%$$

Payroll Percentage	New Jersey	Everywhere
Salaries	300	900

Percentage = 300/900
= 33.33%

Gross Income Percentage	New Jersey	Everywhere
Sales	2,000	4,000

Percentage = 2,000/4,000
= 50%

Total Percentages (Property, Payroll, Gross Income)
= 117.88
Average = 117.88/3
= 39.29%

Net Income Allocable to New Jersey = $1,200,000 ×
39.29%
= $471,480

¹EW means everywhere

If a percentage is missing, you must add the remaining percentages and divide by the number of percentages present. A percentage is missing when both your New Jersey amount and everywhere amount are zero. For example, you may not have a property percentage, since you have no real or personal property inside or outside the state. In this instance, you must add your payroll percentage and gross income percentage and divide by two.

Alternative Method

If you cannot determine your New Jersey income from your books and the formula basis apportionment method does not fairly reflect your New Jersey income, you may use an alternative method to allocate income. Any alternative method used must be approved by the New Jersey Director of Taxation.

> **TAXALERT:** The formula basis apportionment method or alternative method is not applied to income from the rental of real property or gains or losses from the sale of real property. The entire rental income from New Jersey real property or gain from the sale of such property is taxed by New Jersey. Likewise, any loss connected with such property can be deducted on your New Jersey return.

If you are a nonresident who carried on a business both inside and outside New Jersey, you must complete NJ-1040-NR-A, *New Jersey Gross Income Tax Business Apportionment Schedule.* If you carried on more than one business for which an allocation is required, you must prepare a separate Form NJ-1040-NR-A or similar statement for each business. Each schedule must be attached to your Form NJ-1040NR.

NJ-1040-NR-A, Schedule A

If you are a nonresident who carries on business both inside and outside New Jersey, you must complete Schedule A. This is true whether you use separate accounting, formula basis apportionment, or an alternative method to determine your New Jersey income.

In Columns 1 and 2, list all places, both inside and outside New Jersey, where you carry on business. In Column 3, describe all the places you listed in Columns 1 and 2 and state whether you rent or own these places.

If you use the separate accounting method to determine New York income, enter in the space immediately below Schedule A the words "Separate New Jersey accounts maintained."

NJ-1040-NR-A, Schedule B

If you determine your New Jersey income using the formula basis apportionment method or an alternative method, you must complete Schedule B. Do not complete Schedule B if your books and records clearly reflect your New Jersey income.

Enter on Line 1a, Column 2 the average value of real property owned by the business inside and outside New Jersey. Enter in Column 3 the average value of real property located in New Jersey.

Enter on Line 1b, Column 2 the fair market value of real property rented by the business inside and outside New Jersey. Enter in Column 3 the fair market value of real property rented in New Jersey. (Refer to the *Formula Basis Apportionment of Income* section for a explanation of how to determine the fair market value of rented real property.)

Enter on Line 1c, Column 2 the average value of tangible personal property owned by the business inside and outside New Jersey. Enter in Column 3 the average value of tangible personal property located in New York.

Enter on Line 1d, the total of Lines 1a, 1b, and 1c in Column 2 and Column 3. You must divide the Column 3 amount by the Column 2 amount to determine your property percentage. The result should be carried to four decimal places and entered as a percentage in Column 4.

Enter on Line 2, Column 2 the total compensation paid to employees located inside and outside New Jersey. Enter in Column 3 the total compensation paid to your employees in connection with operations carried on in New Jersey.

You must divide the Column 3 amount by the Column 2 amount to determine your payroll percentage. The result should be carried to four decimal places and entered as a percentage in Column 4.

Enter on Line 3, Column 2 total gross sales or charges for services performed inside and outside New Jersey. Enter in Column 3 the gross sales or charges performed by or through an office or agency of the business located in New Jersey.

You must divide the Column 3 amount by the Column 2 amount to determine your gross income percentage. The result should be carried to four decimal places and entered as a percentage in Column 4.

Enter on Line 4, Column 4 the total of the percentages from Lines 1d, 2, and 3.

You must divide Line 4 by three or the actual number of percentages if less than three to determine your business apportionment percentage. The result should be carried to four decimal places and entered as a percentage on Line 5.

PART VI—ALLOCATION OF BUSINESS INCOME TO NEW JERSEY, FORM NJ 1040NR

PART VI	ALLOCATION OF BUSINESS INCOME TO NEW JERSEY	(See instructions if other than Formula Basis of allocation is used.)

BUSINESS ALLOCATION PERCENTAGE (From Line 5, Schedule B, Form NJ-1040 NR-A)

Enter below, the line number and amount of each item of business income reported in Column A of Part I which is required to be allocated and multiply by allocation percentage to determine amount of income from New Jersey sources.

From Line No. _____ Part I $ _____ X _____ % = $ _____
From Line No. _____ Part I $ _____ X _____ % = $ _____

The Business Apportionment Percentage computed on Line 5, Schedule B must be entered in the space provided on Form NJ-1040-NR, Part VI, *Allocation of Business Income to New Jersey*.

The business apportionment percentage is to be applied to Line 36 of Part I, *Net Profits from Business*, and to each other item of business income reported in Column A of Part I which must be apportioned. You should make the proper entries in the spaces provided in Part VI. You may attach an additional sheet if more spaces are needed. Your apportioned New Jersey income is then entered on the appropriate line of Part I in Column B.

Special Problems in Attributing Income

This section discusses the unique items of income, such as deferred compensation and other retirement benefits, income from intangible personal property, and distributions from partnerships and S corporations that affect the New Jersey taxable income of nonresidents.

Deferred Compensation

Deferred compensation generally includes income that is taxed when it is received, rather than when it is earned. For example, contributions made by an employer on behalf of an employee to a qualified pension or retirement plan generally will not be taxed to the employee until the funds are made available for distribution or are distributed to the employee upon retirement.

For tax years beginning after January 1, 1989, pension and annuity income received by nonresidents for work performed in New Jersey is not subject to the New Jersey gross income tax. As a result, you should enter "zero" on Line 40, *Column B* of your New Jersey nonresident return (NJ-1040NR) to reflect the fact that you need not pay tax on this income. However, you are required to report the amount of taxable pension and annuity income you earned from all sources, including New Jersey, on Line 40, *Column A* of your New Jersey nonresident return.

Income From New Jersey Sources

If you are a nonresident, your income from New Jersey sources is any compensation, profits, gains, interest, or other income you earned, received, or acquired from any business activity in New Jersey. You might have such income if you:

1. Owned or sold any interest in real estate or personal property located in New Jersey;
2. Engaged in a trade, profession, or occupation in New Jersey;
3. Performed personal services in the state;
4. Had a share in a partnership, professional association, or other unincorporated entity that performed services or engaged in business in New Jersey; or
5. Owned intangible personal property that was used in a trade, profession, or business carried on in New Jersey.

Example

Holly, a resident of New York, owns 100% of the stock of XYZ corporation, which operates in New Jersey. The corporation pays Holly a salary of $45,000, all of which is earned in New Jersey. Holly's salary of $45,000 is subject to New Jersey tax. She also received a dividend of $5,000 from the company last year. The dividend is not taxable for New Jersey gross income tax purposes. Even though the company pay-ing the dividend owns property in New Jersey, Holly's stock is not considered "used in the business."

Example

Bruce, an amateur rock musician living in Rhode Island, owns a music publishing business located in New Jersey. Over the years, he has acquired copyrights to original scores he has composed and used in his business. Any royalty income he receives from performances of his music by other musicians must be reported on his New Jersey nonresident return.

Flow-Through Entities

Flow-through entities, such as partnerships and S corporations, are forms of doing business in which the entity itself is generally not subject to income tax. Instead, the individual partners and shareholders pay tax on the income of the partnership or S corporation, at the personal income tax rate, rather than the tax rate applicable to corporations. Although New Jersey grants "flow-through" status to partnerships, it does not give the same advantage to S corporations and their shareholders. S corporations must pay the regular corporation business tax, and their resident shareholders must pay tax on any dividends from the corporation. Nonresidents, however, don't pay tax on dividends, unless the stock giving rise to the dividends is employed in a trade or business.

Although a full discussion of flow-through entities is beyond the scope of this book, you may find the following information useful if you are a nonresident partner.

Partnerships

A partnership is not subject to the personal income tax, but the income or gain of a nonresident partner is subject to the gross income tax if it comes from a New Jersey source. The tax is based on the partner's share of the income or gain from New Jersey sources, whether or not it is distributed. This amount should be entered on Line 41, Column B, of your New Jersey nonresident return.

If you received a share of partnership income and reported it on Line 41, Column A, of your nonresident return, New Jersey requires you to attach a copy of Schedule K-1 of federal Form 1065 which you received from the partnership.

If you are a nonresident partner in a New Jersey partnership, you need report only your share of the income or gain of the partnership from activities within New Jersey in Column B. If the partnership's business is carried on both inside and outside New Jersey, use the New Jersey gross income tax allocation schedule (Form NJ-1040-NR-A) to calculate your share of the partnership's New Jersey income that you should report.

S Corporations

New Jersey does not recognize a federal S corporation election. S corporations are subject to the corporate income tax if they do business in New Jersey.

Example

John, a nonresident of New Jersey, received a dividend from an S corporation with a factory in New Jersey. New Jersey does not recognize S corporations for state tax purposes. Instead, they are treated in every way as regular business corporations. Since New Jersey does not tax dividends paid to nonresidents by regular business corporations, John's dividend will not be subject to New Jersey personal income tax unless his stock is considered "used in the business."

Appendix I

Form NJ-1040NR, Part II—Net Gains or Income from Disposition of Property (Lines 45–48)

Part II, Form NJ-1040NR, is reproduced below:

PART II NET GAINS OR INCOME FROM DISPOSITION OF PROPERTY	List the net gains or income, less net loss, derived from the sale, exchange, or other disposition of property including real or personal whether tangible or intangible.				
(a) Kind of property and description	(b) Date acquired (Mo., day, yr.)	(c) Date sold (Mo., day, yr.)	(d) Gross sales price	(e) Cost or other basis as adjusted (see instructions) and expense of sale	(f) Gain or (loss) (d less e)
45.					
46. Capital Gains Distribution				46	
47. Other Net Gains				47	
48. Net Gains (Add Lines 45, 46, and 47) (Enter here and on Line 37) (If Loss, enter ZERO)				48	

NJ-1040NR, *Line 45*

Enter in the appropriate columns on this line the net amount of your gains or losses, derived from the sale, exchange or disposition of property. This includes both real and personal property, whether tangible or intangible.

> ***TaxAlert:*** Distributions by a qualified investment fund are also excluded from gross income to the extent that they are attributable to obligations excluded from federal, state, and local taxes. See the preceding discussion of New Jersey qualified investment funds under *Interest, Line 34* on page NJ-16.

When you compute your net gain or loss, you must use the same method of accounting and tax basis that you used for federal income tax purposes. Gain on certain transactions, that are not recognized or are only partially recognized for federal tax purposes, such as tax-free reorganizations and the sale of your principal residence, may also be excluded from your New Jersey tax computation. Otherwise, all of your capital gains are taxable at their full amount. Gains from installment sales must be reported in the same year that you report them for federal income tax purposes. No deduction from gains or income is allowed for penalties, fines, or damages paid for violations of environmental laws or ordinances. Attach a rider to your return if you need additional space to report your gains or losses.

Capital Gain Distributions: NJ-1040NR, *Line 46*

Enter any capital gain distributions that were not included on Line 45. This includes taxable distributions of capital gain from a mutual fund. However, do not include any distributions you received from a qualified investment fund that are attributable to exempt federal, state, and local obligations. See earlier discussion about New Jersey qualified investment funds under *Interest, Line 34* on page NJ-16.

Other Net Gains: NJ-1040NR, *Line 47*

Enter your net gains or income, less your net losses, from the distribution of property not included in Line 45 or Line 46 above.

Net Gains: NJ-1040NR, *Line 48*

Enter the total of Lines 45, 46, and 47. Also, enter this amount on Line 37, Column A of Part I. If this amount is a loss, enter zero.

> ***TaxAlert:*** New Jersey does not allow carryforward losses that may be reported on federal Schedule D.

Appendix II

Form NJ-1040NR: Part III—Net Gains from Rents, Royalties, Patents, and Copyrights (Lines 49–51)

Part III, Form NJ-1040NR, is reproduced below:

PART III NET GAINS OR INCOME FROM RENTS, ROYALTIES, PATENTS AND COPYRIGHTS	List the net gains or net income, less net loss, derived from or in the form of rents, royalties, patents, and copyrights as reported on your Federal Income Tax Return.			
(a) Kind of property	(b) Net Rental Income (Loss)	(c) Net Income From Royalties	(d) Net Income From Patents	(e) Net Income From Copyrights
49.				
50. Totals	(b)	(c)	(d)	(e)
51. Net Income (Combine Columns b, c, d, and e) (Enter here and on Line 38) (If Loss enter ZERO) 51				

NJ-1040NR, *Line 49*

Enter in the appropriate spaces the kind of property and the net gains (or losses) you derived from rents, royalties, patents, and copyrights as you reported them on your federal return.

TAXALERT: New Jersey does not distinguish between passive and active losses. Carrybacks or carryforwards of losses are not permitted. Therefore, you may deduct federal passive losses in full in the year you incurred them *only if* you have a gain within the same category of income. For example, you can only deduct a net rental loss on a property you own if you have sufficient income from some other property to absorb the loss. Attach a rider to your return if you need additional space.

TAXPLANNER: If you have incurred a loss, and expect to receive income in that category at some time in the future, consider accelerating the income to the current year. You will then be able to take advantage of losses you have incurred to offset otherwise taxable income.

NJ-1040NR, *Line 50*

Enter on this line the individual totals of Columns (b), (c), (d), and (e).

NJ-1040NR, *Line 51*

Enter on this line the combined total of Line 50, Columns (b), (c), (d), and (e), also enter this amount on Line 38, Column A. If this amount is a loss, enter zero.

You have now completed Form NJ-1040NR through Part III. Part IV is discussed in Chapter 3 under *Deductions*. Parts V and VI were discussed in *Attributing Income to New Jersey—Sourcing Rules*.

4 | How to Figure Your Tax

Computation of Tax for Residents

After you have calculated your New Jersey taxable income, you will be ready to calculate your New Jersey "state tax due." This should be distinguished from the amount you pay with your return which is your "tax payment." In order to determine your tax payment you will need to determine how much of this year's tax you have already paid to New Jersey through payroll withholdings, estimated payments, or an overpayment of taxes last year. You may be able to reduce your New Jersey tax by a credit for income taxes paid to another state. You may owe use tax on out-of-state purchases, or wish to make a voluntary contribution to the New Jersey Wildlife Conservation or Children's Trust Fund along with your tax *before* you deduct a credit or previous payments or add any use tax you owe.

Calculating Your State Tax Due

You will need the following information to calculate your New Jersey income tax and New Jersey *total tax* after any credit or use tax:

1. Your New Jersey taxable income from Line 31 of Form NJ-1040;
2. Income taxes you paid to other states or cities (from 1992 state or local income tax returns); and
3. Use tax due on out-of-state purchases (from purchase receipts).

Determining the tax due on your New Jersey taxable income is fairly straightforward. If you are *single* or *married filing separately*, use Table A (which follows) to determine your tax. Enter the result on Line 32 of Form NJ-1040. If you are *married filing jointly*, *head of household*, or a *qualifying widow(er)*, use Table B to determine your tax. Enter the result on Line 32 of Form NJ-1040. Sample tax calculations accompany each table.

The credit for taxes paid to other states or cities is computed on Schedule A of Form NJ-1040. Any credit to which you are entitled will be subtracted from your New Jersey tax due. (See *Credits*, which follows, for a detailed discussion of credits for taxes paid to other states.)

If you purchased any taxable item out of state for delivery into or use in New Jersey, and you did not pay New Jersey sales tax on the purchase, you may be liable for New Jersey use tax. See the section on *Sales and Use Tax* in Chapter 7 for more information.

Once you have determined your New Jersey total tax after your credit and use tax due, you should subtract any taxes you have already paid through payroll withholdings, estimated payments, and credits for overpayments on tax returns from previous years. (See *Payments* to follow.)

Using the Tax Rate Schedules

TABLE A*

If your filing status is *single* or you are *married filing separately*, compute your tax as indicated in Table A below:

If the amount on Line 31 is		
OVER	BUT NOT OVER	ENTER ON LINE 32
$ 0	$20,000	2% of the amount on Line 31
20,000	35,000	$400 plus 2.5% of excess over $20,000
35,000	40,000	$775 plus 5.0% of excess over $35,000
40,000	75,000	$1,025 plus 6.5% of excess over $40,000
75,000	and over	$3,300 plus 7.0% of excess over $75,000

Example

Mike's filing status is single. His New Jersey taxable income from Line 31 of his NJ-1040 is $45,000. Mike is not claiming a credit for taxes paid to other states nor does he owe any use tax on out-of-state purchases. Mike's New Jersey tax liability is calculated as follows:

Filing status	Single	
New Jersey taxable income	$45,000	
Tax on first $40,000		1,025
Tax on excess over $40,000		
New Jersey taxable income	$45,000	
Less	40,000	
Remaining income to tax	5,000	
× 6.5% (.065)		325
New Jersey tax entered on Line 32		1,350

TABLE B*

If you are *married filing jointly* or filing as *head of household* or *qualifying widow(er)* compute your tax as indicated in Table B below:

If the amount on Line 31 is		
OVER	BUT NOT OVER	ENTER ON LINE 32
$ 0	$20,000	2% of the amount on Line 31
20,000	50,000	$400 plus 2.5% of excess over $20,000
50,000	70,000	$1,150 plus 3.5% of excess over $50,000
70,000	80,000	$1,850 plus 5.0% of excess over $70,000
80,000	150,000	$2,350 plus 6.5% of excess over $80,000
150,000	and over	$6,900 plus 7.0% of excess over $150,000

Example

Joe and Debbie are filing a joint return. Their New Jersey taxable income from Line 31 of their Form NJ-1040 is $74,000. Because Debbie is employed in Delaware, she is claiming a credit for taxes paid to other states. She has determined that her allowable credit

*From 1991 Tax Rate Schedules. The 1992 Tax Rate Schedules are reproduced in Chapter 10. Note that New Jersey's income tax rates have not changed.

is $1,000. Their New Jersey tax is calculated as follows:

Filing status..........................	Married filing jointly	
New Jersey taxable income...	$74,000	
Tax on first $70,000...........		1,850
Tax on excess over $70,000		
New Jersey taxable income	$74,000	
Less	70,000	
Remaining Income to tax...	4,000	
× 5.0% (0.5)......................		200
New Jersey tax entered on Line 32		2,050
Credit for taxes paid to other states........................		1,000
New Jersey tax liability		1,050

Computation of Tax for Nonresidents

This section will help you calculate your New Jersey income taxes if you were not a resident of New Jersey but earned money in the state. If you maintained living quarters in New Jersey and spent 183 days there during the year, or if your permanent home is in New Jersey, please refer to the sections on *Determining Residency/Domicile* and *Nonresidents* in Chapter 2, to make sure that you will not be considered a resident for tax purposes. If you qualify as a nonresident for all or part of the year and you have calculated your taxable income as discussed in Chapter 3, you are ready to compute your tax.

Calculating Your Tax

Before you can calculate your tax, you must know your filing status. New Jersey has several different tax rate schedules. Which one you use to determine your tax depends on your filing status. If you are not sure of your filing status, please refer to *Filing Status* in Chapter 2.

To determine your tax, you simply need to find your taxable income on the appropriate tax table. Your taxable income is the amount you entered on Line 21 of Form NJ-1040NR. If your filing status is *single* or *married filing separately*, use Table A. You will use Table B if your filing status is *married filing jointly, head of household*, or *qualifying widow(er)*. The examples on the following pages illustrate how these schedules are used.

Filing Status: Single or Married Filing Separately
TABLE A*

If the amount of your New Jersey taxable income is

OVER	BUT NOT OVER	ENTER ON LINE 22
$ 0	$20,000	2% of the amount on Line 21
20,000	35,000	$400 plus 2.5% of excess over $20,000
35,000	40,000	$775 plus 5.0% of excess over $35,000
40,000	75,000	$1,025 plus 6.5% of excess over $40,000
75,000	and over	$3,300 plus 7.0% of excess over $75,000

Example

Eric's filing status is *married filing separately*. His New Jersey taxable income is $27,000. Using Table A, he will compute his tax as follows:

Tax on $20,000	$400
Tax on Excess over $20,000	
Excess over $20,000	
$27,000	
−20,000	
$ 7,000	
$7,000 × 2.5% (0.25)................................	$175
Total Tax...	$575

Filing Status: Married Filing Jointly, Head of Household, or Qualifying Widow(er)

TABLE B*

If the amount of your taxable income is

OVER	BUT NOT OVER	ENTER ON LINE 22
$ 0	$20,000	2% of the amount on Line 21
20,000	50,000	$400 plus 2.5% of excess over $20,000
50,000	70,000	$1,150 plus 3.5% of excess over $50,000
70,000	80,000	$1,850 plus 5.0% of excess over $70,000
80,000	150,000	$2,350 plus 6.5% of excess over $80,000
150,000	and over	$6,900 plus 7.0% of excess over $150,000

Example

Alan's filing status is *head of household* and his taxable income is $72,000. Using Table B above, he will compute his tax as follows:

$70,000..	$1,850
Excess over $70,000	
$72,000	
−70,000	
$ 2,000	
$2,000 × 5% (.05)	$ 100
Total Tax...	$1,950

Credits

Once you have calculated your state tax due, you may be able to reduce this amount by claiming a tax credit. Residents and part-year residents of New Jersey may reduce their New Jersey tax liability by claiming a credit for income taxes paid to other states or cities. Unlike New York and Connecticut, New Jersey does not allow a credit for taxes paid to Canada or any of its provinces.

Commuters to Pennsylvania

A Reciprocal Personal Income Tax Agreement between Pennsylvania and New Jersey provides that compensation paid to a New Jersey resident who works in Pennsylvania will not be subject to income taxes in Pennsylvania. As a result, you cannot take a credit against New Jersey tax for taxes paid to Pennsylvania on compensation. However, Philadelphia imposes a tax on wages *that is not* included in the reciprocal agreement. A credit for taxes paid to Philadelphia may be claimed on Schedule A of Form NJ-1040.

TaxAlert: Pension income is not considered compensation and is not covered by the reciprocal agreement.

TaxPlanner: If you are a resident of New Jersey who is employed in Pennsylvania, be sure that your employer is *not* withholding Pennsylvania income taxes from your paycheck. You will not receive a tax credit from New Jersey for taxes withheld on wages. So check your pay stubs carefully!

If you are required to file a personal income tax return in any state other than New Jersey, including taxes on unearned income by Pennsylvania that are not covered by the reciprocal agreement, you should claim an income tax credit for income taxes paid to these other states.

*From 1991 Tax Rate Schedules. The 1992 Tax Rate Schedules are reproduced in Chapter 10. Note that New Jersey's income tax rates have not changed.

Completing Schedule A

The resident tax credit is claimed by completing Schedule A of Form NJ-1040. If you are claiming a credit for income taxes paid to more than one jurisdiction, a separate Schedule A must be attached for each state or city. The sum of the allowable credits for each jurisdiction (Line 5 of Schedule A) should be entered on Page 1, Line 33 of Form NJ-1040.

Your resident tax credit may not exceed the percentage of your New Jersey tax on income that is also taxed by the other jurisdiction. Income subject to tax in other jurisdictions means the gross income reported to the other jurisdiction (before personal exemptions or standard itemized deductions) that is also included in New Jersey gross income. The adjusted gross income taxed in the other jurisdiction should be entered on Line 1 of Schedule A. The limitation on the credit can best be expressed by the following formula:

$$\frac{\text{Income Taxed by Other Jurisdiction (from Schedule A, Line 1)}}{\text{Income Subject to Tax by New Jersey (from Schedule A, Line 2)}}$$

$$\times \text{ Tax due to New Jersey (from Form NJ-1040, Line 32)}$$

$$= \text{Resident Tax Credit Limitation Amount}$$

Enter the amount of income tax you actually paid to the other state or city for the tax year on Line 4 of Schedule A.

on each Schedule A you prepared and enter the total on Page 1, Line 33 of Form NJ-1040. Your total resident tax credit claimed on Line 33 may not exceed the tax due on Line 32.

Example

Joe is a New Jersey resident working in New York City. Joe has New Jersey income of $100,000. He completed his New York State and City nonresident tax returns (Forms IT-203 and NYC-203) and has determined that $40,000 of income is subject to tax in New York State and $50,000 of his income is subject to tax in New York City. Joe's New Jersey tax is $2,690. His New York State tax is $2,700 and his New York City tax is $225. Joe calculates his New Jersey resident tax credit in the following manner:

Credit on Income Taxed by New Jersey, New York State, and New York City

Step 1: *Amount of New Jersey tax paid on New York State income.*

$$\frac{\$40,000}{\$100,000} \times \$2,690 = \$1,076$$

Step 2: *Amount of New York State and City Income Tax paid on New York State Income.*

(a) Determine New York City tax on income taxed by both New York City and New York State.

$$\frac{\$40,000}{\$50,000} \times \$225 = \$180$$

New Jersey Resident Tax Credit
Schedule A

Name(s) as shown on Form NJ-1040		Your social security number
Schedule A CREDIT FOR INCOME OR WAGE TAXES PAID TO OTHER JURISDICTION(S)		If you are claiming a credit for income taxes paid to more than one jurisdiction, a separate Schedule A must be attached for each.

A copy of other state(s) or political subdivision tax return(s) must be attached to Form NJ-1040

1.	Income subject to tax by other jurisdiction(s) during tax year (indicate name(s) _____) (DO NOT combine the same income taxed by more than one jurisdiction) (The amount on Line 1 cannot exceed the amount shown on Line 2)	1	
2.	Income subject to tax by New Jersey (From Line 26a or see instructions)	2	
3.	Maximum Allowable Credit 1 _____ X _____ = (Divide Line 2 into Line 1) 2 (New Jersey Tax, Line 32, Page 1)	3	
4.	Income or wage tax paid to other jurisdictions during tax year	4	
5.	Credit allowed (Enter lesser of Line 3 or 4 here and on Line 33, Page 1) (The credit may not exceed your New Jersey Tax on Line 32)	5	

TaxPlanner: If you must file a return and pay tax in more than one state, it is advisable to complete your federal return first, complete the return for each non-resident state second, and complete your New Jersey return last. The reason is that you can only claim a tax credit for taxes paid to other states or cities on your resident tax return. Since your resident state requires that you enter the tax liabilities to the other nonresident states in order to determine your allowable resident credit, you must have calculated those liabilities before attempting to complete your resident return.

Enter the lower of your tax liability to the other jurisdiction or your New Jersey resident tax credit limitation amount on Line 5 of Schedule A. Add the resident tax credit you claim

(b) Add (a) to New York State tax paid.

$$\$180 + \$2,700 = 2880$$

Step 3: *Compare amounts from Step 1 and Step 2. Use lesser of $1,076 or $2,880.*

Step 4: *Amount of New Jersey tax paid on income taxed only in New York City.*

Tax Credit Restrictions on Credit for Taxes Paid to Nonresident States on S Corporation Earnings

S Corporations. New Jersey residents who are shareholders in S corporations doing business in another state may pay a nonresident income tax to that state on their share of the S corporation's undistributed taxable income. A resident tax credit is not allowed on such a tax because New Jersey does not recognize S corporations.

However, if the S corporation makes a distribution that is included as a dividend in New Jersey gross income, a limited credit may be available for a tax paid to another state. Because the resident tax credit is only allowed for taxes imposed for the taxable year, only that part of the taxable dividend that is from the S corporation's current earnings and profits is recognized in calculating the credit. No credit is available for taxes attributable to accumulated earnings and profits, because those amounts are presumed taxed by the other state in prior years.

Payments

Your total payments are comprised of amounts withheld, your estimated payments, payments you may have made with your *Extension of Time to File a New Jersey Gross Income Tax Return* (Form NJ-630), and any overpayment from prior years that you have applied to this year's tax. In addition, you may deduct *excess* withholdings of unemployment insurance or disability insurance from two or more employers. The following is a discussion of the payment section of Form NJ-1040 reproduced below. Corresponding lines on Form NJ-1040NR have been noted.

37.	Total Tax (From Line 36 Page 1)	**37**	
38.	Total N.J. Income Tax Withheld (Attach Forms W-2 and 1099R)	**38**	Check ☐ if Form NJ-2210 is attached
39.	New Jersey Estimated Tax Payments/Credit from 1991 tax return	**39**	If an amount is entered on Line 40 or Line 41 attach Form NJ-2450
40.	EXCESS N.J. Unemployment Insurance Withheld (See instr. p. 15)	**40**	←
41.	EXCESS N.J. Disability Insurance Withheld (See instr. p. 15)	**41**	←
42.	Total Payments/Credits (Add Lines 38 through 41) ..... ENTER TOTAL	**42**	

Homestead Property Tax Rebate Application

Residents whose New Jersey gross income does not exceed $100,000 may be eligible for a rebate of property taxes paid either directly (homeowners) or as part of rent (tenants). You must be domiciled in New Jersey. Statutory residents (see *Determining Residency/Domicile* in Chapter 2) do not qualify for this rebate, and the taxes must have been paid on your principal residence. A vacation home does not qualify.

What You Will Need to Complete Form HR-1040

Homeowners

1. Your NJ-1040, completed at least through Line 26c;
2. The amount of property taxes due and paid in 1992;
3. Your block and lot numbers; and
4. The Social Security numbers of your co-owners (other than your spouse).

Tenants

1. Your NJ-1040, completed at least through Line 26c;
2. The amount of rent you paid in 1992; and
3. The Social Security numbers of your co-tenants (other than your spouse).

If you meet any *one* of the following conditions, you must complete and attach Schedule HR-A to your Homestead Rebate Application:

- You lived in more than one New Jersey residence during the year;
- You shared ownership of your principal residence with anyone other than your spouse;
- Your principal residence consisted of multiple dwelling units; or
- You shared a rental apartment with anyone other than your spouse.

The State of New Jersey will calculate any rebate to which you are entitled.

The filing deadline for the Homestead Property Tax Rebate Application is April 15, 1993. If the filing deadline for your gross income tax return is extended, the filing deadline for your rebate application is also extended. If you are filing your gross income tax return (Form NJ-1040) under an extension, DO NOT submit a Homestead Property Tax Rebate Application (Form HR-1040) until you file your NJ-1040.

Total New Jersey Income Tax Withheld: NJ-1040, Line 38; NJ-1040NR, Line 23.

Enter the total of the amounts shown as New Jersey income tax withheld on your federal Forms W-2, W-2G, 1099R, or equivalent New Jersey statements. These statements must be attached to your return. If you fail to attach them, you will not receive credit for taxes withheld.

TaxALERT: When locating the New Jersey income tax withheld on your W-2 Form, check carefully to see that the amount you report is, in fact, New Jersey *income* tax. *Do not* include amounts withheld as "NJSUI"—New Jersey State Unemployment Insurance—or "NJUC"—New Jersey Unemployment Compensation. These amounts are *not* New Jersey income tax withholdings and may not be included on Line 38. To claim a credit for Excess Unemployment and/or Disability Insurance Benefit payments, you must file Form NJ-2450 in duplicate. See the discussion under Lines 40 and 41 for more information.

New Jersey Estimated Tax Payments/Credit From Prior Year Tax Return: NJ-1040, Line 39; NJ-1040NR, Line 24.

Enter the total of any estimated payments that you made for the taxable year plus any *overpayment* applied as a credit from a previous tax year's tax return. Also include any payment you made if you requested an extension of time to file your tax return.

TaxALERT: Be sure to include any estimated payments you made in 1993 when reporting payments on your 1992 return.

TaxSAVER: If you changed your name during the year because of marriage, divorce, or other reasons, and you made estimated tax payments using your former name, attach a statement to your return explaining the payments you made under different names. If you are filing a joint return, include estimated payments made by your spouse. For each payment, indicate the name(s) and Social Security number(s) under which you made the payment.

Credit For Excess Withholding of Unemployment and/or Disability Insurance: *NJ-1040, Lines 40 and 41; NJ-1040NR, Lines 25 and 26.*

You may deduct *excess* withholdings of unemployment insurance or disability insurance from two or more employers. (See the section, *Withholding*, in Chapter 7 for more information.) You must attach a completed Form NJ-2450, *in duplicate*, to your NJ-1040 or NJ-1040NR tax return in order to claim this credit. The information on Form NJ-2450 must be substantiated by your wage and tax statements or your claim will be denied. In addition, the amounts that were withheld for unemployment and disability insurance must be reported separately on all your wage and tax statements.

NJ-1040, Line 40; NJ-1040NR, Line 25.

Enter the amount of excess unemployment insurance withheld and reported on Line 4 of Form NJ-2450.

NJ-1040, Line 41; NJ-1040NR, Line 26.

Enter the amount of excess disability insurance withheld and reported on Line 5 of Form NJ-2450.

Total Payments/Credits: *NJ-1040, Line 42; NJ-1040NR, Line 27.*

Enter the total of Lines 38–41 (Form NJ-1040NR, Lines 23–27).

Amount of Tax You Owe: *NJ-1040, Line 43; NJ-1040NR, Line 28.*

If your New Jersey Total Tax (Line 37) is greater than your Total Payment (Line 42), subtract Line 42 from Line 37 and enter the difference on Line 43. This is the amount of tax you owe with your return.

Make Your Check Payable to: **"State of New Jersey-TGI."** Be sure to write your Social Security number on the face of your check.

If you owe tax and wish to contribute to the New Jersey funds (see Lines 45B and C), add the amount of your donation to your check amount.

TaxAlert: If you owe interest for the underpayment of estimated tax (Form NJ-2210), include this amount in your check.

TaxPlanner: If you owe more than $100 in tax (Line 43), you may want to increase your estimated payments or contact your employer for Form NJ-W4 to increase your withholdings. (See *Penalties* in Chapter 5 and *Withholding* in Chapter 7 for more information.)

Overpayment: *NJ-1040, Line 44; NJ-1040NR, Line 29.*

If your Total Payments on Line 42 are greater than your New Jersey Tax on Line 37, subtract Line 37 from Line 42 and enter the result on Line 44. This is the amount of your overpayment.

NJ-1040, Line 45A; NJ-1040NR, Line 30A.

Enter the amount of any overpayment from Line 44 above that you wish to have credited against your 1993 tax liability.

Contribution to NJ Endangered and Nongame Wildlife Fund and Children's Trust Fund: *NJ-1040, Lines 45B and C; NJ-1040NR, Lines 30B and C.*

If you wish to make a donation to the Endangered and Nongame Wildlife Fund, the Children's Trust Fund, or the New Jersey Vietnam Veterans Memorial Fund, check the appropriate box or enter the amount you wish to contribute. You may make a deduction regardless of whether you have an overpayment or a balance due. Please note that an entry on Line 45B or C will reduce your refund or increase your tax due.

Total Deductions from Overpayment: *NJ-1040, Line 46; NJ-1040NR, Line 31.*

Enter on Line 46 the total of Lines 45A, 45B, and 45C.

Refund: *NJ-1040, Line 47; NJ-1040NR, Line 32.*

Subtract Line 46 from the amount of any overpayment on Line 44 and enter the amount to be refunded.

TaxAlert: Don't Forget to Sign and Date Your Return!

Note: Both husband and wife must sign a joint return.

Attachments

You may be required to attach other forms or schedules to your New Jersey gross income tax return (Form NJ-1040 or Form NJ-1040NR). These forms or schedules provide additional information to the New Jersey tax authorities that will assist them in processing your return. These attachments may be forms or schedules provided by New Jersey, federal schedules you used in preparing your federal income tax return, or tax returns for other states or localities. The following section discusses what attachments may be required.

New Jersey Tax Forms and Schedules

You may need to prepare the following New Jersey forms and schedules in order to complete your state tax return. These forms should be attached to the back of your Form NJ-1040, *New Jersey Gross Income Tax Resident Return* or NJ-1040-NR, *New Jersey Gross Income Tax Nonresident Return*.

Schedule HR-A. This schedule requests additional information needed to process your *Homstead Property Tax Rebate* on the second page of your New Jersey tax return. You will need to complete this form if any one of the following statements applies to you:

- You lived in more than one New Jersey residence during the year;
- You shared ownership of a principal residence during the year with anyone other than your spouse;
- Your principal residence is in a multiple dwelling unit that you own; or
- Someone other than your spouse occupied an apartment or other rental dwelling with you and shared the rent.

You are not eligible for a Homestead Property Tax Rebate if your gross income is more than $100,000.

Form NJ-2450, Employee's Claim for Credit for Excess Unemployment and Disability Contributions. If you worked for more than one employer during the year, you may be entitled to a credit for excess withholdings of unemployment and disability taxes. You must complete this form to receive your credit. (Please refer to the *Credits* section of this chapter for additional information.)

Form NJ-630, Application for Extension of Time to File New Jersey Gross Income Tax Return. If you were not required to file Form NJ-630, and you are filing your New Jersey tax return within four months of the initial due date, you must attach a copy of the federal extension to your tax return. If you filed Form NJ-630 for your initial or additional extension of time to file, you must attach a copy of this form to your state tax return. (Please refer to the *Extensions* section of Chapter 2 for further information.)

Federal Forms That Were Attached to Your Federal Tax Return

Many of the forms and schedules that you may have completed when you prepared your federal Form 1040, *U.S. Individual Income Tax Return*, must be attached to your state tax return. These forms should be placed in numerical order at the back of your tax return. If you are not sure whether you should have completed these forms when preparing your federal return, please refer to *The Ernst & Young Tax Guide 1993*.

Schedule B, Interest and Dividend Income.

Schedule C, Profit or Loss From Business.

Form 2106, Employee Business Expenses.

Form 3903, Foreign Moving Expenses.

Schedule K-1, Partner's Share of Income, Credits, Deductions, etc.

Form W-2, Wage and Tax Statement.

Form 1099-R, Distributions from Pensions, Annuities, Retirement or Profit Sharing Plans, IRAs, Insurance Contracts, etc.

Form 1099, Misc, Miscellaneous Income.

Form W-2G, Certain Gambling Winnings.

Income Tax Returns That You Filed in Other States

You will also need to attach copies of any income tax returns that you filed in other states if you are claiming a credit for taxes paid to other jurisdictions. (Please refer to the *Credits* section of this chapter for additional information.)

5 | Estimated Taxes

Requirements

The airlines used to have an advertising slogan: "Fly now, pay later!" New Jersey's slogan for paying taxes might be: "Pay as you play." New Jersey, like the federal government, requires that taxpayers pay tax as they earn income. Thus, you must make tax payments throughout the year, in the form of estimated tax payments or withholding of tax from your salary or wages, even though your return is not due until April 15 of the following year.

This chapter discusses estimated tax payments. It explains who must pay estimated taxes, when and how much you must pay, and what forms you must file. Withholding of tax is discussed in Chapter 7.

Who Must Pay Estimated Taxes?

New Jersey requires you to make a declaration of estimated tax if you expect your New Jersey gross income tax to exceed any withholdings of tax by more than $100 (after allowing for credits). However, if you expect that your taxes withheld will equal or exceed 80% of your current New Jersey tax liability, you do not need to file a declaration.

Example

Mary works for a company that withholds New Jersey taxes from her salary. In 1992, Mary had $400 in state taxes withheld from her salary. When Mary files her 1992 New Jersey tax return, she calculates that she actually owes $700 in tax because of other income from babysitting that was not subject to withholding. This is $300 more than the tax that was withheld from her salary. Mary should have filed a declaration of estimated taxes for 1992 because her withholdings ($400) were less than 80% of her current-year liability of $700 ($700 × 0.8 = $560) and she owed more than $100 on her final return.

Estimating the Tax Due

If you think you are liable for estimated taxes after reading the previous discussion, you must estimate your taxes due for 1993. You will need to pay your estimated tax due, less any withholding or tax credits, in four equal installments during the year. Because your first installment will be due by April 15, you must estimate your tax due for the entire year before this date.

Before preparing your estimate for 1993, it's helpful to look at your 1992 return, assuming you have completed it at this point. Although your estimated tax payments must be based on your anticipated tax due for the *current* year, the previous year's return may remind you of what items of income you expect and what deductions and exemptions you usually take.

To prepare your estimate, you can use the Estimated Tax Worksheet in the instructions accompanying Form NJ-1040-ES, *Declaration of Estimated Tax*, or prepare your own estimate.

If you prepare your own estimate, begin by writing down items of income you received from last year's return (e.g., salary, interest, dividends, etc.). Next to each item, write the amount that you estimate you will receive this year. Next, add the income you expect to receive or earn this year that will be subject to tax in New Jersey. Don't forget that New Jersey has a retirement income exclusion. For more information on what you should be reporting as income, see, in Chapter 3, the *Starting Point* sections for both residents and nonresidents.

Next, determine the amount of exemptions to which you are entitled. Again, consulting your 1992 tax return may be helpful. Also refer to *Personal Exemptions and Dependents* in Chapter 2 to determine the number and amount of exemptions to which you are entitled.

Next, estimate the deductions you will take in 1993 for medical expenses and alimony or separate maintenance payments. Remember that medical expenses must exceed 2% of your gross income to be deductible. For more information on deductions, see the *Additions and Subtractions* section of Chapter 3.

At this point, you should have a fairly good idea of what your New Jersey taxable income will be for the coming year. To determine your estimated tax for the year, consult the appropriate (resident/nonresident) *Computation of Tax* section of Chapter 4. Or you can select the appropriate rate of tax for your filing status and level of taxable income from the instructions to Form NJ-1040ES.

Use this rate to determine your total estimated taxes for the year. If you are a New Jersey resident and expect to pay taxes to another state or locality outside New Jersey, you are allowed a tax credit. For more information, see *Credits* in Chapter 4.

When to Make Estimated Payments

Your installments of estimated tax must be paid by April 15, June 15, and September 15 of the current year, and January 15 of the following year.

Fiscal year taxpayers pay estimated taxes by the 15th day of the fourth month, sixth month, ninth month of their taxable year, and first month of the following taxable year.

Installment Amounts

If you are liable for estimated tax payments before April 15, you must pay 25% of the total on each of the four dates listed above.

If you file your *first* installment of estimated tax by June 15, you must pay ⅓ of the tax at that time and pay the same amount on each of the next two due dates.

If you file your *first* installment by September 15, you must pay 50% of your total estimated tax at that time and pay the other half on January 15.

If you do not become liable for estimated taxes until January 15 of the following year, you must pay *all* of your net estimated tax for the year at that time. The only exception is if you file your gross income tax return *and* pay your entire tax due by February 15.

Filing and Paying Quarterly Estimated Taxes

Your installment payments of estimated tax must be accompanied by the proper form. Form NJ-1040ES, *Declaration of Estimated Tax*, consists of four parts, or vouchers, separated by perforations. Each voucher is marked with a due date and should accompany your required payment for that due date. This will insure that your payment is properly credited to your account. If you are *married filing jointly*, don't forget to fill in your spouse's name and Social Security number too. Even if you and your spouse file separate tax returns, you may still make a joint declaration of estimated tax unless you are divorced, separated, or have different taxable years.

Make your check payable to "State of New Jersey—TGI," write your Social Security number on the face of your check, and send your check and completed voucher (Form NJ 1040-ES) to:

State of New Jersey—TGI
CN 222
Trenton, NJ 08646-0222

Use U.S. certified mail, if possible, and retain your receipt as proof that you filed your estimated tax on time.

Penalties

Introduction

As a New Jersey resident you should have paid at least 80% of your income tax during the year, through taxes that are withheld by your employer or through estimated tax payments. New Jersey will assess a penalty for underpayment of estimated tax if you pay *less than* 80% of the estimated tax payment due each quarter or less than 100% of the total tax you paid in 1992.

To calculate the amount of any underpayment for each of the quarterly payment periods, subtract the estimated tax payment you made from the amount actually due on the filing date. If you underpaid your estimated tax, you must complete Form NJ-2210.

Each payment you make must equal at least one-quarter of 80% of the *total* tax liability due for the year. If you fall short of that, there will be a penalty on the underpayment from the due date of the installment until the date you finally make your payment.

Example

Assume you have a total tax due of $2,000 for the year. The amount due for each estimated payment is figured as follows:

1. 80% × $2,000 .... = $1,600
2. Quarterly Payment $\frac{\$1,600}{4}$ .... = $ 400

An *underpayment* on a quarterly installment would result if your payment was *less than* $400. If you only paid $300 each time an installment was due, you would have *underpaid* $100 each time. Therefore, a

penalty would be due on each $100 underpayment from its due date until the date it is paid *or* April 15 (whichever is later).

As an alternative way to determine if you underpaid, New Jersey will consider your payments current if you pay *at least* the same amount of tax as you owed on your preceding year's Gross Income Tax Return, provided that the return covered 12 calendar months.

TaxSaver: New Jersey requires you to pay the *lesser of* 80% of this year's tax due or 100% of the tax paid last year. Even if you received a large increase in income this year, you can still use last year's tax as the basis for making your estimated tax payments and *also* avoid penalties.

Calculating the Penalty

The penalty for underpayment of estimated tax equals the amount of underpayment (see example below) multiplied by the applicable penalty rate on underpayment of tax for the period, multiplied by the fraction of the year during which your estimated taxes were underpaid.

Example

Your total underpayment for the year is $800. That means each installment is underpaid by $200. Assume the penalty is determined as follows:

1. Penalty due on April 15 installment
   $200 × 10% (current rate) × $\frac{365}{365}$ = $20
2. Penalty due on June 15 installment
   $200 × 10% (current rate) × $\frac{304}{365}$ = $16.66
3. Penalty due on September 15 installment
   $200 × 10% (current rate) × $\frac{213}{365}$ = $11.67
4. Penalty due on January 15 installment
   $200 × 10% (current rate) × $\frac{90}{365}$ = $ 4.93

Total Penalty = $53.26

TaxSaver: For New Jersey purposes, the total tax withheld includes not only amounts withheld from your salary, but excess New Jersey unemployment insurance *and* excess New Jersey disability insurance withheld. Don't forget to include these amounts in your estimated tax calculation.

Exceptions

In this section, we will discuss the exceptions to penalties and interest for underpayment of estimated taxes.

TaxAlert: The terms *exceptions* and *safe harbors* are often used interchangeably. Some states call these exceptions *Safe Harbor Provisions* and others, simply *Exceptions*.

In New Jersey, a taxpayer may avoid the imposition of penalties on any underpayment of an installment of estimated taxes paid on or before the due date of the installment if it exceeds any of the four safe harbor amounts.

TaxAlert: These safe harbor provisions for avoiding penalties *do not* apply if the original installment was filed after the return's due date.

The safe harbor provisions are as follows:

1. If you filed a New Jersey Gross Income Tax Return last year, and that return was calculated on a 12 month year, (full-year resident status), no penalties will be owed if each quarterly installment equals at least 25% of the liability you calculated on the prior year's return;

2. No penalty will be due if the total of your installment payments this year is greater than the tax you computed last year, using the current year's tax rates and exemption amounts. Use the rates applicable to your filing status; and

3. New Jersey will not impose a penalty if the amount of estimated payments is equal to 80% of the tax for the tax year computed on an annualized basis for the portion of the tax year ending before the estimated payment is due.

4. No penalty is due if your installments are equal to 90% of last year's tax, computed at the current year's rates. This exception is based on the actual amount of income you received for the months ending before the month the installment is due.

TaxAlert: You should prepare a schedule showing your calculations and attach it to Form NJ-2210.

6 | Refunds (Amended Returns)

At some point, you may conclude that you are owed a refund of taxes you previously paid. To obtain a refund, you will have to file an amended return. This chapter will discuss refund claims and other circumstances in which the filing of an amended return may be required.

Refunds in General

If you paid more taxes on your income than you actually owe, whether through estimated tax payments or withholding, you may be entitled to receive a refund.

You may also be entitled to a refund from New Jersey if the Internal Revenue Service has made changes to your federal income tax return that result in a reduction of your federal adjusted gross income. Or, you may have made an error in New Jersey's favor on your original tax return. In these cases, you will need to file an amended New Jersey State income tax return.

When to Submit an Amended Return

If you already filed your New Jersey income tax return, you should file an amended return if you discover errors or omissions, such as one of the following:

- You did not report some income you received;
- You overstated your income;
- You claimed deductions or tax credits to which you were not entitled;
- You were entitled to deductions or credits you did not take;
- The information on your federal tax return changed, requiring you to file an amended federal tax return; or
- The Internal Revenue Service made changes to your federal return.

There are strict time limits you must follow depending on the reason why you have amended your New Jersey return. Generally, to claim a refund, you must file an amended return within three years from the due date of your original return, including any extensions, or within two years of the date the tax was paid, *whichever is later*. If you filed your return early, it is still deemed to be filed on the due date rather than the actual date you mailed it.

If you or the Internal Revenue Service changes any of the following items, you must amend your New Jersey tax return.

- Federal taxable income;
- Total taxable amount of ordinary income portion of a lump-sum distribution;
- Federal credit for employment-related expenses;
- Income tax withholding; or
- Disallowance of a refund claim.

You must file an amended New Jersey tax return within 90 days from the date you filed the amended federal return, within 90 days of a final determination by the Internal Revenue Service.

See the Chapter 8 section *Statute of Limitations* for further information.

Which Form to Use

If you filed your original return on Form NJ-1040, you must use Form NJ-1040X to amend your return for the corresponding tax year.

If you are a nonresident taxpayer and filed Form NJ-1040NR with New Jersey, use a blank copy of the return you originally filed and write **Amended,** on the top of the front page.

Limits on Amounts of Refunds

If you have three years to file a claim for a refund, your refund will be limited to the tax paid during the three years before the filing of the return. If you file your return early, it is still deemed to be filed on the due date rather than on the date filed.

Example

Tony's 1990 New Jersey income tax return was due on April 15, 1991. He filed it on March 31, 1991. Tony had income tax withheld by his employer of $1,000 and paid estimated income taxes of $2,000 over the course of the tax year. Even though Tony filed his return before April 15 and paid most of his estimated taxes before that date, if he qualifies for the three-year limit, he will have until April 15, 1994, to file an amended return. Therefore, if Tony files his amended return on or before April 15, 1994, he will be entitled to claim a refund up to the total amount of income tax he previously paid, $3,000.

If Tony received a valid extension of time to file his original return, he would have three years from the date he filed the return to claim a refund. For example, if Tony received a four-month extension he would have until August 15, 1994, to file his amended return.

If Tony filed his original return *after* his extended due date, he would only be entitled to a refund of the amount he paid with his original return. He could not claim a refund of amounts originally withheld or paid as estimated taxes. If Tony filed his original return late, and paid an additional $100 with the return, he would only be entitled to receive a refund up to $100.

If you file a claim for a refund after the three-year period, but within two years from the time you paid the tax, your refund is limited to the amount of tax paid within the two years immediately prior to your refund request.

Example

Nicholas filed his 1990 New Jersey income tax return on April 15, 1991. He paid taxes in the amount of $100. The Department of Revenue audited his 1990 return and determined that Nicholas owed an additional $500 for 1990. Nicholas paid the additional tax on December 20, 1992. On June 15, 1994, Nicholas discovers he was entitled to a tax credit of $800 and files an amended return. Since the amended return is filed three years after the original filing date of the return, April 15, 1991, Nicholas will not be entitled to a refund of any amount of tax paid prior to or with the return. Nicholas will only be entitled to receive a refund up to the amount he paid on December 20, 1992.

What if Your Refund Claim is Denied?

If you file an amended return for a refund and your claim is denied, you may write a letter to the person and/or office that responded to your refund claim to further explain the reasons for your refund claim. Include any extra information to support your position. If the tax department still denies your claim, it will respond with a letter explaining the procedures for filing a protest.

Filing Your Amended Return

If you are claiming a refund, send your amended return to:

> Division of Taxation
> Income Tax—CN555
> Trenton, NJ 08647-0555

If your amended return requires the payment of additional taxes, send it to:

> Division of Taxation
> Income Tax—CN222
> Trenton, NJ 08647-0111

In either case, use U.S. certified mail to send your amended return, and be sure to save your receipt.

7 | Other Taxes

Sales and Use Tax

A sales tax is a tax on the sale, exchange, or rental of goods and certain services. For the most part, it is imposed on sales that take place between a merchant or supplier and a customer inside the state. As a New Jersey consumer, you generally pay sales tax directly to the merchant or supplier of the goods or services you purchase. He or she is responsible for collecting the tax from you and paying it to the Division of Taxation. An out-of-state merchant may be required to collect sales tax from New Jersey residents if he or she has some connection with New Jersey. Effective July 1, 1992, New Jersey's sales tax rate was reduced from 7 percent to 6 percent.

A use tax is a complement to the sales tax and is imposed at the same rate as the sales tax. If you are a New Jersey resident, you owe use tax on all taxable goods and services used in New Jersey unless they were taxed at the time of purchase.

Example

Ron, a New Jersey resident, purchases camping equipment from a mail order company located in Maine. The equipment is shipped from Maine to his New Jersey residence. Ron does not pay any sales tax at the time of purchase since the Maine vendor is not required to collect New Jersey sales tax. However, Ron is liable for the use tax on this purchase.

If you are a New Jersey resident who purchases goods outside the state and pays sales tax at a lower rate than the New Jersey rate, you are liable for the *difference* in the sales tax rates when you bring the goods into the state.

If you owe use tax, you must report and pay it on Form ST-18, *New Jersey Use Tax*. The return is due within twenty days after you take possession of the items in New Jersey. If you fail to report and pay use tax due on any purchases you made during the tax year, you may still report and pay the tax on Line 35 of Form NJ-1040, *New Jersey Gross Income Tax Resident Return*.

What is Taxable?

As a consumer, you pay sales tax on many goods and services used in your daily life. In general, the following goods and services are taxed by New Jersey:

- Retail sales and rentals of tangible personal property such as appliances, automobiles, household cleaning agents, video rentals, cosmetics, pet foods and supplies, cigarettes, soft drinks, alcoholic beverages, books and publications, and records and tapes;
- Producing, fabricating, processing, printing, and imprinting tangible personal property;
- Installing, maintaining, and repairing personal property;
- Certain repairs to real property;
- Telecommunication services;

- Advertising services;
- Janitorial services;
- Window cleaning;
- Rodent and pest control;
- Temporary rental of hotel rooms;
- Admission charges to entertainment events; and
- Storage of tangible personal property.

EXCEPTION: Some sales of tangible personal property are exempt from sales tax. Common exempt items include sales for resale, clothing, food other than candy and confections, disposable paper products, bottled water, beverages other than soft drinks and alcoholic beverages, drugs and medicines, over-the-counter pain relievers, corrective eyeglasses, hearing aids, dentures, braces, artificial limbs, prosthetic aids, medical equipment, wheelchairs, newspapers, magazines, and periodicals.

Withholding

If you are an employee, your salary or wages are probably subject to the withholding of income taxes. Also, other forms of compensation or income may be subject to withholding. This section explains who is subject to withholding, how the amount to be withheld is calculated, and how you can adjust the amount of withholding to fit your tax situation. Generally, New Jersey follows the federal government's provision within the Internal Revenue Code for income tax withholding. To learn more about the federal provisions, consult *The Ernst & Young Tax Guide 1993*.

Who is Subject to Withholding?

Residents. If you are a resident of New Jersey, and your employer is located only in New Jersey, he or she is required to withhold income tax for all services you performed, even though the services may have been performed outside the state.

If you work for an employer who is located outside New Jersey and does not transact any business in New Jersey, your employer *will not* be obligated to withhold New Jersey income tax from your wages. However, he or she may be required to withhold income taxes on your wages for the state in which the business is located. You will still be obligated to file a New Jersey resident tax return and pay income taxes. If income taxes are withheld by your out-of-state employer, you may be entitled to claim a credit for these taxes. (See the Chapter 4 section, *Credits.*)

Nonresidents and Part-Year Residents. If you are a nonresident of New Jersey and your employer is located in New Jersey, he or she is only obligated to withhold income taxes on wages paid to you for services you performed in

New Jersey. (See, in Chapter 3, *Attributing Income to New Jersey—Sourcing Rules*.) If your job requires that you perform services only within New Jersey, the tax must be withheld on all wages paid to you.

New Jersey Residents Working in Pennsylvania. New Jersey and Pennsylvania have entered into a reciprocal tax agreement that allows each state to tax its own residents on compensation derived in the other state. Under the agreement, if you are a New Jersey resident, you are liable for New Jersey income tax on any compensation you earned in Pennsylvania. This agreement only applies to wages, salaries, commissions, and other forms of employee compensation.

What Income is Subject to Withholding?

The principal type of income from which taxes must be withheld is wage or salary income. Any supplemental wages you receive are also subject to withholding of tax. Supplemental wages include bonuses, commissions, overtime pay, sales awards, tips, and vacation allowances.

If supplemental wages are paid to you at the same time as your regular wages, your employer should withhold tax on the entire amount at the same rate as the rate applicable to your wages. However, if the supplemental wages are paid to you separately from your regular wages, your employer may withhold income taxes without allowance for withholding exemptions, discussed below. Other income subject to income tax withholding includes taxable fringe benefits, sick pay, pensions and annuities, and certain gambling winnings.

Exemptions From Withholding

If you file federal Form W-4, *Employee's Withholding Allowance Certificate*, certifying that you had no federal income tax liability last year and you anticipate no income tax liability this year, you may claim to be exempt from New Jersey income tax withholding. See *The Ernst & Young Tax Guide 1993* for the requirements to qualify for exemption for withholding for federal tax purposes.

Determining Withholding Taxes

Your employer can determine the amount of income taxes to be withheld from your wages by using the tax tables provided by the state or by calculating the tax. The tax to be withheld depends upon the amount of income you earned for the pay period and the information you give your employer on a withholding allowance certificate (federal Form W-4). A withholding allowance certificate tells your employer the rate at which you want your income tax withheld, if you want any additional amount withheld, and how many withholding allowances you claim.

You will want to calculate as accurately as possible the amount of income tax to be withheld from your earnings so that it will cover your final tax liability at the end of the year. This may enable you to avoid penalties for underpaying your income tax. (See, in Chapter 8, the section on *Penalties*.) Although you may owe interest and penalties if your employer underwithholds your income tax, you do not receive any interest or additional money if he or she overwithholds.

You can choose to have your income tax withheld at a higher tax rate for *single* taxpayers or a lower tax rate for *married* taxpayers. You can choose either tax rate, regardless of your marital status. (However, as discussed above, you may owe interest and penalties if not enough income tax is withheld.) You can also request that your employer withhold additional amounts beyond the income tax calculated at the tax rate you choose. You may wish to have additional withholdings from

tax if you and your spouse both work, you have more than one job, or you have income from interest, dividends, or self-employment. If you choose to have additional withholdings from your paycheck, you must have a written agreement to this effect with your employer.

You are generally entitled to the same number of withholding allowances on your Form W-4 as the number of dependent exemptions you are allowed to take on your New Jersey tax return (Form NJ-1040 Lines 27a and 27b). If you and your spouse both work, each of you must complete a separate Form W-4. You can divide the total number of withholding exemptions you and your spouse are entitled to between yourselves in any combination you wish.

TAXSAVER: You should review your Form W-4 periodically to assure its accuracy with respect to your current tax situation. Examples of changes in your tax situation include the following: you no longer claim a child or other person as a dependent, or you or your spouse reach the age of 65.

TAXALERT: If you do not file a Form W-4 with your employer, your employer will withhold taxes from your pay at the highest rate: Single, no withholding allowances.

Credit for Tax Withheld

You are allowed a credit against your income tax for any withholding of tax during the year. See the section on *Payments* in Chapter 4 for more information.

Your employer is required to supply you with a summary of wages paid and taxes withheld. Typically, you will receive several copies of federal Form W-2, *Wage and Tax Statement*. Attach a designated copy, indicated on Form W-2, to your New Jersey return. You should receive this form from your employer no later than January 31 following the close of the tax year.

Example

John and Eileen are married and two children. They work for different employers. John has filed Form W-4 with his employer, claiming three withholding allowances for himself and his children. Eileen has also filed Form W-4 with her employer. She also wants her taxes to be withheld at the married rate, but claims only one withholding allowance. With this information, their respective employers can determine the amount of taxes to be withheld from each paycheck.

Real Property Transfer and Gains Tax

You may be subject to the Real Property Transfer Tax if you sell real property located in New Jersey. You may also need to pay this tax when you lease property to another person if the leasehold interest is for 99 years or more. *Real Property* that may be subject to this tax includes houses, condominiums, cooperatives, buildings, and land. This tax is imposed on the seller of the real property. It is levied on the *full purchase price*, which includes money, the assumption of a prior mortgage, and the fair market value of other consideration. If you are subject to this tax, you may need to complete Form RTF-1, *Affidavit of Consideration or Exemption*.

Exemptions

You will not have to pay the Real Property Transfer Tax if your transaction meets one of the following requirements:

- The money or other consideration you receive is less than $100;
- You sell your property to or buy property from the United States of America, New Jersey, or any federal or state instrumentality, agency, or subdivision;
- You are transferring a deed to release collateral for a debt;
- You are correcting a deed that was previously recorded;
- Your realty is sold to pay delinquent taxes or assessments;
- You are merely dividing your realty into separate shares or units. (If you sell one or more of these shares or units, you will be subject to tax.);
- The realty is transferred as a result of a bankruptcy or liquidation for the benefit of your creditors;
- Your realty is transferred to your spouse, parent, or child;
- You are conveying a cemetery plot or lot;
- The transfer is required by a court in specific performance of a final judgment;
- You are merely releasing your right to future possession of the property;
- You recorded the transfer in another county and paid the transfer fee there;
- The property was transferred by a decedent's estate; or
- You transferred property as a result of a divorce and the deed is recorded within 90 days following the entry of your divorce decree.

Example

Martha sold a tract of land to the Parking Authority of a New Jersey municipality. This transaction is exempt from tax.

Calculation of Tax

New Jersey has three different tax rates for transfers of real property. The one you should use depends upon the nature of your transaction.

If you are a senior citizen or blind or disabled and you are transferring a one- or two-family residence that you owned and occupied immediately before the transfer, your tax rate will be 50¢ per $500 on the first $150,000 of the purchase price and $1.25 per $500 on any amount over $150,000. The same tax rate applies if you are selling low or moderate income housing. Such housing must be "affordable" according to the federal Department of Housing or another recognized standard. If you are selling new construction which was not previously occupied or used for any purpose, your tax rate will be 75¢ per $500 on the first $150,000 of the purchase price and $2.50 per $500 on any amount over $150,000. All others must use a tax rate of $1.75 per $500 on the first $150,000 of the purchase price and $2.50 per $500 on any amount over $150,000.

Example

Jerry built a house and sold it for $175,000. His tax is computed as follows:

Tax on $150,000:
$150,000 ÷ 500 = $300 × 75¢ = $225
Tax on amount greater than $150,000:
           $175,000
         −150,000
        $ 25,000 ÷ 500
        = $50 × $2.50 = $125
Total Tax $350

Estate and Gift Tax

This section will provide you with an overview of the inheritance tax on the transfer of New Jersey real and tangible personal property at death or within three years before death by a resident or nonresident decedent. The estate of a resident decedent also must pay inheritance tax on transfers of intangible property, regardless of where the property is located. In addition to the inheritance tax, an estate tax is also imposed on the estate of a resident to absorb the federal credit allowed for state estate taxes. This tax is equal to the maximum federal credit less state inheritance and estate taxes paid.

Inheritance Tax

Transfers of a "material part" of an estate made by a resident or nonresident decedent within three years of death for which an insignificant price was paid are considered to have been made in contemplation of death. Such transfers are added back to the estate when computing the inheritance tax. The estate is given the chance to prove that the transfer was not made in contemplation of death. If successful, the transfer will not be subject to the tax.

Transfers by a decedent to a surviving spouse, parent, grandparent, child, or grandchild are exempt from inheritance tax, as are transfers to certain charitable, religious, and educational institutions or to New Jersey or one of its political subdivisions.

Filing the Return

Form IT-R (resident decedent) or Form IT-NR (nonresident decedent) must be filed by one of the following:

- The estate's executor or administrator;
- A beneficiary of the estate;
- A surviving joint tenant if the estate passes to the surviving joint tenant by operation of law; or
- The director of a county welfare board if there is no executor, and no next of kin can be found.

The inheritance tax return, with payment, is due within eight months of the death of the decedent. An extension of time to file the return can be granted by the Division of Taxation if good cause is shown. However, this only extends the time for filing. The tax payment must be made on time, or a penalty may be assessed. Generally, interest of 10% per year will also be due on any late payments of tax.

Estate Tax

In addition to the inheritance tax, New Jersey also imposes an estate tax on the estates of resident decedents. This tax is only imposed if the death taxes paid by the estate to New Jersey and other states are less than the federal credit allowed for state death taxes. Estates that are exempt from the inheritance tax may still be subject to the estate tax.

Filing the Return

The executor of the estate of a resident decedent must file a *New Jersey Estate Tax Return*, Form IT-Estate, within 60 days after receiving notification from the Internal Revenue Service setting the amount of federal estate tax and the amount of the credit for state death taxes. The executor of the estate is not required to file Form IT-Estate if the estate was not required to file federal Form 706, or no estate tax is due.

8 | What to Do If Your Return Is Examined

Audits

The word "audit" strikes fear into the hearts of taxpayers. The thought of a tax official knocking at your door is a nightmare many begin to have soon after April 15th. This chapter will explain what an audit is, how an audit is triggered, and how to survive an audit with the least amount of pain and suffering.

What is an Audit?

An audit is, simply, a review of your tax return by the taxing authorities. New Jersey conducts audits through the mail, in district offices around the state, and at the homes or places of business of its taxpayers. Simple computational errors on your return are corrected by computer. You are notified by mail of any resulting correction in the tax due (or refund).

The most common audit procedure practiced in New Jersey is the desk audit. The desk audit is conducted through the mail. These audits originate from the Division of Taxation in Trenton. Typically these audits revolve around simple issues requiring documentary substantiation that is easily handled through the mail.

If more complex issues are examined, a field audit is conducted at the Division's district office in your area of the state. You may be asked to appear at the auditor's office to provide information or discuss the issues under examination. The scope of inquiry generally revolves around your books, records, and property.

Whose Return is Audited?

Many taxpayers wonder how New Jersey's taxing authorities determine which returns will be audited. Generally, tax returns are selected for audit either by computer or by hand. Sometimes a random selection by computer triggers an audit; at other times, it is triggered because a return involves certain issues or deductions. The most common ways the state determines which return gets audited are as follows:

Issues That May Trigger an Audit:

1. Errors made in filling out a return that require a taxpayer's explanation before a computational correction can be made.
2. Changes on federal audits. changes made on your federal Form 1040 that are reported to New Jersey under the Federal-State Exchange Agreement. This is an information exchange agreement between the state and federal government aimed at consistency in return filings. You are required to report changes in your federal taxable income that result from a federal audit or an amended return on Form 1040.
3. Other exchange-of-information programs with the Internal Revenue Service (e.g., matching Forms 1099, tax shelter information, partnership Schedule K-1 and other forms). New Jersey is also planning to join with other states in exchanging income tax information with respect to individuals, estates, and trusts. States are now able to check whether a taxpayer has established residency in another state, filed as a nonresident in two or more states, or improperly claimed income in another state in order to reduce his or her residence taxes illegally.
4. Computer selection based on built-in norms for certain income deductions. The computer is a significant new auditing tool.
5. State issue areas. These are specific New Jersey issues more likely to be audited by the state than items of income and deductions that are also reported on federal Form 1040. Due to New Jersey's unique Gross Income Tax, the taxing authorities often examine each item of gross income separately.
6. Residency issues. Nonresident and part-year resident returns are especially susceptible to audit. New Jersey's taxing authorities look first at whether a taxpayer filing as a nonresident or part-year resident should have filed a resident return. Next, for part-year residents, they look at whether the taxpayer properly reported income to his or her resident period. Because of the potential loss of revenue from improper filing, auditing of residency issues is a major audit concern. For more information about filing as a resident or nonresident, consult Chapter 2.
7. Special Audit projects of the Division of Taxation. State audit projects focus on auditing certain groups of individual taxpayers. These may include limited partners, or persons with exceptionally high amounts of income.
8. Multi-audit. Being audited for another state tax may result in audit of a personal income tax issue. For example, simultaneous audits of a taxpayer and his or her business, consisting of an individual income tax and sales tax audit, may be conducted.
9. Special requests for returns made by District Office auditors based on their personal knowledge of particular taxpayers or their prior dealings with those taxpayers. If you have been audited before, chances are that you will be audited again.

TAX*ALERT:* At this stage, it may be advisable to contact your accountant or retain competent legal representation. If you determine that representation is warranted, you must assign your representative the right to speak on your behalf by executing a Power of Attorney. This must be given to the auditor before the meeting.

The auditor may send you a written list of items and documents he or she wishes to examine. If you have retained representation, be sure that he or she is present at any meeting with an auditor and that he or she sees the auditor's information request before releasing any documents or signing any papers.

Documents the agent may request include the following:

1. Your home address and phone number, as well as any business address and phone number;
2. The name and address of your tax preparer;
3. Whether a Power of Attorney has been executed;
4. A copy of your federal Form 1040, with any attachments and schedules;
5. The names and addresses of your dependents;
6. The sources of any amounts entered on your return, either income or loss;
7. Proof of withholding payments, estimated tax payments, copies of wage and income statements;
8. Statements from brokerage accounts and other property;
9. Checking and savings account statements held individually or in joint name; and
10. Results of any previous audits by federal or New Jersey authorities.

During the audit, the auditor will assess the information he or she receives. Generally, documents associated with income and loss or medical expenses will be examined in detail.

If income from a partnership is at issue, the auditor may request copies of partnership agreements, accounting records, or federal returns, such as federal Form 1065.

The Closing Conference. Once the auditor has concluded the examination, he or she will notify you of his or her proposed assessment. You are entitled to meet with the auditor and his or her supervisor at a closing conference. At this conference, the auditor will explain any adjustments made to your return. This is the stage in which any disagreement may be expressed, compromises worked out, or concessions made.

If all issues connected with the audit are not satisfactorily resolved, you will receive at the closing conference, a *Notice of Tax Deficiency*. You have ninety days in which to request a formal appeal of this notice to the New Jersey Tax Court.

For more information on protesting the Notice of Tax Deficiency, please consult the following section. As we will discuss there, filing the right documents *on time* is critical to the outcome of your protest.

Protesting the Audit

This section will discuss how to protest a gross income tax audit and explain your legal remedies as a taxpayer.

Notice of Tax Deficiency

You're opening your mail and to your surprise, a *Notice of Tax Deficiency* from the New Jersey Division of Taxation is staring you right in the face. Your adrenaline starts flowing and thoughts of imprisonment and stiff penalties run rapidly through your mind. What should you do? Clearly, do not panic.

If you don't consent to the income tax adjustments proposed by the Division of Taxation, the next step in the process is the issuance of a formal Notice of Tax Deficiency.

From here on, your rights to protest any additional tax and penalty assessments are strictly governed by New Jersey law.

TAX*ALERT:* It is of the *utmost* importance that you pay strict attention to time limits and proper filing requirements. Your right to protest a *Notice of Tax Deficiency* can be lost if you are late in filing a required petition by even one day! There are requirements that the state must fulfill, too. For example, the Notice of Tax Deficiency must be mailed to your *last known address*. This is usually the address on your last tax return, unless you've since notified the Division of Taxation that you've moved.

Appeals

If you decide to protest your Notice of Tax Deficiency, your first recourse is to file a petition with the Director of Taxation for a redetermination of the tax deficiency within 90 days (150 days if you are living outside the U.S.) from the date of the Notice of Tax Deficiency.

Example

John received a Notice of Tax Deficiency from the New Jersey Division of Taxation. The notice was dated April 4, 1990. John had until July 3, 1990, to file a petition with the Director of Taxation for a redetermination of his tax deficiency.

The appeals process provides you with an inexpensive and relatively informal way of resolving your dispute with the taxing authorities. In this type of proceeding, you or your representatives will meet with the Audit Division's agents in an attempt to resolve the controversy. A mediator, called a Conferee, will oversee the proceeding. The Conferee may request additional information from you if he or she thinks it would be helpful in clarifying the issues or resolving the dispute. If you are unable to resolve your dispute, the Conferee will issue a final determination. The final determination is binding upon both parties unless an appeal is filed by *you* within 90 days after the final determination in the Tax Court. The Division cannot appeal an adverse determination.

TAX*ALERT:* You must file a petition for redetermination within 90 days from the date of your Notice of Tax Deficiency. If you fail to file this petition on time, you will lose your opportunity to appeal. Unlike the laws of New York and many other states, New Jersey's law prohibits you from filing a refund claim *after* you pay the deficiency.

Tax Court

If you are not satisfied with the Division's final determination, you can file an appeal to Tax Court. You must file your appeal to this formal forum within 90 days after the Division's final determination is rendered.

TAX*SAVER:* It is recommended that you obtain legal representation if you are appealing a matter to the Tax Court, because formal courtroom procedures will be followed.

Penalties

Introduction

By law, you are required to file a New Jersey tax return and pay your fair share of taxes. If you do not file and pay the correct amount of tax by the due date, you can incur substantial penalties and interest. Failure to file on time and pay the tax can be costly. This section will describe the penalties New Jersey imposes on delinquent taxpayers.

Penalties and Interest

A tax "penalty" is an addition to the tax you owe if you fail to file a New Jersey tax return on time or fail to pay a tax that is due. Interest, on the other hand, is an amount you owe because you had the use of money that properly belonged to New Jersey. Some people confuse interest and penalties, but the interest you owe New Jersey for a late payment of tax is no different from the interest you owe your credit card company if you fail to pay your monthly balance. Both represent a charge for extending credit. If you extend "credit" to New Jersey by overpaying your tax, the state must refund your tax with interest (subject to certain limitations and differences in rate). Also, New Jersey may waive a penalty if you show "reasonable cause" for your failure to pay the tax. Interest, however, cannot be waived under any circumstances.

Interest. New Jersey imposes interest at a rate equal to 5% above the prime rate, compounded daily, on any unpaid tax. If you receive an authorization of extension to pay tax, interest is reduced to a rate of 3% above the prime rate. If you do not pay all of the tax during the extension period, interest is imposed on any unpaid tax at the rate of 5% above the prime rate from the time it is due to the time you finally pay it. However, the New Jersey tax authorities may reduce the interest to 3% above prime, if you show "reasonable cause" for failing to pay the tax on time.

> *TaxAlert:* Interest is compounded daily. It is calculated on any unpaid tax, penalties, and previously accrued interest.

Late Payment Penalty. If you do not pay your tax on time, New Jersey will assess you a late payment penalty. The late payment penalty is equal to 5% of any tax balance paid late.

Late Filing Penalty. If you file a return late, a penalty is imposed of $100 per month plus 5% of the tax per month or fraction of a month (up to a maximum of 25%) for the time your return remains unfiled.

If you still fail to file a return, the state may make an arbitrary assessment of tax. The tax authorities will make an estimate of the tax you owe and send you the bill, or *Notice of Tax Deficiency.* You will have 15 days from the date on the notice to pay all taxes, interest, and penalties. If you do not pay within that period, an additional penalty of 5% of the tax may be imposed. The state may also bill you for any costs the tax authorities incur in collecting the tax due.

Reasonable Cause

Under certain circumstances, you may be able to request a waiver of penalties and a reduction in interest charges. You will need to demonstrate "reasonable cause" if you fail to file a return or pay your tax when it is due. The New Jersey Director of Taxation is authorized to waive all or part of a penalty and to reduce interest charges from 5% to 3% above the prime rate. Generally, "reasonable cause" means that you acted in good faith and were not intentionally negligent. "Reasonable cause" may include the following:

- Extreme circumstances such as serious illness, death, destruction of a place of business, or business records;
- An inability to assemble the information necessary to file a return, for reasons beyond your control;
- An honest misunderstanding of the law, or a computation or transcription error; or
- Reliance in good faith on the written advice of an office of the New Jersey Division of Taxation, or other professional tax advice, provided the advice was reasonable and you had no reason to suspect it was wrong.

It is your responsibility to prove that your deliquency was due to "reasonable cause." You must submit a written statement to the Director of Taxation that presents all relevant facts as clearly as possible.

Criminal Penalties

Most criminal tax offenses involve reckless or fraudulent intent. Remember that the obligation to pay tax and file a return is a *law,* and if you grossly or recklessly fail to comply with the state's requirements, you could be sent to prison, receive a substantial fine, or both.

Statute of Limitations

General Rule

The period of time during which the New Jersey Department of Revenue can assess a tax deficiency is limited by a statute called the *statute of limitations.* As a general rule, the statute of limitations allows New Jersey's taxing authorities to make an assessment of additional taxes at any time within three years after the date you actually filed your return. This section will discuss the statute of limitations and exceptions.

The Three-Year Rule

If you file your income tax return before April 15 (or August 15 if you have an extension), the three-year statute of limitations period does not start running until the last day on which you could have filed your return. However, if you file your income tax return late, the three-year statute of limitations does not start to run until the date you actually file your return.

No Income Tax Return Filed or Fraudulent Return Filed

The general three-year rule does not apply if you fail to file your New Jersey income tax return or if you file a state tax return with information that you know to be false or fraudulent. In these instances, the state can assess you additional taxes, penalties, and interest at any time. However, the taxing authority must have reason to believe that you intentionally withheld information in the interest of avoiding or evading your fair share of income taxes.

Extension by Agreement

New Jersey can extend the time to assess additional taxes beyond the statutory three years if you agree in writing to the extension. This written agreement to extend the statute of limitations must be signed by you and the taxing officials before the expiration of the statutory three-year period. An agreement to extend the statute of limitations is always limited to a particular tax and specific filing year(s). It extends the time during which New Jersey can assess you for a limited period—usually, one year. Additional extensions may be granted by agreement.

You may wonder why anyone would willingly consent to let the taxing authorities have more time in which to make an assessment. Usually, such agreements are made in connection with an audit or a review of a refund request. It may well be in the interest of *both* parties to allow the state more time to complete its examination. The extra time may enable a taxpayer to present new facts that support a refund claim or reduce a proposed assessment.

Report of Federal Change

The statute of limitations will be extended if you amend your federal income tax return or consent to a federal income tax adjustment. If a change in your federal income tax causes you to owe additional taxes to New Jersey, the taxing authorities are deemed to have made a valid assessment of those additional taxes on the date you file your federal amended return. Amended federal returns, whether filed by choice or because you conceded to an adjustment, automatically extend New Jersey's normal three-year statute of limitations. If you fail to report your federal change or file an amended state return within the required 90-day period, New Jersey may assess additional income tax (plus penalties and interest) on the amount attributable to the federal changes or amended return at any time. The statute of limitations does not run in such cases.

TaxAlert: If you file an amended federal return showing any change in your taxable income, you must also file an amended New Jersey return within 90 days from the date you amend your federal return.

If the assessment is made during a period extended beyond the normal three-year assessment period by a report of federal changes, New Jersey cannot review or assess more than the amount attributable to the federal changes on your amended return.

Omission of Income

If your New Jersey income tax return omits more than 25% of the income that should have been properly included, New Jersey's assessment period is extended to six years. This assessment period will not be extended if the amount which your have omitted on your return is adequately disclosed in the return or on a supporting statement attached to the return.

Erroneous Refund

If your receive an erroneous refund of tax, it is treated as an underpayment of tax on the date you received the payment. The tax deficiency created by this erroneous refund may be assessed within three years after the refund is made. However, if the refund was as result of fraud or misrepresentation of important facts, then New Jersey has five years in which to make an assessment. An *erroneous refund* is a refund given to you by mistake.

9 | New Jersey Sample Forms

This chapter provides filled-in examples of the principal personal income tax forms used by New Jersey residents and nonresidents for you to refer to when preparing your own return. To ensure that you have the most complete and accurate information, we advise you to use this book in conjunction with the official 1992 New Jersey forms and instructions.

The forms included in this chapter are:

Form NJ-1040: State of New Jersey Income Tax—Resident Return Homestead Property Tax Rebate Application

Form NJ-1040NR: State of New Jersey Income Tax—Nonresident Return

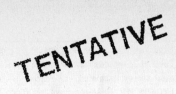

NJ-1040
1992

STATE OF NEW JERSEY
INCOME TAX—RESIDENT RETURN
HOMESTEAD PROPERTY TAX
REBATE APPLICATION

For Tax Year Jan.-Dec. 31, 1992 Or Other Tax Year Beginning _____ , 1992, Ending _____ , 19___

5R Check block ☐ if application for Federal extension is attached.

Your Social Security Number	Last Name, First Name and Initial (Joint filers enter first name and initial of each—Enter spouse last name ONLY if different)	Please place label on form you file. Make all necessary changes on label.
300 30 3000	*Kirk James T. and Judy L*	
Spouse's Social Security Number	Home address (Number and Street, including apartment number or rural route)	
400 40 4000	*100 Enterprise Lane*	
County/Municipality Code (See Table p. 22)	City, Town, Post Office *Jupiter* State *N.J.* Zip Code *66666*	
1810		

For Privacy Act Notification See Instructions

Please Print or Type

FILING STATUS

(Check only ONE box)

1. ☐ Single
2. ☑ Married, filing joint return
3. ☐ Married, filing separate return

_____ Name and Social Security No. of Spouse _____

4. ☐ Head of Household
5. ☐ Qualifying Widow(er)

EXEMPTIONS

				ENTER NUMBERS HERE
6. Regular	☒ Yourself	☑ Spouse	6	*2*
7. Age 65 or Over	☐ Yourself	☐ Spouse	7	
8. Blind or Disabled	☐ Yourself	☐ Spouse	8	
9. Number of your qualified dependent children			9	*1*
10. Number of other dependents			10	
11. Dependents attending colleges		11		
12. Totals (For Line 12a—Add Lines 6, 7, 8 and 11)		12a *2*	12b *1*	
(For Line 12b—Add Line 9 and Line 10)				

RESIDENCY STATUS

13. If you were a New Jersey resident for ONLY part of the taxable year, give the period of New Jersey residency:

From _____ MONTH DAY YEAR   To _____ MONTH DAY YEAR

GUBERNATORIAL ELECTIONS FUND ➤ Do you wish to designate $1 of your taxes for this fund? ✔ Yes / No
If joint return, does your spouse wish to designate $1? ✔ Yes / No

Note if you check the Yes box(es) it will not increase your tax or reduce your refund.

Please Attach W-2/1099R Forms Here

14. Wages, salaries, tips, and other employee compensation (Attach W-2)	14	*100,000*
15a. Taxable interest income	15a	*10,000*
15b. Tax exempt interest income. DO NOT include on Line 15a. 15b *1000*		
16. Dividends	16	*5,000*
17. Net profits from business (Attach copy of Federal Schedule C, Form 1040)	17	
18. Net gains or income from disposition of property (Schedule B, Line 4)	18	
19. Pensions, Annuities a. Taxable Amount Received 19a *1200*		
and IRA Withdrawals b. Less New Jersey Pension Exclusion 19b *0*		
c. Subtract Line 19b from Line 19a	19c	*1,200*
20. Distributive Share of Partnership Income (Attach copy of Schedule K-1 Federal Form 1065) ...	20	*5,000*
21. Net gain or income from rents, royalties, patents & copyrights (Sch. C, Line 3)	21	
22. Net Gambling Winnings	22	
23. Alimony and separate maintenance payments received	23	
24. Other (See instr. p. 12)	24	
25. Total Other Income (Add Lines 21 through 24)	25	
26a. Total Income (Add Lines 14, 15a, 16, 17, 18, 19c, 20 and 25)	26a	*121,200*
26b. Other Retirement Income Exclusion (See Worksheet and instr. p. 13)	26b	
26c. **New Jersey Gross Income** (Subtract Line 26b from Line 26a). If $3,000 or less see instr. p. 13. ..	26c	*121,200*
27a. Exemptions: From Line 12a ___*2*___ x $1,000 = *2000*		
27b. From Line 12b ___*1*___ x $1,500 = *1500*		
27c. Total Exemption Amount (Add Line 27a and Line 27b) 27c *3500*		
28. Medical Expenses (See Worksheet and instr. p. 13) 28 *3000*		
29. Alimony & Separate Maintenance Payments 29		
30. Total Exemptions and Deductions (Add Lines 27c, 28, and 29) .... ENTER TOTAL ➤	30	*6,500*
31. **NEW JERSEY TAXABLE INCOME** (Subtract Line 30 from Line 26c) If zero or less, enter ZERO	31	*114,700*
32. TAX: (From Tax Rate Schedules, p. 14)	32	*4,605*
33. Credit For Income Taxes Paid To Other Jurisdictions (From Schedule A, Line 5)	33	*3,800*
34. Balance of Tax (Subtract Line 33 from Line 32)	34	*805*
35. Use Tax Due on Out-of-State Purchases (See instr. p. 15)	35	
36. Total Tax (Add Line 34 and Line 35) Also enter on Line 37	36	*805*

Net losses in one category of income (Lines 14 through 25) cannot be applied against income in another. In case of a net loss in any category, enter ZERO for the category.

⬅ Part Year Residents See instr. p. 3

Please Attach Check or Money Order Here

NJ-45

37.	Total Tax (From Line 36 Page 1)	37	805
38.	**Total N.J. Income Tax Withheld** (Attach Forms W-2 and 1099R) 38 4,400	Check ☐ if Form NJ-2210	

38. **Total N.J. Income Tax Withheld** (Attach Forms W-2 and 1099R) .... | 38 | 4,400 | Check ☐ if Form NJ-2210 is attached
39. New Jersey Estimated Tax Payments/Credit from 1991 tax return .... | 39 | | If an amount is entered on Line 40 or Line 41 attach
40. EXCESS N.J. Unemployment Insurance Withheld (See instr. p. 15) .... | 40 | | ← Form NJ-2450
41. EXCESS N.J. Disability Insurance Withheld (See instr. p. 15) .... | 41 | | ←
42. **Total Payments/Credits** (Add Lines 38 through 41) .... **ENTER TOTAL** | 42 | 4,400 |
43. If payments (Line 42) are LESS THAN tax (Line 37) enter AMOUNT OF TAX YOU OWE .... | 43 | |

If you owe tax, you may make a donation by entering an amount on Lines 45B, 45C and/or 45D and adding this to your check amount.

44. If payments (Line 42) are MORE THAN tax (Line 37) enter OVERPAYMENT .... | 44 | 3,595 |
45. Deductions from Overpayment on Line 44 which you elect to credit to:

(A) Your 1993 Tax .... | 45A |

(B) The N.J. Endangered Wildlife Fund   ☐ $5, ☐ $10, Other $ _____ | 45B |

(C) The Children's Trust Fund   ☐ $5, ☐ $10, Other $ _____ | 45C |

(D) The N.J. Vietnam Veterans' Memorial Fund   ☐ $5, ☐ $10, Other $ _____ | 45D |

NOTE: AN ENTRY ON LINE 45A, B, C or D WILL REDUCE YOUR TAX REFUND

46. Total Deductions From Overpayment (Add Lines 45A, B, C and D) .... **ENTER TOTAL →** | 46 | |
47. REFUND (Amount to be sent to you, Line 44 LESS Line 46) .... | 47 | 3,595 |

Form HR-1040   HOMESTEAD PROPERTY TAX REBATE APPLICATION   1992

1. Enter the GROSS INCOME you reported on Line 26c, Form NJ-1040 (Part year residents see instr. p. 20) | 1 | 121,200 |

2. If your filing status is MARRIED, FILING SEPARATE RETURN and you and your spouse MAINTAIN THE SAME PRINCIPAL RESIDENCE enter the gross income reported on your spouse's return (Line 26c Form NJ-1040) and **check this box** ──────────► ☐ .... | 2 | |

3. TOTAL GROSS INCOME (Add Line 1 and Line 2) .... | 3 | 121,200 |

4. Enter your **New Jersey** residence on December 31, 1992 if different than indicated on Page 1. If you were not a resident on December 31, 1992 enter your last **New Jersey** residence.
Street Address _____   Municipality _____

5. Check your residency status during 1992:   a. ☑ HOMEOWNER   b. ☐ TENANT   c. ☐ BOTH

6. If you checked "Homeowner" or "Both" on Line 5, enter the block and lot number of the residence for which the rebate is claimed.

Block [C][0][0][0] - [0][0][0][0]   Lot [2][0][0][0] - [0][0][0][0]   Qualifier [ ][ ][ ][ ]

7a. ☐ Yes ☑ No   Did you live at more than one New Jersey residence during the year?

b. ☐ Yes ☑ No   Did you share ownership of a principal residence during the year with anyone, other than your spouse?

c. ☐ Yes ☑ No   Did any principal residence you owned during the year consist of multiple dwelling units?

d. ☐ Yes ☑ No   Did anyone, other than your spouse, occupy and share rent with you for an apartment or other rental dwelling during the year?

If you answered "Yes" to any of the above, you MUST complete and submit Schedule HR-A.

HOMEOWNER

8. Enter the total 1992 property taxes you (and your spouse) paid on your principal residence in New Jersey during 1992 .... | 8 | 5,000 |

IF YOU COMPLETED SCHEDULE HR-A, Part I, enter:

9a. Total Property taxes paid (Sch. HR-A, PART I, Line 5) .... | 9a | |

9b. Number of days as an owner (Sch. HR-A, PART I, Line 4) .... | 9b | Days |

TENANT

10. Enter the total rent you (and your spouse) paid on your principal residence in New Jersey during 1992 | 10 | |

IF YOU COMPLETED SCHEDULE HR-A, Part II, enter:

11a. Total Rent Paid (Sch. HR-A, PART II, Line 11) .... | 11a | |

11b. Number of days as a tenant (Sch. HR-A, PART II, Line 10) .... | 11b | Days |

SIGN HERE

Under the penalties of perjury, I declare that I have examined this income tax return and Homestead Property Tax Rebate Application, including accompanying schedules and statements, and to the best of my knowledge and belief, it is true, correct, and complete. If prepared by a person other than taxpayer, this declaration is based on all information of which the preparer has any knowledge.

► *James T. Kirk*   4-14-92   ► *Judy L. Kirk*
Your signature   Date   Spouse's signature (if filing jointly, BOTH must sign.)

Paid Preparer's Signature _____   Federal Identification Number _____

Firm's Name _____   Federal Employer Identification Number _____

Pay amount on line 43 in full. Write social security number on check or money order and make payable to: State of New Jersey-TGI Mail your return to: Division of Taxation, Lakewood Processing Center, 895 Towbin Rd., Suite A, Lakewood, N.J. 08701
If REFUND: Division of Taxation, Income Tax—CN-555, Trenton, NJ 08647-0555

(REV. 10-92)

Division Use   1 _____ 2 _____ 3 _____ 4 _____ 5 _____ 6 _____ 7 _____

Name(s) as shown on Form NJ-1040	Your social security number
Kirk, James T. and Judy L.	300 30 3000

Schedule A — CREDIT FOR INCOME OR WAGE TAXES PAID TO OTHER JURISDICTION(S)

If you are claiming a credit for income taxes paid to more than one jurisdiction, a separate Schedule A must be attached for each.

A copy of other state(s) or political subdivision tax return(s) must be attached to Form NJ-1040

1.	Income subject to tax by other jurisdiction(s) during tax year (indicate name(s) __New York__) (DO NOT combine the same income taxed by more than one jurisdiction) (The amount on Line 1 cannot exceed the amount shown on Line 2)	1	100,000
2.	Income subject to tax by New Jersey (From Line 26a or see instructions)	2	121,200
3.	Maximum Allowable Credit $\dfrac{1\ \ 100,000}{2\ \ 121,200}$ x $\underset{\text{(New Jersey Tax, Line 32, Page 1)}}{4605}$ = (Divide Line 2 into Line 1)	3	3,800
4.	Income or wage tax paid to other jurisdictions during tax year	4	8,000
5.	Credit allowed (Enter lesser of Line 3 or 4 here and on Line 33, Page 1 .... (The credit may not exceed your New Jersey Tax on Line 32)	5	3,800

Schedule B — NET GAINS OR INCOME FROM DISPOSITION OF PROPERTY

List the net gains or income, less net loss, derived from the sale, exchange, or other disposition of property including real or personal whether tangible or intangible.

	a. Kind of property and description	b. Date acquired (Mo., day, yr)	c. Date sold (Mo., day, yr)	d. Gross sales price	e. Cost or other basis as adjusted (see instructions) and expense of sale	f. Gain or (loss) (d less e)	
1.							
2.	Capital Gains Distributions					2	
3.	Other Net Gains					3	
4.	Net Gains (Add Lines 1, 2, and 3) (Enter here and on Line 18, if loss enter ZERO)					4	

Schedule C — NET GAIN OR INCOME FROM RENTS, ROYALTIES, PATENTS AND COPYRIGHTS

List the net gains or net income, less net loss, derived from or in the form of rents, royalties, patents, and copyrights as reported on your Federal Income Tax Return. If you have passive losses for Federal purposes, see instructions.

	a. Kind of Property	b. Net Rental Income (Loss)	c. Net Income From Royalties	d. Net Income From Patents	e. Net Income From Copyrights
1.					
2.	Totals	b.	c.	d.	e.
3.	Net Income (Combine Columns b, c, d, and e) (Enter here and on Line 21, if loss enter ZERO)			3	

Rev. 91

NJ-1040NR

STATE OF NEW JERSEY
INCOME TAX—NONRESIDENT RETURN

1992

For Tax Year Jan.-Dec. 31, 1992 Or Other Tax Year Beginning _____, 1992, Ending _____, 19 ____

5-N Check block ☐ if application for Federal extension is attached.

Please Print or Type

For Privacy Act Notification See Instructions

Your Social Security Number	Last Name, First Name and Initial (Joint filers enter first name and initial of each—Enter spouse last name ONLY if different)	
500	50	5000	Stein, Carol	

Please place label on form you file. Make all necessary changes on label.

Spouse's Social Security Number | Home address (Number and Street, including apartment number or rural route)
52 Lindy Avenue

State of Residency: New York

City, Town, Post Office	State	Zip Code
Yonkers,	NY	10701

(Check only ONE box)

1. ☑ Single
2. ☐ Married, filing joint return
3. ☐ Married, filing separate return

Name and Social Security No. of Spouse

4. ☐ Head of Household
5. ☐ Qualifying Widow(er)

EXEMPTIONS

6.	Regular	☑ Yourself	☐ Spouse	6	1	
7.	Age 65 or Over	☐ Yourself	☐ Spouse	7		
8.	Blind or Disabled	☐ Yourself	☐ Spouse	8		
9.	Number of your qualified dependent children					9
10.	Number of other dependents					10
11.	Dependents attending colleges		11			
12.	Totals (For Line 12a—Add Lines 6, 7, 8 and 11)			12a	1	12b
	(For Line 12b—Add Line 9 and Line 10)					

RESIDENCY STATUS 13. If you were a New Jersey resident for ONLY part of the taxable year, give the period of New Jersey residency.

From _____ (MONTH DAY YEAR) To _____ (MONTH DAY YEAR)

GUBERNATORIAL ELECTIONS FUND ►

Do you wish to designate $1 of your taxes for this fund? .... ☑ Yes ☐ No

If joint return, does your spouse wish to designate $1? .... ☐ Yes ☐ No

Note: If you check the "Yes" box(es) it will not increase your tax or reduce your refund

NOTE: Retirement Income Exclusion is computed by completing the worksheet on page 6 of the instructions.

			(Column A) AMOUNT OF GROSS INCOME (EVERYWHERE)	(Column B) AMOUNT FROM NEW JERSEY SOURCES
14a.	Total Income (From Line 44, Part 1)	14a	30,000	14a 24,000
14b.	Other Retirement Income Exclusion (See Worksheet and Instructions)	14b		14b
14c.	Gross Income (Subtract Line 14b from Line 14a)	14c Ⓐ	30,000	14c Ⓑ 24,000
15.	Limitation Percentage Ⓑ (Line 14c) / Ⓐ (Line 14c) = 80.0 %			NOTE: If amount at Ⓐ on Line 14c exceeds the amount at Ⓑ by more than $100, complete formula on Line 15 and apply to Line 20.
16a.	Exemptions: From Line 12a 1 x $1,000 = 1,000			
16b.	From Line 12b x $1,500 =			
16c.	Total Exemption Amount (Add Line 16a and Line 16b)	16c	1,000	
	NOTE: Part-year residents—See Instructions			
17.	Medical Expenses (From Line 54)	17		
18.	Alimony & separate maintenance payments	18		
19.	Total Exemptions and Deductions (Add Lines 16c, 17, and 18)	19	1,000	
20.	Enter amount from Line 19 1,000 x 80.0 % (from Line 15) =			20 800
21.	NEW JERSEY TAXABLE INCOME (Subtract Line 20 from Line 14c, Column B)			21 23,200
22.	TAX (From Tax Rate Schedules on Page 7)			22 480
23.	Total New Jersey Tax Withheld (Attach Form W-2)	23	400	Check ☐ If Form NJ-2210 is attached.
24.	New Jersey Estimated Tax Payments/Credit from 1991 tax return	24		← If an amount is entered on Line 25 or Line 26 attach Form NJ-2450
25.	EXCESS N.J. Unemployment Insurance Withheld (See Instructions)	25		
26.	EXCESS N.J. Disability Insurance Withheld (See Instructions)	26		
27.	Total Payments/Credits (Add Lines 23 through 26) .... ENTER TOTAL ►	27		400
28.	If payments (Line 27) are LESS THAN tax (Line 22) enter AMOUNT OF TAX YOU OWE	28		80
29.	If payments (Line 27) are MORE THAN tax (Line 22) enter OVERPAYMENT	29		
30.	Deductions from Overpayment on Line 29 which you elect to credit to:			NOTE: AN ENTRY ON LINE 30A, B, C OR D WILL REDUCE YOUR TAX REFUND
	(A) Your 1993 Tax	30A		
	(B) The N.J. Endangered Wildlife Fund ☐$5, ☐$10, Other $____	30B		
	(C) The Children's Trust Fund ☐$5, ☐$10, Other $____	30C		
	(D) The N.J. Vietnam Veterans' Memorial Fund ☐$5, ☐$10, Other $____	30D		
31.	Total Deductions From Overpayment (Add Lines 30A, B, C and D) .... ENTER TOTAL ►	31		
32.	REFUND (Amount to be sent to you, Line 29 LESS 31)	32		

Under penalties of perjury, I declare that I have examined this return, including accompanying schedules and statements, and to the best of my knowledge and belief, it is true, correct, and complete. If prepared by a person other than taxpayer, this declaration is based on all information of which the preparer has any knowledge.

► *Carol Stein* 4/14/93 ►

Your signature | Date | Spouse's signature (if filing jointly, BOTH must sign.)

Paid Preparer's Signature | Federal Identification Number

Firm's name | Federal Employer Identification Number

Pay amount on Line 28 in full. Write social security number on check or money order and make payable to:
Division of Taxation Income Tax CN-244 Trenton, N.J. 08646-0244

SIGN HERE

Please Attach Check or Money Order Here | Please Attach W-2 Forms Here

Division Use | 1 ____ 2 ____ 3 ____ 4 ____ 5 ____ 6 ____ 7 ____

PART I	TOTAL INCOME	Net losses in one category cannot be applied against income in another. In case of a net loss in any category, enter "zero" for that category		(Column A) AMOUNT OF GROSS INCOME (EVERYWHERE)		(Column B) AMOUNT FROM NEW JERSEY SOURCES	
33.	Wages, salaries, tips, and other employee compensation		33	20,000		18,000	
34.	Interest		34	3,000			
35.	Dividends		35	1,000			
36.	Net profits from business (Attach copy of Federal Schedule C, Form 1040)		36				
37.	Net gains or income from disposition of property (From line 48)		37	6,000		6,000	
38.	Net gains or income from rents, royalties, patents, and copyrights (From Line 51)		38				
39.	Net Gambling winnings		39				
40.	Pensions, Annuities and IRA Withdrawals, Less New Jersey Exclusion		40				
41.	Distributive Share of Partnership Income		41				
42.	Alimony and separate maintenance payments received		42				
43.	Other—State Nature and Source _____		43				
44.	TOTAL INCOME (Add Line 33 thru 43) (Enter here and on Line 14a, Page 1)		44	30,000		24,000	

PART II	NET GAINS OR INCOME FROM DISPOSITION OF PROPERTY	List the net gains or income, less net loss, derived from the sale, exchange, or other disposition of property including real or personal whether tangible or intangible.

(a) Kind of property and description	(b) Date acquired (Mo., day, yr.)	(c) Date sold (Mo., day, yr.)	(d) Gross sales price	(e) Cost or other basis as adjusted (see instructions) and expense of sale		(f) Gain or (loss) (d less e)
45. Land Trenton, NJ	2/14/87	3/17/92	10,000	4,000		6,000
46. Capital Gains Distribution					46	
47. Other Net Gains					47	
48. Net Gains (Add Lines 45, 46, and 47) (Enter here and on Line 37) (If Loss, enter ZERO)					48	6,000

PART III	NET GAINS OR INCOME FROM RENTS, ROYALTIES, PATENTS AND COPYRIGHTS	List the net gains or net income, less net loss, derived from or in the form of rents, royalties, patents, and copyrights as reported on your Federal Income Tax Return.		

(a) Kind of property	(b) Net Rental Income (Loss)	(c) Net Income From Royalties	(d) Net Income From Patents	(e) Net Income From Copyrights
49.				
50. Totals	(b)	(c)	(d)	(e)
51. Net Income (Combine Columns b, c, d, and e) (Enter here and on Line 38) (If Loss enter ZERO) 51				

PART IV	MEDICAL EXPENSES (Not compensation for by insurance or otherwise)	
52.	Total Medical Expenses	52
53.	Enter 2% (.02) of Line 14c, Column A, Page 1	53
54.	Subtract Line 53 from Line 52. (Enter here and on Line 17, Page 1) if less than zero enter zero	54

PART V	ALLOCATION OF WAGE AND SALARY INCOME EARNED PARTLY INSIDE AND OUTSIDE NEW JERSEY	(See instructions if compensation depends entirely on volume of business transacted or if other basis of allocation is used.)	
55.	Amount reported on Line 33 in Column A of Part I required to be allocated	55	20,000
56.	Total days in taxable year	56	365
57.	Deduct non-working days (Sundays, Saturdays, holidays, sick leave, vacation, etc.)	57	125
58.	Total days worked in taxable year (Line 56 minus Line 57)	58	240
59.	Deduct days worked outside New Jersey	59	24
60.	Days worked in New Jersey (Line 58 less Line 59)	60	216

61. ALLOCATION FORMULA   (Line 60) 216 / (Line 58) 240 x 20,000 (Enter amount from Line 55) = 19,000 (Salary earned inside N.J.)   (Include this amount on Line 33, Col. B, Part I)

PART VI	ALLOCATION OF BUSINESS INCOME TO NEW JERSEY	(See instructions if other than Formula Basis of allocation is used.)

BUSINESS ALLOCATION PERCENTAGE (From Line 5, Schedule B, Form NJ-1040 NR-A)

Enter below, the line number and amount of each item of business income reported in Column A of Part I which is required to be allocated and multiply by allocation percentage to determine amount of income from New Jersey sources.

From Line No. _____ Part I $ _____ X _____ % = $ _____

From Line No. _____ Part I $ _____ X _____ % = $ _____

10 | New Jersey Tax Rate Schedules (1992)

Unlike New York and Connecticut, New Jersey does not use tax tables for the calculation of tax, but uses Tax Rate Schedules instead. These Tax Rate Schedules have been repro-duced below. For more information on how to use the Tax Rate Schedules, see Chapter 4, *How to Figure Your Tax*.

New Jersey Tax Rate Schedules

Table A — For Filing Status: Single / Married, filing separate return

If Taxable Income (Line 21) is: Over	But not over	Your Line 21	Multiply Line 21 by:		Subtract		Your Tax (Line 22)
0	$20,000		X .02 =		- $0	=	
$20,000	$35,000		X .025 =		- $100	=	
$35,000	$40,000		X .05 =		- $975	=	
$40,000	$75,000		X .065 =		- $1,575	=	
$75,000	and over		X .07 =		- $1,950	=	

Table B — For Filing Status: Married, filing joint return / Head of Household / Qualifying Widow(er)

If Taxable Income (Line 21) is: Over	But not over	Your Line 21	Multiply Line 21 by:		Subtract		Your Tax (Line 22)
0	$20,000		X .02 =		- $0	=	
$20,000	$50,000		X .025 =		- $100	=	
$50,000	$70,000		X .035 =		- $600	=	
$70,000	$80,000		X .05 =		- $1,650	=	
$80,000	$150,000		X .065 =		- $2,850	=	
$150,000	and over		X .07 =		- $3,600	=	

NOTE: The New Jersey Income tax rates have NOT changed. The new tables were developed to make your calculations easier.

7

III | Connecticut

1 | Changes in the Tax Law

This chapter summarizes and highlights recent personal income tax developments in Connecticut. These changes are effective beginning January 1, 1992.

Income Modifications
The following *additional* items must be added to your federal adjusted gross income in determining your Connecticut adjusted gross income:

- Any loss from the sale or exchange of obligations issued by Connecticut or its political subdivisions that you included in determining your net gain or loss from the sale of capital assets for federal income tax purposes;
- Any Connecticut income taxes that you deducted for federal income tax purposes;
- Any interest expense you paid on debt incurred to purchase obligations that generate income which is exempt from Connecticut personal income taxes, if you deducted this expense for federal income tax purposes;
- Any expenses paid or incurred during the year for the production or collection of income that is exempt from Connecticut personal income taxes, if you deducted these expenses for federal income tax purposes; and
- To the extent included in gross income for federal purposes, the total taxable amount of a lump-sum distribution that is deductible from federal gross income.

The following items may be subtracted from federal adjusted gross income in determining your Connecticut adjusted gross income:

- Any interest income earned from obligations issued by Connecticut or its political subdivisions, if you included the interest in your gross income for federal income tax purposes. Formerly, taxpayers were only allowed to deduct interest income earned from U.S. obligations;
- Any gain from the sale or exchange of obligations issued by Connecticut or its political subdivisions that you included in determining your net gain or loss from the sale of capital assets for federal income tax purposes;
- Any interest paid on debt incurred to purchase obligations that generate income subject to Connecticut personal income tax, if you did not deduct this expense for federal purposes and it is related to your trade or business; and
- Any ordinary and necessary expenses paid or incurred during the year for the production or collection of income that is subject to Connecticut income tax but exempt from federal income tax, if you did not deduct them for federal purposes and they are related to your trade or business.

Credits

Income Taxes Paid to Another Jurisdiction. You may not claim a credit for income taxes paid to another jurisdiction if you claimed or will claim a credit in the other jurisdiction for taxes paid to Connecticut.

If the tax you are required to pay to another jurisdiction is different from the amount you used to determine your credit, you must notify the Commissioner of Revenue Services within 30 days after the final amount is determined. You must pay any additional tax redetermined by the Commissioner.

Foreign Tax Credit. If you elect to claim a foreign tax credit on your federal return, you will be allowed to claim a credit for any portion of income taxes paid to a Province of Canada, which you did not claim on your federal return during the current tax year or a previous tax year. However, if for federal purposes you claim the tax credit in a later tax year, it must be added back to Connecticut adjusted gross income in the year in which you claimed the federal credit.

Estimated Taxes
Connecticut now requires you to make estimated tax payments when your Connecticut income tax liability can reasonably be expected to exceed $200. Previously, the threshold was $1,000.

Required installments of estimated taxes based on the current year's tax have been reduced as follows:

- First installment due April 15 is reduced from 25% to 22.5% of the current year's tax;
- Second installment due June 15 is reduced from 50% to 45% of the current year's tax;
- Third installment due September 15 is reduced from 75% to 67½% of the current year's tax; and
- Fourth installment due January 15 of succeeding year (January 18 of 1994) is reduced from 100% to 90% of the current year's tax.

No interest or penalty will be imposed for an installment of estimated tax due after a taxpayer's death. (For information about payments based on your 1991 tax, see Chapter 5.)

Nonresidents
If married nonresidents file a joint tax return for federal purposes, and only one spouse has Connecticut source income, that spouse alone needs to file a Connecticut return. Unless the couple elects to determine their joint Connecticut taxable income as if both had Connecticut source income, the tax will be computed on a separate filing basis.

Nonresidents, other than dealers in securities, will not be

considered to be carrying on a trade or business in Connecticut solely by reason of purchasing or selling intangible property or purchasing, selling, or writing stock options for their own account.

Trusts

The calculation of Connecticut taxable income for a trust not created by the will of a decedent is changed effective January 1, 1993. If such a trust has both resident and nonresident noncontingent beneficiaries, Connecticut taxable income of the trust will be the trust's Connecticut source income, plus a portion of the trust's other income based on the percentage of noncontingent beneficiaries who are residents.

Partnerships

Income tax returns are now only required of every partnership having income derived from Connecticut sources. Previously, every partnership having a resident partner in Connecticut was also required to file a return. The partnership now must furnish every partner with a copy of the partnership return before it is filed.

2 | The Income Tax Return

Who Must File

The following individuals or groups may be required to file a Connecticut income tax return:

- Resident individuals;
- Nonresident individuals with income from Connecticut sources;
- Part-year resident individuals;
- Partners with income from a partnership doing business in Connecticut;
- Shareholders in S corporations that do business in Connecticut; and
- Trusts or estates with Connecticut income.

The easiest way to determine if you must file a Connecticut income tax return is to complete your federal income tax forms first. Your Connecticut tax is based on your federal adjusted gross income.

Individual Taxpayers

If you are a Connecticut resident, part-year resident, or nonresident working in the state, you are required to file a Connecticut income tax return if your gross income for the year exceeds:

- $12,000 for a single or married person filing separately;
- $19,000 for the head of a household; or
- $24,000 for married persons filing jointly.

(For more information on filing statuses, see the section *Filing Status* which follows.)

Your gross income is the amount you reported on your federal individual schedules (Schedules B, C, and D). This figure is not necessarily the same as the net amount reported on Line 23 of your federal tax return (Form 1040). It includes all income you received during the year, including wages, rental income, and the value of any goods or services you received.

Example

John is a Connecticut resident who is married and files a joint return. His only income is from a shoe repair business that he owns. His income from self-employment is reported on federal Schedule C, as follows:

Gross Income	$100,000
Expenses	– 92,000
Net Income	$ 8,000

Since the gross income that John reported on his federal income tax return is $100,000, he is required to file a Connecticut income tax return.

Partnerships

Partnerships are not subject to the Connecticut personal income tax. However, an individual partner may be subject to state income tax on his or her share of the partnership's income. If you are a partner in a partnership and a Connecticut state resident, your share of the partnership's income is included in Connecticut taxable income, regardless of where your partnership does business. If you are a nonresident partner in a partnership that has business activity in Connecticut, Connecticut can tax you on the partnership income derived from Connecticut sources. If the partnership earns any income connected with a Connecticut activity, it is required to file a partnership information return (Form CT-1065). The items of income or loss, deduction, or adjustment shown by the partnership on its Form CT-1065 are transferred to each partner's individual resident or nonresident return, based on the partner's share of the partnership.

Shareholders in S Corporations

Nonresident Shareholder of S Corporation. In Connecticut an S corporation shareholder assumes the obligation to individually pay tax on S corporation income. Therefore if you are a Connecticut nonresident shareholder of a Connecticut S corporation, you must file a nonresident Connecticut income tax return. On this return you must include in your Connecticut adjusted gross income your pro rata share of the S corporation's income, loss, and deduction.

When an Individual Dies

An executor, administrator, or spouse must file and sign a Connecticut income tax return for a taxpayer who died before filing a 1992 return. If the deceased person and his or her surviving spouse filed a joint federal income tax return, a joint Connecticut return, Form CT-1040 or Form CT-1040 NR/PY, must be filed. Your Connecticut filing status must be the same as your federal filing status. This includes the two years following the date of death in which the filing status of "surviving spouse" may be used.

TaxAlert: The date of the taxpayer's death must be clearly stated at the top of the return in the area designated as "other tax years ending _____, 1992." If a surviving spouse is filing the return, the words "filing as a surviving spouse" must be written in the box reserved for the taxpayer's signature.

TaxAlert: A copy of a completed federal Form 1310, Statement of Person Claiming Refund Due a Deceased Taxpayer, must be attached to the Connecticut return of a deceased taxpayer if you are requesting a refund due to the decedent and you are not that person's surviving spouse. In addition, a surviving spouse is required to attach Form 1310 if a federal refund is not claimed.

Members of the Armed Forces

If you are a member of the Armed Forces and a Connecticut resident, the amount of your military pay that is subject to federal income tax is also subject to Connecticut tax. This is true even if you are based outside the state of Connecticut. However, if your permanent home was outside Connecticut when you entered the military, you do not need to file in Connecticut merely because you are assigned to duty in Connecticut and establish a place to live there while on duty. A nonresident's military pay is not subject to Connecticut income tax.

TaxAlert: If you are a Connecticut nonresident on assigned military duty, any income you earn in Connecticut other than your military pay may be subject to Connecticut income tax. This may include your nonmilitary spouse's income or any money you earn from an off-duty civilian job.

TaxAlert: If you are in the U.S. Armed Forces and are serving in a combat zone, or you were injured and hospitalized while serving in a combat zone, your return is not due until 180 days after your return from the combat zone or hospital. No penalty or interest charges will apply.

TaxAlert: If a Connecticut taxpayer dies while on active duty in the Armed Forces and the death occurred while the person was serving in a combat zone or as a result of wounds, disease, or injury incurred while so serving, any income tax for the year in which he or she died is waived.

Estates and Trusts

The fiduciary of a Connecticut resident estate or trust or part-year resident trust must file a return on Form CT-1041 if the estate or trust:

1. Is required to file a federal income tax return for the taxable year; or
2. Had any income earned in Connecticut for the taxable year.

A resident trust or estate is the estate of a person who at the time of his death was a resident of the state of Connecticut. A part-year resident trust is any trust which the person who established it was not either a resident or a nonresident for the entire taxable year.

The fiduciary of a nonresident estate or trust must file a return on Form CT-1041 if the estate or trust had income earned within Connecticut.

TaxAlert: The place in which either the fiduciary or beneficiary resides does not affect the status of an estate or trust as resident or nonresident.

If you live in Connecticut and are a beneficiary of any trust or estate you must increase or decrease your federal adjusted gross income by your share.

Determining Residency/Domicile

Connecticut's rules concerning residency and domicile are generally comparable to those of New York State. Please refer to the New York section on *Determining Residency/ Domicile* for a more detailed discussion. Also, see the *Abandoning Your Domicile Checklist* for New York for guidance on abandoning a Connecticut domicile and determining your residency status.

The Connecticut Tax Department has provided a list of items that will be considered in determining domicile. The list, which is not all-inclusive, includes the following:

1. Location of your domicile for past years;
2. Place where you vote or are registered to vote;
3. Your status as a student;
4. Location where you are employed;
5. Classification of your employment as temporary or permanent;
6. Location of any newly acquired living quarters, whether owned or rented;
7. The present status of your former living quarters. For example, was your home sold, offered for sale, rented or made available for rent to another person?
8. Whether you claimed a Connecticut veteran's exemption for real or personal property tax;
9. The location of other real property you own;
10. The jurisdiction in which a valid driver's license was issued and type of license;
11. The jurisdiction from which any professional licenses were issued to you;
12. The location of your union membership;
13. The jurisdiction from which any motor vehicle registration was issued to you and the actual physical location of the vehicle;
14. Whether you purchased a resident or nonresident fishing or hunting license;
15. Whether you filed an income tax return as a resident or nonresident;
16. Whether you fulfilled the tax obligations required of a resident;
17. The location of any bank accounts you may have, especially the location of your most active checking account;
18. The location of any other transactions with financial institutions that you may have, including rental of a safe deposit box;
19. The location of your place of worship;
20. The location of your business relationships and the place where you transact business;
21. The location of any social, fraternal, or athletic organizations, lodges or country clubs, of which you are a member;
22. The address where you receive mail;
23. The percentage of time, excluding hours of employment, that you are present in Connecticut, compared to the percentage of time, excluding hours of employment, that you are physically present outside Connecticut;
24. The location from which you receive any unemployment compensation benefits;
25. The location of the schools that your children or spouse attend and whether the school charges you resident or nonresident tuition;
26. Statements that you made to any insurance company concerning your residence;
27. The location of your professional contacts with physicians, attorneys, and other professionals; and
28. The location where your pets are licensed.

EXCEPTION: Students are not usually considered residents of the state in which they attend school, as long as they have a permanent home somewhere else.

Nonresidents

If you are a nonresident or part-year resident of Connecticut and have income taxes withheld by a Connecticut employer or make estimated tax payments to Connecticut, you must file a Connecticut nonresident return, Form CT-1040 NR/PY. You must also file a Connecticut nonresident return if you are a nonresident and have income from the sale of real property located in Connecticut.

You must file a Connecticut nonresident or part-year resident return if you have Connecticut source income and your gross income from *all* sources exceeds:

Amount	and	Your Filing Status is:
$12,000		Single or married filing separately
$19,000		Head of household
$24,000		Married filing jointly

Gross income includes, but is not limited to:

1. Compensation for services, including wages, fees, commissions, taxable fringe benefits, and similar items;
2. Gross income from a business;
3. Capital gains;
4. Interest and dividends;
5. Gross rental income;
6. Gambling winnings;
7. Alimony;
8. Taxable pensions and annuities, including lump-sum distributions from qualified retirement plans;
9. Your pro rata share of income from partnerships, S corporations, estates, and trusts; and
10. IRA distributions.

Connecticut Source Income—Nonresidents

If you are a nonresident taxpayer, your Connecticut source income is:

- Income attributable to ownership or disposition of real or tangible personal property within Connecticut;
- Income attributable to wages for services performed in Connecticut, or to a business, trade, profession, or occupation carried on in Connecticut;
- Your pro rata share of Connecticut source income from a partnership doing business in Connecticut;
- Your pro rata share of income from an S corporation doing business in Connecticut, multiplied by the S corporation's Connecticut apportionment factor; or
- Income you received because you were a beneficiary of a trust or estate with income derived from or connected with sources in Connecticut.

EXCEPTION: Connecticut source income of a nonresident does not include the following income, even if it was included in your federal adjusted gross income:

- Distributions from federally qualified pension plans;
- Interest, dividends, or gains from the sale or exchange of intangible personal property, unless the property was used in connection with a business, trade, profession, or occupation in Connecticut;
- Compensation you received for active service in the United States military;
- Dividends from a corporation, other than an S corporation, doing business in Connecticut;
- Compensation you received from an interstate private carrier when you worked in more than one state;
- Prizes or awards; or
- Interest from a Connecticut bank, unless earned in connection with a business conducted in Connecticut.

Connecticut source income of a part-year resident is all income you received while you were a resident of Connecticut, plus any special accruals you are required to make, *and* any Connecticut source income you received for the period you were a nonresident. See the section *Attributing Income to Connecticut—Sourcing Income* in Chapter 3.

Nonresident and Part-Year Resident—Election of Filing Status for Married Taxpayers

If one spouse is a resident and the other is a nonresident, you must file separate returns unless you file jointly for federal income tax purposes and elect to be treated as if you were both residents of Connecticut. If one spouse is a resident and the other is a part-year resident, separate returns must be filed unless you file jointly for federal income tax purposes and elect to be treated as if both were full-year residents. If you are a part-year resident and your spouse is either a nonresident or a part-year resident, you must file separate returns. If both of you are nonresidents and only one spouse has Connecticut-source income, that spouse may file a separate return, regardless of how you filed for federal purposes.

Special Rules for Members of the Armed Forces

If you are a member of the United States Armed Forces, your residency status depends upon where your permanent home or domicile is located. Generally, your domicile does not change if you are serving temporarily in the Armed Forces.

If your domicile was in Connecticut when you entered the military, you are still considered a Connecticut resident, even if you are stationed in another country or state. You must file your return as a Connecticut resident. However, if you did not maintain a permanent home in Connecticut during any part of the year, but maintained your home outside Connecticut and spent fewer than 30 days during the year in Connecticut, you may file as a nonresident. (See preceding section, *Determining Residency/Domicile*.)

Generally, if your permanent home was outside Connecticut when you entered the Armed Forces, you will not be considered a Connecticut resident, even if you are assigned to duty in Connecticut and rent or buy a place to live there. Any income you receive from the military is not sourced to Connecticut. However, if you receive income from other Connecticut sources, including your spouse's income, you may be subject to tax as a nonresident.

Example

Admiral Adolfo of the U.S. Navy and his wife, Diane, are stationed at a navy base in Hartford, Connecticut. They live on the base. Adolfo and Diane are residents of Montana. To supplement his military pay, Adolfo also works for a military weapons manufacturer. Diane is a physical therapist at a local hospital. Adolfo's military income is not taxable by Connecticut. However, his income from the weapons manufacturer and Diane's income from her job will be taxable by Connecticut. They must file a Connecticut nonresident return.

EXCEPTION: Connecticut does not have the Foreign Country Domicile Exemption in Group B of the New York residency section, but does follow the Group A Domicile Exemption. (See page NY-6, *Determining Residency/Domicile*.)

Deceased Taxpayer

The executor, administrator, or spouse of a deceased nonresident or part-year resident of Connecticut must file a Connecticut nonresident and part-year resident return if the person died before filing his or her tax return and he or she would otherwise have been required to file a return. If an individual dies while on active duty in a "combat zone" or as a result of injuries received in a "combat zone" no income tax or return is due for the year of death. A refund of any estimated or withheld tax previously paid will be provided upon request to the legal representative of the estate or to a surviving spouse. (See Chapter 6, *Refunds (Amended Returns)*.)

Filing Status

Note: The general rules determining filing status discussed in greater detail under New York also apply to Connecticut unless otherwise indicated.

Your choice of filing status determines the effective, or true, rate of tax you will pay on your income. It also determines whether you are entitled to certain *exemptions*, *credits*, and *deductions;* and how much income you can earn before you are taxed at all. It is therefore a crucial element in preparing to file your tax return.

To summarize the rules in determining your Connecticut filing status for purposes of Form CT 1040, CT 1040EZ, and CT 1040 NR/PY, your filing status must generally match your federal filing status for the year. (See *Joint vs. Separate Returns for Married Taxpayers*, which follows.)

The five possible filing statuses for federal and Connecticut purposes are:

1. Single;
2. Married filing jointly;
3. Married filing separately;
4. Head of household (with qualifying person); or
5. Qualifying widow(er) with dependent child.

Your filing status for the *entire* year is determined by your marital and family situation on the last day of the tax year. For individuals, that day is almost always December 31.

Single

Your filing status is *single* if you are unmarried, divorced under a final decree, or legally separated under a separate maintenance decree as of the last day of the taxable year, provided you do not qualify to file as either *head of household* or *qualifying widow(er) with dependent child*. (See discussion of these statuses, which follows.)

Married Filing Jointly

You may choose *married filing jointly* as your filing status if you are married and both you and your spouse agree to file a joint return.

You are considered married for the whole year if on the last day of the tax year you are *either:*

1. Married and living together as husband and wife;
2. Married living apart, but not under a court-ordered decree of divorce or separate maintenance;
3. Separated under an interlocutory (not final) decree of divorce; *or*
4. Your spouse died during the year and you did not remarry before the close of the tax year. If you remarried during the year, you are considered married if you fall under one of the categories listed in 1, 2, or 3 above.

EXCEPTION: Certain married individuals may be considered unmarried and eligible for *head of household* status if his or her spouse was not a member of the household for the last six months of the tax year and if the household is the principal home of a dependent child. (See *Head of Household*, which follows, for more information.) If you qualify to file as *head of household* instead of *married filing separately*, you will be entitled to use the more favorable tax rates that apply to head of household. Additionally, you may benefit from certain exemptions, deductions, and credits not otherwise available.

When you file a joint return, all items of income and expense for you and your spouse are combined. Generally, married taxpayers who file joint returns enjoy more favorable tax rates than married taxpayers who file separately.

Married Filing Separately

You may prefer *married filing separately* for your filing status if you want to be responsible for your own tax or wish to avoid interest and penalties that your spouse may incur. You may be required to use this filing status if your spouse does not agree to file a joint return. Unless you are required to file separately, you should figure your tax under both methods to make sure you are using the method that results in the lower combined tax. Generally, you will pay a greater total combined tax by filing separate returns. This is because there is a higher effective tax rate for married persons filing separately.

If you live apart and meet certain tests, you may be *considered unmarried* for federal and state purposes and file as *head of household* even though you are not divorced or legally separated. (See *Head of Household*, which follows, for more information.)

If you file as *married filing separately*, you must write your spouse's full name and Social Security number in the spaces provided.

Joint vs. Separate Return for Married Taxpayers

Separate Federal Returns. If you and your spouse file separate returns, you must also file separate Connecticut returns. Be sure to enter the name and Social Security number of your spouse on your return.

Joint Federal Returns. If you and your spouse filed a joint federal return, you must also file a joint Connecticut return.

EXCEPTION: Where one spouse is a resident and the other is a nonresident or a part-year resident, separate returns must be filed *unless:*

1. A joint federal return was filed; *and*
2. Both spouses agree to be treated as if they were residents.

If you and your spouse file a joint Connecticut resident income tax return, you will both be jointly and severely liable for the entire tax owed plus any interest or penalty due on your joint return.

EXCEPTION: If you and your spouse are both non-residents and only one of you has income from Connecticut sources, only the spouse with Connecticut sourced income is required to file a Connecticut income tax return. Only that spouse's income will be used as the basis for calculating Connecticut income tax liability. If a separate return is filed in this manner, the income tax liability will likewise be separate.

Head of Household

In order to qualify as *head of household*, you must not be married or a surviving spouse at the close of the tax year. If you are a widow or widower, you may not use the *head of household* rates for tax years in which you are eligible to use the joint tax rates under *qualifying widow(er)*. In addition, you must maintain as your home a household which, for more than one-half of the tax year, is the principal home of one or more of the following:

1. A son or daughter, a stepchild, a grandchild, an adopted child, or a foster child. If any of the foregoing is married on the last day of the tax year, you must qualify to claim him or her as a dependent. (See the following section, *Personal Exemptions and Dependents*.) If the person is unmarried, then it is not necessary that he or she qualify as your dependent in order for you to qualify for head of household status; or
2. Any other relative eligible to be claimed as a dependent, except those eligible to be claimed by virtue of a multiple support agreement.

EXCEPTION: It is still possible for you to qualify as *head of household* if your dependent parent lives elsewhere, such as in a rest home or home for the aged, provided you maintain your parent's household.

You are considered to "maintain a household" only if you furnish, with funds that can be traced to you, more than one-half of the cost of maintaining a home during the year. Costs of maintaining a household include property taxes, mortgage interest, rent, utility charges, upkeep and repairs, property insurance, domestic help, and food consumed on the premises. They do not include the cost of clothing, education, medical treatment, vacations, life insurance, or transportation.

A married taxpayer will be *considered unmarried* and eligible for *head of household* status if his or her spouse was not a member of the household for the last six months of the tax year and if the household is the principal home of a dependent child.

Qualifying Widow(er) with Dependent Child

If you are a surviving spouse with a dependent child, you may be able to use *qualifying widow(er) with dependent child* as your filing status in the next two following years, provided you have not remarried. This filing status entitles you to use joint return tax rates (provided you do not remarry) and other deductions for two years following the death of your spouse.

In order to qualify for this filing status, you must have a child, stepchild, adopted child, or foster child that qualifies as your dependent for the tax year and you must have paid more than half the cost of maintaining a home in which both you and the child resided for the *entire* year, except for temporary absences.

Death or Birth. If the dependent who qualifies you to file using *qualifying widow(er) with dependent child* is born or dies during the year, you may still be able to claim that filing status. You must, however, have provided for more than half of the costs of maintaining a home that was the dependent's main home during the entire part of the year he or she was alive.

Indicate your status by checking the appropriate box (A through D) on your Connecticut tax return. Figure your tax by using the column in the tax tables that corresponds with your filing status. If the tax calculation schedule is used, make sure that you use the proper exemption and personal tax credit for your status.

Personal Exemptions and Dependents

The Connecticut Resident Income Tax Return (CT-1040) and the Connecticut Nonresident or Part-Year Resident Income Tax Return (CT-1040 NR/PY) do not require you to figure your personal or dependent exemptions. Your personal exemptions are included in the Connecticut tax table. No exemptions are allowed for dependents.

Connecticut State Tax Forms

Which Forms to Use

For 1992 and beyond, Connecticut supplies two resident forms for taxpayers and one nonresident/part-year resident form. The 1991 tax year was a transitional one for Connecticut filers. During the year, the former tax on interest, dividend, and capital gains was phased out. A comprehensive new tax on income was put into place. Last year, many Connecticut taxpayers were required to file two income tax returns, one for the newly enacted income tax and the other for the old tax on interest, dividends, and capital gains. This filing season should be much easier on taxpayers, since only one form will need to be filed. Connecticut filers now have a choice of two resident forms (CT-1040 and CT-1040EZ), and one nonresident form (CT-1040 NR/PY).

Form CT-1040EZ. The simplest form you can file as a Connecticut resident is Form CT-1040EZ. This form is similar to federal Form 1040EZ. For 1992, you will be able to file Form CT-1040EZ, if you meet *all* of the following criteria:

1. You *are not* claiming adjustments to federal adjusted gross income for Connecticut income tax purposes. (For example, you did not receive any interest from U.S. government bonds that could be subtracted from your federal adjusted gross income.);
2. You were a resident of Connecticut for the entire year; and
3. You *are not* claiming credit for income taxes paid to another state or locality.

In general, the Connecticut short form has broad appeal and many taxpayers will be able to take advantage of its convenience and simplicity.

Form CT-1040. The CT-1040EZ will be a suitable form for many Connecticut resident filers. However, if you are making adjustments to federal adjusted gross income or you wish to claim a credit for taxes paid to another state, you must file Form CT-1040. This form is essentially the same as Form CT-1040EZ. However, there are two additional schedules on the back of the form. One schedule is used for making adjustments to federal adjusted gross income. The other one is used to figure your credit for income taxes paid to other states or cities.

Example

If you live in Connecticut but work in New York City, you will be liable for New York State and City nonresident taxes. You can claim a credit on your Connecticut income tax return for the taxes you paid to New York, but only if you file the standard resident return, Form CT-1040. If you use Form 1040EZ, you cannot claim the credit.

Most of the information you will need to fill out your Connecticut resident income tax form can be found on your completed federal Form 1040. Even if you must fill out the adjustment or tax credit schedules, they can usually be completed fairly rapidly.

Nonresident/Part-Year Resident Form CT-1040 NR/PY. This form must be filed by all nonresidents with Connecticut source income and all part-year residents. It is virtually identical to Form CT-1040. However, an additional schedule is used to allocate income between Connecticut and non-Connecticut sources. This schedule, Form CT-SI, must be attached to your Form CT-1040 NR/PY. (See *Attributing Income to Connecticut—Sourcing Rules* in Chapter 3.)

> **TAXPLANNER:** A nonresident taxpayer who is a partner in a partnership or a shareholder in an S corporation doing business in Connecticut may not need to file a CT-1040 NR/PY. Connecticut requires a partnership or S corporation to remit personal income taxes on behalf of any nonresident partner or shareholder who does not sign an agreement with Connecticut to file an individual nonresident return. If you wish to file your own return, you must send in an agreement on Form CT-1NA. If you have no other Connecticut source income besides income that is derived from the partnership or S corporation, you may wish to have the partnership or S corporation pay the taxes for you. However, the tax must then be paid at the highest marginal rate for individuals, with no exemptions or credits.

Certain nonresident partners or shareholders may file a group return, using Form CT-1040 NR/PY. If your only Connecticut source income is from a partnership or S corporation, and you agree in writing to let a designated partner or shareholder submit the return on your behalf, you may qualify to file group returns. A minimum of 20 qualified electing partners are required. If you are a partner or shareholder in a partnership or S corporation that is generating Connecticut source income, you should discuss these different filing options with the designated tax partner or shareholder. One major disadvantage of both filing options is that your tax must be computed without the benefit of any exemptions or credits.

Before adopting any strategy, it is important to know your sources of Connecticut income, estimate the amounts you ex-

pect to receive, and discuss your eligibility for a group filing with other partners or shareholders to see if a qualified electing group exists.

The principal additional forms you may need to attach to your tax returns are listed below:

CT-1040TCS — **Tax Calculation Schedule (CT-1040 Filers), (CT-1040 NR/PY Filers)** This form is used to calculate the tax owed. *It does not have to be attached to your return.*

Schedule CT-SI — **Nonresident or Part-Year Resident Schedule of Income from Connecticut Sources** Use this form to detail Connecticut source income if you are a *nonresident* or a *part-year* resident. This form must be attached to Form CT-1040 NR/PY.

CT-1040BA — **Nonresident/Part-Year Business Apportionment Schedule** This form is for *nonresidents* and part-year residents who allocate income from self-employment sourced to Connecticut. This form must be attached to Form CT-SI.

CT-1040AW — **Part-Year Resident Allocation** This form is used by *part-year residents* who need to allocate their income sourced to Connecticut for the period they were residents. A nonresident employee who is not sure how much of his income should be reported as Connecticut-source income should also use this form.

CT-1040EXT — **Application for Extension of Time to File Individual Income Tax Return** Use this form to request an extension to file your income tax return. (See the section on *Extensions*, which follows.)

CT-1NA — **Nonresident Income Tax Agreement** This form is used by nonresidents who are partners or shareholders of a partnership or S corporation that does business in Connecticut. File this form if you plan to be responsible for filing your own CT-1040 NR/PY rather than let the partnership or S corporation remit taxes on your behalf.

Partnerships and S corporations that do business in Connecticut are required by law to furnish tax information to their partners or shareholders. If you are a partner in a partnership or a shareholder in an S corporation, you will receive a copy of an information form from the partnership or S corporation, showing your share of the entity's income, deductions, losses, etc. You should use this information to complete your personal income tax return. These information forms are:

CT-1065 Partnership Return—filed by partnership
CT-1065 Schedule K-1—furnished to resident partners
CT-1065 Schedule K-1-(NR)—furnished to nonresident partners
CT-1120SI—filed by S corporation
CT-1120SI Schedule K-1—furnished to resident shareholders
CT-1120SI Schedule K-1(NR)—furnished to nonresident shareholders.

Where to File

Form Name and Number	To Send a Tax Payment	To Claim a Refund
CT-1040EZ Connecticut EZ Resident Income Tax Return	State of Connecticut Dept. of Revenue Services P.O. Box 2977 Hartford, CT 06104-2977	State of Connecticut Dept. of Revenue Services P.O. Box 2976 Hartford, CT 06104-2976
CT-1040 Connecticut Resident Income Tax Return	State of Connecticut Dept. of Revenue Services P.O. Box 2977 Hartford, CT 06104-2977	State of Connecticut Dept. of Revenue Services P.O. Box 2976 Hartford, CT 06104-2976
CT-1040(NR/PY) Connecticut Nonresident or Part-year Resident Income	State of Connecticut Dept. of Revenue Services P.O. Box 2969 Hartford, CT 06104-2969	State of Connecticut Dept. of Revenue Services P.O. Box 2968 Hartford, CT 06104-2968

Due Dates—When Do I File?

Resident, Nonresident, and Part-Year Resident Individuals. Your Connecticut income tax return is due on or before April 15, 1993, if you file on a calendar year basis. If you file on a fiscal year basis, your return is due on or before the 15th day of the fourth month after the close of your fiscal year. If the due date for filing the return falls on a Saturday, Sunday, or legal holiday, the return becomes due on the next day that is not a Saturday, Sunday or legal holiday. See the following section, *Extensions*, for information about requesting an extension of your return due date.

TaxAlert: Connecticut does not provide an exception for Patriot's Day, a legal holiday in Massachusetts and Maine that falls in mid-April.

Deceased Taxpayers. The due date for filing a return for a taxpayer who died during the taxable year is the 15th day of the fourth month after the end of the decedent's calendar or fiscal year. The Connecticut filing status must be consistent with the federal filing status. The return must be signed and filed by the taxpayer's executor, administrator, or spouse.

No return is due for any individual who died while on active duty in a combat zone or as a result of injuries received in a combat zone. However, a return may be filed to claim a refund.

Partnerships. The partnership return is an information return showing each partner's distributive share in the various classes of partnership income, losses, deductions, and credits. The partnership return is due the 15th day of the fourth month following the close of the tax year.

A nonresident group return filed on behalf of qualified nonresident partners must be filed on or before the 15th day of the fourth month following the close of the qualified electing partner's taxable year.

For nonresident partners not included in a group return, the partnership must file a composite return on the partner's behalf on or before the 15th day of the fourth month following the close of the partnership's taxable year.

Other Taxes. You may be subject to filing requirements for other taxes, such as Sales and Use Tax, Estate and Gift Tax. (Refer to Chapters 7 for a discussion of other taxes.)

Fiduciaries. Persons filing as fiduciaries are subject to the same filing requirements as are applicable to state resident returns.

Extensions

Like New York and New Jersey, Connecticut allows you to extend the due date of your return for reasonable cause. Unlike either New York or New Jersey, Connecticut has a number of different extension forms, depending upon which return you file.

An individual, trust, estate, partnership, or S corporation that has requested a federal extension may receive a six-month Connecticut extension. The entire amount of tax due must be sent with your Connecticut request form. The extension does not extend the time you have to pay your tax. It merely extends the time for filing your return.

If you have not been granted a federal extension, you may still apply for a Connecticut extension, provided you have a good cause for your request. This request must also be filed on or before the date the original return is due. Again, you must pay all of the tax you owe with the extension request and file it on or before the due date of the original return. However, an extension of time to pay your tax may be granted under special circumstances.

TaxAlert: The death of a spouse or missing records are generally considered reasonable causes for requesting an extension.
nt.

TaxAlert: To avoid interest and penalty charges for underpayment of tax, be conservative when estimating your Connecticut income tax liability.

Connecticut has developed special forms for extension requests. The number of the form corresponds to the number of the return, with an "EXT" after the number. For example, if you are requesting an extension of time to file a CT-1040, or CT-1040 NR/PY you must request it on Form CT-1040 EXT. Partnerships filing a CT-1065 must request an extension on Form CT-1065 EXT. The Department of Revenue will not notify you if your request has been accepted. It will only notify you if your request has been denied.

An extension of time to *pay* your tax may be granted if you can demonstrate that it will cause you undue hardship to pay your income tax by the due date of your original return. To request an extension of time to pay, you must file Form CT-1127, *Application For Extension of Time for Payment of Income Tax*, by the original due date (generally, April 15). You will need to explain fully why you are unable to pay your tax on time and provide documentation of your situation.

Partnerships or S corporations filing group or "composite" returns must request an extension on Form CT-1040 EXT. Do not use a CT-1065 EXT or the CT-1120SI-EXT. A partnership request must show the partnership's name and have the word "GROUP" written clearly across the top. It must be signed by a partner with the authority to act as an agent of the partnership. The request is due on or before the date the original nonresident return is due to be filed. The same rules apply to an S corporations filing a composite return. The S corporation's name must be on the form and the word "GROUP" must be written across the top. It must be signed by a shareholder having agent status or authority to sign.

Other than the titles, the forms are generally the same. Each form requires you to fill in your name, address, and Social Security or taxpayer identification number. Each requires you to estimate your tax liability for the year. The forms must be completed, signed, and mailed on or before the date the original return was due. However, different forms must be sent to different mailing addresses. Be sure to write the form number and tax year on any check you send with your extension request. For example, if you are requesting an extension on Form CT-1040 EXT, write "1992 Form CT-1040 EXT" on your check.

Connecticut Extension Request Addresses

CT-1040 EXT:	CT-1127 EXT:
State of Connecticut	State of Connecticut
Department of Revenue	Department of Revenue
Services	Services
P.O. Box 2977	P.O. Box 2977
Hartford, CT 06104-2977	Hartford, CT 06104-2977

CT-1065 EXT:
State of Connecticut
Department of Revenue
Services
P.O. Box 2935
Hartford, CT 06104-2935

An extension request will be considered filed on time if the United States Post Office postmarks the envelope no later than the due date of the return. If the extension request is sent by certified mail, the date stamped on your Post Office receipt is the date it is considered filed. Hand-delivered, overnight delivery, or messenger delivery is considered filed on the date when the Department of Revenue receives the request. If the last day for filing falls on a Saturday, Sunday, or legal holiday, the time to file a request is extended to the next regular business day.

Information Block

The top portion of your income tax return is called the "information block." It requests general information about you and your spouse primarily for the purposes of identification. This section covers the type of information you will need to fill out the information block of Connecticut forms.

Tax Year

If you are filing a return for a period other than January 1, 1992, through December 31, 1992, the calendar year 1992 at the top of your Connecticut return indicates the dates your tax year began and ended. Enter this information on the line starting with the phrase *For the year January 1–December 31, 1992 or other tax year beginning _____*.

Forms CT-1040, CT-1040 EZ, CT-1040 NR/PY: If you re-

ceived a pre-printed label from Connecticut, use it over the sections requesting your name, address, and Social Security number. You may skip to number 4. If the pre-printed label has incorrect information, cross out the incorrect information, and write in the correct information. If you do not have a pre-printed label, continue reading.

Check here for 1992 Resident Status: Form CT-1040 NR/PY only. Part-year residents should check the box for part-year residents. Nonresidents, check the box labelled "Nonresident."

1. *Name*—Enter your first name and middle initial, if you have one, followed by your last name. If you are married *and* filing jointly with your spouse, enter your spouse's name also, with his or her first name followed by a middle initial. If your spouse has a different last name, you must enter that name, as well as your own, in the last name section.

Your First Name and Middle Initial	*Last Name*
Brian D.	Smith

If a joint return, spouse's first name and middle initial	*Last Name*
Katherine M.	Smith

2. *Social Security Number:* Enter your Social Security number. If you are filing jointly, enter your spouse's Social Security number as well. It is critical that you enter the correct number(s) next to the appropriate name, so proofread carefully!

3. *Home Address:* Enter your current home address at which you can receive mail. Students who are only in Connecticut to attend school should use their permanent home address outside of Connecticut, *not* their school address. This is because if you file your return and then leave school at the end of the semester, the state can send your refund, if any, to the correct address.

4. Check the appropriate box if you (a) used a paid preparer to prepare your tax return and no longer wish to receive tax forms or (b) filled out Part 1 of Form CT-2210, *Underpayment of Estimated Income Tax by Individuals and Fiduciaries.*

TaxAlert: Your federal income tax return does not ask you if you were a "resident" of a particular state. It only asks you to fill out your home address. You can still be a "resident" of Connecticut for income tax purposes, even if your home address is somewhere else. To make matters even more confusing, *some* taxpayers list their preparer's address as their home address. Refer to the section on *Determining Residency/Domicile* on page CT-6, to determine if you are a Connecticut resident.

5. *Filing Status*—Generally, you should use the same status as you used on your federal return. However, nonresident married taxpayers may elect to file differently from their federal return. If you choose the filing status of married filing separately, enter your spouse's full name and Social Security number.

3 | Calculating Your Taxable Income

Residents—Starting Point

Introduction

The preceding chapters discussed preliminary matters, such as deciding whether or not you need to file a personal income tax return and whether to file as a resident or a nonresident. By now, you've organized your records, figured out who your dependents are for tax purposes, and made the basic decisions about how to file.

Now it's time to start actually calculating your tax. Don't be nervous. This chapter and the succeeding ones will lead you through the process, step by step and line by line. If you are a *resident*, this chapter will show you how to fill in the first few lines of your return to report your income to Connecticut. If you are a *nonresident*, please skip ahead to the section titled *Nonresidents/Part-Year Residents—Starting Point* on page CT-15.

To begin calculating your Connecticut personal income tax, you must know your federal adjusted gross income.

Income: CT-1040, *Line 1*; CT-1040EZ, *Line 1*

Enter your federal adjusted gross income from Line 31 of federal Form 1040, Line 16 of federal Form 1040A, or Line 3 of federal Form 1040EZ. This is your Connecticut adjusted gross income. No further adjustments are necessary.

TAXALERT: You must attach any wage or income statements you received (Forms W-2) to your Form CT-1040 or CT-1040EZ, whichever one you file.

For assistance in choosing the proper form to file, refer back to the section on *Which Forms to Use* in Chapter 2. See the next section, *Additions and Subtractions*, to determine what modifications to your Connecticut adjusted gross income you will need to make.

Residents—Additions and Subtractions

The preceding chapter explained how to report your federal adjusted gross income to Connecticut. Modifications must be made to federal adjusted gross income to add back certain expenses or subtract certain income items that were deducted or included respectively in federal adjusted gross income.

These modifications are required by Connecticut law. Form CT-1040EZ does not provide for modifications. If you are not required to make any modifications to your federal adjusted gross income, and you meet all the other requirements for filing Form CT-1040EZ, you should use this form. However,

if you are required to make such modifications, you should use Form CT-1040.

Form CT-1040, Schedule 1, lists all of the modifications you may have to make on Lines 2 and 4. The modifications, which must be entered on the appropriate lines on Schedule 1, are as follows:

Additions to Federal Adjusted Gross Income

CT-1040: Schedule 1, Lines 22–29.

1. Interest on state and local obligations other than Connecticut (Schedule 1, Line 22): Enter the total amount of interest income you received from bonds issued by a state other than Connecticut. Include interest from municipal bonds issued by a county, city, town, or other local government unit in a state other than Connecticut including the District of Columbia. The interest income from these bonds is not taxed for federal purposes but must be added back for Connecticut purposes.

TAXPLANNER: If you receive a list of interest income from bonds issued by states or localities other than those in Connecticut, you may wish to consider buying Connecticut bonds or U.S. obligations and selling the others. See the *Subtractions from Federal Adjusted Gross Income* section on the next page for more information on U.S. obligations.

2. Exempt-interest dividends on state or local obligations other than Connecticut (Schedule 1, Line 23). Exempt interest dividends are distributions from qualified mutual funds that invest in state and local bonds, the interest on which is exempt from federal taxation. Enter the total amount of your exempt-interest dividends from state or local obligations, other than those of Connecticut or its municipalities. If you receive dividends from a mutual fund that invests in bonds of many states, enter only the percentage of income derived from non-Connecticut obligations. The fund should supply you with these percentages. Please consult your year-end tax statements or call the mutual fund directly.

Example

Gloria invests in a municipal bond fund and receives dividends. The fund itself invests in bonds of all fifty states. Gloria must report only the portion of her dividends that the fund derived from bonds of states other than Connecticut. If 30% of the dividends is from Connecticut bonds, then Gloria must add back the remaining 70% on her Form CT-1040, Schedule 1.

3. Pro rata share of certain S corporation shareholder's loss (Schedule 1, Line 24). Enter only the Connecticut portion of any loss from your interest in an S corporation that you reported on Schedule E of federal Form 1040.

   If the S corporation apportions its income to other states, use the apportionment percentage reported on the corporation's Connecticut tax return (Form 208S) to apportion the loss.

Example

John is a 20% shareholder in an S corporation. The S corporation reported a loss of $100 on its federal return. The corporation apportioned 60% of the loss ($60) to Connecticut. John will take 20% of the $60, or $12, and enter it on Line 24 of Schedule 1.

4. Ordinary income portion of lump sum distributions from qualified plans (Schedule 1, Line 25). Enter the total of the amounts that you reported on federal Form 4972, Part III, Line 1 and Part IV, Line 1. Attach a copy of federal Form 4972 to the back of Form CT-1040.

5. Beneficiary's share of Connecticut Fiduciary Adjustment (Schedule 1, Line 26). If you have income from an estate or trust, any Connecticut additions or subtractions that apply to that income will be shown as state supplemental information on federal Schedule K-1 or its equivalent. The federal K-1 should be sent to you by the estate or trust. If the adjustment is a net addition, enter that amount. If the adjustment is a net subtraction, refer to the following section, *Subtractions from Federal Adjusted Gross Income*.

   If more than one estate or trust is involved, enter the total amount of all additions.

6. Loss on sale of Connecticut bonds (Schedule 1, Line 27). If you sold Connecticut bonds and notes at a loss, enter the total amount of your losses.

7. Other (Schedule 1, Line 28): Enter any additions to income not listed above and describe them in an attachment to your return. If you think that you may be obligated to make certain additions to income not included in the preceding lines, consult a professional tax advisor. Otherwise, leave this line blank.

Enter your total additions on Line 29 of Schedule 1 and Line 2 of your CT-1040.

Subtractions from Federal Adjusted Gross Income

CT-1040: Schedule 1, Lines 30–39. Items on Form CT-1040, Schedule 1, that may be subtracted from federal adjusted gross income include:

1. Interest on U.S. obligations (Line 30). Enter the total of any interest income you received from such federal obligations as Savings Bonds Series EE and HH, and U.S. Treasury bills and notes. Interest from U.S. government bonds is exempt from Connecticut tax.

   Do *not* enter the amount of interest you earned on Federal National Mortgage Association (Fannie Mae) bonds, Government National Mortgage Association (Ginnie Mae) bonds, and Federal Home Loan Mortgage Corporation (FHLMC) securities. This interest is taxed by Connecticut. If you are unsure of what's taxable and what isn't, consult a professional tax advisor or call Taxpayer Services at 1-800-382-9463 or 203-297-4900. (See *Examples of Taxable and Non-Taxable Securities*, which follows.)

2. Dividends from certain mutual funds consisting of U.S. obligations (Line 31). Enter the total amount of exempt dividends you received from a mutual fund(s) if the fund invests 50% or more of its assets in tax-exempt federal obligations. Your mutual fund statement should tell you if any or all of the dividends are tax-exempt. If you need assistance, call your mutual fund directly.

Example

Larry owns shares in a mutual fund that invests all of its funds in U.S. Treasury bonds. The dividends Larry received from the fund will be exempt from Connecticut tax because more than 50% of the fund's assets are made up of direct federal obligations.

3. Reimbursed moving expenses (Line 32). Enter the total reimbursed moving expenses that were reported on your W-2. These amounts should have been reported to you on federal Form 4782, Line 9, or an equivalent statement provided by your employer.

4. Refunds of state and local taxes (Line 33). Enter the refunds of state and local income taxes you reported on federal Form 1040. The amount includes refunds of state taxes that you received from other states.

5. Tier 1 Railroad Retirement Benefits (Line 34). If you received any Tier 1 Railroad Retirement Benefits during 1992, you may deduct the taxable amount you received from your federal adjusted gross income. Enter the total amount of Tier 1 railroad retirement benefits you reported on your federal Form 1040 or 1040A.

6. Pro rata share of certain S corporation shareholder's income (Line 35). Enter only the Connecticut portion of any income you reported on your Schedule E of federal Form 1040 which you received from the S corporation.

   If the S corporation apportions its income to other states, you may use the apportionment percentage reported on the corporation's Connecticut Form 208S to determine your share of the income.

Example

Katherine owns 20% of a S corporation. The corporation apportions its income to New York (60%) and to Connecticut (40%). In 1992, the corporation had $100 in income and it apportioned 40% or $40 to Connecticut. Katherine may deduct 20% of $40, or $8, on her CT-1040.

7. Beneficiary's share of Connecticut fiduciary adjustment (Line 36). If you received any income from an estate or trust, any Connecticut additions and subtractions that apply to that income will be shown as state supplemental information on a federal Form K-1 or its equivalent. The federal Form K-1 should be sent to you by the trust or estate. If the adjustment is a net subtraction, enter the amount on this line.

   If more than one estate or trust is involved, enter the sum of all the subtractions on this line.

8. Gain on sale of Connecticut bonds (Line 37). Enter the total amount of all gains from the sale or exchange of Connecticut notes, bonds or other obligations that you received.

9. Other: Enter any subtractions to income that are not listed above. For example, enter any interest income from state of Connecticut state bonds that you reported on your federal form 1040. Although this interest income is taxable for federal income tax purposes, it may be subtracted from your federal adjusted gross income on your Connecticut return. However, if the federal government paid you interest on your federal income tax refund, that income *cannot* be subtracted from your federal adjusted gross income.

Examples of Taxable and Non-Taxable Securities*

Interest Subtracted from Federal Adjusted Gross Income (Interest is Not Taxable)	Interest Added Back to Federal Adjusted Gross Income (Interest is Taxable)
• Commodity Credit Corporation • Federal Home Loan Banks • Federal Savings and Loan Insurance Corporation • Guam, Puerto Rico, and Virgin Islands • Resolution Funding Corporation	• Other States and Municipalities • District of Columbia **Interest is _NOT_ subtracted or added back to Federal Adjusted Gross Income** • Asian Development Bank • Federally chartered financial institutions • Federal Home Loan Mortgage Corporation ("Freddie Mac") • Federal National Mortgage Association ("Fannie Mae") • Government National Mortgage Association ("Ginnie Mae") • Inter-American Development Bank • International Bank for Reconstruction and Redevelopment ("World Bank") • Student Loan Marketing Association ("Sallie Mae")

This list is not exhaustive; it simply illustrates the wide range of exempt and non-exempt securities available.

If you believe that you may be entitled to make other subtractions not listed on Lines 30 through 38, consult your professional tax advisor.

Enter your total subtractions on Line 39, Schedule 1 and Line 4 of your CT-1040.

Deductions

Connecticut takes a different approach to deductions and exemptions from the one reflected on your federal individual income tax return. While your federal return provides for many choices to allow you the most tax savings, Connecticut does not allow any choices.

For most filers, exemptions are built into the tax table that you use to determine your Connecticut income tax. The result is a reduction in the amount of taxes you owe according to your filing and status.

A Connecticut income tax return filer therefore has no decisions to make when it comes to deductions. Connecticut either does not allow them or has already taken them into account. Please turn now to *Computation of Tax for Residents* in Chapter 4, to continue preparation of your CT-1040.

If you are not permitted to use the tax tables, see *Personal Exemptions and Dependents* in Chapter 2, for instructions on how to calculate your exemptions.

Nonresidents/Part-Year Residents— Starting Point

This section is designed to help you determine your Connecticut nonresident or part-year resident income base. This will be the starting point from which you figure the income tax you owe to Connecticut. By now, you should have obtained a copy of Form CT-1040 NR/PY and determined your filing status. If not, review the preceding chapters, and have your federal Form 1040 in front of you.

If you are a part-year resident, you will be taxed on *all* income you received from all sources during the time you were a resident of Connecticut plus income you received from Connecticut sources while you were a nonresident. As a nonresident, you are only taxed on income you received from Connecticut sources. If you look at your CT-1040 NR/PY, you will see that there are really *two* income bases, or starting points, for nonresidents and part-year residents. You will allocate whichever base is larger and pay tax on that base. The first base is your federal adjusted gross income from Line 31 of federal Form 1040 (or Line 16 of Form 1040A). You should enter this amount exactly as it appears on your federal income tax return on Line 1 of your CT-1040 NR/PY.

The second income base is not actually found on Form CT-1040 NR/PY itself, but on Schedule CT-SI, which must be completed by all part-year residents and nonresidents. Look at Line 16 on Schedule CT-SI, *Gross Income from Connecticut Sources.* Then look above at Lines 1 through 15. In contrast to your federal adjusted gross income, which you merely copied from your federal return, you will determine each item of gross income from Connecticut sources separately.

By beginning with federal adjusted gross income, Connecticut has also adopted federal definitions of gross income as well as federal adjustments applied to this income. Gross income includes all payments you received in the form of money, goods, property, or services from all sources.

Filling Out Schedule CT-SI, Part 1

Lines 1–16 of Part 1, Schedule CT-SI contain a summary of the items that make up your gross income from Connecticut sources with modifications discussed below.

Nonresidents. If you are a nonresident, you must report in Part 1 the amount included in your federal items of income that you received from Connecticut sources, with appropriate modifications as discussed below. You should have your federal return and appropriate schedules in front of you when completing this section.

Part-Year Residents. If you moved into or out of Connecticut during the year, you must report the income that you received from *all* sources during the time you were a Connecticut resident, in addition to your Connecticut source income for the part of the year you were a nonresident. Refer to the preceding sections on *Nonresidents/Part-Year Residents.* The Part-Year Resident Allocation Income Worksheet (CT-1040 AW) on page CT-23 will help you figure your Connecticut source income for the entire year.

Wages, Salaries, Tips, etc.: CT-SI, *Line 1*

(See *Attributing Income to Connecticut—Sourcing Rules* later in this chapter in order to determine the amount of your wages, salaries, tips, and other compensation that you earned from services performed in Connecticut.) Your compensation will be attributed, or *sourced*, to Connecticut based on the number of days you worked there.

Interest Income: CT-SI, *Line 2*; and Dividend Income: CT-SI, *Line 3*

(See *Special Problems in Attributing Income*, which follows.) Generally, nonresidents are not taxed on dividends or interest income. However, if you used the securities that gave rise to the income in a trade or business carried on in Connecticut, you must report the dividend or interest income here.

PART I — CONNECTICUT INCOME — Part-Year Residents: Enter all of your income earned while you were a Connecticut resident and your income received from Connecticut sources while you were a nonresident. (Use *Part-Year Resident Income Allocation Worksheet - CT-1040AW*).
Nonresidents: Enter income received from Connecticut sources.

1.	Wages, salaries, tips, etc.	1 _____
2.	Taxable interest income	2 _____
3.	Dividend income	3 _____
4.	Alimony received	4 _____
5.	Business income or (loss) *(from federal Schedule C)*....................	5 _____
6.	Capital gain or (loss) *(from federal Schedule D)*...........................	6 _____
7.	Capital gain distributions not reported on Line 6	7 _____
8.	Other gains or (losses) *(from federal Form 4797)*.........................	8 _____
9.	Taxable amount of IRA distributions	9 _____
10.	Taxable amount of pensions and annuities	10 _____
11.	Rents, royalties, partnerships, estates, trusts, etc. *(from federal Schedule E)*....	11 _____
12.	Farm income or (loss) *(from federal Schedule F)*..........................	12 _____
13.	Unemployment compensation (insurance)	13 _____
14.	Taxable amount of social security benefits	14 _____
15.	Other income *(including Lump Sum Distributions)*	15 _____
16.	Gross Income from Connecticut sources. (Add Lines 1 through 15) ...	16 _____

Schedule CT-SI

Alimony Received: CT-SI, *Line 4*

This lines does *not* apply if you are a nonresident.

Business Income or (Loss): CT-SI, *Line 5*

(See *Attributing Income to Connecticut—Sourcing Rules*.) If you are self-employed and carrying on a business in Connecticut, or a partner or shareholder in a partnership or S corporation that does business in Connecticut, you may have to report income or losses on this line.

Capital Gain or (Loss): CT-SI, *Line 6*

(See discussion in *Special Problems in Attributing Income* for rules on computing your gain (or loss) from Connecticut sources.) In general, gains or losses are sourced to Connecticut if they arose from real or tangible personal property located in Connecticut. Connecticut follows federal rules in determining capital gains or losses.

Capital Gain or (Loss) from Connecticut Real Property. If you are a nonresident, you must include on this line the amount of any capital gains or losses that you derived from real property located in Connecticut. Gains and losses from the sale or disposition of real property are not subject to apportionment.

CT-SI, *Lines 7–10*

These lines are used to report certain items that were reported on your federal Form 1040 but are not addressed elsewhere on the Connecticut return, such as capital gains not reported on Line 6 or Taxable Individual Retirement Arrangement distributions. (See *Special Problems in Attributing Income* for a discussion on sourcing these categories of income (or loss).)

Rents, Royalties, Partnerships, Estate Trusts, etc.: CT-SI, *Line 11*

Enter the part of your federal amount that represents income (or losses) connected with Connecticut sources on this line.

Rent and Royalty Income. Enter on this line the part of your federal amount of rents and royalties from:

1. Real property in Connecticut;
2. Tangible personal property located in Connecticut;
3. Intangible personal property used in connection with a business, trade, profession, or occupation carried on in Connecticut.

If the business is carried on in other states besides Connecticut, use the business apportionment percentage or alternative allocation method to source income from intangible property to Connecticut. (See *Attributing Income to Connecticut—Sourcing Rules*.)

Partnerships, S Corporations, Estates and Trusts. (See *Special Problems in Attributing Income* for more information on these types of income.) If you are a nonresident partner in a partnership, shareholder in an S corporation, or beneficiary of an estate or trust, you must enter any share of income from the partnership, etc., that arose from Connecticut sources.

Farm Income or (Loss): CT-SI, *Line 12*

Enter on this line the part of the federal amount that represents your income (or loss) from farming carried on in Connecticut.

Unemployment Compensation: CT-SI, *Line 13*

Nonresidents. Because unemployment compensation is a direct result of past employment, the rules for sourcing this income are the same as for any other type of compensation. (See *Attributing Income to Connecticut—Sourcing Rules*.)

Part-Year Residents. Include *all* unemployment compensation you received during your resident period.

Taxable Amount of Social Security Benefits: CT-SI, *Line 14*

This lines does *not* apply if you are a nonresident.

Other Income: CT-SI, *Line 15*

Enter on this line the part of your federal adjusted gross income from other income that you received from or was connected with Connecticut sources.

TaxAlert: If you have a federal net operating loss carryover, do *not* enter any portion on this line.

Gross Income from Connecticut Sources: CT-SI, *Line 16*

Add Lines 1 through 15 and enter the total on Line 16. This is your gross income from Connecticut sources. The remainder of Form CT-SI has to do with modifications to gross income from Connecticut sources. (See *Additions and Subtractions*, which follows, for information on completing Form CT-SI.)

Nonresidents/Part-Year Residents— Additions and Subtractions

This section assumes that you have entered your *federal adjusted gross income* on Line 1 of your Connecticut nonresident and part-year resident tax return, Form CT-1040 NR/PY. If you haven't done this yet, go back and review the preceding section.

Now let's examine how to make the modifications that Connecticut requires to federal adjusted gross income. You will make additions and subtractions required by law to reflect the various differences between income taxed by the federal government and income taxed by Connecticut. The result will be your *Connecticut adjusted gross income*, entered on Line 5 of your return.

Connecticut's modifications are listed on Schedule 1 of your Connecticut nonresident or part-year resident income tax return. Connecticut has seven different lines for adding back items to your *federal adjusted gross income*. To determine your *Connecticut adjusted gross income*, you must add back the following categories of income:

- Interest from state and local obligations other than those Issued by Connecticut or its municipalities;
- Dividends from mutual funds based on state and local obligations other than those of Connecticut or its municipalities;
- Your share of S corporation losses from Connecticut sources;
- Ordinary income portion of lump-sum distributions;
- Beneficiary's share of Connecticut fiduciary adjustment;
- Loss on sale of Connecticut bonds; and
- Other additions.

There are also nine line items that represent income exempt from tax in Connecticut but taxable for federal purposes. The following line items must be subtracted from your *federal adjusted gross income* before you can correctly determine your Connecticut taxable income:

- Interest on U.S. obligations;
- Dividends from qualified mutual funds investing in U.S. obligations;
- Reimbursed moving expenses;
- Refunds of state and local income taxes;
- Tier 1 Railroad Retirement benefits;
- Your share of S corporation income from sources within Connecticut;
- Beneficiary's share of Connecticut fiduciary adjustment;
- Gain on sale of Connecticut bonds; and
- Other subtractions.

TAXALERT: Enter all amounts on Schedule 1 (Lines 26–43) as positive numbers. This is even true for amounts that represent losses.

Additions to Federal Adjusted Gross Income

Interest from State and Local Obligations for Nonresidents: CT-1040 NR/PY, Line 26. If you were not a Connecticut resident during 1992, you do not have to include in your *Connecticut adjusted gross income* any interest income you received from state and local bonds or obligations. The only exception to this rule is if the bonds were used in a business, trade, profession, or occupation carried on in Connecticut.

Example

Sandra is a New York State resident who works in Connecticut. In the beginning of 1992, Sandra purchased one-year obligations from New York State for her personal portfolio. These obligations paid $125 of interest during the year. Sandra is not required to show any interest on Line 26 of her Connecticut nonresident/part-year resident income tax return. The interest from the New York obligation need not be included as part of Connecticut income because it was not earned in connection with a business taking place in Connecticut.

TAXALERT: Interest income received for Connecticut bonds or obligations is always tax-exempt for Connecticut purposes, however the bonds or obligations were used.

Interest from State and Local Obligations for Part-year Residents: CT-1040 NR/PY, Line 26. Special rules apply to interest income if you were a part-year Connecticut resident at any time in 1992. You must include on Line 26, of Form CT-1040 NR/PY, any interest income you received while you were a resident from state and local bonds and obligations issued by any state other than Connecticut and its local governments. This includes interest you had a right to receive but did not collect until you moved out of Connecticut.

Exempt-Interest Dividends From State or Local Obligations: CT-1040 NR/PY, Line 27. If you were a part-year Connecticut resident in 1992 and received exempt-interest dividends from an investment company or mutual fund during that time, you must include that amount on Line 27 of your nonresident/part-year resident return. *Exempt interest dividends* is the amount of income you receive from your regulated investment company or mutual fund account which was not included on your federal return. Any amount of interest dividend you receive in connection with a trade or business located in Connecticut must be included on Line 27, whether you are a nonresident or part-year resident. Federal exempt-interest dividends derived from obligations of Connecticut or its municipalities are also exempt for Connecticut state purposes. You must include this amount on Line 27.

Pro Rata Share of Certain S Corporation Losses: CT-1040 NR/PY, Line 28. If you are a shareholder in an S corporation that does business in Connecticut, you must add back to your federal adjusted gross income your share of the Connecticut portion of any loss reported on Schedule E of your federal income tax return (Form 1040). This amount must be included on Line 28 of your Connecticut nonresident/part-year resident return.

TAXALERT: If the federal S corporation in which you own shares apportions its income to more than one state, the apportionment percentage reported on Connecticut Corporation Tax Form 1120S should be used to determine the loss to be added back on Line 28. This information should be provided to you by the S corporation.

Ordinary Income Portion of Lump-Sum Distributions from Qualified Plans: CT-1040 NR/PY, Line 29. If you were a part-year Connecticut resident, and you received a lump-sum payment from a qualified plan, you must include the amount you have entered on federal Form 4972, Part III, Line 1, and Part IV, Line 1 on Line 29 of your Connecticut income tax return. You must also attach a copy of this form to your Connecticut return.

Beneficiary's Share of Connecticut Fiduciary Adjustment (positive amount): CT-1040 NR/PY, Line 30. If you received income from a Connecticut estate or trust, you must include this income, adjusted by any Connecticut additions and subtractions that apply, on Line 30 of your non-resident or part-year resident Connecticut income tax return.

Loss on Sale of Connecticut Bonds: CT-1040 NR/PY, Line 31. If you incurred any losses on the sale or exchange of notes, bonds, or other obligations of Connecticut, you must add this amount back. Because Connecticut does not tax the gains of these sales, you are not allowed to take a loss.

Other Additions: CT-1040 NR/PY, Line 32. Line 32 was included in case Connecticut passed new laws requiring more adjustments after Form CT-1040 NR/PY was printed.

Total Additions: CT-1040 NR/PY, Line 33. Add your Connecticut addition modifications (Lines 26–32). Enter the total on Line 33 and on Line 2. Add Lines 1 and 2 and enter the result on Line 3. This is your *Connecticut adjusted gross income* plus addition modifications.

Subtractions from Federal Adjusted Gross Income

Interest on United States Government Bonds: CT-1040 NR/PY, Line 34. If you have any interest income from certain United States government bonds, you are allowed to subtract this amount from your federal adjusted gross income. Federal law prohibits states from taxing direct obligations of the United States such as savings bonds, treasury bills, or treasury notes.

Enter the interest income you receive from your United States government bonds and obligations on Line 34 of your return.

Dividends from Certain Mutual Funds Invested in United States Obligations: CT-1040 NR/PY, Line 35. If you receive dividend payments from a mutual fund that invests at least 50% of its assets in United States government obligations, you may subtract the percentage of dividends so invested. Enter the dividends that qualify on Line 36 of your Connecticut return. The portion of dividends that is exempt from state taxation will be shown on your annual statement from the mutual funds.

Example

In 1992, Jill, a New York resident who works in Connecticut, invests $2,500 in a mutual fund. She received $120 in dividends from the mutual fund. At the end of the year, Jill received a statement that the mutual fund invested 80% of its total assets in United States government. Jill may enter 80% of her $120 dividend (or $96) as a subtraction modification on Line 35 of her Connecticut nonresident return.

Reimbursed Moving Expense: CT-1040 NR/PY, Line 36. If you had any reimbursed moving expenses in 1992, you may enter this amount on Line 36 of your Connecticut non-resident part-year resident income tax return. This information may be found on federal Form 478, Line 9, or an equivalent statement provided by your employer.

Refunds of State and Local Income Taxes: CT-1040 NR/PY, Line 37. Enter on Line 37 of your Connecticut non-resident return any state and local income taxes you reported on Line 10 of your federal income tax return (Form 1040).

Tier 1 Railroad Retirement Benefits: CT-1040 NR/PY, Line 38. Enter on Line 38 of your Connecticut non-resident return any amount you received in 1992 from Tier 1 Railroad Retirement Benefits if this amount was included in your federal adjusted gross income. It would be included in Line 21b of federal Form 1040 or Line 13b of federal Form 1040A.

Pro Rata Share of Certain S Corporation Shareholder's Income: CT-1040 NR/PY, Line 39. If you are a shareholder in an S corporation, you are entitled to subtract from your federal adjusted gross income the Connecticut portion of any gain reported on Schedule E of your federal income tax return (Form 1040). Total the Connecticut portion of the gains from all S corporations doing business in Connecticut and enter this number on Line 39 of your Connecticut income tax return.

TaxAlert: If the S corporation in which you own shares apportions its income to more than one state, the apportionment percentage reported on Connecticut Corporation Tax Form 1120S should be used to determine the Connecticut portion of the gain. This information should be provided to you by the S corporation.

Beneficiary's Share of Connecticut Fiduciary Adjustment (negative amount): CT-1040 NR/PY, Line 40. If you received income from one or more Connecticut estates or trusts, you must include this income adjusted by any Connecticut additions and subtractions that apply on Line 40 of your nonresident part-year resident income tax return.

Gain on Sale of Connecticut Bonds: CT-1040 NR/PY, Line 41. If you received any income from the sale or exchange of notes, bonds, or other obligations of Connecticut, you are entitled to subtract this amount from your federal adjusted gross income. Enter this amount on Line 41 of your Connecticut income tax return.

Other Subtractions: CT-1040 NR/PY, Line 42. Enter here any interest you received from Connecticut bonds that was included in your federal adjusted gross income. If you are legally entitled to subtract any other items that you did not subtract elsewhere on Form CT-1040 NR/PY, subtract them here.

Total Subtractions: CT-1040 NR/PY, Line 43. Add your subtraction modifications (Lines 34–42) and enter the total on Line 43 and on Line 4. Subtract Line 4 from Line 3 and enter the result on Line 5. This is your *Connecticut Adjusted Gross Income.*

Attributing Income to Connecticut— Sourcing Rules

Note: The terms allocation and apportionment have the same meaning. In order to be consistent with Connecticut income tax forms, the term *apportionment* is used in this chapter.

Nonresidents

Connecticut's tax laws require nonresidents to compute their taxes using their Connecticut adjusted gross income or their total income from Connecticut sources, whichever is greater. If you are a nonresident employee who performed services both inside and outside the state and you do not know the actual amount of income you earned in Connecticut, you must apportion your income to Connecticut using a percentage. This percentage is determined by the number of days you worked in Connecticut out of *all* the days you worked. You cannot count weekends and holidays as part of your base. If you know the actual amount of your Connecticut source income, you cannot use a percentage of your total working days to apportion your income.

Example

Jack, a resident of New York, is an employee of B-Z Corporation. B-Z's main offices are located in Connecticut but it has other offices located in Pennsylvania and Florida. During 1992, Jack was sent to the Florida office for four months to help establish a new data processing department. Since Jack performed services for his employer both inside and outside the state and does not know the actual amount of his Connecticut source income, he may allocate his income.

The term ''total working days'' does not include:

- Saturdays, Sundays, and holidays;
- Sick days or days lost due to personal injury; and
- Vacation days (paid or unpaid).

Example

Sharon, a resident of New Jersey, is employed by an accounting firm in Stamford, Connecticut at an annual salary of $40,000. During 1992, she spent 75 days performing field audits in New York. All her other work was performed within Connecticut. Her apportionment percentage is determined as follows:

Total days in year		365
Nonworking days		
Saturdays and Sundays	104	
Holidays	10	
Sick days	3	
Vacation	8	
(Total nonworking days)		(125)
Working days		240
Days worked outside Connecticut:		
Field audit days in New York	75	
(Total working days outside		
Connecticut)		(75)
Days worked in Connecticut		165

$$\text{Income Apportionment Percentage} = \frac{165}{240} = 68.75\%$$

TaxPlanner: Maintain adequate records to support those days you count as days worked outside Connecticut. Those days may be questioned by Connecticut if you are audited. Examples of supporting records include work diaries, appointment calendars, expense reports, and trip sheets.

When a working day is spent working partly within Connecticut, you must count it as a half day within Connecticut.

Example

Gloria, a Massachusetts resident, is employed by X Corporation. Her employer is located in Connecticut. During the year, Gloria worked 20 days in which she spent part of each day in Massachusetts and part in Connecticut. Gloria must include ten days (20 × ½) in her total days worked inside Connecticut, in addition to the other days she worked entirely in Connecticut.

If your compensation depends upon sales commissions, you must apportion your income based on the percentage of sales you made in Connecticut out of your total sales. For income apportionment purposes, a sale is considered made within Connecticut if the salesperson takes the order in the state. It does not matter that the formal acceptance of the sales contract may have occurred outside the state.

If your compensation depends upon the miles you traveled, you must apportion your income based on the percentage of amount of miles you traveled within Connecticut out of the total miles you traveled.

If you apportion your income using the working days method, sales method, or mileage method, you must use CT-1040 AW (Part 2), *Employee Apportionment Worksheet*, to apportion your income. If you perform services partly in and partly outside Connecticut for more than one employer you must complete a separate worksheet for each job.

Professional Athletes. Connecticut requires that the entire amount of compensation received by a nonresident professional athlete for games played in Connecticut be included in Connecticut source income. If a nonresident athlete is not paid specifically for a game played in Connecticut, an apportionment percentage must be used. Connecticut requires that you apportion income based on a percentage of the number of exhibition and regular season games that you played or were *obligated* to play in Connecticut out of the total number of exhibition and regular season games you were obligated to play during the year.

Example

James, a nonresident professional golfer, played in one tournament in Connecticut during 1992. He spent only four days in Connecticut, but earned $125,000 in winnings from the tournament. The entire $125,000 should be included in his Connecticut source income. James will not be able to allocate his total income, since he can clearly trace the exact amount of income he received to an event that occurred in Connecticut.

Example

Larry, a nonresident professional hockey player, played or was available to play in 50 exhibition and regular season games for his Pennsylvania-based team before experiencing a season-ending injury. During 1992, his team played four exhibition games and 80 regular season games. Larry played four games in Connecticut before his injury. His team played one more game in Connecticut after his injury. Larry's Connecticut source income is calculated by multiplying his total income by $^5/_{84}$. The game played by the team in Connecticut after Larry's injury is included in the numerator, and all games played by the team after his injury are included in the denominator.

For apportionment purposes, your total income includes salary, incentive payments, and bonuses and extras but does not include signing bonuses and league playoff money. Connecticut requires that you apportion separately your league playoff money earned for playoff games which occurred in Connecticut. You must apportion your playoff earnings based on a ratio of number of playoff games that you played or were available to play in Connecticut during the year over the total number of playoff games your team played during the year. This includes games in which you were excused from playing because of injury or illness.

Entertainers. Connecticut requires that the entire amount received by an entertainer for performances given in the state be included in Connecticut source income. If an entertainer is not paid specifically for performances in Connecticut, an apportionment percentage must be used. This percentage is based on the number of performances in Connecticut over the total number of performances that you were obligated to perform during the year.

Example
Lynn, a nonresident professional dancer, earns an annual salary of $40,000. During 1992, she danced in all 50 of her dance company's performances, five of which were performed in Connecticut. Lynn's Connecticut source income is $4,000 calculated by multiplying $40,000 by 5/50 (10%).

Seamen. Connecticut requires that wages of a nonresident seaman be sourced entirely to Connecticut if the seaman works on a vessel operating exclusively within the state. If you are a nonresident seaman who works on a vessel that operates exclusively between Connecticut and foreign ports, or ports of other states, none of your income is sourced to Connecticut. This is true even though you may work aboard the ship while the ship is docked in a Connecticut port.

Self-Employed Individuals
If you are a nonresident individual who is self-employed and you earn income from a business which is carried on partly inside and outside Connecticut, you must determine your Connecticut source income using one of the following methods:

- Separate accounting;
- Formula basis apportionment of income; or
- An alternative method which fairly and equitably reflects Connecticut source income.

You are considered to be carrying on a business partly outside Connecticut if you occupy or maintain desk space, an office, a shop, a store, a warehouse, a factory, an agency, or other place where your business matters are systematically and regularly carried on outside Connecticut.

TaxAlert: An occasional or isolated business transaction outside Connecticut will not permit an al-

location of income. You are not systematically and regularly carrying on business outside the state. You must have a regular place of business outside Connecticut in order to allocate income for business carried on outside the state.

Separate Accounting
In general, separate accounting is used to source your Connecticut income when you can specifically identify the profits earned from your Connecticut location. If you use this method, you must keep books and records which disclose to the satisfaction of the Tax Commissioner the items of income, gain, loss, and deduction attributable to your business activities carried on inside Connecticut. In addition, your income reported to other states in which you carry on business, where such states permit allocation on the basis of separate accounting, must result in a consistent allocation of income. Otherwise, you must allocate your items of income, gain, loss, and deduction using the formula basis apportionment of income method.

Example
Garrett, a resident of Massachusetts, is a carpenter who carried out business in Connecticut and Massachusetts. During the 1992 tax year, he allocated 70% of his income to Connecticut and 30% to Massachusetts on the basis of separate accounting. On his Massachusetts return, he must also allocate 70% of his income to Connecticut and 30% to Massachusetts, since Massachusetts allows separate accounting.

Formula Basis Apportionment of Income
You must use this method to allocate your income if you cannot determine your Connecticut income from your books and records. Under this method, your income is apportioned using the average of the following percentages:

- Property percentage;
- Payroll percentage; and
- Gross Income percentage.

Property Percentage. The property percentage is computed by dividing the average of the beginning and ending values of real and tangible personal property located in Connecticut by the average of the beginning and ending values of real and tangible personal property located everywhere. Real property also includes real property rented by the business. To determine the fair market values of rented real property both inside and outside Connecticut, you must multiply the gross rents payable during the tax year by eight.
Gross rent includes:

- Any amount payable for the use or possession of real property whether paid as a fixed sum of money or as a percentage of sales, profits, or otherwise;
- Any amount payable as additional rent or instead of rent, such as interest, taxes, insurance, repairs, or any other amount required to be paid by the terms of lease; and
- A proportion of the cost of any improvement to real property made by or on behalf of the business which reverts to the owner or lessor upon termination of a lease or other arrangement; however, if a building is erected on leased land by or on behalf of the business, the value of the building is determined in the same manner as if it were owned by the business.

Payroll Percentage. The payroll percentage is computed by dividing the total compensation paid during the year to employees in connection with operations carried on in Connecticut by the total compensation paid during the year to employees everywhere.

TaxAlert: You should not include payments made to independent contractors, independent sales agents, etc. in the payroll percentage. These individuals are not considered employees of your business.

Gross Income Percentage. The gross income percentage is computed by dividing the gross sales or charges for services performed by or through an office or agency of the business located in Connecticut by the total gross sales or charges for services performed inside and outside Connecticut. The sales or services allocated to Connecticut include sales made or services performed by an employee, agent, or independent contractor connected to or sent out from offices of the business or its agencies located in Connecticut. It does not matter that an employee, agent, or independent contractor may make sales outside the state. The business must allocate all sales made by that individual to Connecticut.

Example

Howard, a New Jersey resident, owns a chain of computer stores inside and outside Connecticut. Howard runs his multistate business from his headquarters located in New Jersey. During 1992, his operating results were as follows:

	-(in thousands)-	
	Connecticut	Total
Revenues	$1,500	$4,000
General Administration		750
Advertising		300
Salaries	200	800
Rent Expenses	100	300
Depreciation		250
Total Expenses		2,400
Net Income		$1,600

Howard owns no real property but does own tangible personal property. The value of the property at the beginning of the year everywhere was $400,000 and at the end of the year was $300,000. The value of the property owned at the beginning of the year in Connecticut was $150,000 and at the end of the year $150,000. Howard would compute his Connecticut income using formula basis apportionment in the following manner:

	-(in thousands)-	
Property Percentage	Connecticut	Everywhere
Rent (Rent Expense × 8)	800	2,400
Average Property Value:		
[1]Beg-EW 400,000		
[1]End-EW 300,000	150	350
Total	950	2,750

Percentage = 950/2,750
= 34.55%

Payroll Percentage	Connecticut	Everywhere
Salaries	200	800

Percentage = 200/800
= 25%

Gross Income Percentage	Connecticut	Everywhere
Revenue	1,500	4,000

Percentage = 1,500/4,000
= 37.50%

Total Percentages (Property, Payroll, Gross Income)
= 97.05
Average = 97.05/3
= 32.35%

Net Income Allocable to Connecticut = $1,600,000
× 32.35% = $517,600

[1]EW means everywhere

If a percentage is missing, you must add the remaining percentages and divide by the number of percentages present. A percentage is missing when both your Connecticut amount and everywhere amount are zero. For example, you may not have a property percentage since you have no real or personal property inside or outside the state. In this instance, you must add your payroll percentage and gross income percentage and divide by two.

Alternative Method

If you cannot determine your Connecticut income from your books and the formula basis apportionment method does not fairly reflect your Connecticut income, you may use an alternative method to allocate income. Any alternative method used must be approved by the Commissioner of the Department of Revenue Services.

TaxAlert: The formula basis apportionment or alternative method is not applied to income from the rental of real property or gains or losses from the sale of real property. The entire rental income from Connecticut real property or gain from the sale of such property is taxed by Connecticut. Likewise, any loss connected with such property can be deducted on your Connecticut return.

If you are a nonresident who carried on a business both inside and outside Connecticut, you must complete Schedule CT-1040 BA, *Connecticut Nonresident Business Apportionment Schedule*. If you carried on more than one business for which an allocation is required, you must prepare a separate CT-1040 BA or similar statement for each business. Each schedule must be attached to your Form CT-1040 NR/PY.

CT-1040 BA, Schedule A

If you are a nonresident who carries on business both inside and outside Connecticut, you must complete Schedule A. This is true whether you use separate accounting, formula basis apportionment, or an alternative method to determine your Connecticut income.

In Columns 1 and 2, list all places, both inside and outside Connecticut, where you carry on business. In Column 3, describe all the places you listed in Columns 1 and 2 and state whether you rent or own these places.

If you use the separate accounting method to determine Connecticut income, enter in the space immediately below Schedule A the words "Connecticut Income determined from books."

CT-1040 BA, Schedule B (Lines 1–8)

If you determine your Connecticut income using the formula basis apportionment method or an alternative method, you must complete Schedule B. Do not complete Schedule B if your books and records clearly reflect your Connecticut income.

Enter on Line 1, Column A the average value of real property owned by the business inside and outside Connecticut. Enter in Column B the average value of real property located in Connecticut.

Enter on Line 2, Column A the fair market value of real property rented by the business inside and outside Connecticut. Enter in Column B the fair market value of real property located in Connecticut. (Refer to the *Formula Basis Apportionment of Income* section for an explanation of how to determine the fair market value of rented property.)

Enter on Line 3, Column A the average value of tangible personal property owned by the business inside and outside Connecticut. Enter in Column B the average value of tangible personal property located in Connecticut.

Enter on Line 4 the total of Lines 1, 2, and 3 in Column A and Column B. You must divide the Column B amount by the Column A amount to determine your property percentage. The result should be carried to four decimal places and entered as a percentage in Column C.

Enter on Line 5, Column A the total compensation paid to employees located inside and outside Connecticut. Enter in Column B the total compensation paid to your employees in connection with operations carried on in Connecticut.

You must divide the Column B amount by the Column A amount to determine your payroll percentage. The result should be carried to four decimal places and entered as a percentage in Column C.

Enter on Line 6, Column A total gross sales or charges for services performed inside and outside Connecticut. Enter in Column B the gross sales or charges performed by or through an office or agency of the business located in Connecticut.

You must divide the Column B amount by the Column A amount to determine your gross income percentage. The result should be carried to four decimal places and entered as a percentage in Column C.

Enter on Line 7, Column C the total of the percentages from Lines 4, 5, and 6.

You must divide Line 7 by three or the actual number of percentages, if fewer than three, to determine your business allocation percentage. The result should be carried to four decimal places and entered as a percentage on Line 8.

Multiply each item of business income (or loss) reported on federal Form 1040, which is required to be apportioned by the percentage from Line 8. This is your Connecticut amount which must be transferred to the proper lines on Schedule CT-SI, *Nonresident or Part-Year Resident Schedule of Income from Connecticut Sources.*

Part-Year Residents

Connecticut requires part-year residents to compute their income tax liability as if they were resident individuals and then apportion the tax based on a percentage of their Connecticut source income out of income received from all sources. Your Connecticut source income includes all income you received plus any special accruals you are required to make while a Connecticut resident and Connecticut source income you received while a nonresident. "Accrual" means recording income when you obtained the *right* to receive it, rather than when you actually receive the cash payment.

Special Accruals. If you move out of Connecticut during the year, you must accrue and report any income, gain, loss, or deduction that you incurred during your residency if you would have to include it in a federal return that you filed for the same period on an accrual basis. This includes any income or gain you elect to report on an installment basis.

Example

On July 1, 1992, Ken, a Connecticut resident, terminated his employment in the state and moved to Wyoming. Before his resignation, Ken earned salary totalling $60,000. He also sold a track of land in New York, realizing a gain of $20,000. Ken elected to report the gain on an installment basis. Ken must include in his Connecticut source income his salary of $60,000, plus the $20,000 gain he realized on the sale of his New York land. Ken cannot defer any of the $20,000 gain for Connecticut purposes, even though he is reporting the gain on a cash basis for federal purposes.

Example

Erin moved from Connecticut to Texas on September 1, 1992. On August 20, 1992, her employer awarded her a guaranteed bonus of $2,000. The bonus was not paid until September 20, 1992. Although the bonus was paid after her move, Erin must include the $2,000 in her Connecticut source income, since this income accrued to her during her resident period.

Accruals are not required if you post a surety bond or other acceptable security with the Department of Revenue Services. The amount you are required to post is an amount equal to or greater than the additional tax that would be due if the accrued items were included on your part-year resident return. If you satisfy the security requirements, you must include the accrued amounts on your Connecticut nonresident return in future tax years as if you had not changed your residence.

The following kinds of security are considered acceptable by Connecticut:

- U.S. treasury bonds;
- Connecticut bonds;
- Certain bonds of political subdivisions of Connecticut;
- Bank passbooks and certificates of deposits;
- Irrevocable standby letters of credit made payable to Connecticut Department of Revenue Services;
- Withholding of Connecticut personal income tax from lottery winning payments made by the Connecticut Division of Special Revenue; and
- Other forms of security acceptable to the Department of Revenue Services.

Part-Year Resident Income Allocation Worksheet, Part 1 (CT-1040AW). If you moved into or out of Connecticut during the year, Lines 1–16 of Part 1 of this worksheet will help you figure your Connecticut source income.

Note: Before beginning Form CT-1040 AW, you should complete Schedule 1 of Form CT-1040 NR/PY.

1.) Column A

Enter the amount of income and adjustments that you reported on your federal return, as modified by amounts on Schedule 1, Form 1040 NR/PY, plus all items you would be required to include if you were filing a federal return using the accrual method. (See the sections on *Additions and Subtractions* and *Attributing Income to Connecticut—Sourcing Rules.*)

2.) Column B

Enter the part of the amount from Column A that you received during the period you were a Connecticut resident.

Part-Year Resident Income Allocation Worksheet

Adjusted Gross Income Married persons filing separate Connecticut State returns should complete separate worksheets		Federal income as modified **Column A** Income from federal return	Connecticut Resident Period **Column B** Income from Column A for this period	Connecticut Nonresident Period	
				Column C Income from Column A for this period	**Column D** Income from Column C from Connecticut State sources
1. Wages, salaries, tips, etc............................	1.				
2. Taxable interest income.............................	2.				
3. Dividend income.......................................	3.				
4. Alimony received	4.				
5. Business income (or loss) (*from federal Schedule C*)	5.				
6. Capital gain (or loss) (*from federal Schedule D*)..	6.				
7. Capital gain distributions not reported on line 6..	7.				
8. Other gains (or losses) (*from federal Form 4797*)...	8.				
9. Taxable amount of IRA distributions............	9.				
10. Taxable amount of pensions and annuities ..	10.				
11. Rents, royalties, partnerships, estates, trusts, etc. (*from federal Schedule E*)............	11.				
12. Farm income (or loss) (*from federal Schedule F*)...	12.				
13. Unemployment compensation (insurance)....	13.				
14. Taxable amount of Social Security benefits..	14.				
15. Other income	15.				
16. Add lines 1 through 15	16.				

ADJUSTMENTS TO INCOME

17. IRA deduction	17.				
18. Deduction for self-employment tax..............	18.				
19. Self-employed health insurance deduction ...	19.				
20. Keogh retirement plan and self-employed SEP deduction	20.				
21. Penalty on early withdrawal of savings........	21.				
22. Alimony paid	22.				
23. Total adjustments—Add lines 17 through 22	18.				
24. Subtract line 23 from line 16......................	19.				

3.) Column C
Enter that part of the amount from Column A that you received while you were a nonresident.

4.) Column D
Enter that part of the amount from Column C that you received from:

• Services you performed in Connecticut;
• Real or tangible personal property located in Connecticut; and
• Business, trades, professions, or occupations conducted in Connecticut.

You should refer to the specific line instruction for Schedule CT-SI in the section on *Nonresidents* earlier in this chapter to determine your income from Connecticut sources during the time you were a nonresident.

Example
Martha moved from Illinois to Connecticut on September 15. On her federal return she reported $45,000 in total wages. Of this amount $15,000 was earned while she was a Connecticut resident. On Line 1, Martha would enter $45,000 in Column A, $15,000 in Column B, $30,000 in Column C and $0 in Column D (she did not earn any income in Connecticut prior to her move).

The amounts in Columns B and D of the worksheet must be added to compute your total Connecticut amount for each line item. Transfer the totals amounts to the corresponding lines on Schedule CT-SI, *Nonresident or Part-Year Resident, Schedule of Income Connecticut Sources.*

Special Problems in Attributing Income

This section considers the unique items of income, such as deferred compensation and other retirement benefits, income from intangible personal property, and distributions from partnerships and S corporations that affect the Connecticut taxable income of nonresidents.

Deferred Compensation

Deferred compensation generally includes income which will be taxed when received and not when earned. For example, contributions made by an employer to a qualified pension plan or retirement plan on behalf of an employee generally will not be taxed to the employee until the funds are made available or distributed to the employee upon retirement.

Unlike New York, Connecticut does not use the term "annuity" in determining whether a nonresident is required to pay personal income tax on a pension or other retirement benefit. Instead, Connecticut does not tax the income received by a nonresident connected with activities within Connecticut if it came from a "qualified pension plan."

The term "qualified pension plan" includes the following plans, if they meet the requirements of the Internal Revenue Code:

- Pension, profit sharing, or stock bonus plan;
- An annuity plan;
- An annuity contract meeting the requirements of Section 403(b) of the Internal Revenue Code;
- An individual retirement account arrangement; and
- An individual retirement annuity meeting the requirements of Section 408(b) of the Internal Revenue Code.

Your employer should be able to tell you if your plan meets one of these requirements or not. If you have difficulty getting this information or want a fuller explanation, consult *The Ernst & Young Tax Guide 1993* or a professional tax advisor.

Sourcing of Income

When a pension or other retirement benefit does not qualify as a qualified pension, it is considered compensation for personal services. If you are a nonresident receiving such benefits, they are taxable to Connecticut to the extent that they are based on services you performed in Connecticut. The term *Compensation for Personal Services* generally includes the following:

- Amounts received in connection with the termination of employment (for example, severance pay).
- Amounts received upon early retirement in consideration of past services performed.
- Amounts received after retirement for consultation services.
- Amounts received upon retirement under a covenant not to compete. A *covenant not to compete* is an agreement in which an employee agrees to refrain after retiring from working in the same line of business as his or her former employer or to sever all ties with his or her employer's client or customer base.

If a pension or other retirement benefit is based solely on services performed outside Connecticut, it is not taxable by Connecticut. However, if you performed services for your employer partly within Connecticut, the amount which is taxable for Connecticut personal income tax purposes is determined by a formula. You need to take the percentage of time you spent working in Connecticut for the part of the year immediately before your retirement date and the percentages that you used to allocate your salary to Connecticut for the three preceding years. Use these percentages to determine, for each of the four periods, the Connecticut portion of your total compensation. Add the Connecticut portion for the four periods together and divide this amount by the sum of your total compensation over the same time. Multiply the resulting fraction by the payments you receive annually under your deferred compensation or retirement plan. The compensation for services performed within Connecticut must be determined separately for each taxable year.

Example

Montgomery Scott, a nonresident of Connecticut, performs services partially within Connecticut for his corporate employer. Under his employment contract, Mr. Scott receives an annual salary of $40,000. He receives an additional $100,000, payable in ten equal annual installments, commencing after his employment terminates. Mr. Scott's employment is terminated on July 1, 1995. The contract between Mr. Scott and his employer is not considered a "qualified plan" and therefore the payments are taxable to Mr. Scott for Connecticut personal income tax purposes. The Connecticut percentages for allocating his salary were 50% for 1992, 60% for 1993, 75% for 1994, and 40% for the first half of 1995. Mr. Scott computes the part of his annual installments that must be included in his income sourced to Connecticut as follows:

	Percentage of Services Performed in Connecticut	Total Compensation	Connecticut Compensation
1992	50%	$40,000	$20,000
1993	60%	40,000	24,000
1994	75%	40,000	30,000
1995 (6 months)	40%	20,000	8,000
		$140,000	$82,000

Connecticut Allocation Fraction: $\dfrac{\$82,000}{\$140,000} = 0.59$ or 59% (approximately)

Mr. Scott would report $5,900 as his income sourced to Connecticut.

($10,000 × 59% = $5,900)

Other Business Income from Connecticut Sources

In addition to wages and pension income, the Connecticut tax base of a nonresident may also include all income, gain, loss, or deduction received from a business, trade, profession, or occupation conducted in Connecticut.

Business, Trade, Profession, or Occupation Conducted in Connecticut

A business, trade, profession, or occupation is considered conducted in Connecticut by a nonresident when he or she occupies or maintains any one of the following business locations within the state:

- A desk;
- An office;
- A shop;
- A store;
- A warehouse;
- A factory;

- An agency; or
- Any other place for carrying on regular business activities.

Example

Tom, a plumber, who is a resident of Rhode Island, maintains a small office in Danielson, Connecticut. His maintenance contracts require him to carry on business within Connecticut. Since Tom carries on business within Connecticut on a regular basis, the income he receives from his plumbing business is subject to Connecticut personal income tax, even though Tom is a nonresident.

Personal Services

If you are a nonresident performing personal services as an employee for a Connecticut employer, you will be subject to Connecticut personal income tax. However, you will be taxed only on income you received for services performed within Connecticut. Compensation for personal services performed by a nonresident outside Connecticut is not subject to Connecticut taxation, even if payment was made from Connecticut and the employer is a resident individual or corporation. If you work only part of the time in Connecticut, the part of your compensation that you receive for services performed in Connecticut is subject to tax. The rules for allocating income to nonresidents are described earlier under *Attributing Income to Connecticut—Sourcing Rules.*

Income from Intangible Personal Property

Income that is generated by intangible personal property owned by a nonresident is generally not subject to Connecticut taxation.

Example

Dana, a resident of Pennsylvania, owns 100% of the stock of ABC Corporation, which operates a store in Connecticut. The corporation pays Dana a salary of $30,000, all of which is earned in Connecticut, and a dividend of $2,500. Dana's salary of $30,000 is subject to Connecticut personal income tax. However, the dividend she receives is not taxable for Connecticut personal income tax purposes. Even though the company paying the dividend owns property in Connecticut, Dana's stock is not considered "used in the business."

TaxSaver: Connecticut's rules concerning sourcing of income, income from intangible property, and income received from business, profession, or occupation carried on in Connecticut are generally the same as those of New York State. (Please refer to *Special Problems in Attributing Income* in Chapter 3, Part I, *New York* for further information.)

Partnerships and S Corporations

Connecticut's treatment of nonresident partners and shareholders in S corporations is generally the same as New York's treatment. (Refer to *Special Problems in Attributing Income* in the New York section for more information.)

4 | How to Figure Your Tax

Computation of Tax for Residents

After you have calculated your Connecticut adjusted gross income (AGI), you will be ready to calculate your Connecticut "state tax due." However, this is not necessarily, or even usually, the same as the tax payment you will owe with this return. This chapter will show you how to calculate your Connecticut state tax due. (See also *Credits* later in this chapter.)

The Connecticut income tax calculation is different from that of most other states because personal exemptions and personal tax credits are built into the tax table. They are not itemized separately as they are in New York and New Jersey. The only tax credit that is shown as a separate line item on the face of the CT-1040 is the credit for taxes paid to taxing jurisdictions other than Connecticut.

Calculating Your State Tax Due

Your state tax due depends on three factors:

1. Your Connecticut adjusted gross income;
2. The amount of personal exemption you are entitled to; and
3. The personal tax credit percentage.

Using the Tax Table. Most taxpayers will be able to use the Connecticut tax table. The tax table is useful because any personal credits and exemptions *are included* in the tax shown for any given amount of Connecticut adjusted gross income up to $96,000. However, if your Connecticut adjusted gross income exceeds $96,000 you *must* use the Connecticut Tax Calculation Schedule shown below. You may also use the tax calculation schedule if your Connecticut adjusted gross income is below $96,000, although you will probably find that using the tax table is much easier.

If you use the tax calculation schedule and are eligible for personal exemptions or credits, you can use schedules of exemptions and credits that are reproduced on the following page to look up the amounts you are entitled to claim. If you are ineligible to receive any personal exemptions or personal tax credits, the calculation is simple. Take your Connecticut adjusted gross income, multiply it by the Connecticut tax rate of 4.5% and the result is your Connecticut income tax.

Once you have figured out your Connecticut income tax, enter this amount on Line 6 of Form CT-1040 or Line 2 of Form CT-1040EZ. For CT-1040 filers, the only additional adjustment that need be considered is the tax credit available for taxes paid to other states. Tax credits and the calculation of the Connecticut credit for taxes paid to other states are discussed in detail in *Credits*, which follows. Any credit you take for taxes paid to other states will reduce the amount of your Connecticut tax payment.

Example

Mary's Connecticut adjusted gross income is $24,745, and her filing status is *single*. Because $24,745 is between $24,701 and $24,750 on the Connecticut tax table, the corresponding tax on this amount, including all personal exemptions and credits, is $525 (rounded to the nearest whole dollar). Mary will enter $525 on Line 6 of Form CT-1040 or on Line 2 of Form CT-1040EZ.

If your CT AGI is—		And you are—		
At least	But less than	Single or Married Filing Separately	Head of Household	Married Filing Jointly*
24,500	24,550	517.33	161.61	5.91
24,550	24,600	519.24	163.07	6.47
24,600	24,650	521.16	164.53	7.03
24,650	24,700	523.07	165.99	7.59
24,700	**24,750**	**524.98**	**167.46**	**8.16**

*or qualifying widow(er)

Using the Tax Calculation Schedule.

1. Enter CONNECTICUT AGI (From CT-1040, Line 5; CT-1040EZ, Line 1)	1	
2. Personal Exemption (From Table A—Exemptions)	2	
3. Connecticut Taxable Income (Subtract Line 2 from Line 1—if less than 0, enter 0)	3	
4. Connecticut Income Tax—4.5% of Line 3 (Line 3 × .045)	4	
5. Enter Credit % from Table B—Personal Tax Credits	5	
6. Multiply the amount on Line 4 by the percentage on Line 5	6	
7. INCOME TAX (Subtract Line 6 from Line 4) *Enter this amount on CT-1040, Line 6; CT-1040EZ, Line 2*	7	

Example

Tom and Sue are married and filing a joint tax return. Their Connecticut adjusted gross income is $66,500. Using the Tax Calculation Schedule, they calculate their tax as follows:

Line 1	Connecticut AGI	$66,500
Line 2	Personal Exemption (from Table A below)	5,000
Line 3	Connecticut Taxable Income	$61,500

Line 4	Connecticut Income Tax (@4.5%)	2,768	2,768
Line 5	Personal Credit % (from Table B below)	10%	
Line 6	Personal Tax Credit Allowed	277	(277)
Line 7	Connecticut Income Tax		2,491

TaxAlert: When determining your tax credit, make sure that you use your taxable income before exemptions and not your net taxable income after exemptions.

Tables of Exemptions and Credits

Note: Use this schedule only if you are using the Tax Calculation Schedule. **Do not** use this schedule if you are using the Connecticut tax tables!

Table A—Exemptions
Use the filing status you indicated on the front of your tax return and your Connecticut adjusted gross income from Line 1 of the tax calculation schedule to determine your personal exemption.

Single/Married Filing Separately		Head of Household		Married Filing Jointly/Qualifying Widow(er)	
CONNECTICUT AGI	EXEMPTION	CONNECTICUT AGI	EXEMPTION	CONNECTICUT AGI	EXEMPTION
$ 0 - $24,000	$12,000	$ 0 - $38,000	$19,000	$ 0 - $48,000	$24,000
$24,001 - $25,000	$11,000	$38,001 - $39,000	$18,000	$48,001 - $49,000	$23,000
$25,001 - $26,000	$10,000	$39,001 - $40,000	$17,000	$49,001 - $50,000	$22,000
$26,001 - $27,000	$ 9,000	$40,001 - $41,000	$16,000	$50,001 - $51,000	$21,000
$27,001 - $28,000	$ 8,000	$41,001 - $42,000	$15,000	$51,001 - $52,000	$20,000
$28,001 - $29,000	$ 7,000	$42,001 - $43,000	$14,000	$52,001 - $53,000	$19,000
$29,001 - $30,000	$ 6,000	$43,001 - $44,000	$13,000	$53,001 - $54,000	$18,000
$30,001 - $31,000	$ 5,000	$44,001 - $45,000	$12,000	$54,001 - $55,000	$17,000
$31,001 - $32,000	$ 4,000	$45,001 - $46,000	$11,000	$55,001 - $56,000	$16,000
$32,001 - $33,000	$ 3,000	$46,001 - $47,000	$10,000	$56,001 - $57,000	$15,000
$33,001 - $34,000	$ 2,000	$47,001 - $48,000	$ 9,000	$57,001 - $58,000	$14,000
$34,001 - $35,000	$ 1,000	$48,001 - $49,000	$ 8,000	$58,001 - $59,000	$13,000
$35,001 - and up	$ 0	$49,001 - $50,000	$ 7,000	$59,001 - $60,000	$12,000
		$50,001 - $51,000	$ 6,000	$60,001 - $61,000	$11,000
		$51,001 - $52,000	$ 5,000	$61,001 - $62,000	$10,000
		$52,001 - $53,000	$ 4,000	$62,001 - $63,000	$ 9,000
		$53,001 - $54,000	$ 3,000	$63,001 - $64,000	$ 8,000
		$54,001 - $55,000	$ 2,000	$64,001 - $65,000	$ 7,000
		$55,001 - $56,000	$ 1,000	$65,001 - $66,000	$ 6,000
		$56,001 - and up	$ 0	$66,001 - $67,000	$ 5,000
				$67,001 - $68,000	$ 4,000
				$68,001 - $69,000	$ 3,000
				$69,001 - $70,000	$ 2,000
				$70,001 - $71,000	$ 1,000
				$71,001 - and up	$ 0

Enter your personal exemption on Line 2 of the tax calculation schedule.

Table B—Personal Tax Credits
Use your filing status shown on the front of your tax return and your Connecticut AGI (from Line 1 of the Tax Calculation Schedule) to determine your personal tax credit percentage.

Single/Married Filing Separately		Head of Household		Married Filing Jointly/Qualifying Widow(er)	
CONNECTICUT AGI	CREDIT %	CONNECTICUT AGI	CREDIT %	CONNECTICUT AGI	CREDIT %
$12,001 - $15,000	75%	$19,001 - $24,000	75%	$24,001 - $30,000	75%
$15,001 - $20,000	35%	$24,001 - $34,000	35%	$30,001 - $40,000	35%
$20,001 - $25,000	15%	$34,001 - $44,000	15%	$40,001 - $50,000	15%
$25,001 - $48,000	10%	$44,001 - $74,000	10%	$50,001 - $96,000	10%
$48,001 - and up	0%	$74,001 - and up	0	$96,001 - and up	0

Enter your personal tax credit percentage on Line 5 of the Tax Calculation Schedule.

Computation of Tax for Nonresidents

This section will help you calculate your Connecticut income tax if you were not a resident of Connecticut, but earned money in the state. You will fall under this category if you were characterized as a nonresident or a part-year resident by the state. If you maintained living quarters in Connecticut and spent 183 days there during the year, or if your permanent home is in Connecticut, refer to *Nonresidents* in Chapter 2 to make sure that you are not considered a resident by the state.

Calculating Your Taxable Income

When you calculated your Connecticut Adjusted Income, as discussed in Chapter 3, your first step was to compute your income as if you were a resident of the state for the entire year. In other words, you reported your income from *all* sources. When you filled out Schedule CT-SI of your tax return, you determined the portion of your income that was derived from Connecticut sources. Now that you are computing your tax, you must use the *larger* of the two numbers. For our purposes, this will be called your *taxable income*.

Example

Mary's *Connecticut Adjusted Gross Income* from page 1 of her Connecticut tax return consists of the following items:

Wages from Connecticut sources	$60,249
Loss from sources outside of Connecticut	(14,000)
Connecticut Adjusted Gross Income	$46,249

Mary's taxable income is the $60,249 of wages from Connecticut sources, since this amount exceeds her *Connecticut Adjusted Gross Income.*

Tax Computation: Step-by-Step Instructions

Now that you have determined your taxable income, you are ready to calculate your tax. To do this, you will either use the tax tables, which are provided with the instructions to your tax return, or the tax calculation schedule discussed in the following section. If your taxable income is less than $96,000, you may use the tax tables. You must use the tax calculation schedule if your taxable income equals or exceeds $96,000.

Using the Tax Table. When you use the tax table, simply remember that the rows represent the different income levels and the columns stand for your filing status. If you are not sure of your correct filing status, refer to *Filing Status* in Chapter 2. The tax shown on the tax table is your net tax due. When you use the tax table, you are given the benefit of all exemptions and credits to which you are entitled. Your next step will be to allocate a portion of this tax to your income from Connecticut sources. The allocation is discussed in a later section of this chapter.

Using the Tax Calculation Schedule. An alternate way to calculate your tax is to use the tax calculation schedule. You do not need to use the tax calculation schedule if you already used the tax table. However, you must use the tax calculation schedule if your taxable income exceeds $96,000.

Connecticut Tax Calculation Schedule

1. Enter greater of Connecticut Adjusted Gross Income or Income from Connecticut Sources   1. _____
2. Personal Exemption (From Table A—Exemptions)   2. _____
3. Connecticut Taxable Income (Subtract Line 2 from Line 1—If less than 0, enter 0)   3. _____
4. Connecticut Income Tax at 4.5% of Line 3 (Line 3 × .045)   4. _____
5. Enter Credit % from Table B—Personal Tax Credits   5. _____
6. Multiply the amount on Line 4 by the percentage on Line 5   6. _____
7. **INCOME TAX** (Subtract Line 6 from Line 4)   7. _____

Exemption: If your taxable income is less than a certain amount, you are entitled to an exemption. Your *Connecticut taxable income* is the amount of income remaining after this exemption. The amount of your exemption is based on your filing status and the amount of your taxable income.

Example

Janet's filing status is *head of household*. Her taxable income is $45,000. Her exemption (found in Table A—Exemptions on the previous page) is $12,000 leaving her with *Connecticut taxable income* of $33,000. Her tax, before credits, is $33,000 multiplied by 4.5%, or $1,485.

Tax Credit. A tax credit is allowed if your income is below a certain level. A tax credit is a dollar-for-dollar reduction of your tax liability. The table below shows the tax credit to which you may be entitled, depending upon your filing status and the amount of your taxable income.

TAXALERT: When determining your tax credit, make sure that you use your taxable income before exemptions and not your net taxable income after exemptions.

Example

Using the same facts as in the previous Example, Janet may claim a tax credit of 10% because her taxable income is $45,000 (See Table B, below.) Her tax credit is 10% of $1,485, or $148.50. Subtracting her tax credit from her tax leaves her with a net tax of $1,336.50 ($1,485 − $148.50).

Table B—Personal Tax Credits

Single/Married Filing Separately		Head of Household		Married Filing Jointly/Qualifying Widow(er)	
TAXABLE INCOME	CREDIT %	TAXABLE INCOME	CREDIT %	TAXABLE INCOME	CREDIT %
$12,001 - $15,000	75%	$19,001 - $24,000	75%	$24,001 - $30,000	75%
$15,001 - $20,000	35%	$24,001 - $34,000	35%	$30,001 - $40,000	35%
$20,001 - $25,000	15%	$34,001 - $44,000	15%	$40,001 - $50,000	15%
$25,001 - $48,000	10%	**$44,001 - $74,000**	**10%**	$50,001 - $96,000	10%
$48,001 - and up	0%	$74,001 - and up	0	$96,001 - and up	0

Allocated Tax

Now that you have determined your net tax, you are ready to allocate a portion of this tax to your income from Connecticut sources. To accomplish this, divide the amount of your *income from Connecticut sources* by your *Connecticut Adjusted Gross Income*. This fraction *may not be greater than one or less than zero*. Multiply this fraction by your net tax to arrive at your allocated tax.

Example

Debbie has $6,000 in income from Connecticut sources. Her Connecticut Adjusted Gross Income is $21,960. Debbie calculates her income tax allocated to Connecticut as follows:

Income from Connecticut Sources

Connecticut Adjusted Gross Income

= Tax Allocation Fraction

$$\frac{\$6,000}{\$21,960} = .27 \text{ (or 27\%)}$$

Net Income Tax After Exemption and Credits
× Tax Allocation Fraction

= Net Income Tax Allocated to Connecticut

$381.54
× .27
$103.02

Debbie's net income tax allocated to Connecticut is $103.02.

Credits

Once your Connecticut tax liability has been calculated, a tax credit can be used to reduce your tax. Connecticut provides a tax credit to residents and part-year residents who have paid income taxes to other states, cities, the District of Columbia, or a province or city in Canada. All other credits are included as part of the tax tables. Hence, only the resident tax credit is available as a separate line item on your Connecticut income tax return.

Example

Denise lives in Greenwich, Connecticut, but works in New York City. She should calculate the tax credit allowable for income taxes paid on wages earned in New York State and City, and claim this credit on her Connecticut income tax return.

The remainder of this section will discuss the calculation of your Connecticut credit for income taxes paid to other states or cities. It will provide line-by-line instructions for completing Schedule 2 of Form CT-1040, as well as sample tax credit calculations.

TAXALERT: If you claim a credit for taxes paid to other states or cities, you *must* use Form CT-1040. You *cannot* claim this credit on the Connecticut short form (Form CT-1040EZ).

TAXPLANNER: If you pay tax in more than one state, it is advisable to complete your federal income tax return first, returns for each nonresident state second, and your Connecticut resident return last. Because you claim a tax credit for taxes paid to other states or cities on your resident tax return, you must calculate your taxes due to the nonresident states before completing your resident return.

Completing Schedule 2 of Your Connecticut Tax Return

The first step in the credit calculation is to add back any net losses that are attributable to non-Connecticut sources to your Connecticut adjusted gross income reported on Line 5 of Form CT-1040. The result is your modified Connecticut adjusted gross income. Enter this number on Line 40 of Schedule 2 shown on the following page.

Line 41 provides two columns (A and B) for calculating your resident tax credit for income taxes paid to other jurisdictions. If you paid taxes in more than two states or cities, photocopy Schedule 2 and fill out a separate column for each jurisdiction. On Line 41, enter the name(s) of the other jurisdiction(s) in which you paid tax. Enter the two-letter code (shown on Form CT-1040) next to the name.

On Line 42 enter the income included on Line 40 that was reported to the other jurisdiction.

Next, divide the amount you entered on Line 42 by the amount you entered on Line 40. Enter this amount in the appropriate column of Line 43. This shows the percentage of income out of your total modified Connecticut adjusted gross income that was sourced to each jurisdiction for which you are claiming a credit.

On Line 44, enter your Connecticut income tax liability from Line 6 of Form CT-1040. The amount of income tax credit you can receive for taxes paid to other jurisdictions cannot exceed the tax that would be imposed on the same income by Connecticut. For example, New York's highest personal income tax is 7.875%, while Connecticut's tax rate is 4.5%. Even though a Connecticut resident may be taxed at the higher New York rate on income sourced to New York, the maximum tax credit allowed by Connecticut cannot exceed the Connecticut tax related to that income.

Multiply Line 43 by Line 44 and enter the result on Line 45. This shows the portion of your Connecticut tax liability that is imposed on income sourced to each additional tax jurisdiction. Enter on Line 46 the amount of income tax you actually paid to the other state or city.

Enter the Connecticut tax on income sourced to another jurisdiction, or the amount of income tax you actually paid on Line 47, whichever amount is smaller. The last step is to add up the amounts entered in each column of Line 47 and enter this number on Line 48 of Schedule 2 and Line 7 of Form CT-1040. This amount is your Connecticut income tax credit for taxes paid to other tax jurisdictions. It reduces the amount of Connecticut income tax that would otherwise have been due. Attach a copy of your nonresident tax return for each jurisdiction for which you are claiming the resident tax credit to Form CT-1040.

Connecticut Resident Working in New York City

Example

Steve is an attorney who lives in Stamford, CT and commutes to New York City to work two or three days a week. He spends the remainder of his week at his firm's Stamford office. He has determined that he earned 50% of his $100,000 salary in New York City. He reports New York State source income of $40,000 on his New York nonresident return. His Connecticut resident tax credit is calculated as follows:

(1) Connecticut adjusted gross
    income $100,000
(2) New York State income   40,000

(3) New York City income   50,000
(4) Common amount of income subject to tax in both jurisdictions   40,000
(5) New York State tax   2,400
(6) New York City tax   225
(7) Connecticut tax   4,500

The following entries must be made on Steve's Connecticut income tax return (CT-1040, Schedule 2—Credit for Income Taxes Paid to Other Jurisdictions, reproduced below.):

Step 1:

COLUMN A: (New York State and New York City)

Line 40	Modified Connecticut AGI	$100,000
Line 42	Non-Connecticut income included on Line 40 and reported on another jurisdiction's income tax return	40,000
Line 43	Divide Line 42 by Line 40	.40
Line 44	Connecticut income tax liability	4,500
Line 45	Multiply Line 43 by Line 44	1,800
Line 46	Income tax paid to another jurisdiction: New York State tax	2,400
	Prorated New York City tax (40,000/ 50,000 × 225)	180
		2,580
Line 47	Enter smaller of Line 45 or Line 46	1,800
	Total credit allowed	1,800

Step 2:

COLUMN B: (New York City excess)

Line 40	Modified Connecticut AGI	$100,000
Line 42	Non-Connecticut income included on Line A and reported on New York nonresident income tax return (the portion of New York City income on which no tax was imposed by New York State)	10,000
Line 43	Divide Line 42 by Line 40	.10
Line 44	Connecticut income tax liability	4,500
Line 45	Multiply Line 43 by Line 44	450
Line 46	Income tax paid to another jurisdiction: Prorated New York City tax (10,000/ 50,000 × 225) = 45	45
Line 47	Enter smaller of Line 45 or Line 46	45
	Total credit allowed	45

Step 3:
*Total credit allowed:

Step 1	$1,800
Step 2	45
Total Credit	$1,845

Steve will enter $1,845 on Line 48 of Schedule 2 and Line 7 of Form CT-1040. He will attach copies of his New York State and City nonresident returns (Forms IT-203 and NYC-203) to Form CT-1040.

Payments

Your total tax payments are comprised of amounts withheld, your estimated payments, payments you may have made with your Application for Extension to File, Form CT-1040EXT, and any overpayment from the prior year that you have applied to this year's tax. The following is a line-by-line discussion of the payment section of Form CT-1040 reproduced on the next page. Corresponding lines on Form CT-1040EZ and Form CT-1040NR/PY have been noted.

SCHEDULE 2 — CREDIT FOR INCOME TAXES PAID TO OTHER JURISDICTIONS

NOTE: Attach copy of return filed with other jurisdiction(s).

40. MODIFIED CONNECTICUT ADJUSTED GROSS INCOME (See Instructions)

FOR EACH COLUMN, ENTER THE FOLLOWING:

	COLUMN A		COLUMN B	
	Name	Code	Name	Code
41. Enter other jurisdiction's name and two-letter code. (See chart below)	►		►	
42. Non-Connecticut income included on Line 40 and reported on another jurisdiction's income tax return (from Schedule 2 Worksheet)				
43. Divide Line 42 by Line 40 (May not exceed 1.00)				
44. Connecticut Income Tax liability (From Line 6)				
45. Multiply Line 43 × Line 44				
46. Income tax paid to another jurisdiction	►		►	
47. Enter the smaller of Line 45 or Line 46				
48. TOTAL CREDIT (Add Line 47, all columns) Enter this amount here and on Line 7				

CT-1040, Schedule 2—Credit for Income Taxes Paid to Other Jurisdictions

9. Connecticut Tax withheld (**Attach all W-2's and certain 1099's;** See Instructions)	▶ 9		
10. All 1992 estimated payments	▶ 10		
11. Payments made with extension request	▶ 11		
12. Total payments (Add Lines 9 through 11)	▶ 12		

Connecticut Income Tax Withheld: CT-1040, Line 9; CT-1040EZ, Line 3; CT-1040NR/PY, Line 13

Enter the total of the amounts shown as withheld for Connecticut on your Forms W-2, W-2G, W-2P, and Form 1099R, or equivalent Connecticut statements. The *state* copies of your Forms W-2, W-2G, etc. must be attached to your return or you will not receive credit for taxes that were withheld. Copies of Form 1099s need only be attached if they show amounts withheld for Connecticut tax.

All Estimated Payments: CT-1040, Line 10; CT-1040EZ, Line 4; CT-1040NR/PY, Line 14

Enter the total of any estimated tax payments or advance payments that you made for the taxable year plus any *overpayment* applied as a credit from your prior year's tax return.

TaxAlert: Be sure to include any estimated payments that you made in the current year for the taxable year covered by your return.

TaxSaver: If you changed your name during the year because of marriage, divorce, or other reasons, and you made estimated tax payments using your former name, attach a statement to your return explaining the payments you made under different names. If you are filing a joint return, include estimated payments made by your spouse. For each payment, indicate the name(s) and Social Security number(s) under which you made the payment.

Payments Made with Extension Requests: CT-1040, Line 11; CT-1040EZ, Line 5; CT-1040NR/PY, Line 15

Enter the amount that you paid with a timely filed Application for Extension of Time to File, (Form CT-1040EXT).

Total Payments: CT-1040, Line 12; CT-1040EZ, Line 6; CT-1040NR/PY, Line 16

Add the preceding three lines of the *Payments* section. Enter the total of these payments here. This amount represents the total of all your Connecticut tax payments made.

Overpayment: CT-1040, Line 13; CT-1040EZ, Line 7; CT-1040NR/PY, Line 17

If your Total Payments are more than your Connecticut Total Tax enter the amount of your overpayment on this line.

Amount of Tax To Be Applied To Your 1993 Estimated Tax: CT-1040, Line 14; CT-1040EZ, Line 8; CT-1040NR/PY, Line 18

Enter the amount of your current-year overpayment from the preceding line that you wish to have applied to your 1993 Connecticut estimated tax.

Amount of Your Refund: CT-1040, Line 15; CT-1040EZ, Line 9; CT-1040NR/PY, Line 19

Enter the amount of your overpayment that you want to have refunded to you.

TaxPlanner: If you are a *nonobligated spouse* who files jointly with a spouse owing past-due child support payments, you may claim a refund for your share of any overpayments of your 1992 tax through withholding or estimated tax payments. You must file Form CT-8379, *Nonobligated Spouse Claim.* A *nonobligated spouse* is one who is not delinquent on payments of child support.

TaxPlanner: If you are receiving a refund, it is to your advantage to file your return early. Early filers get quicker refunds.

Amount of Tax You Owe: CT-1040, Line 16; CT-1040EZ, Line 10; CT-1040NR/PY, Line 20

If your Total Connecticut Tax is greater than your Total Payments, enter the amount of tax you owe on this line.

Late Payment Penalty and Interest: CT-1040, Lines 17 and 18; CT-1040NR/PY, Lines 21 and 22

Calculate any penalty you owe and enter this amount in the space provided. Refer to the section in Chapter 5 entitled *Penalties* and the Chapter 8 section, *Penalties.*

If your payment is late, enter any interest you owe on the late payment on Line 18. Interest is calculated at 1.25% per month of the tax you owe, from the date your payment is due until it is finally paid.

Penalty and Interest for Underpayment of Estimated Tax: CT-1040, Lines 19 and 20; CT-1040 NR/PY, Lines 23 and 24.

Enter any penalty or interest for underpayment of estimated tax from Form CT-2210.

Balance Due With This Return: CT-1040, Line 21; CT-1040NR/PY, Line 25

Enter the total amount due with your return on this line. Make your check payable or Money Order payable to: **Commissioner of Revenue Services.**

Be sure to write your Social Security number(s) and "1992 Form CT-1040;" "Form CT-1040EZ" or "CT-1040NR/PY" on the face of your check or money order in the lower left corner.

TaxAlert: **Don't forget to sign and date your return!**

Attachments

You may be required to attach other forms or schedules to your Connecticut income tax return (Form CT-1040, Form CT-1040NR/PY, or Form CT-1040EZ). These forms or schedules provide additional information to the Connecticut tax authorities that will enable them to process your return. These attachments may be forms or schedules provided by Connecticut, federal schedules you used in preparing your federal income tax return, or tax returns for other states or localities. The following section summarizes what attachments may be required.

Connecticut Tax Forms and Schedules

You may need to prepare the following forms and schedules in order to complete your state tax return. These forms should be attached to the back of your Form CT-1040 *Resident Income Tax Return*, CT-1040NR/PY *Nonresident or Part-Year Resident Income Tax Return*, or CT-1040EZ, *Resident Income Tax Return-Short Form*.

CT-SI, Nonresident or Part-Year Resident Schedule of Income. This form is used by nonresidents and part-year residents to determine the amount of income that is attributable to Connecticut sources. If you are a part-year resident, you will use this schedule in conjunction with CT-1040AW.

CT-1040AW, Part-Year Resident Income Allocation Worksheet. If you moved into or out of Connecticut and you qualify as a part-year resident, you will need to complete Form CT-1040AW. This worksheet will help you to determine your income from Connecticut sources for the taxable year. (If you are not sure whether you are a part-year resident, please refer to *Nonresidents* in Chapter 2.)

CT-1040BA, Nonresident Business Apportionment Schedule. You will need to complete this schedule if you are a nonresident and you carry on business both in and out of Connecticut.

CT-1040-EXT, Application for Extension of Time to File Individual Income Tax Return. This form is used for an initial extension of time to file your tax return.

CT-1127, Application for Extension of Time for Payment of Income Tax. You must attach this form if you cannot pay your tax on time because of "undue hardship." You must also include supporting documentation and explain why you cannot borrow the money you owe.

CT-2210, Underpayment of Estimated Tax by Individuals and Fiduciaries. If you underpaid your estimated tax, use this form to calculate your interest and penalties.

Federal Forms

Form W-2, Wages and Tax Statement.

1099-R, Distributions From Pensions, Annuities, Retirement or Profit Sharing Plans, IRAs, Insurance Contracts, etc.

1099-Misc, Miscellaneous Income

W-2G, Certain Gambling Winnings.

Income Tax Returns That You Filed in Other States

(Please refer to *Credits*, earlier in this chapter, for additional information.)

5 | Estimated Taxes

Requirements

Connecticut, like the federal government, requires that taxpayers pay tax as they earn income. Thus, you must make tax payments throughout the year, in the form of estimated tax payments or withholding of tax from your salary or wages, even though your return is not due until April 15 of the following year.

This chapter discusses estimated tax payments. It explains who must pay estimated taxes, when and how much you must pay, and what forms you must file. Withholding of tax is discussed in Chapter 7.

Who Must Pay Estimated Taxes?

If you are a Connecticut resident, you must make estimated tax payments to Connecticut if you anticipate more than $1,000 of taxable income for the year that is not covered by withholding or taxes paid to other states. Nonresidents must pay estimated taxes if their income from Connecticut sources will exceed $1,000, after any withholding of tax. For a discussion of what constitutes income from Connecticut sources, see Chapter 3.

Example

Dennis is a resident of Massachusetts. For 1993, Dennis anticipates taxable income from Connecticut sources of $2,000. Dennis will not have taxes withheld from his Connecticut income. He will be required to pay estimated taxes.

Filing a Declaration of Estimated Taxes

Taxpayers who are liable for payment of estimated taxes must file a declaration of estimated tax using Form CT1040-ES. If you are married, you may make a joint declaration, even if you file separate returns. You may *not* make a joint declaration if you are separated by a decree of divorce or separate maintenance. You are also prevented from making a joint declaration of estimated tax if you and your spouse have different taxable years or if one of you is a resident and the other a nonresident of Connecticut.

Calculating Your Estimated Tax

Your required annual estimated tax is based on the *smaller* of the following two amounts:

- Last year's tax; or
- 90% of your estimated tax for the current year, based on current year assumptions about income and deductions.

Chapters 3 and 4 explain how to calculate your adjusted gross income, modifications, exemptions, and tax for residents and nonresidents. Credits are explained in Chapter 4. Withholding of tax is discussed in Chapter 7.

When to Make Estimated Payments

Normally, you will make four estimated tax payments on the following dates: April 15, June 15, September 15, and January 18 (1994).

However, you may not be required to pay estimated tax until sometime after April 15. This can happen, for example, if you switch from being a salaried employee to being self-employed. If you are not liable for estimated tax payments before April 15, but become liable at some time later in the year, use the following schedule.

If you meet the requirements	File your first payment by
After April 1 and before June 2	June 15
After June 1 and before September 2	September 15
After September 1	January 18 (1994)

Fiscal-year taxpayers pay estimated taxes by the 15th day of the fourth month, sixth month, ninth month of their taxable year, and first month of the following taxable year.

How Much to Pay

The following schedule shows how much of your annual estimated tax you must pay by each due date to avoid penalties.

Due Date	Minimum Amount of Payment
April 15	30% of 1992 tax or 22.5% of 1993 tax
June 15	25% of 1992 tax or 22.5% of 1993 tax
Sept 15	25% of 1992 tax or 22.5% of 1993 tax
Jan 18	20% of 1992 tax or 22.5% of 1993 tax

If you begin paying estimated taxes after April 15, you must play "catch-up." Make sure you pay the minimum amount due for the date on which you begin making payments.

Example

Suppose you begin paying estimated taxes on June 15. By June 15, you must pay either 55% of your 1992 tax or 45% of your estimated tax for 1993—whichever is less. If $300 is your current-year estimated tax and $200 is your assumed tax for 1993, you must pay either 55% of the current-year tax ($165) or 45% of the assumed tax ($90), whichever is less. Thus, you would pay $90 in estimated taxes by June 15.

TaxPlanner: Despite your best efforts to come up with an accurate estimate of your tax, an unforeseen change in your circumstances may require a new estimate. If your income or deductions change during the year and will cause an increase in your tax not covered by withholding, you must increase the amount of your estimated tax payments to cover the difference. You may also decrease your estimated tax payments if your tax estimate decreases, based on new facts.

Filing and Paying Quarterly Estimated Taxes

You must file CT1040-ES, Connecticut Individual Estimated Payment, whenever you make a payment of your estimated taxes. The form consists of four parts, or vouchers, separated by perforations. Each voucher is marked with a due date and should accompany your payment for that due date.

Make your check payable to the Commissioner of Revenue Services. Send your check and payment voucher to:

Commissioner of Revenue Services
92 Farmington Avenue
Hartford, CT 06105

To insure proper credit to your estimated tax account, write your Social Security number on the check. Also, write the words ''1993 CT1040-ES'' on the check. If you and your spouse filed a joint declaration, include your spouse's Social Security number also. Use U.S. certified mail, if possible, and retain your receipts as proof that you filed your estimated tax on time.

Penalties

Introduction

As a Connecticut resident you must prepay your income tax during the year. This is usually accomplished through taxes that are withheld by your employer. If you have certain income from which tax is not withheld, such as self-employment income, you may be required to make estimated tax payments. If you fail to do so, you may be subject to penalties and interest.

EXCEPTION: You may be able to avoid estimated tax penalties if you paid *at least* 90% of the total tax due for the current year. As an alternative, you can pay an amount equal to last year's tax. See the previous section for further instructions.

Connecticut charges both interest and a penalty on underpayments of estimated taxes, as follows:

1. If you make the payment late (i.e., after the due date) or underpay the amount you owe, interest of 1.25% per month or fraction of a month is charged until the payment is received. If you make a payment after the due date while you have an amount outstanding, the payment will first be applied to the past due portion, and the rest will be applied to the amount currently due.
2. A penalty of 10% of the underpaid or late tax, assessed at the end of the year.

Form CT-2210, *Underpayment of Estimated Tax by Individuals and Fiduciaries,* should be used to calculate penalties and interest on underpayments of estimated tax. Attach a copy of this form to your CT-1040 or CT-1040 NR/PY. If you owe penalties and interest, you cannot use form CT-1040EZ.

TaxSaver: If you underpay an installment of estimated tax or pay it after the due date, you may eventually be assessed the 10% penalty and interest on the balance of estimated tax you owe. Therefore, if you realize you have made an error on a previous quarter's estimated tax payment, be sure to correct your mistake with your next installment. That way, you may be able to avoid a deficiency at year's end.

If you have reasonable circumstances that delayed your payment of estimated taxes, you may ask for a waiver of penalties. A letter explaining the reasons should be sent to:

Connecticut Department of Revenue Services
Tax Review Committee
92 Farmington Avenue
Hartford, CT 06105

Exceptions

As of the date of publication, the Connecticut Legislature has not provided exceptions to the imposition of estimated tax penalties. See the preceding two sections for a description of estimated tax requirements and penalties for failure to pay the proper amount of estimated tax.

6 | Refunds (Amended Returns)

At some point, you may conclude that you are owed a refund of taxes you previously paid. To obtain a refund, you will have to file an amended return. You may also be required to file an amended return with Connecticut if there are changes to your federal income tax. This chapter will discuss refund claims and other circumstances in which the filing of an amended return may be required.

Refunds in General

If you paid more taxes on your income than you actually owe, whether through estimated tax payments or withholding, you may be entitled to receive a refund.

You may be entitled to a refund from Connecticut if the Internal Revenue Service has made changes to your federal income tax return that result in a reduction of your federal adjusted gross income. You may also have made an error in Connecticut's favor on your original tax return. In these cases, you will need to file an amended Connecticut income tax return.

When to Submit an Amended Return

If you already filed your Connecticut income tax return, you should file an amended return if you discover errors or omissions, such as one of the following:

- You did not report some income you received;
- You overstated your income;
- You claimed certain deductions or tax credits to which you were not entitled;
- You were entitled to deductions or tax credits you did not take;
- The information on your federal tax return changed, requiring you to file an amended federal tax return; or
- The Internal Revenue Service made changes to your federal return.

There are strict time limits you must follow depending on the reason why you have amended your Connecticut return. Generally, you must file an amended return within three years from the due date of your original return, taking into account any extensions, or within two years of the date the tax was paid, *whichever is later*.

If you amend your federal tax return, you must file an amended Connecticut tax return within 90 days from the date you filed the amended federal return. If the Internal Revenue Service redetermines your tax, you must file an amended Connecticut tax return within 90 days of a final determination by the Internal Revenue Service.

See the section in Chapter 8 entitled *Statute of Limitations* for further information.

Which Form to Use

If you filed your original return on Form CT-1040EZ or CT-1040, you must amend your original return by filing Form CT-1040X for the corresponding tax year.

If you are a nonresident taxpayer and filed Form CT-1040 NR/PY, use a blank copy of your original return and write **Amended**, on the top of the front page. You *must* also complete Form CT-1040X and attach the amended CT-1040 NR/PY.

Limits on Amounts of Refunds

If you have three years to file a claim for a refund, your refund will be limited to the tax paid during those three years. If you file your return early, it is still deemed to be filed on the original due date.

Example

Steve's 1990 Connecticut income tax return was due on April 15, 1991. He filed it on March 31, 1991. Steve had income tax withheld by his employer of $1,000 and paid estimated income taxes of $2,000 over the course of the tax year. Even though Steve filed his return before April 15 and paid most of his estimated taxes before that date, if he qualifies for the three-year limit, he will have until April 15, 1994, to file an amended return. Therefore, if Steve filed his amended return on or before April 15, 1994, he will be entitled to claim a refund up to the total amount of income tax he previously paid, $3,000.

If Steve received a valid extension of time to file his original return, he would have three years from the date he filed the return to claim a refund. For example, if Steve received a four-month extension from April 15, 1991, he would have until August 15, 1994, to file an amended return for a refund of his full tax liability, $3,000.

If Steve filed his original return *after* the extended due date, he would only be entitled to a refund of the amount he paid with his original return. He could not claim a refund of taxes withheld or paid as estimated taxes. If Steve filed his original return late and paid an additional $100 with the return, he would only be entitled to receive a refund up to a maximum of $100.

State Tax Changes

If you claimed a resident tax credit for income taxes paid to other jurisdictions (see the section on *Credits* in Chapter 4), you must report any changes to these taxes. Any such changes must be reported to Connecticut within 30 days of a final determination by another jurisdiction. Use Form CT-1040X to report the changes.

What if Your Refund is Denied?

If your refund claim is denied, you will receive a written Notice of Disallowance, briefly stating the reasons for the denial. You may request judicial review of the denial within thirty days after the date the Notice of Disallowance was issued.

For information on how to request judicial review of your claim for a refund, see the section entitled *Protesting the Audit* in Chapter 8.

Filing Your Amended Return

Whether you are requesting a refund or not, send all amended returns to:

> Department of Revenue Services
> P.O. Box 2978
> Hartford, CT 06104-2978

As with every other tax return, be sure to sign and date the amended return and send it by U.S. certified mail. Keep a copy for your files.

7 | Other Taxes

Sales and Use Tax

A sales tax is a tax on the sale, exchange, or rental of goods and certain services. For the most part, it is imposed on sales that take place between a merchant or supplier and a customer inside the state. An out-of-state merchant may be required to collect sales tax from Connecticut residents if he or she has some connection with Connecticut. As a Connecticut consumer, you generally pay sales tax directly to the merchant or supplier of the goods or services you purchase. He or she is responsible for collecting the tax from you and paying it to the Department of Revenue Services. The current sales tax is imposed at a general rate of 6 percent.

A use tax is a complement to the sales tax and is imposed at the same rate as the sales tax. If you are a Connecticut resident, you owe use tax on all taxable goods and services used in Connecticut unless they were taxed at the time of purchase.

Example

Renee, a Connecticut resident, purchases stereo equipment from a mail order company located in Maine. The equipment is shipped from Maine to her Connecticut residence. Renee does not pay any sales tax at the time of purchase since the Maine vendor is not required to collect Connecticut sales tax. Renee is liable for the use tax on this purchase.

If you purchased goods outside the state and paid sales tax at a lower rate than the Connecticut rate, you are liable for the difference in the sales tax rates when you bring the goods into the state. You are *only* liable for the difference in tax, however, since Connecticut allows you a credit for the percentage of tax paid to the other state.

If you owe use tax on taxable goods and services purchased for your own use, you must report and pay the tax on Form OP-186, *Connecticut Individual Use Tax Return*. The return must be filed no later than April 15 of the year following purchase. You are not required to pay use tax on purchases brought into the state with a value of $25 or less, in total.

What is Taxable?

As a consumer, you pay sales tax on many goods and services used in your daily life. Unlike most states, Connecticut imposes sales tax not only on tangible goods but on a whole host of services. In general, the following goods and services are taxed by Connecticut:

- Retail sales and rentals of tangible personal property, such as clothing and footwear, appliances, automobiles, household cleaning agents, video rentals, cosmetics, pet foods and supplies, cigarettes, carbonated beverages, alcoholic beverages, books and publications, and records and tapes;

- Producing and fabricating tangible personal property; and
- A number of services, including the following:
  - computer and data processing services
  - credit information and reporting services
  - collection services
  - employment and personnel services
  - private investigation, protection, patrol, watchman, and armored car services
  - sign painting and lettering services
  - interior design and decorating services
  - telephone answering services
  - stenographic services
  - photographic studio services
  - services to industrial, commercial, or income-producing real property
  - business analysis, management, management consulting, and public relations services
  - tax preparation services
  - motor vehicle repairs
  - motor vehicle parking
  - radio or television repair services
  - furniture reupholstering and repair services
  - certain amusement and recreation services
  - telecommunication services
  - cable television services
  - rental of hotel rooms for the first 30 consecutive days or less of occupancy
  - locksmith services
  - janitorial services
  - exterminating services.

EXCEPTION: Some sales of goods are exempt from sales tax. Common exempt items include sales for resale, clothing and footwear costing less than $50, food other than candy and confections, sales of cloth or fabric used in making clothing for personal use, beverages other than carbonated beverages and alcoholic beverages, prescription drugs and certain over-the-counter drugs, corrective eyeglasses, hearing aids, dentures, artificial limbs, prosthetic aids, certain medical equipment, wheelchairs, crutches, telephone equipment for deaf or blind persons, disposable diapers, newspapers, and magazines.

Other purchases that may qualify for an exemption from sales tax include:

- Machinery used or consumed directly in a manufacturing production process;
- Machine parts purchased exclusively for the purpose of assembling a machine for use directly in a manufacturing production process; and
- Property used exclusively in agricultural production.

If you claim an exemption, you must submit a valid certificate at the time of purchase.

TaxPlanner: Keep detailed records of all information you used to prepare your sales tax returns. This will aid you if your sales tax returns are ever challenged on audit. If you are ever subject to audit, you may be asked to provide records such as ledgers, journals, worksheets, sales invoices, purchase invoices, cash register tapes, exemption certificates, etc.

Withholding

If you are an employee and perform services for which you are paid a salary or wages, chances are your salary or wages are subject to the withholding of income taxes. Also, other forms of compensation or income may be subject to withholding. The following section will explain who is subject to withholding, how the amount to be withheld is calculated, and how you can adjust the amount of withholding to fit your tax situation. Generally, Connecticut follows the provisions of the Internal Revenue Code concerning income tax withholding.

Who is Subject to Withholding?

Residents. If you are a resident of Connecticut and your employer is located only in Connecticut, he or she is required to withhold income tax for all services you performed, even though some services may have been performed outside the state.

If you work for an employer who is located outside Connecticut, and he or she does not transact any business in Connecticut, then he or she *will not* be obligated to withhold any Connecticut income tax from your wages, although he or she may be required to withhold income taxes on your wages for the state in which he or she is located. As a resident, you will still be obligated to file a Connecticut resident tax return. You may claim a credit for taxes paid to other states against any income tax you may owe to Connecticut. (See the section, *Credits*, in Chapter 4.)

Nonresidents and Part-Year Residents. If you are a nonresident of Connecticut and your employer is located in Connecticut, he or she is only obligated to withhold income taxes on wages paid to you for services performed in Connecticut. If your job requires that you perform all services within Connecticut, then tax must be withheld on all wages paid to you.

If you perform services both inside and outside Connecticut, your employer is only obligated to withhold income taxes on the portion of income for the services performed within Connecticut. (See, in Chapter 3, *Attributing Income to Connecticut—Sourcing Rules.*)

What Income is Subject to Withholding?

The main category of income from which taxes must be withheld is wage or salary income. Any supplemental wages you receive are also subject to withholding of tax. Supplemental wages include bonuses, commissions, overtime pay, sales awards, tips, and vacation allowances.

If supplemental wages are paid to you at the same time as your regular wages, your employer should withhold tax on the entire amount at the same rate as the rate applicable to your wages. However, if the supplemental wages are paid to you separately from your regular wages, your employer may withhold income taxes at the highest rate, without allowance for withholding exemptions, discussed below. Other income subject to income tax withholding are taxable fringe benefits, sick pay, pensions and annuities, and certain gambling winnings.

Exemptions from Withholding

If you had no federal income tax liability last year and anticipate no federal income tax liability this year, you may claim to be exempt from Connecticut income tax withholding. To claim this exemption, however, you must file Form CT-W4, *Employee's Withholding or Exemption Certificate.* See *The Ernst & Young Tax Guide 1993* for the requirements to qualify for exemption from withholding for federal income tax purposes. Whether or not if you filed federal Form W-4 with your employer, you still must file Form CT-W4.

Determining Withholding Taxes

Your employer can determine the amount of income tax to be withheld from your wages by using the tax tables provided by the state or by calculating the tax himself or herself. The tax withheld depends upon the amount of income you earned for the pay period and the information you gave your employer on Form CT-W4.

You will want to calculate as accurately as possible the amount of income tax to be withheld from your earnings so that it will cover your final tax liability at the end of the year. This may enable you to avoid any potential penalties for underpaying your income tax. (See the section in Chapter 8 on *Penalties.*) Although you may owe interest and penalties if your employer underwithholds your income tax, you will not receive any interest or additional money if he or she overwithholds.

You can choose to have your income tax withheld at a higher tax rate for *single* taxpayers or a lower tax rate for *married* taxpayers, regardless of your marital status. You can also request that your employer withhold additional amounts beyond the income tax calculated at the tax rate you choose. You may wish to have additional withholdings from tax if you and your spouse both work, you have more than one job, or you have income from interest, dividends, alimony, or self-employment. If you choose to have additional withholdings from your paycheck, you must have a written agreement to this effect with your employer.

TaxAlert: If you do not file a Form CT-W4 with your employer, your employer will withhold taxes from your pay at the highest rate: Single, no withholding allowances.

Credit for Tax Withheld

You are allowed a credit against your income tax for any withholding during the year.

Your employer is required to supply you with a summary of wages paid and taxes withheld. Typically, you will receive several copies of a federal Form W-2, *Wage and Tax Statement.* You should attach a designated copy to your federal, state, or local return. You should receive this form from your employer no later than January 31 following the close of the tax year.

Example

John and Eileen are married and have two children. They work for different employers. For Connecticut tax purposes they are entitled to four withholding allowances, one for each one of them and one for each child. John has filed a Form W-4 with his employer claiming three withholding allowances. Eileen also has filed Form W-4 with her employer. She also wants her taxes to be withheld at the married rate, no additional taxes withheld, but only one withholding allowance. With this information their employers can determine the amount of taxes to be withheld from each paycheck.

Real Property Transfer and Gains Tax

You will need to pay the Real Property Transfer Tax if you sell real property in Connecticut. You will also need to pay this tax if you are a lessor and the leasehold interest is for 99 years or more. *Real Property* that may be subject to this tax includes houses, condominiums, cooperatives, buildings, and land. This tax is imposed on the seller of the real property. It is levied on the *full purchase price*, which includes money, the assumption of a prior mortgage, and the fair market value of other consideration transferred to you. Persons subject to this tax must complete Form OP-236, *Real Estate Conveyance Tax Return.*

Connecticut imposes a similar tax called the *Controlling Interest Transfer Tax* on transfers of a controlling interest in a corporation, partnership, association, trust, or other entity that owns an interest in real property located in Connecticut. *Controlling interest* means 50% or more of the voting stock of a corporation or 50% or more of the capital, profits, or beneficial interest in a partnership, association, trust, or other entity. A transfer of a controlling interest may be accomplished through a series of transactions or by a group acting in a combined effort. Persons subject to this tax must complete Form AU 330, *Controlling Interest Transfer Taxes.*

Example
Alan and Brenda each own 30% of the interest in ABC Partnership, which owns property in Connecticut. In a joint effort, they decide to sell their interests in the partnership. This transfer will be subject to tax because their combined efforts result in a transfer of a controlling interest in an entity that owns property in Connecticut.

Exemptions
You will not have to pay the Real Property Transfer Tax if your transaction meets one of the following requirements:

- The money or other consideration transferred to you is less than $2,000;
- You sell property to or buy property from the United States of America, Connecticut, or any instrumentality, agency, or subdivision of these governments;
- You transfer a deed to release security for a debt or obligation;
- You are transferring a deed as collateral for a debt;
- Your realty is transferred to a trustee for the benefit of your creditors. The transfer of the deed from your trustee to your creditor(s) or to any other person is subject to tax;
- Your realty is transferred to your spouse, parent, or child as a gift;
- Your transfer is pursuant to a divorce decree;
- You transfer your realty as a gift. The transfer of real property as a gift may be subject to gift taxes. (See the following section, *Estate and Gift Tax,* for additional information);
- Your property is located in an area designated by any municipality as an enterprise zone;
- Your property is transferred because of delinquent taxes;

- You divide your real property into separate shares or units; or
- You transfer the deed to your principal residence and you are receiving tax relief for the elderly.

Calculation of Tax

Real Property Transfer Tax.

Tax Calculation Schedule

Type of Property	Purchase Price	Tax Rate
Unimproved land residential dwelling	Any amount $800,000 or less over $800,000	0.5% (0.005) 0.5% (0.005) 1% (0.01)
Other residential property	Any amount	0.5% (0.005)
Nonresidential property other than unimproved land	Any amount	1% (0.01)

Controlling Interest Transfer Tax. The Controlling Interest Transfer Tax is imposed at a rate of 1.11% (0.011) on the fair market value of real property in which a controlling interest is transferred.

Estate and Gift Tax

An explanation of all the Connecticut estate tax rules is beyond the scope of this book. However, the following information should help you to determine whether you must pay the estate tax or the gift tax.

Estate Tax
If you are the fiduciary of the estate of a resident decedent, you must file Form OP-231, *Connecticut Estate Tax Return,* if the estate has federal taxable income exceeding $20,000.

If you are the fiduciary of a nonresident's estate, you must file Form OP-231 if the nonresident's estate includes any Connecticut property and the $20,000 threshold is met. For a resident decedent's estate, all real and tangible property located within the state and intangible property located anywhere are included in the estate. For a nonresident decedent's estate, only real and tangible property located in the state is subject to estate tax.

Filing the Return
Form OP-231 is due April 15th of the year following the one in which the individual died. The return is considered timely if the date shown on the U.S. Postal Service postmark falls on or before the due date of the return.

If you are unable to file the return by this date, you can request a four-month extension by filing Form OP-231TA. This will only extend the time for filing the return. It does not extend the time to pay the tax. An extension of time granted by the IRS for filing a federal estate tax return does not extend the time for filing the Connecticut return. If the tax is not paid on time, penalty and interest will be charged. A copy of the first page of federal Form 1041 must be included with the estate tax return.

A duplicate return must be filed with the probate court within six months of the date of death.

Gift Tax
A gift tax is due on gifts made by Connecticut residents of Connecticut real, tangible, or intangible property after September 1, 1991, if the value of the gift to a single individual in a calendar year exceeds $10,000. Nonresidents are taxed

on gifts of Connecticut real or tangible personal property exceeding $10,000 to a single individual in a calendar year.

The tax is based on the fair market value of the property. The giver of the gift must pay the tax, but if the giver does not pay, then the person receiving the gift must pay.

Filing the Return

A Connecticut Gift Tax Return, Form CT-709, must be filed for all taxable gifts made on or after September 1, 1991. The return must be filed and the tax paid by April 15th of the year following the one in which the gift was made.

8 | What to Do If Your Return Is Examined

Audits

Tax returns filed by Connecticut taxpayers will be increasingly subject to the Department of Revenue's scrutiny because of the recent enactment of the Connecticut personal income tax. This chapter will explain how a tax return is chosen for audit, how an audit is conducted, and how it is concluded. You will find information on appeals later in this chapter.

Whose Return is Audited?

The Connecticut Audit Division will randomly select certain returns for examination, either by computer screening or by random sample. If your return is selected for audit, the Audit Division will notify you by mail. As in New York and New Jersey, the Audit Division may conduct the audit through the mail, at a district office, at your home or place of business, or even at your accountant's or attorney's office.

TaxAlert: According to a recent publication, PS 94(2), *Your Rights as a Connecticut Taxpayer*, most audits will be conducted by mail. You may request this publication, which describes all your rights under Connecticut's tax laws, by calling (203) 297-4000 or 1-(800)-382-9463 (toll free within Connecticut).

Preliminary Analysis. In preparation for an audit, the agent will first determine which tax years are open for assessment under the statute of limitations. He or she will examine all information in your tax file related to these years, including your tax returns, supporting schedules, and any correspondence you had with the Department of Taxation and Finance. The agent will then decide which items on your returns need verification or further documentary support. The actual scope of the audit may be expanded later, depending on what information you supply.

Once a preliminary selection of your return is made, the Audit Division will notify you of the information or documents it wishes to review. An agent will evaluate any information you supply. You may request a personal interview with your assigned agent to discuss the issues under examination and to register any disagreement.

TaxPlanner: Although many people believe that saving tax records for three years is sufficient, professional tax advisors are increasingly advising clients to keep all records relating to their tax returns for eight to ten years or longer. Save copies of your filed returns, checks for deductions, receipts, income and wage statements, as well as any substantiation for deductions or income items not covered by checks or receipts you may have. If you change your residence for tax purposes, save adequate proof of the change. See the *Abandoning Your Domicile Checklist* on page NY-9. If you allocate your income based on days in and days out of Connecticut, save the documents showing where you were on any particular day. See Chapter 3 for more information on attributing income to Connecticut. Get into the habit of keeping your tax information in a safe place.

Conducting the Audit

It may be advisable to contact your accountant or retain competent legal representation when dealing with an agent. If you determine that representation is warranted, you must assign your representative the right to speak on your behalf by executing a Power of Attorney and sending it to the agent. Your representative should then contact the agent to discuss the audit.

If any additional assessment is proposed, the state will explain it in writing to you or your appointed representative. At the conclusion of the audit, you will receive a copy of a Tax Determination Report summarizing the adjustments proposed by the agent and including copies of his or her workpapers. The report will also list any penalties and interest that are due. If a refund is to be made for any given year, it will be reflected on the report as well.

Concluding the Audit

If you agree with the Audit Division's findings, the audit will be considered closed and a statement will be sent to you indicating the amount due or to be refunded. You should receive a statement of tax due about one or two months after you receive the Tax Determination Report. Interest on the assessment will continue to accrue until any amount due is paid. This statement, along with a copy of the cancelled check indicating payment, should be kept with all your tax information for the year in a safe place.

TaxSaver: To avoid the accrual of additional interest, you may make advance payment of the assessment before receiving the final statement. If you do so, include a copy of the Tax Determination Report with your check. Mail the report and check to The Department of Revenue Services, Audit Division, Selection and Control Unit, 92 Farmington Avenue, Hartford, CT 05105.

You may make a partial payment of the assessment if you agree with the adjustment of some issues but disagree with the Audit Division on other issues. If you make such a partial payment, any amount you pay will be applied to interest first, penalty second, and then finally to the tax amount. To make a partial payment, you must complete Form LGL-005, in which you will concede the issues no longer in dispute. Form LGL-005 will stop interest from accruing on the partial payment. Interest will still accrue on that part of the assessment still contested.

TaxAlert: By filing Form LGL-005, you also waive your rights to any refund claim for the amount paid.

If you disagree with the adjustments, you may continue to protest the assessment under Connecticut's appeal process, described in the next section.

Protesting the Audit

This section will discuss how to protest a personal income tax audit and explain your legal remedies as a taxpayer.

Notice of Tax Deficiency
If you don't consent to the income tax adjustments proposed by the Department of Revenue Services, the next step in the process is the issuance of a formal *Notice of Tax Deficiency*. From here on, your rights to protest any additional tax and penalty assessments are strictly governed by Connecticut law.

TaxAlert: It is of the *utmost* importance that you pay strict attention to time limits and proper filing requirements. Your right to protest a Notice of Tax Deficiency can be lost if you are late in filing a required protest letter by even one day. There are requirements that the state must fulfill, too. For example, the Notice of Tax Deficiency must be mailed to your *last known address.* This is usually the address on your last tax return, unless you've since notified the Commissioner of Revenue Services that you've moved.

If you decide to protest a Notice of Tax Deficiency, your first recourse is a written protest to the Appellate Division of the Department of Revenue Services. A written protest to the Appellate Division provides you with a rapid, inexpensive, and relatively informal way of resolving your dispute with the taxing authorities.

You have 60 days from the date of your Notice of Tax Deficiency to file a written protest. There is no official form for this purpose; a letter will suffice. The written protest must describe the nature of your grievance and whether you or your representatives would like an opportunity to be heard at an oral hearing. An Appellate Officer, who is employed by the Department of Revenue Services, will review your written protest and decide whether oral arguments will be heard. The Appellate Officer may also request additional information from you if he or she thinks it would be helpful in clarifying the issues or resolving the dispute.

As a practical matter, oral arguments are rarely granted and the entire appeals process is handled through the mail. The Appellate Officer will mail you his or her final determi-

nation, with a summary stating the basis for the decision, generally within 3 to 5 months after receipt of your written protest or submission of additional information.

Example
Beatrice received a Notice of Tax Deficiency from the Connecticut Department of Revenue Services. The notice was dated June 1, 1992. Beatrice has until July 31, 1992, to file a written protest with the Commissioner of Revenue Services.

TaxSaver: You must file a written protest within 60 days from the date your Notice of Tax Deficiency was issued. If you fail to file this request on time, you will lose your opportunity to appeal before you pay the tax deficiency.

Judicial Review
If you are not satisfied with the Appellate Officer's determination of your written protest, you have 30 days from that date to file an appeal with the Superior Court for the judicial district of Hartford-New Britain.

TaxSaver: It is recommended that you obtain legal representation at this level. The reason is that formal courtroom procedures will be followed.

Penalties

Introduction
By law, you are required to file a Connecticut tax return and pay your fair share of taxes. If you do not file and pay the correct amount of tax by the due date, you can incur substantial penalties and interest. This section will describe the penalties Connecticut imposes on delinquent taxpayers.

Penalties and Interest
A tax "penalty" is an addition to the tax you owe if you fail to file a Connecticut tax return on time or fail to pay a tax that is due. Interest, on the other hand, is an amount you owe because you had the use of money that properly belonged to Connecticut. Some people confuse interest and penalties, but the interest you owe Connecticut for a late payment of tax is no different from the interest you owe your credit card company if you fail to pay your monthly balance. Both represent a charge for extending credit. If you extend "credit" to Connecticut by overpaying your tax, the state must refund your tax with interest (subject to certain limitations and differences in rate). Another difference between penalties and interest is that Connecticut may waive a penalty if you show "reasonable cause" for your failure. Interest, however, cannot be waived under any circumstances.

Exception: You will not be liable for interest and penalties if, by the end of the tax year, you have paid *at least* 90% of the total tax due for 1992, or 100% of last year's tax, whichever is less.

The following is a summary of civil penalties and interest if you fail to comply with the requirements for filing a tax return and paying your tax:

- If you fail to pay the amount due on your return on time, a penalty of 10% of the underpayment is added to your tax, along with interest of 1.25%.

- If you fail to file a return, the Commissioner of Revenue may make an estimate of the tax you owe, based on the best available information. A penalty of 10% of the tax due is added. In addition, the unpaid tax will accrue interest at a rate of 1.25% per month, or fraction thereof, from the due date of the tax to the date you finally pay. There is a minimum penalty of $50.
- If you are negligent or intentionally disregard your obligation to pay tax, a penalty is assessed at 10% of the underpayment. Interest is calculated at a rate of 1.25% per month on the unpaid tax.

TaxAlert: The term *negligence* means a failure to make a reasonable attempt to obey the rules. The term *intentional disregard* includes any careless, reckless, or intentional disregard.

Reasonable Cause

You may be entitled to an abatement of all or some of these penalties if you can demonstrate that your failure to pay or file was not intentional and was due to reasonable cause. See the New Jersey section for a discussion of what constitutes "reasonable cause." Your appeal must be made in writing to the Connecticut Commissioner of Revenue. In your correspondence, carefully state your reasons for not paying the required tax or not filing your return. Be sure to provide any copies of documentation which you feel will strengthen your position.

Tax Evasion and Fraud

If you fraudently file a return or deliberately evade Connecticut tax law, the penalty is 25% of the amount of the underpayment, in addition to interest charges. Extreme cases of tax fraud may be punishable by imprisonment, fines, or both.

Deficiency Assessments

After you file a final tax return for the year, the Commissioner of Revenue Services may determine, upon audit, that you underpaid your tax. If this is the case, you will receive a formal *Notice of Deficiency*, which will include additional taxes, penalties, and interest that are due. You must pay the amount due within 60 days of the mailing of the notice unless you protest the assessment. See the preceding section, *Protesting the Audit*, for additional information on filing protests.

Mathematical Error

If you make a mathematical error but otherwise comply with the tax laws, Connecticut may bill you for the additional amount of the error by mailing you a *Notice of Additional Tax Due*. A *mathematical error* means you made a mistake in computing your tax, made an entry on the wrong line, forgot to include proper forms or information, or made improper entries for certain claims or deductions. You will not be assessed a penalty as a result of an unintentional mathematical error or other omission. However, you will have to pay interest on any additional tax you may owe as a result of your error.

Statute of Limitations

General Rule

The period of time during which the Connecticut Department of Revenue can assess a tax deficiency is limited by statute, called the *statute of limitations*. As a general rule, state law allows Connecticut taxing authorities to make an assessment of additional taxes at any time within three years after the date you actually filed your return. This section will discuss rules concerning the statute of limitations and exceptions.

The Three-Year Rule

If you file your return before April 15 (or August 15 if you filed for an extension), the three-year statute of limitations period does not start running until the last day on which you could have filed. If you file your income tax return late, the three-year statute of limitations does not start to run until the date you actually file your return.

No Income Tax Return Filed or Fraudulent Return Filed

The general three-year rule does not apply if you fail to file your Connecticut income tax return or if you file a state tax return with information that you know to be false or fraudulent. In these instances, the state can assess you additional tax, penalties, and interest at any time. However, the taxing authorities must have reason to believe that you intentionally withheld information in the interest of avoiding or evading your fair share of income taxes.

Extension by Agreement

Connecticut can extend the time to assess additional taxes beyond the statutory three years if you agree in writing to the extension. This written agreement to extend the statute of limitations must be signed both by you and the taxing officials before the expiration of the statutory three-year period. An agreement to extend the statute of limitations is always limited to a particular tax and specific filing year(s). It extends the time during which the state can assess you for a limited period of time—usually, one year. Additional extensions may be granted by agreement.

You may wonder why anyone would willingly consent to let the taxing authorities have more time in which to make an assessment. Usually, such agreements are made in connection with an audit or a review of a refund request. It may well be in the interest of *both* parties to allow the state more time to complete its examination. The extra time may enable a taxpayer to present new facts that support a refund claim or reduce a proposed assessment.

Report of Federal Change

The statute of limitations will also be extended if you amend your federal income tax return or consent to a federal income tax adjustment. If a change in your federal income tax causes you to owe additional taxes to Connecticut, the taxing authorities are deemed to have made a valid assessment of those additional taxes on the date you file your federal amended return. This assessment is valid even if made after the normal three-year limitation period has expired. Amended federal returns, whether filed by choice or because you conceded to an adjustment, automatically extend Connecticut's normal three-year statute of limitations.

If you file an amended federal return showing any change in your taxable income, you must also file an amended Connecticut return within 90 days from the date you amend your federal return. You are also required to notify Connecticut of any changes in your federal income made as a result of a federal audit within 90 days of the determination. If you fail to report your federal change within the required 90-day period, Connecticut may assess a tax deficiency on the amount attributable to the federal changes at any time.

If the assessment is made during the extended three-year period, the state cannot review or assess more than the amount attributable to the federal changes on your amended return. If, however, the assessment is made during the normal three-year assessment period, any tax items can be reviewed.

Omission of Income

If your Connecticut income tax return omits more than 25% of the income that should have been properly included, the Connecticut assessment period is extended to six years.

9 | Connecticut Sample Forms

This chapter provides filled-in examples of the principal personal income tax forms used by Connecticut residents and nonresidents for you to refer to when preparing your own return. To ensure that you have the most complete and accurate information, we advise you to use this book in conjunction with the official 1993 Connecticut income tax forms and instructions.

The forms and schedule included in this chapter are:

Form CT-1040EZ: Connecticut EZ Resident Income Tax Return

Form CT-1040: Connecticut Resident Income Tax Return

Form CT-1040NR/PY: Connecticut Nonresident or Part-Year Resident Income Tax Return

Schedule CT-SI: Nonresident or Part-Year Schedule of Income from Connecticut Sources

Form CT-1040EZ

CONNECTICUT EZ RESIDENT INCOME TAX RETURN

EZ
1992

For the year January 1 - December 31, 1992, or other taxable year ►beginning _____, 1992, ►ending _____, 19___.

Name and Address

PLACE LABEL HERE

Your First Name and Middle Initial	Last Name	Your Social Security Number
► ROGER P.	ROSE	► 100 10 1000

If a JOINT Return, Spouse's First Name and Middle Initial	Last Name	Spouse's Social Security Number
► BRENDA M.	ROSE	► 200 20 2000

Home Address Number and Street	Your Telephone Number
► 10 MILL ROAD	(203) 951-3200

City, Town or Post Office	State	Zip Code
► LITTLETON	CT	00000

You may file a CT-1040EZ if you meet ALL of the following conditions: Otherwise file CT-1040 (See Instructions)

   A. You have no modifications to Federal Adjusted Gross Income for Connecticut income tax purposes, and

   B. You were a resident of Connecticut for the entire taxable year, and

   C. You are not claiming credit for income taxes paid to another jurisdiction.

Filing Status

NOTE: Your filing status must be the same as your federal income tax filing status for this year. See instructions for details.

► A. ☐ Single

► B. ☑ Married filing joint return or Qualifying widow(er)

► C. ☐ Married filing SEPARATE returns _____

                                      Spouse's full name   ► ___ ___

► D. ☐ Head of Household   Spouse's Social Security Number

STAPLE W-2's HERE

Income and Tax

1. Federal Adjusted Gross Income (From Federal Form 1040, Line 31 or Form 1040A, Line 16 or Form 1040EZ, Line 3) This is your Connecticut Adjusted Gross Income.	► 1	67,001	00
2. Income Tax: From Tax Table or Tax Calculation Schedule (See instructions) ALL EXEMPTIONS AND CREDITS ARE INCLUDED IN THE TAX TABLE.	► 2	2,552	51
3. Connecticut Tax withheld (Attach all W-2's and certain 1099's; See Instuctions)	► 3	2,922	51
4. All 1992 estimated payments	► 4		
5. Payments made with extension request	► 5		
6. Total payments (Add Lines 3 through 5)	► 6	2,922	51

Refund or Amount Owed

7. If Line 6 is greater than Line 2, enter amount overpaid. (Subtract Line 2 from Line 6)	► 7	370	00
8. Amount of Line 7 you want to be applied to your 1993 estimated tax	► 8		
9. Amount of Line 7 you want to be refunded to you (Subtract Line 8 from Line 7) (See mailing instructions below) REFUND	► 9	370	00
10. If Line 2 is greater than Line 6, enter amount of tax you owe. (Subtract Line 6 from Line 2) BALANCE DUE	► 10		

NOTE: IF YOU OWE PENALTY AND INTEREST FOR A LATE FILED RETURN OR FOR UNDERPAYMENT OF 1992 ESTIMATES AND YOU WANT TO PAY THE AMOUNT WITH YOUR RETURN, YOU MUST FILE FORM CT-1040. IF YOU FILE FORM CT-1040EZ, THE DEPARTMENT WILL CALCULATE ANY APPLICABLE PENALTY AND INTEREST. YOU WILL EITHER BE BILLED SEPARATELY FOR THIS AMOUNT, OR, IF YOU ARE DUE A REFUND, IT WILL BE SUBTRACTED FROM YOUR REFUND.

DUE DATE: April 15, 1993

Make your check payable to: COMMISSIONER OF REVENUE SERVICES
Write your Social Security Number(s) and "1992 Form CT-1040EZ" on your check.
Attach a copy of all applicable schedules and forms to this return.
Mail in the envelope provided to you with this return or to the address shown at right.

FOR REFUNDS, MAIL TO:
Department of Revenue Services
P.O. Box 2976
Hartford, CT 06104-2976

FOR PAYMENTS AND NO TAX DUE, MAIL TO:
Department of Revenue Services
P.O. Box 2977
Hartford, CT 06104-2977

DECLARATION: I declare under the penalties of false statement that this return (including any accompanying schedules and statements) has been examined by me and, to the best of my knowledge and belief, it is a true, correct and complete return. Declaration of preparer (other than taxpayer) is based on all information of which preparer has any knowledge.

CLIP CHECK HERE (DO NOT STAPLE)

Sign Your Return

Your Signature	Date	Spouse's Signature (if joint return)	Date
Roger P. Rose	4/14/93	Brenda M. Rose	4/14/93

Paid Preparer's Signature	Date	Federal Employer I.D. Number
		►

Firm Name and Address	CT Sales Tax Registration Number
	►

Was a fee charged either for the preparation of this return or for advice in the preparation of this return? ☐ YES ☐ NO

CT-1040
1992

Form CT-1040

CONNECTICUT RESIDENT INCOME TAX RETURN

For the year January 1 - December 31, 1992, or other taxable year ▶beginning _____ , 1992, ▶ending _____ , 19___

Name and Address (PLACE LABEL HERE)

Your First Name and Middle Initial ▶ PAUL	Last Name de MAINE	Your Social Security Number ▶ 100 | 10 | 1000
If a JOINT Return, Spouse's First Name and Middle Initial ▶ DENISE B.	Last Name de MAINE	Spouse's Social Security Number ▶ 200 | 20 | 2000
Home Address Number and Street ▶ 3 FAIRLAWN AVENUE		Your Telephone Number (203) 951-3487
City, Town or Post Office ▶ ANYTOWN	State CT	Zip Code 00000

Check if you used a preparer and do not want forms sent to you next year. Checking this box does not relieve you of your responsibility to file.. ▶ ☐

Check here if you completed Part I of Form CT-2210. (See instructions for Form CT-2210).................... ▶ ☐

Filing Status

NOTE: Your filing status must be the same as your federal income tax filing status for this year. See instructions for details.

▶ A. ☐ Single
▶ B. ☑ Married filing joint return or Qualifying widow(er)
▶ C. ☐ Married filing *SEPARATE* returns _____
▶ D. ☐ Head of Household   Spouse's full name

▶ ___ — ___ — ___ Spouse's Social Security Number

Income and Tax (STAPLE W-2's HERE)

		$	
1. Federal Adjusted Gross Income (From Federal Form 1040, Line 31 or Form 1040A, Line 16, or Form 1040EZ, Line 3) ▶ 1		50,000	00
2. Additions, if any (From Schedule 1, Line 29) ▶ 2		1,500	00
3. Add Lines 1 and 2 ▶ 3		51,500	00
4. Subtractions, if any (From Schedule 1, Line 39) ▶ 4		600	00
5. Connecticut Adjusted Gross Income (Subtract Line 4 from Line 3) ▶ 5		50,900	00
6. Income Tax: From Tax Table or Tax Calculation Schedule (See Instructions) ALL EXEMPTIONS AND CREDITS ARE INCLUDED IN THE TAX TABLE ▶ 6		1,211	96
7. Credit for Income Tax paid to other jurisdictions (From Schedule 2, Line 48) ▶ 7			
8. Total Income Tax (Subtract Line 7 from Line 6. If Line 7 is greater than Line 6, enter 0) ▶ 8		1,211	96
9. Connecticut Tax withheld (**Attach all W-2's and certain 1099's;** See Instructions) ▶ 9		1,311	96
10. All 1992 estimated payments ▶ 10			
11. Payments made with extension request ▶ 11			
12. Total payments (Add Lines 9 through 11) ▶ 12		1,311	96

Refund or Amount Owed

13. If Line 12 is greater than Line 8, enter amount overpaid. (Subtract Line 8 from Line 12) ▶ 13		100	00
14. Amount of Line 13 you want to be **applied to your 1993 estimated tax** ▶ 14			
15. Amount of Line 13 you want to be **refunded** to you (Subtract Line 14 from Line 13) (See mailing instructions below) **REFUND** ▶ 15		100	00
16. If Line 8 is greater than Line 12, enter the amount of tax you owe. (Subtract Line 12 from Line 8) ▶ 16			
17. If late: Enter Penalty (10% × amount on Line 16 OR if Line 16 is zero, enter $50) ▶ 17			
18. If late: Enter Interest (1¼% × number of months late, or fraction thereof × amount on Line 16) ▶ 18			
19. Penalty for Underpayment of Estimated Tax (From Form CT-2210) ▶ 19			
20. Interest for Underpayment of Estimated Tax (From Form CT-2210) ▶ 20			
21. **Balance due** with this return (Add Lines 16 through 20) **BALANCE DUE** ▶ 21			

DUE DATE: April 15, 1993.
Make your check payable to: COMMISSIONER OF REVENUE SERVICES
Write your Social Security Number(s) and "1992 Form CT-1040" on your check.
Attach a copy of all applicable schedules and forms to this return.
Mail in the envelope provided to you with this return or to the address shown at right.

FOR REFUNDS, MAIL TO:
Department of Revenue Services
P.O. Box 2976
Hartford, CT 06104-2976

FOR PAYMENTS AND NO TAX DUE, MAIL TO:
Department of Revenue Services
P.O. Box 2977
Hartford, CT 06104-2977

DECLARATION: I declare under the penalties of false statement that I have examined this return (including any accompanying schedules and statements) and, to the best of my knowledge and belief, it is true, complete and correct. Declaration of preparer (other than the taxpayer) is based on all information of which preparer has any knowledge.

Sign Your Return (CLIP CHECK HERE (DO NOT STAPLE))

Your Signature Paul de Maine	Date 4/14/93	Spouse's Signature (if joint return) Denise B. de Maine Date 4/14/93
Paid Preparer's Signature ▶	Date	Federal Employer I.D. Number
Firm Name and Address		CT Sales Tax Registration Number

Was a fee charged either for the preparation of this return or for advice in the preparation of this return?   ☐ YES   ☐ NO

CT-47

SCHEDULE 1 — MODIFICATIONS TO FEDERAL ADJUSTED GROSS INCOME (SEE INSTRUCTIONS)

Additions To Federal Adjusted Gross Income - Enter All Amounts as Positive Numbers

22. Interest on state and local obligations other than Connecticut	► 22	900
23. Exempt-interest dividends from a mutual fund derived from state and local obligations other than Connecticut	► 23	
24. Shareholder's pro rata share of S corporation nonseparately computed loss	► 24	100
25. Total taxable amount of lump sum distributions from qualified plans not included in Federal Adjusted Gross Income	► 25	
26. Beneficiary's share of Connecticut fiduciary adjustment (enter only if greater than 0)	► 26	
27. Loss on sale of Connecticut state and local government bonds	► 27	500
28. Other - specify:	► 28	
29. Total Additions (Add Lines 22 through 28) Enter here and on Line 2 on the front of this form)	► 29	1500

Subtractions From Federal Adjusted Gross Income - Enter All Amounts as Positive Numbers

30. Interest on U.S. government obligations	► 30	500
31. Exempt dividends from certain mutual funds derived from U.S. government obligations	► 31	
32. Reimbursed moving expenses deducted on federal Form 1040, Schedule A	► 32	
33. Refunds of state and local income taxes	► 33	100
34. Tier 1 Railroad Retirement benefits	► 34	
35. Shareholder's pro rata share of S corporation nonseparately computed income	► 35	
36. Beneficiary's share of Connecticut fiduciary adjustment (enter only if less than 0)	► 36	
37. Gain on sale of Connecticut state and local government bonds	► 37	
38. Other — specify: _____	► 38	
39. Total Subtractions (Add Lines 30 through 38) Enter here and on Line 4 on the front of this form)	► 39	600

SCHEDULE 2 — CREDIT FOR INCOME TAXES PAID TO OTHER JURISDICTIONS

NOTE: Attach copy of return filed with other jurisdiction(s).

40. MODIFIED CONNECTICUT ADJUSTED GROSS INCOME (See Instructions)   40 [   ]

FOR EACH COLUMN, ENTER THE FOLLOWING:

	COLUMN A		COLUMN B	
	Name	Code	Name	Code
41. Enter other jurisdiction's name and two-letter code. (See chart below)	41 ►		►	
42. Non-Connecticut income included on Line 40 and reported on another jurisdiction's income tax return (from Schedule 2 Worksheet)	42			
43. Divide Line 42 by Line 40 (May not exceed 1.00)	43			
44. Connecticut Income Tax liability (From Line 6)	44			
45. Multiply Line 43 × Line 44	45			
46. Income tax paid to another jurisdiction	46 ►		►	
47. Enter the smaller of Line 45 or Line 46	47			
48. TOTAL CREDIT (Add Line 47, all columns) Enter this amount here and on Line 7		48		

If you claim credit for income taxes paid to a political subdivision of a state or Canadian province, enter the two-letter code of the state or Canadian province, respectively.

STANDARD TWO-LETTER CODES

Alabama	AL	Louisiana	LA	Ohio	OH
Arizona	AZ	Maine	ME	Oklahoma	OK
Arkansas	AR	Maryland	MD	Oregon	OR
California	CA	Massachusetts	MA	Pennsylvania	PA
Colorado	CO	Michigan	MI	Rhode Island	RI
Delaware	DE	Minnesota	MN	South Carolina	SC
District of Columbia	DC	Mississippi	MS	Tennessee	TN
Georgia	GA	Missouri	MO	Utah	UT
Hawaii	HI	Montana	MT	Vermont	VT
Idaho	ID	Nebraska	NE	Virginia	VA
Illinois	IL	New Jersey	NJ	West Virginia	WV
Indiana	IN	New Mexico	NM	Wisconsin	WI
Iowa	IA	New York	NY	Any Canadian Province	OO
Kansas	KS	North Carolina	NC		
Kentucky	KY	North Dakota	ND		

CT-1040 (BACK) Rev. 12/92

STATE OF CONNECTICUT
DEPARTMENT OF REVENUE SERVICES

CT-1040 NR/PY

NR/PY 1992

CONNECTICUT NONRESIDENT OR PART-YEAR RESIDENT INCOME TAX RETURN

Check here for 1992 resident status: ►☑ Nonresident ►☐ Part-Year Resident ☐ Amended

For the year January 1 — December 31, 1992, or other taxable year ►beginning _____, 1992, ►ending _____, 19____.

Name and Address (PLACE LABEL HERE)

Your First Name and Middle Initial	Last Name		Your Social Security Number
► KATHERINE	HALL	►	100 10 1000

If a JOINT return, Spouse's First Name and Middle Initial	Last Name		Your Spouse's Social Security Number
►		►	

Home Address Number and Street		Your Telephone Number
► 50 HOME ROAD		( )

City, Town or Post Office	State	Zip Code
► YOURTOWN	NY	10000

Check if you used a paid preparer and do not want forms sent to you next year. Checking this box does not relieve you of your responsibility to file. ►☐
Check here if you completed Part I of Form CT-2210. (See instructions for Form CT-2210) ►☐

Filing Status

- ►A. ☑ Single
- ►B. ☐ Married filing joint return or Qualifying widow(er)
- ►C. ☐ Married filing SEPARATE returns _____ — _____
- ►D. ☐ Head of household

Spouse's full name   Spouse's Social Security Number

Income

1. Federal Adjusted Gross Income (From federal Form 1040, Line 31 or Form 1040A, Line 16 or Form 1040EZ, Line 3)	►1	25,000	
2. Additions, if any (From Schedule 1, Line 33)	►2	100	
3. Add Lines 1 and 2	►3	25,100	
4. Subtractions, if any (From Schedule 1, Line 43)	►4	1,800	
5. Connecticut Adjusted Gross Income (Subtract Line 4 from Line 3)	►5	23,300	

Tax Computation and Credits

6. Income from Connecticut sources (From Schedule CT-SI, Line 24)	►6	21,600	
7. Enter the greater of Line 5 or Line 6	►7	23,300	
8. Income Tax: From Tax Table or Calculation Schedule (See Instructions) **ALL EXEMPTIONS AND CREDITS ARE INCLUDED IN THE TAX TABLE**	►8	432	22
9. Divide Line 6 by Line 5 (If Line 6 is equal to or greater than Line 5, enter 1.0000)	►9	0.9270	
10. Allocated Connecticut Income Tax (Multiply Line 9 by Line 8)	►10	400	67
11. Credit for Income Tax paid to other jurisdictions by Part-Year residents only (From Schedule 2, Line 52)	►11		
12. Total Income Tax (Subtract Line 11 from Line 10)	►12	400	67
13. Connecticut Tax withheld (Attach State copies of all W-2's and certain 1099's; See Instructions)	►13	520	67
14. All 1992 estimated payments	►14		
15. Payments made with extension request	►15		
16. Total payments (Add Lines 13 through 15)	►16	520	67

Refund or Amount You Owe

17. If Line 16 is greater than Line 12, enter amount overpaid. (Subtract Line 12 from Line 16)	►17	120	00
18. Amount of Line 17 you want to be applied to your 1993 estimated tax	►18		
19. Amount of Line 17 you want to be refunded to you (Subtract Line 18 from Line 17) (See mailing instructions below) **REFUND** ►	19	120	00
20. If Line 12 is greater than Line 16, enter the amount of tax you owe. (Subtract Line 16 from Line 12)	►20		
21. If late: Enter Penalty (10% × amount on line 20 OR if Line 20 is zero, enter $50)	►21		
22. If late: Enter Interest (1¼% × number of months late, or fraction thereof × amount on Line 20)	►22		
23. Penalty for Underpayment of Estimated Tax (From Form CT-2210)	►23		
24. Interest for Underpayment of Estimated Tax (From Form CT-2210)	►24		
25. Balance due with this return (Add Lines 20 through 24) **BALANCE DUE** ►	25		

DUE DATE: April 15, 1992

Make check payable to: COMMISSIONER OF REVENUE SERVICES
Write your Social Security Number(s) and "1992 Form CT-1040 NR/PY" on your check.
Attach a copy of all applicable schedules and forms to this return.
Mail in the envelope provided to you with this return or to the address shown at right.

For **REFUNDS**, Mail to:
Department of Revenue Services
P.O. Box 2968
Hartford, CT 06104-2968

For **PAYMENTS** and **NO TAX DUE**, Mail to:
Department of Revenue Services
P.O. Box 2969
Hartford, CT 06104-2969

(CLIP CHECK HERE (DO NOT STAPLE))
(STAPLE W-2's HERE)

TAXPAYERS MUST SIGN DECLARATION ON PAGE 2

Page 1

CT-49

SCHEDULE 1 — MODIFICATIONS TO FEDERAL ADJUSTED GROSS INCOME (SEE INSTRUCTIONS)

Additions To Federal Adjusted Gross Income - Enter All Amounts as Positive Numbers

26. Interest on state and local obligations other than Connecticut	► 26	100 00
27. Exempt-interest dividends from a mutual fund derived from state and local obligations other than Connecticut	► 27	
28. Shareholder's pro rata share of certain S corporation nonseparately computed loss	► 28	
29. Total taxable amount of lump sum distributions from qualified plans not included in Federal Adjusted Gross Income	► 29	
30. Beneficiary's share of Connecticut fiduciary adjustment (enter only if greater than 0)	► 30	
31. Loss on sale of Connecticut state and local government bonds	► 31	
32. Other - specify: _____	► 32	
33. Total Additions (Add Lines 26 through 32) Enter here and on Line 2 on the front of this form	► 33	100 00

Subtractions From Federal Adjusted Gross Income - Enter All Amounts as Positive Numbers

34. Interest on U.S. government obligations	► 34	500 00
35. Exempt dividends from certain mutual funds derived from U.S. government obligations	► 35	300 00
36. Reimbursed moving expenses deducted on federal Form 1040, Schedule A	► 36	
37. Refunds of state and local income taxes	► 37	
38. Tier 1 Railroad Retirement benefits	► 38	
39. Shareholder's pro rata share of certain S corporation nonseparately computed income	► 39	1,000 00
40. Beneficiary's share of Connecticut fiduciary adjustment (enter only if less than 0)	► 40	
41. Gain on sale of Connecticut state and local government bonds	► 41	
42. Other — specify: _____	► 42	
43. Total Subtractions (Add Lines 34 through 42) Enter here and on Line 4 on the front of this form	► 43	1,800 00

SCHEDULE 2 — CREDIT FOR INCOME TAXES PAID TO OTHER JURISDICTIONS (FOR PART-YEAR RESIDENTS ONLY)

NOTE: Attach copy of return filed with other jurisdiction(s).

44. Connecticut AGI during the residency portion of the taxable year only (See Instructions) | 44 | |

FOR EACH COLUMN, ENTER THE FOLLOWING:

		COLUMN A		COLUMN B	
		Name	Code	Name	Code
45. Enter other jurisdiction's name and two-letter code. (See chart below)	45	►		►	
46. Non-Connecticut income included on Line 44 and reported on another jurisdiction's income tax return (Attach copy)	46				
47. Divide Line 46 by Line 44 (May not exceed 1.00)	47				
48. Apportioned Income Tax (See Instructions)	48				
49. Multiply Line 48 × Line 47	49				
50. Income tax paid to another jurisdiction	50	►		►	
51. Enter the lesser of Line 49 or Line 50	51				
52. TOTAL CREDIT (Add Line 51, all columns) Enter this amount here and on Line 11		52			

If you claim credit for income taxes paid to a political subdivision of a state or Canadian province, enter the two-letter code of the state or Canadian province, respectively.

STANDARD TWO-LETTER CODES

Alabama	AL	Louisiana	LA	Ohio	OH
Arizona	AZ	Maine	ME	Oklahoma	OK
Arkansas	AR	Maryland	MD	Oregon	OR
California	CA	Massachusetts	MA	Pennsylvania	PA
Colorado	CO	Michigan	MI	Rhode Island	RI
Delaware	DE	Minnesota	MN	South Carolina	SC
District of Columbia	DC	Mississippi	MS	Tennessee	TN
Georgia	GA	Missouri	MO	Utah	UT
Hawaii	HI	Montana	MT	Vermont	VT
Idaho	ID	Nebraska	NE	Virginia	VA
Illinois	IL	New Jersey	NJ	West Virginia	WV
Indiana	IN	New Mexico	NM	Wisconsin	WI
Iowa	IA	New York	NY	Any Canadian Province	OO
Kansas	KS	North Carolina	NC		
Kentucky	KY	North Dakota	ND		

DECLARATION: I declare under the penalties of false statement that I have examined this return (including any accompanying schedules and statements) and to the best of my knowledge and belief, it is true, complete and correct. Declaration of preparer (other than the taxpayer) is based on all information of which preparer has any knowledge.

Sign Here

Your Signature *Katherine Hall*	Date 4/14/93	Spouse's Signature (If a joint return)	Date
Paid Preparer's Signature ►		Date ►	Federal Employer I.D. Number
Firm Name and Address ►			CT Sales Tax Registration Number

Keep a copy of this return for your records

Was a fee charged either for the preparation of this return or for advice in the preparation of this return? ☐ YES ☒ NO

CT-1040NR/PY (BACK) Rev. 11/92

CT-50

Schedule CT-SI

NONRESIDENT OR PART-YEAR RESIDENT
SCHEDULE OF INCOME FROM CONNECTICUT SOURCES

1992

USE THIS SCHEDULE IF YOU WERE A NONRESIDENT OR PART-YEAR RESIDENT OF CONNECTICUT IN 1992.
ATTACH TO FORM CT-1040 NR/PY.

Your first name and middle initial	Last Name	Your Social Security Number
KATHERINE	HALL	100 10 1000
If a joint return, spouse's first name and middle initial	Last Name	Spouse's Social Security Number

IMPORTANT: SEE INSTRUCTIONS BEFORE COMPLETING THIS SCHEDULE

PART I — CONNECTICUT INCOME — Part-Year Residents: Enter all of your income earned while you were a Connecticut resident and your income received from Connecticut sources while you were a nonresident. (Use *Part-Year Resident Income Allocation Worksheet - CT-1040AW*).
Nonresidents: Enter income received from Connecticut sources.

1.	Wages, salaries, tips, etc.	1	21,600
2.	Taxable interest income	2	
3.	Dividend income	3	
4.	Alimony received	4	
5.	Business income or (loss) *(from federal Schedule C)*	5	
6.	Capital gain or (loss) *(from federal Schedule D)*	6	
7.	Capital gain distributions not reported on Line 6	7	
8.	Other gains or (losses) *(from federal Form 4797)*	8	
9.	Taxable amount of IRA distributions	9	
10.	Taxable amount of pensions and annuities	10	
11.	Rents, royalties, partnerships, estates, trusts, etc. *(from federal Schedule E)*	11	
12.	Farm income or (loss) *(from federal Schedule F)*	12	
13.	Unemployment compensation (insurance)	13	
14.	Taxable amount of social security benefits	14	
15.	Other income *(including Lump Sum Distributions)*	15	
16.	Gross Income from Connecticut sources. (Add Lines 1 through 15)	16	21,600

PART 2 — ADJUSTMENTS TO CONNECTICUT INCOME — Enter adjustments that are directly related to income reported above.

17.	IRA deduction: You $_____ Spouse $_____	17	
18.	Deduction for self-employment tax	18	
19.	Self-employed health insurance deduction	19	
20.	Keogh retirement plan and self-employed SEP deduction	20	
21.	Penalty on early withdrawal of savings	21	
22.	Alimony paid. Recipient's last name: _____ & Social Security # ____-__-____	22	
23.	Total adjustments - Add Lines 17 through 22	23	
24.	**Income from Connecticut sources.** Subtract Line 23 from Line 16. Enter the amount here and on Form CT-1040 NR/PY, Page 1, Line 6	24	21,600

PART 3 — Check the appropriate boxes below and enter the appropriate information that applies to you and your spouse.

Part-year residents: If you were a Connecticut resident for only part of the year, check the box which describes your situation on the last day of the taxable year:

(1) moved into Connecticut: date / / .... ☐

(2) moved out of Connecticut and received income from Connecticut sources during your nonresident period .... ☐

(3) moved out of Connecticut and received no income from Connecticut sources during your nonresident period .... ☐

For (2) or (3), enter date of move: / /

ATTACH THIS SCHEDULE TO FORM CT-1040 NR/PY

CT-51

TAX CALCULATION SCHEDULE

1. Enter CONNECTICUT AGI (From CT-1040, Line 5; CT-1040EZ, Line 1 or CT-1040NR/PY, Line 7)	1	23,300	
2. Personal Exemption (From Table A - Exemptions)	2	12,000	
3. Connecticut Taxable Income (Subtract Line 2 from Line 1 - If less than 0, enter 0)	3	11,300	
4. Connecticut Income Tax - (Line 3 × .045)	4	508	50
5. Enter Credit % from Table B - Personal Tax Credits (0.75, 0.35, 0.15, 0.10)	5	.	15
6. Multiply the amount on Line 4 by the percentage on Line 5	6	76	28
7. INCOME TAX (Subtract Line 6 from Line 4) Enter this amount on CT-1040, Line 6; CT-1040EZ, Line 2 or CT-1040NR/PY, Line 8	7	432	22

TABLE A - EXEMPTIONS

Use your filing status shown on the front of your tax return and your CONNECTICUT AGI (From Line 1 above) to determine your exemption.

Single/Married Filing Separately			Head of Household			Married Filing Jointly/Qualifying Widow(er)		
CONNECTICUT AGI		EXEMPTION	CONNECTICUT AGI		EXEMPTION	CONNECTICUT AGI		EXEMPTION
MORE THAN	LESS THAN OR EQUAL TO		MORE THAN	LESS THAN OR EQUAL TO		MORE THAN	LESS THAN OR EQUAL TO	
$ 0	$24,000	$12,000	$ 0	$38,000	$19,000	$ 0	$48,000	$24,000
$24,000	$25,000	$11,000	$38,000	$39,000	$18,000	$48,000	$49,000	$23,000
$25,000	$26,000	$10,000	$39,000	$40,000	$17,000	$49,000	$50,000	$22,000
$26,000	$27,000	$ 9,000	$40,000	$41,000	$16,000	$50,000	$51,000	$21,000
$27,000	$28,000	$ 8,000	$41,000	$42,000	$15,000	$51,000	$52,000	$20,000
$28,000	$29,000	$ 7,000	$42,000	$43,000	$14,000	$52,000	$53,000	$19,000
$29,000	$30,000	$ 6,000	$43,000	$44,000	$13,000	$53,000	$54,000	$18,000
$30,000	$31,000	$ 5,000	$44,000	$45,000	$12,000	$54,000	$55,000	$17,000
$31,000	$32,000	$ 4,000	$45,000	$46,000	$11,000	$55,000	$56,000	$16,000
$32,000	$33,000	$ 3,000	$46,000	$47,000	$10,000	$56,000	$57,000	$15,000
$33,000	$34,000	$ 2,000	$47,000	$48,000	$ 9,000	$57,000	$58,000	$14,000
$34,000	$35,000	$ 1,000	$48,000	$49,000	$ 8,000	$58,000	$59,000	$13,000
$35,000	and up	$ 0	$49,000	$50,000	$ 7,000	$59,000	$60,000	$12,000
			$50,000	$51,000	$ 6,000	$60,000	$61,000	$11,000
			$51,000	$52,000	$ 5,000	$61,000	$62,000	$10,000
			$52,000	$53,000	$ 4,000	$62,000	$63,000	$ 9,000
			$53,000	$54,000	$ 3,000	$63,000	$64,000	$ 8,000
			$54,000	$55,000	$ 2,000	$64,000	$65,000	$ 7,000
			$55,000	$56,000	$ 1,000	$65,000	$66,000	$ 6,000
			$56,000	and up	$ 0	$66,000	$67,000	$ 5,000
						$67,000	$68,000	$ 4,000
						$68,000	$69,000	$ 3,000
						$69,000	$70,000	$ 2,000
						$70,000	$71,000	$ 1,000
						$71,000	and up	$ 0

TABLE B - PERSONAL TAX CREDITS

Use your filing status shown on the front of this return and your CONNECTICUT AGI (From Line 1 above) to determine your credit %. Enter this percentage on Line 5.

Single/Married Filing Separately			Head of Household			Married Filing Jointly/Qualifying Widow(er)		
CONNECTICUT AGI		CREDIT %	CONNECTICUT AGI		CREDIT %	CONNECTICUT AGI		CREDIT %
MORE THAN	LESS THAN OR EQUAL TO		MORE THAN	LESS THAN OR EQUAL TO		MORE THAN	LESS THAN OR EQUAL TO	
$12,000	$15,000	75%	$19,000	$24,000	75%	$24,000	$30,000	75%
$15,000	$20,000	35%	$24,000	$34,000	35%	$30,000	$40,000	35%
$20,000	$25,000	15%	$34,000	$44,000	15%	$40,000	$50,000	15%
$25,000	$48,000	10%	$44,000	$74,000	10%	$50,000	$96,000	10%
$48,000	and up	0%	$74,000	and up	0	$96,000	and up	0

KEEP THIS WORKSHEET FOR YOUR RECORDS

DO NOT ATTACH TO YOUR TAX RETURN

Form CT-1040TCS
Rev. 10/92

10 | Connecticut Tax Table (1992)

This chapter includes the official 1992 Connecticut Tax Table. This tax table is used to determine tax on *adjusted gross income* of up to $96,000. For an example of how to use the tax tables, see Chapter 4, *How to Figure Your Tax.*

If CT AGI is -		And you are -			If CT AGI is -		And you are -		
more than	less than or equal to	Single or Married Filing Separately	Head of Household	Married Filing Jointly *	more than	less than or equal to	Single or Married Filing Separately	Head of Household	Married Filing Jointly *
12,000					**15,000**				
12,000	12,050	0.28	0.00	0.00	15,000	15,050	88.48	0.00	0.00
12,050	12,100	0.84	0.00	0.00	15,050	15,100	89.94	0.00	0.00
12,100	12,150	1.41	0.00	0.00	15,100	15,150	91.41	0.00	0.00
12,150	12,200	1.97	0.00	0.00	15,150	15,200	92.87	0.00	0.00
12,200	12,250	2.53	0.00	0.00	15,200	15,250	94.33	0.00	0.00
12,250	12,300	3.09	0.00	0.00	15,250	15,300	95.79	0.00	0.00
12,300	12,350	3.66	0.00	0.00	15,300	15,350	97.26	0.00	0.00
12,350	12,400	4.22	0.00	0.00	15,350	15,400	98.72	0.00	0.00
12,400	12,450	4.78	0.00	0.00	15,400	15,450	100.18	0.00	0.00
12,450	12,500	5.34	0.00	0.00	15,450	15,500	101.64	0.00	0.00
12,500	12,550	5.91	0.00	0.00	15,500	15,550	103.11	0.00	0.00
12,550	12,600	6.47	0.00	0.00	15,550	15,600	104.57	0.00	0.00
12,600	12,650	7.03	0.00	0.00	15,600	15,650	106.03	0.00	0.00
12,650	12,700	7.59	0.00	0.00	15,650	15,700	107.49	0.00	0.00
12,700	12,750	8.16	0.00	0.00	15,700	15,750	108.96	0.00	0.00
12,750	12,800	8.72	0.00	0.00	15,750	15,800	110.42	0.00	0.00
12,800	12,850	9.28	0.00	0.00	15,800	15,850	111.88	0.00	0.00
12,850	12,900	9.84	0.00	0.00	15,850	15,900	113.34	0.00	0.00
12,900	12,950	10.41	0.00	0.00	15,900	15,950	114.81	0.00	0.00
12,950	13,000	10.97	0.00	0.00	15,950	16,000	116.27	0.00	0.00
13,000					**16,000**				
13,000	13,050	11.53	0.00	0.00	16,000	16,050	117.73	0.00	0.00
13,050	13,100	12.09	0.00	0.00	16,050	16,100	119.19	0.00	0.00
13,100	13,150	12.66	0.00	0.00	16,100	16,150	120.66	0.00	0.00
13,150	13,200	13.22	0.00	0.00	16,150	16,200	122.12	0.00	0.00
13,200	13,250	13.78	0.00	0.00	16,200	16,250	123.58	0.00	0.00
13,250	13,300	14.34	0.00	0.00	16,250	16,300	125.04	0.00	0.00
13,300	13,350	14.91	0.00	0.00	16,300	16,350	126.51	0.00	0.00
13,350	13,400	15.47	0.00	0.00	16,350	16,400	127.97	0.00	0.00
13,400	13,450	16.03	0.00	0.00	16,400	16,450	129.43	0.00	0.00
13,450	13,500	16.59	0.00	0.00	16,450	16,500	130.89	0.00	0.00
13,500	13,550	17.16	0.00	0.00	16,500	16,550	132.36	0.00	0.00
13,550	13,600	17.72	0.00	0.00	16,550	16,600	133.82	0.00	0.00
13,600	13,650	18.28	0.00	0.00	16,600	16,650	135.28	0.00	0.00
13,650	13,700	18.84	0.00	0.00	16,650	16,700	136.74	0.00	0.00
13,700	13,750	19.41	0.00	0.00	16,700	16,750	138.21	0.00	0.00
13,750	13,800	19.97	0.00	0.00	16,750	16,800	139.67	0.00	0.00
13,800	13,850	20.53	0.00	0.00	16,800	16,850	141.13	0.00	0.00
13,850	13,900	21.09	0.00	0.00	16,850	16,900	142.59	0.00	0.00
13,900	13,950	21.66	0.00	0.00	16,900	16,950	144.06	0.00	0.00
13,950	14,000	22.22	0.00	0.00	16,950	17,000	145.52	0.00	0.00
14,000					**17,000**				
14,000	14,050	22.78	0.00	0.00	17,000	17,050	146.98	0.00	0.00
14,050	14,100	23.34	0.00	0.00	17,050	17,100	148.44	0.00	0.00
14,100	14,150	23.91	0.00	0.00	17,100	17,150	149.91	0.00	0.00
14,150	14,200	24.47	0.00	0.00	17,150	17,200	151.37	0.00	0.00
14,200	14,250	25.03	0.00	0.00	17,200	17,250	152.83	0.00	0.00
14,250	14,300	25.59	0.00	0.00	17,250	17,300	154.29	0.00	0.00
14,300	14,350	26.16	0.00	0.00	17,300	17,350	155.76	0.00	0.00
14,350	14,400	26.72	0.00	0.00	17,350	17,400	157.22	0.00	0.00
14,400	14,450	27.28	0.00	0.00	17,400	17,450	158.68	0.00	0.00
14,450	14,500	27.84	0.00	0.00	17,450	17,500	160.14	0.00	0.00
14,500	14,550	28.41	0.00	0.00	17,500	17,550	161.61	0.00	0.00
14,550	14,600	28.97	0.00	0.00	17,550	17,600	163.07	0.00	0.00
14,600	14,650	29.53	0.00	0.00	17,600	17,650	164.53	0.00	0.00
14,650	14,700	30.09	0.00	0.00	17,650	17,700	165.99	0.00	0.00
14,700	14,750	30.66	0.00	0.00	17,700	17,750	167.46	0.00	0.00
14,750	14,800	31.22	0.00	0.00	17,750	17,800	168.92	0.00	0.00
14,800	14,850	31.78	0.00	0.00	17,800	17,850	170.38	0.00	0.00
14,850	14,900	32.34	0.00	0.00	17,850	17,900	171.84	0.00	0.00
14,900	14,950	32.91	0.00	0.00	17,900	17,950	173.31	0.00	0.00
14,950	15,000	33.47	0.00	0.00	17,950	18,000	174.77	0.00	0.00

* This column must also be used by a qualifying widow(er)

Continued on next page

If CT AGI is more than	less than or equal to	Single or Married Filing Separately	Head of Household	Married Filing Jointly *
18,000				
18,000	18,050	176.23	0.00	0.00
18,050	18,100	177.69	0.00	0.00
18,100	18,150	179.16	0.00	0.00
18,150	18,200	180.62	0.00	0.00
18,200	18,250	182.08	0.00	0.00
18,250	18,300	183.54	0.00	0.00
18,300	18,350	185.01	0.00	0.00
18,350	18,400	186.47	0.00	0.00
18,400	18,450	187.93	0.00	0.00
18,450	18,500	189.39	0.00	0.00
18,500	18,550	190.86	0.00	0.00
18,550	18,600	192.32	0.00	0.00
18,600	18,650	193.78	0.00	0.00
18,650	18,700	195.24	0.00	0.00
18,700	18,750	196.71	0.00	0.00
18,750	18,800	198.17	0.00	0.00
18,800	18,850	199.63	0.00	0.00
18,850	18,900	201.09	0.00	0.00
18,900	18,950	202.56	0.00	0.00
18,950	19,000	204.02	0.00	0.00
19,000				
19,000	19,050	205.48	0.28	0.00
19,050	19,100	206.94	0.84	0.00
19,100	19,150	208.41	1.41	0.00
19,150	19,200	209.87	1.97	0.00
19,200	19,250	211.33	2.53	0.00
19,250	19,300	212.79	3.09	0.00
19,300	19,350	214.26	3.66	0.00
19,350	19,400	215.72	4.22	0.00
19,400	19,450	217.18	4.78	0.00
19,450	19,500	218.64	5.34	0.00
19,500	19,550	220.11	5.91	0.00
19,550	19,600	221.57	6.47	0.00
19,600	19,650	223.03	7.03	0.00
19,650	19,700	224.49	7.59	0.00
19,700	19,750	225.96	8.16	0.00
19,750	19,800	227.42	8.72	0.00
19,800	19,850	228.88	9.28	0.00
19,850	19,900	230.34	9.84	0.00
19,900	19,950	231.81	10.41	0.00
19,950	20,000	233.27	10.97	0.00
20,000				
20,000	20,050	306.96	11.53	0.00
20,050	20,100	308.87	12.09	0.00
20,100	20,150	310.78	12.66	0.00
20,150	20,200	312.69	13.22	0.00
20,200	20,250	314.61	13.78	0.00
20,250	20,300	316.52	14.34	0.00
20,300	20,350	318.43	14.91	0.00
20,350	20,400	320.34	15.47	0.00
20,400	20,450	322.26	16.03	0.00
20,450	20,500	324.17	16.59	0.00
20,500	20,550	326.08	17.16	0.00
20,550	20,600	327.99	17.72	0.00
20,600	20,650	329.91	18.28	0.00
20,650	20,700	331.82	18.84	0.00
20,700	20,750	333.73	19.41	0.00
20,750	20,800	335.64	19.97	0.00
20,800	20,850	337.56	20.53	0.00
20,850	20,900	339.47	21.09	0.00
20,900	20,950	341.38	21.66	0.00
20,950	21,000	343.29	22.22	0.00

If CT AGI is more than	less than or equal to	Single or Married Filing Separately	Head of Household	Married Filing Jointly *
21,000				
21,000	21,050	345.21	22.78	0.00
21,050	21,100	347.12	23.34	0.00
21,100	21,150	349.03	23.91	0.00
21,150	21,200	350.94	24.47	0.00
21,200	21,250	352.86	25.03	0.00
21,250	21,300	354.77	25.59	0.00
21,300	21,350	356.68	26.16	0.00
21,350	21,400	358.59	26.72	0.00
21,400	21,450	360.51	27.28	0.00
21,450	21,500	362.42	27.84	0.00
21,500	21,550	364.33	28.41	0.00
21,550	21,600	366.24	28.97	0.00
21,600	21,650	368.16	29.53	0.00
21,650	21,700	370.07	30.09	0.00
21,700	21,750	371.98	30.66	0.00
21,750	21,800	373.89	31.22	0.00
21,800	21,850	375.81	31.78	0.00
21,850	21,900	377.72	32.34	0.00
21,900	21,950	379.63	32.91	0.00
21,950	22,000	381.54	33.47	0.00
22,000				
22,000	22,050	383.46	34.03	0.00
22,050	22,100	385.37	34.59	0.00
22,100	22,150	387.28	35.16	0.00
22,150	22,200	389.19	35.72	0.00
22,200	22,250	391.11	36.28	0.00
22,250	22,300	393.02	36.84	0.00
22,300	22,350	394.93	37.41	0.00
22,350	22,400	396.84	37.97	0.00
22,400	22,450	398.76	38.53	0.00
22,450	22,500	400.67	39.09	0.00
22,500	22,550	402.58	39.66	0.00
22,550	22,600	404.49	40.22	0.00
22,600	22,650	406.41	40.78	0.00
22,650	22,700	408.32	41.34	0.00
22,700	22,750	410.23	41.91	0.00
22,750	22,800	412.14	42.47	0.00
22,800	22,850	414.06	43.03	0.00
22,850	22,900	415.97	43.59	0.00
22,900	22,950	417.88	44.16	0.00
22,950	23,000	419.79	44.72	0.00
23,000				
23,000	23,050	421.71	45.28	0.00
23,050	23,100	423.62	45.84	0.00
23,100	23,150	425.53	46.41	0.00
23,150	23,200	427.44	46.97	0.00
23,200	23,250	429.36	47.53	0.00
23,250	23,300	431.27	48.09	0.00
23,300	23,350	433.18	48.66	0.00
23,350	23,400	435.09	49.22	0.00
23,400	23,450	437.01	49.78	0.00
23,450	23,500	438.92	50.34	0.00
23,500	23,550	440.83	50.91	0.00
23,550	23,600	442.74	51.47	0.00
23,600	23,650	444.66	52.03	0.00
23,650	23,700	446.57	52.59	0.00
23,700	23,750	448.48	53.16	0.00
23,750	23,800	450.39	53.72	0.00
23,800	23,850	452.31	54.28	0.00
23,850	23,900	454.22	54.84	0.00
23,900	23,950	456.13	55.41	0.00
23,950	24,000	458.04	55.97	0.00

* This column must also be used by a qualifying widow(er)

Continued on next page

If CT AGI is - more than	less than or equal to	Single or Married Filing Separately	Head of Household	Married Filing Jointly *
24,000				
24,000	24,050	498.21	146.98	0.28
24,050	24,100	500.12	148.44	0.84
24,100	24,150	502.03	149.91	1.41
24,150	24,200	503.94	151.37	1.97
24,200	24,250	505.86	152.83	2.53
24,250	24,300	507.77	154.29	3.09
24,300	24,350	509.68	155.76	3.66
24,350	24,400	511.59	157.22	4.22
24,400	24,450	513.5i	158.68	4.78
24,450	24,500	515.42	160.14	5.34
24,500	24,550	517.33	161.61	5.91
24,550	24,600	519.24	163.07	6.47
24,600	24,650	521.16	164.53	7.03
24,650	24,700	523.07	165.99	7.59
24,700	24,750	524.98	167.46	8.16
24,750	24,800	526.89	168.92	8.72
24,800	24,850	528.81	170.38	9.28
24,850	24,900	530.72	171.84	9.84
24,900	24,950	532.63	173.31	10.41
24,950	25,000	534.54	174.77	10.97
25,000				
25,000	25,050	608.51	176.23	11.53
25,050	25,100	610.54	177.69	12.09
25,100	25,150	612.56	179.16	12.66
25,150	25,200	614.59	180.62	13.22
25,200	25,250	616.61	182.08	13.78
25,250	25,300	618.64	183.54	14.34
25,300	25,350	620.66	185.01	14.91
25,350	25,400	622.69	186.47	15.47
25,400	25,450	624.71	187.93	16.03
25,450	25,500	626.74	189.39	16.59
25,500	25,550	628.76	190.86	17.16
25,550	25,600	630.79	192.32	17.72
25,600	25,650	632.81	193.78	18.28
25,650	25,700	634.84	195.24	18.84
25,700	25,750	636.86	196.71	19.41
25,750	25,800	638.89	198.17	19.97
25,800	25,850	640.91	199.63	20.53
25,850	25,900	642.94	201.09	21.09
25,900	25,950	644.96	202.56	21.66
25,950	26,000	646.99	204.02	22.22
26,000				
26,000	26,050	689.51	205.48	22.78
26,050	26,100	691.54	206.94	23.34
26,100	26,150	693.56	208.41	23.91
26,150	26,200	695.59	209.87	24.47
26,200	26,250	697.61	211.33	25.03
26,250	26,300	699.64	212.79	25.59
26,300	26,350	701.66	214.26	26.16
26,350	26,400	703.69	215.72	26.72
26,400	26,450	705.71	217.18	27.28
26,450	26,500	707.74	218.64	27.84
26,500	26,550	709.76	220.11	28.41
26,550	26,600	711.79	221.57	28.97
26,600	26,650	713.81	223.03	29.53
26,650	26,700	715.84	224.49	30.09
26,700	26,750	717.86	225.96	30.66
26,750	26,800	719.89	227.42	31.22
26,800	26,850	721.91	228.88	31.78
26,850	26,900	723.94	230.34	32.34
26,900	26,950	725.96	231.81	32.91
26,950	27,000	727.99	233.27	33.47

If CT AGI is - more than	less than or equal to	Single or Married Filing Separately	Head of Household	Married Filing Jointly *
27,000				
27,000	27,050	770.51	234.73	34.03
27,050	27,100	772.54	236.19	34.59
27,100	27,150	774.56	237.66	35.16
27,150	27,200	776.59	239.12	35.72
27,200	27,250	778.61	240.58	36.28
27,250	27,300	780.64	242.04	36.84
27,300	27,350	782.66	243.51	37.41
27,350	27,400	784.69	244.97	37.97
27,400	27,450	786.71	246.43	38.53
27,450	27,500	788.74	247.89	39.09
27,500	27,550	790.76	249.36	39.66
27,550	27,600	792.79	250.82	40.22
27,600	27,650	794.81	252.28	40.78
27,650	27,700	796.84	253.74	41.34
27,700	27,750	798.86	255.21	41.91
27,750	27,800	800.89	256.67	42.47
27,800	27,850	802.91	258.13	43.03
27,850	27,900	804.94	259.59	43.59
27,900	27,950	806.96	261.06	44.16
27,950	28,000	808.99	262.52	44.72
28,000				
28,000	28,050	851.51	263.98	45.28
28,050	28,100	853.54	265.44	45.84
28,100	28,150	855.56	266.91	46.41
28,150	28,200	857.59	268.37	46.97
28,200	28,250	859.61	269.83	47.53
28,250	28,300	861.64	271.29	48.09
28,300	28,350	863.66	272.76	48.66
28,350	28,400	865.69	274.22	49.22
28,400	28,450	867.71	275.68	49.78
28,450	28,500	869.74	277.14	50.34
28,500	28,550	871.76	278.61	50.91
28,550	28,600	873.79	280.07	51.47
28,600	28,650	875.81	281.53	52.03
28,650	28,700	877.84	282.99	52.59
28,700	28,750	879.86	284.46	53.16
28,750	28,800	881.89	285.92	53.72
28,800	28,850	883.91	287.38	54.28
28,850	28,900	885.94	288.84	54.84
28,900	28,950	887.96	290.31	55.41
28,950	29,000	889.99	291.77	55.97
29,000				
29,000	29,050	932.51	293.23	56.53
29,050	29,100	934.54	294.69	57.09
29,100	29,150	936.56	296.16	57.66
29,150	29,200	938.59	297.62	58.22
29,200	29,250	940.61	299.08	58.78
29,250	29,300	942.64	300.54	59.34
29,300	29,350	944.66	302.01	59.91
29,350	29,400	946.69	303.47	60.47
29,400	29,450	948.71	304.93	61.03
29,450	29,500	950.74	306.39	61.59
29,500	29,550	952.76	307.86	62.16
29,550	29,600	954.79	309.32	62.72
29,600	29,650	956.81	310.78	63.28
29,650	29,700	958.84	312.24	63.84
29,700	29,750	960.86	313.71	64.41
29,750	29,800	962.89	315.17	64.97
29,800	29,850	964.91	316.63	65.53
29,850	29,900	966.94	318.09	66.09
29,900	29,950	968.96	319.56	66.66
29,950	30,000	970.99	321.02	67.22

* This column must also be used by a qualifying widow(er)

Continued on next page

If CT AGI is - more than	less than or equal to	Single or Married Filing Separately	Head of Household	Married Filing Jointly *
30,000				
30,000	30,050	1,013.51	322.48	176.23
30,050	30,100	1,015.54	323.94	177.69
30,100	30,150	1,017.56	325.41	179.16
30,150	30,200	1,019.59	326.87	180.62
30,200	30,250	1,021.61	328.33	182.08
30,250	30,300	1,023.64	329.79	183.54
30,300	30,350	1,025.66	331.26	185.01
30,350	30,400	1,027.69	332.72	186.47
30,400	30,450	1,029.71	334.18	187.93
30,450	30,500	1,031.74	335.64	189.39
30,500	30,550	1,033.76	337.11	190.86
30,550	30,600	1,035.79	338.57	192.32
30,600	30,650	1,037.81	340.03	193.78
30,650	30,700	1,039.84	341.49	195.24
30,700	30,750	1,041.86	342.96	196.71
30,750	30,800	1,043.89	344.42	198.17
30,800	30,850	1,045.91	345.88	199.63
30,850	30,900	1,047.94	347.34	201.09
30,900	30,950	1,049.96	348.81	202.56
30,950	31,000	1,051.99	350.27	204.02
31,000				
31,000	31,050	1,094.51	351.73	205.48
31,050	31,100	1,096.54	353.19	206.94
31,100	31,150	1,098.56	354.66	208.41
31,150	31,200	1,100.59	356.12	209.87
31,200	31,250	1,102.61	357.58	211.33
31,250	31,300	1,104.64	359.04	212.79
31,300	31,350	1,106.66	360.51	214.26
31,350	31,400	1,108.69	361.97	215.72
31,400	31,450	1,110.71	363.43	217.18
31,450	31,500	1,112.74	364.89	218.64
31,500	31,550	1,114.76	366.36	220.11
31,550	31,600	1,116.79	367.82	221.57
31,600	31,650	1,118.81	369.28	223.03
31,650	31,700	1,120.84	370.74	224.49
31,700	31,750	1,122.86	372.21	225.96
31,750	31,800	1,124.89	373.67	227.42
31,800	31,850	1,126.91	375.13	228.88
31,850	31,900	1,128.94	376.59	230.34
31,900	31,950	1,130.96	378.06	231.81
31,950	32,000	1,132.99	379.52	233.27
32,000				
32,000	32,050	1,175.51	380.98	234.73
32,050	32,100	1,177.54	382.44	236.19
32,100	32,150	1,179.56	383.91	237.66
32,150	32,200	1,181.59	385.37	239.12
32,200	32,250	1,183.61	386.83	240.58
32,250	32,300	1,185.64	388.29	242.04
32,300	32,350	1,187.66	389.76	243.51
32,350	32,400	1,189.69	391.22	244.97
32,400	32,450	1,191.71	392.68	246.43
32,450	32,500	1,193.74	394.14	247.89
32,500	32,550	1,195.76	395.61	249.36
32,550	32,600	1,197.79	397.07	250.82
32,600	32,650	1,199.81	398.53	252.28
32,650	32,700	1,201.84	399.99	253.74
32,700	32,750	1,203.86	401.46	255.21
32,750	32,800	1,205.89	402.92	256.67
32,800	32,850	1,207.91	404.38	258.13
32,850	32,900	1,209.94	405.84	259.59
32,900	32,950	1,211.96	407.31	261.06
32,950	33,000	1,213.99	408.77	262.52

If CT AGI is - more than	less than or equal to	Single or Married Filing Separately	Head of Household	Married Filing Jointly *
33,000				
33,000	33,050	1,256.51	410.23	263.98
33,050	33,100	1,258.54	411.69	265.44
33,100	33,150	1,260.56	413.16	266.91
33,150	33,200	1,262.59	414.62	268.37
33,200	33,250	1,264.61	416.08	269.83
33,250	33,300	1,266.64	417.54	271.29
33,300	33,350	1,268.66	419.01	272.76
33,350	33,400	1,270.69	420.47	274.22
33,400	33,450	1,272.71	421.93	275.68
33,450	33,500	1,274.74	423.39	277.14
33,500	33,550	1,276.76	424.86	278.61
33,550	33,600	1,278.79	426.32	280.07
33,600	33,650	1,280.81	427.78	281.53
33,650	33,700	1,282.84	429.24	282.99
33,700	33,750	1,284.86	430.71	284.46
33,750	33,800	1,286.89	432.17	285.92
33,800	33,850	1,288.91	433.63	287.38
33,850	33,900	1,290.94	435.09	288.84
33,900	33,950	1,292.96	436.56	290.31
33,950	34,000	1,294.99	438.02	291.77
34,000				
34,000	34,050	1,337.51	574.71	293.23
34,050	34,100	1,339.54	576.62	294.69
34,100	34,150	1,341.56	578.53	296.16
34,150	34,200	1,343.59	580.44	297.62
34,200	34,250	1,345.61	582.36	299.08
34,250	34,300	1,347.64	584.27	300.54
34,300	34,350	1,349.66	586.18	302.01
34,350	34,400	1,351.69	588.09	303.47
34,400	34,450	1,353.71	590.01	304.93
34,450	34,500	1,355.74	591.92	306.39
34,500	34,550	1,357.76	593.83	307.86
34,550	34,600	1,359.79	595.74	309.32
34,600	34,650	1,361.81	597.66	310.78
34,650	34,700	1,363.84	599.57	312.24
34,700	34,750	1,365.86	601.48	313.71
34,750	34,800	1,367.89	603.39	315.17
34,800	34,850	1,369.91	605.31	316.63
34,850	34,900	1,371.94	607.22	318.09
34,900	34,950	1,373.96	609.13	319.56
34,950	35,000	1,375.99	611.04	321.02
35,000				
35,000	35,050	1,418.51	612.96	322.48
35,050	35,100	1,420.54	614.87	323.94
35,100	35,150	1,422.56	616.78	325.41
35,150	35,200	1,424.59	618.69	326.87
35,200	35,250	1,426.61	620.61	328.33
35,250	35,300	1,428.64	622.52	329.79
35,300	35,350	1,430.66	624.43	331.26
35,350	35,400	1,432.69	626.34	332.72
35,400	35,450	1,434.71	628.26	334.18
35,450	35,500	1,436.74	630.17	335.64
35,500	35,550	1,438.76	632.08	337.11
35,550	35,600	1,440.79	633.99	338.57
35,600	35,650	1,442.81	635.91	340.03
35,650	35,700	1,444.84	637.82	341.49
35,700	35,750	1,446.86	639.73	342.96
35,750	35,800	1,448.89	641.64	344.42
35,800	35,850	1,450.91	643.56	345.88
35,850	35,900	1,452.94	645.47	347.34
35,900	35,950	1,454.96	647.38	348.81
35,950	36,000	1,456.99	649.29	350.27

* This column must also be used by a qualifying widow(er)

Continued on next page

ALL EXEMPTIONS AND CREDITS ARE INCLUDED

If CT AGI is more than	less than or equal to	Single or Married Filing Separately	Head of Household	Married Filing Jointly *
36,000				
36,000	36,050	1,459.01	651.21	351.73
36,050	36,100	1,461.04	653.12	353.19
36,100	36,150	1,463.06	655.03	354.66
36,150	36,200	1,465.09	656.94	356.12
36,200	36,250	1,467.11	658.86	357.58
36,250	36,300	1,469.14	660.77	359.04
36,300	36,350	1,471.16	662.68	360.51
36,350	36,400	1,473.19	664.59	361.97
36,400	36,450	1,475.21	666.51	363.43
36,450	36,500	1,477.24	668.42	364.89
36,500	36,550	1,479.26	670.33	366.36
36,550	36,600	1,481.29	672.24	367.82
36,600	36,650	1,483.31	674.16	369.28
36,650	36,700	1,485.34	676.07	370.74
36,700	36,750	1,487.36	677.98	372.21
36,750	36,800	1,489.39	679.89	373.67
36,800	36,850	1,491.41	681.81	375.13
36,850	36,900	1,493.44	683.72	376.59
36,900	36,950	1,495.46	685.63	378.06
36,950	37,000	1,497.49	687.54	379.52
37,000				
37,000	37,050	1,499.51	689.46	380.98
37,050	37,100	1,501.54	691.37	382.44
37,100	37,150	1,503.56	693.28	383.91
37,150	37,200	1,505.59	695.19	385.37
37,200	37,250	1,507.61	697.11	386.83
37,250	37,300	1,509.64	699.02	388.29
37,300	37,350	1,511.66	700.93	389.76
37,350	37,400	1,513.69	702.84	391.22
37,400	37,450	1,515.71	704.76	392.68
37,450	37,500	1,517.74	706.67	394.14
37,500	37,550	1,519.76	708.58	395.61
37,550	37,600	1,521.79	710.49	397.07
37,600	37,650	1,523.81	712.41	398.53
37,650	37,700	1,525.84	714.32	399.99
37,700	37,750	1,527.86	716.23	401.46
37,750	37,800	1,529.89	718.14	402.92
37,800	37,850	1,531.91	720.06	404.38
37,850	37,900	1,533.94	721.97	405.84
37,900	37,950	1,535.96	723.88	407.31
37,950	38,000	1,537.99	725.79	408.77
38,000				
38,000	38,050	1,540.01	765.96	410.23
38,050	38,100	1,542.04	767.87	411.69
38,100	38,150	1,544.06	769.78	413.16
38,150	38,200	1,546.09	771.69	414.62
38,200	38,250	1,548.11	773.61	416.08
38,250	38,300	1,550.14	775.52	417.54
38,300	38,350	1,552.16	777.43	419.01
38,350	38,400	1,554.19	779.34	420.47
38,400	38,450	1,556.21	781.26	421.93
38,450	38,500	1,558.24	783.17	423.39
38,500	38,550	1,560.26	785.08	424.86
38,550	38,600	1,562.29	786.99	426.32
38,600	38,650	1,564.31	788.91	427.78
38,650	38,700	1,566.34	790.82	429.24
38,700	38,750	1,568.36	792.73	430.71
38,750	38,800	1,570.39	794.64	432.17
38,800	38,850	1,572.41	796.56	433.63
38,850	38,900	1,574.44	798.47	435.09
38,900	38,950	1,576.46	800.38	436.56
38,950	39,000	1,578.49	802.29	438.02

If CT AGI is more than	less than or equal to	Single or Married Filing Separately	Head of Household	Married Filing Jointly *
39,000				
39,000	39,050	1,580.51	842.46	439.48
39,050	39,100	1,582.54	844.37	440.94
39,100	39,150	1,584.56	846.28	442.41
39,150	39,200	1,586.59	848.19	443.87
39,200	39,250	1,588.61	850.11	445.33
39,250	39,300	1,590.64	852.02	446.79
39,300	39,350	1,592.66	853.93	448.26
39,350	39,400	1,594.69	855.84	449.72
39,400	39,450	1,596.71	857.76	451.18
39,450	39,500	1,598.74	859.67	452.64
39,500	39,550	1,600.76	861.58	454.11
39,550	39,600	1,602.79	863.49	455.57
39,600	39,650	1,604.81	865.41	457.03
39,650	39,700	1,606.84	867.32	458.49
39,700	39,750	1,608.86	869.23	459.96
39,750	39,800	1,610.89	871.14	461.42
39,800	39,850	1,612.91	873.06	462.88
39,850	39,900	1,614.94	874.97	464.34
39,900	39,950	1,616.96	876.88	465.81
39,950	40,000	1,618.99	878.79	467.27
40,000				
40,000	40,050	1,621.01	918.96	612.96
40,050	40,100	1,623.04	920.87	614.87
40,100	40,150	1,625.06	922.78	616.78
40,150	40,200	1,627.09	924.69	618.69
40,200	40,250	1,629.11	926.61	620.61
40,250	40,300	1,631.14	928.52	622.52
40,300	40,350	1,633.16	930.43	624.43
40,350	40,400	1,635.19	932.34	626.34
40,400	40,450	1,637.21	934.26	628.26
40,450	40,500	1,639.24	936.17	630.17
40,500	40,550	1,641.26	938.08	632.08
40,550	40,600	1,643.29	939.99	633.99
40,600	40,650	1,645.31	941.91	635.91
40,650	40,700	1,647.34	943.82	637.82
40,700	40,750	1,649.36	945.73	639.73
40,750	40,800	1,651.39	947.64	641.64
40,800	40,850	1,653.41	949.56	643.56
40,850	40,900	1,655.44	951.47	645.47
40,900	40,950	1,657.46	953.38	647.38
40,950	41,000	1,659.49	955.29	649.29
41,000				
41,000	41,050	1,661.51	995.46	651.21
41,050	41,100	1,663.54	997.37	653.12
41,100	41,150	1,665.56	999.28	655.03
41,150	41,200	1,667.59	1,001.19	656.94
41,200	41,250	1,669.61	1,003.11	658.86
41,250	41,300	1,671.64	1,005.02	660.77
41,300	41,350	1,673.66	1,006.93	662.68
41,350	41,400	1,675.69	1,008.84	664.59
41,400	41,450	1,677.71	1,010.76	666.51
41,450	41,500	1,679.74	1,012.67	668.42
41,500	41,550	1,681.76	1,014.58	670.33
41,550	41,600	1,683.79	1,016.49	672.24
41,600	41,650	1,685.81	1,018.41	674.16
41,650	41,700	1,687.84	1,020.32	676.07
41,700	41,750	1,689.86	1,022.23	677.98
41,750	41,800	1,691.89	1,024.14	679.89
41,800	41,850	1,693.91	1,026.06	681.81
41,850	41,900	1,695.94	1,027.97	683.72
41,900	41,950	1,697.96	1,029.88	685.63
41,950	42,000	1,699.99	1,031.79	687.54

* This column must also be used by a qualifying widow(er)

Continued on next page

If CT AGI is -		And you are -			If CT AGI is -		And you are -		
more than	less than or equal to	Single or Married Filing Separately	Head of Household	Married Filing Jointly *	more than	less than or equal to	Single or Married Filing Separately	Head of Household	Married Filing Jointly *
42,000					**45,000**				
42,000	42,050	1,702.01	1,071.96	689.46	45,000	45,050	1,823.51	1,378.01	804.21
42,050	42,100	1,704.04	1,073.87	691.37	45,050	45,100	1,825.54	1,380.04	806.12
42,100	42,150	1,706.06	1,075.78	693.28	45,100	45,150	1,827.56	1,382.06	808.03
42,150	42,200	1,708.09	1,077.69	695.19	45,150	45,200	1,829.59	1,384.09	809.94
42,200	42,250	1,710.11	1,079.61	697.11	45,200	45,250	1,831.61	1,386.11	811.86
42,250	42,300	1,712.14	1,081.52	699.02	45,250	45,300	1,833.64	1,388.14	813.77
42,300	42,350	1,714.16	1,083.43	700.93	45,300	45,350	1,835.66	1,390.16	815.68
42,350	42,400	1,716.19	1,085.34	702.84	45,350	45,400	1,837.69	1,392.19	817.59
42,400	42,450	1,718.21	1,087.26	704.76	45,400	45,450	1,839.71	1,394.21	819.51
42,450	42,500	1,720.24	1,089.17	706.67	45,450	45,500	1,841.74	1,396.24	821.42
42,500	42,550	1,722.26	1,091.08	708.58	45,500	45,550	1,843.76	1,398.26	823.33
42,550	42,600	1,724.29	1,092.99	710.49	45,550	45,600	1,845.79	1,400.29	825.24
42,600	42,650	1,726.31	1,094.91	712.41	45,600	45,650	1,847.81	1,402.31	827.16
42,650	42,700	1,728.34	1,096.82	714.32	45,650	45,700	1,849.84	1,404.34	829.07
42,700	42,750	1,730.36	1,098.73	716.23	45,700	45,750	1,851.86	1,406.36	830.98
42,750	42,800	1,732.39	1,100.64	718.14	45,750	45,800	1,853.89	1,408.39	832.89
42,800	42,850	1,734.41	1,102.56	720.06	45,800	45,850	1,855.91	1,410.41	834.81
42,850	42,900	1,736.44	1,104.47	721.97	45,850	45,900	1,857.94	1,412.44	836.72
42,900	42,950	1,738.46	1,106.38	723.88	45,900	45,950	1,859.96	1,414.46	838.63
42,950	43,000	1,740.49	1,108.29	725.79	45,950	46,000	1,861.99	1,416.49	840.54
43,000					**46,000**				
43,000	43,050	1,742.51	1,148.46	727.71	46,000	46,050	1,864.01	1,459.01	842.46
43,050	43,100	1,744.54	1,150.37	729.62	46,050	46,100	1,866.04	1,461.04	844.37
43,100	43,150	1,746.56	1,152.28	731.53	46,100	46,150	1,868.06	1,463.06	846.28
43,150	43,200	1,748.59	1,154.19	733.44	46,150	46,200	1,870.09	1,465.09	848.19
43,200	43,250	1,750.61	1,156.11	735.36	46,200	46,250	1,872.11	1,467.11	850.11
43,250	43,300	1,752.64	1,158.02	737.27	46,250	46,300	1,874.14	1,469.14	852.02
43,300	43,350	1,754.66	1,159.93	739.18	46,300	46,350	1,876.16	1,471.16	853.93
43,350	43,400	1,756.69	1,161.84	741.09	46,350	46,400	1,878.19	1,473.19	855.84
43,400	43,450	1,758.71	1,163.76	743.01	46,400	46,450	1,880.21	1,475.21	857.76
43,450	43,500	1,760.74	1,165.67	744.92	46,450	46,500	1,882.24	1,477.24	859.67
43,500	43,550	1,762.76	1,167.58	746.83	46,500	46,550	1,884.26	1,479.26	861.58
43,550	43,600	1,764.79	1,169.49	748.74	46,550	46,600	1,886.29	1,481.29	863.49
43,600	43,650	1,766.81	1,171.41	750.66	46,600	46,650	1,888.31	1,483.31	865.41
43,650	43,700	1,768.84	1,173.32	752.57	46,650	46,700	1,890.34	1,485.34	867.32
43,700	43,750	1,770.86	1,175.23	754.48	46,700	46,750	1,892.36	1,487.36	869.23
43,750	43,800	1,772.89	1,177.14	756.39	46,750	46,800	1,894.39	1,489.39	871.14
43,800	43,850	1,774.91	1,179.06	758.31	46,800	46,850	1,896.41	1,491.41	873.06
43,850	43,900	1,776.94	1,180.97	760.22	46,850	46,900	1,898.44	1,493.44	874.97
43,900	43,950	1,778.96	1,182.88	762.13	46,900	46,950	1,900.46	1,495.46	876.88
43,950	44,000	1,780.99	1,184.79	764.04	46,950	47,000	1,902.49	1,497.49	878.79
44,000					**47,000**				
44,000	44,050	1,783.01	1,297.01	765.96	47,000	47,050	1,904.51	1,540.01	880.71
44,050	44,100	1,785.04	1,299.04	767.87	47,050	47,100	1,906.54	1,542.04	882.62
44,100	44,150	1,787.06	1,301.06	769.78	47,100	47,150	1,908.56	1,544.06	884.53
44,150	44,200	1,789.09	1,303.09	771.69	47,150	47,200	1,910.59	1,546.09	886.44
44,200	44,250	1,791.11	1,305.11	773.61	47,200	47,250	1,912.61	1,548.11	888.36
44,250	44,300	1,793.14	1,307.14	775.52	47,250	47,300	1,914.64	1,550.14	890.27
44,300	44,350	1,795.16	1,309.16	777.43	47,300	47,350	1,916.66	1,552.16	892.18
44,350	44,400	1,797.19	1,311.19	779.34	47,350	47,400	1,918.69	1,554.19	894.09
44,400	44,450	1,799.21	1,313.21	781.26	47,400	47,450	1,920.71	1,556.21	896.01
44,450	44,500	1,801.24	1,315.24	783.17	47,450	47,500	1,922.74	1,558.24	897.92
44,500	44,550	1,803.26	1,317.26	785.08	47,500	47,550	1,924.76	1,560.26	899.83
44,550	44,600	1,805.29	1,319.29	786.99	47,550	47,600	1,926.79	1,562.29	901.74
44,600	44,650	1,807.31	1,321.31	788.91	47,600	47,650	1,928.81	1,564.31	903.66
44,650	44,700	1,809.34	1,323.34	790.82	47,650	47,700	1,930.84	1,566.34	905.57
44,700	44,750	1,811.36	1,325.36	792.73	47,700	47,750	1,932.86	1,568.36	907.48
44,750	44,800	1,813.39	1,327.39	794.64	47,750	47,800	1,934.89	1,570.39	909.39
44,800	44,850	1,815.41	1,329.41	796.56	47,800	47,850	1,936.91	1,572.41	911.31
44,850	44,900	1,817.44	1,331.44	798.47	47,850	47,900	1,938.94	1,574.44	913.22
44,900	44,950	1,819.46	1,333.46	800.38	47,900	47,950	1,940.96	1,576.46	915.13
44,950	45,000	1,821.49	1,335.49	802.29	47,950	48,000	1,942.99	1,578.49	917.04

* This column must also be used by a qualifying widow(er)

Continued on next page

If CT AGI is - more than	less than or equal to	Single or Married Filing Separately	Head of Household	Married Filing Jointly *	If CT AGI is - more than	less than or equal to	Single or Married Filing Separately	Head of Household	Married Filing Jointly *
48,000					**51,000**				
48,000	48,050	2,161.13	1,621.01	957.21	51,000	51,050	2,296.13	1,864.01	1,256.51
48,050	48,100	2,163.38	1,623.04	959.12	51,050	51,100	2,298.38	1,866.04	1,258.54
48,100	48,150	2,165.63	1,625.06	961.03	51,100	51,150	2,300.63	1,868.06	1,260.56
48,150	48,200	2,167.88	1,627.09	962.94	51,150	51,200	2,302.88	1,870.09	1,262.59
48,200	48,250	2,170.13	1,629.11	964.86	51,200	51,250	2,305.13	1,872.11	1,264.61
48,250	48,300	2,172.38	1,631.14	966.77	51,250	51,300	2,307.38	1,874.14	1,266.64
48,300	48,350	2,174.63	1,633.16	968.68	51,300	51,350	2,309.63	1,876.16	1,268.66
48,350	48,400	2,176.88	1,635.19	970.59	51,350	51,400	2,311.88	1,878.19	1,270.69
48,400	48,450	2,179.13	1,637.21	972.51	51,400	51,450	2,314.13	1,880.21	1,272.71
48,450	48,500	2,181.38	1,639.24	974.42	51,450	51,500	2,316.38	1,882.24	1,274.74
48,500	48,550	2,183.63	1,641.26	976.33	51,500	51,550	2,318.63	1,884.26	1,276.76
48,550	48,600	2,185.88	1,643.29	978.24	51,550	51,600	2,320.88	1,886.29	1,278.79
48,600	48,650	2,188.13	1,645.31	980.16	51,600	51,650	2,323.13	1,888.31	1,280.81
48,650	48,700	2,190.38	1,647.34	982.07	51,650	51,700	2,325.38	1,890.34	1,282.84
48,700	48,750	2,192.63	1,649.36	983.98	51,700	51,750	2,327.63	1,892.36	1,284.86
48,750	48,800	2,194.88	1,651.39	985.89	51,750	51,800	2,329.88	1,894.39	1,286.89
48,800	48,850	2,197.13	1,653.41	987.81	51,800	51,850	2,332.13	1,896.41	1,288.91
48,850	48,900	2,199.38	1,655.44	989.72	51,850	51,900	2,334.38	1,898.44	1,290.94
48,900	48,950	2,201.63	1,657.46	991.63	51,900	51,950	2,336.63	1,900.46	1,292.96
48,950	49,000	2,203.88	1,659.49	993.54	51,950	52,000	2,338.88	1,902.49	1,294.99
49,000					**52,000**				
49,000	49,050	2,206.13	1,702.01	1,033.71	52,000	52,050	2,341.13	1,945.01	1,337.51
49,050	49,100	2,208.38	1,704.04	1,035.62	52,050	52,100	2,343.38	1,947.04	1,339.54
49,100	49,150	2,210.63	1,706.06	1,037.53	52,100	52,150	2,345.63	1,949.06	1,341.56
49,150	49,200	2,212.88	1,708.09	1,039.44	52,150	52,200	2,347.88	1,951.09	1,343.59
49,200	49,250	2,215.13	1,710.11	1,041.36	52,200	52,250	2,350.13	1,953.11	1,345.61
49,250	49,300	2,217.38	1,712.14	1,043.27	52,250	52,300	2,352.38	1,955.14	1,347.64
49,300	49,350	2,219.63	1,714.16	1,045.18	52,300	52,350	2,354.63	1,957.16	1,349.66
49,350	49,400	2,221.88	1,716.19	1,047.09	52,350	52,400	2,356.88	1,959.19	1,351.69
49,400	49,450	2,224.13	1,718.21	1,049.01	52,400	52,450	2,359.13	1,961.21	1,353.71
49,450	49,500	2,226.38	1,720.24	1,050.92	52,450	52,500	2,361.38	1,963.24	1,355.74
49,500	49,550	2,228.63	1,722.26	1,052.83	52,500	52,550	2,363.63	1,965.26	1,357.76
49,550	49,600	2,230.88	1,724.29	1,054.74	52,550	52,600	2,365.88	1,967.29	1,359.79
49,600	49,650	2,233.13	1,726.31	1,056.66	52,600	52,650	2,368.13	1,969.31	1,361.81
49,650	49,700	2,235.38	1,728.34	1,058.57	52,650	52,700	2,370.38	1,971.34	1,363.84
49,700	49,750	2,237.63	1,730.36	1,060.48	52,700	52,750	2,372.63	1,973.36	1,365.86
49,750	49,800	2,239.88	1,732.39	1,062.39	52,750	52,800	2,374.88	1,975.39	1,367.89
49,800	49,850	2,242.13	1,734.41	1,064.31	52,800	52,850	2,377.13	1,977.41	1,369.91
49,850	49,900	2,244.38	1,736.44	1,066.22	52,850	52,900	2,379.38	1,979.44	1,371.94
49,900	49,950	2,246.63	1,738.46	1,068.13	52,900	52,950	2,381.63	1,981.46	1,373.96
49,950	50,000	2,248.88	1,740.49	1,070.04	52,950	53,000	2,383.88	1,983.49	1,375.99
50,000					**53,000**				
50,000	50,050	2,251.13	1,783.01	1,175.51	53,000	53,050	2,386.13	2,026.01	1,418.51
50,050	50,100	2,253.38	1,785.04	1,177.54	53,050	53,100	2,388.38	2,028.04	1,420.54
50,100	50,150	2,255.63	1,787.06	1,179.56	53,100	53,150	2,390.63	2,030.06	1,422.56
50,150	50,200	2,257.88	1,789.09	1,181.59	53,150	53,200	2,392.88	2,032.09	1,424.59
50,200	50,250	2,260.13	1,791.11	1,183.61	53,200	53,250	2,395.13	2,034.11	1,426.61
50,250	50,300	2,262.38	1,793.14	1,185.64	53,250	53,300	2,397.38	2,036.14	1,428.64
50,300	50,350	2,264.63	1,795.16	1,187.66	53,300	53,350	2,399.63	2,038.16	1,430.66
50,350	50,400	2,266.88	1,797.19	1,189.69	53,350	53,400	2,401.88	2,040.19	1,432.69
50,400	50,450	2,269.13	1,799.21	1,191.71	53,400	53,450	2,404.13	2,042.21	1,434.71
50,450	50,500	2,271.38	1,801.24	1,193.74	53,450	53,500	2,406.38	2,044.24	1,436.74
50,500	50,550	2,273.63	1,803.26	1,195.76	53,500	53,550	2,408.63	2,046.26	1,438.76
50,550	50,600	2,275.88	1,805.29	1,197.79	53,550	53,600	2,410.88	2,048.29	1,440.79
50,600	50,650	2,278.13	1,807.31	1,199.81	53,600	53,650	2,413.13	2,050.31	1,442.81
50,650	50,700	2,280.38	1,809.34	1,201.84	53,650	53,700	2,415.38	2,052.34	1,444.84
50,700	50,750	2,282.63	1,811.36	1,203.86	53,700	53,750	2,417.63	2,054.36	1,446.86
50,750	50,800	2,284.88	1,813.39	1,205.89	53,750	53,800	2,419.88	2,056.39	1,448.89
50,800	50,850	2,287.13	1,815.41	1,207.91	53,800	53,850	2,422.13	2,058.41	1,450.91
50,850	50,900	2,289.38	1,817.44	1,209.94	53,850	53,900	2,424.38	2,060.44	1,452.94
50,900	50,950	2,291.63	1,819.46	1,211.96	53,900	53,950	2,426.63	2,062.46	1,454.96
50,950	51,000	2,293.88	1,821.49	1,213.99	53,950	54,000	2,428.88	2,064.49	1,456.99

* This column must also be used by a qualifying widow(er)

Continued on next page

If CT AGI is - more than	less than or equal to	Single or Married Filing Separately	Head of Household	Married Filing Jointly *	If CT AGI is - more than	less than or equal to	Single or Married Filing Separately	Head of Household	Married Filing Jointly *
54,000					**57,000**				
54,000	54,050	2,431.13	2,107.01	1,499.51	57,000	57,050	2,566.13	2,309.51	1,742.51
54,050	54,100	2,433.38	2,109.04	1,501.54	57,050	57,100	2,568.38	2,311.54	1,744.54
54,100	54,150	2,435.63	2,111.06	1,503.56	57,100	57,150	2,570.63	2,313.56	1,746.56
54,150	54,200	2,437.88	2,113.09	1,505.59	57,150	57,200	2,572.88	2,315.59	1,748.59
54,200	54,250	2,440.13	2,115.11	1,507.61	57,200	57,250	2,575.13	2,317.61	1,750.61
54,250	54,300	2,442.38	2,117.14	1,509.64	57,250	57,300	2,577.38	2,319.64	1,752.64
54,300	54,350	2,444.63	2,119.16	1,511.66	57,300	57,350	2,579.63	2,321.66	1,754.66
54,350	54,400	2,446.88	2,121.19	1,513.69	57,350	57,400	2,581.88	2,323.69	1,756.69
54,400	54,450	2,449.13	2,123.21	1,515.71	57,400	57,450	2,584.13	2,325.71	1,758.71
54,450	54,500	2,451.38	2,125.24	1,517.74	57,450	57,500	2,586.38	2,327.74	1,760.74
54,500	54,550	2,453.63	2,127.26	1,519.76	57,500	57,550	2,588.63	2,329.76	1,762.76
54,550	54,600	2,455.88	2,129.29	1,521.79	57,550	57,600	2,590.88	2,331.79	1,764.79
54,600	54,650	2,458.13	2,131.31	1,523.81	57,600	57,650	2,593.13	2,333.81	1,766.81
54,650	54,700	2,460.38	2,133.34	1,525.84	57,650	57,700	2,595.38	2,335.84	1,768.84
54,700	54,750	2,462.63	2,135.36	1,527.86	57,700	57,750	2,597.63	2,337.86	1,770.86
54,750	54,800	2,464.88	2,137.39	1,529.89	57,750	57,800	2,599.88	2,339.89	1,772.89
54,800	54,850	2,467.13	2,139.41	1,531.91	57,800	57,850	2,602.13	2,341.91	1,774.91
54,850	54,900	2,469.38	2,141.44	1,533.94	57,850	57,900	2,604.38	2,343.94	1,776.94
54,900	54,950	2,471.63	2,143.46	1,535.96	57,900	57,950	2,606.63	2,345.96	1,778.96
54,950	55,000	2,473.88	2,145.49	1,537.99	57,950	58,000	2,608.88	2,347.99	1,780.99
55,000					**58,000**				
55,000	55,050	2,476.13	2,188.01	1,580.51	58,000	58,050	2,611.13	2,350.01	1,823.51
55,050	55,100	2,478.38	2,190.04	1,582.54	58,050	58,100	2,613.38	2,352.04	1,825.54
55,100	55,150	2,480.63	2,192.06	1,584.56	58,100	58,150	2,615.63	2,354.06	1,827.56
55,150	55,200	2,482.88	2,194.09	1,586.59	58,150	58,200	2,617.88	2,356.09	1,829.59
55,200	55,250	2,485.13	2,196.11	1,588.61	58,200	58,250	2,620.13	2,358.11	1,831.61
55,250	55,300	2,487.38	2,198.14	1,590.64	58,250	58,300	2,622.38	2,360.14	1,833.64
55,300	55,350	2,489.63	2,200.16	1,592.66	58,300	58,350	2,624.63	2,362.16	1,835.66
55,350	55,400	2,491.88	2,202.19	1,594.69	58,350	58,400	2,626.88	2,364.19	1,837.69
55,400	55,450	2,494.13	2,204.21	1,596.71	58,400	58,450	2,629.13	2,366.21	1,839.71
55,450	55,500	2,496.38	2,206.24	1,598.74	58,450	58,500	2,631.38	2,368.24	1,841.74
55,500	55,550	2,498.63	2,208.26	1,600.76	58,500	58,550	2,633.63	2,370.26	1,843.76
55,550	55,600	2,500.88	2,210.29	1,602.79	58,550	58,600	2,635.88	2,372.29	1,845.79
55,600	55,650	2,503.13	2,212.31	1,604.81	58,600	58,650	2,638.13	2,374.31	1,847.81
55,650	55,700	2,505.38	2,214.34	1,606.84	58,650	58,700	2,640.38	2,376.34	1,849.84
55,700	55,750	2,507.63	2,216.36	1,608.86	58,700	58,750	2,642.63	2,378.36	1,851.86
55,750	55,800	2,509.88	2,218.39	1,610.89	58,750	58,800	2,644.88	2,380.39	1,853.89
55,800	55,850	2,512.13	2,220.41	1,612.91	58,800	58,850	2,647.13	2,382.41	1,855.91
55,850	55,900	2,514.38	2,222.44	1,614.94	58,850	58,900	2,649.38	2,384.44	1,857.94
55,900	55,950	2,516.63	2,224.46	1,616.96	58,900	58,950	2,651.63	2,386.46	1,859.96
55,950	56,000	2,518.88	2,226.49	1,618.99	58,950	59,000	2,653.88	2,388.49	1,861.99
56,000					**59,000**				
56,000	56,050	2,521.13	2,269.01	1,661.51	59,000	59,050	2,656.13	2,390.51	1,904.51
56,050	56,100	2,523.38	2,271.04	1,663.54	59,050	59,100	2,658.38	2,392.54	1,906.54
56,100	56,150	2,525.63	2,273.06	1,665.56	59,100	59,150	2,660.63	2,394.56	1,908.56
56,150	56,200	2,527.88	2,275.09	1,667.59	59,150	59,200	2,662.88	2,396.59	1,910.59
56,200	56,250	2,530.13	2,277.11	1,669.61	59,200	59,250	2,665.13	2,398.61	1,912.61
56,250	56,300	2,532.38	2,279.14	1,671.64	59,250	59,300	2,667.38	2,400.64	1,914.64
56,300	56,350	2,534.63	2,281.16	1,673.66	59,300	59,350	2,669.63	2,402.66	1,916.66
56,350	56,400	2,536.88	2,283.19	1,675.69	59,350	59,400	2,671.88	2,404.69	1,918.69
56,400	56,450	2,539.13	2,285.21	1,677.71	59,400	59,450	2,674.13	2,406.71	1,920.71
56,450	56,500	2,541.38	2,287.24	1,679.74	59,450	59,500	2,676.38	2,408.74	1,922.74
56,500	56,550	2,543.63	2,289.26	1,681.76	59,500	59,550	2,678.63	2,410.76	1,924.76
56,550	56,600	2,545.88	2,291.29	1,683.79	59,550	59,600	2,680.88	2,412.79	1,926.79
56,600	56,650	2,548.13	2,293.31	1,685.81	59,600	59,650	2,683.13	2,414.81	1,928.81
56,650	56,700	2,550.38	2,295.34	1,687.84	59,650	59,700	2,685.38	2,416.84	1,930.84
56,700	56,750	2,552.63	2,297.36	1,689.86	59,700	59,750	2,687.63	2,418.86	1,932.86
56,750	56,800	2,554.88	2,299.39	1,691.89	59,750	59,800	2,689.88	2,420.89	1,934.89
56,800	56,850	2,557.13	2,301.41	1,693.91	59,800	59,850	2,692.13	2,422.91	1,936.91
56,850	56,900	2,559.38	2,303.44	1,695.94	59,850	59,900	2,694.38	2,424.94	1,938.94
56,900	56,950	2,561.63	2,305.46	1,697.96	59,900	59,950	2,696.63	2,426.96	1,940.96
56,950	57,000	2,563.88	2,307.49	1,699.99	59,950	60,000	2,698.88	2,428.99	1,942.99

* This column must also be used by a qualifying widow(er)

Continued on next page

If CT AGI is -		And you are -			If CT AGI is -		And you are -		
more than	less than or equal to	Single or Married Filing Separately	Head of Household	Married Filing Jointly *	more than	less than or equal to	Single or Married Filing Separately	Head of Household	Married Filing Jointly *
60,000					**63,000**				
60,000	60,050	2,701.13	2,431.01	1,985.51	63,000	63,050	2,836.13	2,552.51	2,228.51
60,050	60,100	2,703.38	2,433.04	1,987.54	63,050	63,100	2,838.38	2,554.54	2,230.54
60,100	60,150	2,705.63	2,435.06	1,989.56	63,100	63,150	2,840.63	2,556.56	2,232.56
60,150	60,200	2,707.88	2,437.09	1,991.59	63,150	63,200	2,842.88	2,558.59	2,234.59
60,200	60,250	2,710.13	2,439.11	1,993.61	63,200	63,250	2,845.13	2,560.61	2,236.61
60,250	60,300	2,712.38	2,441.14	1,995.64	63,250	63,300	2,847.38	2,562.64	2,238.64
60,300	60,350	2,714.63	2,443.16	1,997.66	63,300	63,350	2,849.63	2,564.66	2,240.66
60,350	60,400	2,716.88	2,445.19	1,999.69	63,350	63,400	2,851.88	2,566.69	2,242.69
60,400	60,450	2,719.13	2,447.21	2,001.71	63,400	63,450	2,854.13	2,568.71	2,244.71
60,450	60,500	2,721.38	2,449.24	2,003.74	63,450	63,500	2,856.38	2,570.74	2,246.74
60,500	60,550	2,723.63	2,451.26	2,005.76	63,500	63,550	2,858.63	2,572.76	2,248.76
60,550	60,600	2,725.88	2,453.29	2,007.79	63,550	63,600	2,860.88	2,574.79	2,250.79
60,600	60,650	2,728.13	2,455.31	2,009.81	63,600	63,650	2,863.13	2,576.81	2,252.81
60,650	60,700	2,730.38	2,457.34	2,011.84	63,650	63,700	2,865.38	2,578.84	2,254.84
60,700	60,750	2,732.63	2,459.36	2,013.86	63,700	63,750	2,867.63	2,580.86	2,256.86
60,750	60,800	2,734.88	2,461.39	2,015.89	63,750	63,800	2,869.88	2,582.89	2,258.89
60,800	60,850	2,737.13	2,463.41	2,017.91	63,800	63,850	2,872.13	2,584.91	2,260.91
60,850	60,900	2,739.38	2,465.44	2,019.94	63,850	63,900	2,874.38	2,586.94	2,262.94
60,900	60,950	2,741.63	2,467.46	2,021.96	63,900	63,950	2,876.63	2,588.96	2,264.96
60,950	61,000	2,743.88	2,469.49	2,023.99	63,950	64,000	2,878.88	2,590.99	2,266.99
61,000					**64,000**				
61,000	61,050	2,746.13	2,471.51	2,066.51	64,000	64,050	2,881.13	2,593.01	2,309.51
61,050	61,100	2,748.38	2,473.54	2,068.54	64,050	64,100	2,883.38	2,595.04	2,311.54
61,100	61,150	2,750.63	2,475.56	2,070.56	64,100	64,150	2,885.63	2,597.06	2,313.56
61,150	61,200	2,752.88	2,477.59	2,072.59	64,150	64,200	2,887.88	2,599.09	2,315.59
61,200	61,250	2,755.13	2,479.61	2,074.61	64,200	64,250	2,890.13	2,601.11	2,317.61
61,250	61,300	2,757.38	2,481.64	2,076.64	64,250	64,300	2,892.38	2,603.14	2,319.64
61,300	61,350	2,759.63	2,483.66	2,078.66	64,300	64,350	2,894.63	2,605.16	2,321.66
61,350	61,400	2,761.88	2,485.69	2,080.69	64,350	64,400	2,896.88	2,607.19	2,323.69
61,400	61,450	2,764.13	2,487.71	2,082.71	64,400	64,450	2,899.13	2,609.21	2,325.71
61,450	61,500	2,766.38	2,489.74	2,084.74	64,450	64,500	2,901.38	2,611.24	2,327.74
61,500	61,550	2,768.63	2,491.76	2,086.76	64,500	64,550	2,903.63	2,613.26	2,329.76
61,550	61,600	2,770.88	2,493.79	2,088.79	64,550	64,600	2,905.88	2,615.29	2,331.79
61,600	61,650	2,773.13	2,495.81	2,090.81	64,600	64,650	2,908.13	2,617.31	2,333.81
61,650	61,700	2,775.38	2,497.84	2,092.84	64,650	64,700	2,910.38	2,619.34	2,335.84
61,700	61,750	2,777.63	2,499.86	2,094.86	64,700	64,750	2,912.63	2,621.36	2,337.86
61,750	61,800	2,779.88	2,501.89	2,096.89	64,750	64,800	2,914.88	2,623.39	2,339.89
61,800	61,850	2,782.13	2,503.91	2,098.91	64,800	64,850	2,917.13	2,625.41	2,341.91
61,850	61,900	2,784.38	2,505.94	2,100.94	64,850	64,900	2,919.38	2,627.44	2,343.94
61,900	61,950	2,786.63	2,507.96	2,102.96	64,900	64,950	2,921.63	2,629.46	2,345.96
61,950	62,000	2,788.88	2,509.99	2,104.99	64,950	65,000	2,923.88	2,631.49	2,347.99
62,000					**65,000**				
62,000	62,050	2,791.13	2,512.01	2,147.51	65,000	65,050	2,926.13	2,633.51	2,390.51
62,050	62,100	2,793.38	2,514.04	2,149.54	65,050	65,100	2,928.38	2,635.54	2,392.54
62,100	62,150	2,795.63	2,516.06	2,151.56	65,100	65,150	2,930.63	2,637.56	2,394.56
62,150	62,200	2,797.88	2,518.09	2,153.59	65,150	65,200	2,932.88	2,639.59	2,396.59
62,200	62,250	2,800.13	2,520.11	2,155.61	65,200	65,250	2,935.13	2,641.61	2,398.61
62,250	62,300	2,802.38	2,522.14	2,157.64	65,250	65,300	2,937.38	2,643.64	2,400.64
62,300	62,350	2,804.63	2,524.16	2,159.66	65,300	65,350	2,939.63	2,645.66	2,402.66
62,350	62,400	2,806.88	2,526.19	2,161.69	65,350	65,400	2,941.88	2,647.69	2,404.69
62,400	62,450	2,809.13	2,528.21	2,163.71	65,400	65,450	2,944.13	2,649.71	2,406.71
62,450	62,500	2,811.38	2,530.24	2,165.74	65,450	65,500	2,946.38	2,651.74	2,408.74
62,500	62,550	2,813.63	2,532.26	2,167.76	65,500	65,550	2,948.63	2,653.76	2,410.76
62,550	62,600	2,815.88	2,534.29	2,169.79	65,550	65,600	2,950.88	2,655.79	2,412.79
62,600	62,650	2,818.13	2,536.31	2,171.81	65,600	65,650	2,953.13	2,657.81	2,414.81
62,650	62,700	2,820.38	2,538.34	2,173.84	65,650	65,700	2,955.38	2,659.84	2,416.84
62,700	62,750	2,822.63	2,540.36	2,175.86	65,700	65,750	2,957.63	2,661.86	2,418.86
62,750	62,800	2,824.88	2,542.39	2,177.89	65,750	65,800	2,959.88	2,663.89	2,420.89
62,800	62,850	2,827.13	2,544.41	2,179.91	65,800	65,850	2,962.13	2,665.91	2,422.91
62,850	62,900	2,829.38	2,546.44	2,181.94	65,850	65,900	2,964.38	2,667.94	2,424.94
62,900	62,950	2,831.63	2,548.46	2,183.96	65,900	65,950	2,966.63	2,669.96	2,426.96
62,950	63,000	2,833.88	2,550.49	2,185.99	65,950	66,000	2,968.88	2,671.99	2,428.99

* This column must also be used by a qualifying widow(er)

Continued on next page

CT-62

66,000

If CT AGI is - more than	less than or equal to	Single or Married Filing Separately	Head of Household	Married Filing Jointly *
66,000	66,050	2,971.13	2,674.01	2,471.51
66,050	66,100	2,973.38	2,676.04	2,473.54
66,100	66,150	2,975.63	2,678.06	2,475.56
66,150	66,200	2,977.88	2,680.09	2,477.59
66,200	66,250	2,980.13	2,682.11	2,479.61
66,250	66,300	2,982.38	2,684.14	2,481.64
66,300	66,350	2,984.63	2,686.16	2,483.66
66,350	66,400	2,986.88	2,688.19	2,485.69
66,400	66,450	2,989.13	2,690.21	2,487.71
66,450	66,500	2,991.38	2,692.24	2,489.74
66,500	66,550	2,993.63	2,694.26	2,491.76
66,550	66,600	2,995.88	2,696.29	2,493.79
66,600	66,650	2,998.13	2,698.31	2,495.81
66,650	66,700	3,000.38	2,700.34	2,497.84
66,700	66,750	3,002.63	2,702.36	2,499.86
66,750	66,800	3,004.88	2,704.39	2,501.89
66,800	66,850	3,007.13	2,706.41	2,503.91
66,850	66,900	3,009.38	2,708.44	2,505.94
66,900	66,950	3,011.63	2,710.46	2,507.96
66,950	67,000	3,013.88	2,712.49	2,509.99

67,000

If CT AGI is - more than	less than or equal to	Single or Married Filing Separately	Head of Household	Married Filing Jointly *
67,000	67,050	3,016.13	2,714.51	2,552.51
67,050	67,100	3,018.38	2,716.54	2,554.54
67,100	67,150	3,020.63	2,718.56	2,556.56
67,150	67,200	3,022.88	2,720.59	2,558.59
67,200	67,250	3,025.13	2,722.61	2,560.61
67,250	67,300	3,027.38	2,724.64	2,562.64
67,300	67,350	3,029.63	2,726.66	2,564.66
67,350	67,400	3,031.88	2,728.69	2,566.69
67,400	67,450	3,034.13	2,730.71	2,568.71
67,450	67,500	3,036.38	2,732.74	2,570.74
67,500	67,550	3,038.63	2,734.76	2,572.76
67,550	67,600	3,040.88	2,736.79	2,574.79
67,600	67,650	3,043.13	2,738.81	2,576.81
67,650	67,700	3,045.38	2,740.84	2,578.84
67,700	67,750	3,047.63	2,742.86	2,580.86
67,750	67,800	3,049.88	2,744.89	2,582.89
67,800	67,850	3,052.13	2,746.91	2,584.91
67,850	67,900	3,054.38	2,748.94	2,586.94
67,900	67,950	3,056.63	2,750.96	2,588.96
67,950	68,000	3,058.88	2,752.99	2,590.99

68,000

If CT AGI is - more than	less than or equal to	Single or Married Filing Separately	Head of Household	Married Filing Jointly *
68,000	68,050	3,061.13	2,755.01	2,633.51
68,050	68,100	3,063.38	2,757.04	2,635.54
68,100	68,150	3,065.63	2,759.06	2,637.56
68,150	68,200	3,067.88	2,761.09	2,639.59
68,200	68,250	3,070.13	2,763.11	2,641.61
68,250	68,300	3,072.38	2,765.14	2,643.64
68,300	68,350	3,074.63	2,767.16	2,645.66
68,350	68,400	3,076.88	2,769.19	2,647.69
68,400	68,450	3,079.13	2,771.21	2,649.71
68,450	68,500	3,081.38	2,773.24	2,651.74
68,500	68,550	3,083.63	2,775.26	2,653.76
68,550	68,600	3,085.88	2,777.29	2,655.79
68,600	68,650	3,088.13	2,779.31	2,657.81
68,650	68,700	3,090.38	2,781.34	2,659.84
68,700	68,750	3,092.63	2,783.36	2,661.86
68,750	68,800	3,094.88	2,785.39	2,663.89
68,800	68,850	3,097.13	2,787.41	2,665.91
68,850	68,900	3,099.38	2,789.44	2,667.94
68,900	68,950	3,101.63	2,791.46	2,669.96
68,950	69,000	3,103.88	2,793.49	2,671.99

69,000

If CT AGI is - more than	less than or equal to	Single or Married Filing Separately	Head of Household	Married Filing Jointly *
69,000	69,050	3,106.13	2,795.51	2,714.51
69,050	69,100	3,108.38	2,797.54	2,716.54
69,100	69,150	3,110.63	2,799.56	2,718.56
69,150	69,200	3,112.88	2,801.59	2,720.59
69,200	69,250	3,115.13	2,803.61	2,722.61
69,250	69,300	3,117.38	2,805.64	2,724.64
69,300	69,350	3,119.63	2,807.66	2,726.66
69,350	69,400	3,121.88	2,809.69	2,728.69
69,400	69,450	3,124.13	2,811.71	2,730.71
69,450	69,500	3,126.38	2,813.74	2,732.74
69,500	69,550	3,128.63	2,815.76	2,734.76
69,550	69,600	3,130.88	2,817.79	2,736.79
69,600	69,650	3,133.13	2,819.81	2,738.81
69,650	69,700	3,135.38	2,821.84	2,740.84
69,700	69,750	3,137.63	2,823.86	2,742.86
69,750	69,800	3,139.88	2,825.89	2,744.89
69,800	69,850	3,142.13	2,827.91	2,746.91
69,850	69,900	3,144.38	2,829.94	2,748.94
69,900	69,950	3,146.63	2,831.96	2,750.96
69,950	70,000	3,148.88	2,833.99	2,752.99

70,000

If CT AGI is - more than	less than or equal to	Single or Married Filing Separately	Head of Household	Married Filing Jointly *
70,000	70,050	3,151.13	2,836.01	2,795.51
70,050	70,100	3,153.38	2,838.04	2,797.54
70,100	70,150	3,155.63	2,840.06	2,799.56
70,150	70,200	3,157.88	2,842.09	2,801.59
70,200	70,250	3,160.13	2,844.11	2,803.61
70,250	70,300	3,162.38	2,846.14	2,805.64
70,300	70,350	3,164.63	2,848.16	2,807.66
70,350	70,400	3,166.88	2,850.19	2,809.69
70,400	70,450	3,169.13	2,852.21	2,811.71
70,450	70,500	3,171.38	2,854.24	2,813.74
70,500	70,550	3,173.63	2,856.26	2,815.76
70,550	70,600	3,175.88	2,858.29	2,817.79
70,600	70,650	3,178.13	2,860.31	2,819.81
70,650	70,700	3,180.38	2,862.34	2,821.84
70,700	70,750	3,182.63	2,864.36	2,823.86
70,750	70,800	3,184.88	2,866.39	2,825.89
70,800	70,850	3,187.13	2,868.41	2,827.91
70,850	70,900	3,189.38	2,870.44	2,829.94
70,900	70,950	3,191.63	2,872.46	2,831.96
70,950	71,000	3,193.88	2,874.49	2,833.99

71,000

If CT AGI is - more than	less than or equal to	Single or Married Filing Separately	Head of Household	Married Filing Jointly *
71,000	71,050	3,196.13	2,876.51	2,876.51
71,050	71,100	3,198.38	2,878.54	2,878.54
71,100	71,150	3,200.63	2,880.56	2,880.56
71,150	71,200	3,202.88	2,882.59	2,882.59
71,200	71,250	3,205.13	2,884.61	2,884.61
71,250	71,300	3,207.38	2,886.64	2,886.64
71,300	71,350	3,209.63	2,888.66	2,888.66
71,350	71,400	3,211.88	2,890.69	2,890.69
71,400	71,450	3,214.13	2,892.71	2,892.71
71,450	71,500	3,216.38	2,894.74	2,894.74
71,500	71,550	3,218.63	2,896.76	2,896.76
71,550	71,600	3,220.88	2,898.79	2,898.79
71,600	71,650	3,223.13	2,900.81	2,900.81
71,650	71,700	3,225.38	2,902.84	2,902.84
71,700	71,750	3,227.63	2,904.86	2,904.86
71,750	71,800	3,229.88	2,906.89	2,906.89
71,800	71,850	3,232.13	2,908.91	2,908.91
71,850	71,900	3,234.38	2,910.94	2,910.94
71,900	71,950	3,236.63	2,912.96	2,912.96
71,950	72,000	3,238.88	2,914.99	2,914.99

* This column must also be used by a qualifying widow(er)

Continued on next page

If CT AGI is -		And you are -			If CT AGI is -		And you are -		
more than	less than or equal to	Single or Married Filing Separately	Head of Household	Married Filing Jointly *	more than	less than or equal to	Single or Married Filing Separately	Head of Household	Married Filing Jointly *
72,000					**75,000**				
72,000	72,050	3,241.13	2,917.01	2,917.01	75,000	75,050	3,376.13	3,376.13	3,038.51
72,050	72,100	3,243.38	2,919.04	2,919.04	75,050	75,100	3,378.38	3,378.38	3,040.54
72,100	72,150	3,245.63	2,921.06	2,921.06	75,100	75,150	3,380.63	3,380.63	3,042.56
72,150	72,200	3,247.88	2,923.09	2,923.09	75,150	75,200	3,382.88	3,382.88	3,044.59
72,200	72,250	3,250.13	2,925.11	2,925.11	75,200	75,250	3,385.13	3,385.13	3,046.61
72,250	72,300	3,252.38	2,927.14	2,927.14	75,250	75,300	3,387.38	3,387.38	3,048.64
72,300	72,350	3,254.63	2,929.16	2,929.16	75,300	75,350	3,389.63	3,389.63	3,050.66
72,350	72,400	3,256.88	2,931.19	2,931.19	75,350	75,400	3,391.88	3,391.88	3,052.69
72,400	72,450	3,259.13	2,933.21	2,933.21	75,400	75,450	3,394.13	3,394.13	3,054.71
72,450	72,500	3,261.38	2,935.24	2,935.24	75,450	75,500	3,396.38	3,396.38	3,056.74
72,500	72,550	3,263.63	2,937.26	2,937.26	75,500	75,550	3,398.63	3,398.63	3,058.76
72,550	72,600	3,265.88	2,939.29	2,939.29	75,550	75,600	3,400.88	3,400.88	3,060.79
72,600	72,650	3,268.13	2,941.31	2,941.31	75,600	75,650	3,403.13	3,403.13	3,062.81
72,650	72,700	3,270.38	2,943.34	2,943.34	75,650	75,700	3,405.38	3,405.38	3,064.84
72,700	72,750	3,272.63	2,945.36	2,945.36	75,700	75,750	3,407.63	3,407.63	3,066.86
72,750	72,800	3,274.88	2,947.39	2,947.39	75,750	75,800	3,409.88	3,409.88	3,068.89
72,800	72,850	3,277.13	2,949.41	2,949.41	75,800	75,850	3,412.13	3,412.13	3,070.91
72,850	72,900	3,279.38	2,951.44	2,951.44	75,850	75,900	3,414.38	3,414.38	3,072.94
72,900	72,950	3,281.63	2,953.46	2,953.46	75,900	75,950	3,416.63	3,416.63	3,074.96
72,950	73,000	3,283.88	2,955.49	2,955.49	75,950	76,000	3,418.88	3,418.88	3,076.99
73,000					**76,000**				
73,000	73,050	3,286.13	2,957.51	2,957.51	76,000	76,050	3,421.13	3,421.13	3,079.01
73,050	73,100	3,288.38	2,959.54	2,959.54	76,050	76,100	3,423.38	3,423.38	3,081.04
73,100	73,150	3,290.63	2,961.56	2,961.56	76,100	76,150	3,425.63	3,425.63	3,083.06
73,150	73,200	3,292.88	2,963.59	2,963.59	76,150	76,200	3,427.88	3,427.88	3,085.09
73,200	73,250	3,295.13	2,965.61	2,965.61	76,200	76,250	3,430.13	3,430.13	3,087.11
73,250	73,300	3,297.38	2,967.64	2,967.64	76,250	76,300	3,432.38	3,432.38	3,089.14
73,300	73,350	3,299.63	2,969.66	2,969.66	76,300	76,350	3,434.63	3,434.63	3,091.16
73,350	73,400	3,301.88	2,971.69	2,971.69	76,350	76,400	3,436.88	3,436.88	3,093.19
73,400	73,450	3,304.13	2,973.71	2,973.71	76,400	76,450	3,439.13	3,439.13	3,095.21
73,450	73,500	3,306.38	2,975.74	2,975.74	76,450	76,500	3,441.38	3,441.38	3,097.24
73,500	73,550	3,308.63	2,977.76	2,977.76	76,500	76,550	3,443.63	3,443.63	3,099.26
73,550	73,600	3,310.88	2,979.79	2,979.79	76,550	76,600	3,445.88	3,445.88	3,101.29
73,600	73,650	3,313.13	2,981.81	2,981.81	76,600	76,650	3,448.13	3,448.13	3,103.31
73,650	73,700	3,315.38	2,983.84	2,983.84	76,650	76,700	3,450.38	3,450.38	3,105.34
73,700	73,750	3,317.63	2,985.86	2,985.86	76,700	76,750	3,452.63	3,452.63	3,107.36
73,750	73,800	3,319.88	2,987.89	2,987.89	76,750	76,800	3,454.88	3,454.88	3,109.39
73,800	73,850	3,322.13	2,989.91	2,989.91	76,800	76,850	3,457.13	3,457.13	3,111.41
73,850	73,900	3,324.38	2,991.94	2,991.94	76,850	76,900	3,459.38	3,459.38	3,113.44
73,900	73,950	3,326.63	2,993.96	2,993.96	76,900	76,950	3,461.63	3,461.63	3,115.46
73,950	74,000	3,328.88	2,995.99	2,995.99	76,950	77,000	3,463.88	3,463.88	3,117.49
74,000					**77,000**				
74,000	74,050	3,331.13	3,331.13	2,998.01	77,000	77,050	3,466.13	3,466.13	3,119.51
74,050	74,100	3,333.38	3,333.38	3,000.04	77,050	77,100	3,468.38	3,468.38	3,121.54
74,100	74,150	3,335.63	3,335.63	3,002.06	77,100	77,150	3,470.63	3,470.63	3,123.56
74,150	74,200	3,337.88	3,337.88	3,004.09	77,150	77,200	3,472.88	3,472.88	3,125.59
74,200	74,250	3,340.13	3,340.13	3,006.11	77,200	77,250	3,475.13	3,475.13	3,127.61
74,250	74,300	3,342.38	3,342.38	3,008.14	77,250	77,300	3,477.38	3,477.38	3,129.64
74,300	74,350	3,344.63	3,344.63	3,010.16	77,300	77,350	3,479.63	3,479.63	3,131.66
74,350	74,400	3,346.88	3,346.88	3,012.19	77,350	77,400	3,481.88	3,481.88	3,133.69
74,400	74,450	3,349.13	3,349.13	3,014.21	77,400	77,450	3,484.13	3,484.13	3,135.71
74,450	74,500	3,351.38	3,351.38	3,016.24	77,450	77,500	3,486.38	3,486.38	3,137.74
74,500	74,550	3,353.63	3,353.63	3,018.26	77,500	77,550	3,488.63	3,488.63	3,139.76
74,550	74,600	3,355.88	3,355.88	3,020.29	77,550	77,600	3,490.88	3,490.88	3,141.79
74,600	74,650	3,358.13	3,358.13	3,022.31	77,600	77,650	3,493.13	3,493.13	3,143.81
74,650	74,700	3,360.38	3,360.38	3,024.34	77,650	77,700	3,495.38	3,495.38	3,145.84
74,700	74,750	3,362.63	3,362.63	3,026.36	77,700	77,750	3,497.63	3,497.63	3,147.86
74,750	74,800	3,364.88	3,364.88	3,028.39	77,750	77,800	3,499.88	3,499.88	3,149.89
74,800	74,850	3,367.13	3,367.13	3,030.41	77,800	77,850	3,502.13	3,502.13	3,151.91
74,850	74,900	3,369.38	3,369.38	3,032.44	77,850	77,900	3,504.38	3,504.38	3,153.94
74,900	74,950	3,371.63	3,371.63	3,034.46	77,900	77,950	3,506.63	3,506.63	3,155.96
74,950	75,000	3,373.88	3,373.88	3,036.49	77,950	78,000	3,508.88	3,508.88	3,157.99

* This column must also be used by a qualifying widow(er)   Continued on next page

If CT AGI is -		And you are -			If CT AGI is -		And you are -		
more than	less than or equal to	Single or Married Filing Separately	Head of Household	Married Filing Jointly *	more than	less than or equal to	Single or Married Filing Separately	Head of Household	Married Filing Jointly *
78,000					**81,000**				
78,000	78,050	3,511.13	3,511.13	3,160.01	81,000	81,050	3,646.13	3,646.13	3,281.51
78,050	78,100	3,513.38	3,513.38	3,162.04	81,050	81,100	3,648.38	3,648.38	3,283.54
78,100	78,150	3,515.63	3,515.63	3,164.06	81,100	81,150	3,650.63	3,650.63	3,285.56
78,150	78,200	3,517.88	3,517.88	3,166.09	81,150	81,200	3,652.88	3,652.88	3,287.59
78,200	78,250	3,520.13	3,520.13	3,168.11	81,200	81,250	3,655.13	3,655.13	3,289.61
78,250	78,300	3,522.38	3,522.38	3,170.14	81,250	81,300	3,657.38	3,657.38	3,291.64
78,300	78,350	3,524.63	3,524.63	3,172.16	81,300	81,350	3,659.63	3,659.63	3,293.66
78,350	78,400	3,526.88	3,526.88	3,174.19	81,350	81,400	3,661.88	3,661.88	3,295.69
78,400	78,450	3,529.13	3,529.13	3,176.21	81,400	81,450	3,664.13	3,664.13	3,297.71
78,450	78,500	3,531.38	3,531.38	3,178.24	81,450	81,500	3,666.38	3,666.38	3,299.74
78,500	78,550	3,533.63	3,533.63	3,180.26	81,500	81,550	3,668.63	3,668.63	3,301.76
78,550	78,600	3,535.88	3,535.88	3,182.29	81,550	81,600	3,670.88	3,670.88	3,303.79
78,600	78,650	3,538.13	3,538.13	3,184.31	81,600	81,650	3,673.13	3,673.13	3,305.81
78,650	78,700	3,540.38	3,540.38	3,186.34	81,650	81,700	3,675.38	3,675.38	3,307.84
78,700	78,750	3,542.63	3,542.63	3,188.36	81,700	81,750	3,677.63	3,677.63	3,309.86
78,750	78,800	3,544.88	3,544.88	3,190.39	81,750	81,800	3,679.88	3,679.88	3,311.89
78,800	78,850	3,547.13	3,547.13	3,192.41	81,800	81,850	3,682.13	3,682.13	3,313.91
78,850	78,900	3,549.38	3,549.38	3,194.44	81,850	81,900	3,684.38	3,684.38	3,315.94
78,900	78,950	3,551.63	3,551.63	3,196.46	81,900	81,950	3,686.63	3,686.63	3,317.96
78,950	79,000	3,553.88	3,553.88	3,198.49	81,950	82,000	3,688.88	3,688.88	3,319.99
79,000					**82,000**				
79,000	79,050	3,556.13	3,556.13	3,200.51	82,000	82,050	3,691.13	3,691.13	3,322.01
79,050	79,100	3,558.38	3,558.38	3,202.54	82,050	82,100	3,693.38	3,693.38	3,324.04
79,100	79,150	3,560.63	3,560.63	3,204.56	82,100	82,150	3,695.63	3,695.63	3,326.06
79,150	79,200	3,562.88	3,562.88	3,206.59	82,150	82,200	3,697.88	3,697.88	3,328.09
79,200	79,250	3,565.13	3,565.13	3,208.61	82,200	82,250	3,700.13	3,700.13	3,330.11
79,250	79,300	3,567.38	3,567.38	3,210.64	82,250	82,300	3,702.38	3,702.38	3,332.14
79,300	79,350	3,569.63	3,569.63	3,212.66	82,300	82,350	3,704.63	3,704.63	3,334.16
79,350	79,400	3,571.88	3,571.88	3,214.69	82,350	82,400	3,706.88	3,706.88	3,336.19
79,400	79,450	3,574.13	3,574.13	3,216.71	82,400	82,450	3,709.13	3,709.13	3,338.21
79,450	79,500	3,576.38	3,576.38	3,218.74	82,450	82,500	3,711.38	3,711.38	3,340.24
79,500	79,550	3,578.63	3,578.63	3,220.76	82,500	82,550	3,713.63	3,713.63	3,342.26
79,550	79,600	3,580.88	3,580.88	3,222.79	82,550	82,600	3,715.88	3,715.88	3,344.29
79,600	79,650	3,583.13	3,583.13	3,224.81	82,600	82,650	3,718.13	3,718.13	3,346.31
79,650	79,700	3,585.38	3,585.38	3,226.84	82,650	82,700	3,720.38	3,720.38	3,348.34
79,700	79,750	3,587.63	3,587.63	3,228.86	82,700	82,750	3,722.63	3,722.63	3,350.36
79,750	79,800	3,589.88	3,589.88	3,230.89	82,750	82,800	3,724.88	3,724.88	3,352.39
79,800	79,850	3,592.13	3,592.13	3,232.91	82,800	82,850	3,727.13	3,727.13	3,354.41
79,850	79,900	3,594.38	3,594.38	3,234.94	82,850	82,900	3,729.38	3,729.38	3,356.44
79,900	79,950	3,596.63	3,596.63	3,236.96	82,900	82,950	3,731.63	3,731.63	3,358.46
79,950	80,000	3,598.88	3,598.88	3,238.99	82,950	83,000	3,733.88	3,733.88	3,360.49
80,000					**83,000**				
80,000	80,050	3,601.13	3,601.13	3,241.01	83,000	83,050	3,736.13	3,736.13	3,362.51
80,050	80,100	3,603.38	3,603.38	3,243.04	83,050	83,100	3,738.38	3,738.38	3,364.54
80,100	80,150	3,605.63	3,605.63	3,245.06	83,100	83,150	3,740.63	3,740.63	3,366.56
80,150	80,200	3,607.88	3,607.88	3,247.09	83,150	83,200	3,742.88	3,742.88	3,368.59
80,200	80,250	3,610.13	3,610.13	3,249.11	83,200	83,250	3,745.13	3,745.13	3,370.61
80,250	80,300	3,612.38	3,612.38	3,251.14	83,250	83,300	3,747.38	3,747.38	3,372.64
80,300	80,350	3,614.63	3,614.63	3,253.16	83,300	83,350	3,749.63	3,749.63	3,374.66
80,350	80,400	3,616.88	3,616.88	3,255.19	83,350	83,400	3,751.88	3,751.88	3,376.69
80,400	80,450	3,619.13	3,619.13	3,257.21	83,400	83,450	3,754.13	3,754.13	3,378.71
80,450	80,500	3,621.38	3,621.38	3,259.24	83,450	83,500	3,756.38	3,756.38	3,380.74
80,500	80,550	3,623.63	3,623.63	3,261.26	83,500	83,550	3,758.63	3,758.63	3,382.76
80,550	80,600	3,625.88	3,625.88	3,263.29	83,550	83,600	3,760.88	3,760.88	3,384.79
80,600	80,650	3,628.13	3,628.13	3,265.31	83,600	83,650	3,763.13	3,763.13	3,386.81
80,650	80,700	3,630.38	3,630.38	3,267.34	83,650	83,700	3,765.38	3,765.38	3,388.84
80,700	80,750	3,632.63	3,632.63	3,269.36	83,700	83,750	3,767.63	3,767.63	3,390.86
80,750	80,800	3,634.88	3,634.88	3,271.39	83,750	83,800	3,769.88	3,769.88	3,392.89
80,800	80,850	3,637.13	3,637.13	3,273.41	83,800	83,850	3,772.13	3,772.13	3,394.91
80,850	80,900	3,639.38	3,639.38	3,275.44	83,850	83,900	3,774.38	3,774.38	3,396.94
80,900	80,950	3,641.63	3,641.63	3,277.46	83,900	83,950	3,776.63	3,776.63	3,398.96
80,950	81,000	3,643.88	3,643.88	3,279.49	83,950	84,000	3,778.88	3,778.88	3,400.99

* This column must also be used by a qualifying widow(er)

Continued on next page

If CT AGI is -		And you are -			If CT AGI is -		And you are -		
more than	less than or equal to	Single or Married Filing Separately	Head of Household	Married Filing Jointly *	more than	less than or equal to	Single or Married Filing Separately	Head of Household	Married Filing Jointly *
84,000					**87,000**				
84,000	84,050	3,781.13	3,781.13	3,403.01	87,000	87,050	3,916.13	3,916.13	3,524.51
84,050	84,100	3,783.38	3,783.38	3,405.04	87,050	87,100	3,918.38	3,918.38	3,526.54
84,100	84,150	3,785.63	3,785.63	3,407.06	87,100	87,150	3,920.63	3,920.63	3,528.56
84,150	84,200	3,787.88	3,787.88	3,409.09	87,150	87,200	3,922.88	3,922.88	3,530.59
84,200	84,250	3,790.13	3,790.13	3,411.11	87,200	87,250	3,925.13	3,925.13	3,532.61
84,250	84,300	3,792.38	3,792.38	3,413.14	87,250	87,300	3,927.38	3,927.38	3,534.64
84,300	84,350	3,794.63	3,794.63	3,415.16	87,300	87,350	3,929.63	3,929.63	3,536.66
84,350	84,400	3,796.88	3,796.88	3,417.19	87,350	87,400	3,931.88	3,931.88	3,538.69
84,400	84,450	3,799.13	3,799.13	3,419.21	87,400	87,450	3,934.13	3,934.13	3,540.71
84,450	84,500	3,801.38	3,801.38	3,421.24	87,450	87,500	3,936.38	3,936.38	3,542.74
84,500	84,550	3,803.63	3,803.63	3,423.26	87,500	87,550	3,938.63	3,938.63	3,544.76
84,550	84,600	3,805.88	3,805.88	3,425.29	87,550	87,600	3,940.88	3,940.88	3,546.79
84,600	84,650	3,808.13	3,808.13	3,427.31	87,600	87,650	3,943.13	3,943.13	3,548.81
84,650	84,700	3,810.38	3,810.38	3,429.34	87,650	87,700	3,945.38	3,945.38	3,550.84
84,700	84,750	3,812.63	3,812.63	3,431.36	87,700	87,750	3,947.63	3,947.63	3,552.86
84,750	84,800	3,814.88	3,814.88	3,433.39	87,750	87,800	3,949.88	3,949.88	3,554.89
84,800	84,850	3,817.13	3,817.13	3,435.41	87,800	87,850	3,952.13	3,952.13	3,556.91
84,850	84,900	3,819.38	3,819.38	3,437.44	87,850	87,900	3,954.38	3,954.38	3,558.94
84,900	84,950	3,821.63	3,821.63	3,439.46	87,900	87,950	3,956.63	3,956.63	3,560.96
84,950	85,000	3,823.88	3,823.88	3,441.49	87,950	88,000	3,958.88	3,958.88	3,562.99
85,000					**88,000**				
85,000	85,050	3,826.13	3,826.13	3,443.51	88,000	88,050	3,961.13	3,961.13	3,565.01
85,050	85,100	3,828.38	3,828.38	3,445.54	88,050	88,100	3,963.38	3,963.38	3,567.04
85,100	85,150	3,830.63	3,830.63	3,447.56	88,100	88,150	3,965.63	3,965.63	3,569.06
85,150	85,200	3,832.88	3,832.88	3,449.59	88,150	88,200	3,967.88	3,967.88	3,571.09
85,200	85,250	3,835.13	3,835.13	3,451.61	88,200	88,250	3,970.13	3,970.13	3,573.11
85,250	85,300	3,837.38	3,837.38	3,453.64	88,250	88,300	3,972.38	3,972.38	3,575.14
85,300	85,350	3,839.63	3,839.63	3,455.66	88,300	88,350	3,974.63	3,974.63	3,577.16
85,350	85,400	3,841.88	3,841.88	3,457.69	88,350	88,400	3,976.88	3,976.88	3,579.19
85,400	85,450	3,844.13	3,844.13	3,459.71	88,400	88,450	3,979.13	3,979.13	3,581.21
85,450	85,500	3,846.38	3,846.38	3,461.74	88,450	88,500	3,981.38	3,981.38	3,583.24
85,500	85,550	3,848.63	3,848.63	3,463.76	88,500	88,550	3,983.63	3,983.63	3,585.26
85,550	85,600	3,850.88	3,850.88	3,465.79	88,550	88,600	3,985.88	3,985.88	3,587.29
85,600	85,650	3,853.13	3,853.13	3,467.81	88,600	88,650	3,988.13	3,988.13	3,589.31
85,650	85,700	3,855.38	3,855.38	3,469.84	88,650	88,700	3,990.38	3,990.38	3,591.34
85,700	85,750	3,857.63	3,857.63	3,471.86	88,700	88,750	3,992.63	3,992.63	3,593.36
85,750	85,800	3,859.88	3,859.88	3,473.89	88,750	88,800	3,994.88	3,994.88	3,595.39
85,800	85,850	3,862.13	3,862.13	3,475.91	88,800	88,850	3,997.13	3,997.13	3,597.41
85,850	85,900	3,864.38	3,864.38	3,477.94	88,850	88,900	3,999.38	3,999.38	3,599.44
85,900	85,950	3,866.63	3,866.63	3,479.96	88,900	88,950	4,001.63	4,001.63	3,601.46
85,950	86,000	3,868.88	3,868.88	3,481.99	88,950	89,000	4,003.88	4,003.88	3,603.49
86,000					**89,000**				
86,000	86,050	3,871.13	3,871.13	3,484.01	89,000	89,050	4,006.13	4,006.13	3,605.51
86,050	86,100	3,873.38	3,873.38	3,486.04	89,050	89,100	4,008.38	4,008.38	3,607.54
86,100	86,150	3,875.63	3,875.63	3,488.06	89,100	89,150	4,010.63	4,010.63	3,609.56
86,150	86,200	3,877.88	3,877.88	3,490.09	89,150	89,200	4,012.88	4,012.88	3,611.59
86,200	86,250	3,880.13	3,880.13	3,492.11	89,200	89,250	4,015.13	4,015.13	3,613.61
86,250	86,300	3,882.38	3,882.38	3,494.14	89,250	89,300	4,017.38	4,017.38	3,615.64
86,300	86,350	3,884.63	3,884.63	3,496.16	89,300	89,350	4,019.63	4,019.63	3,617.66
86,350	86,400	3,886.88	3,886.88	3,498.19	89,350	89,400	4,021.88	4,021.88	3,619.69
86,400	86,450	3,889.13	3,889.13	3,500.21	89,400	89,450	4,024.13	4,024.13	3,621.71
86,450	86,500	3,891.38	3,891.38	3,502.24	89,450	89,500	4,026.38	4,026.38	3,623.74
86,500	86,550	3,893.63	3,893.63	3,504.26	89,500	89,550	4,028.63	4,028.63	3,625.76
86,550	86,600	3,895.88	3,895.88	3,506.29	89,550	89,600	4,030.88	4,030.88	3,627.79
86,600	86,650	3,898.13	3,898.13	3,508.31	89,600	89,650	4,033.13	4,033.13	3,629.81
86,650	86,700	3,900.38	3,900.38	3,510.34	89,650	89,700	4,035.38	4,035.38	3,631.84
86,700	86,750	3,902.63	3,902.63	3,512.36	89,700	89,750	4,037.63	4,037.63	3,633.86
86,750	86,800	3,904.88	3,904.88	3,514.39	89,750	89,800	4,039.88	4,039.88	3,635.89
86,800	86,850	3,907.13	3,907.13	3,516.41	89,800	89,850	4,042.13	4,042.13	3,637.91
86,850	86,900	3,909.38	3,909.38	3,518.44	89,850	89,900	4,044.38	4,044.38	3,639.94
86,900	86,950	3,911.63	3,911.63	3,520.46	89,900	89,950	4,046.63	4,046.63	3,641.96
86,950	87,000	3,913.88	3,913.88	3,522.49	89,950	90,000	4,048.88	4,048.88	3,643.99

* This column must also be used by a qualifying widow(er)

Continued on next page

If CT AGI is - more than	less than or equal to	And you are - Single or Married Filing Separately	Head of Household	Married Filing Jointly *
90,000				
90,000	90,050	4,051.13	4,051.13	3,646.01
90,050	90,100	4,053.38	4,053.38	3,648.04
90,100	90,150	4,055.63	4,055.63	3,650.06
90,150	90,200	4,057.88	4,057.88	3,652.09
90,200	90,250	4,060.13	4,060.13	3,654.11
90,250	90,300	4,062.38	4,062.38	3,656.14
90,300	90,350	4,064.63	4,064.63	3,658.16
90,350	90,400	4,066.88	4,066.88	3,660.19
90,400	90,450	4,069.13	4,069.13	3,662.21
90,450	90,500	4,071.38	4,071.38	3,664.24
90,500	90,550	4,073.63	4,073.63	3,666.26
90,550	90,600	4,075.88	4,075.88	3,668.29
90,600	90,650	4,078.13	4,078.13	3,670.31
90,650	90,700	4,080.38	4,080.38	3,672.34
90,700	90,750	4,082.63	4,082.63	3,674.36
90,750	90,800	4,084.88	4,084.88	3,676.39
90,800	90,850	4,087.13	4,087.13	3,678.41
90,850	90,900	4,089.38	4,089.38	3,680.44
90,900	90,950	4,091.63	4,091.63	3,682.46
90,950	91,000	4,093.88	4,093.88	3,684.49
91,000				
91,000	91,050	4,096.13	4,096.13	3,686.51
91,050	91,100	4,098.38	4,098.38	3,688.54
91,100	91,150	4,100.63	4,100.63	3,690.56
91,150	91,200	4,102.88	4,102.88	3,692.59
91,200	91,250	4,105.13	4,105.13	3,694.61
91,250	91,300	4,107.38	4,107.38	3,696.64
91,300	91,350	4,109.63	4,109.63	3,698.66
91,350	91,400	4,111.88	4,111.88	3,700.69
91,400	91,450	4,114.13	4,114.13	3,702.71
91,450	91,500	4,116.38	4,116.38	3,704.74
91,500	91,550	4,118.63	4,118.63	3,706.76
91,550	91,600	4,120.88	4,120.88	3,708.79
91,600	91,650	4,123.13	4,123.13	3,710.81
91,650	91,700	4,125.38	4,125.38	3,712.84
91,700	91,750	4,127.63	4,127.63	3,714.86
91,750	91,800	4,129.88	4,129.88	3,716.89
91,800	91,850	4,132.13	4,132.13	3,718.91
91,850	91,900	4,134.38	4,134.38	3,720.94
91,900	91,950	4,136.63	4,136.63	3,722.96
91,950	92,000	4,138.88	4,138.88	3,724.99
92,000				
92,000	92,050	4,141.13	4,141.13	3,727.01
92,050	92,100	4,143.38	4,143.38	3,729.04
92,100	92,150	4,145.63	4,145.63	3,731.06
92,150	92,200	4,147.88	4,147.88	3,733.09
92,200	92,250	4,150.13	4,150.13	3,735.11
92,250	92,300	4,152.38	4,152.38	3,737.14
92,300	92,350	4,154.63	4,154.63	3,739.16
92,350	92,400	4,156.88	4,156.88	3,741.19
92,400	92,450	4,159.13	4,159.13	3,743.21
92,450	92,500	4,161.38	4,161.38	3,745.24
92,500	92,550	4,163.63	4,163.63	3,747.26
92,550	92,600	4,165.88	4,165.88	3,749.29
92,600	92,650	4,168.13	4,168.13	3,751.31
92,650	92,700	4,170.38	4,170.38	3,753.34
92,700	92,750	4,172.63	4,172.63	3,755.36
92,750	92,800	4,174.88	4,174.88	3,757.39
92,800	92,850	4,177.13	4,177.13	3,759.41
92,850	92,900	4,179.38	4,179.38	3,761.44
92,900	92,950	4,181.63	4,181.63	3,763.46
92,950	93,000	4,183.88	4,183.88	3,765.49

If CT AGI is - more than	less than or equal to	And you are - Single or Married Filing Separately	Head of Household	Married Filing Jointly *
93,000				
93,000	93,050	4,186.13	4,186.13	3,767.51
93,050	93,100	4,188.38	4,188.38	3,769.54
93,100	93,150	4,190.63	4,190.63	3,771.56
93,150	93,200	4,192.88	4,192.88	3,773.59
93,200	93,250	4,195.13	4,195.13	3,775.61
93,250	93,300	4,197.38	4,197.38	3,777.64
93,300	93,350	4,199.63	4,199.63	3,779.66
93,350	93,400	4,201.88	4,201.88	3,781.69
93,400	93,450	4,204.13	4,204.13	3,783.71
93,450	93,500	4,206.38	4,206.38	3,785.74
93,500	93,550	4,208.63	4,208.63	3,787.76
93,550	93,600	4,210.88	4,210.88	3,789.79
93,600	93,650	4,213.13	4,213.13	3,791.81
93,650	93,700	4,215.38	4,215.38	3,793.84
93,700	93,750	4,217.63	4,217.63	3,795.86
93,750	93,800	4,219.88	4,219.88	3,797.89
93,800	93,850	4,222.13	4,222.13	3,799.91
93,850	93,900	4,224.38	4,224.38	3,801.94
93,900	93,950	4,226.63	4,226.63	3,803.96
93,950	94,000	4,228.88	4,228.88	3,805.99
94,000				
94,000	94,050	4,231.13	4,231.13	3,808.01
94,050	94,100	4,233.38	4,233.38	3,810.04
94,100	94,150	4,235.63	4,235.63	3,812.06
94,150	94,200	4,237.88	4,237.88	3,814.09
94,200	94,250	4,240.13	4,240.13	3,816.11
94,250	94,300	4,242.38	4,242.38	3,818.14
94,300	94,350	4,244.63	4,244.63	3,820.16
94,350	94,400	4,246.88	4,246.88	3,822.19
94,400	94,450	4,249.13	4,249.13	3,824.21
94,450	94,500	4,251.38	4,251.38	3,826.24
94,500	94,550	4,253.63	4,253.63	3,828.26
94,550	94,600	4,255.88	4,255.88	3,830.29
94,600	94,650	4,258.13	4,258.13	3,832.31
94,650	94,700	4,260.38	4,260.38	3,834.34
94,700	94,750	4,262.63	4,262.63	3,836.36
94,750	94,800	4,264.88	4,264.88	3,838.39
94,800	94,850	4,267.13	4,267.13	3,840.41
94,850	94,900	4,269.38	4,269.38	3,842.44
94,900	94,950	4,271.63	4,271.63	3,844.46
94,950	95,000	4,273.88	4,273.88	3,846.49
95,000				
95,000	95,050	4,276.13	4,276.13	3,848.51
95,050	95,100	4,278.38	4,278.38	3,850.54
95,100	95,150	4,280.63	4,280.63	3,852.56
95,150	95,200	4,282.88	4,282.88	3,854.59
95,200	95,250	4,285.13	4,285.13	3,856.61
95,250	95,300	4,287.38	4,287.38	3,858.64
95,300	95,350	4,289.63	4,289.63	3,860.66
95,350	95,400	4,291.88	4,291.88	3,862.69
95,400	95,450	4,294.13	4,294.13	3,864.71
95,450	95,500	4,296.38	4,296.38	3,866.74
95,500	95,550	4,298.63	4,298.63	3,868.76
95,550	95,600	4,300.88	4,300.88	3,870.79
95,600	95,650	4,303.13	4,303.13	3,872.81
95,650	95,700	4,305.38	4,305.38	3,874.84
95,700	95,750	4,307.63	4,307.63	3,876.86
95,750	95,800	4,309.88	4,309.88	3,878.89
95,800	95,850	4,312.13	4,312.13	3,880.91
95,850	95,900	4,314.38	4,314.38	3,882.94
95,900	95,950	4,316.63	4,316.63	3,884.96
95,950	96,000	4,318.88	4,318.88	3,886.99

* This column must also be used by a qualifying widow(er)

Index

Save $5.00 When You File Your Return Electronically.

Take advantage of the speed, accuracy and convenience of electronic filing and save $5.00!

Present the attached coupon to your tax preparer to receive $5.00 off the price of electronic filing when the SPEED>FILING system is used.

If your preparer does not offer electronic filing, or if you prepare your own return, call 1-800-532-5320 to receive an information packet containing all the materials you need to have us electronically file your return swiftly and securely.

Your error-free prepared return will be entered into our computers and filed directly with the IRS within 24 hours after we receive it. As soon as the IRS accepts your return (usually within 24 hours of transmission) SPEED>FILING will send you a postcard confirming the date you can expect your refund. Returns received containing errors may take longer to process.

ELECTRONIC FILING OF TAX RETURNS

1-800-532-5320

SPECIAL MONEY-SAVING OFFERS

TURN PAGE FOR DETAILS... ☞

SPECIAL CONSUMER OFFERS!

Get a one dollar rebate on your purchase
of each of the following tax guides. Increase your
dollar value of the rebate (up to $3.00)
if you buy more than one book.

For Year-Round Planning

$1.00 Rebate for The Ernst & Young
Tax-Saving Strategies Guide 1993

For Preparing Federal Tax Returns

$1.00 Rebate for The Ernst & Young
Tax Guide 1993

For Preparing NY, NJ, and CT State Tax Returns

$1.00 Rebate for The Ernst & Young
New York, New Jersey, Connecticut
State Tax Guide 1993

OFFICIAL REFUND CERTIFICATE

I have purchased the Ernst & Young guides checked below and have enclosed the purchase receipt with the
books' prices circled. Please send me the appropiate refund.

(1 Book)	(2 Books)	(3 Books)
❏ $1 Refund	❏ $2 Refund	❏ $3 Refund

Mail to: The Ernst & Young Rebate Offer
P.O. Box 1177
Grand Rapids, MN 55745-1177

_____

Name (Please Print)

_____

Address

_____

City

_____

State   Zip

_____

Signature

_____

Store Where Purchased

This certificate must accompany your request. No duplications accepted. Offer good only in the United States. Offer invited one refund to a family, group or organization. Void where prohibited, taxed or restricted. Allow 4-6 weeks for mailing of your rebate. Offer expires June 30, 1993.